Curriculum
Planning
A NEW APPROACH

Curriculum Planning
A NEW APPROACH

GLEN HASS
Professor of Education
University of Florida

JOSEPH BONDI
Associate Professor of Education
University of South Florida

JON WILES
Assistant Professor of Education
George Peabody College for Teachers

ALLYN AND BACON, INC. · BOSTON

Contents

Contributors

ABRAMOWITZ, MILDRED W., Principal, Niles Junior High School, Bronx, New York

ALEXANDER, WILLIAM M., Professor of Education, University of Florida

ANDERSON, ROBERT H., Professor of Education, Harvard University

AUSUBEL, DAVID P., Professor of Education, City University of New York

AVILA, DONALD, Professor of Education, University of Florida

BELLACK, ARNO A., Professor of Education, Teachers College, Columbia University

BILLINGS, ZILPHA W., Curriculum Specialist, Idlewilde, South Hero, Vermont

BONDI, JOSEPH, Associate Professor of Education, University of South Florida

BOSS, RICHARD, Director, Portland Residential Manpower Training System, Portland Public Schools, Portland, Oregon

BOYER, ERNEST L., Chancellor, State University of New York, Albany

BROWN, HARRISON, Professor of Science and Government, California Institute of Technology

BRUNER, JEROME S., Professor of Psychology and Director of Center for Cognitive Studies, Harvard University

BURNS, JAMES A., Administrative Assistant, Metropolitan Public Schools, Nashville, Tennessee

CLAYTON, MARILYN, Project Director, Exploring Childhood, Education Development Center, Cambridge, Massachusetts

COHEN, DONALD, Special Assistant to the Director, Office of Child Development, U.S. Office of Education

COHODES, AARON, President, Superintendents Only, Chicago, Illinois

COLEMAN, JULIE BROWN, Social Studies Teacher, Lewis and Clark Junior High School, Billings, Montana

COMBS, ARTHUR W., Professor of Education, University of Florida

COMMAGER, HENRY STEELE, Simpson Lecturer, Amherst College

Contributors

CULKIN, JOHN M., S.J., Director, Center for Communications, Fordham University

DEANS, EDWINA, Former Specialist for Elementary School Mathematics, U.S. Office of Education

DOW, PETER, Director, Social Studies Program, Education Development Center, Cambridge, Massachusetts

ELKIND, DAVID, Professor of Psychology, University of Rochester, Rochester, New York

EMPEY, DONALD W., Deputy Superintendent, Lave Washington School District No. 414, Kirkland, Washington

ERICKSON, RALPH, Educational Writer

FANTINI, MARIO D., Dean of Education, State University College, New Paltz, New York

FINCHER, GLEN, Director, Federal Programs, Canton City Schools, Canton, Ohio

GAGNÉ, ROBERT M., Professor of Educational Research and Testing, Florida State University

GANTT, WALTER N., Associate Professor, Early Childhood Elementary Education, University of Maryland

GEARING, FREDERICK O., Professor of Anthropology, State University of New York at Buffalo

GORDON, IRA J., Professor of Education, University of Florida

HARLACHER, ERVIN L., President, Brookdale Community College, Lincrost, New Jersey

HARRIS, DONALD, Executive Educational Specialist, United States Senate Select Committee on Equal Educational Opportunity

HASS, GLEN, Professor of Education, University of Florida

HAVIGHURST, ROBERT J., Professor of Education and Human Development, University of Chicago

HEFFERNAN, HELEN, Retired, Former Assistant Chief, Division of Instruction in Charge of Elementary Education, California State Department of Education

HOUNSHELL, PAUL B., Associate Professor of Education, University of North Carolina

HYMES, JAMES L., JR., Specialist in Early Childhood Education, Carmel Valley, California

IANNI, FRANCIS A. J., Director, Horace-Mann-Lincoln Institute, Chairman Department of Educational Administration and Director Division of Educational Institutions and Programs, Teachers College, Columbia University

KARNES, MERLE B., Professor of Special Education, Institute for Research on Exceptional Children, University of Illinois

KELLER, GEORGE C., Assistant to the Chancellor, State University of New York, Albany

KNELLER, GEORGE F., Professor of Education, Graduate School of Education, University of California, Los Angeles

LEVINE, DANIEL U., Director, Center for the Study of Metropolitan Problems in Education, University of Missouri at Kansas City

LEVINE, SOL, Principal, John Dewey High School, Brooklyn, New York

LEWIS, BILL RAY, Assistant Superintendent, Center School District (Public Schools) Kansas City, Missouri

McCarthy, Robert J., Superintendent of Schools, East Greenwich School Department, East Greenwich, Rhode Island

McGuire, Carson, Professor of Educational Psychology, University of Texas, Austin (Deceased)

Macari, Claudia, Assistant Principal for Guidance, Niles Junior High School, Bronx, New York

Madsen, Charles H., Jr., Associate Professor, Department of Psychology, Florida State University

Madsen, Clifford K., Associate Professor, School of Music, Florida State University

Martin, Marie Y., Director, Community College Education, United States Office of Education

Measel, Wes, Director, Lathrop Team-Teaching Project, Canton City Schools, Canton, Ohio

Moore, William, Jr., Professor, Ohio State University

Nader, Ralph, Consumer Advocate and Writer

Nash, Samuel, Director, Special Projects and Program Planning, New Haven, Connecticut

Ohme, Herman, Principal, Cubberley High School, Palo Alto, California

Otto, Herbert A., Psychologist and Educator, Chairman, National Center for The Exploration of Human Potential, La Jolla, California

Purkey, William, Professor of Education, University of Florida

Quayle, Therald P., Division Head, Science and Math, Weber High School, Ogden, Utah

Resnik, Henry S., Educational Writer

Richards, Catherine V., Chief Youth Specialist, Office of Child Development, U.S. Office of Education

Roberts, Edwin A., Jr., Senior Editor, *National Observer*

Roberts, Thomas B., Assistant Professor, Secondary Education, North Illinois University

Rogers, Vincent R., Professor of Education, School of Education, University of Connecticut

Rowland, G. Thomas, Chancellor, The Institute for Epistemic Studies, Fort Worth, Texas

Schultz, Raymond E., Professor of Community College Education, Washington State University

Senn, Milton J. E., M.D., Sterling Professor Emeritus, Pediatrics and Psychiatry, Yale University

Shane, Harold G., Professor of Education, Indiana University

Smith, Nila Banton, Distinguished Professor, School of Education, University of Southern California, Los Angeles

Sussman, Marvin, Selah Chamberlain Professor of Sociology and Director, Institute on Family and Bureaucratic Society, Case Western Reserve University, Cleveland

Thornburg, Hershel, Associate Professor of Educational Psychology, University of Arizona

Tillman, Rodney, Dean, School of Education, George Washington University, Washington, D.C.

VAN TIL, WILLIAM, Coffman Distinguished Professor in Education, Indiana State University

WARD, SPENCER A., M.D., Staff Psychiatrist, Mental Health Study Center, National Institute of Mental Health

WATSON, GOODWIN, Professor of Social Psychology and Education, Teachers College, Columbia University, and Distinguished Professor, Newark State College

WEINSTEIN, GERALD, Professor of Education, University of Massachusetts

WELDEN, J. EUGENE, Chief, Program Development, Community Service and Continuing Education Program, U.S. Office of Education

WEST, EDWIN L., JR., Science Consultant, North Carolina State Department of Public Instruction

WILES, KIMBALL (Deceased), formerly Dean, College of Education, University of Florida

WILES, JON, Assistant Professor of Education, George Peabody College for Teachers, Nashville

WILLIAMS, ROGER J., Professor of Biochemistry, Clayton Foundation Biochemical Institute, University of Texas

WILSON, IAN H., Consultant, Business Environment Studies, General Electric Company

YETTER, CLYDE C., Director of Public Information, Research for Better Schools, Inc., Philadelphia

Preface

Curriculum Planning: A New Approach offers a combination of methods, and approaches for studying curriculum improvement and planning that is particularly appropriate for the 1970s. This approach to studying curriculum planning includes the following:

1. A "modular approach" to the presentation of each of the nine major topics in the book, including prerequisites for the topic, the rationale, the student's objectives stated as performance competencies, a preassessment (to be used as a diagnostic self-test), alternative learning activities, and a postassessment. By using the modular approach, many students may be able to pursue each topic to a substantial degree through independent study.
2. A case study method of learning that includes the study of real school programs.
3. An emphasis on the achievement of performance competencies as the objective for the study of curriculum planning. Linking the performance competencies to the case study method enables the student to demonstrate to himself, as well as to others, the degree to which he has achieved the desired competencies, either as a preassessment prior to study or as a postassessment.
4. A new definition of *curriculum* that seeks to distinguish *education* from *schooling* and that emphasizes the *role of teachers, as well as others,* as curriculum planners.
5. An emphasis on a multidimensional approach, rather than a linear approach, to curriculum planning that uses what we know about the individual, the society, and the group. This multidimensional approach should distinguish the *professional in curriculum planning* from other professionals, such as the human development or learning or group sensitivity specialist (all of whom are important to the curriculum planner).
6. The development of the following competencies:
   (1) To describe and analyze a curriculum or teaching plan with respect to its relationship to objectives; current social aims, forces, and problems; human development knowledge and theories; knowledge about how learning occurs; and knowledge of the nature of knowledge.

(2) To formulate and justify a set of criteria for evaluating a curriculum or teaching plan.

(3) To identify the various roles in curriculum planning, including the role of the teacher.

(4) To identify, describe, and evaluate characteristic features, trends, and innovations of programs of education at all age levels.

7. The presentation of the positions of more than eighty contributing authors on the nine topics being studied. By this means the reader conveniently obtains the views of writers with competing or special viewpoints. The writings of these authors also expand on the positions presented in the rationale for each topic.

8. The inclusion of problem-oriented, competency-developing "additional learning activities" for each topic studied.

Curriculum Planning: A New Approach is the successor to *Readings in Curriculum,* first published in 1965, by Allyn and Bacon, Inc., and revised in 1970. But the present book is much more than a book of readings. Hence the need for the new title.

Acknowledgment is given to the many authors who have granted access to their writings. Their willingness to permit others to republish their ideas is an indication of their dedication to the continuous improvement of curriculum and instruction as a field of study.

All three of the editors participated in the search for, and the selection of, articles for reprinting. All of the section introductions were written by Glen Hass. The three editors also shared in preparing the material for the "additional learning activities" at the end of each section.

Curriculum Planning: A New Approach may be used either as a text for the usual course or as a guide to independent study, with the instructor available as a consultant, guide, or resource person.

Introduction

The purpose of *Curriculum Planning: A New Approach* is to help you to develop many of the performance competencies that you need in order to engage in curriculum planning and decision-making as a teacher, principal, supervisor, or other curriculum leader. The competencies that you may attain through the resources offered in this book are as follows:

1. To describe and analyze a curriculum or teaching plan with respect to its relationship to (a) current social aims, forces, and problems; (b) human development knowledge and theories; (c) knowledge about how learning occurs; and (d) knowledge of the nature of knowledge.
2. To formulate and justify a set of criteria for evaluating a curriculum or teaching plan.
3. To explain and use the roles of various persons in curriculum planning and change, including teachers, parents, other citizens, specialists in the disciplines, school principals, etc.
4. To identify, describe, and evaluate characteristic features, trends, and innovations of programs of education at all age levels, pre-school through the university.

Part 1, "Bases and Criteria for the Curriculum," will help you perfect the first three performance competencies. Part 2, "The Curriculum," will help you attain competency four.

You must be a student of society, human development and learning, and knowledge if you are to be competent in curriculum planning and decision-making. You must be able to interrelate your understandings in each of these areas appropriately as you plan programs of education for groups of learners or for an individual learner.

Because this procedure is difficult until you have mastered all the knowledge involved, Part 1 presents social forces, human development, learning, and knowledge as separate topics. Part 1 concludes with a section on curriculum criteria that will teach you how to interrelate the competencies learned with the objectives of a curriculum or teaching plan.

Part 2 will help you to use objectives of education, curriculum bases and criteria, and current trends in education in evaluating curriculum plans at all levels of education including elementary, middle, and high school, as well as those in community colleges and universities. Even though this may be your first opportunity to study curriculum planning, you should find it possible to develop the competencies involved so that you can describe and analyze curriculum plans at each level and suggest improvements.

Before beginning Part 1, you should have answers to the following questions:

1. What is meant by the term *curriculum?*
2. What is mean by *instruction?*
3. Why are social forces, human development, the nature of learning, and the nature of knowledge called the "bases of the curriculum"?

Each of these questions will now be discussed.

CURRICULUM AND INSTRUCTION: DEFINITIONS AND DISCUSSION

The word *curriculum* has been used in a variety of ways. It has been used to mean:

1. A school's written courses of study and other curriculum materials
2. The subject-matter taught to the students
3. The courses offered in a school
4. The planned experiences of the learners under the guidance of the school

The definition of curriculum in this book incorporates all of those definitions and more.

When the term *curriculum* includes all of the planned experiences of the learners under the school's guidance, curriculum and instruction cannot be regarded as separate entities. The learners' planned experiences in the school will of course include the planning of instruction by the teachers and the methods used by them in teaching. This is a helpful conceptualization of *curriculum* and *instruction* because it shows clearly that the curriculum bases are important both for guiding decision-making in teaching and for curriculum planning and evaluation. The planning of a curriculum and teaching are part of the same process: the planning of learning opportunities and engagements. And the most creative teachers are often those who engage in all the steps of the process—the preplanning of the curriculum and the planning of instruction as well (for an example of this, see "The Self-Selection Classroom," by Zilpha W. Billings, in Section 6 of this book).

When the curriculum is defined as "all of the planned experiences that learners have under the school's guidance," it includes, of course, all school activities and planned school services such as the library, health care, assemblies, the food services and lunchrooms, and field trips. Indeed the school is then seen as a social system designed to provide planned learning experiences for the students who attend the school. All of the aspects of the learners' experiences in school should be examined in terms of the appropriate curriculum bases—social forces, human development, learning, and knowledge—by the school principal, the teachers, other staff members, and the learners themselves.

But none of the above definitions are adequate in terms of present needs and trends. The definition of curriculum we use is as follows:

> The curriculum is all of the experiences that individual learners have in a program of education, which is planned in terms of a framework of theory and research or past and present practice used in the program planning.

The phrase "program of education," has major significance in this definition. It means that the curriculum is a planned program based in part on prepared curriculum materials and planning by teachers and other professional staff members. The words "program of education" are utilized instead of "under the direction of the school" to indicate that the planned experiences may take place in the community, in the learner's home, in a school, or in any other suitable place. This definition emphasizes that all of the following factors should be included in our thinking when we consider the meaning of *curriculum*.

1. The curriculum is preplanned.
2. Planned objectives, and theories and research concerning social forces, human development, learning, and knowledge should guide the preplanning at all levels including the school system, the school, the instructional group, and the individual learner.
3. Planning of instruction by teachers is a major part of curriculum planning, since it often has greater influence on the learners than the preplanned curriculum, which may be used or ignored by the teacher as he plans. This is as it should be, since the teacher is usually in a better position to know the learner and his needs than the other persons who engage in preplanning at the national, state, school system, or school levels. But in planning his instruction, the teacher should be guided by his knowledge of planned objectives and of theories and research concerning the four bases of the curriculum and curriculum criteria.
4. For each learner, the actual curriculum is his experiences as he participates in the learning opportunities provided and as he shares in the planning of the program of education.
5. As the curriculum focuses to a greater extent on programs of education rather than programs of schooling, the teacher's role in the planning becomes increasingly important, since the uniqueness of each individual and of the local community as a classroom becomes more important. In such programs of education, the importance of preplanning flexible arrangements and learning alternatives also increases. To make skillful, professional decisions in such a setting, the teacher should make them in terms of the bases and criteria of the curriculum. (See "High School With No Walls," by Henry S. Resnik, in Section 8.) Programs have failed in the past when teachers and other curriculum planners failed to recognize the need for adequate planning.

The "framework of theory and research or past and present practice used in the program planning" is made part of the definition of the curriculum because it is the presence or absence of this framework of theory that may determine the quality of the curriculum or teaching. Implicit ideas and views about social forces, human development, knowledge, and learners and learning should be made explicit by each person who engages in curriculum planning. What is implied is professional accountability in the planning of both curricula and instruction.

When a need is felt for a distinction between *curriculum* and *instruction,* then the following definitions may be useful:

> The *curriculum* is considered to encompass the instructional activities planned and provided for pupils by the school or school system. The curriculum, therefore, is the planned interaction of pupils with instructional *content,* instructional *resources,* and instructional *processes* for the attainment of educational objectives. . . .
>
> *Instruction* includes the activities dealing directly with the teaching of pupils and with improving the quality of teaching. . . .
>
> In summarizing the meaning of the two terms *curriculum* and *instruction,* one might consider that the *curriculum* is *what is taught* and instruction is *how it is taught.*[1]

THE BASES OF THE CURRICULUM: DEFINITION AND DISCUSSION

In this book we will study the four bases of the curriculum as a major source of guidance for decision-making in curriculum planning and the planning of teaching. The four bases are social forces, human development, the nature of learning, and the nature of knowledge. Most of Part 1 is devoted to the study of these four bases and how they should be used in the planning of curricula and teaching.

All civilized societies establish schools and programs of education in order to induct the young into the culture and to transmit the culture and values of the society. But today the work of the school must be constantly conducted in the midst of social and economic pressures and changes. Thus, one of the major areas of consideration in all curriculum planning must be *social forces* as reflected in (1) social goals, (2) cultural uniformity and diversity, (3) social pressures, and (4) social change.

The graded school and the curriculum organization based on it were adopted in the United States before we knew about human development and individual differences. However, *human development* knowledge and scientific research have been accumulating for nearly seventy-five years. Children are not small adults, we have learned. Human beings are qualitatively different at the different age levels for which we must provide in curriculum planning and in the planning of teaching. Knowledge of human development helps the curriculum planner provide for both age and individual differences among learners. Therefore, knowledge of human development research is an essential aspect of curriculum planning.

Knowledge about the *ways human beings learn* has also been accumulating for approximately seventy-five years. Because of the complexity of learning and because of individual differences in learning, a number of *theories of learning* have been developed and tested through scientific studies and research during this period. Today, the curriculum planner is guided by several approaches to learning that have been described in the theories. Each of the scientific learning theories appears to describe a different kind of learning. There are many differences among

---

[1] HEW, National Center for Educational Statistics, *Standard Terminology for Curriculum and Instruction in Local and State School Systems* (Washington, D.C., 1970), p. 3.

learners, and the various learning theories support the development of approaches to curriculum planning that can help to provide for these differences.

Today *knowledge* must be considered one of the bases of the curriculum. A major question is, What knowledge is of most worth? What to exclude from the curriculum is as difficult to determine as what to include. Another question is, How shall knowledge be organized in the curriculum? A number of theories about knowledge can assist the curriculum planner in making these decisions.

All four curriculum bases are needed for making decisions regarding *individual differences* among learners and for providing *balance* in a curriculum. Knowledge about human development is necessary in order to provide for *continuity* in learning and for the development of *self-understanding*. And knowledge about the nature of knowledge enables the curriculum planner to provide for learning that is useful, or *problem-oriented*, or that will be most likely to be *transferred* by the learner from one situation to another.

In the planning of curricula and instruction, we should use what we know about society, human development, learning, and knowledge. That is why Part 1 of this book is devoted to assisting you to develop the performance competencies that are needed to do this planning. This *multi-dimensional approach* to planning will distinguish you, as a professional in curriculum and instructional planning, from other professionals in education such as specialists in human development, or learning, or social structure, or group sensitivity, or knowledge (all of whom assist the curriculum planner).

CURRICULUM OBJECTIVES

The objectives being sought are another major consideration in curriculum planning and in the planning of teaching. Unfortunately, the goals of a curriculum are often forgotten or left unplanned as teachers engage in teaching.

Without having a set of objectives clearly in mind, teachers and curriculum planners cannot make professional judgments about choices of materials, procedures, or content on any planned basis.

Both broad, general objectives and specific objectives are needed to guide curriculum planning and the planning of teaching. In this introduction we will consider only the need for general objectives.

Broad, general objectives define the need for various courses, activities, and experiences. They should be limited in number so that they can readily be kept in mind.

We have found it useful to consider four general goals in curriculum planning: education for *citizenship*, *self-realization*, *vocation*, and *critical thinking*. Often the same program of learning can contribute to several of these goals, which should be kept in mind at all levels of education. (See, for example, "Occupational Preparation in the Elementary School" by Walter N. Gantt, in Section 6).

A MODULAR, CASE STUDY APPROACH

To introduce the study of each of the nine major topics, we have used a modular approach and the case study method. Each of the sections is opened by a module that includes the following parts: prerequisites, rationale, objectives, preassessment, learning activities, and postassessment.

The prerequisites at the beginning of each module refer to other sections of this book that should be studied before that module and section are attempted. For example, the study of this Introduction is listed as a prerequisite to each of the other sections.

The rationale in each module should be studied carefully. It includes the guiding principles and concepts for that topic. It enables you to relate the various articles and study sources to each other and to the topic.

The objectives are stated as performance competencies—what you should be able to do as a curriculum planner or teacher in relation to the topic of the module. They help you to focus your efforts and to check whether you have achieved the performance competencies.

The preassessment suggests ways you can test yourself, before studying the topic, to see whether you already possess some or all of the competencies. A case study about a real school is used as a major part of each preassessment.

Learning activities are the articles related to the topic that are included in this book. Additional learning problems and activities are suggested at the end of each section. The purpose of the learning activities is to develop skill in the performance competencies that are listed as the objectives of the module.

The postassessment is intended as a test of your degree of skill in the performance competencies following the learning activities. The case problem method and a real school program are again used for the postassessment.

The major question in each module is, "Do I possess, or have I attained, the performance competencies in curriculum planning or the planning of teaching that are my goals in the study of this topic?"

SUMMARY

This introduction raises many topics and questions that will, of course, be treated in detail throughout the book. The introduction is intended not to settle the questions, but to help you see where we are going together. It is intended also to suggest the ways in which we can professionalize decision-making in curriculum planning and teaching.

Much has been written and said recently about "accountability." To enable teachers and other curriculum planners to be professionally accountable when they make instructional decisions or prepare curriculum materials is a goal of *Curriculum Planning: A New Approach.* To be "professionally accountable," teachers and curriculum planners should be able to use objectives, the bases of the curriculum, and critical knowledge of trends in decision-making whether the decisions are about teaching science at the high school level or preparing materials to aid in dealing with human relationships at all levels of education. To be professionally accountable means to be able to use the knowledge, methods, and skills that the profession has developed through past experience, theories, and research. You are about to begin, or to continue, the development of some of the necessary performance competencies.

PART ONE

Bases and Criteria for the Curriculum

Social Forces

PREREQUISITE

Reading of the Introduction to this book.

RATIONALE

To understand schools and school systems, one must relate them to the surrounding cultural, economic, historical, philosophical, and political circumstances. Since education is always an expression of a civilization and of a political and economic system, schools must harmonize with the lives and ideas of men in a particular time and place. Since the social environment today is in a state of change, descriptions of society in the nineteenth century or in the fifties or sixties no longer suffice. As a major element in curriculum planning and teaching, present social forces and future trends must be regularly reconsidered.

Today our nation is faced with a crisis of purpose such as we never faced in the past. Perhaps it is because of our seeming inability to control our technology or the weight of corporate power that often seems to override individual rights and public interests. Whatever the cause, there is a crisis of values and purposes in our society.

Lined up behind these questions, like so many planes on a runway, are other major contemporary problems of American society: environment, generation gap, changing values and morality, the family, urban and suburban crises, and equal rights.

1. *Environment.* Man has become increasingly proficient in his attempt to control and use nature for his safety, comfort, and convenience. The advances in science and technology and the increased industrialization of America led many

to believe that man could indeed control and use nature as he pleased. We are now realizing that such is not the case. A computer at MIT predicted that we are doomed if we don't make some drastic changes. Ecological experts disagree about the seriousness of the problem. Some believe that we have already passed the "point of no return"—that we have so polluted our air and water and plundered our natural resources that it is only a matter of time before we perish, regardless of what corrective measures we now take. The federal government has admitted that beginning the clean-up in earnest will produce the following results: expenditure of billions of dollars, rise in unemployment, increase in the price of products, the closing of many plants, and a seriously damaging impact on the economic welfare of many communities.

2. *Generation Gap.* Some people believe that there has always been a basic difference in outlook between older and younger people and that today's so-called generation gap is a perfectly natural phenomenon. However, the differences today are much more real and difficult than ever before. Margaret Mead believes that there is a basic split between older and younger generations that we have never before experienced. She feels that, to a large extent, communication between generations has broken down.[1] Many parents now admit that they do not understand their own children's thinking and actions. Many young people now say that adults are not capable of understanding their own children.

3. *Changing Values and Morality.* The percentage of Americans who attend churches is lower today than it has been since before World War II. A significant percentage of youth admit to smoking marijuana and using a vast array of other drugs. The surgeon general has expressed alarm at the problem of alcoholism, primarily among adults. People now live together openly without getting married. Venereal disease is rising so rapidly that statisticians are hard pressed to keep up with it. An increasing number of young people feel that it is patriotic to refuse to serve in the armed forces. There is increasing pressure for passage of liberalized abortion and divorce laws. There has been a proliferation of violence, sex, and nudity on stage, screen, and printed page.

4. *The Family.* The family has traditionally been one of the most important institutions in American society. But in many cases today, the family no longer functions as a closely-knit unit. There is great mobility among a large segment of the population—the family is not tied closely to the community, and family members are spread out over a wide geographical area. Other segments of the population are trapped in the inner city. More and more children are raised without benefit of their natural father's or mother's presence. The roles of the father and mother have undergone change. Population control has become extremely important and controversial. Some see control as necessary, others see it as threat.

5. *Urban and Suburban Crises.* A higher and higher percentage of the American population has moved into the urban areas. Whites have been moving to the suburbs, leaving the inner city to minority groups. The tax base for the inner city has been seriously eroded, making it difficult for the government to provide adequate services. Crime has continued to rise at a seemingly unstoppable pace, spreading from the central city into the suburbs. Slums and ghettos are evident in every major city, and providing adequate housing is a major problem. The

[1] Mead's position is presented in her book *Culture and Commitment: A Study of the Generation Gap* (New York: Natural History Press, 1970).

transportation system has also become a problem of major proportions, as it relates to both the inner city and the suburban commuter.

6. *Equal Rights.* Minority groups in America have become more vocal and more active in demanding equal rights. Blacks, Chicanos, Indians, Puerto Ricans, and other racial groups often do not agree among themselves about how to proceed, but they share in a common cause of fighting back against years of inequality, inferior status, and often inhumane treatment. Those who know poverty, regardless of race, also clamor for a better life. Some middle-class Americans rebel against such groups and feel that their own "hard earned" rights are being violated in favor of other groups. The women's lib movement is getting increasing recognition of its goals.

The articles in this section, dealing with these and other social forces, should help you examine your own views regarding current social forces. Are there other social forces that you consider as important as, or more important than, the ones discussed in this section?

One way to see the close relationship between an understanding of the social environment and the development of an appropriate educational program is to view the social setting from the standpoint of the individual. Some claim that in our society the role of each person is determined by his *occupation.* His friends are often drawn from those with whom he works, and the whole tone of his life is related to this reference group. Moreover, a democratic society requires *citizens* who are prepared to deal with the current issues of government. Finally, each person faces problems of *self-fulfillment* and *self-development.* Thus, from the individual learner's standpoint, the rationally developed school program must provide for his *vocational demands and requirements,* the *demands of citizenship,* and the *demands of self-fulfillment.* In every society the nature of these demands on the individual is different. And because all industrial civilizations are undergoing rapid change, the demands are subject to constant modification within each society.

One of the difficult problems is that the social forces are constantly changing, and the curriculum should change with them. Few of the social forces exist independent of each other. They are interrelated to a large degree, and each individual in the society has most, and sometimes all, of them acting upon him to a greater or lesser degree at the same time. This point can be illustrated by the following hypothetical situation.

Liza is a black girl who lives in the ghetto of a large city. She is fourteen years old. She is the oldest of a family of nine children. Her father left the family five years ago because he could not find employment and knew that his children could receive more financial support from the government if he left home. Liza's mother works during the evening, so Liza is expected to care for the apartment and children when she gets home from school. The apartment has only two rooms and is infested with rats. It has poor plumbing and toilet facilities, and the heating system works only occasionally. The children get only one real meal a day and have no money to spend at school. Their clothing is old and worn.

Kevin is a white boy who lives in a middle-class suburb. He is fourteen years old. He has a seventeen-year-old sister. His father is a lawyer who works downtown and commutes daily, often arriving home very late in the evening. Kevin's mother attends many social functions and has a serious drinking problem. His parents often have loud arguments and are openly talking about divorce. Kevin's sister smokes marijuana and takes LSD. She often spends the weekend with her boy friend. Kevin is well fed, lives in an attractive home with a good-sized yard, and is given a generous allowance to spend at school.

Roy is a white boy who lives near a factory on the outer fringe of the city. He is fourteen years old. He has one older brother and one older sister. His father is employed at the nearby factory as a blue collar worker. Roy lives in a small, but comfortable, house. His family does not have many luxuries, but their needs are well satisfied. His parents are deeply religious and take Roy to church with them twice on Sunday and again on Wednesday evening. His father is a veteran and proudly displays several medals. He also belongs to the local VFW. Roy's parents spend much time with their children. He often hears them talk about how the hippies and the minority groups are taking over the country.

All three of these young people attend the same school and most of the same classes. Roy walks three blocks to school, but both Liza and Kevin ride the bus. Consider these questions and try to formulate some answers to them in your own mind.

1. How are all three of these young people alike?
2. How are they different?
3. What social forces have played a significant part in their lives?
4. How can the school curriculum plan for meeting the needs of these students, considering the social setting from which they come?
5. How would you, as the teacher of these three students, deal with the similarities and differences they bring from diverse social backgrounds?

It is obvious that each person is unique in the way that social forces have affected his life, and the school curriculum is challenged to deal with that individuality. But the curriculum is also asked to meet the needs of the total society. This problem can be seen as you consider the following questions:

1. How actively involved should the school become in dealing with social forces? (Should the faculty lead the students in picket lines?)
2. What percentage of the curriculum should be devoted to learning about and discussing social issues?
3. How should the school respond to parents who feel that the curriculum is either overemphasizing or underemphasizing particular social issues?

We must formulate curricula and plan teaching that takes into account the preceding points. One suggestion is now offered to get you started in that direction. One key word suggests something that the school and its educators must have in order to deal with social forces; that word is AWARENESS. The point is somewhat general, but it surely must be the starting place. The school and its faculty should know and understand intimately the social setting of the surrounding community and each teacher should make a strong effort to know and understand each of his students. If such awareness is not evident, it is not likely that positive, constructive action can be taken. Do you agree?

OBJECTIVES

Your objectives in studying social forces as one of the bases of curriculum planning should be as follows:

1. To be able to analyze a curriculum plan with respect to its relationships to current social forces and problems.
2. To be able to suggest changes and improvements in a curriculum plan that are based on an understanding of current social forces.
3. To be able to consider and use social forces and community influences in planning for teaching.

PREASSESSMENT

The purpose of the preassessment is to enable you to determine whether you already possess the performance competencies in curriculum planning that are listed under "objectives," above.

1. List no more than ten social forces that have implications for planning the curriculum of the public schools of today. For example, rapid population growth is said to have meaning for curriculum planning. It is assumed that this will be your own list and that it may not have precisely the same social forces as those listed in the preceding Rationale.
2. Taking each of the social forces you have listed, tell how you believe it should influence or change curriculum planning and planning for teaching in the 1970s.
3. Select any curriculum plan of your choice, at any school level, and examine it in the light of the social forces you have selected. This could be done by visiting and studying a school or by analyzing a written statement regarding the school's program or the instruction in one classroom. You might choose some part of the school's curriculum, such as the science curriculum, if you prefer to do so.
4. Suggest improvements or changes in the curriculum plan as a result of your analysis in number 3.

Do not be surprised if the curriculum plan of your choice does not appear to consider social forces. Many curriculum plans don't. Suggest improvements in the planning on the basis of social forces that you believe should be considered in today's curriculum.

In answering number 3 of the preassessment, you might choose to consider the use of social forces in the curriculum described in "High School With No Walls," by Henry S. Resnik. Or you might consider "An Innovative High School in a Midwestern Suburb," by Bill Ray Lewis. Both of these articles are in Section 8.

LEARNING ACTIVITIES

Articles in this section will assist you in defining the current social forces of importance in curriculum planning. They may cause you to ask whether a curriculum focused only on planning for *experiences in schools* can adequately meet the needs of learners who must cope with many social forces outside the school.

Other learning alternatives are suggested at the end of this section.

POSTASSESSMENT

After attempting the preassessment you may do *one or more* of the following:

1. See your instructor to determine whether he believes that you are ready for a postassessment evaluation on social forces and the curriculum. Most students will need further work on this curriculum base.
2. Read the articles on social forces in this section and try to determine how the social forces being discussed in each article should be considered in curriculum planning and teaching.
3. Choose additional activities and readings or films and videotapes from those listed at the end of this section.
4. Look for other films, books, or articles on social forces in your library or media center.
5. With your fellow students, discuss the reading you have done and the films you have viewed. The key questions: How should the social forces you've studied affect a school's curriculum? How should they be considered in planning for teaching?
6. When you are ready, ask your instructor for advice on a suitable postassessment for you for this topic. Satisfactory completion of number 2 under Problems and Projects at the end of this section might be one possibility. Or written completion of the preassessment for this section, after completing other learning activities, might be a satsifactory postassessment. Consult your instructor about this. Determine whether you can do either or both of these activities before seeing the instructor.

Up Against the Corporate Wall

Ralph Nader

A popular American myth is that progress and efficiency are linked to size. Business corporations have interpreted this to mean that the bigger the corporation, the better. Consequently, ever greater expansion has been one of their most cherished goals, as is seen by the establishment of giant conglomerates over the past two decades. This has led to an alarming concentration of economic power.

From *AAUW Journal,* LXV, no. 5 (April 1972): 3–6. Used by permission of the author and the publisher.

Today, some 200 corporations dominate the American economy. Unlike the trusts of the turn of the century, modern conglomerates control not just a single industry but dominate several. Often the industries within a single conglomerate are vastly different. They may range from the manufacture of aircraft parts to soda crackers.

Guided by the concept of "synergism," which holds that greater business efficiency is achieved through cooperation rather than competition among companies (or that the whole is greater than the sum of its parts), the giants have swallowed up smaller companies. At the same time, they have rationalized their actions to the public with the argument that a larger corporation provides more services at lower prices. Corporate executives further claim that only giant corporations can properly utilize the fruits of modern technology. The facts prove otherwise. Several studies conclusively show that modern technological innovation not only does not need giantism but can actually be thwarted by it. Unless prodded by competition, highly concentrated industries tend to resist the applications of technology if they do not show an immediate and clear profit, or if, as in the case of the internal combustion engine, they threaten to displace long invested capital and habits— even though the result is a cleaner, more efficient automobile engine. In recent years, some hints of the corporate reality have begun to reach public ears. Congressional hearings, court testimony and critical pieces by investigative reporters, not to mention the effects of inflation, have helped to discredit the mystique of synergism with its notion that conglomerates mean superior management. One recent investigation of the social, political and economic effects of acquisitions and mergers by giant corporations found that many of the claims made by conglomerates are fraudulent. Initiated by Emanuel Celler, chairman of the House Antitrust Subcommittee, the Celler Report, filling 703 pages and based on hearings that take up seven volumes, impressively documents the fact that large, inefficient companies often buy up smaller, more efficient ones with the result that the American public is forced to pay higher prices for products of lower quality.

HOW FREE IS THE CONSUMER?

Another myth holds that the individual consumer is free to make rational choices that will result in the provision of superior products and services in lieu of inferior products and services. But at the same time that they proclaim consumer sovereignty, corporations mount expensive advertising campaigns that are aimed at the deception of consumers. Instead of supplying accurate and essential information, advertising rests increasingly upon sloganeering and deliberate misinformation. The message that Ultra Brite "gives your mouth sex appeal," is not only irrelevant but perverts the message of the American Dental Association that "whitener" toothpastes may be too abrasive and may in fact cause decay.

Along with media advertising, the packaging revolution includes not only colorful styling but deliberate obfuscation of product quality, price and warranty. Its purpose is to subvert the consumer's choice of products on the basis of need, and to replace it with product buying tied to sex appeal or childish fantasies.

Even worse are the undetected, hidden hazards and frauds to which consumers are daily subjected. Because of the "marvels" of chemical doctoring and deep-freeze storage, for instance, the consumer can no longer depend on his sense of taste, smell, or sight to warn him of impurities. As a result, the public consumes large quantities of food containing harmful additives such as seasoning agents, preservatives, antibiotics and a supplementary battery of chemical adulterants. Add to this the recent barrage of facts about drug hazards, unsafe automobiles, vicious credit practices, insurance abuses, price-fixing and industrial pollution, and it becomes clear that the consumer is defenseless in the modern marketplace.

Two essential elements of a healthy enterprise system are a free market and competition, based on the consumer's knowledge of competing goods and services. Conglomerates, however, have effectively blunted the healthy forces of a freely competitive market economy—in part by absorbing or intimidating smaller competitors, and in part by engaging in secret deals and reciprocal favoritism. The result is a controlled market in place of a free one, and product and price-fixing in place of competition. The cost to consumers has been staggering. Not only are prices higher during periods of high demand and low supply, but they fail to go down as demand decreases and supply stays constant. Thus, corporate concentration subverts the "laws" of supply and demand, together with the usual tools for combating inflation, with the result that the nation is saddled with high unemployment, high taxes, high interest rates and inflation.

HOW INDEPENDENT IS THE GOVERNMENT?

A third myth is that the federal government acts as a countervailing force to corporate power. Certainly, there is a long record of legislation to set limits on such power. The need for consumer protection in the United States was first recognized in 1872 with the passage of the criminal fraud statute. In 1887, the Interstate Commerce Commission was created to regulate the railroads. In 1906, Upton Sinclair's novel *The Jungle* brought public attention to the need for regulation of packing plants and led to the Federal Meat Inspection Act. The Food and Drug Administration was created the same year, and the Federal Trade Commission was set up in 1915 to maintain "free competitive enterprise" and to prevent "unfair or deceptive trade practices." Following the stock market crash in the late 1920s, the Securities and Exchange Commission was founded to regulate the securities market. In addition, antitrust laws were designed to prevent the aggregation of economic and political power.

There are now about 40 government agencies and bureaus in this country, hundreds of laws, and a special assistant to the President for Consumer Affairs— all pledged to the consumers' interests. But the passage of a law or the creation of a regulatory agency does not by any means automatically assure the consumer of protection. On the contrary, it is now commonplace knowledge that many regulatory agencies have become apologists, if not overt supporters of the industries they are assigned to regulate, and have failed to enforce public laws.

Over the years, industries have learned how to "handle" their regulators. One device, political patronage, has consistently undermined local and state consumer protection agencies as well as federal agencies. Business lobbying— including campaign contributions, powerful law firms, trade and professional associations and public relations—has worked very effectively against vigorous enforcement. Finally, so many regulatory officials resign from their agencies to go into high-paying jobs in the industries they were once supposed to regulate that these government posts are viewed as on-the-job training by coldly realistic employees.

The evidence of favoritism shown by regulatory agencies to their respective industries is abundant. The Department of the Interior, for example, leases public land to the gas and oil industries at absurdly low prices; it further protects these industries by imposing rigid import quotas on less expensive oil from foreign countries that could save home owners and motorists $6 billion every year. And so it goes, for nearly every agency. Their failure is not so much due to outright corruption, though it certainly exists, as it is to the government's irresponsibility to the consumer. This irresponsibility becomes normal procedure whenever decision making is so far removed from any accountability for its consequences.

Since World War II, government contracts, particularly in the Department of Defense, have provided corporations with vast sums of public monies and capital equipment. Defense contracting has helped to create such giants as Lockheed, and to sustain others even when their own administrative mismanagement places them in economic peril. Subsidies, tax privileges and depletion allowances are still other ways in which government aids big business. In 1970, though Congress failed to provide a food stamp program to feed some of the nation's hungry and bickered with no result over a rat-control bill, it managed to vote $199.5 million in subsidies to shipbuilders, most of which are owned by conglomerates. Thus, the countervailing power of government turns out to be mostly an accommodating power that transfers the ill effects of corporate avarice and mismanagement to the point of least resistance—the consumer-citizen-taxpayer.

CORPORATE-INDUCED VIOLENCE

It is clear that regulatory agencies and antitrust laws have proven to be more hollow symbols than stalwart defenses of the American economy. In part this can be attributed to a national failure to make the necessary legal and moral distinctions between individual crimes and corporate crimes. (Crime statistics, in fact, almost wholly ignore corporate or business crime.)

The law determines responsibility for a crime on the basis of a cause and effect sequence, i.e., when A strikes B, A is held responsible. The law gets into difficulty, however, where the style of violence and the harm done are "invisible" or "silent." Much corporate-induced violence, such as pollution, comes under the heading of "silent" crime, but corporate power has effectively prevented its punishment. In some cases, legal accountability is hard to pinpoint, even when a crime is known. When dozens of industrial plants are spewing forth waste into the air and water, it is difficult to find out who is spewing what and in what quantity.

But even clear violations of existing laws go ignored and unenforced. Corporations daily commit acts that would be swiftly punished if committed by an individual, such as willful and knowing violations of pollution, drug, insurance, auto, tire, radiation and gas pipeline safety standards. Although such acts dwarf other crimes in terms of damage done and lives lost, they are usually not considered crimes under the relevant statutes. And even on the rare occasions in which the law is invoked against corporate violence, the penalty is applied to the corporate shell, not to the insulated executives who make corporate policy.

REFORM AND VIGILANT CITIZENSHIP

Clearly, a distinction must also be made between individual rights and corporate rights. A corporation, for example, does not have the same right to privacy that an individual does. Much information that should be made public is veiled behind the guise of "trade secrets" which usually turn out to be secrets not from competitors but from consumers. Secrecy has multiple uses for both business and government; since it has multiple uses, it has multiple supports to preserve it. Ironically, we have a burgeoning technology with many potential applications for the benefit of mankind. But it is dominated by the traditional holders of power. The computer, for example, is by all accounts the technology of the century. Since information these days is power, the computer should be the great equalizer, not a force toward greater concentration. But while credit associations and other government and corporate agencies make use of computerized dossiers on individuals, raising legitimate fears about the invasion of privacy, the system of citizen access to governmental and corporate information gets steadily worse.

Computerized data banks for consumers can have a solid impact for corporate reform by encouraging competition based on quality. At present, the capability for gathering and providing information about products and services for consumers is about as primitive as the Gutenberg printing press.

The central question is, of course, what can be done to break up the power of conglomerates and redirect their resources to serve consumer interests? In addition to vigorous antitrust enforcement, the replacement of state chartering of corporations with federal chartering is a first step. Abused for over a century, state chartering has now reached the point where states, following the examples of Delaware and New Jersey, compete with one another to see whose tax laws can be the most lax. A rewriting of the rules at the federal level can make the grant of corporate status conditional on a responsiveness to well-defined public interest. It could also establish mechanisms for accountability and procedures for detailed disclosure. Moreover, it would clarify the appropriate roles of government and corporations and limit the scope of conglomerate or monopolistic companies.

But even if solid structural changes and effective reforms are forthcoming, it will only be a beginning. A far more important move is toward the development of a new kind of vigilant citizenship. Only through a continual assertion and defense of individual rights and responsibilities on the part of professionals and laymen working both within the corporation and outside will there be some assurance that the public interest will be served.

The Roots of Lawlessness

Henry Steele Commager

It was in 1838 that the young Abraham Lincoln—he was not yet twenty-nine—delivered an address at Springfield, Illinois, on "The Perpetuation of Our Political Institutions." What he had to say is curiously relevant today. Like many of us, Lincoln was by no means sure that our institutions could be perpetuated; unlike some of us, he was convinced that they should be.

What, after all, threatened American political institutions? There was no threat from outside, for "all the armies of Europe, Asia, and Africa combined could not by force take a drink from the Ohio or make a track on the Blue Ridge in a thousand years." No, the danger was from within. "If destruction be our lot, we must ourselves be its author and finisher. As a nation of freemen, we must live through all time or die by suicide."

This, Lincoln asserted, was not outside the realm of possibility; as he looked about him, he saw everywhere a lawlessness that, if persisted in, would surely destroy both law and Constitution and eventually the nation itself. In the end, lawlessness *did* do that—lawlessness in official guise that refused to abide by the Constitutional processes of election or by the will of the Constitutional majority. It was to be Lincoln's fate to be called upon to frustrate that lawless attack on the nation, and to be remembered as the savior of the Union. And it has been our fate to be so bemused by that particular threat to unity—the threat of sectional fragmentation—that we have failed to appreciate the danger that so deeply disturbed Lincoln at the threshold of his political career.

The explanation of our confusion is rooted in history. The United States invented, or developed, a new kind of nationalism, one that differed in important ways from the nationalism that flourished in the Old World. One difference was the enormous emphasis that Americans, from the beginning, put on territory and the extent to which American nationalism came to be bound up with the acquisition of all the territory west to the Pacific and with the notion of territorial integrity on a continental scale. The idea that a nation should "round out" its territory, or take over all unoccupied territory, was not prominent in the nationalism of the Old World. Territory there, after all, was pretty well pre-empted, and there was no compelling urge to acquire neighboring land for its own sake.

In the Old World, threats to unity had been, for the most part, dynastic or religious rather than territorial. As proximity did not dictate assimilation, distance did not require separation. But in America space and distance appeared to pose

From *Saturday Review*, LIV, no. 7 (February 13, 1971):17–19, 63–64. Copyright 1971 Saturday Review, Inc. Used by permission of the author and the publisher.

threats to the Union from the beginning. Some of the Founding Fathers, to be sure, continued to think of unity and disunion in Old World terms of interests and factions, rather than in terms of territory. This was perhaps because they had little choice in the matter or none that they could publicly acknowledge, for the United States was born the largest nation in the Western world, and the Framers had to put a good face on the matter. But Europeans generally, and some Americans, long familiar with Montesquieu's dictum that, while a republic could flourish in a small territory, a large territory required a despotism, assumed that the new United States, with boundaries so extensive, could not survive.

Jefferson and his associates were determined to prove Montesquieu mistaken. From the beginning, they formulated a counter-argument that size would strengthen rather than weaken the nation. Brushing aside the warnings of such men as Gouverneur Morris, they boldly added new states west of the Alleghenies. They made the Louisiana Purchase, seized West Florida, and looked with confidence to acquiring all the territory west to the Pacific; thus, the Lewis and Clark expedition into foreign territory, something we would not tolerate today in our territory. Territorial expansion and integrity became a prime test of the American experiment, and within a few years what had been a test became, no less, a providential command: Manifest Destiny. From this flowed naturally the principle that the proof of union was territorial, and the threat to union territorial.

A second American contribution to the ideology of nationalism was, in time, to become its most prominent characteristic: the notion that national unity required not merely territorial unity but social and cultural. In the Old World, the only cultural unity that had any meaning was religious: The principle *Cuius regio eius religio* was dictated by the fact that the ruler's religion determined the religion of the state. But class distinctions were taken for granted, as were profound differences in cultural and social habits—in speech, for example, or in such simple things as food and drink and dress and games.

Americans changed this pattern around. They rejected the principle of religious unity—doubtless in large part because they had no alternative—and then substituted cultural for religious unity. Americans were not expected to pray alike, but they were expected to talk alike, dress alike, work alike, profess the same moral code, and subscribe to the same legal code. Eventually, as we know, they were expected to eat the same food, drink the same liquors, play the same games, read the same journals, watch the same television programs, and even have the same political ideas—expectations never seriously entertained by, say, German or Italian nationalists.

American nationalism thus became, at a very early stage, a self-conscious affair of imposing unity upon a vast territory, a heterogeneous population, and a miscellaneous culture. Because there was indeed land enough to absorb some forty million immigrants, because those immigrants were so heterogeneous that (with the exception of the Germans and, in modern times, the Negroes) they were unable to maintain a cultural identity counter to the prevailing American culture, and because, in provisions for naturalization and opportunities for active participation, the political system was the most hospitable of any in the world, an artificial unity became, in time, a real unity. Americans managed to achieve a single language with fewer deviations than were to be found in England, Germany, or Italy; to achieve a common education—not universal, to be sure, but

more nearly universal than elsewhere in the nineteenth-c
common political system, each state like every other s
to conjure up a common history and a common past.

The threat to union, as Lincoln saw it in 1838, was
or social or even moral; it was quite simply the "spiri
as *Notes on Virginia* (1782), Thomas Jefferson had c
for his country when he reflected that "God is just a
forever," and throughout his life Jefferson saw slavery as a ....
this he was more farsighted than most. The threat to union posed by slavery
was unprecedented; it was a product of that elementary fact by now so familiar
that we take it for granted: that deep economic, social, and moral differences
assumed a geographical pattern, and that the American Constitutional system,
namely federalism, permitted them to take a political pattern as well. As it happened, the sectional pattern of slavery was in mortal conflict with a very different
sectional pattern, and it was this conflict that proved in the end fatal to the thrust
for Southern independence: the sectionalism created by the Mississippi River and
its tributaries. That, as it turned out, was the decisive fact that preserved the
Union; when, in the summer of 1863, Lincoln wrote that "the signs look better,"
what he noted first was that "the Father of Waters goes again unvexed to the
sea."

Suppose slavery had rooted itself vertically in the Mississippi Valley rather
than horizontally across the South from the Atlantic to Texas. That would have
given sectionalism a more rational base than it had in the South—a base that in
all likelihood would have been impregnable.

Here we have one of the assumptions about American history that gets in
the way of an appreciation of our distinctive characteristics. Because thirteen
American states, hugging the Atlantic seaboard, became a single nation spanning
a continent, we either take American unity for granted or consider fragmentation
only in terms of the experiment in Southern nationalism, which misfired. But
there was nothing foreordained about the triumph of unity. Why did not the
vast American territory between Canada and the Gulf of Mexico go the way of
Latin America, which, with a common religion, language, and territory, nevertheless fragmented into numerous independent states?

The spectacular nature of the American achievement has bemused almost
all students of American nationalism and dictated most interpretations of the
problem of American unity. The transcendent fact of slavery and of the Negro
—so largely responsible for creating a sectionalism that did not yield to the
ameliorating influences of economy, social mobility, cultural uniformity, and
political compromise—has distracted our attention from other threats, if not to
union then to unity. Because we had a civil war, precipitated by sectional fragmentation, we did not imagine that we could have a revolution based on social
fragmentation.

We are tempted to say of Lincoln's Springfield address that it was short-
sighted of him not to have seen that the threats to union were slavery and sectionalism—something he learned, in time. We should say rather that he was
farsighted in imagining the possibility of a very different threat to union: an
internal dissension and lawlessness that bespoke a breakdown in cultural and moral
unity. This is what confronts us today: blacks against whites, old against young,

against eggheads, militarists against doves, the cities against the suburbs countryside—hostilities that more and more frequently erupt into open ice.

Two considerations warrant attention. First, that what Lincoln described was in fact normal—we have always been a lawless and a violent people. Thus, our almost unbroken record of violence against the Indians and all others who got in our way—the Spaniards in the Floridas, the Mexicans in Texas; the violence of the vigilantes on a hundred frontiers; the pervasive violence of slavery (a "perpetual exercise," Jefferson called it, "of the most boisterous passions"); the lawlessness of the Ku Klux Klan during Reconstruction and after; and of scores of race riots from those of New Orleans in the 1860s to those of Chicago in 1919. Yet, all this violence, shocking as it doubtless was, no more threatened the fabric of our society or the integrity of the Union than did the lawlessness of Prohibition back in the Twenties. The explanation for this is to be found in the embarrassing fact that most of it was official, quasi-official, or countenanced by public opinion: exterminating the Indian; flogging the slave; lynching the outlaw; exploiting women and children in textile mills and sweatshops; hiring Pinkertons to shoot down strikers; condemning immigrants to fetid ghettos; punishing Negroes who tried to exercise their civil or political rights. Most of this was socially acceptable —or at least not wholly unacceptable—just as so much of our current violence is socially acceptable: the 50,000 automobile deaths every year; the mortality rate for Negro babies twice that for white; the deaths from cancer induced by cigarettes or by air pollution; the sadism of our penal system and the horrors of our prisons; the violence of the police against what Theodore Parker called the "perishing and dangerous classes of society."

What we have now is the emergence of violence that is not acceptable either to the Establishment, which is frightened and alarmed, or to the victims of the Establishment, who are no longer submissive and who are numerous and powerful. This is the now familiar "crime in the streets," or it is the revolt of the young against the economy, the politics, and the wars of the established order, or it is the convulsive reaction of the blacks to a century of injustice. But now, too, official violence is no longer acceptable to its victims—or to their ever more numerous sympathizers: the violence of great corporations and of government itself against the natural resources of the nation; the long-drawn-out violence of the white majority against Negroes and other minorities; the violence of the police and the National Guard against the young; the massive and never-ending violence of the military against the peoples of Vietnam and Cambodia. These acts can no longer be absorbed by large segments of our society. It is this new polarization that threatens the body politic and the social fabric much as religious dissent threatened them in the Europe of the sixteenth and seventeenth centuries.

A second consideration is this: The center of gravity has shifted from "obedience" to "enforcement." This shift in vocabulary is doubtless unconscious but nonetheless revealing. Obedience is the vocabulary of democracy, for it recognizes that the responsibility for the commonwealth is in the people and appeals to the people to recognize and fulfill their responsibility. Enforcement is the language of authority prepared to impose its will on the people. Lincoln knew instinctively that a democracy flourishes when men obey and revere the law; he did not invoke the language of authority. We are no longer confident of the virtue or good will of the people; so it is natural that we fall back on force. The resort to lawless force

—by the Weathermen, the Black Panthers, the Ku Klux Klan, the hardhats; by the police in Chicago; by the National Guard at Orangeburg, South Carolina, and Kent, Ohio; or by highway police at Jackson, Mississippi—is a confession that both the people and their government have lost faith in the law, and that the political and social fabric that has held our society together is unraveling: "By such examples," said Lincoln at Springfield, "the lawless in spirit are encouraged to become lawless in practice."

It has long been our boast—repeated by the President's Commission on Violence—that notwithstanding our lengthy history of violence we have never had a "revolution," and that our political system appears to be more stable than those of other nations. Our only real revolution took a sectional pattern and was not called revolution but rebellion; since it was rationalized by high-minded rhetoric, led by honorable men, and fought with gallantry, it speedily took on an aura of respectability, and to this day Southerners who would be outraged by the display of the red flag of rebellion proudly wave the Stars and Bars of rebellion.

Thus, like most of our violence, violence against the Constitution and the Union, and by implication against the blacks who were to be kept in slavery, is socially approved. Where such violence has been dramatic (as in lynching or industrial warfare), it has not been widespread or prolonged; where it has been widespread and prolonged (as in slavery and the persistent humiliation of the Negro), it has not been dramatic. Where its victims were desperate, they were not numerous enough or strong enough to revolt; where they were numerous (never strong), they did not appear to be desperate, and it was easy to ignore their despair. Now this situation is changing. Lawlessness is more pervasive than ever; the sense of outrage against the malpractices of those in power is more widespread and articulate; and the divisions in society are both deeper and more diverse, and the response to them more intractable.

One explanation of our current malaise is that it seems to belong to the Old World pattern rather than that of the New. Much of the rhetoric of the conflict between generations is that of class or religious wars—class war on the part of, let us say, Vice President Agnew; religious protest on the part of Professor Charles Reich and those involved in what he calls "the greening of America." If this is so, it goes far toward explaining some of our current confusion and blundering: the almost convulsive efforts to distract attention from the genuine problems of environment, social injustice, and war, and to fasten it on such phony issues as campus unrest or social permissiveness or pornography. What this implies is ominous: Our society is not prepared, either by history or philosophy, for the kind of lawlessness and violence and alienation that now afflict us.

Why is this so ominous?

Traditionally, our federal system could and did absorb regionalism and particularism, or channel these into political conduits. More accurately than in any other political system, our representatives represent geographical places—a specific Congressional district or a state—and our parties, too, are organized atop and through states. Our system is not designed to absorb or to dissipate such internal animosities as those of class against class, race against race, or generation against generation.

A people confident of progress, with a social philosophy that assumed that what counted most was children and that took for granted that each new generation would be bigger, stronger, brighter, and better educated than its predecessor, could afford to indulge the young. "Permissiveness" is not an invention of Dr. Spock but of the first settlers in America. Today, a people that has lost faith in progress and in the future, and that has lost confidence in the ameliorating influence of education, indulges instead in convulsive counter-attacks upon the young.

A nation with, in Jefferson's glowing words, "land enough for our descendants to the thousandth and thousandth generation" could indulge itself in reckless exploitation of that land—the mining of natural resources, the destruction of deer and bison and beavers, of the birds in the skies and the fish in the streams, and could even (this was a risky business from the beginning) afford to ignore its fiduciary obligations to coming generations without exciting dangerous resentment. But a nation of more than two hundred million, working through giant corporations and giant governments that ravage, pollute, and destroy on a scale heretofore unimagined, cannot afford such self-indulgence. Nor can it persist in its habit of violating its fiduciary obligations without outraging those who are its legal and moral legatees.

A nation that had more and better land available for its people than any other in history and that, for the first time, equated civilization with the pastoral life and exalted the farmer over the denizen of the city could take urban development in its stride, confident that the city would never get the upper hand, as it were. Modern America seems wholly unable to adapt its institutions or its psychology to massive urbanization, but proceeds instead to the fateful policy of reducing its farm population to a fraction and, at the same time, destroying its cities and turning them into ghettos that are breeding places for crime and violence.

A system that maintained and respected the principle of the superiority of the civil power over that of the military could afford to fight even such great conflicts as the Civil War, the First World War, and the Second World War without danger to its Constitution or its moral character. It cannot absorb the kind of war we are now fighting in Southeast Asia without irreparable damage to its moral values, nor can it exercise power on a world scale without moving the military to the center of power.

No nation could afford slavery, certainly not one that thought itself dedicated to equality and justice. The issue of slavery tore the nation asunder and left wounds still unhealed. Here is our greatest failure: that we destroyed slavery but not racism, promised legal equality but retained a dual citizenship, did away with legal exploitation of a whole race but substituted for it an economic exploitation almost as cruel. And this political and legal failure reflects a deeper psychological and moral failure.

Unlike some of our contemporary politicians, Lincoln was not content with decrying lawlessness. He inquired into its causes and, less perspicaciously, into its cure. In this inquiry, he identified two explanations that illuminated the problem. These—translated into modern vocabulary—are the decline of the sense of fiduciary obligation and the evaporation of political resourcefulness and creativity. Both are still with us.

No one who immerses himself in the writings of the Revolutionary generation—a generation still in command when Lincoln was born—can doubt that the sense of obligation to posterity was pervasive and lively. Recall Tom Paine's plea for independence: " 'Tis not the concern of a day, a year, or an age; *Posterity* are virtually involved in the contest and will be . . . affected to the end of time." Or John Adam's moving letter to his beloved Abigail when he had signed the Declaration of Independence: "Through all the gloom I can see the rays of ravishing light and glory. *Posterity* will triumph in this day's transaction." Or Dr. Benjamin Rush's confession, after his signing, that "I was animated constantly by a belief that I was acting for the benefit of the whole world and of future ages." So were they all.

The decline of the awareness of posterity and of the fiduciary principle is a complex phenomenon not unconnected with the hostility to the young that animates many older Americans today. It is to be explained, in part, by the concept of an equality that had to be vindicated by each individual; in part, by the fragmentation of the Old World concepts of family and community relationships, which was an almost inevitable consequence of the uprooting from the Old World and the transplanting to the New; in part, by the seeming infinity of resources and the seeming advantages of rapid exploitation and rapid aggrandizement; in part, by the weakness of governmental and institutional controls; in part, by the ostentatious potentialities of industry and technology, the advent of which coincided with the emergence of nationalism in the United States; and, in part, by the triumph of private enterprise over public.

However complex the explanation, the fact is simple enough: We have wasted our natural resources more recklessly than has any other people in modern history and are persisting in this waste and destruction even though we are fully aware that our children will pay for our folly and our greed.

Lincoln's second explanation—if it can be called that—was that we had suffered a decline of the creativity and resourcefulness that had been the special distinction of the Founding Fathers. "The field of glory is harvested," he said, "the crop is already appropriated." Other leaders would emerge, no doubt, and would "seek regions hitherto unexplored." At a time when Martin Van Buren was in the White House, to be succeeded by Harrison, Tylor, Polk, Taylor, Fillmore, Pierce, and Buchanan, that expectation doubtless represented the triumph of hope over history. But the decline of political creativity and leadership was not confined to this somewhat dismal period of our history; it has persisted into our own day. We can no more afford it than could Lincoln's generation. At a time when the white population of English America was less than three million, it produced Franklin and Washington, Jefferson and Madison, John Adams and Hamilton, John Jay and James Wilson, George Wythe and John Marshall, and Tom Paine, who emerged, first, in America. We have not done that well since.

Even more arresting is the undeniable fact that this Revolutionary generation produced not only many of our major leaders but all of our major political institutions, among them federalism, the Constitutional convention, the Bill of Rights, the effective separation of powers, judicial review, the new colonial system, the political party. It is no exaggeration to say that we have been living on that political capital ever since.

Here again the explanation is obscure. There is the consoling consideration that the Founding Fathers did the job so well that it did not need to be done over; the depressing consideration that American talent has gone, for the past century or so, more into private than into public enterprise; and the sobering consideration that at a time when our chief preoccupation appears to be with extension of power rather than with wise application of resources, those "regions hitherto unexplored" appear to be in the global arena rather than the domestic. Whatever the explanation, lack of leadership is the most prominent feature on our political landscape, and lack of creativity the most striking characteristic of our political life.

It is still true that, "if destruction be our lot, we must ourselves be its author" —that the danger is not from without but from within. But

> . . . passions spin the plot;
> We are betrayed by what is false within.

For, paradoxically, the danger from within is rooted in and precipitated by foreign adventures that we seem unable either to understand or to control. We have not been attacked from Latin America or from Asia; we have attacked ourselves by our own ventures into these areas.

The problem Lincoln faced in 1838 is with us once again: the breakdown of the social fabric and its overt expression in the breakdown of the law. Lincoln's solution, if greatly oversimplified, is still valid: reverence for the law. A people will revere the law when it is just and is seen to be just. But no matter how many litanies we intone, we will not induce our people to obey laws that those in authority do not themselves obey. The most striking feature of lawlessness in America today is that it is encouraged by public examples. It is no use telling a Mississippi Negro to revere the law that is palpably an instrument of injustice to him and his race. It is no use exhorting the young to obey the law when most of the major institutions of our society—the great corporations, the powerful trade unions, the very instruments of government—flout the law whenever it gets in their way. It is of little use to admonish a young man about to be drafted to revere the law when he knows that he is to be an instrument for the violation of international law on a massive scale by his own government. It is futile to celebrate the rule of law and the sanctity of life when our own armies engage in ghoulish "body counts," burn unoffending villages, and massacre civilians. While governments, corporations, and respectable elements in our society not only countenance lawlessness and violence but actively engage in it, violence will spread and lawlessness will flourish. We are betrayed by what is false within.

After the Population Explosion

Harrison Brown

At one time or another almost all of us have asked: How many human beings can the Earth support? When this question is put to me, I find it necessary to

From *Saturday Review*, LIV, no. 26 (June 26, 1971):11–13, 29. Copyright 1971 Saturday Review, Inc. Used by permission of the author and publisher.

respond with another question: In what kind of world are you willing to live? In the eyes of those who care about their environment, we have perhaps already passed the limits of growth. In the eyes of those who don't care how they live or what dangers they create for posterity, the limits of growth lie far ahead.

The populations of all biological species are limited by environmental factors, and man's is no exception. Food supplies and the presence of predators are of prime importance. When two rabbits of opposite sex are placed in a fenced-in field of grass, they will go forth and multiply, but the population will eventually be limited by the grass supply. If predators are placed in the field, the rabbit population will either stabilize at a new level or possibly become extinct. Given no predators and no restrictions on food, but circumscribed space, the number of rabbits will still be limited, either by the psychological and biological effects of overcrowding, or by being buried in their own refuse.

When man, endowed with the power of conceptual thought, appeared upon the Earth scene, something new was introduced into the evolutionary process. Biological evolution, which had dominated all living species for billions of years, gave way to cultural evolution. As man gradually learned how to control various elements of his environment, he succeeded in modifying a number of the factors that limited his population. Clothing, fire, and crude shelters extended the range of habitable climate. Tools of increasing sophistication helped man gather edible vegetation, hunt animals more effectively, and protect himself from predators.

But no matter how effective the tools, there is a limit to the number of food gatherers who can inhabit a given area of land. One cannot kill more animals than are born or pick more fruit than trees bear. The maximum population of a worldwide food-gathering society was about ten million persons. Once that level was reached, numerous cultural patterns emerged that caused worldwide birth rates and death rates to become equal. In some societies, the natural death rate was elevated by malnutrition and disease; in others, the death rate was increased artificially by such practices as infanticide or the waging of war. In some cases, certain sex taboos and rituals appear to have lowered the birth rate. But, however birth and death rates came into balance, we can be confident that for a long time prior to the agricultural revolution the human population remained virtually constant.

With the introduction of agriculture about 10,000 years ago, the levels of population that had been imposed by limited supplies of food were raised significantly. Even in the earliest agricultural societies, several hundred times as much food could be produced from a given area of fertile land than could be collected by food gatherers. As the technology of agriculture spread, population grew rapidly. This new technology dramatically affected the entire fabric of human culture. Man gave up the nomad life and settled in villages, some of which became cities. Sufficient food could be grown to make it possible for about 10 percent of the population to engage in activities other than farming.

The development of iron technology and improved transportation accelerated the spread of this peasant-village culture. Indeed, had new technological developments ceased to appear after 1700, it is nevertheless likely that the peasant-village culture would have spread to all inhabitable parts of the Earth, eventually to reach a level of roughly five billion persons, some 500 million of whom would live in cities. But long before the population had reached anything close to that level, the emergence of new technologies leading up to the Industrial Revolution markedly changed the course of history. The steam engine for the first time gave man a means of concentrating enormous quantities of inanimate mechanical energy, and the newly found power was quickly applied.

During the nineteenth century in western Europe, improved transportation, increased food supplies, and a generally improved environment decreased the morbidity of a number of infectious diseases and virtually eliminated the large fluctuations in mortality rates that had been so characteristic of the seventeenth and eighteenth centuries. As mortality rates declined and the birth rate remained unchanged, populations in these areas increased rapidly. But as industrialization spread, a multiplicity of factors combined to lessen the desirability of large families. After about 1870, the size of families decreased, at first slowly and then more rapidly; eventually, the rate of population growth declined.

During the nineteenth and early twentieth centuries, some of the new technologies were gradually transplanted to the non-industrialized parts of the world, but in a very one-sided manner. Death rates were reduced appreciably, and, with birth rates unchanged, populations in these poorer countries increased rapidly and are still growing.

In spite of the fact that the annual rate of population growth in the industrialized countries has dropped to less than 1 percent, the worldwide rate is now close to 2 percent, the highest it has ever been. This rate represents a doubling of population about every thirty-five years. The human population is now 3.5 billion and at the present rate of increase is destined to reach 6.5 billion by the turn of the century and ten billion fifty years from now. Beyond that point, how much further can population grow?

An analysis of modern technology's potential makes its clear that from a long-range, theoretical point of view, food supplies need no longer be the primary factor limiting population growth. Today nearly 10 percent of the land area of the Earth, or about 3.5 billion acres, is under cultivation. It is estimated that with sufficient effort about fifteen billion acres of land could be placed under cultivation —some four times the present area. Such a move would require prodigious effort and investment and would necessitate the use of substantial quantities of desalinated water reclaimed from the sea. Given abundant energy resources, however, it now appears that in principle this can be done economically.

Large as the potential is for increasing the area of agricultural land, the increases in yield that can be obtained through fertilizers, application of supplementary water, and the use of new high-yielding varieties of cereals are even more impressive. Whereas in the past the growth of plants was circumscribed by the availability of nutrients and water, this need no longer be true. Using our new agricultural technology, solar energy can be converted into food with a high degree of efficiency, and even on the world's presently cultivated lands several times as much food can be produced each year than is now being grown.

To accomplish these objectives, however, an enormous amount of industrialization will be required. Fertilizers must be produced; thus, phosphate rock must be mined and processed, and nitrogen fixation plants must be built. Pesticides and herbicides are needed; thus, chemical plants must be built. All this requires steel and concrete, highways, railroads, and trucks. To be sure, the people of India, for example, might not need to attain Japan's level of industrialization in order to obtain Japanese levels of crop yield (which are about the highest in the world), but they will nevertheless need a level of industrialization that turns out to be surprisingly high.

Colin Clark, the director of the Agricultural Economics Research Institute of Oxford and a noted enthusiast for large populations, estimates that, given this new agricultural land and a level of industrialization sufficiently high to apply Japanese standards of farming, close to thirty billion persons could be supported on a Western European diet. Were people to content themselves with a Japanese diet, which contains little animal protein, he estimates that 100 billion persons could be supported.

To those who feel that life under such circumstances might be rather crowded, I should like to point out that even at the higher population level, the mean density of human beings over the land areas of the Earth would be no more than that which exists today in the belt along the Eastern Seaboard between Boston and Washington, D.C., where the average density is now 2,000 persons per square mile and where many people live quite comfortably. After all, Hong Kong has a population density of about 13,000 persons per square mile (nearly six times greater), and I understand that there are numerous happy people there.

Of course, such a society would need to expend a great deal of energy in order to manufacture, transport, and distribute the fertilizers, pesticides, herbicides, water, foodstuffs, and countless associated raw materials and products that would be necessary.

In the United States we currently consume energy equivalent to the burning of twelve-and-a-half short tons of coal per person per year. This quantity is bound to increase in the future as we find it necessary to process lower-grade ores, as we expend greater effort on controlling pollution (which would otherwise increase enormously), and as we recover additional quantities of potable water from the sea. Dr. Alvin Weinberg, director of the Oak Ridge National Laboratory, and his associates estimate that such activities will cost several additional tons of coal per person per year, and they suggest that for safety we budget twenty-five tons of coal per person per year in order to maintain our present material standard of living. Since we are a magnanimous people, we would not tolerate a double standard of living (a rich one for us and a poor one for others); so I will assume that this per capita level of energy expenditure will be characteristic of the world as a whole.

It has been estimated that the world's total usable coal reserve is on the order of 7,600 billion tons. This amount would last a population of thirty billion persons only ten years and a population of 100 billion only three years. Clearly, long before such population levels are reached, man must look elsewhere for his energy supplies.

Fortunately, technology once again gets us out of our difficulty, for nuclear fuels are available to us in virtually limitless quantities in the form of uranium and thorium for fission, and possibly in the form of deuterium for fusion. The Conway granite in New Hampshire could alone provide fuel for a population of twenty billion persons for 200 years. When we run out of high-grade granites, we can move on to process low-grade granites. Waste rock can be dumped into the holes from which it came and can be used to create new land areas on bays and on the continental shelf. Waste fission products can be stored in old salt mines.

23

Actually, a major shift to nuclear fuel might well be necessary long before our supplies of fossil fuels are exhausted. The carbon dioxide concentration in our atmosphere is rapidly increasing as a result of our burning of coal, petroleum, and natural gas, and it is destined to increase still more rapidly in the future. More than likely, any such increase will have a deleterious effect upon our climate, and if this turns out to be the case, use of those fuels will probably be restricted.

Thus, we see that in theory there should be little difficulty in feeding a world population of thirty billion or even 100 billion persons and in providing it with the necessities of life. But can we go even further?

With respect to food, once again technology can come to our rescue, for we have vast areas of the seas to fertilize and farm. Even more important, we will be able to produce synthetic foods in quantity. The constituents of our common oils and fats can already be manufactured on a substantial scale for human consumption and animal feeds. In the not too distant future, we should be able to synthetically produce complete, wholesome foods, thus bypassing the rather cumbersome process of photosynthesis.

Far more difficult than the task of feeding people will be that of cooling the Earth, of dissipating the heat generated by nuclear power plants. It has been suggested that if we were to limit our total energy generation to no more than 5 percent of the incident solar radiation, little harm would be done. The mean surface temperature of the Earth would rise by about 6 degrees F. A temperature rise much greater than this could be extremely dangerous and should not be permitted until we have learned more about the behavior of our ocean/atmosphere system.

Of course, there will be local heating problems in the vicinity of the power stations. Dr. Weinberg suggests a system of "nuclear parks," each producing about forty million kilowatts of electricity and located on the coast or offshore. A population of 333 billion persons would require 65,000 such parks. The continental United States, with a projected population of close to twenty-five billion persons, would require nearly 5,000 parks spaced at twenty-mile intervals along its coastline.

Again, I want to allay the fears of those who worry about crowding. A population of 333 billion spread uniformly over the land areas of the Earth would give up a population density of only 6,000 persons per square mile, which, after all, is only somewhat greater than the population density in the city of Los Angeles. Just imagine the thrill of flying from Los Angeles to New York and having the landscape look like Los Angeles all the way. Imagine the excitement of driving from Los Angeles to New York on a Santa Monica Freeway 2,800 miles long.

A few years ago Dr. J. H. Fremlin of the University of Birmingham analyzed the problem of population density and concluded that several stages of development might be possible beyond the several-hundred-billion-person level of population. He conceives of hermetically sealing the outer surface of the planet and of using pumps to transfer heat to the solid outer skin from which it would be radiated directly into space. Combining this with a roof over the oceans to prevent excessive evaporation of water and to provide additional living space, he feels it would be possible to accommodate about 100 persons per square yard, thus giving a total population of about sixty million billion persons. But, frankly, I consider this proposal visionary. Being basically conservative, I doubt that the human population will ever get much above the 333-billion-person level.

Now some readers might be thinking that I am writing nonsense, and they are right. My facts are correct; the conclusions I have drawn from those facts are correct. Yet, I have truthfully been writing nonsense. Specifically, I have given only some of the facts. Those facts that I have omitted alter the conclusions considerably.

I have presented only what is deemed possible by scientists from an energetic or thermodynamic point of view. An analogy would be for me to announce that I have calculated that in principle all men should be able to leap ten feet into the air. Obviously, such an announcement would not be followed by a sudden, frenzied, worldwide demonstration of people showing their leaping capabilities. Some people have sore feet; others have inadequate muscles; most haven't the slightest desire to leap into the air. The calculation might be correct, but the enthusiasm for jumping and the ability to jump might be very low. The problem is the behavior of people rather than that of inanimate matter.

We are confronted by the brutal fact that humanity today doesn't really know how to cope with the problems presented by the three-and-a-half billion persons, let alone 333 billion. More than two-thirds of the present human population is poor in the material sense and is malnourished. The affluent one-third is, with breathtaking rapidity, becoming even more affluent. Two separate and distinct societies have emerged in the world, and they are becoming increasingly distinct and separated. Numerically the largest is the culture of the poor, composed of some 2,500 million persons. Numerically the smallest is the culture of the rich, composed of some 1,000 million persons. On the surface, the rich countries would appear to have it made; in historical perspective, their average per capita incomes are enormous. Their technological competence is unprecedented. Yet, they have problems that might well prove insoluble.

The most serious problem confronting the rich countries today is nationalism. We fight among each other and arm ourselves in order to do so more effectively. The Cold War has become a way of life, as is reflected in military budgets. Today the governments of the United States and the Soviet Union spend more on their respective military establishments than they do on either education or health— indeed a scandalous situation but, even worse, an explosive one.

All of the rich countries are suffering from problems of growth. Although the rates of population proliferation in these areas are not large, per capita consumption is increasing rapidly. Today an average "population unit" in the United States is quite different from one in the primitive world. Originally, a unit of population was simply a human being whose needs could be met by "eating" 2,500 calories and 60 grams of protein a day. Add to this some simple shelter, some clothing, and a small fire, and his needs were taken care of. A population unit today consists of a human being wrapped in tons of steel, copper, aluminum, lead, tin, zinc, and plastics. This new creature requires far more than food to keep it alive and functioning. Each day it gobbles up sixty pounds of coal or its equivalent, three pounds of raw steel, plus many pounds of other materials. Far from getting all of this food from his own depleted resources, he ranges abroad, much as the hunters of old, and obtains raw supplies in other parts of the world, more often than not in the poorer countries.

Industrial societies the world over are changing with unprecedented speed as the result of accelerated technological change, and they are becoming increasingly complex. All of them are encountering severe problems with their cities, which were designed within the framework of one technology and are falling apart at the seams within the framework of another.

The technological and social complexities of industrial society—composed as it is of vast interlocking networks of mines, factories, transportation systems, power grids, and communication networks, all operated by people—make it extremely vulnerable to disruption. Indeed, during the past year we have seen that the United States is far more vulnerable to labor strikes than North Vietnam is to air strikes. This vulnerability may eventually prove to be our undoing.

A concomitant of our affluence has been pollution. That which goes into a system must eventually come out; as our society has consumed more, it has excreted more. Given adequate supplies of energy and the necessary technology, such problems can be handled from a technical point of view. But it is by no means clear that we are about to solve these problems from a social or political point of view.

Although we know that theoretically we can derive our sustenance from the leanest of earth substances, such as seawater and rock, the fact remains that with respect to the raw materials needed for a highly industrialized society the research essential to the development of the necessary technology has hardly begun. Besides, it is less expensive for the rich countries to extract their sustenance from the poor ones.

As to the poor countries with their rapidly increasing populations, I fail to see how, in the long run, they can lift themselves up by their own bootstraps. In the absence of outside help commensurate with their needs, I suspect they will fail, and the world will become permanently divided into the rich and the poor—at least until such time as the rich, in their stupidity, blow themselves up.

One of the most difficult problems in the poor countries is that of extremely rapid population growth. If an economy grows only as fast as its population, the average well-being of the people does not improve—and indeed this situation prevails in many parts of the world. Equally important, rapid growth produces tremendous dislocations—physical, social, and economic. It is important to understand that the major population problem confronting the poor countries today is not so much the actual number of people as it is rapid growth rates. Clearly, if development is to take place, birth rates must be reduced.

Unfortunately, it is not clear just how birth rates can be brought down in these areas. Even with perfect contraceptives, there must be motivation upon the part of individuals, and in many areas this appears to be lacking. Some people say that economic development is necessary to produce the motivation, and they might be right. In any event, the solution will not be a simple one.

Although I am pessimistic about the future, I do not consider the situation to be by any means hopeless. I am convinced that our problems both here and abroad are soluble. But if they are ever solved, it will be because all of us reorient our attitudes away from those of our parents and more toward those of our children. I am convinced that young people today more often than not have a clearer picture of the world and its problems than do their elders. They are questioning our vast military expenditures and ask whether the Cold War is really necessary. They question the hot war in which we have become so deeply involved. They are questioning our concepts of nationalism, materialism, and laissez faire. It is just such questioning on the part of the young that gives me hope.

If this questioning persists, I foresee the emergence of a new human attitude in which people the world over work together to transform anarchy into law, to decrease dramatically military expenditures, to lower rates of population growth to zero, and to build an equitable world economy, so that all people can lead free and abundant lives in harmony with nature and with each other.

The Middle Class Does the Work, Pays the Bills, and Gets Blamed for Everything

Edwin A. Roberts, Jr.

The middle class is today under attack in America as it hasn't been in years, if ever. The assault force is a kind of international brigade composed of dissenting students, black revolutionaries, inventive bohemians, liberal extremists, and a fair complement of writers and scholars. The attackers don't have identical goals, but they are of one mind about the central objective—the elimination of the country's mores, the denigration and destruction of what are generally referred to as middle-class values.

When we speak of middle-class values, we are not really speaking about values associated with a particular income level. The values under attack today derive from the Protestant ethic. The foundations for American society were not laid down by diverse cultures. The melting pot would come later. The foundations were framed and poured by Protestant Englishmen who believed in the inherent rightness and efficiency of self-discipline, hard work, thrift, and the sanctity of contracts.

The values can be followed back much further, of course. Since the dawn of civilization, men have found that no community can survive without general adherence to certain standards of behavior. Sometimes these standards were written as laws. Sometimes they took the form of customs, and customs are hardly less effective than laws in regulating behavior.

Specifically, the middle class values hard work because hard work produces a higher standard of living. Middle-class men may admire the commuter train little more than the hippies do, but it is the commuter train that permits men to get to the work that provides their families with homes, gardens, and play areas. However dreary one may think the commuter's routine, it makes possible countless other life satisfactions. That millions of middle-class people live culturally narrow lives does not diminish their contribution to the economy.

Nor can reasonable critics put this down as a phony value. An artist's brush,

From *Today's Education*, LVIX, no. 1 (January 1970):20–23, as reprinted from *The National Observer*. Used by permission of the authors and publisher.

a bohemian's guitar, a poet's paper, a hippie's amulet—every artifact costs money. The economy pays the bills for everything.

The mistake bohemians make is inferring that life styles must be adopted on an either-or basis. Because their parents might have failed to take advantage of life's spiritual graces, they conclude that only by withdrawing from society can they experience the great intellectual and emotional joys available to almost everybody. What they eventually discover is that a sure way to miss happiness is to take dead aim at it. I am sure the hippies will find this to be the case with drugs and casual sex.

This brings up the middle-class value of marriage and sexual discipline. The function of the marital state in society is obvious. Marriage permits the orderly rearing of children. It helps hold society together. Sex in marriage not only satisfies a fundamental human appetite, it also cements the relationship between a man and a woman so that they have an incomparable reason for continuing to live together and care for their young.

Many young people today are experimenting with alternative arrangements. Some are aggressively seeking sexual experience at every opportunity. Some young people are simply playing house without benefit of matrimony. This arrangement is generally convenient for the man and futile for the girl. As a practical matter, a woman's greatest asset in winning the total interest of a man is the mystery of her body. When she casually discards this mystery, she is much like the magician who reveals his secrets before his performance. The audience gets bored before it has a chance to get interested.

Whatever its weaknesses as a human institution, marriage, like hard work, strengthens the social fabric. And a strong social fabric makes life more reasonable, more secure, and more satisfying.

Other middle-class values frequently belittled are thrift, which only means a careful handling of resources; the acquisition of "material" things like home appliances, which commit no greater crime than to reduce household drudgery; and social and business competition, which occurs when people try to improve themselves.

Wait a minute, say the critics. What we object to is the plastic character of American life (dissenters use the term *plastic* to mean synthetic).

According to Bennett M. Berger, former chairman of the Sociology Department at the University of California at Davis, who has talked with many dissenters, "from the perspective of the disaffected young, to be middle class these days means to have your achievements and your aspirations so adjusted that you always want or need a little more than you've got, but are so dependent upon what you *have* got—and so vulnerable to its being taken away—that threats to it compound your anxiety and put you, in the parlance of the young, uptight."

What the dissenters are saying, then, is that they have no freedom of choice when it comes to setting their own goals. No freedom of choice? Surely they have enough character to eschew a college education if that smacks too much of conformity. Do they want to spend their lives sitting in the top of a tree writing sonnets? That can be arranged. If the pace of modern living and its rewards are judged unsatisfactory, there are ways to get out of the mainstream. But if the great middle-class majority feels differently, then perhaps the dissenters should be content to do their own thing, and not insist that everyone else must do it. However, the acceptance of dissent is also a middle-class value.

As for anxiety, some anxiety is the lot of anyone with wit enough to imagine adversity. When a society becomes complicated, tensions increase because the possibilities for mishap increase. Nevertheless, it's more satisfying to send a spacecraft to the moon than to burrow under a bush to hide from the night.

What of "middle-class hypocrisy"? American society is indeed hypocritical—most societies are. Hypocrisy is necessary, especially in a pluralistic society, where people of divergent cultures are attempting to live at peace with one another. The serious hypocrisy in this nation concerns white society's treatment of the Negro. But customs change. Whites and Negroes are both maturing with a speed that could not have been predicted 15 years ago. Pluralistic America has had more opportunities for ethnic conflict than any other nation in history. That our society has been able to hold together while so many antagonistic forces have pushed and shoved is something of a miracle.

To blame the contemporary middle class for the plight of the Negro is absurd. By the accident of birth a man becomes the product and prisoner of a culture, and this is as true of whites as of blacks. Cultural differences in a society take time to fade; men can do no more than try to accelerate the process.

The admitted responsibility of the American middle class—admitted in the form of acts of Congress, presidential declarations, state and municipal laws, and enlightened business policies—is to work hard at clearing a path for Negroes. That's what the country is doing. It's a very expensive job but there is no choice, either from the standpoint of internal peace or from the standpoint of the Protestant ethic. It's the right thing to do, and the middle class knows it.

The American middle class, being composed of human beings, is not short on hostilities, but it doesn't deserve to be damned as racist when it exists in a racist world. The middle class didn't chart the course of civilization, nor did it invent those cultural phenomena that make relations between the races difficult.

The attack on the middle class, when it has been nonviolent, has performed a useful service. Change is the order of the universe and as man expands his horizons, he should be ready to review all his attitudes. But customs and values are deeply embedded in the social structure; they change by being sanded down and reshaped, not by being discarded whole.

It would be a dreary world without the dissenters. It's too easy for middle-class people to work themselves into a rut, especially in a highly organized society of specialists. We all need to be jolted once in a while. But having absorbed the jolt, we are still free to place competing values on the scales of reason.

Is it preferable to seek inner satisfaction by turning one's best efforts upon a difficult task or by seeking immediate gratification through drugs? Is it better to bear up under the commuter's burden and thereby earn leisure and the means to use it or to lounge in a loft all day and then beg for a meal? Is a shirt and tie more plastic than a psychedelic kimono? Is it more rational to promote a continuing dialogue between students and campus authorities or to come to school with guns and tools for vandalizing buildings? Is some hypocrisy a useful social lubricant or is it a sin against mankind? Are security and respectability less desirable than their opposites? Is the Negro making more progress today in America than he has ever made anywhere else at any time in history? Do middle-class values serve the general welfare?

The middle class does the work, pays the bills, and gets blamed for everything. But, though the dissidents might deny it, the middle class is susceptible to rational, civilized argument. It is willing to change—however joltingly hypocritical this may seem.

"Many Student Activists Feel that Middle-Class Society Needlessly Blocks Personal Growth"

Thomas Bradford Roberts

Stronger than the economic and social values that Edwin Roberts attributes to the middle class is a value that stands behind them and is central to those he mentions. I believe that an understanding of this value helps clarify what he sees as American middle-class values and helps explain why he interprets the central objective of the attackers of those values to be the elimination of the country's mores and why he seems to me to misunderstand student critics in the particular way he does.

Middle-class values and orientation to life can largely be understood in terms of sociability—smooth social relations, getting along with others, being friendly with as many people as possible, and fitting into one's community. A typical middle-class person interprets the world and himself in terms of family and friends, neighborhood, town, and nation.

We see this, for example, in middle-class parents' strong concern with their children's social development. If the teacher says that Johnny can't read, that is cause for some concern, but if he reports, "Johnny is unable to get along with others," that is cause for alarm. When these parents prepare their children for school, they stress getting along with the other children and cooperating with the teacher. Thus, in middle-class schools, we see a whole social philosophy of education that emphasizes smooth social relations, popularity, and joining clubs and activities.

A different emphasis, interpretation, and view of the world comes from a large segment of students—the activists—who regard individual development and expression as their primary values. They ask, "Does this make sense to me personally? Does this aid my own and others' *individual* development?" Because such a point of view is especially characteristic of young people in the upper-middle

From *Today's Education*, LVIX, no. 1 (January 1970):22–23. Used by permission of the author and the publisher.

and upper classes, this type of activism occurs frequently in upper-middle-class schools and universities and among children of well-educated and economically well-off parents.

With subjective self-development and self-expression as a goal, how do these young people react to the norms, customs, and values of society? They feel that society often needlessly blocks personal growth. When a school enforces dress or appearance codes, for instance, they see this as an example of the middle-class addiction to getting along with others, to uniformity, to social acceptance. Student activists don't mind if people want to conform, but believe that the standards people conform to ought to be of their personal selection, not forced upon them.

This is the problem as the activists see it: We have a predominantly middle-class society. The high value that the middle class assigns to norms and conformity results in a society that places too much emphasis on its laws and customs. These constraints limit personal freedom more than is necessary. In the long run, they also endanger society, because they limit the renewal, adaptation, and evolution that come from experimentation with new values and new ways of living.

A healthy society ought to encourage social experimentation and invention just as it encourages technological research and development. Cultural and social diversity is a measure of society's wealth just as much as are GNP and material things like home appliances. But to make progress in this direction, the middle class will have to give up its notion that there is one American way of life and one sort of social organization that is best for all the people all the time. There are many.

According to Edwin Roberts, the activists "are of one mind about the central objective—the elimination of the country's mores." When we keep in mind the fact that middle-class people are very sensitive to norms and interpret the world through the idea of social acceptance, we can understand that Edwin Roberts is a spokesman for this point of view. It seems to me that people of this persuasion misinterpret the desire for personal growth and its subsidiary disaffection with norms as primarily an attack on the norms. Actually, the so-called attack is merely an attempt to remove an impediment to self-growth.

The issue the established middle class sees is an attack on middle-class mores; the issue student social critics see is a restriction of human potential.

For example, middle-class defense of middle-class values is based on the fact that they contribute to the economy, not that they lead to a richer, fuller life. They talk as if those who are critics of society are attacking society's affluence. The fact is that the critics are attacking the misuse of affluence and the view that sees man as predominantly an economic animal rather than as a human being with immense potentials. It is the apparent infatuation with goods and services and the seeming disregard of man's higher states that student critics of society object to. "Couldn't some of these resources be used for purposes better than protection against imagined political, economic, and social enemies?" they ask.

Edwin Roberts says that the middle class values hard work because "hard work produces a higher standard of living," and adds "That millions of middle-class people live culturally narrow lives does not diminish their contributions to the economy." This sounds to the activists as though, to the middle class, the higher standard of living is a goal in itself.

Thank God the Holy Economy isn't affected! Anything but that! If millions of people don't contribute to the cultural richness of society, so what? So what, if they live culturally impoverished lives? So what, as long as the GNP keeps compounding? The student activists are asking the unthinkable question: *Now that our standard of living is high enough, what do we do with the surplus economy?*

More important than the middle class's conception of man as predominantly economic and spurred on by economic goals are its shockingly immoral views toward women and sex. It seems to regard women as some sort of mysteriously performing sex machine. When the magical performance is over, they are useless. It overlooks the problem of what that point of view forecasts when, after the first year of marriage, the "mystery of her body" is a fact of everyday life. It doesn't face the problem of what happens when age makes her body less appealing.

To today's young people, sex relationships are no longer based on the ephemeral "mystery of her body"; instead, they are based on more enduring and important qualities, such as compatibility of character, personality, interests and hopes, sense of humor and taste, the joys of sharing life, values.

Restricting half of society to lower status on the grounds that their greatest asset is only the mystery of their bodies, an asset soon lost, is degrading not only to the denigrated half but also to the half that perpetuates these demeaning, immoral attitudes. Regardless of whether sex, skin color, or any other physiological difference provides the grounds for debasement, the prejudice, restriction of individual liberty, and pinioning of the human potential are just as immoral. On this basis, at least, the battle for women's rights and for minority rights is the same.

The middle-class emphasis on social acceptance and social norms weakens its appreciation of divergent views and ideas—makes it blind to social problems, especially those stemming from its own middle-class norms. Unfortunately, many middle-class institutions, especially schools, persist in forcing these values on the whole society, ignoring the fact that they are amputating individual liberty under the slogan "Socially Acceptable Standards."

The middle class may value a money-minded, socially acquiescent nation, but this won't build the world or the educational system that the self-growth type of student activists want. It will stunt, not nourish, the human potential.

Changing Values and Institutional Goals

Ian H. Wilson

We find ourselves today at the opening of a New Reformation—a major re-formation or re-ordering, of our public and private value systems. Powered by the forces of affluence, education, and technology, and forged in the crucible of our tense and changing times, this values reformation—perhaps more than any economic or technical change—is becoming perhaps the most distinctive, certainly the most pervasive, feature of the newly emerging "post-industrial society."

For society as a whole, a major implication of these trends is that the seventies will be a decade of questioning, uncertainty, potential turmoil, and confrontation. There will be substantial restructuring of many institutions; an effort to rethink their social purpose and objectives and reshape their operations and relationships, both internal and external. For business in particular, there will be the need to face up to the consequences of real questioning, challenge, and modification of many basic business concepts—growth, technology, efficiency, profit, work, the legitimacy and authority of management.

It is important to stress at the outset, first, that we are not talking about "new" values, but rather about a restructuring of values systems; second, that we should not associate this movement merely with the new college generation, though they may be its cutting edge, but rather with a broader societal thrust.

It would, indeed, be remarkable if, after many millennia on this earth, mankind had discovered a new value. The more modest, but still revolutionary assertion that we are moving toward a greater stress on the qualitative, rather than the purely quantitative, aspects of our economy and society reflects the developing picture more accurately.

Then, too, this movement is not limited to college students; nor are college students a monolithic body, with identical values, attitudes and and opinions. It remains a fact, however, that it was the emergence of the "post-war generation" (the babies of 1946–49) on campus—a generation large in numbers, and significantly different in values—that brought into unified focus, in conspicuous locations, many of the diverse issues and problems of the sixties.

There can be no doubt that the escalation of the Vietnam War, the urban explosions of minority groups, and student unrest, were the events that catalyzed the turmoil, doubts, and polarization of the late sixties. The outbreaks in the cities and on the campuses might be interpreted as continuations of slowly growing disaffection—in one case, with progress toward integration and the elimination of poverty; in the other, with authoritarian structures and "irrelevant" education—

A paper presented at World Future Society General Assembly Session on "Goals and Values of Mankind," May 13, 1971. Used by permission of the author.

...d into an explosive burst. In varying degrees, both were
...attention on, major discrepancies between the American
...realities—equality, individual dignity, the "melting pot,"
...er cities."

...youth might, therefore, be said to have started a major re-
...ial and individual values, even beyond the specific issues and
den... ...causes. Thus, the minority rights movement, focusing on the
issue of m... ...es, has opened the way for, and lent momentum to, the women's
rights movement (though the two may clash at particular points). The riots have
also finally riveted public attention on the general deterioration of urban living
(for whites as well as blacks), and so been responsible for the initial escalation
of efforts at urban renewal. And the youth movement, by focusing on the issues
of materialism and individual choice, has led to some major questioning about
the adequacy of the provisions made by "the system" (political, educational,
business, etc.) for individual rights and choice.

Though it is an undoubted oversimplification, there is some justification for
seeing the mood of the late sixties as setting the stage for new goals and new
policies based on a recognition of current societal limitations:

The limitations of power: both of U.S. nuclear power in policing the world, and
of domestic authority in preserving "law and order"

The limitations of affluence: in personal terms, awareness of the impact of inflation and (among some) a disenchantment with materialistic satisfactions; in
public terms, a recognition that even an affluent society cannot afford "guns
and butter," but has to make critical choices among national goals

The limitations of technology: doubts about the benefits of unrestricted technological development, with its potential for social instability and environmental
damage

The limitations of our infrastructure: an awareness that a problem which had
been supposed to be limited to underdeveloped countries also applied to the
U.S.

The limitations on equality: a broader recognition of the extent to which large
segments of our population—women and nonwhites—did not enjoy true equality of opportunity

The limitations on individualism: a questioning of whether there is an equitable
"trade-off" between individual rights and institutional needs, and of whether
organizations truly serve human needs

The limitations of "the old values," or more accurately of the sincerity and adequacy of individual and social *performance* against these basic values.

For the future we may safely conjecture that the new challenge to our national will is in the *qualitative* sector of public expectations. It is not much of an
exaggeration to say that we have largely solved the *quantitative* problems of our
society: two years ago the London *Economist* put it this way:

The United States in this last third of the twentieth century is the place
where man's long economic problem is ending, but where his social problems still gape. On any rational view, the enormous fact of that approach to
economic consummation should rivet all attention. It is almost certainly the
most momentous news story so far in the history of the world. But people
in the United States are at present wracked by the stretching to snapping

point of too many of their temporary social tensions, so that this society which represents man's greatest secular achievement sometimes seems to be on the edge of a national nervous breakdown. [The article, incidentally, was entitled "The Neurotic Trillionaire."]

It is because of this probable future emphasis on quality that we, as futurists, need to be more keenly sensitive to social forces, and in particular to the attitudinal shifts of our population. It is these less tangible, more subtle forces that may work greater changes in our society than will the more obvious physical changes that we can expect. Some of the attitudinal shifts that we should prepare for are:

An emphasis on the "quality of life," from the quality of products to the quality of our environment

Some modification of the old Puritan work ethic, and a growing belief that leisure is a valid activity in its own right

A new "self-image" that a rising level of education bestows on its graduates

A rejection of authoritarianism as an acceptable style

A growing belief in the values of pluralism, decentralization, participation, involvement

A heightened respect for individual conscience and dignity

An increased public impatience, a "lower frustration tolerance," with many forms of economic hardship (such as poverty and unemployment), and with social injustice in all its forms.

In sum, these (and other) changes would quite radically reorder our public and private values. Particularly among the young and the better-educated, we are likely to see a shift in emphasis:

From considerations of quantity ("more"), toward considerations of quality ("better")

From the concept of independence, toward the concept of interdependence

From the satisfaction of private material needs, toward meeting public needs

From the primacy of technical efficiency, toward considerations of social justice and equity

From the dictates of organizational convenience, toward the aspirations of self-development of an organization's members

From authoritarianism, toward participation

From uniformity and centralization, toward pluralism and diversity

From preservation of the system's status quo and routine, toward promotion and acceptance of change.

What we are, and shall be, experiencing on a national scale is a progression up Maslow's hierarchy of needs. The late Abraham Maslow of Brandeis University postulated that man's needs could be arranged in a hierarchy of five levels—from the lowest level of the purely physiological needs (for food, clothing, shelter, rest), through security, social and ego needs, to the highest level of self-actualization needs (mental and spiritual growth, self-development, the fullest expression of all one's human potential). Viewed in this light, this New Reformation takes on a new significance. We can begin, I think, not merely to explain the present, but to predict the future.

When discussing shifts on a national scale, some gross generalizations and over-simplifications have to be made. Yet it should be possible to predict major trends and changes in emphasis. In a society as complex and varied as the United States, the population cannot be slotted at one level only, for there are people operating at all levels. A profile of the population make-up, with its various modes of living, will thus be needed to represent the full range of needs; and future changes in this profile will be indicative of shifting value-systems.

As a start, it is possible to predict that by 1980 there will be fewer people in the poverty class, and so a reduction of emphasis on survival and security needs nationally. At the other end of the spectrum, increasing affluence, more education, and the changing composition of the work force will mean a rise in the number of high-income individuals, college graduates, professional and managerial personnel, and so an increase in emphasis on social, ego, and (particularly) self-actualization needs.

The importance of this interpretation for our discussion this morning lies in the seemingly simple statement that:

Needs determine values; and values determine goals.

At any given level, we tend to value what we need. If we are operating at the level of physiological needs, then we tend to value food and shelter. Attaining them becomes our goal. At the self-actualization level, we will be "turned on" by opportunities for self-expression, self-development, outreach. It is not, of course, that we need food, shelter or any of the other intermediate needs any the less; but they are assumed or subsumed in the larger goal, rather than valued for themselves.

One conclusion that we may draw from all the foregoing is that there will be greater importance, and greater complexity, attached both to the articulation of values and the formulation of more explicit goals—for ourselves, for our institutions, for our society. It should be evident, I think, that, as the "quality of life" becomes more and more our aim, so it becomes increasingly important that we identify and debate our values (an exercise in which few of us are adept or happy), for these will be major determinants of the specific goals we set.

"Better" requires more philosophizing, if you will, than "more." So long as our goals were mainly quantitative, there was less need to debate about the nature of the next steps for our society and economy. The immediate, physical needs had an obviousness and compulsion to them that made philosophizing largely irrelevant: they also, incidentally, generated a powerful unifying force in our society. To be sure, we have debated values-laden issues of the distribution of wealth and, increasingly, of the ordering of our economic priorities.

As a society we are not yet—and shall not be within the foreseeable future—so affluent that we can afford to do everything at once: we have, in other words, to make choices. Indeed, it can be argued that increasing affluence and technology will enlarge our range of options, by bringing more of man's historical aspirations within the realm of the possible, and so make choices more, not less, difficult and important than in a poorer society in which options are strictly limited.

Establishing explicit goals will be a way of making these choices explicit, whether for the nation or for an institution. They will also be needed to create institutional focus and identity in an era of change. A search for meaning, purpose and identity—which we now think of primarily as an individual quest—will become necessary for organizational, and even national, vitality and self-renewal.

This need for identity and purpose was stressed by Max Ways in a recent *Fortune* article.

> To a modern nation, especially one as fast-moving as the U.S., a sense of direction becomes the indispensable touchstone of the society's character, its identity. Specific issues of what is right for a modern society can no longer be referred back to some preceding condition considered as ideal. *The "normality" of a modern society has to be found in the unfolding of its fundamental values and principles,* in the pattern of its movement, *in the broad characteristics of its forward reach.* [Emphasis added.]

It is perhaps worth stressing the obvious point that this new concern with values and goals does *not* usher in an era of tranquility, sweetness, and light. To the contrary, as values have to be made more explicit, goals established, and priorities selected, the potential for confrontation, conflict, and polarization will be *increased.* Though I do not want to take issue too strongly with Daniel Bell, I have the feeling that reports of the death of ideology have been greatly exaggerated.

Not only do we face the problem of how to define goals in a pluralistic, democratic setting, but we need to find answers to the question of how to bring about the degree of institutional change that I suspect our values and goals will call for. The answer, my friends, is not blowin' in the wind; we will not find it on the Beatles' magical mystery tour; it will not come to us with the dawning of the Age of Aquarius or the onset of Consciousness III. Indeed, if we rely on the presumed panacea of Charles Reich's phenomenon, we shall more likely experience the groaning than the greening of America. The developing tensions in our society cannot wait that long.

We must work, with speed, with passion, with competence, to build into our institutional systems the possibilities for a fuller expression of the values I have discussed. "The tasks of social change," John Gardner said, "are tasks for the tough-minded and competent." He added that "those who come to the task with the currently fashionable mixture of passion and incompetence only add to the confusion."

There is a valid question to be raised about the outcome of this venture. For centuries man has wondered, "Is there intelligent life on other planets?" However, when one considers the disarray in international relations, the tensions in our society, and the physical decay of our cities, I feel there is a prior question we should ask ourselves: "Is there intelligent life on *this* planet?" I do not mean to sound cynical. I know that in this most educated of all societies there is an abundance of *individual* intelligence. But we all must question whether we have the same degree of *collective* intelligence to bring about the needed process of self-renewal and change required by the accelerated aging and rigidity of our institutions.

Yet we must make a beginning. And the beginning, I suggest, can be found in making this type of values-analysis and then building these newly-stressed values into the day-to-day working of our institutional systems. We are not perhaps fully aware of the extent to which these systems currently reflect certain values. We are more used to thinking of them as delivering a product or service than as reflections of our values. The current trouble—the trouble that puts so many of our institutions on a collision course with the future—is that they reflect almost exclusively organizational values such as order, routine, output, authority, efficiency. They reflect inadequately such other values as individualism, self-development, personal relationships, due process, equality.

Contrasting Educative Environments in the Metropolitan Area

Daniel U. Levine

Living in a school five or six hours a day five days a week does strange things to people. It leads educators to behave, in many cases, as if the school were the world, as if education only takes place in the setting that educators know best—the school. What happens to young people outside the school is not so easily discernible; hence, it is difficult to remember that a young person's educational environment is his total environment, and to constantly assess education in the school for its congruence with his experience outside the school.

Of course, there is a sense in which a teacher or administrator is all too well aware that a student's experience outside the school strongly affects how he behaves and reacts in the classroom. A great deal of time is spent discussing—and frequently complaining about—the homes and families from which students come and the degree of motivation and preparation for learning which they bring to the classroom. One might think that the propensity to trade information about students' behavior in their neighborhoods or peer groups and about the strengths and weaknesses of their family situations indicates a profound understanding and awareness of the nature and influence of educative environments outside the school. But does it really?

Before responding to this question, it is necessary to review some of the fundamental characteristics of the educative environment in which the young people in metropolitan areas live and grow up. By definition, the metropolitan area is a place where people of diverse groups and habits live interdependently but also in communities which differ in definable ways from one another according to physical and social characteristics associated with the evolution of urban society. Thus, there is not one but many educative environments in the metropolitan area. To facilitate analysis and comparison, this paper will be concerned only with

From *Educational Horizons*, XLVIII, no. 1 (Fall 1969):5–12. Used by permisson of the author and publisher.

two of the most contrasting parts of the metropolitan area, namely, the inner core poverty area in the central city and the middle-income suburban area outside the central city. Although this approach tends to exaggerate the differences which exist between the two types of communities, it also underlines the most salient of the characteristics which have direct implications for the educator.

THE INNER CITY

Since everyone knows there are serious problems of poverty, poor housing, and crime in the inner core parts of the big city, it is not necessary to belabor the obvious—most people in a slum are poor and many are unhappy.

It is not easy for people outside the inner city, however, to realize what living in a poverty ghetto means to the families which are trying to raise children there. The inner city of a generation ago, for one thing, is not the same as the inner city today, and the American who boasts of his own origins and escape from the slums is not describing (whether he knows it or not) the problems of surviving in the inner city in the 1960's and 1970's. The American of middle-class origins, for his part, tends to have much indirect but little personal knowledge of conditions in the inner city. Neither background is conducive to gaining a visceral as contrasted to a verbal understanding of the educative environment of the inner city today.

As a step toward understanding the environment of the inner city and some of its implications for education, it is useful to consider two myths commonly encountered in discussions of the big city slums.

Myth One—Conditions in the inner city have been improving as residents of the slums have learned to take advantage of opportunities in the big city.

Fact—It is true that many residents of the inner city escaped from poverty (as defined by Labor Department criteria) between 1960 and 1969. For example, there were one million fewer "nonwhites" below the official "poverty line" in 1967 than in 1966. However, data from special studies in Cleveland, Los Angeles, and from other sources also indicate that conditions in the poorest core parts of the inner cities have, if anything, deteriorated rather than improved in the 1960's.[1] Although there may have been a decline in the total population living in poverty areas, figures on crime, unemployment, school dropouts, family breakdown, and other measures of social disorganization in these areas indicate that hundreds of thousands of people are trapped in an environment in which poverty and alienation are being perpetuated from one generation to the next. Possibly for the first time, United States society has produced an "underclass" of citizens mired in pervasive hopelessness and despair.

Myth Two—Most people who live in an urban slum are so boxed in to a "culture of poverty" that they no longer hold the values of the wider society. Few parents care very much about the education of their children, and fewer still try very hard to give their children a good start in life.

Fact—Even in the most run-down sections of the inner city ghetto, the majority of parents strive to obtain just what middle-class parents strive to obtain

---

[1] U.S. Bureau of the Census, "Trends in Social and Economic Conditions in Metropolitan Areas," *Current Population Reports*, Series P-23, no. 27 (February 7, 1969).

—economic security, good health, and peaceful, stable family relationships for themselves and their children. Many work desperately hard to maintain and improve their communities, to keep their children out of trouble, and to convince their children of the value of a good education. As two reporters recently summarized the situation in describing the intensive study of one of the most depressed blocks in Spanish Harlem:

> It is easy to see crime and evil when you look at a block. It is harder to see the good, since the good people are often 'good' merely in a negative sense—that is, refrain from performing certain acts. Yet the good people on this block are often good positively and overtly—even though what they do is still overlooked . . . They have organized social clubs to keep the children occupied, manned anti-poverty agencies, and in a hundred of quiet ways are trying to change the block.[2]

It may be something of a paradox to conclude on the one hand that most families in the inner city are trying hard to "make it" in American society and to give their children the advantage of a good start in life but on the other hand to note that so many parents are experiencing little but failure in this desperate effort. But it is this same discrepancy between what parents are trying to give their children and what is actually happening to their children which accounts for the plaintive admissions that "I can't do anything with that child" commonly heard among the people of the inner city. The paradox dissolves when we realize that segregation by economic class and race in the United States has created inner city areas larger and more socially damaging than any we have heretofore seen in the United States.

The simple fact is that economic and racial segregation have created poverty ghettoes in which it is proving almost impossible for many families to raise children successfully. Space limitations do not allow for an exhaustive treatment of the many conditions which destroy the human potential of young people in the inner city, but a few of the most salient ones should be at least briefly discussed.

1. Density

In a time of rapid population growth, large-scale migration of the poor to the cities, and restrictions imposed by poverty and racial discrimination on the geographic mobility of people in the slums, one of the "natural" outcomes has been increasing population density in the inner city.

A few statistics illustrate the high densities which exist in the inner core parts of the central cities.

Housing density in the poverty areas of central cities recently surveyed in a special Census Bureau study were 100 times as great as in poverty areas in the suburbs, or 3,071 units per square mile as against 30 units per square mile. Within the central cities, average density in non-poverty areas was only 61 percent of that in poverty areas.[3]

"In 1960 Negroes made up almost a quarter of Chicago's population . . . but 67 percent lived in Negro tracts covering a mere 4 percent of the city's total

---

[2] David and Sophy Burnham, "El Barrio's Worst Block Is Not All Bad," *The New York Times Magazine*, January 5, 1969, 75.

[3] Donald Canty, Editor, *The Ill-Housed* (Washington, D.C.: Urban America, 1969), p. 16.

area . . . in Washington, D.C., half the Negro population [which was 54 percent of the total population] was spread over only 5 percent of the city."[4] Even though such figures include many middle-class black residents who do not live in poverty areas, they obviously reflect the overcrowding characteristic of the poverty ghettoes of the big cities.

Neither social nor natural scientists completely understand the effects of high density on animals much less on humans. In general, however, there is a widespread and growing belief that overcrowding in itself often has undesirable effects on the social behavior of human beings. As one example, Robert H. Wood, director of the Harvard-M.I.T. Joint Urban Studies Center, has expressed the opinion that high density is the single most important factor in generating the social problems of the big city.[5] And in testimony to the Joint Economics Committee of the Congress summarizing their review of research on the effects of density, Leo Levy and Harold M. Visotsky have stated that:

> While living arrangements are quite varied crossculturally and even within a culture, we believe certain principles obtain in all such arrangements. . . . It would appear that even beyond culturally relative (learned) values in this regard, there is a biologically determined distancing mechanism in people. Where physical distancing becomes impossible as in prisons, concentration camps, army barracks, slum apartments, etc., it would appear that people make use of psychological distancing mechanisms . . . such emotional distancing in crowded city areas may contribute to indifference to the suffering of others and unwillingness to 'get involved' with neighbors or people who may be attacked on the street by hoodlums.[6]

In a still more specific analysis of the high-rise public housing projects and the multi-story tenements which house a significant proportion of the inner-city poor in many of the big cities, anthropologist Edward T. Hall has observed that:

> If one looks at human beings in the same way that the early slave traders did, conceiving of their space requirements simply in terms of the limits of the body, one pays very little attention to the effects of crowding. . . . [People] find themselves forced into behavior, relationships, or emotional outlets that are overly stressful. . . . When stress increases, sensitivity to crowding rises—people get more on edge—so that more and more space is required as less and less is available.
>
> Consider the public housing constructed for low income groups in Chicago which has tended to dress up and hide the basic problem. . . . Row after row of high-rise apartments is less distressing to look at than slums but more disturbing to live in than much of what it replaced. . . . The high rise fails to solve many basic human problems. As one tenant described his building to me: 'It's no place to raise a family. A mother can't look out for her kids if they are fifteen floors down in the playground. They

[4] Sydney M. Wilhelm, "Red Man, Black Man, and White America," Catalyst (Spring, 1969), p. 33.
[5] Speech presented at the University of Missouri Inter-campus Seminar on Urban Problem Solving, Clayton, Missouri, April 10, 1969.
[6] Leo Levy and Harold M. Visotsky, "The Quality of Urban Life: An Analysis from the Perspective of Mental Health," in Urban America: Goals and Problems (Washington, D.C.: U.S. Government Printing Office, 1967), pp. 104–5.

get beaten up by the rough ones, the elevators are unsafe and full of filth
. . . are slow and break down. When I want to go home I think twice because it may take me a half an hour to get the elevator.[7]

To increase density in a rat population and maintain healthy specimens,
put them in boxes so they can't see each other, clean their cages, and give
them enough to eat. You can pile the boxes up as many stories as you wish.
Unfortunately, caged animals become stupid, which is a very heavy price
to pay for a super filing system. The question we must ask ourselves is, How
far can we afford to travel down the road of sensory deprivation in order to
file people away? One of man's most critical needs, therefore, is for principles for designing spaces that will maintain a healthy density, a healthy
interaction rate, a proper amount of involvement, and a continuing sense
of ethnic identification.[8]

It was knowledge of considerations such as those which led Jeno F. Paulucci,
chairman of the board of Jeno's Inc., and the New Cities Program Committee
to publish a full two-page "Open Letter to President Nixon and Our Nation's
Leaders" in the New York Times which said, "How can we expect legislation to
solve our problems unless we realize that their real root is in congestion? It Is
Congestion That Breeds Violence, And In Turn Breeds Revolt, Social Or
Armed."[9]

Perhaps teachers, as well as anyone, know something about the debilitating
effects of density on social institutions in the inner city. As waves of youngsters
have entered inner city schools in the 1950's and 1960's, teachers have been
driven to exasperation by classes of thirty, forty, and even fifty pupils many of
whom are unprepared to succeed in our schools as they are organized and operated
today. But have we really understood what it means for a family to try to raise a
child when instead of eight or ten peers in his immediate neighborhood, there
are fifty or one-hundred or two-hundred peers who may be influencing him in a
different direction than his parents?[10] Do we really understand what it is like for
a family to try to supervise a child in an environment where high population
densities bring him in daily contact with a large number of negative—but often
attractive—adult models? Probably not, or teachers would not so often be heard
disparaging the families of urban disadvantaged students and blaming the problems of the inner city school on the "intractability" of the students themselves.

---

[7] Edward T. Hall, The Human Dimension (New York: Doubleday, 1966), pp. 121,
158–59.
[8] Edward T. Hall, "The Hidden Dimension," in Urban America: Goals and Prospects,
pp. 2, 7.
[9] The New York Times, Sunday, April 27, 1969, 10-E-11-E.
[10] An editor of The Economist recently pointed out that
    It is a statistical and sociological fact that . . . a youth is particularly liable to become
    delinquent if he is living in dilapidated housing near the center of a big metropolitan
    area, without a father in the house, with low-income, unstable employment, little edu-
    cation, and in a culture that has a grievance against society and its police. The United
    States has now managed to create exactly these conditions in most of its big cities with
    over one million population . . . Moreover, the age structure in the ghettoes is not
    going to get better. In the immediate future it is going to get much worse. . . . be-
    tween 1966 and 1975 the number of young Negroes in the ghettoes aged from 15 to
    24 will rise by 1.6 million, or 40.1 percent.
Norman Macrae, "The Problems of Impacted Ghettos," Current (August, 1969), 26.

2. Racial Segregation

The volume of literature in which black and other minority-group Americans describe the problems they have experienced growing up in a big city ghetto is large and growing larger. Rather than offering a formal analysis and survey of the many books and articles currently available, it may be useful to quote one major writer who has eloquently described—and protested—the conditions which cripple so many families which have been confined within these ghettoes:

My father is dead. And he had a terrible life. He was defeated long before he died because at the bottom of his heart he really believed what the white people said about him. He believed he was a nigger. This belief made him bitter and cruel, and he died hating and fearing every living soul, including his children, who had betrayed him too by reaching toward the world which despised him.

. . . My life had begun . . . in the invincible and indescribable squalor of Harlem. Here in this ghetto I was born and here it was intended by my countrymen that I should live and perish . . . I loathed it because I couldn't get out and I knew I couldn't get out . . .

Everywhere, everything was falling down and going to pieces, and no one cared. They had spelled out to me with brutal clarity and in every possible way that I was a worthless human being. You don't accept it, because it is literally unacceptable. Those who accepted it are all, without exception, dead. They're either criminals, which is one way to die, or they're junkies, or they're drunkards. Or they're like my father was—fanatically self-righteous and cold.[11]

3. Drug Addiction

Whatever the disagreements about marijuana, "speed," and other drugs whose addictive qualities are not fully known, heroin—the bane of the ghetto— clearly is a horrible destructive influence on young people in the inner city. It is not simply the drug itself, of course, which is cause for concern in the ghetto, though the number of young people who die from an overdose is shockingly high, but also its association with crime and depravity and its revelation of conditions which the Reverend Andrew Young of the Southern Christian Leadership Conference has described as follows:

There is a constant war being waged in the ghetto between the people and the forces which would enslave them, and narcotics is probably the most deadly of these forces.

There's a legitimate paranoia in the ghetto, brought on by the loan shark on the corner, the door-to-door salesman, the numbers racketeer, the kids peddling hot merchandise—somebody is always offering these people 'a deal.' These are all obstacles—temptations that have to be overcome in order for the black man in the ghetto to live a decent, productive life and get out. But there's always somebody offering the good life now. Why wait? Get it on credit. These are things the middle-class white people don't come in contact with. They don't have to make a conscious moral decision every day of their lives.[12]

[11] James Baldwin, "My Childhood," *The Listener*, 81, no. 2078 (January 23, 1969), 102.
[12] Gail Miller, "Narcotics: A Study in Black and White," *City*, 3 (June, 1969), 6.

Although the percentage of young people in the ghetto who fall victim to heroin ebbs and flows over time, the dimensions of the problem vary only from dreadful to more dreadful. Thus when a recent survey in New York showed a steep increase in heroin use, *New York Post* reporter Leonard Katz concluded his story by pointing out that, "As things stand now, the number of addicts under sixteen is increasing greatly, and no one seems to be doing anything about it."[13] And when a team of researchers from three universities completed an intensive study of social conditions on a single block in Spanish Harlem, one of the researchers described the fluctuating use of heroin among young people and then told a *New York Times* reporter that:

The curious thing we noticed during the last two years . . . is that kids from families with the greatest economic and social stability seem to be more interested in drugs than kids from less stable families. I don't know why this is happening, but perhaps it is because the kids from the stronger families are better able to see the world they will never succeed in.[14]

A community plagued by relatively widespread use of addictive drugs teaches not just deviancy but also disrespect for the law and hatred for the entire outside society which the law is supposed to represent. What must one conclude, for example, about the educative influence of an environment in which "Anyone who has been around," as the Reverend Channing Phillips of Washington, D.C., has pointed out:

has seen a policeman turn his head at a dope transaction, or accept a payoff from a pusher. With the sophisticated investigative devices we have, I don't see how anyone could believe for a minute that law enforcement officials don't know who's behind the dope traffic. It's not a lack of knowledge; it's a lack of will to move against it. Look, if the FBI can bug Martin Luther King's phone right after the day of his death, you can bet they can bug the Mafia's—unless they're saying Martin Luther was a more dangerous guy than the dope peddlers.[15]

The high incidence of heroin addiction in the inner city is a particularly instructive topic for consideration because it returns us to and helps us understand the bitterness of ghetto parents who try every conceivable means—even to locking youngsters into the home—to shut out the social disorganization of the streets, but whose children still fall victim to the heroin culture by the time they are fifteen or sixteen years old. Noting that studies of the proportion of ghetto youngsters who are or have been heroin addicts yield estimated percentages of 10 and 20 percent for Saint Louis and New York,[16] respectively, one might ask such questions as:

How high a minority of deviant youngsters in a community is enough to exercise strong negative influence on the development of most other youngsters

[13] Leonard Katz, "Children and Heroin: A Post Survey," *New York Post*, April 28, 1969, p. 1.
[14] David Burnham, "Heroin Traps 33 Per Cent on Harlem 'Addict Block,'" *The New York Times*, October 13, 1968, p. 1.
[15] Gail Miller, *op. cit.*, 7.
[16] *Ibid.*, 6.

in the community and thus swing the balance of forces against the efforts of parents, teachers, and others working to prevent social disorganization? Five percent? Ten percent? Fifteen percent?

At what point does the influence of deviants make it impossible for a social institution to function effectively? For example, most teachers can cope with one or two "acting out" youngsters in their classrooms, but very few can cope with five or six, which may be just about the difference in conditions one encounters between the typical middle-class school and the typical inner-city school.

At what point does a high incidence of overt delinquency in a community reinforce a tendency for police to treat all youth in the community (particularly a minority community) as if they were delinquents? Ten percent? Twenty percent? What percent of prejudiced police officers (or school teachers, or social workers) does it take to reinforce a tendency for children in the ghetto to perceive all police officers (or school teachers, or social workers) as prejudiced? Five percent? Ten percent?

The question marks running through this analysis signify that no one knows, or can know, the exact percentages, which undoubtedly vary and shift from community to community in accordance with local conditions and national trends. What is clear is that the delicate line which differentiates between a community where conditions are favorable to the socialization of young people and one where they are not is easily crossed. Congestion, the psychological effects of segregation, the drug culture, and other forces originating, in one way or another, this discrimination has created poverty ghettoes in which the overall educative environment works against positive socialization of the young. "The ghetto," social planner Harvey S. Perloff has said, "is not just a place with many unemployed and subemployed persons; it is a place that saps motivation, erodes the capacity to learn, pulls young people out of national mainstream activities by overwhelming them with human temptation and risk."[17] Such is the pathology of racial and social class prejudice and discrimination.

THE MIDDLE-INCOME SUBURB

Although there has been a good deal of speculation and exchanging of opinions about suburban youth and their problems, hardly any systematic research has been carried out to determine what happens to suburban young people in their communities or whether their reactions and experiences are different from those of city youth. Thus, despite the fact that more than half the metropolitan population now lives in suburban areas outside the central cities, the amount of information we possess about the educative environment in which suburban youngsters group up is inexplicably small.

It is important to stress that there are many types of suburbs. For example, some suburbs have mostly poor families, some are exclusive communities for the very rich, and many have a mixed-class population of working class, lower middle-

---

[17] Harvey S. Perloff, "What Economic Future for the Inner City Ghetto?", in Science and Technology and the Cities. A Compilation of Papers Prepared for the Tenth Meeting of the Panel on Science and Technology (Washington, D.C., U.S. Government Printing Office, 1969), p. 13.

class, and upper middle-class families. The focus of discussion here will be on the predominantly middle-income suburb with many upper middle-class families.

Increasingly, parents in middle-income suburbs say they are alarmed about the behavior of their children, particularly teenagers and young adults. Rebellion and lack of interest in school, drug use, dropping out of college, sexual promiscuity, and petty delinquency rank high on any list of parental concerns. One knowledgeable observer in a large middle-income suburban area of the East estimated that at least 50 percent of the high school students use marijuana or other drugs, and similar estimates could hold true in some other parts of the country. During the past year disturbing reports have been circulating about the beginnings of a serious heroin problem in some eastern suburbs. What is going on?

To a significant degree, signs of rebellion in the suburbs reflect primarily a generation gap, a change in values between the old generation and the new. Much of the behavior which disturbs parents is really only the young trying to transcend what they see as hypocrisy among adults whose actions often are highly discrepant with their professed values and beliefs. But recognizing that these developments are literally tearing families apart and that many young people are destroying themselves trying to cope with the situation, more must be said than that.

One major root of the problem is associated with the motivations that have generated the flow of families to the suburbs since the second world war. Middle-class parents, as do parents of other social groups, typically move to the suburbs at least partly in order to provide a wholesome environment for their children, one in which they can protect their children from danger and guide them to become responsible, happy adults. Thus motivated, it perhaps is natural for parents to provide close supervision for their children and to confine a large share of their children's contacts and experiences to a relatively limited area centering on the home and the immediate neighborhood. In many cases such efforts constitute a systematic attempt to isolate children from negative influences in the outside world. This motivation is an admirable one and has much to recommend it. The trouble is that it often doesn't work beyond the point that a youngster is no longer a child.

Herbert Gans' participant-observer study of Levittown, New Jersey, is one of the few studies of suburbia in which appreciable attention was given to the circumstances and problems of children and young people. While Gans did not find much evidence to support many of the common stereotypes of the suburbs, he did find that Levittown was "child-centered" in the sense that it was much more suited to the needs of children than of teenagers. Although Levittown is a mixed suburb whose residents have a variety of social backgrounds, Gans' remarks on the adequacy of Levittown's environment for older children and young adults probably hold equally well for many if not most middle-income suburbs:

> The adult conception of Levittown's vitality is not shared by its adolescents. Many consider it a dull place to which they have been brought involuntarily by their parents. Often there is no place to go and nothing to do after school . . .
>
> Specifically, adolescent malcontent stems from two sources: Levittown was not designed for them, and adults are reluctant to provide the recreational facilities and gathering places they want. Like most suburban com-

munities, Levittown was planned for families with young children . . .
Shopping centers are intended for car-owning adults, and in accord with
the desire of property owners, are kept away from residential areas . . .

The schools were not designed for after-hours use, except for adults
and student activities which entertain adults, such as varsity athletics . . .

Recreational and social facilities are not enough, however. Part of the
adolescents' dissatisfaction with the community—as with adult society in
general—is their functionlessness outside of school. . . . They are trying
to learn to be adults, but since the community and the larger society want
them to be children, they learn adulthood only at school—and there im-
perfectly.[18]

Another adolescent need which is not well-satisfied, or even capable of being
satisfied, in the middle-income suburb is the necessity to feel part of the real
world. Adolescence is *par excellence* the time of life when a person must establish
a firm identity which seems comfortable and subjectively suited to enable one to
participate fully in adult society. It is understandable that a middle-class adult
male should want to retreat into the isolation and privacy of a sheltered, homogeneous suburb at the end of a day struggling to survive the pressures and frictions
of a diverse and competitive urban society. But his sons and daughters who are
searching for their own appropriate roles in life may not feel the same way.

Roles and identities, as Orrin E. Klapp,[19] Erik H. Erikson,[20] and others
have been pointing out, require testing and evaluation before oneself and others,
but the testing of an identity hardly can seem very authentic if it is done in a
context which a youngster knows reflects too small a part of reality. But in many
middle-income suburbs there are few opportunities, even in the school, to feel
"plugged in" to reality; thus the widespread unrest among middle-class youth
epitomized by a seventeen-year-old girl who responded to a reporter's question
about her suburban community with the statement, "Oh, I feel so sheltered . . .
And I just *hate* it. I don't think I've seen anything or done anything really unusual in my whole life. I love my parents, but I'm so dependent on them."[21]

Leaving extended analysis of identity problems, the bomb, the pill, the place
of rock music in youth culture, and related matters to others, this section cannot
be concluded without stressing the role of television and other mass media in
providing youngsters with some awareness that the genteel environment of the
middle-class suburb is not the real world. "The subjectivism of so many of today's
youth," H. L. Neiburg wrote recently, "is a search for firsthand experience and a
rejection not only of soap, but also of soap opera"[22]—but the soap opera being
rejected is not just that of radio or television but also the overly-inward-looking
orientation of the predominantly middle-income suburb. Thus it should be no
surprise that widespread unrest and deviancy have appeared most strikingly in
the middle-income suburbs whose young people feel most cut off from reality

[18] Herbert J. Gans, *The Levittowners* (New York: Pantheon, 1967), pp. 206–15.
[19] Orrin E. Klapp, *Collective Search for Identity* (New York: Holt, Rinehart, and Winston, 1969).
[20] Erik H. Erikson, *Identity: Youth and Crisis* (New York: W. W. Norton, 1968).
[21] Lois Wille, "The Suburb That Turned Its Back," *McCall's* (July, 1968), 14.
[22] H. L. Neiburg, "The Tech-fix and the City," in Henry J. Schmandt and Warner Bloom-
berg, Jr. (Eds.) *The Quality of Urban Life*, Volume Three, Urban Affairs Annual Reviews
(Beverly Hills, California: Sage, 1969), p. 238.

and at the same time are best qualified by education to perceive the gap between the news they read and see on television and the world around them. It probably will be another three-to-five years, by way of comparison, before manifestations of student unrest and rejection of current adult values become as serious a problem in working-class and mixed-class suburbs.

IMPLICATIONS

Educators certainly do not need to be told that the educative environments of the inner city students and the middle-income suburban students influence their behavior in the school; we experience this every day in our classrooms. But, to return to the question with which this paper started, do educators really understand how important the student's total educative environment is in determining how much he can be taught and whether he will accept or reject the educational opportunities that the school offers him?

In many cases they do not. If there were a better understanding, would professional behavior not indicate a greater awareness of the inseparability between what happens to students inside and outside the school and of the actions that might be taken to make education a more powerful influence in the lives of students?

In the inner city, for example, teachers and administrators would be found picketing boards of education and other public bodies to demand that families have a chance to live elsewhere than in poverty ghettoes and that students have a chance to attend schools outside the inner city. They would be in the forefront of movements to gain more effective economic and political power for people in the inner city. They would be working to initiate and implement comprehensive programs to overcome the racial prejudices ultimately responsible for the creation of the poverty ghetto.

In middle-income suburbs, they would be frantically reexamining and revising curricula to eliminate dated materials and replace them with experiences that help students understand and find a place in contemporary society. They would take the lead in increasing recreational and social facilities and programs inside and outside the school. They would be giving young people greater freedom and responsibility in the school, and they would be systematically challenging students to identify and work out solutions to the real problems in their lives. They would be much more active in changing the schools into "prototypes of our culture, posing real obstacles, real threats, and real conflicts . . . The schoolhouse, after all, is a place to learn, and one ought to be able there to learn about life the way it is."[23]

If educators do not take the lead in such matters, does that inaction not belie a claim to understanding?

[23] Bruno Bettelheim, "Autonomy and Inner Freedom: Skills of Emotional Management," *Life Skills in School and Society.* 1969 Yearbook of the Association for Supervision of Curriculum Development (Washington, D.C.: ASCD, 1969), pp. 92–93.

The Changing American Family

Marvin Sussman

There is a need to make visible the increased variability in family forms and to recognize the right of individuals to live in any family form they feel will increase their options for self-fulfillment. Although we recognize that the majority of children can find the conditions for character and personality development in the nuclear family, we do not favor any particular family form. Our central concern is that family conditions foster healthy physiological, emotional and social growth of children.

—Forum 14

The nuclear family of procreation, husband, wife and issue living in a separate household apart from other kin, is being subjected to its severest test in this age of Aquarius. Wholly an invention of man, the nuclear family—as it has evolved in recent history—is said to induce separation and isolation from other families.

One of the leading exponents of this argument, Margaret Mead, says, "We also have had a form of marriage that is probably one of the more precarious and fragile forms of marriage that people have ever tried. That form—the Nuclear Family—was not named after the bomb. It was just named after the physical analogy, but calling it the Nuclear Family is very good because it is just about as dangerous as the bomb."[1]

Dr. Mead's main theme, and one that I share, is that people, especially children, need a lot of other people. It may be that a form of group family such as those found in some types of communes may be the answer. But since the bulk of people in our society do not live in communes and do not plan to, some other forms of neighborhood organization may be required to build a psychologically sound "people-oriented" society, especially one that would be good for children.

The report of Forum 14 of the 1970 White House Conference on Children supported the thesis that diversity in family structure is present and "here to stay." Pluralism in family forms resembles the variation in racial, ethnic and religious groups which compose our salad-bowl culture. These diverse forms are increasing and family watchers are confused as to what this phenomenon means.

The popular press has examined, damned and praised these new family structures. The expression "alternative lifestyle" indicates something radically different and even exotic, and the commune family is most frequently exhorted as the ideal. What is misleading about all this is the stress placed on the unique and rare case.

From *AAUW Journal*, LXV, no. 2 (November 1971):10–12. Used by permission of the publisher.
[1] Margaret Mead, "Future Families," *Transaction*, 8 (September 1971), pp. 52–53.

To better understand what "pluralism of family structures" is all about, to differentiate between variations on the traditional nuclear form and emerging experimental ones which get the best press, let's consider a beginning typology which contains the principal but by no means all the forms. They are:

1. Nuclear family—husband, wife and offspring living in a common household.
   a. Single career
   b. Dual career
      1) Wife's career continuous
      2) Wife's career interrupted
2. Nuclear dyad—husband and wife alone: childless, or no children living at home.
   a. Single career
   b. Dual career
      1) Wife's career continuous
      2) Wife's career interrupted
3. Single-parent family—one head, as a consequence of divorce, abandonment, or separation (with financial aid rarely coming from the second parent), and usually including preschool and/or school-age children.
   a. Career
   b. Non-career
4. Single adult living alone.
5. Three-generation family—may characterize any variant of family forms 1, 2 or 3 living in a common household.
6. Middle-aged or elderly couple—husband as provider, wife at home (children have been "launched" into college, career or marriage).
7. Kin network—nuclear households or unmarried members living in close geographical proximity and operating within a reciprocal system of exchange of goods and services.
8. "Second-career" family—the wife enters the work force when the children are in school or have left the parental home.

Emerging experimental structures which have an effect on children include:

1. Commune family
   a. Household of more than one monogamous couple with children, sharing common facilities, resources and experiences; socialization of the child is a group activity.
   b. Household of adults and offspring—a "group marriage" known as one family—where all individuals are "married" to each other and all are "parents" to the children. Usually develops a status system with leaders believed to have charisma.
2. Unmarried parent and child family—usually mother and child, where marriage is not desired or possible.
3. Unmarried couple and child family—usually a common-law type of marriage with the child their biological issue or informally adopted.[2]

---

[2] Marvin B. Sussman et al., Forum 14 in *Report to the President: White House Conference on Children.* Margaret P. Brooks, research associate, Institute on the Family and the Bureaucratic Society, has suggested a modification of the original typology which is incorporated into this presentation.

NUCLEAR FAMILY AND ITS VARIANTS

All of us know of persons living in variations of the nuclear family presented in the first grouping; what we may not have appreciated is this growing diversity in family style and how it affects children.

The salient question is whether family members have been "pushed" or "pulled" into a variant or experimental form. There is a world of difference in the way one responds to children, friends, kin, helping professionals of human service systems, etc.—if the individual was "pulled," i.e., elected to take a job or was "pushed," that is, forced to because of economic need. The woman with small children who goes it alone because she chooses to and not because her husband dropped her is a single parent with a different set of perceptions, motivations and uses of options than her counterpart who was "pushed" into single parenthood.

The majority of persons who live in family forms that deviate from the traditional nuclear family do so as a consequence of uncontrolled events—a divorce or death, father abandoning the family or economic deprivation forcing the mother to seek employment.

Data from the latest census make strikingly clear the changing pattern of American family life, the growing incidence of such family forms as the single-parent family and the dual-work family. From 1948 to 1969, the percentage of mothers in the labor force with children less than six years old increased from 13 to 30 percent and with children aged six to seventeen, the percentage increased 31 to 51 percent. This increased incidence of family forms that vary from the traditional nuclear one is largely attributed to changing societal structures and values and less to deliberate selection of them.

What is clear is that each of the variant forms of family life have different needs for support from kin and human service systems; they have varying ability to cope with demands placed upon them by school, church and work. Various family structures, in turn, place differing stresses upon individual family members, especially children, to "make it" in society.

A second point is that each of these family forms has different problems to solve if it is to continue as a going concern. The most pressing immediate problem is that of allocation of roles so that the family can function in its day-to-day activities, allowing the self-fulfillment of the family members with their varying capabilities, motivations and aspirations. Another important requirement is flexibility which will allow easy movement from one family form to another, an event which is likely to occur at an average of two to three times over the life span of most Americans.

EXPERIMENTAL FAMILY

The experimental family forms are a genre of a different order. Some of today's youth declare the nuclear family form obsolete and seek an alternative lifestyle, one counter to their parents' with its boredom, tastelessness, meaninglessness and even agony. They seek some form of communal living.

Now that the excitement of the communal movement revival has abated, some critics have attacked the commune idea as a cop-out to the establishment, denigrating of women and ideologically unsound. "The counter-culture [most characteristically represented by the communes] turns the seeds of revolt into endless self-criticism, self-blame: just what the ruling class ordered. To think seriously of seizing power is not only out of the question but the height of immorality . . . the counter-culture does a thorough job in preventing all real material change."[3]

There have been many explanations of the increasing incidence of experimental family forms, but our interest is more in the consequences. However, the confusion and ambiguity over the purposes of these new forms and the lack of time to study them makes it impossible to theorize on how they will affect human relationships, particularly for the children raised in communes.

BUILT-IN ENVIRONMENT

With the growing pluralism in American family structures and the increasing incidence of experimental ones, it is essential, I believe, that we focus on the family's environment—the arrangement of social and physical space and the utilization of material resources and human services that should be built to meet the needs of the different kinds of families. *The family should be given the center position on the stage. The environment should be built around the family rather than fitting the family into a preconceived, standardized and often unimaginative and unexciting physical and social space.* These services should be the servants of the family, rather than the other way around.

For instance, for the young family where both parents work and there are small children, it is important that they have day care and after-school services. Instead of following the traditional pattern of locating "mother-helper" activities in a settlement house, church or other centrally located area of the community, such services in a model community would be integrated with the apartment, townhouse, duplex or single-family home style of living.

Medical care, marketing, dining, recreational and work facilities would be easily available in this family-centered environment. Those who provide services through schools, social agencies, eating establishments and day care centers would function as consultants to the family rather than as salesmen or surrogates. Whatever may be the package of services, it would be determined by the families themselves. They should know best what they need to have rich and exciting lives.

Pluralism in family structures is one major reason for urging this traditionectomy in thinking and practice. Another is the emerging value of the '70s that everyone has a right to do his "own thing" and that parents and children have the competence to decide what they need to enjoy a sense of fulfillment and excitement, to "make out" in this very complex society. A good example of this is that of providing options for the self-fulfillment of young, educated mothers whose personal satisfaction may rest on a job outside the home.

In short, the built-in environment should be so constructed that it optimizes the possibility of each family member achieving what he wishes with a minimum of frustration.

[3] Lynn O'Connor, "Alternative Life Styles: The Monster in Disguise," Supplement to the *Radical Therapist*. Hillsdale, N.Y., June, 1971, section 3.

STRONG RECOMMENDATION

Because of lack of information about the incidence and prevalance of variant and experimental family forms and because we know so little about the significance of these forms for human development, Forum 14 (Changing Families in a Changing Society) of the White House Conference on Children strongly recommended the establishment of a "People-Oriented National Institute for the Family for Action, Implementation, Legislation and Research," Among its many proposed functions are:

1. Develop and support demonstration, action, research and evaluation programs which focus on building new environments for families and children; reorder existing services and programs to fit around desires and aspirations of families, and to involve families in their development and implementation.
2. Examine existing legislation for its effects on variant family forms.
3. Take action against legislation, regulations and practices which are punitive to children because of their discriminatory policies against the integrity of families or variant forms of parenting.

SECTION 1   ADDITIONAL LEARNING ACTIVITIES

Problems and Projects

1. Describe the social forces in one community that *do affect*, and those that *should affect* the school curriculum and teaching in the community. Discuss them with your fellow students, community leaders, school principals, and others.
2. Begin to develop a "case problem" about one school and the curriculum and teaching in that school. Select a real school that you know well, and describe how its social setting affects the school and individual learners in that school. Then try to suggest how these forces should be reflected in the curriculum and teaching in that school. You will, of course, be suggesting changes in the curriculum and in teaching. You can add to this study as you work on each of the bases of the curriculum and the criteria.
3. Read *Our Children Are Dying*, by Nat Hentoff, Viking Press, 1966, for its description of P. S. 119 in Harlem—a school that has an "organic" relationship with its community. How do the curriculum and teaching in this school reflect the school's social setting?
4. Today the social forces that should be considered in curriculum planning often *change very rapidly*. In the article on pages 33-38, the author states that we have "largely solved the quantitative problems of our society." Is this still true today? Should the energy crisis now be included as one of the major contemporary problems of American society that should be considered in curriculum planning? Are there other changes in social forces that should be considered in planning and teaching that have occurred since the authors in this section wrote their articles?
5. Try the preassessment again, examining a different school or curriculum plan in the light of the social forces you have selected for study.

Films

Cities in Crisis: What's Happening, 16mm., color, 21 mins. Presents an exploratory view of a modern city by means of fast photography. Includes present day problems. Universal Education Visual Arts, 221 Park Avenue, S., New York, New York 10003.

Society and You, 16mm., color, 14 mins. Questions whether disenchantment with parents and discontentment with the way things are is to be considered valid. Distributed by Sterling Educational Films, P. O. Box 8497, Universal City, California 91608.

Videotapes

Overview of Human Relations Problems—A Series. Describes progress in human relations by developing goals for interpersonal behavior consistent with democratic ideals and by making an analysis of the central concept of democracy. Titles include *The Acting Crowd, The American Dream—Progress in Making It, Education for the Culturally Deprived, Public Opinion and the Power Structure*. Forty-five minutes each, black and white. Distributed by Great Plains Instructional T. V. Library, University of Nebraska, Lincoln, Nebraska 68508.

Books to Review

Alexander, W. M. *The High School of the Future: A Memorial To Kimball Wiles*. Columbus, Ohio: Charles E. Merrill Publishing Company, 1968 (part 2, "The Society of the Future and Its School").

Bennis, Warren; Benne, Kenneth; and Chin, Robert. *The Planning of Change,* 2d ed. New York: Holt, Rinehart and Winston, 1969.

Cuban, Larry. *To Make a Difference: Teaching in the Inner City.* New York: The Free Press, 1970.

Drucker, Peter F. *The Age of Discontinuity: Guidelines to Our Changing Society.* Harper and Row, Publishers, 1969.

Eddy, Elizabeth. *Walk the White Line: A Profile of Urban Education.* Garden City, New York: Doubleday and Co., 1967.

Fantini, Maria, and Weinstein, Gerald. *Making Urban Schools Work.* New York: Holt, Rinehart and Winston, 1968.

Finifter, Ada W., ed. *Alienation and the Social System.* New York: John Wiley and Sons, 1972.

Greer, Germaine. *The Female Eunuch.* New York: McGraw-Hill Book Company, 1971.

Havighurst, Robert J. *Education in Metropolitan Areas,* 2d ed. Boston: Allyn and Bacon, 1971.

Martin, John Henry, and Harrison, Charles. *Free To Learn: Unlocking and Ungrading American Education.* Englewood Cliffs, New Jersey: Prentice-Hall, 1972.

Miller, Harry L., and Smiley, Marjorie, eds. *Education in the Metropolis.* New York: The Free Press, 1967.

Muller, Herbert J. *The Children of Frankenstein: A Primer on Modern Technology and Human Values.* Bloomington: Indiana University Press, 1970.

Mintz, Morton, and Cohen, Jerry S. *America, Inc.: Who Owns and Operates the United States.* New York: The Dial Press, 1971.

Raths, Louis E.; Harmin, M.; and Simon, S. B. *Values and Teaching: Working With Values in the Classroom.* Columbus, Ohio: Charles E. Merrill Publishing Co., 1966.

Reich, Charles A. *The Greening of America.* New York: Random House, 1970.

Rich, John Martin. *Conflict and Decision: Analyzing Educational Issues.* New York: Harper and Row, Publishers, 1972.

Schneider, Kenneth R. *Destiny of Change: How Relevant Is Man in the Age of Development?* New York: Holt, Rinehart and Winston, 1968.

Smiley, Marjorie, and Miller, Harry L., eds. *Policy Issues in Urban Education.* New York: The Free Press, 1968.

Smith, Kline and French Laboratories. *Drug Abuse: Escape to Nowhere: A Guide for Educators.* Philadelphia: Smith, Kline and French Laboratories, 1969, 104 pp.

Toffler, Alvin. *Future Shock.* New York: Random House, 1970.

Wasserman, Miriam. *The School Fix, N.Y.C., U.S.A.* New York: Simon and Schuster, 1970.

Woock, Roger R. *Education and the Urban Crisis.* Scranton, Pennsylvania: International Textbook Company, 1970.

Human Development

PREREQUISITE

Reading of the Introduction to this book and Section 1.

RATIONALE

Human development is generally accepted as one of the bases of the curriculum. The study of child and adolescent development is regarded as one of the basic sciences underlying education.

The human development approach to the curriculum and to teaching includes a body of knowledge about human growth. It also includes a point of view with reference to learners: they should be studied as individuals, so that the program of instruction can be shaped, in part, by the individual's own nature and needs.

There are a number of generally accepted stages of human development, including infancy, childhood, early adolescence, middle adolescence, and late adolescence. The elementary school years correspond roughly to the stage known as childhood. Early, middle, and late adolescence correspond roughly to the middle school, high school, and community college levels of the school. The stage concept is useful as a rough rule of thumb but it cannot define the development of any one learner at a particular age.

Several theorists and their research studies have had particular influence on curriculum planning. They include Havighurst and the "developmental tasks" concept; Erikson and his stages of "growth toward a mature personality"; and Piaget and his four stages of growth in intelligence through "assimilation" and "accommodation." Articles concerning all three of these theorists and their theories are included in this section.

Curriculum planning should be guided by five aspects of development:

1. The biological basis of individual development
2. Physical maturation
3. Intellectual development and achievement
4. Emotional growth and development
5. Cultural pressures

Havighurst's and Piaget's theories consider the biological, psychological, and cultural aspects of development. Erikson's theory emphasizes emotional growth and development.

Ausubel discusses several concepts of significance in curriculum planning that he relates to human growth and development: *readiness,* which is based on both maturation and learning; *breadth and depth of the curriculum;* the *learner's voice in curriculum planning;* and *organization and cognitive development.*

Maturation and change in human development occur over the whole life span, providing one of the bases for curriculum and instruction planning at all age levels, including university and adult education. Havighurst's developmental tasks include those of adult and later life. Erikson's theory also examines human development during adult and later life.

Maturation follows different courses of development for the different kinds of development and behavior. One of the guidelines for curriculum planning to be derived from the study of human development is the "problem of the match." Some sort of fitting or matching between the development stage and the program of learning is needed by each individual. The goal of curriculum makers and teachers is to see that the proper match is accomplished.

OBJECTIVES

Your objectives in studying human development as one of the bases of curriculum planning should be as follows:

1. To be able to analyze a curriculum plan with respect to its relationship to human development research and theories.
2. To be able to suggest changes and improvements in the curriculum plan that are based on an understanding of human development theories and research.
3. To be able to plan for teaching in terms of human development stages and individual needs and development.

PREASSESSMENT

The purpose of the preassessment is to enable you to determine whether you already possess the performance competencies in curriculum planning that are listed under "Objectives" above.

1. Select three aspects of human development and tell how each can be applied to planning a curriculum or teaching.
2. Describe each of the following human development concepts and how they may be applied to curriculum planning and teaching: stages of development; developmental tasks; readiness; assimilation and accommodation; growth toward a mature personality.

3. Select any curriculum plan, at any school level, and examine it in the light of human development concepts, theories, and research. This could be done by visiting and studying a school, or by analyzing a written statement regarding a school's program or the instruction in one classroom. You might choose some part of the school's curriculum, such as the social studies curriculum.
4. Suggest improvements or changes in the curriculum plan as a result of your analysis in number 3.

If you find that the school of your choice does not consider human development in its curriculum planning, suggest improvements in the planning on the basis of knowledge about human development. Begin by checking the developmental tasks of the age group in the school (in terms of Havighurst's theory described in "Developmental Tasks" in this section). Then see what other theories, such as Erikson's and Piaget's (see their articles in this section), suggest for this age level. Remember that individual variations must be considered in providing for individual learners.

In answering number 3 of the preassessment, you might choose to analyze the curriculum of the non-graded middle school at Liverpool, New York, described by Robert J. McCartney in Section 7 of this book.

LEARNING ACTIVITIES

Articles in this section will assist you in identifying and understanding human development concepts, theories, and research that are important in curriculum planning and in planning for teaching.

Other learning activities are suggested at the end of this section.

POSTASSESSMENT

After attempting the preassessment you may do one or more of the following:

1. See if your instructor believes that you are ready for a postassessment evaluation on human development and the curriculum. Most students will need further work on this curriculum base.
2. Read the articles on human development in this section and try to determine how the theories and research being discussed in each article should be considered in curriculum planning and teaching.
3. Choose additional activities and readings or films and videotapes from those listed at the end of this section under "Additional Learning Activities."
4. Look for other films, books, or articles on human development in your library or media center.
5. Discuss the reading you have done and the films you have viewed with your fellow students. The key questions: How should the human development theories and research you've studied affect a school's curriculum? How should they be considered in planning for teaching?
6. When you are ready, ask your instructor for advice on a suitable postassessment for you for this topic. Satisfactory completion of number 3 or 4 under "Problems and Projects" at the end of this section might be one possibility. Or written completion of the preassessment for this section, after completing

other learning activities, might be a satisfactory postassessment. Consult your instructor about this. You can evaluate your own ability to do these activities before you see the instructor.

The Biology of Behavior

Roger J. Williams

The prevalence of student rebellions throughout the world makes one wonder just how effectively modern education relates to real human problems. To approach the problems of generic man from a biological standpoint may be far too superficial in this scientific age with its tremendous advances in technology; yet, could not the general weakness of human science be the basis for the comment by Robert Frost: "Poets like Shakespeare knew more about psychiatry than any $25-an-hour man"?

Biologically, each member of the human family possesses inborn differences based on his brain structure and on his vast mosaic of endocrine glands—in fact, on every aspect of his physical being. Each of us has a distinctive set of drives— for physical activity, for food, for sexual expression, for power. Each one has his own mind qualities: abilities, ways of thinking, and patterns of mental conditions. Each one has his own emotional setup and his leanings toward music and art in its various forms, including literature. All these leanings are subject to change and development, but there is certainly no mass movement toward uniformity. No one ever "recovers" from the fact that he was born an individual.

When a husband and wife disagree on the temperature of the soup or on the amount of bed coverings, or if their sleep patterns do not jibe, this is evidence of inborn differences in physiology. If one child loves to read or is interested in science and another has strong likings for sports or for art, this is probably due to inborn differences in makeup. If two people disagree about food or drink, they should not disregard the fact that taste and smell reactions often widely differ and are inherited. If we see a person wearing loud clothing without apparent taste, we need to remember, in line with the investigations of Pickford in England, that each individual has a color vision all his own; some may deviate markedly from the pack.

The inborn leanings of Mozart were evident by age three, and he began composing when he was four. Capablanca was already a good chess player—good enough to beat his father—when at age five he played his first game. For many centuries, Indian philosophers have recognized innate individuality, which they explain on the basis of experience in previous incarnations.

Biology has always recognized inborn individuality. If this inborn distinctiveness had not always been the rule in biology, evolution could never have happened. It is a commonplace fact in biology that every living organism needs a heredity and a suitable environment. Unfortunately, in the minds of most intellectuals biological considerations have been pushed aside.

Professor Jerry Hirsch, a psychologist at the University of Illinois, has protested in *Science* that "the opinion makers of two generations have literally excommunicated heredity from the behavioral sciences." This neglect of the study of heredity has effectively produced a wide gap between biology and psychology. Biology deals with living things, and psychology is logically an important phase of biology.

Bernard Rimland, director of the Institute for Child Behavior Research in San Diego, in reviewing my book *You Are Extraordinary* in *American Psychologist*, wrote: "Since between-group differences are commonly a small fraction of the enormous, important, and very interesting within-group (individual) difference, psychology's focus on average values for heterogenous groups represents, as Williams indicates, a chronic case of throwing out the babies with the bath water. 'Throwing out the babies' is bad enough, but we psychologists have the dubious distinction of making this error not only repeatedly but *on purpose*."

Social solidarity exists and social problems are pressing, but we cannot hope to deal with these successfully by considering only generic man, that is, average values for heterogenous groups. We need a better understanding of *men*.

The basic problem of generic man is how to achieve "life, liberty, and the pursuit of happiness." The writers of our Declaration of Independence were on solid ground, biologically speaking, when they took the position that each human being has inalienable rights and that no one has, by virtue of his imagined "royal blood," the right to rule over another. In their emphasis on mankind as individuals, Jefferson and his co-authors were closer to biological reality than are those of our time who divorce psychology from biology and center their attention on that statistical artifact, the average man.

Because each of us is distinctive, we lean in different directions in achieving life, liberty, and the pursuit of happiness. Happiness may come to individual people in vastly different ways, and so the human problem of achieving life and the pursuit of happiness resolves itself, more than it is comfortable to admit, into a series of highly individual human problems. We need to take this consideration into account in attempting to build an advanced society.

In understanding the scope of human desires, it is worthwhile to consider briefly the problems that real—as opposed to theoretical—people face. These may be grouped under four headings: 1) making a livelihood; 2) maintaining health; 3) getting along with others; and 4) getting along with one's self. These four categories, singly or in combination, cover most of the familiar human problems—marriage and divorce, crime, disease, war, housing, and water pollution, urban congestion, race relations, poverty, the population explosion, the all-pervading problem of education, and the building of an abundant life.

The importance of approaching the problem of making a livelihood from the individual's standpoint lies in the fact that in our complex society a multitude of ways exist—an estimated 23,000—in which people can make a living. People are not by any means interchangeable parts in society. While some might function well in any one of a large number of capacities, many others might be highly restricted in their capabilities and yet be extremely valuable members of society. The idea that it is all a matter of education and training cannot possibly be squared with the hard biological facts in inborn individuality. This perversion of education perpetuates the banishment of heredity—an ever present biological fact—from our thinking. Fitting together people and jobs is just as real and compelling as fitting shoes to people. People sometimes suffer from ill-fitting shoes; they suffer more often from ill-fitting jobs.

The maintenance of health—both physical and mental—involves individual problems to such a degree that it is difficult to exaggerate their role. Ever since the days of Hippocrates it has been known in a vague way that "different sorts of people have different maladies," but we are only beginning to learn how to sort people on the basis of their inborn individual characteristics. When we have become expert in this area, vast progress will result, particularly in the prevention of metabolic and psychosomatic diseases, i.e., those not resulting from infection. As long as we dodge the biological fact of inborn individuality, we remain relatively impotent in the handling of diseases that arise from within individual constitutions.

The problem of getting along with others is a very broad one, in which individual problems are basic. If husbands and wives and members of the same family always get along well together, we would have some reason to be surprised when squabbles break out within business, religious, or political groups. If all these kinds of squabbles were non-existent, we would have a basis for being surprised at the phenomenon of war.

While self-interest and differences in training are vital factors in these common conflicts, another factor should not be overlooked: the inborn individuality of the participants. There is a mass of evidence to support the thesis that every individual, by virtue of his or her unique brain structure and peripheral nervous system, is psychologically conditionable in a distinctive manner. Thus, a person's unique nervous system picks up distinctive sets of impulses, and because his interpretive apparatus is also unique he learns different things and interprets the world in a distinctive manner. Even if two individuals were to have exactly the same learning opportunities, each would think differently and not quite like anyone else. This is the basis for the observation by Santayana: "Friendship is almost always the union of a part of one mind with another; people are friends in spots."

In spite of our attempts to do so, individual minds cannot be compared on a quantitative basis. The minds of Shakespeare and Einstein cannot be weighed one against the other; there were many facets to the minds of each. At birth the two minds were equally blank, but as they matured, each saw, perceived, and paid attention to different aspects of the world around it. Each was conditionable in a unique way.

The recognition of the uniqueness of human minds is essential to human understanding. By developing expertness in this area, psychology will eventually become far more valuable. In an advanced society with a growing population and closer associations, it is obviously essential that we learn better how to get along with each other. When we are unaware of the innate differences that reside within each of us, it becomes very easy to think of one who disagrees with us as a "nitwit" or a "jerk," or perhaps as belonging to the "lunatic fringe." When we appreciate the existence of innate differences, we are far more likely to be understanding and charitable. Strife will not be automatically eliminated, but tensions can be decreased immeasurably.

Individual problems are at the root of the problem of crime. Many years ago, James Devon placed his finger on the crucial point. "There is only one principle in penology that is worth any consideration: It is to find out why a man does wrong and make it not worth his while." The question "Why does a particular man commit crime?" is a cogent one; the question "Why does man turn to crime?" is relatively nonsensical.

Since all human beings are individual by nature, they do not tick in a uniform way nor for the same reasons. Broadly speaking, however, many doubtless turn to crime because society has not provided other outlets for their energies. If we could find a suitable job for every individual, the problem of crime would largely vanish. The problem of crime is thoroughly permeated with individual problems; it cannot be blamed solely on social conditions, because as the studies of Sheldon and Eleanor Glueck have shown, highly respected citizens may come from areas where these conditions are the worst.

Racial relations would ease tremendously if we faced squarely the biological facts of individuality. If we were all educated to know that all whites are not the same, that all Negroes do not fit in the same pattern, that all Latins are not identical, that all American Indians are individuals, and that all Jews do not fit a stereotype, it would help us to treat every member of the human race as an individual.

It is no denial of the existence of racial problems to assert that individual problems need to be stressed more than they are. For individual Negroes and individual whites, the pursuit of happiness is by no means a uniform pursuit. Doubtlessly, although there are whites and Negroes who would think they had reached Utopia if they had a decent shelter and were assured three meals a day, this would not satisfy millions of others for whom striving and a sense of accomplishment are paramount. "The Negro problem" or "the white problem"—depending on one's point of view—is shot through with a host of individual problems.

Learning to live with one's self is certainly an individual problem, and will be greatly eased by recognition of inborn individuality. Much unhappiness and many suicides can be traced to misguided desire to be something other than one's self. Each of us as an individual has the problem of finding his way through life as best he can. Knowing one's self as a distinctive individual should be an important goal of education; it will help pave the road each of us travels in his pursuit of happiness.

Why have these facts of individuality not been generally accepted as a backdrop in every consideration of human problems? For one thing, many people, including scholars, like being grandiose and self-inflationary. To make sweeping pronouncements about "man" sounds more impressive than to express more limited concerns. Simplicity, too, has an attractiveness; if life could be made to fit a simple formula, this might be regarded as a happy outcome.

One excuse for excommunicating inheritance from the behavioral sciences for two generations has been the fact that inheritance in mammals is recognized by careful students as being exceedingly complex and difficult to interpret. It is true that some few characteristics may be inherited through the operation of single genes or a few recognizable ones. But other characteristics—those that differ in quantity—are considered to be inherited in obscure and indefinable ways commonly ascribed to multiple genes of indefinite number and character. These multiple-gene characteristics include, to quote the geneticists Snyder and David, "the more deep-seated characters of a race, such as form, yield, intelligence, speed, fertility, strength, development of parts, and so on." To say that a particular characteristic is inherited through the mediation of multiple genes is to admit that we are largely ignorant of how this inheritance comes about.

Recently, some light has been thrown on this problem by experiments carried out in our laboratories. These experiments involved armadillos, which are unusual mammals in that they commonly produce litters of four monozygous ("identical") quadruplets that are necessarily all males or all females.

By making measurements and studying sixteen sets of these animals at birth, it became evident that although they develop from identical genes, they are not identical at all. Organ weights may differ by as much as twofold, the free amino acids in the brain may vary fivefold, and certain hormone levels may vary as much as seven-, sixteen-, or even thirty-twofold. These findings clearly suggest that inheritance comes not by genes alone but by cytoplasmic factors that help govern the size of organs (including endocrine glands) and the cellular makeup of the central nervous system. "Identical" twins are not identical except with respect to the genes in the nucleus of the egg cell from which they developed.

One of the most interesting suggestions arising out of this study is the probability that individual brain structures, which have been known to have "enormous" differences since the investigations of Lashley more than twenty years ago, are made distinctive by the same mechanisms that make for differences in organ weights. The size, number, and distributions of neurons in normal brains vary greatly; this is biologically in line with the uniqueness of human minds. The further elucidation of this type of inheritance should help to focus more attention on heredity.

If this line of thought is valid it makes even more ridiculous the invitation issued by the Ford Foundation to the biological sciences to stay out of the precinct of human behavior. The expression "behavioral science" came into being many years ago as a result of the formulation of the Ford Foundation-supported programs. Biochemistry and genetics, for example, were kept apart from the "scientific activities designed to increase knowledge of factors which influence or determine human conduct."

What can be done to bridge the gap between psychology and biology? More importantly, how can we develop expertise in dealing with the human problems that plague us but at present go unsolved?

A broad, long-range, and practical strategy for learning how to deal more effectively with human problems is to explore, problem by problem, the inborn human characteristics that are pertinent to each one. Differential psychology, for example, needs to be intensified and greatly expanded; this can probably be done most effectively in connection with a series of problem-centered explorations.

Some of the specific problem-areas that require study from the standpoint of how inborn characteristics come into play are: delinquency and crime, alcoholism, drug addiction, unemployability, accident proneness, cancer, heart disease, arthritic disease, mental disease, and, broadest of all, education. Each of these problems could be vastly better understood as the result of interdisciplinary study of the influences of inborn characteristics. Such study would include differential psychology when applicable, combined with extensive and intensive biochemical and physiological examinations, for example, of blood, saliva, urine, and biopsy materials. To expedite these investigations, automated equipment and computer techniques would be used extensively to help interpret the complex data.

It is not likely that these explorations will find that some individuals are born criminals, others alcoholics, etc. Once we recognize the unique leanings that are a part of each of us, we will see how, by adjusting the environment, these leanings can be turned toward ends that are socially constructive. Every inherited factor can be influenced by an appropriate adjustment of the environment. All this should not be made to sound too easy; it may be more difficult than going to the moon, but it will be far more worthwhile.

One of these specific problems—alcoholism—has been of special interest to me. After about twenty-five years of study, I am convinced that inborn biochemical characteristics are basic to this disease, but that expert application of knowledge about cellular nutrition (which is not far off) will make it scientifically possible to prevent the disease completely and to correct the condition if the application of corrective measures is not too long delayed.

Inborn inherited characteristics have a direct bearing on the current revolt against the Establishment. If biology had not been banished from behavioral science, and if students and other intellectuals were well aware of the biological roots of their existence, it would be taken for granted that conformity is not a rule of life.

If all that we human beings inherit is our humanity, then we all should be reaching for the same uniform goal: becoming a thoroughly representative and respectable specimen of Homo sapiens. There is rebellion against this idea. Revolters want to do "their thing." The revolt takes on many forms because many unique individuals are involved.

If non-conformity had a better status in the eyes of the Establishment (and it would have if our thinking were more biologically oriented), exhibitionism would be diminished and the desire of each individual to live his own life could be fostered in a natural way.

Human beings are not carbon copies of one another. Students and others who are in revolt have found this out. Perhaps without fully recognizing it, they are pleading for a recognition of inborn individuality. This is essentially a legitimate plea, but it can take the form of disastrous anarchy. A peaceful means of helping resolve the ideological mess we are in is to recognize heredity by having a happy marriage of biology and behavioral science.

New Light on the Human Potential

Herbert A. Otto

William James once estimated that the healthy human being is functioning at less than 10 percent of his capacity. It took more than half a century before this idea found acceptance among a small proportion of behavioral scientists. In 1954, the highly respected and widely known psychologist Gardner Murphy published his pioneering volume *Human Potentialities*. The early Sixties saw the beginnings of the human potentialities research project at the University of Utah and the organization of Esalen Institute in California, the first of a series of "Growth Centers" that were later to be referred to as the Human Potentialities Movement.

Today, many well-known scientists such as Abraham Maslow, Margaret Mead, Gardner Murphy, O. Spurgeon English, and Carl Rogers subscribe to the hypothesis that man is using a very small fraction of his capacities. Margaret Mead quotes a 6 percent figure, and my own estimate is 5 percent or less. Commitment to the hypothesis is not restricted to the United States. Scientists in the U.S.S.R. and other countries are also at work. Surprisingly, the so-called human potentialities hypothesis is still largely unknown.

What are the dimensions of the human potential? The knowledge we do have about man is minimal and has not as yet been brought together with the human potentialities hypothesis as an organizing force and synthesizing element. Of course, we know more about man today than we did fifty years ago, but this is like the very small part of the iceberg we see above the water. Man essentially remains a mystery. From the depths of this mystery there are numerous indicators of the human potential.

Certain indicators of man's potential are revealed to us in childhood. They become "lost" or submerged as we succumb to the imprinting of the cultural mold in the "growing up" process. Do you remember when you were a child and it rained after a dry spell and there was a very particular, intensive earthy smell in the air? Do you remember how people smelled when they hugged you? Do you recall the brilliant colors of leaves, flowers, grass, and even brick surfaces and lighted signs that you experienced as a child? Furthermore, do you recall that when father and mother stepped into the room you *knew* how they felt about themselves, about life, and about you—at that moment.

Today we know that man's sense of smell, one of the most powerful and primitive senses, is highly developed. In the average man this capacity has been suppressed except for very occasional use. Some scientists claim that man's sense of smell is almost as keen as a hunting dog's. Some connoisseurs of wines, for

From *Saturday Review* LII, no. 51 (December 20, 1969):14–17. Copyright 1969 by Saturday Review, Inc. Used by permission of author and publisher.

example, can tell by the bouquet not only the type of grape and locality where they were grown but even the vintage year and vineyard. Perfume mixers can often detect fantastically minute amounts in mixed essences; finally there are considerable data on odor discrimination from the laboratory. It is also clear that, since the air has become an overcrowded garbage dump for industrial wastes and the internal combustion engine, it is easier to turn off our sense of smell than to keep it functioning. The capacity to experience the environment more fully through our olfactory organs remains a potential.

It is possible to regain these capacities through training. In a similar manner, sensory and other capacities, including visual, kinesthetic, and tactile abilities, have become stunted and dulled. We perceive less clearly, and as a result we feel less—we use our dulled senses to close ourselves off from both our physical and interpersonal environments. Today we also dull our perceptions of how other people feel and we consistently shut off awareness of our own feelings. For many who put their senses to sleep it is a sleep that lasts unto death. Again, through sensory and other training the doors of perception can be cleansed (to use Blake's words) and our capacities reawakened. Anthropological research abounds with reports of primitive tribes that have developed exceptional sensory and perceptive abilities as a result of training. Utilization of these capacities by modern man for life-enrichment purposes awaits the furture.

Neurological research has shed new light on man's potential. Work at the UCLA Brain Research Institute points to enormous abilities latent in everyone by suggesting an incredible hypothesis: The ultimate brain may be, for all practical purposes, infinite. To use the computer analogy, man is a vast storehouse of data, but we have not learned how to program ourselves to utilize these data for problem-solving purposes. Recall of experiential data is extremely spotty and selective for most adults. My own research has convinced me that the recall of experiences can be vastly improved by use of certain simple training techniques, provided sufficient motivation is present.

Under emergency conditions, man is capable of prodigious feats of physical strength. For example, a middle-aged California woman with various ailments lifted a car just enough to let her son roll out from under it after it had collapsed on him. According to newspaper reports the car weighed in excess of 2,000 pounds. There are numerous similar accounts indicating that every person has vast physical reserve capacities that can be tapped. Similarly, the extraordinary feats of athletes and acrobats—involving the conscious and specialized development of certain parts of the human organism as a result of consistent application and a high degree of motivation—point to the fantastic plasticity and capabilities of the human being.

Until World War II, the field of hypnosis was not regarded as respectable by many scientists and was associated with stage performances and charlatanism. Since that time hypnosis has attained a measure of scientific respectability. Medical and therapeutic applications of hypnosis include the use of this technique in surgery and anesthesiology (hypnoanesthesia for major and minor surgery), gynecology (infertility, frigidity, menopausal conditions), pediatrics (enuresis, tics, asthma in children, etc.), and in dentistry. Scores of texts on medical and dental hypnosis are available. Dr. William S. Kroger, one of the specialists in the field and author of the well-known text *Clinical and Experimental Hypnosis*, writes that hypnotherapy is "directed to the patient's needs and is a methodology to tap the 'forgotten assets' of the *hidden potentials* of behavior and response that so often lead to new learnings and understanding."(My italics.) As far as we know now, the possibilities opened by hypnosis for the potential functioning of the human organism are not brought about by the hypnotist. Changes are induced by the subject, utilizing his belief-structure, with the hypnotist operating as an "enabler," making it possible for the subject to tap some of his unrealized potential.

The whole area of parapsychology that deals with extrasensory perception (ESP), "mental telepathy," and other paranormal phenomena, and that owes much of its development to the work of Dr. J. B. Rhine and others is still regarded by much of the scientific establishment with the same measure of suspicion accorded hypnosis in the pre-World War II days. It is of interest that a number of laboratories in the U.S.S.R. are devoted to the study of telepathy as a physical phenomenon, with research conducted under the heading "cerebral radio-communication" and "bioelectronics." The work is supported by the Soviet government. The reluctance to accept findings from this field of research is perhaps best summarized by an observation of Carl C. Jung's in 1958:

> (Some) people deny the findings of parapsychology outright, either for philosophical reasons or from intellectual laziness. This can hardly be considered a scientifically responsible attitude, even though it is a popular way out of quite extraordinary intellectual difficulty.

Although the intensive study of creativity had its beginnings in fairly recent times, much of value has been discovered about man's creative potential. There is evidence that every person has creative abilities that can be developed. A considerable number of studies indicate that much in our educational system—including conformity pressures exerted by teachers, emphasis on memory development, and rote learning, plus the overcrowding of classrooms—militates against the development of creative capacities. Research has established that children between the ages of two and three can learn to read, tape record a story, and type it as it is played back. Hundreds of children between the ages of four and six have been taught by the Japanese pedagogue Suzuki to play violin concertos. Japanese research with infants and small children also suggests the value of early "maximum input" (music, color, verbal, tactile stimuli) in the personality development of infants. My own observations tend to confirm this. We have consistently underestimated the child's capacity to learn and his ability to realize his potential while enjoying both the play elements and the discipline involved in this process.

In contrast to the Japanese work, much recent Russian research appears to be concentrated in the area of mentation, with special emphasis on extending and enlarging man's mental processes and his capacity for learning. As early as 1964 the following appeared in *Soviet Life Today*, a U.S.S.R. English language magazine:

> The latest findings in anthropology, psychology, logic, and physiology show that the potential of the human mind is very great indeed. "As soon as modern science gave us some understanding of the structure and work of the human brain, we were struck with its enormous reserve capacity," writes Yefremov (Ivan Yefremov, eminent Soviet scholar and writer). "Man, under average conditions of work and life, uses only a small part of his thinking

equipment. . . . If we were able to force our brain to work at only half its capacity, we could, without any difficulty whatever, learn forty languages, memorize the large Soviet Encyclopedia from cover to cover, and complete the required courses of dozens of colleges."

The statement is hardly an exaggeration. It is the generally accepted theoretical view of man's mental potentialities.

How can we tap this gigantic potential? It is a big and very complex problem with many ramifications.

Another signpost of man's potential is what I have come to call the "Grandma Moses effect." This artist's experience indicates that artistic talents can be discovered and brought to full flowering in the latter part of the life cycle. In every retirement community there can be found similar examples of residents who did not use latent artistic abilities or other talents until after retirement. In many instances the presence of a talent is suspected or known but allowed to remain fallow for the best part of a lifetime.

Reasons why well-functioning mature adults do not use specific abilities are complex. Studies conducted at the University of Utah as a part of the Human Potentialities Research Project revealed that unconscious blocks are often present. In a number of instances a person with definite evidence that he has a specific talent (let's say he won a state-wide contest in sculpture while in high school) may not wish to realize this talent at a later time because he fears this would introduce a change in life-style. Sometimes fear of the passion of creation is another roadblock in self-actualization. On the basis of work at Utah it became clear that persons who live close to their capacity, who continue to activate their potential, have a pronounced sense of well-being and considerable energy and see themselves as leading purposeful and creative lives.

Most people are unaware of their strengths and potentialities. If a person with some college background is handed a form and asked to write out his personality strengths, he will list, on an average, five or six strengths. Asked to do the same thing for his weaknesses, the list will be two to three times as long. There are a number of reasons for this low self-assessment. Many participants in my classes and marathon group weekends have pointed out that "listing your strengths feels like bragging about yourself. It's something that just isn't done." Paradoxically, in a group, people feel more comfortable about sharing problem areas and hang-ups than they do about personality resources and latent abilities. This is traceable to the fact that we are members of a pathology-oriented culture. Psychological and psychiatric jargon dealing with emotional dysfunction and mental illness has become the parlance of the man in the street. In addition, from early childhood in our educational system we learn largely by our mistakes—by having them pointed out to us repeatedly. All this results in early "negative conditioning" and influences our attitude and perception of ourselves and other people. An attitudinal climate has become established which is continually fed and reinforced.

As a part of this negative conditioning there is the heavy emphasis by communications media on violence in television programs and motion pictures. The current American news format of radio, television, and newspapers—the widely prevalent idea of what constitutes news—results from a narrow, brutalizing concept thirty or forty years behind the times and is inimical to the development of human potential.

The news media give much time and prominent space to violence and consistently underplay "good" news. This gives the consumer the impression that important things that happen are various types of destructive activities. Consistent and repeated emphasis on bad news not only creates anxiety and tension but instills the belief that there is little except violence, disasters, accidents, and mayhem abroad in the world. As a consequence, the consumer of such news gradually experiences a shift in his outlook about the world leading to the formation of feelings of alienation and separation. The world is increasingly perceived as a threat, as the viewer becomes anxious that violence and mayhem may be perpetrated on him from somewhere out of the strange and unpredictable environment in which he lives. There slowly grows a conviction that it is safer to withdraw from such a world, to isolate himself from its struggles, and to let others make the decisions and become involved.

As a result of the steady diet of violence in the media, an even more fundamental and insidious erosion in man's self-system takes place. The erosion affects what I call the "trust factor." If we have been given a certain amount of affection, love, and understanding in our formative years, we are able to place a certain amount of trust in our fellow man. Trust is one of the most important elements in today's society although we tend to minimize its importance. We *basically trust people.* For example, we place an enormous amount of trust in our fellow man when driving on a freeway or in an express lane. We trust those with whom we are associated to fulfill their obligations and responsibilities. The element of trust is the basic rule in human relations. When we distrust people, they usually sense our attitude and reciprocate in kind.

The consistent emphasis in the news on criminal violence, burglarizing, and assault makes slow but pervasive inroads into our reservoir of trust. As we hear and read much about the acts of violence and injury men perpetrate upon one another, year after year, with so little emphasis placed on the loving, caring, and humanitarian acts of man, we begin to trust our fellow man less, and we thereby diminish ourselves. It is my conclusion the media's excessive emphasis on violence, like the drop of water on the stone, erodes and wears away the trust factor in man. By undermining the trust factor in man, media contribute to man's estrangement from man and prevent the full flourishing and deeper development of a sense of community and communion with all men.

Our self-concept, how we feel about ourselves and our fellow man and the world, is determined to a considerable extent by the inputs from the physical and interpersonal environment to which we are exposed. In the physical environment, there are the irritants in the air, i.e., air pollution plus the ugliness and noise of megapolis. Our interpersonal environment is characterized by estrangement and distance from others (and self), and by the artificiality and superficiality of our social encounters and the resultant violation of authenticity. Existing in a setting that provides as consistent inputs multiple irritants, ugliness and violence, and lack of close and meaningful relationships, man is in danger of becoming increasingly irritated, ugly, and violent.

As work in the area of human potentialities progressed, it has become ever clearer that personality, to a much greater degree than previously suspected, functions in response to the environment. This is additional confirmation of what field theorists and proponents of the holistic approach to the study of man have long suspected.

Perhaps the most important task facing us today is the regeneration of our environment and institutional structures such as school, government, church, etc. With increasing sophistication has come the recognition that institutions are not sacrosanct and that they have but one purpose and function—to serve as a framework for the actualization of human potential. It is possible to evaluate both the institution and the contribution of the institution by asking this question: "To what extent does the function of the institution foster the realization of human potential?"

Experimental groups consistently have found that the more a person's environment can be involved in the process of realizing potential, the greater the gains. It is understandable why scientists concerned with the study of personality have been reluctant to consider the importance of here-and-now inputs in relation to personality functioning. To do so would open a Pandora's box of possibilities and complex forces that until fairly recently were considered to be the exclusive domain of the social scientist. Many scientists and professionals, particularly psychotherapists, feel they have acquired a certain familiarity with the topography of "intra-psychic forces" and are reluctant to admit the reality of additional complex factors in the functioning of the personality.

It is significant that an increasing number of psychologists, psychiatrists, and social workers now realize that over and beyond keeping up with developments in their respective fields, the best way to acquire additional professional competence is through group experiences designed for personal growth and that focus on the unfolding of individual possibilities. From this group of aware professionals and others came much of the initial support and interest in Esalen Institute and similar "Growth Centers" later referred to as the Human Potentialities Movement.

Esalen Institute in Big Sur, California, was organized in 1962 by Michael Murphy and his partner, Dick Price. Under their imaginative management the institute experienced a phenomenal growth, established a branch in San Francisco, and is now famous for its seminars and weekend experiences offered by pioneering professionals. Since 1962 more than 100,000 persons have enrolled for one of these activities.

The past three years have seen a rapid mushrooming of Growth Centers. There are more than fifty such organizations ranging from Esalen and Kairos Institutes in California to Oasis in Chicago and Aureon Institute in New York. The experiences offered at these Growth Centers are based on several hypotheses: 1) that the average healthy person functions at a fraction of his capacity; 2) that man's most exciting life-long adventure is actualizing his potential; 3) that the group environment is one of the best settings in which to achieve growth; and 4) that personality growth can be achieved by anyone willing to invest in this process.

Human potentialities is rapidly emerging as a discrete field of scientific inquiry. Exploring the human potential can become the meeting ground for a wide range of disciplines, offering a dynamic synthesis for seemingly divergent areas of research. It is possible that the field of human potentialities offers an answer to the long search for a synthe zing and organizing principle which will unify the sciences. The explosive growth of the Human Potentialities Movement is indicative of a growing public interest. Although there exist a considerable number of methods—all designed to tap human potential—work on assessment or evaluation of these methods has in most instances not progressed beyond field testing and informal feedback of results. The need for research in the area of human potentialities has never been more pressing. The National Center for the Exploration of Human Potential in La Jolla, California, has recently been organized for this purpose. A nonprofit organization, the center will act as a clearing house of information for current and past approaches that have been successful in fostering personal growth. One of the main purposes of the center will be to conduct and coordinate basic and applied research concerning the expansion of human potential.

Among the many fascinating questions posed by researchers are some of the following: What is the relationship of body-rhythms, biorhythms, and the expansion of sensory awareness to the uncovering of human potential? What are the applications of methods and approaches from other cultures such as yoga techniques, Sufi methods, types of meditation, etc.? What is the role of ecstasy and play vis-à-vis the realizing of human possibilities? The exploration of these and similar questions can help us create a society truly devoted to the full development of human capacities—particularly the capacities for love, joy, creativity, spiritual experiencing. This is the challenge and promise of our lifetime.

Developmental Tasks

Robert J. Havighurst

    I. Outline for Analysis of a Developmental Task (p. 17): *Title of Task*
       1. The Nature of the Task
       2. Biological Basis
       3. Psychological Basis
       4. Cultural Basis
       5. Educational Implications
    II. Definition—Developmental Task: A developmental task is a task which arises at or about a certain period in the life of the individual, successful achievement of which leads to his happiness and to success with later tasks, while failure leads to unhappiness in the individual, disapproval by the society, and difficulty with later tasks. (p. 2)
   III. Developmental Tasks: Infancy to Old Age
      A. Developmental Tasks of Infancy and Early Childhood
        1. Learning to Walk
        2. Learning to Take Solid Food
        3. Learning to Talk

      4. Learning to Control the Elimination of Body Wastes
      5. Learning Sex Differences and Sexual Modesty
      6. Achieving Physiological Stability
      7. Forming Simple Concepts of Social and Physical Reality
      8. Learning to Relate Oneself Emotionally to Parents, Siblings, and Other People
      9. Learning to Distinguish Right and Wrong and Developing a Conscience (pp. 9–17)

B. Developmental Tasks of Middle Childhood
      1. Learning Physical Skills Necessary for Ordinary Games
      2. Building Wholesome Attitudes Toward Oneself as a Growing Organism
      3. Learning to Get Along with Age-Mates
      4. Learning an Appropriate Masculine or Feminine Social Role
      5. Developing Fundamental Skills in Reading, Writing, and Calculating
      6. Developing Concepts Necessary for Everyday Living
      7. Developing Conscience, Morality, and a Scale of Values
      8. Achieving Personal Independence
      9. Developing Attitudes Toward Social Groups and Institutions (pp. 25–41)

C. Developmental Tasks of Adolescence (pp. 111–202)
      1. Achieving New and More Mature Relations with Age-Mates of Both Sexes
      2. Achieving a Masculine or Feminine Social Role
      3. Accepting One's Physique and Using the Body Effectively
      4. Achieving Emotional Independence of Parents and Other Adults
      5. Achieving Assurance of Economic Independence
      6. Selecting and Preparing for an Occupation
      7. Preparing for Marriage and Family Life
      8. Developing Intellectual Skills and Concepts Necessary for Civic Competence
      9. Desiring and Achieving Socially Responsible Behavior
    10. Acquiring a Set of Values and an Ethical System as a Guide to Behavior

D. Developmental Tasks of Early Adulthood (pp. 257–267)
      1. Selecting a Mate
      2. Learning to Live with a Marriage Partner
      3. Starting a Family
      4. Rearing Children
      5. Managing a Home
      6. Getting Started in an Occupation
      7. Taking on Civic Responsibility
      8. Finding a Congenial Social Group

E. Developmental Tasks of Middle Age (pp. 268–277)
      1. Achieving Adult Civic and Social Responsibility
      2. Establishing and Maintaining an Economic Standard of Living
      3. Assisting Teen-age Children to Become Responsible and Happy Adults

4. Developing Adult Leisure-Time Activities
5. Relating Oneself to One's Spouse as a Person
6. Accepting and Adjusting to the Physiological Changes of Middle Age
7. Adjusting to Ageing Parents

F. Developmental Tasks of Later Maturity (pp. 277–283)
1. Adjusting to Decreasing Physical Strength and Health
2. Adjustment to Retirement and Reduced Income
3. Adjusting to Death of Spouse
4. Establishing an Explicit Affiliation with One's Age Group
5. Meeting Social and Civic Obligations
6. Establishing Satisfactory Physical Living Arrangements

IV. The "Teachable Moment" (p. 5)

There are two reasons why the concept of developmental tasks is useful to educators. First, it helps in discovering and stating the purposes of education in the schools. Education may be conceived as the effort of the society, through the school, to help the individual achieve certain of his developmental tasks.

The second use of the concept is in the timing of educational efforts. When the body is ripe, and society requires, and the self is ready to achieve a certain task, the teachable moment has come. Efforts at teaching which would have been largely wasted if they had come earlier, give gratifying results when they come at the teachable moment, when the task should be learned. For example, the best times to teach reading, the care of children, and adjustment to retire from one's job can be discovered by studying human development, and finding out when conditions are most favorable for learning these tasks.

V. Developmental Tasks as Objectives of Elementary Education (pp. 92–108)

The elementary-school program contributes in one way or another to the child's achievement of every one of his developmental tasks. Whether consciously designed for the purpose or not, the school curriculum helps or hinders the accomplishment of every task, and every school is a laboratory for the working-out of these tasks.

Consequently, it seems useful to regard the developmental tasks as objectives or goals of elementary education, some more important in the school program than others, of course. Successful achievement of these tasks can be described in terms of observable behavior, and these descriptions may be used in evaluating the progress of a child.

VI. Behavior Descriptions of Developmental Tasks As Outcomes of Secondary Education (pp. 139–141; pp. 156–158)

VII. Developmental Tasks and The School Curriculum (pp. 175–176)

A. Evaluating the School Program

A good school program is one that makes a maximum contribution to the performance by children of their developmental tasks. In a good school program the staff will know which developmental tasks they wish to emphasize. There will be general agreement that the family and other institutions do a good job helping children with certain tasks, and that the school should specialize with certain other tasks.

The questions we might ask, in evaluating the program of a particular school are:

1. Does the school know where each child stands in his achievement of his developmental tasks? And does the school assist each child where his need is greater?
2. Does the school have a clear policy and program for assisting children especially with certain developmental tasks, based on discussions with parents, churches, and youth-serving organizations, while these institutions take more responsibility for assisting with other tasks?
3. Does the school understand the strengths and weaknesses of other community institutions in assisting children with their developmental tasks, and does it aim to help where help is most needed?
4. Do the teachers and other school personnel exert an effective informal influence by their examples as people and through their relations with children so as to help children with their developmental tasks?
5. Does the school definitely and systematically teach reflective thinking in the performance of developmental tasks?

A Healthy Personality for Every Child

Many attempts have been made to describe the attributes of healthy personality. They have been put succinctly as the ability to love and the ability to work. A recent review of the literature suggests that the individual with a healthy personality is one who actively masters his environment, shows a unity of personality, and is able to perceive the world and himself correctly. Clearly, none of these criteria applies to a child. It seemed to us best, then, to present for the Conference's consideration an outline that has the merit of indicating at one and the same time the main course of personality development and the attributes of a healthy personality.

This developmental outline was worked out by Erik H. Erikson, a psychologist and practicing psychoanalyst who has made anthropological field studies and has had much experience with children. It is an analysis that derives from psychological theory, to which is added knowledge from the fields of child development and cultural anthropology. The whole is infused with the author's insight and personal philosophy.

In each stage of child development, the author says, there is a central problem that has to be solved, temporarily at least, if the child is to proceed with vigor and confidence to the next stage. These problems, these conflicts of feeling

From a digest of the Fact Finding Report to the Midcentury White House Conference on Children and Youth, 1951, 6–25.

and desire, are never solved in entirety. Each shift in experience and environment presents them in a new form. It is held, however, that each type of conflict appears in its purest, most unequivocal form at a particular stage of child development, and that if the problem is well solved at that time the basis for progress to the next stage is well laid.

In a sense personality development follows biological principles. Biologists have found that everything that grows has a groundplan that is laid out at its start. Out of this groundplan the parts arise, each part having its time of special ascendancy. Together these parts form a functioning whole. If a part does not arise at its appointed time, it will never be able to form fully, since the moment for the rapid outgrowth of some other part will have arrived. Moreover, a part that misses its time of ascendancy or is severely damaged during its formative period is apt to doom, in turn, the whole hierarchy of organs. Proper rate and normal sequence is necessary if functional harmony is to be secured.

Personality represents the most complicated functioning of the human organism and does not consist of parts in the organic sense. Instead of the development of organs, there is the development of locomotor, sensory, and social capacities and the development of individual modes of dealing with experience. Nevertheless, proper rate and proper sequence are as important here as in physical growth, and functional harmony is achieved only if development proceeds according to the groundplan.

In all this it is encouraging for parents and others who have children in charge to realize that in the sequence of his most personal experiences, just as in the sequence of organ formation, the child can be trusted to follow inner laws of development, and needs from adults chiefly love, encouragement, and guidance.

The operation of biological laws is seen, also, in the fact that there is constant interplay between organism and environment and that problems of personality functioning are never solved once and for all. Each of the components of the healthy personality to be described below is present in some form from the beginning, and the struggle to maintain it continues throughout life.

For example, a baby may show something like "autonomy" or a will of his own in the way he angrily tries to free his head when he is tightly held. Nevertheless, it is not until the second year of life that he begins to experience the whole conflict between being an autonomous creature and a dependent one. It is not until then that he is ready for a decisive encounter with the people around him, and it is not until then that they feel called upon to train him or otherwise curb his free-questing spirit. The struggle goes on for months and finally, under favorable circumstances, some compromise between dependence and independence is reached that gives the child a sense of well-being.

The sense of autonomy thus achieved is not a permanent possession, however. There will be other challenges to that sense and other solutions more in keeping with later stages of development. Nevertheless, once established at two or three years of age, this early sense of autonomy will be a bulwark against later frustrations and will permit the emergence of the next developmental problem at a time that is most favorable for its solution.

So it is with all the personality components to be described. They appear in miniature early in life. The struggle to secure them against tendencies to act otherwise comes to a climax at a time determined by emergence of the necessary physical and mental abilities. There are, throughout life, other challenges and other responses but they are seldom so serious and seldom so decisive as those of the critical years.

In all this, it must be noted in addition, there is not the strict dichotomy that the analysis given below suggests. With each of the personality components to be described, it is not all or nothing: trust or mistrust, autonomy or doubt, and so on. Instead, each individual has some of each. His health of personality is determined by the preponderance of the favorable over the unfavorable, as well as by what manner of compensations he develops to cope with his disabilities.

THE SENSE OF TRUST

The component of the healthy personality that is the first to develop is the sense of trust. The crucial time for its emergence is the first year of life. As with the other personality components to be described, the sense of trust is not something that develops independent of other manifestations of growth. It is not that the infant learns how to use his body for purposeful movement, learns to recognize people and objects around him, and also develops a sense of trust. Rather, the concept "sense of trust" is a short-cut expression intended to convey the characteristic flavor of all the child's satisfying experiences at this early age. Or, to say it another way, this psychological formulation serves to condense, summarize, and synthesize the most important underlying changes that give meaning to the infant's concrete and diversified experience.

Trust can exist only in relation to something. Consequently a sense of trust cannot develop until the infant is old enough to be aware of objects and persons and to have some feeling that he is a separate individual. At about three months of age a baby is likely to smile if somebody comes close and talks to him. This shows that he is aware of the approach of the other person, that pleasurable sensations are aroused. If, however, the person moves too quickly or speaks too sharply the baby may look apprehensive or cry. He will not "trust" the unusual situation but will have a feeling of uneasiness, of mistrust, instead.

Experiences connected with feeding are a prime source for the development of trust. At around four months of age a hungry baby will grow quiet and show signs of pleasure at the sound of an approaching footstep, anticipating (trusting) that he will be held and fed. This repeated experience of being hungry, seeing food, receiving food, and feeling relieved and comforted assures the baby that the world is a dependable place.

Later experiences, starting at around five months of age, add another dimension to the sense of trust. Through endless repetitions of attempts to grasp for and hold objects, the baby is finally successful in controlling and adapting his movements in such a way as to reach his goal. Through these and other feats of muscular coordination the baby is gradually able to trust his own body to do his bidding.

The baby's trust-mistrust problem is symbolized in the game of peek-a-boo. In this game, which babies begin to like at about four months of age, an object disappears and then reappears. There is a slightly tense expression on the baby's face when the object goes away; its reappearance is greeted by wriggles and smiles. Only gradually does a baby learn that things continue to exist even though he does not see them, that there is order and stability in his universe. Peek-a-boo proves the point by playful repetition.

Studies of mentally ill individuals and observations of infants who have been grossly deprived of affection suggest that trust is an early-formed and important element in the healthy personality. Psychiatrists find again and again that the most serious illnesses occur in patients who have been sorely neglected or abused or otherwise deprived of love in infancy. Similarly, it is a common finding of psychological and social investigators that individuals diagnosed as a "psychopathic personality" were so unloved in infancy that they have no reason to trust the human race and, therefore, no sense of responsibility toward their fellow men.

Observations of infants brought up in emotionally unfavorable institutions or removed to hospitals with inadequate facilities for psychological care support these findings. A recent report says: "Infants under six months of age who have been in an institution for some time present a well-defined picture. The outstanding features are listlessness, emaciation and pallor, relative immobility, quietness, unresponsiveness to stimuli like a smile or a coo, indifferent appetite, failure to gain weight properly despite ingestion of diets which are entirely adequate, frequent stools, poor sleep, an appearance of unhappiness, proneness to febrile episodes, absence of sucking habits."[1]

Another investigation of children separated from their mothers at six to twelve months and not provided with an adequate substitute comes to much the same conclusion: "The emotional tone is one of apprehension and sadness, there is withdrawal from the environment amounting to rejection of it, there is no attempt to contact a stranger and no brightening if a stranger contacts him. Activities are retarded and the child often sits or lies inert in a dazed stupor. Insomnia is common and lack of appetite universal. Weight is lost, and the child becomes prone to current infections."[2]

Most significant for our present point, these reactions are most likely to occur in children who up to the time of separation at six to nine months of age had a happy relation with their mothers, while those whose relations were unhappy are relatively unaffected. It is at about this age that the struggle between trusting and mistrusting the world comes to a climax, for it is then that the child first perceives clearly that he and his environment are things apart. That at this time formerly happy infants should react so badly to separation suggests, indeed, that they had a faith which now was shattered. Happily, there is usually spectacular change for the better when the maternal presence and love are restored.

It is probably unnecessary to describe the numerous ways in which stimuli from without and from within may cause an infant distress. Birth is believed by some experts to be a painful experience for the baby. Until fairly recently doctors were likely to advise that babies be fed on schedule and that little attention be paid to their cries of hunger at other times. Many infants spent many of the waking hours of the first four months doubled up with colic. All of them had to be bathed and dressed at stated times, whether they liked it or not. Add to these usual discomforts the fact that some infants are handled rather roughly by their

[1] Harry Bakwin, "Emotional Deprivation in Infants," *Journal of Pediatrics*, October, 1949, 35, 512–529.
[2] John Bowlby, M.D., Summary of Dr. René Spitz's observations, unpublished manuscript.

parents, that others hear angry words and loud voices, and that a few are really mistreated, and it will not be difficult to understand why some infants may feel the world is a place that cannot be trusted.

In most primitive societies and in some sections of our own society the attention accorded infants is more in line with natural processes. In such societies separation from the mother is less abrupt, in that for some time after birth the baby is kept close to the warmth and comfort of its mother's body and at its least cry the breast is produced. Throughout infancy the baby is surrounded by people who are ready to feed it, fondle it, otherwise comfort it at a moment's notice. Moreover, these ministrations are given spontaneously, wholeheartedly, and without that element of nervous concern that may characterize the efforts of young mothers made self-conscious and insecure by our scientific age.

We must not exaggerate, however. Most infants in our society, too, find smiles and the comfort of mother's soft, warm body accompanying their intake of food, whether from breast or bottle. Coldness, wetness, pain, and boredom— for each misfortune there is prompt and comforting relief. As their own bodies come to be more dependable, there is added to the pleasures of increasing sensory response and motor control the pleasure of the mother's encouragement.

Moreover, babies are rather hardy creatures and are not to be discouraged by inexperienced mothers' mistakes. Even a mother cat has to learn, and the kittens endure gracefully her first clumsy efforts to carry them away from danger. Then, too, psychologists tell us that mothers create a sense of trust in their children not by the particular techniques they employ but by the sensitiveness with which they respond to the children's needs and by their over-all attitude.

For most infants, then, a sense of trust is not difficult to come by. It is the most important element in the personality. It emerges at the most vulnerable period of a child's life. Yet it is the least likely to suffer harm, perhaps because both nature and culture work toward making mothers most maternal at that time.

THE SENSE OF AUTONOMY

The sense of trust once firmly established, the struggle for the next component of the healthy personality begins. The child is now twelve to fifteen months old. Much of his energy for the next two years will center around asserting that he is a human being with a mind and will of his own. A list of some of the items discussed by Spock under the heading, "The One Year Old," will serve to remind us of the characteristics of that age and the problems they create for parents. "Feeling his oats." "The passion to explore." "He gets more dependent and more independent at the same time." "Arranging the house for the wandering baby." "Avoiding accidents." "How do you make him leave certain things alone?" "Dropping and throwing things." "Biting humans." "The small child who won't stay in bed at night."

What is at stake throughout the struggle of these years is the child's sense of autonomy, the sense that he is an independent human being and yet one who is able to use the help and guidance of others in important matters. This stage of development becomes decisive for the ratio between love and hate, between cooperation and wilfulness, for freedom of self-expression and its renunciation in the make-up of the individual. The favorable outcome is self-control without loss of self-esteem. The unfavorable outcome is doubt and shame.

Before the sense of autonomy can develop, the sense of trust must be reasonably well established and must continue to pervade the child's feeling about himself and his world. Only so dare he respond with confidence to his new-felt desire to assert himself boldly, to appropriate demandingly, and to hurl away without let or hindrance.

As with the previous stage, there is a physiological basis for this characteristic behavior. This is the period of muscle-system maturation and the consequent ability (and doubly felt inability) to coordinate a number of highly conflicting action patterns, such as those of holding on and letting go, walking, talking, and manipulating objects in ever more complicated ways. With these abilities come pressing needs to use them: to handle, to explore, to seize and to drop, to withhold and to expel. And, with all, there is the dominant will, the insistent "Me do" that defies help and yet is so easily frustrated by the inabilities of the hands and feet.

For a child to develop this sense of self-reliance and adequacy that Erikson calls autonomy, it is necessary that he experience over and over again that he is a person who is permitted to make choices. He has to have the right to choose, for example, whether to sit or whether to stand, whether to approach a visitor or to lean against his mother's knee, whether to accept offered food or whether to reject it, whether to use the toilet or to wet his pants. At the same time he must learn some of the boundaries of self-determination. He inevitably finds that there are walls he cannot climb, that there are objects out of reach, that, above all, there are innumerable commands enforced by powerful adults. His experience is much too small to enable him to know what he can and cannot do with respect to the physical environment, and it will take him years to discover the boundaries that mark off what is approved, what is tolerated, and what is forbidden by his elders whom he finds so hard to understand.

As problems of this period, some psychologists have concentrated particularly on bladder and bowel control. Emphasis is put upon the need for care in both timing and mode of training children in the performance of these functions. If parental control is too rigid or if training is started too early, the child is robbed of his opportunity to develop, by his own free choice, gradual control of the contradictory impulses of retention and elimination.

To others who study child development, this matter of toilet training is but a prototype of all the problems of this age-range. The sphincters are only part of the whole muscle system, with its general ambiguity of rigidity and relaxation, of flexion and extension. To hold and to relinquish refer to much more than the bowels. As the child acquires the ability to stand on his two feet and move around, he delineates his world as me and you. He can be astonishingly pliable once he has decided that he wants to do what he is supposed to do, but there is no reliable formula for assuring that he will relinquish when he wants to hold on.

The matter of mutual regulation between parent and child (for fathers have now entered the picture to an extent that was rare in the earlier stage) now faces its severest task. The task is indeed one to challenge the most resourceful and the most calm adult. Firmness is necessary, for the child must be protected against the potential anarchy of his as yet untrained sense of discrimination. Yet the adult must back him up in his wish to "stand on his own feet," lest he be overcome by shame that he has exposed himself foolishly and by doubt in his self-worth. Perhaps the most constructive rule a parent can follow is to forbid only what "really matters" and, in such forbidding, to be clear and consistent.

Shame and doubt are emotions that many primitive peoples and some of the less sophisticated individuals in our own society utilize in training children. Shaming exploits the child's sense of being small. Used to excess it misses its objective and may result in open shamelessness, or, at least, in the child's secret determination to do as he pleases when not observed. Such defiance is a normal, even healthy response to demands that a child consider himself, his body, his needs, or his wishes evil and dirty and that he regard those who pass judgment as infallible. Young delinquents may be produced by this means, and others who are oblivious to the opinion of society.

Those who would guide the growing child wisely, then, will avoid shaming him and avoid causing him to doubt that he is a person of worth. They will be firm and tolerant with him so that he can rejoice in being a person of independence and can grant independence to others. As to detailed procedures, it is impossible to prescribe, not only because we do not know and because every situation is different but also because the kind and degree of autonomy that parents are able to grant their small children depends on feelings about themselves that they derive from society. Just as the child's sense of trust is a reflection of the mother's sturdy and realistic faith, so the child's sense of autonomy is a reflection of the parents' personal dignity. Such appears to be the teaching of the comparative study of cultures.

Personal autonomy, independence of the individual, is an especially outstanding feature of the American way of life. American parents, accordingly, are in a particularly favorable position to transmit the sense of autonomy to their children. They themselves resent being bossed, being pushed around; they maintain that everybody has the right to express his opinion and to be in control of his affairs. More easily than people who live according to an authoritarian pattern, they can appreciate a little child's vigorous desire to assert his independence and they can give him the leeway he needs in order to grow up into the upstanding, look-you-in-the-eye kind of individual that Americans admire.

It is not only in early childhood, however, that this attitude toward growing children must be maintained. As was said at the outset, these components of the healthy personality cannot be established once and for all. The period of life in which they first come into being is the most crucial, it is true. But threats to their maintenance occur throughout life. Not only parents, then, but everybody who has significant contact with children and young people must respect their desire for self-assertion, help them hold it within bounds, and avoid treating them in ways that arouse shame or doubt.

This attitude toward children, toward all people, must be maintained in institutional arrangements as well. Great differences in educational and economic opportunity and in access to the law, discrimination of all kinds are threats to this ingredient of mental health. So, too, may be the over-mechanization of our society, the depersonalization of human relations that is likely to accompany large-scale endeavor of all kinds.

Parents, as well as children, are affected by these matters. In fact, parents' ability to grant children the kind of autonomy Americans think desirable depends in part on the way they are treated as employees and citizens. Throughout, the relation must be such as affirms personal dignity. Much of the shame and doubt aroused in children result from the indignity and uncertainty that are an expression of parents' frustrations in love and work. Special attention must be paid to all these matters, then, if we are to avoid destroying the autonomy that Americans have always set store by.

THE SENSE OF INITIATIVE

Having become sure, for the time being, that he is a person in his own right and having enjoyed that feeling for a year or so, the child of four or five wants to find out what kind of person he can be. To be any particular kind of person, he sees clearly, involves being able to do particular kinds of things. So he observes with keen attention what all manner of interesting adults do (his parents, the milkman, the truck driver, and so on), tries to imitate their behavior, and yearns for a share in their activities.

This is the period of enterprise and imagination, an ebullient, creative period when phantasy substitutes for literal execution of desires and the meagerest equipment provides material for high imaginings. It is a period of intrusive, vigorous learning, learning that leads away from the child's own limitations into future possibilities. There is intrusion into other people's bodies by physical attack, into other people's ears and minds by loud and aggressive talking. There is intrusion into space by vigorous locomotion and intrusion into the unknown by consuming curiosity.

By this age, too, conscience has developed. The child is no longer guided only by outsiders; there is installed within him a voice that comments on his deeds, and warns and threatens. Close attention to the remarks of any child of this age will confirm this statement. Less obvious, however, are experts' observations that children now begin to feel guilty for mere thoughts, for deeds that have been imagined but never executed. This, they say, is the explanation for the characteristic nightmares of this age period and for the over-reaction to slight punishment.

The problem to be worked out in this stage of development, accordingly, is how to will without too great a sense of guilt. The fortunate outcome of the struggle is a sense of initiative. Failure to win through to that outcome leaves the personality overburdened, and possibly over-restricted by guilt.

It is easy to see how the child's developing sense of initiative may be discouraged. So many of the projects dreamed up at this age are of a kind which cannot be permitted that the child may come to feel he is faced by a universal "No." In addition he finds that many of the projects are impossible of execution and others, even if not forbidden, fail to win the approval of the adults whom he has come to love. Moreover, since he does not always distinguish clearly between actuality and phantasy, his over-zealous conscience may disapprove of even imaginary deeds.

It is very important, therefore, for healthy personality development that much leeway and encouragement be given to the child's show of enterprise and imagination and that punishment be kept at a minimum. Boys and girls at this stage are extraordinarily appreciative of any convincing promise that someday they will be able to do things as well, or maybe better, than father and mother. They enjoy competition (especially if they can win) and insistence on goal; they get great pleasure from conquest. They need numerous examples of the kinds of roles adults assume, and they need a chance to try them out in play.

The ability that is in the making is that of selecting social goals and persevering in the attempt to reach them.

If enterprise and imagination are too greatly curbed, if severe rebukes accompany the frequently necessary denial of permission to carry out desires, a personality may result that is over-constricted. Such a personality cannot live up to its inner capacities for imagination, feeling, or performance, though it may overcompensate by immense activity and find relaxation impossible.

Constriction of personality is a self-imposed constriction, an act of the child's over-zealous conscience. "If I may not do this, I will not even think it," says conscience, "for even thinking it is dangerous." Resentment and bitterness and a vindictive attitude toward the world that forces the restriction may accompany this decision, however, and become unconscious but functioning parts of the personality. Such, at least, is the warning of psychiatrists who have learned to know the inmost feelings of emotionally handicapped children and adults.

This developmental stage has great assets as well as great dangers. At no time in life is the individual more ready to learn avidly and quickly, to become big in the sense of sharing obligation and performance. If during this pre-school period the child can get some sense of the various roles and functions that he can perform as an adult, he will be ready to progress joyfully to the next stage, in which he will find pleasurable accomplishment in activities less fraught with phantasy and fear.

There is a lesson in this for later periods of personality development as well. As has been said before, these conflicts that come to a head at particular periods of a child's life are not settled once and for all. The sense of initiative, then, is one that must be continually fostered, and great care must be taken that youngsters and young people do not have to feel guilty for having dared to dream.

Just as we Americans prize autonomy, so too do we prize initiative; in fact, we regard it as the cornerstone of our economic system. There is much in the present industrial and political mode of life that may discourage initiative, that may make a young person think he had best pull in his horns. What these tendencies are and what they may do to youngsters and to their parents, who too must feel free if they are to cultivate the sense of initiative in their children, is a subject that warrants much serious discussion.

THE SENSE OF ACCOMPLISHMENT

The three stages so far described probably are the most important for personality development. With a sense of trust, a sense of autonomy, and a sense of initiative achieved, progress through the later stages is pretty well assured. Whether this is because children who have a good environment in their early years are likely to continue to be so favored, or whether it is because they have attained such strength of personality that they can successfully handle later difficulties, research has not yet made clear. We do know that nearly all children who get a good start continue to develop very well, and we know that some of those who start off poorly continue to be handicapped. Observations of this sort seem to support psychological theory in the conclusion that personality is pretty well set by about six years of age. Since, however, some children develop into psychological healthy adults in spite of a bad start, and since some who start well run into difficulties later, it is clear that much research is needed before this conclusion can be accepted as wholly correct.

To return to the developmental analysis, the fourth stage, which begins somewhere around six years of age and extends over five or six years, has as its achievement what Erikson calls the sense of industry. Perhaps "sense of accomplishment" would make the meaning clearer. At any rate, this is the period in which preoccupation with phantasy subsides, and the child wants to be engaged in real tasks that he can carry through to completion. As with the other developmental stages, there are foreshadowings of this kind of interest long before six years of age. Moreover, in some societies and in some parts of our own society children are trained very early to perform socially useful tasks. The exact age is not the point at issue. What is to be pointed out is that children, after a period characterized by exuberant imagination, want to settle down to learning exactly how to do things and how to do them well.

In contrast to the preceding stages and to the succeeding ones, this stage does not consist of a swing from a violent inner upheaval to a new mastery. Under reasonably favorable circumstances this is a period of calm, steady growth, especially if the problems of the previous stages have been well worked through. Despite its unspectacular character, this is a very important period, for in it is laid a firm basis for responsible citizenship. It is during this period that children acquire not only knowledge and skills that make for good workmanship but also the ability to cooperate and play fair and otherwise follow the rules of the larger social game.

The chief danger of this period is the presence of conditions that may lead to the development of a sense of inadequacy and inferiority. This may be the outcome if the child has not yet achieved a sense of initiative, or if his experiences at home have not prepared him for entering school happily, or if he finds school a place where his previous accomplishments are disregarded or his latent abilities are not challenged. Even with a good start the child may later lapse into discouragement and lack of interest if at home or school his individual needs are overlooked—if too much is expected of him, or if he is made to feel that achievement is beyond his ability.

It is most important for health of personality, therefore, that schools be conducted well, that methods and courses of instruction be such as will give every child the feeling of successful accomplishment. Autobiographies of juvenile delinquents show time and again a boy who hated school—hated the fact that he was marked out as stupid or awkward, as one who was not as good as the rest. Some such boys find in jobs the sense of accomplishment they miss at school and consequently give up their delinquent ways. Others, however, are handicapped in job finding and keeping by the very fact that in school they did not develop the sense of industry; hence they have work failure added to their other insecurities. Nor is delinquency the only or the most likely outcome of lack of success in school. Many children respond in a quieter way, by passive acceptance of their inferiority. Psychologically they are perhaps even more harmed.

Our Puritan tradition maintains that children will not work except under the spur of competition, so we tend to fear the suggestion that all should succeed. To help children develop a sense of accomplishment does not mean, however, merely giving all of them good marks and passing them on to the next grade. Children need and want real achievement. How to help them secure it, despite differences in native capacity and differences in emotional development, is one of the school's most serious challenges.

School, of course, is not the only place in which children at this stage of development can secure the sense of industry. In work at home there are many opportunities for a child to get a feeling of mastery and worthwhile endeavor. Rural youth groups and their urban counterparts cater to this need, and many recreation programs put as much emphasis on work as on play. School, however, is the legally constituted arrangement for giving instruction to the young, so it is upon teachers that the professional responsibility for helping all children achieve a sense of industry and accomplishment rests.

In addition to aiding personality development in this way, teachers have many opportunities for reconfirming their pupils' sense of trust, autonomy, and initiative or for encouraging its growth in children who have been somewhat hampered by previous life experiences. Teachers cannot work alone, of course, either in aiding a child in the development of new capacities or in strengthening old ones. Jointly with parents and others they can do much, not only for children of already healthy personality but also for many whose development has been handicapped.

THE SENSE OF IDENTITY

With the onset of adolescence another period of personality development begins. As is well known, adolescence is a period of storm and stress for many young people, a period in which previous certainties are questioned and previous continuities no longer relied upon. Physiological changes and rapid physical growth provide the somatic base for the turmoil and indecision. It may be that cultural factors also play a part, for it has been observed that adolescence is less upsetting in some societies than in others.

The central problem of the period is the establishment of a sense of identity. The identity the adolescent seeks to clarify is who he is, what his role in society is to be. Is he a child or is he an adult? Does he have it in him to be someday a husband and father? What is he to be as a worker and an earner of money? Can he feel self-confident in spite of the fact that his race or religion or national background makes him a person some people look down upon? Over all, will he be a success or a failure? By reason of these questions adolescents are sometimes morbidly preoccupied with how they appear in the eyes of others as compared with their own conception of themselves, and with how they can make the roles and skills learned earlier jibe with what is currently in style.

In primitive societies adolescents are perhaps spared these doubts and indecisions. Through initiation rites, often seemingly cruel in character, young people are tested out (and test themselves out) and are then welcomed into a socially recognized age category in which rights and duties and mode of living are clearly defined. In our society there are few rituals or ceremonies that mark the change in status from childhood to youth. For those who have religious affiliations, confirmation, joining the church, may serve this purpose in part, since the young people are thereby admitted, in this one segment of their lives at least, to the company of adults. Such ceremonies serve, in addition, to reaffirm to youth that the universe is trustworthy and stable and that a way of life is clearly laid out.

Graduation ceremonies might play a part in marking a new status were it not that, in present-day America, status is so ill defined. What rules of law and custom exist are too diverse to be of much help. For example, legal regulations governing age of "consent," age at which marriage is permitted, age for leaving school, for driving a car, for joining (or being required to join) the Army or Navy mark no logical progressions in rights and duties. As to custom, there is so much variation in what even families who live next door to each other expect or permit that adolescents, eager to be on their way, are practically forced into standardizing themselves in their search for status. In this they are ably abetted by advertisers and entertainers who seek their patronage, as well as by well-meaning magazine writers who describe in great detail the means by which uniformity can be achieved.

In this urge to find comfort through similarity, adolescents are likely to become stereotyped in behavior and ideals. They tend to form cliques for self-protection and fasten on petty similarities of dress and gesture to assure themselves that they are really somebody. In these cliques they may be intolerant and even cruel toward those they label as different. Unfortunate as such behavior is and not to be condoned, intolerance serves the important purpose of giving the group members at least the negative assurance that there is something they are not.

The danger of this developmental period is self-diffusion. As Biff puts it in The Death of a Salesman, "I just can't take hold, Mom. I can't take hold of some kind of a life." A boy or girl can scarcely help feeling somewhat diffuse when the body changes in size and shape so rapidly, when genital maturity floods body and imagination with forbidden desires, when adult life lies ahead with such a diversity of conflicting possibilities and choices.

Whether this feeling of self-diffusion is fairly easily mastered or whether, in extreme, it leads to delinquency, neurosis or outright psychosis, depends to a considerable extent on what has gone before. If the course of personality development has been a healthy one, a feeling of self-esteem has accrued from the numerous experiences of succeeding in a task and sensing its cultural meaning. Along with this, the child has come to the conviction that he is moving toward an understandable future in which he will have a definite role to play. Adolescence may upset this assurance for a time or to a degree but fairly soon a new integration is achieved, and the boy or girl sees again (and with clearer vision) that he belongs and that he is on his way.

The course is not so easy for adolescents who have not had so fortunate a part or for those whose earlier security is broken by a sudden awareness that as members of minority groups their way of life sets them apart. The former, already unsure of themselves, find their earlier doubt and mistrust reactivated by the physiological and social changes that adolescence brings. The latter, once secure, may feel that they must disavow their past and try to develop an "American" personality.

Much has been learned and written about the adolescent problems of the boys and girls whose early personality development has been impaired. How they can be helped, if their disorders are not too severe, is also fairly well known. The full implications of these findings for parents, teachers, and others who would guide youth are still to be worked out but, even so, there is considerable information.

Less well understood are the difficulties and the ways of helping adolescents who grew up in cultures that are not of the usual run. These boys and girls may have been privileged in having had a childhood in which there was little inhibition of sensual pleasures, and in which development proceeded by easy, unselfconscious stages. For them, difficulties arise if their parents lose trust in themselves or if their teachers apply sudden correctives, or if they themselves reject their past and try to act like the others. The new role of middle-class adolescent is often too hard to play. Delinquency or bizarre behavior marks the failure.

How to reach these boys and girls, how to help them attain their desire, is a matter not well understood. It is clear, however, that they should not be typed by pat diagnoses and social judgments, for they are ever ready to become the "bums" that they are called. Those who would guide them must understand both the psychology of adolescence and the cultural realities of the day. There is trust to be restored and doubt and guilt and feelings of inferiority to be overcome. The science of how to do this is still pretty much lacking, though here and there teachers, clergymen, probation officers and the like are highly successful in the task.

Hard though it be to achieve, the sense of identity is the individual's only safeguard against the lawlessness of his biological drives and the authority of an over-weening conscience. Loss of identity, loss of the sense that there is some continuity, sameness, and meaning to life, exposes the individual to his childhood conflicts and leads to emotional upsets. This outcome was observed time and again among men hard pressed by the dangers of war. It is clear, then, that if health of personality is to be preserved much attention must be given to assuring that America makes good on its promises to youth.

THE SENSE OF INTIMACY

After the sense of identity, to a greater or less extent, is achieved it becomes possible for the next component of the healthy personality to develop. This is the sense of intimacy, intimacy with persons of the same sex or of the opposite sex or with one's self. The youth who is not fairly sure of his identity shies away from interpersonal relations and is afraid of close communion with himself. The surer he becomes of himself, the more he seeks intimacy, in the form of friendship, love and inspiration.

In view of the early age at which boy and girl attachments are encouraged today, it may seem strange to put the critical period for the development of the sense of intimacy late in adolescence. The explanation is that, on the one hand, sexual intimacy is only one part of what is involved, and, on the other, boy-girl attachments of earlier age periods are likely to be of a somewhat different order. Regarding the latter point, it has been observed by those who know young people well that high-school age boys and girls often use each other's company for an endless verbal examination of what the other thinks, feels, and wants to do. In other words, these attachments are one means of defining one's identity.

In contrast to this use of friendship and companionship, boys and girls late in adolescence usually have need for a kind of fusion with the essence of other people and for a communion with their own inner resources. If, by reason of inadequacies in previous personality development, this sense of intimacy cannot be achieved, the youth may retire into psychological isolation and keep his relations with people on a formal stereotyped level that is lacking in spontaneity and warmth or he may keep trying again and again to get close to others, only to meet with repeated failure. Under this compulsion he may even marry, but the role of mate is one he can rarely sustain, for the condition of true two-ness is that each individual must first become himself.

In this area of personality development as in the others, cultural factors play a part in sustaining or in discouraging the individual in his development. American culture is unusually successful in encouraging the development of the feelings of independence, initiative, industry, and identity. It is somewhat less successful in the area of intimacy, for the culture's ideal is the subordination of sexuality and sensuality to a life of work, duty, and worship.

Consequently, American adolescents are likely to be unsupported by their parents and to find little confirmation in story or song for their desire to sense intimately the full flavor of the personality of others. In many of them, then, the sense of intimacy does not develop highly and they have difficulty in finding in close personal relations the outlet for tension that they need.

There is some evidence that a change in conventions and customs in this respect is in the making, however. Too abrupt change in any such cultural matter is not to be urged, but it is to be hoped that gradual, frank discussion can bring about gradual alteration in attitude and overcome the dangers inherent in the traditional rigidity.

THE PARENTAL SENSE

"Parental sense" designates somewhat the same capacity as that implied in the words, creativity or productivity. The individual has normally come to adulthood before this sense can develop fully.

The parental sense is indicated most clearly by interest in producing and caring for children of one's own. It may also be exhibited in relation to other people's children or by a parental kind of responsibility toward the products of creative activity of other sorts. The mere desire for or possession of children does not indicate that this component of the healthy personality has developed. In fact, many parents who bring their children to child guidance clinics are found not to have reached this stage of personality development.

The essential element is the desire to nourish and nurture what has been produced. It is the ability to regard one's children as a trust of the community, rather than as extensions of one's own personality or merely as beings that one happens to live with.

Failure to develop this component of the healthy personality often results in a condition which has not been adequately categorized clinically. Although a true sense of intimacy has not developed, the individual may obsessively seek companionship. There is something of egotism in this as in his other activities, a kind of self-absorption. The individual is inclined to treat himself as a child and to be rivalrous with his children, if he has any. He indulges himself, expects to be indulged, and in general behaves in an infantile or immature manner.

There are both individual and social explanations of the failure to develop an adequate parental sense. Individually, the explanation may be found in the inadequate development of the personality components previously described. In some people this failure goes far back. Because of unfortunate experiences in childhood they did not arrive at a firm sense of trust, autonomy, and the rest. In others it is only inadequacies in later stages, especially in the development of the sense of intimacy, that are at fault.

Socially, as has been suggested throughout this analysis, healthy personality development depends upon the culture's ideals and upon the economic arrangements of the society. In order that most people may develop fully the sense of being a parent, the role of parent, both mother and father, must be a respected one in the society. Giving must rank higher than getting, and loving than being loved. The economy must be such that the future can be depended upon and each person can feel assured that he has a meaningful and respected part to play. Only so can most individuals afford to renounce selfish aims and derive much of their satisfaction from rearing children.

THE SENSE OF INTEGRITY

The final component of the healthy personality is the sense of integrity. In every culture the dominant ideals, honor, courage, faith, purity, grace, fairness, self-discipline, become at this stage the core of the healthy personality's integration. The individual, in Erikson's words, "becomes able to accept his individual life cycle and the people who have become significant to it as meaningful within the segment of history in which he lives."

To continue Erikson's description, "Integrity thus means a new and different love of one's parents, free of the wish that they should have been different, and an acceptance of the fact that one's life is one's own responsibility. It is a sense of comradeship with men and women of distant times and of different pursuits, who have created orders and objects and sayings conveying human dignity and love. Although aware of the relativity of all the various life styles that have given meaning to human striving, the possessor of integrity is ready to defend the dignity of his own life style against all physical and economic threats. For he knows that, for him, all human dignity stands or falls with the one style of integrity of which he partakes."

The adult who lacks integrity in this sense may wish that he could live life again. He feels that if at one time he had made a different decision he could have been a different person and his ventures would have been successful. He fears death and cannot accept his one and only life cycle as the ultimate of life. In the extreme, he experiences disgust and despair. Despair expresses the feeling that time is too short to try out new roads to integrity. Disgust is a means of hiding the despair, a chronic, contemptuous displeasure with the way life is run. As with the dangers and the solutions of previous periods, doubt and despair are not difficulties that are overcome once and for all, nor is integrity so achieved. Most people fluctuate between the two extremes. Most, also, at no point, either attain to the heights of unalloyed integrity or fall to the depths of complete disgust and despair.

Even in adulthood a reasonably healthy personality is sometimes secured in spite of previous misfortunes in the developmental sequence. New sources of trust may be found. Fortunate events and circumstances may aid the individual in his struggle to feel autonomous. Imagination and initiative may be spurred by new responsibilities, and feelings of inferiority be overcome by successful achievement. Even late in life an individual may arrive at a true sense of who he is and what he has to do and may be able to win through to a feeling of intimacy with others and to joy in producing and giving.

Evidence of such changes is found in the case records of psychiatrists and social workers. Common sense observation attests that similar changes in health of personality are sometimes accomplished without benefit of any form of psychotherapy. Much remains to be learned about this, however, especially about how life itself may serve as therapeusis.

For the healthy personality development of children and youth it is necessary that a large proportion of adults attain a sense of integrity to a considerable degree. Not only parents but all who deal with children have need of this quality if they are to help children maintain the feeling that the universe is dependable and trustworthy. Integrity is relatively easily attained and sustained when the culture itself gives support, when a meaning to life is clearly spelled out in tradition and ceremony, and roles are clearly defined. Our culture, with its rapidly changing technology and its diversity of value standards, leaves much for the individual to work out for himself. In the American dream, however, and the Judaeo-Christian tradition on which it is based there are values and ideals aplenty. In the interest of the welfare of children and youth, in order that a generation of happy individuals and responsible citizens be reared, it is highly important that these values and ideals be brought into prominence and that the promise of American life be kept.

The Development of Intelligent Behavior: Jean Piaget

Thomas Rowland
Carson McGuire

For many years, Piaget's work was almost unknown to American psychologists, primarily it seems because of the lack of adequate translations into English

From *Psychology in the Schools* V, no. 1 (January 1968):47–52. Used by permission of the author and publisher.

of his elegant but difficult French. D. E. Berlyne was one of the earliest to recognize this inadequacy and to take positive action. Berlyne with Percy (1950) translated Piaget's *Psychology of Intelligence*. Later, he spent the year 1958–59 with Piaget in Geneva. Berlyne's book, *Structure and Direction in Thinking* (1965) introduces a system of neobehavioristic concepts to permit an integrative conceptualization of thinking. In this recent volume, Berlyne discusses curiosity as a motive and learning through discovery, as well as the Geneva research and recent developments in Russian psychology.

As a result of such work as Berlyne's and others, the current influence of Piaget's research and writing can be discerned in the ideas of a host of important psychologists, including such diverse figures as D. P. Ausubel (1963) and J. S. Bruner (1965). Today most of his works are available to students, many in inexpensive paperback editions. One such edition, *Psychology of Intelligence*, has been reviewed by Carson McGuire (1967). The review is a highly condensed form of much of the essence of Piaget's work, written in technical terms. This paper, however, further amplifies what is said below:

> Piaget views intelligence as a mental *adaptation* to new circumstances, both "*accommodation*" to stimuli from the environment and modification of environment by imposing upon it a structure of its own, i.e., "*assimilation*." Thus intelligence as adaptation involves an *equilibrium* toward which the cognitive processes tend (the act of "*equilibration*"). The equilibration is between the action of the organism on the environment and vice versa. Remember that language is a partial substitute for action. Symbols, particularly those of mathematics (which are free of the deception of imagery), refer to an action which could be realized. When such symbols take the form of internalized actions they may be interpreted as operations of thought; i.e., an internal action translatable into behavior. Piaget relates affect and cognition—all behavior "implies an energizer or an 'economy' forming its affective aspect." The interaction with the environment which behavior instigates requires a form or structure to determine the possible circuits between subject and object—the cognitive aspect of behavior (schemata). *Similarly, a perception . . . , sensory-motor learning (i.e., habit . . .), insight and judgment all amount, in one way or another to a structuring of the relations between the environment and the organism* [p. 29].

Hunt (1961) identifies five main themes which he says dominate Piaget's theoretical formulations, namely: (a) the continual and progressive change in the structure of behavior and thought in the developing child; (b) the fixed nature of the order of the stages; (c) the invariant functions of *accommodation* (adaptive change to outer circumstances) and of *assimilation* (incorporation of the external into the inner organization with transfer or generalization to new circumstances) that operate in the child's continuous interaction with the environment; (d) the relation of thought to action; and (e) the logical properties of thought processes.

Roger Brown (1965) attributes to Piaget some 25 books and 160 articles, identifying the goal of the Geneva program as the discovery of *the successive stages* in the development of intelligence. Much current American research, such as that at the University of Chicago, reported by Fowler (1966) and Kohlberg (1966), lends strong support to the goals of Piaget's approach to the development of intelligence, while making an important clarification with their insistence that while the stages of Piaget are real and the sequence is constant, the "American misinterpretation" which attributes to time per se the status of a significant variable is to be denied. The prospective teacher should grasp this concept of sequence without the chains of time boundaries, especially in view of the longstanding force in American psychology: the Gessellian interpretation of stages with firm upper and lower time limits. *This maturationist view of fixed intelligence and predetermined development is no longer considered valid.* Stages, as identified by Piaget, appear to occur in a constant, invariant sequence, but there are no time boundaries. To support this viewpoint, Smedslund (1961) and Wallach (1963) independently designed a program with the specific intention of accelerating a child's development. Both discovered that acceleration appeared to be successful only if the child was approaching readiness at the time of intensive intervention; otherwise it had no significant effect. Piaget (1953) indicated that this would be the case, saying: "When adults try to impose mathematical concepts on a child prematurely, his learning is merely verbal; true understanding of them comes only with his mental growth." Because many of the conceptions studied by Piaget seem resistant to change by training, there would seem to be a substantial readiness factor involved. Probably readiness is at least partially a matter of varied sensory stimulation (Bruner, 1959; and/or Brown, 1965). Readiness, like "stage," should not be linked to time per se.[1]

Piaget has hypothesized four distinct but chronologically successive models of intelligence; namely, (a) sensory motor, (b) preoperational, (c) concretely operational, and (d) formally operational. Imaginal thought, Piaget (1947, trans. 1950) believes, begins at the end of sensory motor and facilitates a transition into the preoperational stage. Bruner (1964), in what seems to be a related concept concerning the development of intelligence, identifies three stages in cognitive representation of experience; namely: (a) enactive, (b) iconic, and (c) symbolic.

The Geneva research begins with some aspect of common *adult* knowledge. The method of inquiry is to ask questions; and data are the responses of the children. An example of this first method of research is reported in many of Piaget's early works such as *Judgment and Reasoning in the Child* (1924). A different approach was used primarily with his own children, when Piaget employed as the starting point a *set of performances*. His method was *naturalistic observation of infant behavior with experimental interventions.* This second approach is demonstrated most effectively in *The Origins of Intelligence in Children* (1936).

Later Geneva studies began with *systematic adult knowledge*, asked questions and provided materials for manipulation. The resultant data included the *manipulations and verbal responses* of the children. In America there is an increasing tendency to set up contrived experiences which parallel Piaget's research. For example, Bruner and his associates (Bruner, Oliver, Greenfield, Hornsby, Kenney, Maccaby, Modiano, Mosher, Olson, Potter, Reich and Sonstroem, 1966) in their book, dedicated to Piaget, report many experiences designed for children which are directly related to the Geneva program, such as Olson's (Bruner, et al., 1966, pp. 135–153) experiment on the development of conceptual strategies with ninety-

---

[1] At the University of Texas we prefer to use the term "development" instead of "growth" which is felt to be redundant. Development is understood to include: (a) increase in mass; (b) differentiation of parts; and (c) coordination of parts.
Rosenzweig (1966) in his research with brains of rats suggests that feedback from learning experiences influences development.

five children. Of striking similarity is the experiment on multiple ordering conducted by Bruner and Kenney (Bruner, et al., pp. 154–167).

An important understanding brought out in the research and writings of Piaget and others (Kohlberg, 1966; Fowler, 1966; and Brown, 1965) is that typically the child's intelligence turns out to be qualitatively different from adult intelligence. As a result the child simply does not see nor understand things as an adult would.

Answers of children, which appear to be "incorrect" from an adult point of view, are not viewed as ignorance. They are regarded as imperfect understandings of various intellectual matters. Much importance is attached to the observation that the imperfect responses often are alike across a sample of children. Nevertheless, the order in which the stages succeed one another usually is constant. The word "usually" should be stressed since a range of crosscultural research has not yet been carried out. A beginning has been made by Goodnow (1962, p. 1) who worked with children in Hong Kong. She began her research with the stated intention of determining if children from other milieus would produce results similar to those obtained by Piaget and his associates in Geneva. Combinatorial reasoning, conservation of space, weight and volume tasks of the Geneva program were administered to approximately 500 European and Chinese boys between the ages of 10–13. Ravens Progressive Matrices also were administered. Chinese boys had almost no formal education. Goodnow (1962) summarizes:

> Similarities across milieus were more striking than differences: there was an odd difference between the combinatorial task . . . and the conservation tasks . . ; replication of the Geneva results was fair to good; the differences occurring suggest a need for a closer look at the concept "stability of reasoning" and at the expected interrelationships among various tasks [p. 21].

Piaget believes the child in the period of sensory-motor intelligence does not have internal representations of the world, even though he acts and perceives. With the development of imagery, the most primitive form of central representation (the beginning of the second stage), the sensory-motor period ends.

For the adult, an object has an identity which is preserved through various transformations by perceptual constancies, namely: size constancy, shape constancy, and color constancy. Other aspects of the object's invariant identity, regardless of changes of appearance, are dependent on knowledge of certain reversible operations, e.g. the adult does not suppose that a car is a different car because the rear does not have the appearance of the front. For adults, disappearance from sight does not imply the cessation of existence, and objects are continuous in time and space. To an adult, an object retains its identity through changes of position and illumination, and exists outside the domain of personal experience, as Viet Nam exists even though we may not have been there.

Piaget holds that the adult's aspects of identity and perceptual constancies are learned, e.g. one of the most difficult things to understand about the infant's conception of an object is that he does not realize that it exists independently of himself. For example, during the period of sensory-motor intelligence, where the child is governed by his perceptions (what he touches, hears, particularly what he traces), he begins to develop the fundamental categories of experience and a conception of causality begins.

The first signs of imagery are a particular kind of imitation and play. *Deferred imitation* is imitation of an absent model, and Piaget postulates the existence of a *central representation* that guides the performance of the child. *Imagery* is also suggested by representational play; and it is imagery, according to Piaget, which makes the development of highly symbolic language possible.

Preoperational and concretely operational levels of intelligence are essentially two levels of response to a common array of tasks; the preoperational being (from an adult point of view) less adequate. Though the preoperational child uses language to identify things, ask questions, issue commands, and assert propositions, he does not distinguish between mental, physical, and social reality. He may believe that anything that moves is alive, such as a cloud, and will likely believe that a plant will feel a pin prick. He may expect to command the inanimate and have it obey. To the preoperational child everything is originally made or created —all things are *artifacts*. The parents, as sources for everything, may serve as *models* who make and create things. Close-tied parental figures also may become models for the child's spontaneous conception of a deity. He sees the parents as infinitely knowing and powerful as well as eternal. The preoperational child is enslaved to his own viewpoint, completely unaware of other perspectives and thereby unaware of himself as a viewer. Things are just the way they are. They are unquestioned. This *egocentrism* is reflected in the child's difficulty in explaining verbally anything to another person. The egocentric child assumes his listener understands everything in advance. It appears that the egocentric child is moving out of his egocentrism in the later developments of the preoperational stage. As the onset of imagery begins this period, so the movement from egocentrism seems to end the preoperational stage and the child begins to function intellectually in the concretely operational stage.

The intelligence of the older child, who has accumulated learning experiences, is more adult-like in its separation of the mental and physical world. He grasps the points-of-view of others as well as relational concepts which tie objects and ideas together. The preoperational child has begun to develop the constancies (space, time, size, shape, color) necessary for survival. For example, the child who cannot tell the difference perceptually between an oncoming auto a block away and one ten feet away is not likely to survive. To survive in a world of moving vehicles, he has to learn to understand some of the underlying invariance behind the world of shifting appearances. Yet, to a large degree, he is still controlled by perception. Piaget believes that the preoperational child, despite his limitations from an adult viewpoint, operates with an intelligence that is of a different order from that of the concretely operational child, who depends less on perception. This dependence on perception often leads the preoperational child to focus upon a single dimension of a problem. He is unable to *decenter*, i.e. he is able to recognize a view which he has just experienced, but not able to pick out views he might experience from different positions. The preoperational child cannot treat relations as left or right, before or behind. Compared to his elders, he is lacking in operations—the central events which do not imitate perception as does the image. Piaget believes that *operations are derived from overt operations*—interaction between the organism and environments (see McGuire review, Piaget, 1967). Piaget is convinced that *intelligence develops out of motor activity*, not just out of passive observation—the wider the range of the activity, the more diversified will be the intellectual operations of the developing child.

The *concretely operational* child can deal to a degree with potentiality as well as actuality to which the preoperational child is limited. The *formally operational* child approaches what is to Piaget the highest level of intelligence: the ability to represent, in advance of the actual problem, a full set of possibilities. The consequences of formally operational intelligence are identified as "characteristics of adolescence" by Brown (1965), who attributes to Piaget and Inhelder the belief that the reformism of the adolescent is a temporary return to egocentrism. Inhelder and Piaget (1958), and Brown (1965, p. 236), identify as "cultural variation" the phenomenon of primitive societies in which *no one attains formally operational intelligence.*

Piaget finds evidence for his theories in the study of the games and the rules for games as children play them, since the understanding of rules appears to reflect the level of intelligence. The child who plays egocentrically holds the rules to be inviolable, and may feel that they have always existed. In a transitional stage (late concrete operations) boys begin to play elaborately articulated social games. His observations of this stage caused Piaget to poke fun at educators who think children of this age are not capable of learning abstract subject matter. For this level of intelligence, a rule can be changed if consensus of the participants is obtained.

Another aspect of the Geneva studies (Piaget, 1948), the *development of moral conceptions,* begins with the understanding that adults judge naughtiness or wickedness on a *basis of intentions,* and can make independent judgments of seriousness as opposed or related to wickedness. In the preoperational child, however, most often naughtiness was judged in terms of perceived *objective damage;* on the other hand, older children judged naughtiness by the intentions of the offender. Similarly, studies of the child's conception of a lie seem to reflect the level of intellectual development. Young children said a lie was "naughty words" while older children believed a lie to be a statement not in accord with fact, for them reprehensibility is proportional to the variance between the false-hood and truth. Too great a departure became a joke instead of a lie, because no one would believe it. Much older children simply saw a lie as an untruth with the intent to deceive. Piaget asserts that in these developmental sequences a child's morality becomes increasingly inward, a process which Brown calls "enculturation" (1965, p. 241).

REFERENCES

AUSUBEL, D. P. A teaching strategy for culturally deprived pupils: Cognitive and motivational considerations. *School Review,* 1963, 71, 454–463.

BERLYNE, D. E. *Structure and direction of thinking.* New York: Wiley, 1965.

BROWN, R. *Social psychology.* New York: Free Press, 1965.

BRUNER, J. S. The course of cognitive growth. *American Psychologist,* 1964, 1, 1–15.

BRUNER, J. S. The growth of mind. President's address to the Seventy-Third Annual Convention of the American Psychological Association, Chicago, September 1965.

BRUNER, J. S. *Toward a theory of instruction.* Cambridge: Belknap, 1966.

BRUNER, J. S., GOODNOW, JACQUELINE J., & AUSTIN, G. A. *A study of thinking.* New York: Science Editions (Wiley), 1959.

BRUNER, J. S., OLIVER, ROSE R., GREENFIELD, PATRICIA M., HORNSBY, JOAN R. KENNEY, HELEN J., MACCOBY, M., MODIANO, NANCY, MOSHER, F. A., OLSON, D. R., POTTER, MARY C., REICH, L. C., & SONSTROEM, ANNE MCK. *Studies in cognitive growth.* New York: Wiley, 1966.

FOWLER, W. Dimensions and directions in the development of affecto-cognitive systems. *Human Development,* 1966, 9, 18–29.

GOODNOW, JACQUELINE J. A test of milieu effects with some of Piaget's tasks. *Psychological Monographs,* 1962, 76, No. 36 (Whole No. 555).

HUNT, J. McV. *Intelligence and experience.* New York: Ronald Press, 1961.

INHELDER, B., & PIAGET, J. *The growth of logical thinking.* New York: Basic Books, 1958.

KOHLBERG, L. Cognitive stages and preschool education. *Human Development,* 1966, 9, 5–17.

MCGUIRE, C. Commentaries. In Mary Jane Aschner & C. E. Bish (Eds.), *Productive thinking in education, Part II: Motivation, personality, productive thinking.* Washington, D.C.: N.E.A., 1965, pp. 180–190.

MCGUIRE, C. Behavioral Science Memorandum #13, Part B, of the Research and Development Center for Teacher Education at the University of Texas. Mimeograph. Austin, Texas, 1967.

PIAGET, J. *Judgment and reasoning in the child.* (1st ed., 1924) New York: Humanities Press, 1952.

PIAGET, J. *The moral judgment of the child.* (1st ed., 1932) New York: Free Press, 1948.

PIAGET, J. *The origins of intelligence in children.* (1st ed., 1936) New York: International University Press, 1952.

PIAGET, J. *Psychology of intelligence.* (Paris: Alcan, 1947; trans. by M. Piercy & D. E. Berlyne. London: Routledge & Kegan Paul, 1950). Totowa, N.J.: Littlefield, Adams, 1966 (ILP Paperback #222, $1.75).

PIAGET, J. How children form mathematical concepts. *Scientific American,* November 1953. (Reprinted in P. H. Mussen, J. J. Conger, & J. Kagan (Eds.), *Readings in child development and personality.* New York: Harper & Row, 1965.)

ROSENZWEIG, M. R. Environmental complexity, cerebral change and behavior. *American Psychologist,* 1966, 21, 321–332.

SMEDSLUND, J. The acquisition of conservation of substance and weight in children. III. Extinction of conservation of weight acquired "normally" and by means of empirical controls on a balance scale. *Scandinavian Journal of Psychology,* 1961, 2, 85–87. (Reprinted in R. C. Anderson & D. P. Ausubel (Eds.), *Readings in the psychology of cognition.* New York: Holt, 1966. Pp. 602–605.)

WALLACH, M. A. Research on children's thinking. In National Society for the Study of Education 62nd Yearbook, *Child Psychology.* Chicago: University of Chicago Press, 1963.

The New World of the Adolescent

Ralph Erickson

After the relative calm of the pre-teen years, comes the storm and stress of adolescence. The child reexamines previously held ideas and even remodels his personality, sometimes drastically. His body shows a new form and silhouette. Endocrine changes may bring skin eruptions, feelings of apathy, and a tendency towards introspection. Cultural factors are important; it is only in industrialized societies that we have invented or discovered adolescence.

The adolescent questions himself: What do I believe in? What will I stand for? What will I do? Who am I? He parades a bewildering variety of ideas before friends and adults. Through observing their reactions, he can take thought to modify his understanding of himself. His personality is not an unfolding of innate characteristics, but is built up and refined through contact with others.

Often the primary reference groups of adults and youth are so opposed to each other that the adolescent feels compelled to hide his own beliefs, concealing himself within the teen-age group, slavishly conforming to every whim, style, or attitude it espouses.

Adult society finds it difficult to agree on the age of accountability for adolescents. Separate chronological ages are established at which one can marry, drive automobiles, be drafted, vote, sign contracts, or discontinue school. Yet age is among the least important factors in one's ability to perform these actions satisfactorily. But notice how fervently the 14-year-olds wish to become 16, while 16-year-olds, in turn, expect that something magical will happen on their 21st birthdays.

Conflicting forces impinging upon the adolescent may allow him to develop a distinctive sense of identity and worth. Rarely, before this time, did he find it profitable or even interesting to question himself. Such questions could shatter his ego. Success in dealing with such questions, if he has it, provides the adolescent with status and self-esteem. Adults must not be put off by the appearance of youngsters. Their behavior should not conceal the fact that they have real concerns, problems, and worries.

Basic to the development of a good self-image are the adolescent's responses to his own body. Changes in size, shape, and sensitiveness center attention upon this physical self. Too often, these developments are considered proof that adulthood has been reached, whereas they are merely more vivid landmarks on a journey that ends only with death. Adulthood is not a matter of age, or experi-

From *Clearing House* XLVI, no. 4 (December 1971):227–230. Used by permission of the author and publisher.

ences, or privileges received, but is an emotional state wherein one accepts responsibility for perpetuating the on-going process of civilization.

Each subculture views the body differently, but none is able to ignore it. In middle-class America we value pre-marital chastity, cleanliness, balanced diets, regular bowel movements, and the concept that self-denial produces strong characters. If left to himself, the young child probably never would come to value such beliefs.

As the child leaves the home for longer and longer periods while becoming an adult, he discovers that the outside world is not so much of a "piece" as he had anticipated. Some attitudes he encounters support the family positions; others raise doubts and conflicts or allow him to reconcile opposing philosophies. Parental teachings are no longer simply accepted; now they are tested in daily living and often are found to be no longer valid and tenable. In defense, many parents simply try to shield their children from problems rather than attempt to teach them to handle such difficulties effectively.

Only an individual who is certain of his own identity, or one who doesn't care for other people, can ignore the demands of his groups. But few adolescents are wholly certain of themselves, and practically none are unconcerned about the opinions of others. They can only somewhat repudiate the opinions of adults. More commonly they interpret them in what they understand to be unique situations. To the adolescent, the problems are new, although everything he does or wants to do his parents have already considered.

Human nature does change, but in a single generation or two the changes are only superficial.

Youths may become impatient with their parents for not understanding them. The older generation becomes disgusted with adolescents who seem determined to make every mistake their parents did. Love and respect may enable reconciliations to take place, but some disagreements are inevitable in a fast-moving world.

The world outside the home may appear as a jungle to a sensitive child. This discrepancy between what is officially valued and what is actually practiced may be too great to be reconciled. The virtues of decency, good manners, chastity, self-effacement, and hard work are regularly violated by adults who appear happy and successful when doing so. No wonder many children who at first accept home moral values become adolescents who consider that parents are squares and rules are for fools. Others take flight from such a seething maelstrom and withdraw, run away, or regress to childhood behavior. Personality disorders, caused by the inability to accept the world for what it is, are far more common among teen-agers than is ordinarily realized.

Yet constantly new ideas must be fitted within old frames of reference. The adolescent discovers that others have problems also. Adults are not as competent and adequate as they profess to be. The youth has extensive exploratory contacts with others now; later he will eliminate many peripheral activities and narrow his range of interest.

Life-styles become identifiable as the child selects preferred activities from those available. At this point adults mold personality, not by setting up rigid patterns to be followed, but by increasing the number of acceptable and attractive alternatives for the adolescent. Finally, the adolescent's customary ways of acting become not just something he does; they are inseparable from the person; they are his personality.

The blurring of sex distinctions has accompanied the demand for female equality. More and more women are reaching for fulfillment in the workaday world while intending to retain their favored position in other areas. Most men are more comfortable dealing with men on the job; women, they feel, tend to vacillate between being a woman and being career persons. The woman who wishes to achieve equality with a man on the job must be noticeably better than he is.

Often the black female must work outside the home in order to survive. Many black families have no resident adult male. College educated black females are sought by employers, since they are not likely to challenge white males for power. The black protest movement is dominated by males who are partially protesting their own status in the black matriarchal society.

Girls find it easy to identify with the adult society, as they find female exemplars all about them in school and in the home. A boy may have only a vague idea as to his father's occupational activity. The characterizations he sees in television, films, or written word are hardly true pictures of typical adults. The systemic lack of concern for others, the violation of their rights, the belief that misunderstandings can only be settled by violence, and that poor manners are acceptable substitutes for intelligence, make dramatic effects, but are not the marks of a mature adult. There is much to be said for the quiet virtues, but they are often so quiet that they are overlooked by the adolescent.

Many parents are uncertain as to what they believe in, wanting the child to grow up, yet conspiring to keep him immature. He is constantly put down and protected from major responsibilities. He is not allowed to participate in adult life. The result may be feelings of inferiority, inadequacy, loneliness, and irritability. He may show his alienation by bizarre clothing, hairstyles, and habits. His heroes become those who are eternally adolescent (as the Beatles) or themselves antagonistic to the Establishment (as Cleaver or McCarthy).

SUMMARY AND RECOMMENDATIONS

Adolescence is best understood as a process rather than as a period. Not every good home for children will automatically produce adolescents that can grow into contributing adults. All about us are older persons who have the form of adults but the emotions of children.

Adults help the adolescent to mature by providing a relatively constant but not static community as a standard. Of course, throughout the world, conditions, values, and cultures are inconsistent and varying, but it is the adolescents' locality that is of primary importance. Many adults have not integrated their own beliefs and perceptions into a uniform whole, so cannot readily serve as good models for youth generally, or even for their own children.

Teachers must design day-to-day class activities employing programs that are interesting, worthwhile, and technically correct. Children must generally be successful in what they are doing. The adolescent may have many doubts about the value of much of the adult society, as indeed many adults do, but it is prefer-

able for him to feel that reforms should come from within the
him to attack it in a wholesale manner or become disgusted with i

Big business, big government, big labor, and the military-indust
now provide the leaders that the colleges formerly did. Student revo
such superpowers are futile if done individually. Adolescents must band t
if they would be heard.

Colleges just have not prepared students to deal effectively with such co
centrations of power. This is the basis for the student complaint that colleges
are removed from the problems of this world. College instructors teach as if the
material is sacred in itself, forgetful of the personality and concerns of the one
who is expected to do the learning.

While often neglected in practice, central to every school and college should
be a development of the student as an effective practitioner in the art of human
relations. No other of society's institutions can have this kind of emphasis. It
includes personality reconstruction. This means that a radical revision of the role
of the college is needed. Failure to achieve this will cause the opportunity to be
lost by default to the charlatans, the star-gazers, the barroom barristers, the newspaper columnists, and the ignorant or uninformed. Such a tragic waste of our
greatest natural resource is nothing less than criminal.

Viewpoints from Related Disciplines: Human Growth and Development

David P. Ausubel

What light can the field of human growth and development throw on the
issue "What shall the schools teach?" I only wish it were possible for me to list
and discuss a dozen or more instances in which developmental principles have
been validly utilized in providing definitive answers to questions dealing with the
content and organization of the curriculum. Unfortunately, however, it must
be admitted that at present our discipline can offer only a limited number of very
crude generalizations and highly tentative suggestions bearing on this issue. In a
very general sense, of course, it is undeniable that concern with child development
has had a salutary effect on the educational enterprise. It alerted school administrators to the fact that certain minimal levels of intellectual maturity were necessary before various subjects could be taught with a reasonable degree of efficiency
and hope of success; and it encouraged teachers in presenting their subject matter

From *Teachers College Record* LX, no. 5 (February 1959):245–254. Used by permission
of the author and publisher.

Human Development

erests of pupils, to consider their point of view, and
limitations in command of language and grasp of
premature and wholesale extension of develop-
ial theory and practice has caused incalculable
eration for teachers to unlearn some of the more
se overgeneralized and unwarranted applications.
ied difficulty proceeds from failure to appreciate
pment is a pure rather than an applied science.
d with the discovery of general laws about the
human development *as an end in itself*. Ultimately, of
course, these laws have self-evident implications for the realization of practical
goals in such fields as education, child rearing, and guidance. In a very general
sense they indicate the effects of different interpersonal and social climates on
personality development and the kinds of methods and subject-matter content
that are most compatible with developmental capacity and mode of functioning
at a given stage of growth. Thus, because it offers important insights about the
changing intellectual and emotional capacities of children as developing human
beings, child development may legitimately be considered one of the basic sciences
underlying education and guidance and as part of the necessary professional preparation of teachers—in much the same sense that anatomy and bacteriology are
basic sciences for medicine and surgery.

Actual application to practical problems of teaching and curriculum, however, is quite another matter. Before the educational implications of developmental findings can become explicitly useful in everyday school situations, much
additional research at the engineering level of operations is necessary. Knowledge
about nuclear fission, for example, does not tell us how to make an atomic bomb
or an atomic-powered submarine, antibiotic reactions that take place in petri
dishes do not necessarily take place in living systems, and methods of learning
employed by animals in mazes do not necessarily correspond to methods of learning that children use in grappling with verbal materials in classrooms. Many of
the better-known generalizations in child development—the principle of readiness,
the cephalocaudal trend, the abstract to concrete trend in conceptualizing the
environment, and others—fit these analogies perfectly. They are interesting and
potentially useful ideas to curriculum specialists but will have little practical
utility in designing a social studies or physical education curriculum unless they
are rendered more specific in terms of the actual operations involved in teaching
these subjects. This lack of fruitful particularization, although unfortunate and
regrettable, does not in itself give rise to damaging consequences except insofar
as many beginning teachers tend to nurture vague illusions about the current
usefulness of these principles, and subsequently, after undergoing acute disillusion-
ment, lose the confidence they may have left in the value of a developmental
approach to educational problems.

Much more detrimental in their effects on pupils and teachers have been the
consequences of far-fetched and uncritical application to educational practice of
developmental generalizations that either have not been adequately validated or
only apply to a very restricted age segment of the total span of children's development. Two illustrations of the latter category of highly limited generalizations—
the "internal ripening" theory of maturation and the principle of self-selection
—will be given later in this discussion. A widely accepted but inadequately vali-

dated developmental principle frequently cited to justify general or over-all ability grouping of pupils is that a child's growth and achievement show a "going-togetherness." Actually, except for a spuriously high correlation during infancy, the relationship between physical status and motor ability on the one hand and intelligence and intellectual achievement on the other is negligible and declines consistently with increasing age. Even among the different subtests of intelligence and among the different areas of intellectual achievement, the weight of the evidence indicates that as a child grows older his component rates of growth in these various functions tend increasingly to diverge.

Keeping these qualifications about the relevance of child development for educational practice in mind, I propose briefly to consider from the standpoint of developmental psychology the following aspects of the issue under discussion: (1) readiness as a criterion for curricular placement; (2) developmental factors affecting breadth of the curriculum; (3) the child's voice in determining the curriculum; and (4) the content and goals of instruction in relation to the organization and growth of the intellect.

READINESS AND GRADE PLACEMENT

There is little disagreement about the fact that readiness always crucially influences the efficiency of the learning process and often determines whether a given intellectual skill or type of school material is learnable at all at a particular stage of development. Most educators implicitly accept also the proposition that an *optimal* age exists for every kind of learning. Postponement of learning experience beyond the age of optimal readiness wastes valuable and often unsuspected learning opportunities, thereby unnecessarily reducing the amount and complexity of subject-matter content that can be mastered in a designated period of schooling. It is also conceivable that beyond a certain critical age the learning of various intellectual skills becomes more difficult for an older than for a younger child. On the other hand, when a pupil is prematurely exposed to a learning task before he is ready for it, he not only fails to learn the task in question but even learns from the experience of failure to fear, dislike, and avoid it.

Up to this point, the principle of readiness—the idea that attained capacity limits and influences an individual's ability to profit from current experience or practice—is empirically demonstrable and conceptually unambiguous. Difficulty first arises when it is confused with the concept of *maturation* and when the latter concept in turn is equated with a process of "internal ripening." The concept of readiness simply refers to the adequacy of existing capacity in relation to the demands of a given learning task. No specification is made as to *how* this capacity is achieved—whether through prior practice of a specific nature (learning), through incidental experience, through genically regulated structural and functional changes occurring independently of environmental influences, or through various combinations of these factors. Maturation, on the other hand, has a different and much more restricted meaning. It encompasses those increments in capacity that take place in the demonstrable absence of specific practice experience—those that are attributable to genic influences and/or incidental experience. Maturation, therefore, is not the same as readiness but is merely one of the two principal factors (the other being learning) that contribute to or determine the organism's readiness to cope with new experience. Whether or not readiness exists, in other words, does not necessarily depend on maturation alone but in many instances is solely a function of prior learning experience and most typically depends on varying proportions of maturation and learning.

To equate the principles of readiness and maturation not only muddies the conceptual waters but also makes it difficult for the school to appreciate that insufficient readiness may reflect inadequate prior learning on the part of pupils because of inappropriate or inefficient instructional methods. Lack of maturation can thus become a convenient scapegoat whenever children manifest insufficient readiness to learn, and the school, which is thereby automatically absolved of all responsibility in the matter, consequently fails to subject its instructional practices to the degree of self-critical scrutiny necessary for continued educational progress. In short, while it is important to appreciate that the current readiness of pupils determines the school's current choice of instructional methods and materials, it is equally important to bear in mind that this readiness itself is partly determined by the appropriateness and efficiency of the previous instructional practices to which they have been subjected.

The conceptual confusion is further compounded when maturation is interpreted as a process of "internal ripening" essentially independent of all environmental influences, that is, of both specific practice and incidental experience. Readiness then becomes a matter of simple genic regulation unfolding in accordance with a predetermined and immutable timetable; and the school, by definition, becomes powerless to influence readiness either through its particular way of arranging specific learning experiences or through a more general program of providing incidental or nonspecific background experience preparatory to the introduction of more formal academic activities.

Actually, the embryological model of development implicit in the "internal ripening" thesis fits quite well when applied to human sensorimotor and neuromuscular sequences taking place during the prenatal period and early infancy. In the acquisition of simple behavioral functions (for example, locomotion, prehension) that characterize all members of the human species irrespective of cultural or other environmental differences, it is reasonable to suppose that for all practical purposes genic factors alone determine the direction of development. Environmental factors only enter the picture if they are extremely deviant, and then serve more to disrupt or arrest the ongoing course of development than to generate distinctive developmental progressions of their own. Thus, the only truly objectionable aspect of this point of view is its unwarranted extrapolation to those more complex and variable components of later cognitive and behavioral development where unique factors of individual experience and cultural environment make important contributions to the direction, patterning, and sequential order of all developmental changes.

It is hardly surprising, therefore, in view of the tremendous influence on professional and lay opinion wielded by Gesell and his colleagues, that many people conceive of readiness in absolute and immutable terms, and thus fail to appreciate that except for such traits as walking and grasping, the mean ages of readiness can never be specified apart from relevant environmental conditions. Although the modal child in contemporary America may first be ready to read at the age of six and one-half, the age of reading readiness is always influenced by cultural, subcultural, and individual differences in background experience, and in any case varies with the method of instruction employed and the child's IQ. Middle-class children, for example, are ready to read at an earlier age than lower-class children because of the greater availability of books in the home and because they are read to and taken places more frequently.

The need for particularizing developmental generalizations before they can become useful in educational practice is nowhere more glaringly evident than in the field of readiness. At present we can only speculate what curricular sequences might conceivably be if they took into account precise and detailed (but currently unavailable) research findings on the emergence of readiness for different subject-matter areas, for different sub-areas and levels of difficulty within an area, and for different techniques of teaching the same material. Because of the unpredictable specificity of readiness as shown, for example, by the fact that four- and five-year-olds can profit from training in pitch but not in rhythm, valid answers to such questions cannot be derived from logical extrapolation but require meticulous empirical research in a school setting. The next step would involve the development of appropriate teaching methods and materials to take optimal advantage of existing degrees of readiness and to increase readiness wherever necessary and desirable. But since we generally do not have this type of research data available, except perhaps in the field of reading, we can only pay lip service to the principle of readiness in curriculum planning.

BREADTH OF CURRICULUM

One of the chief complaints of the critics of public education, both in the United States and in New Zealand, is that modern children fail to learn the fundamentals because of the broadening of the elementary school curriculum to include such subjects as social studies, art, science, music, and manual arts in addition to the traditional three R's. This, of course, would be a very serious charge if it were true, because the wisdom of expanding a child's intellectual horizons at the expense of making him a cripple in the basic intellectual skills is highly questionable to say the least. Fortunately, however, the benefits of an expanded curriculum have thus far not been accompanied by a corresponding deterioration in the standard of the three R's. Evidently the decreased amount of time spent on the latter subjects has been more than compensated for by the development of more efficient methods of teaching and by the incidental learning of the fundamentals in the course of studying these other subjects. Nevertheless, the issue of breadth versus depth still remains because there is obviously a point beyond which increased breadth could only be attained by sacrificing mastery of the fundamental skills; and even if we agreed to maintain or improve the present standard of the three R's, we would still have to choose between breadth and depth in relation to other components of the curriculum, particularly at the junior and senior high school levels. It is at these points of choice that developmental criteria can be profitably applied.

Generally speaking, maximal breadth of the curriculum consistent with adequate mastery of its constituent parts is developmentally desirable at all ages because of the tremendously wide scope of human abilities. The wider the range of intellectual stimulation to which pupils are exposed, the greater are the chances that all of the diverse potentialities both within a group of children and within a single child will be brought to fruition. By the same token, a broad curriculum makes it possible for more pupils to experience success in the performance of school activities and thus to develop the necessary self-confidence and motivation for continued academic striving and achievement. The very fact that elementary school children are able to make significant progress in science and social studies also indicates that myopic concentration on the three R's would waste much available readiness for these types of learnings and thus compel junior and senior high schools to devote much of their instructional time to materials that are easily learnable in the lower grades. In fact, one of the major failings of the secondary school curriculum today is that because it still has not adequately adjusted to the expansion of the elementary school syllabus, entering pupils are subjected to much stultifying repetition and fail to break the new ground for which they are obviously ready.

The relationship between breadth and depth must also take into account the progressive differentiation of intelligence, interests, and personality structure with increasing age. The elementary school child is a "generalist" because both his intellect and his personality are still relatively unstable and uncrystallized and lack impressive internal consistency. Thus, many different varieties of subject matter are equally compatible with his interest and ability patterns. Furthermore, unless he has experience with many different fields of knowledge and gives each a provisional try, he is in no position to judge which kinds of intellectual pursuits are most congruent with his major ability and value systems. Hence, quite apart from the future life adjustment values of a broad educational background, it is appropriate on developmental grounds for elementary and early high school curricula to stress breadth rather than depth.

Toward the latter portion of the high school period, however, precisely the opposite kind of situation begins to emerge. Interests have crystallized and abilities have undergone differentiation to the point where greater depth and specialization are possible and desirable. Many students at this stage of intellectual development are ready to sink their teeth into more serious and solid academic fare, but unfortunately suitable instructional programs geared at an advanced level of critical and independent thinking are rarely available. The changes that have taken place in secondary school curricula since the academy days have been primarily characterized by the belated and half-hearted addition of more up-to-date and topical information. Very little has been done in the way of providing the student with a meaningful, integrated, systematic view of the major ideas in a given field of knowledge.

THE CHILD'S VOICE IN CURRICULUM PLANNING

One extreme point of view associated with the child-centered approach to education is the notion that children are innately equipped in some mysterious fashion for knowing precisely what is best for them. This idea is obviously an outgrowth of predeterministic theories (for example, those of Rousseau and Gesell) that conceive of development as a series of internally regulated sequential steps that unfold in accordance with a prearranged design. According to these theorists, the environment facilitates development best by providing a maximally permissive field that does not interfere with the predetermined processes of spontaneous maturation. From these assumptions it is but a short step to the claim that the child himself must be in the most strategic position to *know* and *select* those components of the environment that correspond most closely with his current developmental needs and hence are most conducive to optimal growth. Empirical "proof" of this proposition is adduced from the fact that nutrition is adequately maintained and existing deficiency conditions are spontaneously corrected when infants are permitted to select their own diets. If the child can successfully choose his diet, he must certainly know what is best for him in all areas of growth and should therefore be permitted to select everything, including his curriculum.

In the first place, and refuting this theory, even if development were primarily a matter of internal ripening, there would still be no good reason for supposing that the child is therefore implicitly conversant with the current direction and facilitating conditions of development and hence axiomatically equipped to make the most appropriate choices. Because the individual is sensitive in early childhood to internal cues of physiological need we cannot conclude that he is similarly sensitive to cues reflective of psychological and other developmental needs; even in the area of nutrition, selection is a reliable criterion of need only during early infancy.

Second, unless one assigns a sacrosanct status to endogenous motivations, there is little warrant for believing either that they alone are truly reflective of the child's *genuine* developmental requirements or that environmentally derived needs are "imposed," authoritarian in spirit, and inevitably fated to thwart the actualization of his developmental potentialities. Actually, most needs originate from without and are internalized in the course of the child's interaction and identification with significant persons in his family and cultural environments.

Third, one can never assume that the child's *spontaneously* expressed interests and activities are completely reflective of *all* of his important needs and capacities. Just because capacities can potentially provide their own motivation does not mean that they always or necessarily do so. It is not the possession of capacities that is motivating, but the anticipation of future satisfactions once they have been successfully exercised. But because of such factors as inertia, lack of opportunity, lack of appreciation, and preoccupation with other activities, many capacities may never be exercised in the first place. Thus, children typically develop only *some* of their potential capacities, and their expressed interests cannot be considered coextensive with the potential range of interests they are capable of developing with appropriate stimulation.

In conclusion, therefore, the current interests and spontaneous desires of immature pupils can hardly be considered reliable guideposts and adequate substitutes for specialized knowledge and seasoned judgment in designing a curriculum. Recognition of the role of pupil needs in school learning does not mean that the scope of the syllabus should be restricted to the existing concerns and spontaneously expressed interests that happen to be present in a group of children growing up under particular conditions of intellectual and social class stimulation. In fact, one of the primary functions of education should be to stimulate the development of motivations that are currently nonexistent. It is true that academic achievement is greatest when pupils manifest felt needs to acquire knowledge as an end in itself. Such needs, however, are not endogenous but acquired—and largely through exposure to provocative, meaningful, developmental, appropriate instruction. Hence, while it is reasonable to consider the views of pupils and even, under certain circumstances, to solicit their participation in the planning of the curriculum, it makes little developmental or administrative sense to entrust them with responsibility for significant policy or operational decisions.

ORGANIZATION AND COGNITIVE DEVELOPMENT

The curriculum specialist is concerned with more than the appropriate grade placement of different subjects and subject-matter content in accordance with such criteria as readiness and relative significance for intellectual, vocational, or current adjustment purposes. More important than what pupils know at the end of the sixth, eighth, and twelfth grades is the extent of their knowledge at the ages of twenty-five, forty, and sixty as well as their ability and desire both to learn more and to apply their knowledge fruitfully in adult life. In light of these latter criteria, in comparing, for example, the quantity and quality of our national research output in the pure and applied sciences with those of European countries, the American educational system stands up relatively well even though our school children apparently absorb less academic material. We are dealing here with the ultimate intellectual objectives of schooling, namely, with the long-term acquisition of stable and usable bodies of knowledge and intellectual skills and with the development of ability to think creatively, systematically, independently, and with depth in particular fields of inquiry. Instruction obviously influences the outcome of these objectives—not so much in the substantive content of subject matter but in the organization, sequence, and manner of presenting learning experiences, their degree of meaningfulness, and the relative balance between conceptual and factual materials.

But obviously, before we could ever hope to structure effectively such instructional variables for the optimal realization of these designated objectives, we would have to know a great deal more about the organizational and developmental principles whereby human beings acquire and retain stable bodies of knowledge and develop the power of critical and productive thinking. This type of knowledge, however, will forever elude us unless we abandon the untenable assumption that there is no real distinction either between the logic of a proposition and how the mind apprehends it or between the logical structure of subject-matter organization and the actual series of cognitive processes through which an immature and developing individual incorporates facts and concepts into a stable body of knowledge. It is perfectly logical from the standpoint of a mature scholar, for example, to write a textbook in which topically homogeneous materials are segregated into discrete chapters and treated throughout at a uniform level of conceptualization. But how closely does this approach correspond with highly suggestive findings that one of the major cognitive processes involved in the learning of any new subject is progressive differentiation of an originally undifferentiated field? Once we learn more about cognitive development than the crude generalizations that developmental psychology can currently offer, it will be possible to employ organizational and sequential principles in the presentation of subject matter that actually parallel developmental changes in the growth and organization of the intellect. In the meantime let us examine briefly how such generalizations as the concrete-to-abstract trend, the importance of meaningfulness, and the principle of retroactive inhibition have been used and abused in educational practice.

Many features of the activity program are based on the premise that the elementary school child perceives the world in relatively specific and concrete terms and requires considerable firsthand experience with diverse concrete instances of a given set of relationships before he can abstract genuinely meaningful concepts. Thus, an attempt is made to teach factual information and intellectual skills in the real-life functional contexts in which they are customarily encountered rather than through the medium of verbal exposition supplemented by artificially contrived drills and exercises. This approach has real merit, if a fetish is not made of naturalism and incidental learning, if drills and exercises are provided in instances where opportunities for acquiring skills do not occur frequently and repetitively enough in more natural settings, and if deliberate or guided effort is not regarded as incompatible with incidental learning. Even more important, however, is the realization that in older children, once a sufficient number of basic concepts are consolidated, new concepts are primarily abstracted from verbal rather than from concrete experience. Hence in secondary school it may be desirable to reverse both the sequence and the relative balance between abstract concepts and supportive data. There is good reason for believing, therefore, that much of the time presently spent in cook-book laboratory exercises in the sciences could be much more advantageously employed in formulating precise definitions, making explicit verbal distinctions between concepts, generalizing from hypothetical situations, and in other ways.

Another underlying assumption of activity and project methods is that concepts and factual data are retained much longer when they are meaningful, genuinely understood, and taught as larger units of interrelated materials than when they are presented as fragmented bits of isolated information and committed to rote memory. This, of course, does not preclude the advisability of rote learning for certain kinds of learning (for example, multiplication tables) *after* a functional understanding of the underlying concepts has been acquired. Unfortunately, however, these principles have made relatively few inroads on the high school instructional program, where they are still applicable. The teaching of mathematics and science, for example, still relies heavily on rote learning of formulas and procedural steps, on recognition of traditional "type problems," and on mechanical manipulation of symbols. In the absence of clear and stable concepts which serve as anchoring points and organizing foci for the assimilation of new material, secondary school students are trapped in a morass of confusion and seldom retain rotely memorized materials much beyond final exam time.

This brings us finally to a consideration of the mechanisms of accretion and long-term retention of large bodies of ideational material. Why do high school and university students tend to forget so readily previous day-to-day learnings as they are exposed to new lessons? The traditional answer of educational psychology, based upon studies of short-term rote learning in animal and human subjects, has been that subsequent learning experiences which are similar to but not identical with previously learned materials exert a retroactively inhibitory effect on the retention of the latter. But wouldn't it be reasonable to suppose that all of the existing, cumulatively established ideational systems which an individual brings with him to any learning situation have more of an interfering effect on the retention of new learning material (proactive inhibition) than brief exposure to subsequently introduced materials of a similar nature (retroactive inhibition)? Because it is cognitively most economical and least burdensome for an individual to subsume as much new experience as possible under existing concepts that are inclusive and stable, the import of many specific illustrative items in later experience is assimilated by the generalized meaning of these more firmly established and highly conceptualized subsuming foci. When this happens the latter items lose their identity and are said to be "forgotten." Hence, if proactive rather than retroactive inhibition turned out to be the principal mechanism affecting the longevity with which school materials were retained, it would behoove us to identify those factors that counteract it and to employ such measures in our instructional procedures.

SECTION 2 ADDITIONAL LEARNING ACTIVITIES

Problems and Projects
1. Visit a Headstart program and classrooms in an elementary school, a middle school, and a high school. Note differences in learners that are due to their stages of human development, and determine how the differences affect learning.
2. Visit any classroom in an elementary school, middle school, or high school. Note the differences in development among learners in any one class. How should they affect the curriculum and teaching? These differences are most noticeable in groups ranging in age from ten, when the first girl may attain puberty, to sixteen, when the last boy may attain it.
3. Continue to develop a "case problem" about one school you know well. Describe the curriculum and teaching in that school as it may be related to human development. Consider the human development theories presented in this section and ask whether they are being used or ought to be used in curriculum planning in that school. You can add to your study of this school as you work on each of the bases of the curriculum and the criteria.
4. Try the preassessment again, examining a different school or curriculum plan in the light of human development theories and research (such as the theories of Havighurst, Erikson, or Piaget).
5. Read *Developing a Curriculum for Modern Living*, 2nd ed., by Florence Stratemeyer and others, in order to see how "persistent life situations" can be made the basis of curriculum planning at all levels of the school. Compare the concept of "persistent life situations" with the "developmental task" concept developed by Robert J. Havighurst (See article in this section and Robert J. Havighurst, *Developmental Tasks and Education*, New York: Longman, Green and Co., 1953). See also the new paperback edition of *Developmental Tasks and Education* published by David McKay and Co., Inc. in 1972.

Films
The Child Watchers, 16mm., color, 30 mins. Explains that children are learning more at a faster rate than most parents realize. Describes behavior patterns that parents can learn to observe in their child's development. Distributed by McGraw-Hill Text Films, 330 W. 42nd St., New York, New York 10036.

Viedotapes
Man—His Growth and Development, Birth Through Adolescence, 2-inch, black and white, 44 mins. Discusses and demonstrates the continuity of development from infancy to adolescence. Distributed by Video Nursing, Inc., 2645 Girsid Avenue, Evanston, Illinois 60201.

Film Strips
Emotional Development, sound, color. Explains emotional development in adolescents and its relationship to bodily changes. Distributed by Eye Gate House, Inc., 146–01 Archer Avenue, Jamaica, New York 11435.

Books to Review

Adams, James F. *Understanding Adolescence: Current Developments in Adolescent Psychology.* Boston: Allyn and Bacon, 1968.

Cruickshank, W. M., and Johnson, G. O., eds. *Education of Exceptional Children and Youth,* 2nd ed. Englewood Cliffs, New Jersey: Prentice-Hall, 1968.

Ebel, Robert, ed. *Encyclopedia of Educational Research,* 4th ed. The Macmillan Company, 1969. See articles on Developmental Psychology; Early Childhood; Childhood; Adolescence; Adulthood.

Erikson, Erik. *Childhood and Society.* New York: W. W. Norton and Company, 1964.

Havighurst, Robert J. *Human Development and Education,* New York: Longmans, Green and Co., 1953. (See also paperback edition published in 1972 by David McKay and Co., Inc.)

Hurlock, Elizabeth. *Child Development,* 5th ed. New York: McGraw-Hill Book Company, 1972.

Maier, Henry W. *Three Theories of Child Development.* New York: Harper and Row, Publishers, 1969.

Mussen, P. H.; Conger, J. J.; and Kagan, J. *Child Development and Personality,* 3rd ed. New York: Harper and Row, Publishers, 1969.

Piaget, Jean, and Inhelder, Bärbell. *The Psychology of the Child.* New York: Basic Books, 1969.

Stone, L. J., and Church, J. *Childhood and Adolescence,* 2d ed. New York: Random House, 1968.

Stratemeyer, F.; Forkner, Hamden; McKim, Margaret G.; and Passow, A. Harry. *Developing a Curriculum for Modern Living,* 2d ed. New York: Bureau of Publications, Teachers College, Columbia University, 1957.

The Nature of Learning

PREREQUISITE

Reading of the Introduction to this book and Sections 1 and 2.

RATIONALE

The third basis of the curriculum is the nature of learning. An understanding of how learning occurs in human beings is obviously of central importance for planning the curriculum and for teaching.

Today, there are three major families, or groupings, of learning theory. There are many subgroupings within these families, but for the curriculum worker or teacher who is seeking to clarify his thinking in this area, it is usually enough to be aware of the three families of theory and then to base further generalizations on them. Understanding of each of the three families is important for the curriculum planner and teacher because each defines the curriculum differently, and each leads to or supports different teaching practices. Thus, curriculum content and organization and teaching practices may be based on S–R conditioning, the field theories, or Freudian theory. Teaching and curriculum practices may include ideas from each of these families of theories because of the needs of different learners, because there are different kinds of learning, or because there are different kinds of knowledge to be learned.

The first learning-theory position stresses stimulus-response association. It includes all the reinforcement and conditioning theories of learning. The key word in these theories is experience. Thinking is a part of an S–R sequence that begins and ends outside the individual learner. Learning is a conditioning process by which a person acquires a new response. Motivation is the urge to act, which results from a stimulus. Behavior is directed by stimuli from the environment. A person selects one response instead of another because of the particular combination of prior conditioning and physiological drives operating at the moment of action. A person does not have to want to learn something in order to learn it. Anyone can learn anything of which he is capable if he will allow himself to be put through the pattern of activity necessary for conditioning to take place.

The S–R learning theories include theories identified by the following names: stimulus-response; behaviorism; associationist; connectionist; conditioning; reward; pleasure or pain. These theories state that learning takes place through transfer. Transfer is defined as "a general term for change in ability to perform a general act as a direct consequence of having performed another act relevant or related to it." It is essential that the *learner* see the relevance. Another definition of transfer is "the gain in mastery of other activities after having obtained mastery in one particular task." Transfer is thought to be brought about by emphasizing *identical elements* in different situations. A major construct of S–R theory is that learning is *rewarded responses.* Another major construct is that teaching should emphasize particular *elements* of the learning tasks.

Each learning theory seeks "basic units" of learning. The basic unit in S–R theories is *rewarded response.* You must reward the response to have learning take place. What is a reward? It is different from instance to instance and from learner to learner. It has to be important to the learner. Reward is often especially useful for certain types of learners: slow-learners, those less prepared for the learning task, and those in need of step-by-step learning.

In "Freedom and the Control of Men," Skinner describes some of the advantages and possibilities of the S–R approach to learning, as he sees them.[1] He states that science insists that man's actions are initiated by forces impinging upon him from the outside. In turning to external conditions that shape and maintain the behavior of men, while questioning the reality of inner qualities and faculties, we turn from the ill-defined and remote to the observable and manipulable. Science can serve humanitarian aims and can play an important role in making a better world for everyone. Notions about man's freedom based on an eighteenth-century political philosophy should not be allowed to interfere with the application of the methods of science to human affairs. In "What Is Behavior Modification?" Madsen and Madsen describe specific teaching practices based on S–R theory.

The second of the three learning theory families important in curriculum planning is "field" theory—the Gestalt-field, cognitive-field, and perceptual-field group of learning theories. In these theories "wholeness" is primary: one should start with the total aspects of a learning situation and then move to particulars in the light of the whole. Obtaining an "overview" is often important in learning. Without this, frequently we cannot see the forest for the trees.

Another major idea in these theories is that the whole is always greater than the sum of its parts. Experiencing a beautiful musical selection is more than hearing the separate notes; seeing a moving picture is more than the thousands of still pictures that make up the movie.

A particularly important field-group learning theory is the one known as perceptual psychology, phenomenological theory, or self-concept learning theory.

[1] See *The American Scholar* xxv, No. 1 (Winter, 1955–56), 47–65.

In this theory the *self-concept* is central. Behavior and learning are functions of *perception*. What most affects learning are the *meanings* that exist for the individual as a result of his unique perceptions.

Basic units of learning in the cognitive-perceptual-gestalt-field learning theories are the *meaningfulness of the whole; the importance of generalizations, principles and organization in learning;* and the *significance of self-concept and personal meaning.*

Perceptual-cognitive field theories are represented in this section in articles by Combs and Gordon.

In the cognitive-perceptual field learning position, man acts, originates, and thinks, and this is the most important source of his learning. In the S–R conditioning theory, man learns by reacting to forces outside himself.

The third family of learning theories consists of those views of learning that have grown out of the work and ideas of Sigmund Freud as well as his numerous present-day followers. Donald W. Robinson ("Psychoanalysis and Education") describes the impact of Freud on learning theory. The Freudian learning theories are utilized freely and compatibly by the exponents of the S–R associationism and cognitive-field learning positions. It would be a major step forward if a more abstract viewpoint might be found that could successfully incorporate the associationist and the cognitive-field viewpoints, as well as the Freudian.

Basic units of learning in Freudian learning theory include *awareness,* which is *freedom or self-understanding; identification;* and *imitation.* The other learning theories make use of these Freudian learning concepts.

A number of theorists assist us in seeking ways to use these learning theories together. They are represented in this section in an article by Avila and Purkey and an article by Watson.

Curriculum planners and teachers need many ways to encourage learning. Each learning theory position appears to describe a different kind of learning. There are many individual differences among learners, and the various learning theories support different approaches to curriculum planning to provide for the differences in learners. For instance, slow learners learn differently from gifted learners. (See "The Slow Learner," by Karnes, in this section).

There are different kinds of knowledge and human activities. One learning theory approach is probably best for teaching mathematics and another for teaching the humanities or the social sciences.

There is active and passive, meaningful and rote, part and whole, individual and social learning. Some learning occurs as a result of outside forces; other learning is the result of inner meaning. Curriculum planners need to know how to encourage each of these kinds of learning in individuals by basing instruction on individual learning styles and needs.

Concepts from each of these learning theories are in use in curriculum planning and teaching today. They include the following:

1. Identification. Children learn by and through identification with others, including their parents, peers, and teachers. Thus, it is important that they have good models.
2. Discovery. Obtaining knowledge for oneself by the use of one's own mind frequently has advantages for motivation, organization of what is learned, retention, and meaningfulness.

3. Empathy. Openness, trust, and security in human relationships free intelligence and enable boys and girls, and teachers as well, to learn more and to be successful in activities in which they are jointly engaged.
4. Culture Potential. Anthropological studies have emphasized that different societies and cultures cultivate different qualities and capacities. Learning experiences that build on the cultural capacities of individuals and groups are particularly successful.
5. Knowledge about Learners. Research has shown that students learn more when teachers know them as individuals.
6. Methods of Increasing Transfer. When the teacher points out the possibility of transfer and develops and applies generalizations with the learner, transfer is more likely to occur.
7. Zeal for Learning and Knowledge. Students learn to like learning from teachers who love knowledge, from communities that provide resources for learning, and from a home environment that supports the search for knowledge by example and by providing materials.

OBJECTIVES

Your objectives in studying learning theories as one of the bases of curriculum planning should be the following:

1. To be able to analyze curricula or teaching practices with reference to the learning theories involved.
2. To be able to suggest changes and improvements in a curriculum or in the planning of teaching based on an understanding of the kinds of learning that are developed most successfully by each of the learning theories.

PREASSESSMENT

The purpose of the preassessment is to determine whether you already possess the performance competencies in curriculum planning listed under "Objectives," above.

1. Explain how S–R learning theory might be applied to curriculum planning or the planning of teaching to the advantage of the learners involved or the knowledge being taught.
2. Do the same for cognitive-field and perceptual-field learning theories.
3. Explain how you might use the principles of Freudian learning theory in teaching or curriculum planning.
4. Select any curriculum plan, at any school level, and examine curriculum or teaching practices in different subjects or by different teachers in the light of learning theories. You could do this by visiting a school and studying curriculum plans and teaching practices or by analyzing a written statement regarding a school's program or the instruction in one classroom.
5. Suggest improvements or changes in the curriculum plan as a result of your analysis in number 4.

In responding to number 4, do not be surprised if learning theories do not appear to be considered in the curriculum planning done at the school or in the classroom that you study. Often they are not. Therefore, suggest improvements in the planning of curriculum or instruction at that school. Knowledge and use of the various learning theories in planning offers important guidelines in providing for individual differences and instructional alternatives. Remember that there are different kinds of learners, different kinds of learning, and different kinds of knowledge. Each can be the basis of significant decisions or alternatives provided for in curriculum and instruction planning.

In answering number 4 of the preassessment, you might choose to analyze the curriculum and teaching practices described in either "The Self-Selection Classroom" by Zilpha W. Billings (Section 6 of this book), or "Youths as Advocates" by Cohen and Richards (Section 8).

LEARNING ACTIVITIES

Articles in this section will assist you in identifying and understanding the various learning theories and how they may be applied to advantage in curriculum planning and in teaching.

Other learning activities are suggested at the end of this section.

POSTASSESSMENT

After attempting the preassessment you may do one or more of the following:

1. See if your instructor believes that you are ready for a postassessment evaluation on learning theories and the curriculum. Most students will need further work on this curriculum base.
2. Read the articles on learning in this section and try to determine how theories and research being discussed in each article should be considered in curriculum planning and teaching.
3. Choose additional activities and readings or films and videotapes from those listed at the end of this section.
4. Look for other films, books, or articles on learning in your library or media center.
5. Discuss the reading you have done and the films you have viewed with your fellow students. The key questions: How should the learning theories you've studied affect a school's curriculum? How should they be considered in planning for teaching?
6. When you are ready, ask your instructor for advice on a suitable postassessment for you for this topic. Satisfactory completion of number 3 under "Problems and Projects" at the end of this section might be one possibility. Or satisfactory written completion of the preassessment for this section, after completing other learning activities, might be a satisfactory postassessment. Consult your instructor about this.

What is Behavior Modification?

Clifford K. Madsen
Charles H. Madsen, Jr.

Stripped to basics, behavior modification means changing behavior by rewarding the kind you want to encourage and ignoring or disapproving the kind you want to discourage. Used with understanding, it is an effective, caring way to control behavior in school.

When we talk about controlling behavior, most teachers think first of the noisy, disruptive child. Behavior modification is useful for such children, but its use is not limited to them; it is for all behaviors of all children. The story of Paul, however, illustrates most behavior modification principles.

Paul yelled, scuffled, pinched, fidgeted, and drummed his heels all day. He seldom concentrated on anything, much less his schoolwork. Scolding, extra attention, acting disappointed, had short-lived results.

In desperation, his teacher Miss Starr decided to try behavior modification. She first needed to find out how many disturbances Paul made in a day. Ticking them off on a sheet of paper, she counted twenty-three incidents, which averaged about one every fifteen minutes. She did this for several days.

Miss Starr knew Paul liked to use the tape recorder more than anything else. "Paul," she said, "Fifteen minutes shouldn't be too long for you to behave. For every fifteen minutes that you pay attention to what you are doing and don't disturb other children at work, I'll let you use the tape recorder for one minute at the end of the day. You can earn up to fifteen minutes of using the tape recorder all by yourself. If you don't earn any time, you can't use it at all. I'll set the timer every fifteen minutes." She made sure Paul had tasks he could do if he tried and that he understood them. She also checked often to see if he was on the right track, and made sure that he knew his efforts were appreciated.

The next day Paul earned seven minutes with the tape recorder. This meant he'd spent an unprecedented hour and three quarters doing his work! Miss Starr resolutely waited out the other outbursts, saying and doing nothing. Once or twice she sharply reminded him, "Paul, you've just lost another minute!" Her judgments between acceptable and nonacceptable behavior were somewhat lenient at first.

It wasn't long before Paul's disturbances became fewer and less intense. The interval was lengthened first to a half hour, then to an hour. One day Paul said, "I want to use the tape recorder for a project. Do I still need to earn the time?" "Do you need to?" asked Miss Starr. Paul

From *Instructor* LXXXI, no. 2 (October 1971):48–49, 51–56. Used by permission of the author and publisher.

grinned and said, "I'll let you know if I do!" Paul remained an excitable child, but his behavior now consistently stayed well within the normal classroom range.

Paul's teacher knew that behavioral scientists believe that all behavior is learned, and that it is learned as a consequence of being associated with a pleasant experience. Paul's behavior was the only way he knew to earn something of value to him, probably simple attention. Where and when he had made this unfortunate association of behavior/reward was not important. His behavior didn't cause the problem; it was the problem. Miss Starr didn't try to change his attitude. She worked with an observable piece of behavior that needed to be changed. She didn't try to change Paul's basic personality. She could and did help Paul learn to control his actions so he and his classmates could settle down to their job of learning.

This teacher went through four steps of behavior modification, which can be boiled down to one word each: (1) pinpoint; (2) record; (3) consequate (set up consequences for); and (4) evaluate. She also made use of the learning steps of experience, discrimination, and association. First she structured the situation so Paul would experience good behavior, then so he would learn to discriminate his behavior, and finally to associate his appropriate behavior with reward. The task was geared to allow him success, and the reward was paired with signs of approval. Soon he could give up the extrinsic reward and function in the regular classroom reward system.

The techniques of behavior modification, also called "reinforcement theory" and other names as well, are highly efficient. Based mainly on the work of B. F. Skinner, they have a simple, scientific cause-and-effect basis that has been used with dramatic results in teaching, overcoming learning disabilities, behavioral research, and clinical psychology.

This dependable relationship of cause and effect makes it possible for a behavioral scientist, given time for observation, to break down and classify any behavior that he can observe, directly or indirectly. Behavior, as he uses the word, means anything a person does, says, or even thinks as long as his thinking is manifested in action. It includes all behaviors: emotional responses, attitudes, reading, doing math, looking into a mirror, liking a person, becoming frustrated, staying on task, getting off task, disturbing one's neighbors, and so on, to include all of children's "good" and "bad" behaviors.

These behaviors have all been learned. They can be changed by giving the child a reason for changing. Specifically, children change behaviors for things that bring them pleasure. They work for approval from people they love and/or respect; they work to satisfy the desires they have been taught to value; they avoid behaviors they associate with unpleasantness; they act in ways that have been reinforced, whether by chance or by design.

Some teachers who have not had experience with this teaching technique feel it smacks of "cold-blooded manipulation." Well, yes, if that phrase means "conscious management," not really of children but of their environment. A teacher (or parent) in charge of children can't help conditioning them, since they make constant associations with the other people or things in their environments. Even in the most open education, a teacher conditions his students by his approval or lack of it, his attention or lack of it, his very presence or absence.

So why shirk the job? You chose the responsibility of changing children's behavior when you chose to teach. It's your job to learn to do it well.

When a child does not learn, or demonstrates other inappropriate school behavior, it is because he is suffering an error in association or reinforcement. He has made an inappropriate association or has not made an appropriate one, because the reinforcement was incorrect or lacking. You are already working with associations when you use teaching games (learning = fun), and when, in your own words, you try to "make learning a rewarding experience."

With a knowledge of behavioral techniques, a teacher can make these reinforcements deliberately and effectively instead of just hoping they will happen. He can also learn to recognize the frequent errors of association and reinforcement for the purpose of avoiding them. Sarcasm, for example, is an error. "Why don't you just yell louder, Jimmy?" can at best create confusion in the child's mind; you may also find he has taken you literally. The chance of being taken literally is the price one always pays for sarcasm with children or adults.

Behavior modification is a technique for shaping behavior; teachers use it to help children learn because that is their job. The values that it promotes in children are the values the teacher intends them to learn, because that is another part of his job. . . .

WHAT IS A "PAYOFF"?
THAT WHICH KEEPS ANY BEHAVIOR ALIVE

One of the discoveries of behavioral science is that it doesn't matter how or where an inappropriate behavior association got started. What does matter is that the behavior is being kept alive by a "payoff" in the present.

The principle can be stated, "Behavior that goes unrewarded will be extinguished," and, conversely, behavior that does not become extinguished is in some way being rewarded. Although saying so goes against much present-day thinking, looking back is not only unnecessary, it is almost always unproductive. This is especially true when unearthing the "reason" for the behavior is used as a substitute for action.

When you want to change a specific behavior, you must first find the payoff and eliminate it. The possibilities are good that you will be able to do so. Some reinforcements, such as those from the child's family or from his own idea of himself, you can't control and so can't change. But many you can.

The teacher must watch the child carefully to find the payoff in each specific case. This is often not easy. Once again, many of us try to simplify our problem by grouping behaviors together or by categorizing children as "types." This is no more successful than other simplistic solutions for inappropriate behavior, such as "These children came from a disadvantaged background and just need experiences," or "This class just needs a teacher with a firm hand." There are too many differences in the behavior of individuals for such thinking to be of any real use.

Individual differences among children can even result in the same behaviors being dependent on different payoffs. For example, Jim, Alex, and Pete are all acting up in class on the same day. They finally become so disruptive that the teacher sends them all to the principal's office. Jim is delighted; his payoff is that he caused the teacher to lose his cool. Alex's payoff is that he maintained his reputation among the rest of the class for being a tough guy. Pete doesn't care anything about the teacher or the class; the people he wants to impress are Jim and Alex, and he's happy because their friendship and approval are his payoff. Behaviorally, the teacher's response should have been to ignore them. Consistently ignoring a behavior will go far toward extinguishing it. When the teacher doesn't get angry or disturbed, the problem is focused back where it belongs: on the children, not on the teacher. He has not allowed his students to manipulate him.

In extinguishing behavior by means of this technique, you must be prepared for the next development, which is that the behavior will initially become worse rather than better! Remember that the child desires the payoff very much, and has learned this particular behavior as the way to get it. When the payoff is not forthcoming, he will redouble his efforts to earn it the only way he knows. It is not until the child realizes once and for all that the payoff is not going to happen that he will stop the behavior. This may happen quickly, and it may happen slowly. Many teachers give up at this stage, saying, "I've tried ignoring, but the child misbehaved more." Of course.

For this reason, ignoring is not an easy technique. You have to be sure of what you are doing. Sometimes even colleagues or parents won't understand why you're doing it. Explain your reasons and ask for time to achieve results. Stick to your guns. You are extinguishing inappropriate behavior in the child because you care.

WHAT CONSTITUTES REWARD?
THAT WHICH THE CHILD WILL WORK TOWARD

Rewards form pleasant associations and promote the behavior being rewarded. To change a child's inappropriate behavior, often it is enough to track down the payoff and eliminate the specific unwanted behavior. It can be even more effective to institute at the same time a reward or system of rewards for desirable behavior, to form a new association.

Just as it is necessary to extinguish a behavior, it is necessary to pinpoint the specific behavior to be rewarded. For example, you can't try to reward Lucy for "changing her attitude toward her schoolwork." You must look at the overall picture, assign a hierarchy to Lucy's problems, and decide what behavior you can best work with. You might decide that Lucy's worst problem is the fact that she fiddles around before getting to work, so she gets rushed and never finishes her tasks. The behavior you decide to promote is getting down to work in a reasonable time. You wouldn't at first insist that Lucy start everything immediately, and have her reward contingent on that. You'd allow her five minutes. The five minutes could gradually be cut down until, by buckling quickly down to necessary tasks, Lucy shows that she has learned that it's much better not to procrastinate.

When you have a child with multiple problems, as usually is the case, or when you have many children with problems, your decision about what behaviors to work with first will depend on several factors. You may decide to work with what you judge to be the basic behavior problem. Again, you may choose the problem that is most acute; or you may choose to work on the most accessible problem, considering the time and help you have available.

Extinguishing is best done on an individual basis. A reward system, however, can often be set up for an entire group. This can be helpful if a problem of jealousy develops. This does not happen as often as you might think, once the children recognize that the rewarded child needs help, but the possibility is there.

Any system of rewards, whether individual or group, should be set up so each child knows specifically what he must do to earn the reward. What he must do should be enough like his present behavior to enable him to realize that it is within his power. The reward should be something the child desires, the more strongly the better. The reward should be given consistently for each performance of the desired behavior. At first, the reward should be tangible, occur quickly as well as surely, and be generous even to the point of being overly so.

Do your best to catch the child being good, even for a moment. It is important to get the child winning as soon as possible.

We suggest that you write the rules in a conspicuous place or have them easily available. Explain the rules every day. If the reward involves a toy, game, or piece of equipment, hold it up or point to it. If there's a choice of rewards, ask each of several children which one he is working for.

Rewards can be anything a child desires. Obviously, the rewards you choose must be within your resources of money, time, and freedom from restrictive school policies. A teacher who is setting up a reward system on his own probably won't be able to use the more dramatic types of reward. He can make use of what he has with imagination and ingenuity.

The first tangible, quick reward can be as simple as food. For young children, it may be small candies (M&M's are a popular choice), presweetened cereal, or small glasses of juice. Older children may work for candy bars, ice-cream bars, or soft drinks. Rewards can involve toys, games, or puzzles, either the ownership of small ones or time to play with larger ones. One effective reward is simply time for a child to do what he pleases. Another is listening to music of his choice. Some children will grab the chance just to read. Be sure to have available music and reading material they want to hear and read.

Some of these rewards depend for their effect on the fact that you usually can't do them in school. Schools with flexible, individualized programs where all children can move around freely will obviously have to find other types of rewards.

Especially with older children, a token system can be highly effective. Actual tokens can be given out, or points marked down in an appropriate place where the child can see how they are accumulating. Specific numbers of points earn specific awards of varying values. The similarity of a token system to our monetary system makes it familiar; it has the added advantage of giving the child the idea that money is earned as a reward for work. Some schools let children earn enough points to take a trip, or to take off an entire day. There are experimental programs that are using commercial trading stamps and even money itself as contingency rewards. You've probably read about some of these, usually reported as "paying children to go to school."

As a variation, a teacher may sometimes point out a child who is doing a particular task well and say, "You can earn a reward if you concentrate on your work as well as Sheila."

You may also at times make effective use of group approval or disapproval, with a special group bonus reward. "If everyone in the math group can work at least one of these programs in a half hour, we'll have a party!" is a powerful stimulus for individual and cooperative work. Such interaction can develop into group self-discipline, and even eventually into a self-governing class and school.

Once the initial stage of behavior/reward is over, the teacher can begin to pair the tangible rewards with approving behavior such as praise, smiles, and pats. Once more you are making use of the principles of association. The time needed between behavior and the original reward will grow longer, and the need for the reward will become less. Eventually teacher approval will begin to function as a reward. The time before this begins to happen is hard to predict. Sometimes it is surprisingly short, sometimes very long.

Traditional teaching takes it for granted that children can be motivated from the beginning by teacher approval. In many cases it's true. But it doesn't work for the problem children, both the ones you notice and those you don't. You must start with the child where he is. You motivate him by what will work, not by what you think ought to work.

After teacher approval, and combined with it, can come the intrinsic rewards of skill achievement and academic achievement. Finally, the skillful teacher can structure the classroom environment in such a way that the child can use self-approval as a reward. Motivation by this means is the ultimate purpose of any kind of discipline, but it isn't going to just happen. It is a goal to be worked toward, knowingly and steadily.

CAN BEHAVIOR BE MEASURED?
IT CAN BE MEASURED EASILY

As a teacher, you are used to spending a good deal of time in devising and employing tests, both formal and informal, for academic skills. To do the same thing for social skills probably seems a formidable task. Although it takes a little effort, it is not so difficult or time-consuming as it might seem, once the behavior you want to test for has been pinpointed as we have suggested. Any specific behavior is observable and occurs over a period of time.

Unlike academic tasks, in behavior modification we are concerned about measuring the number of times a behavior occurs in a given period. To do so, you must set up your criteria as to the extent or quality of the behavior to be measured. For example, the length of time crying goes on before it is counted might be set at two seconds. A noisy disturbance may be considered one that causes other children's heads to turn; a child's getting out of his seat may be counted only when he has no legitimate reason.

Even to start the process of behavior modification, the pinpointed behavior must be counted and recorded. Knowing exactly how many times the behavior occurs helps you set the consequences. It also, of course, tells you when you record again whether the behavior is happening less, more, or at the same rate.

The time period to be counted across will have to be estimated at first. If the occurrences happen over quite a long period, you may find it necessary to take samplings and average them. An aide, team member, or outside observer can be of great help, especially to check on the results of your interaction with the children. Another observer can also verify your count.

Testing tools consist of pencil, paper, and a watch or clock. Numbers of behaviors can be ticked off and any comments noted. A simple form is adaptable to any behavior you want to record.

Videotaping is another method of recording children's behavior. It enables you to watch the results of your manipulation of the classroom environment. It also often happens that children's behaviors are obvious on tape that you were too busy to notice when you were on the spot. The videotape makes an original record from which the behaviors to be recorded can be counted or rechecked.

We'd like here to stress one of the reasons why it's important to record over a time interval. When you speak to children, they will often do what you say for a short time but only until your eye is somewhere else. You say, "Sit down, Diane," and she does; but about a minute later she is up and wandering around the room again. The children are conditioning you by seeming to obey; your handling of the situation is reinforced but you have not done anything to solve the problem.

You don't have time for so much record-keeping? Consider all the time you spend repeating directions, scolding, and nagging. One teacher we know absolutely refused to "waste time with all that book work." Our observer checked her as saying, "Now stop that talking!" 143 times in one morning!

CAN THE CLASSROOM BE STRUCTURED?
IT CAN—AND MUST

Experiments with children have shown that if a child knows specifically what is expected of him, if it is within his power to do it, and he wants to do it, he probably will. As we have discussed, the classroom climate can be structured to make use of this basic premise. You can arrange things so the child will want to do what you want him to.

As the chart shows in summary, the teacher really has five techniques for

Teacher Behavior	Student Behavior (Social and Academic)	
	Appropriate	Inappropriate
Approval	Yes	No
Withholding of Approval	No	Yes
Ignoring	No	Yes (unless dangerous)
Disapproval	No	Yes (unless "payoff")
Threat of Disapproval	No	Yes

behavior shaping. Approval is easy to understand; it is a way of acting that gives the child happiness. Giving rewards, whether as concrete as a piece of candy or as intangible as proximity, demonstrates approval. Withholding of approval is another possible technique; it is effective after the expectation of approval is established—especially so if you hold out hope. The simple act of ignoring, just not paying attention to the child, is a technique much used in behavior modification. Disapproval is generally synonymous with the child's unhappiness; it is punishment. The threat of disapproval or punishment results in the child's changing his behavior through fear.

The chart demonstrates quite clearly that when we talk about being consistent in reinforcing behavior, we don't always mean rewarding. It also shows that fear and punishment are not the only alternatives to giving approval and rewards.

The first three techniques, approval, withholding, and ignoring, are all considered positive methods of reinforcement, even though the last two can be construed as a mild form of punishment. It is this that allows us to refute the objections of those who feel that "praising all the time" is false and saccharine, and that it thus soon loses all its effectiveness. Research indicates, however, that children can benefit from a great deal of praise as long as it is earned. All too many teachers spend most of their time in scolding and punishment by means of words, gestures, bad reports, and depriving students of activities that would benefit them. ("No recess for you today, young man!") This is in fact one of the major reasons so many teachers are shocked to see themselves on videotape. "Can that cross, nagging teacher be me?" It can actually come as a great relief to know that you don't have to be that kind of teacher—that there is a better way to control children's behavior.

Disapproval and threats of disapproval are negative methods of behavior reinforcement, and should be used sparingly. The most effective proportion of positive to negative reinforcements seems to be about 80 to 20 percent. The extreme forms of negative techniques, heavy corporal punishment and resulting terror, should be avoided. For one reason, a teacher who uses disapproval techniques alone may discover that the child has made an unfortunate and even perverted association: "I get a kick out of making the teacher mad," "I can take anything they can dish out," "There isn't anybody who is worse than I am!" It is in fact quite difficult to find a punishment that doesn't have some sort of payoff. Fear, or the threat of punishment, can be an even more effective behavior suppressant. Neither of these techniques, however, does anything to establish the joy of living and learning. Children who are motivated entirely by these negative techniques pay a high price in guilt, compulsiveness, generalized anxiety, and even ulcers. They do not become the kind of adults any teacher of good sense and sensitivity is trying to produce.

There is some evidence to indicate that positive approaches are a little more effective than negative ones. Even more important to the teacher who has the welfare of his charges at heart is the fact that positive reinforcements do not damage. This doesn't mean that the teacher is being overly permissive, as the term is so often used. The use of such reinforcement methods means that the teacher has recognized the need to structure the learning environment so that the child can reach his highest potential, not only of achievement but of happiness.

We sometimes hear people express fear of the "wrong kind of teacher" learning to use these efficient methods of structuring the classroom. It is true that an insensitive teacher can make very effective use of behavioral principles in a way that raises some serious questions about the other associations his students acquire. We know of one seventh-grade teacher who controlled her class by having the most deviant children—"if they are very, very bad"—participate in a mock wedding ceremony. When the children involved changed their behavior, they were allowed to "get a divorce." An art teacher teaches children to color within the lines by behavioral techniques, a procedure damaging to children's creativity. Another person working with eight- and nine-year-olds said, "When one of the boys misbehaves, I make him wear a girl's hair ribbon." This same person thought it "terrible" to suggest to parents that they occasionally send a problem child to school without breakfast so he will be hungry for rewards of cereal, milk, and cookies. No matter how many "behavioral recipes" there are, there can be no substitute for taste and sensitivity in a teacher.

IF AT FIRST YOU DON'T SUCCEED?
WELL—YOU KNOW!

Sometimes a teacher who understands behavioral principles and has even successfully applied them will run into trouble. He should first review the way he has carried out the four steps of behavior modification.

(1) Pinpoint: Is the behavior you are trying to extinguish or promote too general? Have you isolated a single behavior sufficiently? Does the behavior you are working with depend on another which you should deal with first? Have you discovered the real payoff? Does the behavior you are building in the child reflect the idea you are trying to get across?

(2) Record: Have you chosen the best length of time to record across? Does it indicate the true picture of the frequency of the behavior? If you can't record for the full cycle, have you taken different samplings and averaged them? Have you included all necessary data on your sheet or form? Was your recording technique precise? Did every observer understand and use the criteria correctly?

(3) Consequate: Have you made sure that what you think of as a reward really is one for the child? Is a punishment really a punishment? Does the child understand clearly what he has to do to earn the reward? Does he remember what the reward is? Does the reward need to be changed to add variety? Have you been imaginative in planning rewards? Are you pairing approval techniques with rewards?

(4) Evaluate: Have you stayed with your original program long enough to see whether it is actually working or not? Did you remember that behavior you are ignoring will worsen before is disappears, sometimes for a long time? Were the intervals before re-recording long enough? When you became certain one technique wasn't effective, did you go back and try another?

There are a few more behavioral principles that can help when you seem to have come to a dead end. One of these maxims is that it is impossible to maintain contradictory responses at the same time. Interrupting a stimulus-response chain by postponing the response can help break the conditioning. For example, the child won't cry if you can make him laugh, or just stop to take three deep breaths. He can't jump out of his seat if he is picking up a pencil, or pretending to. He can't stare out the window if you walk in front of him, pull the shade, or ask him to pass out papers. "Count ten before you get angry" is a famous example of this technique. "Speak softly so we can have a 'soft' argument" and "Let's take a break so we can begin fresh" are effective in class.

Another useful and very important hint is not to try to get the child to agree that his present behavior is wrong or that different behavior would be more desirable. It is much easier for a child *to act his way into a new way of thinking than to think his way into a new way of acting.* That's why we work with present, observable behavior rather than causes or attitudes. Causes and attitudes are not the problem; the behavior is. Causes will be irrelevant when the behavior changes. Attitudes will change when behavior changes.

There's no reason to get discouraged if you make mistakes in behavioral shaping. Remember that behaviors are learned, and so can be unlearned or relearned. Behavioral techniques *do* work; their success with severely handicapped children in school and institutions for the retarded and mentally ill shows that even these children can learn more and learn faster than we ever believed possible. What shouldn't you be able to do, then, for even the child whom you consider your worst problem?

Some Basic Concepts in Perceptual Psychology

Arthur W. Combs

Perceptual psychology is one expression of the great humanistic movement which seems to me to be going on, not only in psychology, but in all of the social sciences and in human affairs generally. Abe Maslow has called this movement in psychology "Third Force" psychology. Perceptual psychology it seems to me is one of the expressions of that force in operation. It is a humanistic, phenomenological, personalistic, existential view of behavior which sees man engaged in a continuous process of being and becoming.

There are two frames of reference for looking at human behavior available to us. One of these is the external or objective approach familiar to most of us as the traditional view of American psychology. Seen from this frame of reference, behavior is described from the point of view of the outside observer, someone looking on at the process. Its classic expression is to be found in the various forms of stimulus-response psychology which seeks the explanation of behavior in the observable forces exerted upon the individual. The perceptual

From an address presented at the American Personnel and Guidance Association Convention, 1965. Used by permission of the author.

psychologist takes a different view. He seeks to understand the behavior of people from the point of view of the behaver himself. His is a phenomenological understanding of human behavior, emphasizing the meaning of events to the person.

Perceptual psychology is basically a field theory and its primary principle is this: *All behavior, without exception, is a function of the behaver's perceptual field at the instant of behaving.* I am using the term perceptual here in its broadest sense as practically synonymous with meaning. Thus, the individual's behavior is seen as the direct consequence, not of the fact or stimulus with which he is confronted, but the meaning of events in his peculiar economy. That people behave according to how things seem to them seems a simple enough proposition. Each of us as he looks at his own behavior can observe that it is true for him. Self evident as this proposition seems at first glance, however, its ramifications for human interaction are tremendous and its implications for a theory of behavior calls for an entire new psychology. It provides us with a new frame of reference for dealing with some of our most difficult problems. Perceptual psychology is not a denial of former psychologies, let me hasten to say. Rather, it provides us with an additional explanation of particular value to practitioners and to those of us who are confronted with the practical problems of dealing with people, not as subjects in an experiment but as striving, seeking human beings. It does not deny what we have known before. It extends beyond to give us a new string to our bow.

When the perceptual psychologist speaks of the perceptual field he is referring to all those perceptions existing for the individual at the moment of behaving. This includes all aspects of his awareness, not only those perceptions in clear figure which the person may be able to tell us about but, also, those perceptions he has at lower levels of differentiation which he may be incapable of describing. Freud used the terms "conscious" and "unconscious" to describe these levels of awareness. Such designations, however, seem to give the impression of a clear cut dichotomy so the perceptual psychologist prefers to speak of levels of awareness instead. This is a point often misunderstood by some critics of perceptual psychology who have equated "awareness" with "conscious." They have assumed that the term perception referred only to those events the individual was able to report on demand. Such a point of view would make perceptual psychology extraordinarily naive! To understand the behavior of the individual the perceptual psychologist says, it is necessary for us to understand the field of meaning or perceptions existing for him at the instant of his behavior. This includes all perceptions from those in clearest and sharpest figure to those so deeply imbedded in the ground of the field as to be quite unreportable.

If behavior is a function of perception, it follows that to understand behavior it will be necessary to study the factors influencing perception in the individual. Some of the variables affecting perception with which the perceptual psychologist is concerned are familiar to all of us from more orthodox psychologies. Among these are:

1. *The Effect of the Physical Organism.* Perception depends upon the possession of the necessary equipment to make it possible. One must have eyes to see, ears to hear, olfactory organs to smell and so on.
2. *The Effect of Time.* Perception takes time. What is perceived is dependent upon the time of exposure and the length of time one has lived in the world.

3. *The Effect of Opportunity or Environment.* Perceptions are learned. To perceive one must have had opportunity to experience the events that make them possible. Eskimos do not normally comprehend bananas, nor Hottentots, snow. What meanings exist for the individual are a consequence of his unique experience in the process of his growing up.

These effects of the physical organism, time and opportunity have long been considered in traditional psychology. They are equally important for the perceptual approach. But perceptual psychology adds some additional variables to the picture among the most important of which is the self concept.

THE SELF CONCEPT

Of all the perceptions existing in the perceptual or phenomenal field those pertaining to the individual's self play a crucial role. How a person behaves at any moment is always the result of two kinds of perceptions; how he sees the situation he is in and how he sees himself. By the self concept is meant all those aspects of the perceptual field to which we refer when we say "I" or "me." It is that organization of perceptions about self or awareness of self which seems to the individual to be who he is. It is composed of thousands of perceptions about self varying in clarity, precision and importance in the individual's peculiar economy. Taken altogether these concepts of self are described by the perceptual psychologist as the self concept.

The more we study the self concept, the more it becomes apparent how crucial it is to any understanding of behavior. It is at the very center of the individual's personal organization and the frame of reference for his every act. The self concept is learned especially from the experience of the individual with the significant people in his world in the course of growing up. It is both product and process.

The self concept is the product of past experience but, once established, exerts its influence on the behavior of its possessor ever after. It is apparent that we have but barely scratched the surface of the full implications of the self concept for every aspect of human existence. Educators, for example, have discovered that faulty self concepts are often responsible for children's failures in basic school subjects, like reading, spelling, arithmetic and language. Modern counseling theory holds that the practice of counseling is primarily a problem in self exploration. Adjustment and maladjustment turn out on examination to be largely questions of healthy or faulty self concepts. The role of the self concept is equally important in social psychology. Recent work with the mentally retarded and the culturally deprived even seems to indicate that the self concept is basic to intelligence and human capacity.

Since the self concept is learned as a consequence of experience, it can therefore presumably be taught. The implications of this idea have vast importance for education, counseling, social work, and all of the helping professions. It provides the basis for a belief that programs aimed at the defeat of poverty and human degradation have a chance for success.

In recent years the self concept has become one of the most popular topics for research even for some psychologists who would rather be caught dead than described as perceptualists. Researches on the self concept now number in the hundreds. Dozens more are completed every week. Many of these, unfortunately, are mislabeled self concept studies when they are nothing of the kind. Most of them turn out on closer examination to be studies of the self report which is not the same thing at all. The self concept is what a person perceives himself to be, it is what he *believes* about himself. The self report, on the other hand, is what a person is willing, able, or can be tricked into *saying* about himself when he is asked to do so. The assumption that these two concepts are synonymous is naïve and represents a return to introspection which psychology gave up sixty years ago. The basic research technique of perceptual psychology is inference. Introspection is no more acceptable to perceptual approaches than to more orthodox psychologies.

Despite the confusion currently existing in the research on the self, it is apparent that this concept is an extraordinarily useful device for understanding behavior. It makes it possible for us to deal much more effectively with many problems we have not adequately understood before. Among the most exciting aspects of self concept theory, for me, are those having to do with self fulfillment, self realization or actualization. In these ideas we have new definitions of what it means to be well adjusted. These descriptions are not couched in terms of bell shaped curves in which the well adjusted turn out to be average. It describes them in terms of what it means to be truly living to the fullest of one's potentialities. Better still, these concepts do not simply tell us what such fortunate people are like, they point the way to what we must do to get about the business of producing more of them! In this respect they set the goals for counseling, teaching, social action, and all of the helping professions, for whatever we decide is what man can become, must automatically become the goal of all our institutions.

For example, one of the things we have been finding out about self actualizing people is that they tend to see themselves in essentially positive ways. They believe they are basically liked, wanted, acceptable, able, dignified, worthy and the like. Psychologically sick people on the other hand see themselves as unliked, unwanted, unacceptable, unable, unworthy and so on. It follows if this is true that the helping professions must find ways of helping clients, students, patients, or colleagues to feel more positively about themselves. Furthermore, since perceptions are learned from experience, it points the way to what we need to do to help other people to greater health and productivity; clearly, it is necessary to provide them with experiences which will help them feel more positively about self. And the ways to do this are almost self evident. They are suggested by the very descriptions of self actualization:

How can a person feel liked unless somebody likes him?
How can a person feel acceptable unless somewhere he is accepted?
How can a person feel he has dignity unless someone treats him so?
How can a person feel able unless somewhere he has some success?

In the answers to these simple questions lie the guidelines to the conditions for teaching, therapy, social action, supervision and the encouragement of growth and development everywhere.   •

THE PERCEPTUAL VIEW OF MOTIVES

If behavior is seen as a function of the perception of self and the world in perceptual psychology, what, then, provides the motive force? For perceptual psychology this is a given. The characteristic of all things to maintain organization finds its expression in human beings in an insatiable need for the maintenance and enhancement of the self; not the physical self—but the phenomenal self, the self of which the individual is aware, his self concept.

All human beings are seen as continuously engaged in a search for self actualization or self fulfillment, even, sometimes, at the cost of destruction of the physical body itself. The drive for self fulfillment provides the motive power for behavior. It finds its expression through goals which seem to the individual from time to time, to provide the means for actualization. This basic drive for maintenance expressed physically is the drive on which the physician depends to restore his patient to health. Physiologically it has been called the drive to health, the wisdom of the body, etc. Psychologically, it provides the motive power for human growth and development, recovery from psychological illness and the stretch for human achievement.

In the light of this drive, the problem of motivation disappears for the perceptual psychologist, for people are always motivated. Indeed, they are never unmotivated! The motive is always there in the individual's search for the maintenance and enhancement of self. He always does what it seems to him he needs to from his point of view. The problem of motivation as we have usually conceived it is an external problem concerned with the question of how to get somebody else to do something we would like him to do.

Such a view of motivation as I have been describing leads to quite different approaches to dealing with people than those of traditional S–R psychologies. A stimulus-response psychology calls for methods of changing behavior based upon techniques of force, coercion, reward, punishment, or some form of manipulation. The perceptual view of human need places both helper and helpee on the same team. Both are seeking the optimum development of the helpee and the problem is one of facilitation, encouragement and the freeing of forces already in existence to operate at maximum strength. This is a conception of the nature of man basic to some of the most promising conceptions of human interaction, in counseling, education, social work, medicine, nursing and the practice of the clergy. It lends itself to a hopeful view of man concerned with being and becoming and the basic democratic belief that when men are free they can find their own best ways.

In summary, then, the perceptual psychologist attempts to understand behavior from the point of view of the behaver rather than the outsider. He sees the individual behaving in terms of the peculiar field of personal meanings or perceptions existing for him at the moment of acting and motivated by the person's own need for self fulfillment. In the light of this interpretation, human failures are mostly understood as problems in faulty perception of self, others, and the world. The reasons for faulty perceptions may lie in the world but far more often lie in the individual himself. This means that persons engaged in human relations activities, whatever their nature, as supervisors, administrators, parents, counselors, teachers, social workers, nurses, or whatever are likely to be successful in the degree to which they understand the perceptual worlds of those they seek to work with and become skillful in helping others to change their perceptions of themselves and their surroundings.

There is even evidence lately to suggest that the essence of successful professional work is itself a matter of the use of the self as an effective instrument rather than a question of methods or information.

But whether or not a worker is able to use himself as an instrument well in the helping professions is also a function of the helper's own perceptions.

In a series of researches we have been carrying on at the University of Florida we have even been finding that the success of various kinds of "helpers" is a function of their perceptual organization. Hundreds of previous researches on good teaching and counseling have been unable to find clear cut differences between good practitioners and poor ones either on the basis of the knowledge they possess or the methods they use. Nevertheless in four studies to date, we have been able to show clear cut differences between "good" helpers and "poor" ones in the ways these workers typically perceive themselves, their clients and their purposes. What is more, this difference obtains in all three groups we have so far investigated: teachers, counselors and episcopal priests!

One of the most exciting contributions of perceptual psychology, in my experience, is its provision of an immediate frame of reference for understanding behavior to add to the historical one we have lived with so long. Let me clarify what I mean.

Stimulus-response psychology originally taught us that human behavior was a consequence of the stimulus and so we were led to look for the causes of behavior in the forces exerted on the individual. Freud and his students added to this concept by expanding the notion of the stimulus to include all those stimuli to which the individual had been subjected in the course of his growing up. This led us to seek for the causes of behavior in the person's past. Accordingly, for several generations now we have been almost exclusively preoccupied with the nature of behavior as seen from this historical frame of reference. Such a point of view about human behavior has been immensely useful to us in providing guidelines for the construction of programs, social action, and a thousand other applications. But a historic point of view about behavior is essentially descriptive. It tells us how an individual got like this, but frequently offers the practitioner very little in the way of clues as to what to do about it. In Freud's own use, of course, it led to a method of psychotherapy which required digging about in the patient's past history in search of an understanding of causes that was often more helpful to the psychologist than to the patient. For several generations we have been so preoccupied with this historical view as to hardly recognize that any other existed. This is particularly true of professional workers charged with the responsibility of helping the adjustment of others. Unhappily, the historic view of causation has often been more useful for diagnosis than for treatment.

In my own practice of psychotherapy, for example, I find that the clients I have who spend long hours exploring their past, are almost exclusively graduate students in psychology! They have thoroughly learned that their behavior is the function of their past so, when they come for help, they engage in its exploration. Sooner or later, however, they arrive at the conclusion "Well now I *know why* I feel like I do" but almost at once this statement is followed by "But darn it all, I still feel that way!"

Perceptual psychology provides us with a much more adequate treatment orientation. In addition to understanding how the individual got the way he is, it provides us with an understanding of the present dynamics from which we may more adequately derive effective methods of teaching, counseling, persuasion, and solutions to human interaction of many sorts. Perceptual psychology provides us with another frame of reference which makes it possible to deal with behavior in the present.

Perceptions exist in the present. If behavior is a function of perception, then it should be possible to modify behavior by changing perceptions in the present. Thus, it may be possible to help an individual to better adjustment even if we do not have any knowledge of his past whatever! For many psychologists this is a startling, shocking, almost irresponsible, idea. For many non-psychologists, however, it is good news and comes as a great refreshing breeze. It means that teachers, administrators, counselors, social workers and parents who have to deal with human behavior because their roles demand it can hope to do so with some chance of success without the necessity for being skilled psychologists. It means that if such people can become sensitive enough to how their charges are perceiving and feeling they can find effective ways of being helpful. A teacher who understands that a child feels unliked, unwanted, unacceptable and unable can do things to help such a child even without a knowledge of how he got to feel this way. If this seems to anyone to lessen the importance of psychologists, it should not. The purpose of psychology is not, after all, to run the world. It is to help provide the understanding so that others whose job it is can learn to do it better.

The immediate frame of reference, of course, is not a new conception in the field of practice, for beginning with Carl Rogers' early work with client-centered therapy and running through all of the new psychotherapies we have seen in the past twenty years, all are predicated on the notion that it is possible to help clients, even without a full knowledge of the past. What perceptual psychology does for us is to provide a theoretical framework which explains why this is so and thus provides us with a valuable new tool for the understanding of behavior to add to those which traditional psychology has provided us in the past.

Many of the principles of perceptual psychology are deceptively simple. They have an "of course" feeling about them and often fit one's own experience so closely as to seem like one has always known them. This is very upsetting to some psychologists who feel it can't be accurate if it is that simple. Yet, it is necessary to remind ourselves that simplicity is the *goal* of science. What could be simpler, for example, than the physical formula $E=mc^2$? Furthermore, the simple and the "obvious" can have vast implications. Take, for example, the simple fact that reality for each individual lies, not in the outside world, but in his own perceptions. This principle is basic to the problems of communication and human misunderstandings everywhere. People just do not behave according to the "facts" as others see them. They behave in terms of what seems so to them. So we pass each other like ships in the night—not only as individuals but as nations as well.

Perceptual psychology is especially valuable as a practitioner's psychology. It is particularly pertinent to the problems of individual behavior with which the teacher, counselor, social worker, supervisor and therapist must deal. It is particularly appropriate to the helping professions and fits the needs of such workers like hand and glove.

As I indicated at the start of this paper I regard perceptual psychology as a basic expression of the great humanistic, phenomenological, existential movement currently sweeping the social sciences. When Donald Snygg and I stumbled on these concepts twenty years ago, we were certain a perceptual psychology was inevitable. Since then we have attempted to set down in two editions of *Individual Behavior*, a systematic framework for a comprehensive perceptual psychology. The response to that effort has been deeply gratifying and has strengthened the hope we expressed in the preface of the first edition that, "as fallible human beings we can only hope that this is if not the truth, then very like the truth."

Psychoanalysis and Education

Donald W. Robinson

THE IMPACT OF PSYCHOANALYSIS ON OUR CULTURE

The influence of psychoanalysis on education is as indefinable as it is undeniable, because it has been indirect. Sigmund Freud wrote in 1909 that the purpose of education is "to enable the individual to take part in culture and to achieve this with the smallest loss of original energy." However, neither he nor the later analytic theorists have had very much to say about how learning takes place or about what should be taught or how it should be taught. They are primarily concerned with the emotions, while the teacher has traditionally been more concerned with the intellect. Relating the former concern to the latter is the task recently assumed by the psychologist.

Sigmund Freud is often mentioned, along with Charles Darwin and Albert Einstein, as one of the great creative thinkers of modern times. Like the others, he formulated a new way of looking at things that has profoundly altered the way we think about man and his relations to other men and to the universe.

His writings constitute a body of doctrine commonly called psychoanalysis, a doctrine based on the concepts of unconscious motivation, conflict, and symbolism. In this paper the word psychoanalysis will refer to this theory of human behavior set forth by Freud and his disciples.

The profound influence of the theories which Freud presented in books and essays from 1888 to 1938, and which he personally introduced to this country in a series of lectures in 1908, has been especially felt in the fields of psychology, sociology, anthropology, psychiatry, and psychosomatic medicine.

Increasingly this influence is extending to the non-academic world. The

From *Phi Delta Kappan* XLIII, no. 7 (April 1962):292–299. Used by permission of the author and publisher.

growing stream of popular books, the evident Freudian approach by writers on child care and marriage counseling, the prevalence of Freudian allusions in popular literature and drama, and the appeal of analytic speculations about the cause of any human frailty or deviation, all confirm the fact that we cannot escape the influence of Sigmund Freud.

A leading psychologist who resists the Freudian influence nevertheless admits that, "It would be difficult to overestimate the impact of Freud's thoughts on the thinking of our times, especially among the classes which may be considered as supplying the intellectual leadership for the nation."

The impact on the schools has been no less important. It is readily apparent in the current school jargon. Teachers are threatened. Students have guilt feelings, aggressive tendencies, frustrations. Teachers stand as parent symbols, help students to recognize identification and projection and deal with anxiety and tension. These terms and the attitudes they represent are direct outgrowths of the concepts formulated by Freud.

The American Handbook of Psychiatry acknowledges the influence of psychoanalysis on education in these words, "In education, there has been a continuous trend toward the introduction of mental health principles in schools and a greater acceptance of the principles of individual, familial, and social dynamics. The importance of a wholesome school atmosphere, leading the pupil to a greater security and a feeling of belonging, or worth, and of dignity, as well as the importance of the teacher-child and the teacher-family relationships have been generally recognized. Progressive methods of education have been studied in relation to mental health aspects, and such extensive projects as 'human relation classes' have been highly successful. Psychiatric attention is being extended to every school level, including colleges and universities."

The card catalogue in the education library of a typical state college contains, under the heading *Psychoanalysis*, over 200 book titles. Goodwin Watson reports that psychology textbooks published in the 1920's averaged four pages devoted to unconscious factors in motivation, while books published in the 1950's averaged forty-six pages on the same topic. Texts published in the earlier period devoted an average of seven pages to mental hygiene, while the more recent books averaged fifty-seven. The trend is well established.

The reaction of teachers to this trend is naturally mixed. Younger teachers may accept the Freudian orientation more wholeheartedly because their exposure to it has begun earlier and they have not had to overcome a previously established viewpoint. Some teachers resist the whole psychological approach with a blunt insistence that "our job is to teach our subject; let the parents and the doctors take care of the emotional problems. The schools do too much psychologizing already." Others are responsive to the mental health approach, recognizing that establishing emotional health in the child will enhance his intellectual learning, but are unaware of the debt this approach owes to Freud and psychoanalysis.

The origins of this reluctance are easy to find.

Man will resist any new idea which seems to contradict notions long held and accepted as "true," especially such a notion as the complete freedom of man totally to control his actions by sheer willpower. Men have held so tightly to this illusion that it has seemed immoral to suggest, as Freud did, that a man's power to control his actions is limited by forces which he is normally incapable of controlling or even recognizing. We do not actually believe that a person can by sheer determination control his emotions, but we know that in our culture he is expected to do so.

A conscious determination to exercise control is necessary, but not always sufficient, for effective living. Anyone who has been the victim of blushing, stuttering, claustrophobia, forgetfulness, overeating, alcoholism, migraine headaches, insomnia, hypochondria, excessive worry, or any of a hundred other unconsciously-induced torments, will testify that willpower, even when adroitly applied, is often not enough.

The early years are so dominated by the constant urging by parents to "try," to "control," and to "master yourself" that the ego is unable easily to admit defeat by conceding that we are unable by sheer willpower to conquer the disability that plagues us. All people bear some degree of disability, whether it is a compulsive urge to talk or merely being ill at ease in certain situations. Fortunate are those who can adjust to their own idiosyncrasies, accept them, and prevent them from becoming disabling or disqualifying.

Resistance to the full acceptance or Freudian analytic ideas is normal and often assumes one of these rational forms: 1. *That psychoanalysis reduces the self-reliance of man by encouraging him to find explanations in circumstances beyond his control.* (The answer is that the Freudian approach is to discover what influences may be beyond the individual's conscious control and to offer a method for bringing these too within his control. An extension of consciousness can lead to higher levels of self-control, based on self-knowledge. Psychoanalysis seeks to replace the question "Does man possess free will?" with "How much free will does he possess?" and then seeks to enlarge the area in which he can exercise free will by revealing to him the source of some of his problems.)

2. *That the Freudian doctrine is unverifiable and unscientific.* (This is partly true, but the fact does not reduce the effectiveness of analysis. It might be difficult to demonstrate that Christianity or democracy are scientific, but that does not reduce their usefulness. And the power of the unconscious is clearly demonstrable, as in posthypnotic suggestion.)

3. *That Freudian literature is filled with bizarre, if not obscene, overemphasis on sex and sexual symbolism.* (The explanation is that the ever-recurring phallic and vaginal symbols are expressions of the powerful libidinal forces which eventually find fulfillment, if they are not thwarted, in heterosexual activity. Some persons find this symbolism repulsive because it violates the rigid code they were taught that one does not talk about sex except in hospitals and bars, because it is dirty. Is the dream symbolism suggested by Freud more bizarre than everyday occurrences such as blushing and stuttering *without* an explanation?)

Novelists long before Freud knew and exploited the power of the unconscious and the compelling importance of libidinal drives. Scientists too had underlined the instinctive urge to reproduce or the inherent urge for race survival. It is inconceivable that such a powerful urge should not influence the lives of individuals, even beyond their specific sexual acts. In this light Freud's emphasis on sex (which he defines in a far broader way than mere genital associations) is normal and desirable.

A different kind of resistance is engendered in persons who have had the misfortune to gain their first impressions of analysis from charlatans, quacks, or incompetents. Every complex social or psychological theory inevitably becomes altered as it becomes popularized. As the ripples of information circle out from the original source they become ever weaker and more easily distorted. This is equally true of Deweyism, Christianity, psychoanalysis, or any doctrine. The farther the gospel is spread the less it resembles the preachings of the master.

Most people probably adopt new ideas by bits and snatches. With respect to psychoanalysis some accept the concept of the unconscious while rejecting the notion of the sexual stages of development. Some accept the idea of dreams as concealed expressions of unconscious urges while scoffing at the Oedipus complex. As a result, the popular notion of psychoanalysis, as of every complex system, becomes a mishmash of distortions, dilutions, and eclecticisms.

The aversion that many teachers display toward Freudian doctrines results largely from this kind of peripheral misconception. Extremists who associated themselves with Freudian thought as well as with the fringe groups of ultra-progressives have given analysis an undeserved reputation for sanctioning the removal of all control and restraint from the child. Neither Freud nor any reputable analyst recommended the absence of controls.

It is not surprising that some of Freud's emancipatory discoveries, like some of Dewey's, became the vehicles for extremist movements of permissiveness. The early extremist works were published during the late Victorian era when a reaction against excessive authoritarianism was beginning and every possible scrap of evidence was marshaled in favor of the new spirit of freedom. Freud was aware of the unhappy effect of excessive repression and inhibition, as today he would be equally aware of the tragic consequences of insufficient control and direction of children. Both extremes are equally at variance with his theory and with the ideas of reputable analysis today.

THE INFLUENCE OF PSYCHOANALYSIS ON EDUCATION

A generation ago the obstreperous youngster was described as acting up. Today he is diagnosed as acting out. If the effect of the psychological emphasis had been no more than to create a new terminology it would not warrant our serious attention. Some partisans are certain that the psychological impact has rescued the schools from utter collapse, while others are equally convinced that the effect has been nearly disastrous.

The teachers of this country have welcomed the psychologists, though frequently unaware of their debt to psychoanalysis, and have eagerly attempted to incorporate their ideas into school practice. This is not surprising, since, with the extension of compulsory school attendance through high school, teachers have been unduly preoccupied with the problems of the emotionally disturbed students. Any new knowledge from psychology was welcomed if it promised hope of assistance in understanding and dealing with the mass of students who would once have been eliminated from school by virtue of their intellectual and emotional limitations, but who now must remain until graduation or until they reach age sixteen or seventeen.

The direct influence of psychoanalysis on school curriculum is apparent and significant. Teaching units on mental health and sex education have been introduced and psychological testing has mushroomed in importance, as have the guidance and counseling services. Important as these influences have been, we are not here concerned as much with them as with the over-all changes in educational philosophy and the resultant effect on teaching methods.

Psychoanalysis and Progressive Education

Psychoanalysis has been frequently equated with progressive education. It has been extravagantly praised and vehemently damned for introducing the permissiveness which has so conspicuously marked our child-rearing in the past generation. It deserves neither the praise nor the blame.

Three brief quotations should help to clarify the analytic position:

Dr. Peter Neubauer says, in an article in The Atlantic in July, 1961, "Freud pointed out that denial and conflict were as essential a part of the process of growth as gratification, and he never minimized the child's need for direction."

Anna Freud wrote, "The task of a pedagogy based upon analytic data is to find a via media between these extremes—that is to say, allow to each state in the child's life the right proportion of instinct gratification and instinct restriction."

Dr. Pearson, whose 1954 volume, Psychoanalysis and the Education of the Child, is probably the most comprehensive book on this subject, says, "Every individual must learn that he is affected by two fields of influence, the external world of sensory perception and the inner world of instincts. The influence of the latter far outshadows the former and in case of conflict takes precedence. Both too much frustration and too much gratification will hamper the development of the ego."

Excessive authority neglects to train the youngster for emancipation from dependence on the parent figures. Extreme permissiveness in the early years fails to provide the needed authority figures whom the child can use as models in developing his own personality.

If this sounds like a truism known by every experienced teacher, it is. And one of the reassuring aspects of psychoanalysis is that it does confirm the common-sense wisdom of the best of human experience. Psychoanalysis, like education, has for its major goal the freeing of individuals for rational living, unhampered by the bonds of ignorance or emotional thralldom.

Dr. Pearson dwells at length on the importance for teachers of the reality principle. He says, "Every opportunity to test reality is useful in helping the child solve his intrapsychic conflicts. During the latency period there should be ample opportunities for unsupervised and unrestricted play so that each child may have the chance to work out his specific conflicts in the make believe of play." Note that this is a very different thing than suggesting that the child should never be supervised, directed, or corrected. It is interesting to note, as Lilli Peller reminds us, that the child often takes his play just as seriously as the adult takes his work.

Pearson continues, "In reality human life consists more of hard and tedious work than of pleasurable experience, and if the individual wishes to lead a pleasurable life he must develop the capacity to accept and adjust to reality—to the realities of the physical world, the needs and desires of other people in this world, and the customs and mores of the world in which he lives. Only when the individual has this capacity will he be able to attempt to change any part of the environment—the physical work, the other members of his social group, or the prevailing customs and mores."

It is recognized that a child is far more likely to attain a satisfactory adjustment to reality if he is exposed to teachers who operate from reality, for the child incorporates not only what the teacher teaches but all aspects of the teacher's personality.

If the teacher has an extremely rigid personality, or is sadistic, or too inhibited, the child may incorporate some of this quality.

Pearson suggests that this may benefit the child if it happens to be the opposite of extreme parental traits, or harm him if it reinforces parental extremes.

Psychiatric Examinations for Teachers

It is self-evident today that emotional "maturity" is especially essential in a teacher. Pearson and many others urge that student teachers be required to undergo a period of direct psychoanalysis, and, where this is impossible, that applicants for teaching be screened by a rigid psychiatric examination.

It is tempting to speculate on the emotional stability of teachers. Dr. Shipley presents data from a 1948 study of admissions records at the Mayo Clinic showing that while 17 percent of the physicians admitted to the clinic were found to have emotional illness, 19 percent of the farmers, 30 percent of the dentists, and 36 percent of the lawyers and housewives, 55 percent of the teachers admitted were suffering from emotional illnesses! The assumption that teaching harbors a higher percentage of neurotics than other occupations is a popular one. Although it cannot be thoroughly proved or disproved, it can be supported by logical inference, based both on the emotional wear and tear of the job itself and on the attraction of teaching for persons emotionally reluctant to compete in the hurly-burly adult world.

It is just possible that the influence of psychoanalysis on our culture has helped to determine the type of person who tends to become a teacher. If the extreme traditional school with its "this hurts me more than that does you" spirit attracted and then aggravated the "hard" or sadistic personality, the newer, more "progressive" school may appeal to the "soft" or philanthropic personality. Although the analytic approach requires neither "hard" nor "soft" but reality-based teachers, still an indulgent school, spawned in a permissive community, may tend to recruit overly sentimental teachers, who in turn will extend the permissive atmosphere still further.

At present no way exists to determine accurately how many teachers have unconsciously selected teaching as a solution for some deep-seated personal conflict, especially a conflict involving authority.

Analysts recognize this hazard among themselves and attempted some years ago a substantial study of the unconscious reasons why some analysts elected to concentrate in *child analysis*. Although the study was never formally completed, the evidence that was collected indicated three unconscious motives that prompted the choice of child analysis. It is evident that these motives *might* operate equally in the choice of teaching as a career. They are:

1. Fear of overaggressive impulses toward adults, consciously controlled by feelings of marked inferiority with adults and feeling more comfortable with children.
2. Unconscious desire to get even with hated siblings by being in a position where they can control children.

3. Conscious or unconscious hatred of parents, expressed as a determination, "when I grow up I'll show you how children should be treated."

No implication is intended that unconscious motivations are necessarily bad, but they can be unfortunate if they are too intense, and especially if they are not recognized and understood.

THREE PITFALLS FACED BY THE ANALYTICALLY ORIENTED TEACHER

Warnings should be advanced about three danger areas where the well-meaning teacher frequently errs in his efforts to promote mental and emotional health in his students. These three errors occur and are frequently cited by critics as failures of the psychological viewpoint.

The first of the three pitfalls is overemphasis on the developmental aspects of the child's personality at the expense of his intellectual development. Properly handled, teacher attention to the psychological problems of the child, with all of the interviews, tests, sociograms, play therapy, or whatever techniques are indicated, can be helpful in freeing the child from emotional blocks, and enhancing his ego so that he becomes a more effective learner as well as a happier person. If, however, so much time and attention is directed to the study of the psychological problems that too little is left for planning and directing the program of intellectual accomplishment, the child's education suffers. Perhaps there cannot be an overemphasis on emotional adjustment, but there can be an underemphasis on essential factual learning. Teachers are sometimes accused of over-psychologizing. This charge makes little sense as stated, for no teacher can know too much about the psychological problems of his students, but he can know too little or care too little about the learning that results from his instruction. If he goes overboard in his enthusiasm for psychology to the neglect of his subjects, he is justifying the charge that the schools are producing well-adjusted ignoramuses.

If the teacher's enthusiasm for helping the youngsters with obvious emotional problems leads to the neglect of the healthy average child, who also requires attention, he is derelict in his responsibility.

In addition to the general danger of overenthusiasm, a teacher who is familiar with analytic concepts is susceptible to *special* enthusiasms which can be harmful. One of these is the excessive interest and anxiety sometimes aroused in the teacher for the welfare of the problem student. For example, the teacher may know that the lonely child may be queer and that the distance between queerness and schizophrenia may be short, and so may go overboard in his anxious efforts to help the child to socialize. The teacher, in his fear that the child may overdo fantasy or day-dreaming, may prevent the child from working or playing alone, when the child very much needs the constructive values which he can only find alone. This concern about children's day-dreaming has sometimes led to an over-emphasis on togetherness that makes children almost incapable of remaining alone.

So long as interest in psychology and personality development of the child demonstrably contributes to the improvement of his intellectual performance it will receive general support. When it becomes a movement to substitute the development of the personality for the development of the mind it contradicts a long-held and deeply cherished notion of the purposes of education. When the concept of the power of the unconscious is overstated it becomes in effect a kind of anti-intellectualism (or at least anti-academicism), which has been the target of recent attacks on the public schools.

The Teacher as a Behavior Model

A second and equally serious pitfall is neglecting to fulfill the child's need for a satisfying parent figure by being a "real person." The extreme progressive era encouraged the teacher to seek the background, to be inconspicuous and non-directive, so that the child might develop freedom, self-confidence and initiative. Again common sense tells us that the advice might be an excellent antidote for extreme teacher domination, but that the opposite extreme can be equally unfortunate. Children at every stage need the teacher partly as a model of behavior after which to pattern their own conduct. The teacher who remains inconspicuous provides no pattern. At the same time, on the strictly conscious level, students need teachers to tell them what they should learn and show them how to learn it—in short, to teach them.

Teachers who simply let children grow by self-expression are, it is true, avoiding the error of overdomination, but they are not teaching. It seems likely that a share of the apparent neurosis and insecurity today results from the fact that young people have had insufficient direction from adults. They have anxieties because they have not been given standards by which to measure their own conduct. A major function of the teacher is to lead. As a parent symbol he should afford the child the security which the child can derive from the knowledge that he is accepted as a loved child, even while he is corrected for his mistakes and is punished for his wrongdoing. The child seeks this security, both consciously and unconsciously, from the teacher's admonitions and examples. Without it he cannot learn as much.

Lilli Peller is referring to this function when she writes, "The teacher who puts herself on the child's level all the time, who encourages indulgence, who shows lavish admiration for any scribble—this teacher fails to inspire the child's wish to identify himself with her. Much as she tries to captivate the child's interest, she fails to get it. This does not imply that the so-called old-fashioned school has the most effective ways to promote learning and growth, it only indicates that conditions are more complicated than we thought." A school program must be geared to children's abilities and interests, but the child also expects the teacher to make demands and is disappointed when he receives no assistance from her in dealing with his instinctual pressures. Teachers themselves retain enough of the childish need for parent figures so that they frequently place the very concept of learning, or more often a specific new formulation of ideas, such as the Freudian concept, in a parent role. Their intellectual reaction to it is very much colored by their emotional reaction, which betrays a striking similarity to the manner of a child reacting to a parent, either prostrating himself completely to the new demands or rebelling violently against them. The role of the parent symbol is always present, and it is a role that the teacher cannot refuse to play.

Dealing With Resistance to Learning

The third weakness that sometimes comes into teaching with those who profess the mental health point of view is the failure to recognize the importance of resistance. Resistance to learning in the classroom is just as normal and inescapable as is resistance in the analyst's office. Man has a deep-seated human instinct to keep what is his own, especially his beliefs and feelings. Learning, if it is to be meaningful, must alter some cherished misconceptions of the learner, and these he will relinquish only slowly and reluctantly. Therefore when certain of the progressive teachers interpret students' resistance to learning as unacceptable or as evidence that the learning situation has been badly planned, they are missing a major analytic point. If the learning is significant some students *must* resist it and be unhappy about it. This does not make either the teacher or the lesson wrong. Teachers who feel that all learning must be gay and pleasant, almost to the point of being carefree and effortless, are denying the essence of learning. It would probably be an indefensible overstatement to assert that without discomfort and resistance no valuable learning can take place, but this statement is valid if we accept literally the popular dictum that the only learning that is truly worthwhile is that learning which results in changed behavior.

This proposition too can be tested by reference to adults. If we observe teachers or others discussing the relative merits of traditional versus progressive methods of teaching it will soon become apparent that for most of them something more is involved than a rational desire to share viewpoints and discover the best way to teach. What is more powerfully though unconsciously involved is a resistance to having their notions of teaching challenged. The concept of resistance is as significant in learning as the notion of the parent image, and should be thoroughly understood by the teacher.

It now becomes apparent that the three separate dangers inherent in the analytic approach all result in the same damage. The teacher who emphasizes the psychological approach at the sacrifice of subject matter, the teacher who neglects the role of the demanding parent figure, and the teacher who tries to eliminate or avoid pupil resistance, are all playing into the hands of "easy learning" to the long-range disadvantage of the child.

The reader should of course beware of interpreting the three warnings as being pleas for a return to authoritarian methods, or for more homework for students, or for more attention to academic requirements, or any other prescription. If they are pleas at all, they plead for keeping psychological and intellectual goals in balance, for having the teacher understand his psychological as well as his academic role, and for recognizing the inescapability of student resistance to learning.

In exonerating Freud and psychoanalysis of responsibility for the errors and excesses of well-meaning but misdirected disciples, we do not intend to excuse the teachers who perpetuate the damaging excesses.

Analytic theory in the hands of incompetent teachers is dangerous, but no more dangerous than psychological ignorance in the hands of incompetents. Where there has been incompetent teaching by analytically oriented teachers, let us blame the incompetence, not the philosophy.

SUMMARY

Despite the pitfalls, we must learn to make the best possible use of all the available tools and techniques that give promise of aiding in the herculean task of educating all the children of all the people. We must master the psychological contributions in order to improve the excellence of our intellectual accomplishments. And we need some other emphases in the school also. Excellence in imagination, in persuasion, and in artistic creativity are not to be scorned. The point is simply that excellence can seldom be attained by teachers who are unaware of their own emotional limitations and who stoutly resist self-knowledge by asserting that intellectual content is all that matters.

Psychoanalysis seeks for its followers the rational life, through the control and understanding of the emotions. Education too has as its goal the rational life, and seeks to promote a way of life directed by reason rather than by emotion. The cooperation of education and psychoanalysis in the attainment of their common goal seems natural and desirable.

Teachers cannot be trained as psychoanalysts. They cannot attempt the reconstruction of pupil personality. Nevertheless in dealing with emotionally deficient children the teacher is compelled to make some effort to minimize the effects of the child's personality disorders, as well as to prevent their aggravation, if she is to have any hope of teaching the student.

Consequently the teacher who is equipped with an understanding of the child's normal and abnormal behavior is more likely to succeed.

The master teacher who can recognize compulsions, fantasies, projection, identification, and other similarly emotionally dictated behavior can no more eliminate them than the master mariner can eliminate the adverse winds and tides. Neither would be called a master if he failed to recognize the adverse influences and guide his teaching or his navigation accordingly. It is important to have teachers who are analytically sophisticated as long as we have students who are immature and unstable. Otherwise, teachers in positions of authority over children who are unable to respond wholesomely will cause still more maladjustment. A few rare souls learn this without recourse to analysis, as they did before Freud began the systematic study of the unconscious. Unfortunately, still fewer of these rare souls find their way into public school teaching.

Analytic sophistication by teachers is obviously not the only need. Attention to mental health at every level is called for. Dr. Neubauer says, "Perhaps the greatest lag in the field of mental health is the relative lack of action to implement our conviction that emotional health and pathology are determined in early childhood. More than half of all hospital beds in the U.S. are occupied by mentally ill patients, yet there exist almost no institutional facilities for the emotionally disturbed preschool child. As long as we neglect the needs of the very young, we will continue to have a large population of adolescents and adults suffering from neurosis or the acuter forms of mental sickness."

Four-fifths of all counties in the U.S. still have no psychiatric service whatsoever. Studies of school children indicate that from 7 to 12 percent—between two and four million—are in need of psychiatric treatment.

The mental health problem is immense. It is not the school's problem, but the school cannot escape responsibility for doing everything in its power to avoid aggravating it.

The various statements of the role of the teacher in handling this problem have this in common: they are all predicated on a continually increasing awareness and sophistication of psychoanalytic concepts. This is all that can be safely suggested, for psychoanalysis is not prescriptive.

Dr. Lawrence S. Kubie presents a convincing case for the importance of psychoanalysis to education in his introduction to *An Application of Psychoanalysis to Education*, by Richard M. Jones. Dr. Kubie reminds us of the necessity for making emotional maturation a part of the educational process by a continuous concern from kindergarten to university for making self-knowledge in depth part of the main stream of education. He does not urge that teachers play at being analysts, but only that education take place in an atmosphere in which emotional disturbances can be recognized and resolved instead of being repressed and aggravated. He goes on to say:

"The child's fifth freedom is the right to know what he feels; but this does not carry with it any right to act out his feelings blindly. This will require a new set of mores for our schools, one which will enable young people from early years to understand and feel and put into words all the hidden things which go on inside of them, thus ending the conspiracy of silence with which the development of the child is now distorted both at home and at school. If the conspiracy of silence is to be replaced by the fifth freedom, children must be encouraged and helped to attend to their forbidden thoughts, and to put them into words, i.e., to talk out loud about love and hate and jealousy and fear, about curiosity over the body, its products and its apertures; about what goes in and what comes out; about their dim and confused feelings about sex itself; about the strained and stressful relationships within families, which are transplanted into schools."

Dr. Kubie's plea, and it was Sigmund Freud's foremost plea, is for awareness. If teachers are aware of the deepest needs and feelings of their students, and if the students are encouraged to become aware of their own thoughts and feelings, far more effective learning will take place.

Traditionalists and progressivists stand together in abstract acceptance of the notion that the proper study of mankind is man. Increasingly they are sharing the awareness that Sigmund Freud contributed greatly to this study and that teachers have much to learn from him that will make them better teachers by making their students better learners.

Affect and Cognition: A Reciprocal Relationship

Ira J. Gordon

Cognitive psychologists have been fond of quoting Piaget as a major source of our ideas about how intellectual development occurs. We have been busy attempting to engineer this profound developmental theory into an instructional

From *Educational Leadership* 27(7):661–64; April 1970. Reprinted with permission of the Association for Supervision and Curriculum Development and Ira J. Gordon. Copyright © 1970 by the Association for Supervision and Curriculum Development.

theory. We have, however, focused on only some aspects of the theory, and have usually singled out the classes of behaviors, such as conservation, which mark transitions from stage to stage, as the basis for curriculum innovation.

Piaget's book (Piaget and Inhelder, 1969) may come as a surprise to those of us who have had such tunnel vision. The dichotomy between cognition and affect is destroyed in such statements as, "There is no behavior pattern, however intellectual, which does not involve affective factors as motives. . . . Behavior is therefore of a piece. . . . The two aspects, affective and cognitive, are at the same time inseparable and irreducible" (p. 158). I see (with the affective components of joy, excitement, and relief) that Piaget depicts a fully integrated developing child. He helps us get out of our trap of cognition versus affect, and gives us the subject of this paper, affect implies cognition, cognition implies affect.

Many who were involved in education reform treated affect and cognition as though they were mutually exclusive territories of human behavior. The "new curricula" were seen by friend and foe as stressing cognition. The recommendations emerging from developmental psychologists and others concerned with the young child were assailed by early childhood educators because they were "cognitive."

Somehow cognition was viewed as cold, distant, mechanistic, and therefore "bad" by those who saw themselves as warm, loving, and accepting.

Correspondingly, "cognitive" people made equally nasty comments about those whom they saw as concerned "only" with the self-esteem and personal-social development of the child. In effect, this split destroyed what used to be a central notion in progressive education, the concept of the "whole" child. I should like to put the body back together again.

THE SYNTHESIS

The synthesis of affect and cognition is first demonstrated in the infancy period in the way the child relates to the objects and people in his environment. There is a very close connection between the discovery by the infant of the cognitive principle that objects have permanence and his affective ties to people who now begin to take on a life of their own (Guin-Decarie, 1965). The mother, for example, is an object who attains some permanence, is assigned a host of meanings, and influences the emergence of further object relations.

A special tie between affect and cognition exists in the development of language and symbolism. The years from two to six are the time in which the child, through fantasy, imagery, and the acquisition of language, all of which are cognitive tasks, learns to see himself as separate and unique and finds ways to cope with the conflicts that exist between his needs and the demands of the environment. In this effort, affect and cognition serve each other. The child uses language not only to communicate with those around him but also to enable him to comprehend what is happening, to role-play, to talk to himself, to think out loud. Language and thought processes develop from these efforts to assimilate and accommodate; the growth in turn creates new tensions which require further cognitive development.

The human being is a meaning-seeking animal and has strong needs to order and organize the environment so as to deal effectively with it. The child is constantly engaged in ordering and reordering his experience (Gordon, 1969). The existence of disequilibrium created from the transactional relationship between internal growth and external social pressures acts as a motivating force for development. "The formation of personality is dominated by the search for coherence" (Piaget and Inhelder, 1969, p. 158).

A product of this transactional process of inner ⟷ outer and, within the inner, affect ⟷ cognition, is the emergence of concepts of self, which are inseparable syntheses of cognition and affect, subject and object, actor and evaluator, internal and external. The child moves along the egocentric → decentered dimension as he grows in ability to reconcile the inner and external worlds. The growth of intelligence proceeds along this transactional exchange point. As the child incorporates aspects of the external world to fit his views, and as he changes some of his ideas and patterns because of his contacts with reality, he grows in competence and in self-esteem. He becomes more able to search for (and build) coherence.

This search goes on not only in the infancy and childhood periods, but also during adolescence when youngsters are able, because of their cognitive development, to examine their world through language and logical systems but are faced with the discrepancy between neat, intellectual propositions and disorderly patterns of social action which surround and overwhelm them. Their search for coherence is an affective search, which provides the motive power which can be used in schools for cognitive growth, provided the cognitive demands and tasks are so organized and instituted that they are seen by youth as relevant to their affective strivings.

At all ages, from birth to death, cognitive organization, development, and change are inspired and fed by a search for meaning which is affective. As cognitive development takes place, the person moves toward resolutions of states of disequilibrium, but each resolution, because of the cognitive element, is at a higher and more complex level of organization. Each resolution is thus both inseparably affective and cognitive.

APPLICATION TO EDUCATION

So what? What does this contribute to school organization or teacher behavior? It means that a good classroom cannot be understood if we take apart these two elements and focus only on one. It means that any teaching act or learning behavior is an inextricable mix. It means that the child or learner is an active agent who will seek out, master, and devour intellectual activities when they are matched to his present resolution and so challenge him because they create some disequilibrium in his present system. As Don Snygg (1966) indicated, "The optimum level of difficulty is one which allows a student to win success after difficulty" (1966, p. 93).

What do we know about the "mix" in the classroom? First, data show relationships between affective climate and cognitive development. Soar (1967) showed that various patterns of teacher affective behaviors related differentially to pupil growth in reading and vocabulary. Schaefer's (1969) analysis revealed that maternal affective behavior at home was predictive of intellectual perfor-

mance on the Stanford-Binet at age three. Children whose mothers were classified as "hostile—noninvolved" did poorest. What is striking is the close
relationship between Soar's teacher dimensions and Shaefer's maternal dimensions. Adult behavior which was both aloof and hostile produced deleterious
effects on cognitive learning in both home and classroom. If these studies had
focused only on cognitive elements, they would not have yielded the information
on adult affective behavior which relates highly to intellectual growth.

Second, data show the predictive relationship between self-esteem and attitudes toward self in relation to school (affective) and academic performance
(cognitive). Wattenberg and Clifford (1962) and Lamy (1965) report that the
best single predictor of beginning reading achievement in first grade was children's
perceptions of self in kindergarten. The best single predictor of freshman grade
point averages of black male junior college students was their perceptions of self
in relation to teachers and school. Those favorably disposed to teachers and school
tended to have higher grade point averages, regardless of achievement test scores,
than those who did not have this view (Clarke, 1968).

Third, Sears and Sherman (1964) present a model depicting the linkages
between affective and cognitive variables and demonstrate, through case studies,
how these function in both directions.

Any way in which children learn a skill, can demonstrate adequacy, or are
treated as adequate in real-life settings has both affective as well as cognitive payoff. The entry point can be along either the affective or the cognitive dimension.
Children are not easily fooled by phony situations. They learn best when learning
is "real" and respects their integrity. Heightened arousal and affective drive for
learning are most likely to occur when what is to be learned is interesting, exciting,
worthwhile, and real, and provides the child with some measuring rods against
which he can assess himself. Watch the concentration of a kindergartner doing a
difficult jigsaw puzzle. Note his facial expression, note his body movements, and
especially note the smile, the glee, the handclapping, the reward he gives his own
performance when he succeeds. This is the mix.

If we can provide the high schooler with that intensity of experience in
facing the social problems of his day, if we can approach the beginning reader
in ways that create the same excitement, then the reciprocal relationship of affect
and cognition will lead to effective learning. In these examples the learner is
faced with something real outside himself to which he must accommodate, with
which he must cope. This type of challenge stretches him and relates to Snygg's
optimum level of difficulty. In this type of setting, possibilities and goals are
unlimited and cognitive power enhanced. It does not stress affect as precursor of
cognition nor does it stress a dry, intellectual, flat affect exercise. It is a far cry
from turning inward or turning off; it capitalizes instead on the motive power of
the learner's presently developed intellectual organization and his urge to comprehend his world.

The reciprocal relationship of affect and cognition requires the types of
learning tasks in school which turn youngsters on and outward. Their minds can
then expand from contact with the world, not from drugs. They go forward to
the world; they do not retreat into themselves. To be competent is motive to
behave competently. Knowing self and world heightens affect and creates that
measure of discontent which, in turn, can spur us on to achieve our human
potentialities.

REFERENCES

CLARKE, J. R. *Identification of Disadvantaged Junior College Students and Diagnosis of Their Disabilities.* Final Report, July 1968, St. Petersburg Junior College, Grant No. OEG-1-7-070020-3905, Project No. 7-D-020, U.S. Office of Education.

GORDON, I. J. *Human Development: From Birth Through Adolescence.* Second edition. New York: Harper & Row, Publishers, 1969.

GUIN-DECARIE, T. *Intelligence and Affectivity in Early Childhood.* Translated by Elizabeth and Lewis Brandt. New York: International Universities Press, Inc., 1965.

LAMY, M. W. "Relationship of Self-Perceptions of Early Primary Children to Achievement in Reading." In: I. J. Gordon, editor. *Human Development: Readings in Research.* Chicago: Scott, Foresman and Company, 1965. pp. 251–52.

PIAGET, J. AND INHELDER, B. *The Psychology of the Child.* Translated by Helen Weaver. New York: Basic Books, Inc., Publishers, 1969.

SCHAEFER, E. "Home Tutoring, Maternal Behavior and Infant Intellectual Development." Paper presented at the meeting of the American Psychological Association, Washington, D.C., September 4, 1969.

SEARS, P. and SHERMAN, V. *In Pursuit of Self-Esteem.* Belmont, California: Wadsworth Publishing Company, Inc., 1964.

SNYGG, D. "A Cognitive Field Theory of Learning." In: Walter Waetjen, editor. *Learning and Mental Health in the School.* 1966 Yearbook. Washington, D.C.: Association for Supervision and Curriculum Development, 1966. pp. 77–98.

SOAR, R. S. "Optimum Teacher-Pupil Interaction for Pupil Growth." *Educational Leadership* 26 (3):275–80; December 1967.

WATTENBERG, W. and CLIFFORD, C. *Relationships of Self-Concept to Beginning Achievement in Reading.* Final Report, 1962, Wayne State University, C.R.P. No. 377, U.S. Office of Education.

Self-theory and Behaviorism: A Rapprochement

Donald Avila
William Purkey

From the point of view of these authors a sad state of affairs presently exists in psychology and education. Central to this problem is the notion that to accept either behaviorism or self-theory as one's major psychological orientation automatically excludes acceptance of the other. That this assumption is all too prevalent is evidenced by Hitt's description of a recent symposium on behaviorism

From *Psychology in the Schools* IX, no. 2 (April 1972):124–126. Used by permission of the authors and publisher.

vs. phenomenology, which included some of the most prominent psychologists in the nation:

> The presentations dealt with two distinct models of man and the scientific methodology associated with each Model. The discussions following each presentation may be described as aggressive, hostile, and rather emotional; they would suggest that there is little likelihood of a reconciliation between the two schools of thought represented at the symposium . . . [1969, p. 651].

We contend that this either-or state of affairs is destructive, self-deluding and, if we read the temper of the younger psychologists and educators correctly, a position held only by those who look to the past rather than to the future.

Both self-theory and behaviorism offer important contributions to psychology and education. To make them mutually exclusive automatically blinds us to the significant contributions that each can make to our understanding of man. To be half blind is bad enough, but when an antagonistic situation develops that is characterized by aggression, hostility and anger, our vision is distorted even more.

We submit that to view self-theory and behaviorism as mutually exclusive and antagonistic is not only fruitless, but also misleading. Modern behaviorists recognize central processes as essential to an understanding of behavior, while self-theorists are fully aware of the documented power of reinforcement to modify human behavior. It is becoming increasingly evident that both approaches are parts of a single continuum in the incredibly complex processes of understanding people and influencing their behavior. The purpose of this paper is to explain how we have been able to include both behaviorism and self-theory in our thinking about the dynamics of human activity.

First, we see self-theory as a valuable working hypothesis about the nature of man—in fact, self-theory could serve as a framework for a basic philosophy of life. Thanks to the writing and research of self-theorists, we have valuable insights about the nature of individuals, their perceptions, their needs, and their goals. Further, emerging evidence (Murphy & Spohn, 1968; Purkey, 1970) supports the common-sense notion that behavior is determined by the individual's subjective perceptions of the situation rather than by the situation itself. Thus, we have the indispensable construct of the phenomenological world.

Central to the phenomenological world is one's self-awareness. All of the beliefs, opinions, and attitudes that an individual holds about himself have come to be called self-concept. This concept of self and its related facets of self-esteem, self-enhancement, self-consistency, and self-actualization provide rich hypotheses for researchers and valuable guides for those in the helping professions (Combs, Avila, & Purkey, 1971).

People who work in helping relationships have pointed out the importance of a warm, accepting environment in which a person is treated with respect, dignity, warmth, and care. Furthermore, they have shown that the individual who is being helped needs to accept mutual responsibility for the helping relationship. Finally, the research of self-theorists has demonstrated that the way a professional helper feels about himself and his client or student has as much to do with the outcome of the interaction as the specific technique used, if not more. (Combs, Soper, Gooding, Benton, Dickman, & Usher, 1969).

In sum, self-theory provides heuristic guidelines by which to fulfill our professional responsibilities, be they counseling, therapy, teaching, or research. On the other hand, self-theory does seem to have difficulty when it comes to the question of "how." How does one change a self-concept, a perception, or a particular bit of behavior? How can one set up conditions and provide experiences for one's clients and students that will prove to be self-enhancing? This is the point at which we believe behaviorism enters the scene.

Behaviorism, after all, is not a theory, although a person certainly can develop a theoretical position from the approach. Behaviorism is a process and a method (essentially the scientific method) from which psychologists and educators have developed many useful principles and techniques. These principles and techniques can be used to accomplish the purpose of self-theory: *to convince each individual that he is valuable, responsible, and capable of influencing his own destiny.*

The behaviorist has little trouble with the "how" aspects of a given problem. For example, what better way is there to help a person to have positive experiences than to set up situations full of positive contingencies of reinforcement, i.e., situations in which the individual has an excellent chance of success. If a person who has been a failure begins to experience success, he also will begin to change his feelings about himself and others and his perception of the world. This is exactly what the self-theorists want to accomplish. The point has been clarified by Andrews and Karlin (1971), who demonstrated that behavioristic processes can be used to build autonomy in the individual, facilitate his freedom, and strengthen his self-image. Rice (1970) also has demonstrated that the goals of self-theory can be realized by use of behavior modification.

Thus it seems to these authors that enhancement and reinforcement, changing self-concepts and behavior modification are related closely and may sometimes be the same thing. Furthermore, the authors believe that the future of psychology lies in a unification of these two positions, not in the wasted energy of continued conflict.

REFERENCES

ANDREWS, L. M. & KARLIN, M. Requiem for democracy? New York: Holt, Rinehart, & Winston, 1971.

COMBS, A. W., AVILA, D. L. & PURKEY, W. W. Helping relationships: basic concepts for the helping professions. Boston: Allyn & Bacon, 1971.

COMB, A. W., SOPER, D. W., GOODING, C. T., BENTON, J. A., JR., DICKMAN, J. F., & USHER, R. H. Florida Studies in the Helping Professions. University of Florida Social Science Monograph No. 37. Gainesville: University of Florida Press, 1969.

HITT, W. D. Two models of man. American Psychologist, 1969, 24, 651–658.

MURPHY, G. & SPOHN, H. E. Encounter with reality. Boston: Houghton Mifflin, 1968.

PURKEY, W. W. Self concept and school achievement. Englewood Cliffs, N.J.: Prentice-Hall, 1970.

RICE, D. R. Educo-therapy: a new approach to delinquent behavior. Journal of Learning Disabilities, 1970, 3, 16–23.

What Do We Know About Learning?

Goodwin Watson

What do we really know today about learning? Although no scientific "truths" are established beyond the possibility of revision, knowledgeable psychologists generally agree on a number of propositions about learning which are important for education. The educator who bases his program on the propositions presented below is entitled, therefore, to feel that he is on solid psychological ground and not on shifting sands.

Behaviors which are rewarded (reinforced) are more likely to recur.

This most fundamental law of learning has been demonstrated in literally thousands of experiments. It seems to hold for every sort of animal from earthworms to highly intelligent adults. The behavior most likely to emerge in any situation is that which the subject found successful or satisfying previously in a similar situation. No other variable affects learning so powerfully. The best-planned learning provides for a steady, cumulative sequence of successful behaviors.

Reward (reinforcement), to be most effective in learning, must follow almost immediately after the desired behavior and be clearly connected with that behavior in the mind of the learner.

The simple word, "Right," coming directly after a given response, will have more influence on learning than any big reward which comes much later or which is dimly connected with many responses so that it can't really reinforce any of them. Much of the effectiveness of programmed self-instruction lies in 'the fact that information about success is fed back immediately for each learner response. A total mark on a test the day after it is administered has little or no reinforcement value for the specific answers.

Sheer repetition without indications of improvement or any kind of reinforcement (reward) is a poor way to attempt to learn.

Practice is not enough. The learner cannot improve by repeated efforts unless he is informed whether or not each effort has been successful.

Threat and punishment have variable and uncertain effects upon learning: They may make the punished response more likely or less likely to recur; they may set up avoidance tendencies which prevent further learning.

Punishment is not, psychologically, the reverse of reward. It disturbs the relationship of the learner to the situation and the teacher. It does not assist the learner in finding and fixing the correct response.

From *NEA Journal* LII, no. 3 (March 1963):20–22. Used by permission of the author and publisher.

Readiness for any new learning is a complex product of interaction among such factors as (a) sufficient physiological and psychological maturity, (b) sense of the importance of the new learning for the learner in his world, (c) mastery of prerequisites providing a fair chance of success, and (d) freedom from discouragement (expectation of failure) or threat (sense of danger).

Conversely, the learner will not be ready to try new responses which are beyond his powers or are seen as valueless or too dangerous.

Opportunity for fresh, novel, stimulating experience is a kind of reward which is quite effective in conditioning and learning.

Experiments indicate that lower animals (rats, dogs, monkeys) will learn as effectively when they receive rewards of new experience or satisfied curiosity as they will when the rewards gratify physical desires. Similarly, stimulating new insights have been found to be effective as rewards for the learning efforts of human beings.

The sense of satisfaction which results from achievement is the type of reward (reinforcement) which has the greatest transfer value to other life situations.

Any extrinsic reward—candy, or stars on a chart, or commendation—depends on its dispenser. There is no need to strive if the reward-giver is out of the picture. Also, cheating can sometimes win the extrinsic reward. The internal reward system is always present for the learner, and he sees little gain in fooling himself.

Learners progress in an area of learning only as far as they need to in order to achieve their purposes. Often they do only well enough to "get by"; with increased motivation, they improve.

Studies of reading speed show that practice alone will not bring improvement; a person may have read books for years at his customary rate, but with new demands and opportunities he may be able to double that rate.

The most effective effort is put forth by children when they attempt tasks which are not too easy and not too hard—where success seems quite possible but not certain. It is not reasonable to expect a teacher to set an appropriate level of challenge for each pupil in a class; pupils can, however, be helped to set their own goals to bring maximum satisfaction and learning.

Children are more likely to throw themselves wholeheartedly into any learning project if they themselves have participated in the selection and planning of the project.

Genuine participation (not pretended sharing) increases motivation, adaptability, and speed of learning.

Excessive direction by the teacher is likely to result in apathetic conformity, defiance, scapegoating, or escape from the whole affair.

Autocratic leadership has been found to increase dependence of members on the leader and to generate resentment (conscious or unconscious) which finds expression in attacks on weaker figures or even in sabotage of the work.

Overstrict discipline is associated with more conformity, anxiety, shyness, and acquiescence in children; greater permissiveness is associated with more initiative and creativity.

In comparisons of children whose parents were most permissive in home discipline with those whose parents were most strict (both groups of parents loving and concerned), the youngsters from permissive homes showed more enterprise, self-confidence, curiosity, and originality.

Many pupils experience so much criticism, failure, and discouragement in school that their self-confidence, level of aspiration, and sense of worth are damaged.

The pupil who sees himself at his worst in school is likely to place little value on study and to seek his role of importance outside the classroom. He may carry through life a sense of being not good for much. He is likely also to feel resentment at schools, teachers, and books.

When children or adults experience too much frustration, their behavior ceases to be integrated, purposeful, and rational. The threshold of what is "too much" varies; it is lowered by previous failures.

Pupils who have had little success and almost continuous failure at school tasks are in no condition to think, to learn, or even to pay attention. They may turn their anger outward against respectable society or inward against themselves.

Pupils think whenever they encounter an obstacle, difficulty, puzzle, or intellectual challenge which interests them. The process of thinking involves designing and testing plausible solutions for the problem as understood by the thinker.

It is useless to command people to think; they must feel concerned to get somewhere and eager to remove an obstruction on the way.

The best way to help pupils form a general concept is to present the concept in numerous and varied specific situations—contrasting experiences with and without the desired concept—and then to encourage precise formulations of the general idea and its application in situations different from those in which the concept was learned.

For example, the concept of democracy might be illustrated not only in national government but also in familiar situations of home, school, church, jobs, clubs, and local affairs. It is best understood when it is contrasted with other power structures such as autocracy, oligarchy, or laissez faire.

The experience of learning by sudden insight into a previously confused or puzzling situation arises when (a) there has been a sufficient background and preparation, (b) attention is given to the relationships operative in the whole situation, (c) the perceptual structure "frees" the key elements to be shifted into new patterns, (d) the task is meaningful and within the range of ability of the subject.

The term "cognitive reorganization" is sometimes applied to this experience. Suddenly the scene changes into one that seems familiar and can be coped with.

Learning from reading is facilitated more by time spent recalling what has been read than by re-reading.

In one experiment (typical of many), students who spent 80 percent of their learning periods trying to remember what they had read surpassed those who spent only 60 percent of the time on recollection. The students who spent all the time reading and re-reading the assignment made the poorest record.

Forgetting proceeds, rapidly at first—then more and more slowly. Recall shortly after learning reduces the amount forgotten.

Within twenty-four hours after learning something, a large part is forgotten unless efforts are made to prevent forgetting. A thing can be relearned more quickly than it was learned originally, however, and if it is reviewed several times at gradually increasing intervals, it can be retained for some time.

People remember new information which confirms their previous attitudes better than they remember new information which runs counter to their previous attitudes.

Studies consistently show that individuals who feel strongly on a controversial issue, and who are asked to read presentations of both sides, remember the facts and arguments which support their feelings better than they recall those on the opposite side.

What is learned is most likely to be available for use if it is learned in a situation much like that in which it is to be used and immediately preceding the time when it is needed. Learning in childhood, then forgetting, and later relearning when need arises is not an efficient procedure.

The best time to learn is when the learning can be useful. Motivation is then strongest and forgetting less of a problem. Much that is now taught children might be more effective if taught to responsible adults.

If there is a discrepancy between the real objectives and the tests used to measure achievement, the latter become the main influence upon choice of subject matter and method. Curriculum and teaching geared to standardized tests and programmed learning are likely to concentrate only on learnings which can be easily checked and scored.

The more rapid mental growth comes during infancy and early childhood; the average child achieves about half of his total mental growth by age five.

In the first two years a normal child transforms the "big, buzzing, blooming confusion" of his first conscious experience to organized perception of familiar faces, spoken words, surroundings, toys, bed, clothing, and foods. He differentiates himself from others, high from low, many from few, approval from disapproval. He lays a foundation for lifelong tendencies toward trust or mistrust, self-acceptance or shame, initiative or passivity; and these vitally condition further growth.

Not until adolescence do most children develop the sense of time which is required for historical perspective. The so-called facts of history—1492, 1776, and all that—can be learned by children, but without any real grasp of what life was like in another period or in a different country. Most instruction in ancient, medieval, and even modern history is no more real to children than are fairy tales.

Ability to learn increases with age up to adult years. The apparent decline is largely the result of lack of motivation. We can coerce children into school activities; adult education is mostly voluntary. Men and women can, if they wish, master new languages, new ideas, and new ways of acting or problem-solving even at sixty and seventy years of age.

Misunderstandings About How Children Learn

David Elkind

Recently, a young mother of my acquaintance said with some pride: "I insist that my four-year-old daughter watch *Sesame Street*—even when she prefers doing something else." Concerned about the intellectual development of her child, this mother believes that *making* the girl watch the program will eventually help her do better in school.

Many mothers today are pressuring their preschool children to learn numbers, letters, shapes, and so on. Unfortunately, this parental concern for children's intellectual development often seems greater than their concern for children's feelings, interests, and attitudes. What many parents fail to understand is that attempting to force young children to learn specific content may produce an aversive attitude toward academic learning in general. This attitude of distaste may have such serious long-range effects on young children's academic achievement that it completely outweighs the advantages of being familiar with letters, forms, and numbers today or next week.

The foregoing example illustrates one of several common misunderstandings about the thinking and learning of young children that seem to be current today. In this article, I briefly describe five such common misunderstandings that hold particularly true for young children—and a few for older ones as well.

One of the pernicious misunderstandings about young children is that they are most like adults in their thinking and least like us in their feelings. It is just this misconception that prompted the mother mentioned earlier to command her daughter to watch *Sesame Street*. The same woman would not think of insisting that her husband watch a program she thought might "do him some good." Rather, she would realize that this kind of approach would be a sure way to turn him against the program. And yet, because she believes that children's feelings are different from those of adults, she uses a technique with her child she knows would never work with a grown-up.

Parents and teachers are equally prone to regard a child's thinking process as similar to their own. When, for example, a child asks, "Why is the sun hot?" his father is likely to explain that the sun gives off light and that it takes heat to produce the light. The relation between heat and light is not obvious, however, and the young child would hardly understand. Indeed the real intent of the child's question has to do with the *purpose* of the sun's heat. An appropriate reply would be "to keep us warm" or "to give us a suntan." These answers are

From *Today's Education* LXI, no. 3 (March 1972):18–20. Used by permission of the author and publisher.

not entirely incorrect and they correspond to the young child's underlying belief that everything has a purpose.

Because young children are often so capable linguistically, adults often overestimate their capacity to think.

A second misunderstanding about young children is that they learn best while sitting still and listening. This misconception arises because parents tend to generalize from their experiences as adults. It is true that we adults often learn by listening attentively to a lecture or reading a book.

The young child is, however, not capable of mental activity or thinking in the same way as an adult. He learns through engaging in real actions involving tangible objects, such as blocks or dolls.

Thanks to the work of the famed Swiss psychologist, Jean Piaget, we now know that the child's actions upon things are what facilitate his mental activity or thinking. The young child's actions are progressively miniaturized and interiorized until he is able to do in his head what before he had to do with his hands. This internalization of action comes about gradually during early childhood and is completed at age six or seven.

To illustrate this internalization, observe a four-year-old and a six-year-old performing a simple pencil maze. The younger immediately puts pencil to paper and tries to find the right path. The older, in contrast, studies the maze and only after he has mentally decided on the right path does he put pencil to paper.

Accordingly, when we say young children are "active" learners, we must take this in a literal sense. Montessori said: "Play is the child's work." In play, the child is practicing the various actions that he will eventually internalize as thought.

Therefore, however convenient it may be for grownups to think that children learn while sitting still, what they learn in this way is likely to have little lasting value. In contrast, *what children acquire through active manipulation of their environment is the ability to think.*

A third common misunderstanding about young children is the belief that they can learn and operate according to rules. Many parents have had the experience of telling a young child over and over again not to hit his little brother or not to take toys apart or to say thank you when he receives something. Because a young child has not yet internalized thought, he cannot internalize rules either. Consequently, while the child understands the prohibition against hitting his brother and against breaking toys in particular instances, he is unable to generalize to new instances. This is true for learning to say thanks.

The young child's inability to learn rules has special implications for the educational programs prepared for him. We have already noted that the young child learns best through playing with and manipulating materials in his environment. His inability to learn general verbal rules supports this observation and argues against his formal education (involving verbal instruction, a curriculum, and educational objectives). Formal education, whether we speak of reading, arithmetic, or spelling, presupposes the inculcation of rules and thus is inappropriate for the majority of preschool children.

On the other hand, many activities are appropriate educational enterprises for preschoolers. Writing and printing letters is a case in point. Both Montessori and Fernald have pointed out the importance of these for later reading.

Writing as preparation for reading makes good theoretical as well as peda-gogical sense in light of the ideas offered earlier. Thinking is an internalization of action, so reading can be regarded, in part at least, as deriving from the in-ternalization of writing actions. Obviously, reading involves much more than the ability to reproduce letters but such reproduction is an appropriate prereading activity for children not yet ready for formal instruction in that skill.

Another widespread misunderstanding about young children is that ac-*celeration* is preferable to *elaboration*. Many parents, for example, spend a great deal of time trying to teach their young children to read or do mathematics. These parents seem to believe that if children have a head start in these special skills they will have a head start generally. The opposite is more likely to be true.

A child who elaborates the skills he does have, such as the ability to arrange materials according to size on a wide range of materials (blocks, sticks, dolls, dogs, and so on), is likely to be better prepared for future learning than a child who has learned a great deal in a short time but who has not had the chance to assimilate and practice what he has learned.

The situation is not unlike that in which one student crams for a test and another studies regularly throughout a semester. While the two may not per-form too differently on an exam, the one who has been studying regularly is likely to be better prepared for future courses than the one who makes cramming a regular practice. Parents who try to teach their young children special skills and content are, in effect, teaching a cram course, and the results may be as short-lived for the preschooler as for the college student who crams.

A last common misunderstanding about the learning of young children should be mentioned—one involving the belief that parents and teachers can raise children's IQ. To be sure, IQ is affected by environment, but most middle-class children have probably grown intellectually about as rapidly as their en-dowment permits. Further enrichment is not likely to have marked effects upon their intellectual ability, although it may affect how they make use of this ability.

Children who have been intellectually deprived can, however, make signifi-cant gains in intellectual performance as a consequence of intellectual enrich-ment. Just as a child who has grown up with an adequate diet will not benefit much from dietary supplements and a child whose diet has been deficient will, so an intellectually well-nourished child is not likely to benefit markedly from further intellectual enrichment whereas a deprived child will.

In large measure, all of these misunderstandings derive from a contemporary overemphasis on intellectual growth to the exclusion of the personal-social side of development. Although I know it sounds old-fashioned to talk about the whole child and tender loving care, I strongly believe that many problems in child rearing and education could be avoided if concern for a child's achievement as a student were balanced by an equally strong concern for his feelings of self-worth as a person.

The Slow Learner . . . . What Are His Characteristics and Needs?

Merle B. Karnes

Slow learners are children who learn at a less rapid rate than the normal but not as slowly as the educable mentally retarded. They are sometimes referred to as dull-normal or intellectually backward children. One criterion in determining whether or not a child is a slow learner is his intelligence quotient, which may range anywhere from 75 to 90.

In addition to a slow rate of learning, the following characteristics are attributed to slow learners as a group. (Not all slow learners, of course, possess all these characteristics, but it is important to consider them in planning an instructional program for these children.)

The slow learner tends to have more physical defects than the average child. Defects of hearing and speech may interfere with a child's learning. One possible reason for more physical defects among slow learners is that a large percentage come from low-income families where prenatal and postnatal care is inadequate. In addition, when there is a weakness or defect in one area, it is common to find defects in other areas of development. In contrast, an intellectually gifted child is likely to be superior in all aspects of development. Referral to agencies and community resources available to assist the family in correcting physical defects of the child is important.

The slow learner is consistently below grade level in academic progress. Even when the slow learner is working at a level commensurate with his mental age, he can be expected to achieve only about the seventh or eighth grade level when he is 16. He can learn more, but the material to be learned cannot be more difficult. Also, the range of individual differences among slow learners increases with age. Usually, the slow learner lags further and further behind his more able peers, making it more and more difficult for the school to differentiate instruction to meet his specific needs. The higher up the educational ladder this child goes, the more difficulty the school has in changing the regular curriculum to accommodate his slow rate of learning.

The slow learner's reasoning ability is poorer than that of the normal child. He is slow to see cause and effect relationships, to make inferences, to draw logical and valid conclusions, to transfer learning, and to generalize.

Slow learners need meaningful educational experiences geared to their stage of development and ample opportunity to develop reasoning skills. They also

From *Today's Education* LIX, no. 3 (March 1970):42–44. Used by permission of the author and publisher.

need much teacher guidance in order to see meaningful associations. A multi-sensory approach seems to be particularly appropriate in making learning experiences more concrete. The quality of learning experiences is far more important to the slow learner than the quantity of experiences.

Short attention span seems to typify this group of children. However, the short attention span is often due to poor instruction rather than to a defect in the slow learner. When materials are interesting and when success is possible, the attention span of the slow learner tends to be adequate.

Poor retention is still another weakness of slow learners. Slow learners are noticeably below par in both immediate and delayed memory. They need more repetition to reinforce learning. With slow learners, overlearning is especially important. It is crucial that these children have opportunities to practice skills and to use knowledge in various meaningful contexts to ensure permanency of learning.

Unlike brighter children, slow learners do not learn incidentally as a rule. If they are not specifically taught, they are unlikely to learn by themselves. Those learnings felt to be important to current and future academic success and adjustment must never be left to chance but must be taught systematically and sequentially. Careful planning by the teacher is a must to facilitate learning among slow learners.

Poor work habits and poor motivation to learn characterize slow learners, who find it difficult to persist independently until a task is completed. Activities should be carefully chosen so that success is possible and so that a minimum amount of time is required for the completion of a task. Recognition for completion of tasks is important to encourage future efforts. The complexities of the task and the amount of time necessary for completion can be increased as the slow learner matures and progresses.

Slow learners respond to immediate goals rather than to delayed ones. These children must see a reason here and now for engaging in a task. A reward or gratification that is postponed for a week or a month is meaningless. For example, learning arithmetic makes sense to slow learners who need to know arithmetic facts to hold their jobs in certain work-study programs. When they see no immediate, tangible need for learning the facts, they are not likely to apply themselves.

The slow learner has poorly developed language and communication skills. He needs many opportunities to practice language. He learns by talking about meaningful, firsthand experiences involving what he has seen, what he has heard, what he has done, and what he plans to do.

He needs a stimulating school environment where he has many things to talk about. In this way, he increases his vocabulary and improves in his ability to communicate ideas to others. The greater his facility in the use of words, the more effective his thinking will become.

Socially and emotionally, slow learners tend to be less mature than their brighter peers. Approximately 50 percent have poor personal adjustment. Many are discipline problems. They have considerable difficulty controlling their emotions and perceiving how their actions affect others. Acquiring social competence is an important goal for these children throughout their school attendance. They need more counseling services to help them to understand themselves as well as to set realistic goals for themselves. Especially, they need more vocational guidance. The slow learners need teachers who accept them and who provide a warm, friendly atmosphere where they can feel secure and have a sense of belonging.

Slow learners feel less confident and less adequate than average children. To build up feelings of adequacy and personal worth, it is essential to give them immediate feedback as to the correctness of their responses. They need more praise and encouragement than their brighter peers. Tangible evidence of progress should be made available in such forms as graphs, positive notes to pupil and parents, positive verbal evaluations by teachers and other pupils, positive comparisons of present work with previous.

They have a hard time following directions. This problem presents considerable difficulty in school. Since their memory spans are comparatively short, the teacher should make sure that the directions he gives are specific and definite. He should consider carefully how many directions to give at any one time and keep them within each child's ability to follow them successfully.

Slow learners are not as curious and creative as their more able peers. Since achievement and creative thinking have a high correlation, slow learners should be encouraged to develop their creative abilities, especially in language and thinking. They should be encouraged to ask questions and to think through various ways of solving problems. In addition, self-expression through art and music activities can provide outlets that are satisfying and rewarding to them.

A large percentage of slow learners come from disadvantaged homes. These homes often have a multiplicity of problems that affect the child's adjustment. Referral to social agencies can often improve home conditions and thereby help provide the slow learner with an improved atmosphere for learning.

A poor environment can depress a child's intellectual functioning. Teaching parents how to assist their slow learner in developing his potential to the fullest should be a goal of any educational program for slow learners.

Slow learners are capable of being followers but have limited leadership potentials. Schools must aim to help slow learners make valid decisions as to whom they wish to follow. Learning to be good followers is important to them, especially in achieving personal objectives and democratic goals.

Identification of the slow learner should begin early. As a general rule, slow learners are slow in beginning to sit, walk, and talk. While the IQ derived from an individual intelligence test administered by a qualified person is possibly the best single index of a slow rate of learning, it by no means should be considered infallible. Furthermore, in many instances, a psychologist will not be available to administer an individual intelligence test to slow learners. Group intelligence tests, supplemented by cumulative records, information from parents, and objective teacher observations based on a checklist of characteristics of slow learners, can identify almost every slow learner.

Despite their lowered intellectual potential, slow learners are not a homogeneous group. Each has his desires, goals, skills, and differences that make him a unique individual. Planning, programming for, and educating slow learners requires an individualized approach. With such an approach, slow learners can learn academic skills essential for effective daily living. It is up to the schools to respond to the challenge.

SECTION 3 ADDITIONAL LEARNING ACTIVITIES

Problems and Projects

1. Prepare three lesson plans in your subject, each plan based on one of the learning perspectives. How would the classroom program and activities differ in each case? Review the articles in this section by Madsen and Madsen (S–R theorists); Combs and Gordon (cognitive- and perceptual-field theorists); and Robinson (Freudian theorist) to assist you in writing your three lesson plans.
2. Prepare one lesson plan in your subject in which you make use of all three learning theories. Review the articles by Avila and Purkey; Watson; and Elkind to assist you in writing this plan.
3. Continue to develop a "case problem" about one school you know well. Describe the curriculum and teaching in that school as it may be related to each of the three learning theory positions. To do this you may find it necessary to describe the teaching and curriculum in more than one subject field or by more than one teacher. You can add to your study of this school as you work on each of the bases of the curriculum and the criteria.
4. *Dissertation Abstracts* and the *Review of Educational Research* may be used to obtain information on recent studies on learning. The American Educational Research Association (AERA) publishes abstracts of papers presented at annual meetings. These abstracts include much of the current reported research on learning.

Films

Learning by Doing. 16mm., black and white, 30 mins. Asserts that a good school program promotes learning by organizing significant discovery for each child and by confirming and extending his experience. Distributed by Peter Robeck and Co., Inc., 230 Park Avenue, New York, New York 10017.

Learning and Behavior: The Teaching Machine. 16mm., black and white, 29 mins. Presents Drs. B. F. Skinner and J. Herrnstein who demonstrate how to measure the learning process. Distributed by Carousel Films, Inc., 1501 Broadway, New York, New York 10036.

Filmstrips

How We Learn. Color, 50 mins. Filmstrip with script. Explains that all higher animals are capable of learning. Focuses on man and how he learns. Distributed by Warren Schloat Productions, Inc., 115 Tompkins Avenue, Pleasantville, New York 10570.

Books to Review

Allport, G. W. *Pattern and Growth in Personality.* New York: Holt, Rinehart and Winston, 1961.

Ausubel, David. *Educational Psychology, A Cognitive View.* New York: Holt, Rinehart and Winston, 1968.

————. *Learning Theory and Classroom Practice.* Toronto: Ontario Institute for Studies in Education, 1967.

Ausubel, David, ed. *Readings in School Learning.* New York: Holt, Rinehart and Winston, 1969.

Ausubel, David, and Robinson, Floyd C. *School Learning*. New York: Holt, Rinehart and Winston, 1969.

Bigge, Morris L. *Learning Theory for Teachers*, 2d ed. New York: Harper and Row, 1971.

Bugelski, B. R. *The Psychology of Learning Applied to Teaching*, 2d ed. New York: The Bobbs-Merrill Company, 1972.

Combs, Arthur, ed. *Perceiving, Behaving, Becoming*. Washington, D.C.: Association for Supervision and Curriculum Development, N.E.A., 1962.

Combs, Arthur; Avila, Donald; and Purkey, William. *Helping Relationships: Basic Concepts for Helping Professions*. Boston: Allyn and Bacon, 1971.

Combs, Arthur, and Snygg, Donald. *Individual Behavior: A Personal Approach to Behavior*. New York: Harper and Brothers, 1959.

Gagné, Robert M. *The Conditions of Learning*, 2d ed. New York: Holt, Rinehart and Winston, 1970.

Glasser, William. *Schools Without Failure*. New York: Harper and Row, Publishers, 1969.

May, Rollo. *Love and Will*. New York: W. W. Norton and Company, 1969.

Newell, John M. *Student's Guide to Robert M. Gagné*. New York: Holt, Rinehart and Winston, 1970.

Rogers, Carl R. *Freedom to Learn*. Columbus, Ohio: Charles E. Merrill Publishing Company, 1969.

Skinner, B. F. *Beyond Freedom and Dignity*. New York: Alfred A. Knopf, 1971.

Travers, R. M. W. *Essentials of Learning*, 2d ed. New York: Macmillan Company, 1967.

The Nature of Knowledge

PREREQUISITES

Reading of the Introduction to this book and Sections 1, 2, and 3.

RATIONALE

During the decade of the 1960s increasing emphasis was placed on knowledge as a basis for making curriculum decisions. Prior to the 1960s, human development, learning, and the society were seen as the bases of curriculum planning.

In 1961, in his presidential address at the Association for Supervision and Curriculum Development, Arthur W. Foshay pointed out that we were trying to plan curricula without considering formal knowledge. He proposed that when curriculum planners make curriculum decisions, they should take directly into account the nature of organized bodies of knowledge in addition to the nature of the growing child and the nature of our society (see *Educational Leadership,* May, 1961).

Scholars have organized portions of knowledge into disciplines. A discipline consists of a set of generalizations that explain the relationships among a body of facts and concepts. Also, scholars in each discipline have developed methods of inquiry useful in discovering new knowledge. Each discipline is man-made and is subject to revision if a different organization proves more functional.

Some think of knowledge as organized bodies of facts and concepts and believe that all of the knowledge that man has discovered, learned, or invented has been collected, catalogued, and organized into the most useful structures. Further, they often believe that the school's function is to accept the organizations of knowledge that have been made in the past and devise ways of helping each learner acquire as much of it as he can. According to this viewpoint, curriculum workers and teachers must examine each subject or discipline and decide upon a sequence in which the facts, concepts, and generalizations should be learned and the pace and procedures by which learners should be brought into contact with them.

Certain problems have arisen for those who follow this logic. The knowledge available to man has accumulated at an extremely rapid rate and will multiply even faster in the years ahead. It is impossible, and will become even more so, to have any one learner learn all the facts, concepts, generalizations, and methods of inquiry—even in one discipline. Moreover new knowledge constantly makes some other knowledge in each discipline obsolete. What shall be taught? How shall it be taught to enable the learner to use his knowledge to greatest advantage and to be able to accommodate additional knowledge?

Others view knowledge as a much more flexible, fluid product of man's experience. They say that the organization of knowledge produced by the scholars is, more often than not, not functional in life experiences and in new situations or problems. They state that the definition and the structure of a discipline are inventions of man and may be revised in light of new knowledge, and that new disciplines can be formed as needed. And this is happening today to an ever increasing degree.

Those who believe that knowledge should be more functional say that each man attempts to understand himself and the environment about him. In the process, he invents interpretations of his environment and of his own actions. These interpretations are unique to him, and constitute the knowledge that is real and of value to him. Through his attempts to understand himself and his environment, he is brought into contact with facts and concepts that others have discovered and organized. The organization may or may not have meaning for him. He decides. He determines how the newly contacted data will be incorporated into his system of knowledge. His structure of knowledge—his actual structure and not the one he may verbalize—is personally invented and constructed.

Curriculum workers and teachers who hold this second conception of the nature of knowledge approach curriculum construction and teaching in a different manner. They are not sure that the traditional disciplines should be the guides for organizing the curriculum. They want to start with the concerns and needs of the learner, and they want to encourage him to use knowledge from any discipline that will help him. In this section, Fantini and Weinstein ("Reducing the Behavior Gap") represent that position regarding knowledge. It is also the position taken by Bruner in his 1971 article "The Process of Education Reconsidered."

If the curriculum is to be related to present social forces, the subject of Section 1 of this book, then it is not possible to organize the curriculum just according to the separate disciplines. Problems of race, environment, lawlessness, and social change cannot be understood by anything other than interdisciplinary or multi-disciplinary study. And human development theories and research, as presented in Section 2 of this book, suggest the need to organize at least part of what is studied on the basis of the personal-social problems of learners of a particular age level. These personal-social problems are not related to any one discipline but require interdisciplinary or multi-disciplinary study.

A third position regarding knowledge and its uses in curriculum planning and teaching combines the two positions already described. Curriculum and instruction planners who adhere to this position believe that interdisciplinary, multi-disciplinary, and problems approaches, *as well as* structured approaches, to disciplines *are all needed* in curriculum planning. As is stated in the Section 3 Rationale on "Learning," there are different kinds of knowledge and different human needs for knowledge. Transfer in learning is aided when there is structure, order, and configuration in what is learned. Often the structure of the disciplines can aid in providing order, but frequently the learner needs assistance in providing his own structure and order to meet his own problems or to understand society's problems. In this section, this middle position is represented by Bellack ("Conceptions of Knowledge: Their Significance for the Curriculum").

The "medium is the message" seems an important consideration in understanding the nature of knowledge and its relation to curriculum planning. Culkin ("A Schoolman's Guide To Marshall McLuhan") explores the meaning of this dictum for curriculum planning and says that four views of "the medium is the message" should be considered:

1. The medium is the thing to study. We should pay attention to form, structure, framework, and medium as well as content.
2. If you don't know the medium, you don't know the message. Content always exists in some form and is governed by it. Each form has preferences for certain kinds of messages.
3. The medium alters the perceptual habits of its users. Independent of content, the medium gets through. The medium is co-message: it is always content-in-form that is mediated.
4. The media alter the society as well as the individual. The media shape both the content and the consumers, and they do so practically undetected.

Summary of Rationale

The various views of the nature of knowledge provide another important base for curriculum planning. They help the planner decide (a) what to include in the curriculum and how to teach it; (b) how to plan for the different kinds of knowledge to be taught; and (c) how to provide for the individual differences of learners. How the educator views knowledge has major significance for his planning for teaching and curriculum planning.

OBJECTIVES

Your objectives in studying knowledge as one of the bases of curriculum planning should be the following:

1. To be able to analyze a curriculum plan with reference to the theory or position concerning knowledge that is implicit in the plan.
2. To be able to analyze a curriculum plan or a teaching plan on the bases of the various views concerning knowledge and its nature and uses that are described in the rationale.
3. To be able to suggest changes and improvements in a curriculum plan or a teaching plan that are based on the various approaches to knowledge and its structure and uses.

PREASSESSMENT

The purpose of the preassessment is to enable you to determine whether you already possess the performance competencies in curriculum planning that are listed under "Objectives," above.

1. Name three approaches to deciding what knowledge should be included in the school curriculum and how it should be organized.
2. Taking each of the three approaches to knowledge that you have named, tell how each would affect curriculum planning.
3. Select any curriculum plan of your choice, in any subject or at any school level, and examine it in the light of the approaches to knowledge you have named in number 1. You can do this by visiting a school, or by analyzing a written statement about some part of a school's curriculum or the instruction in one classroom.
4. Suggest changes or improvements in the curriculum plan as a result of your analysis.

Often, curriculum plans do not give conscious attention to the best approach to selecting and organizing knowledge. If that is true in the school you selected, suggest improvements on the basis of the nature of knowledge.

In answering number 3 of the preassessment, you might choose to analyze one of the approaches to the selection and organization of knowledge in the curriculum that are found in the following four articles in this book:

"Trends In The Teaching of Science," by Hounshell and West, in Section 5.
"Toward a Mankind Curriculum," by Gearing, in this section.
"Values Clarification in Junior High School," by Abramowitz and Macari, in Section 7.
"Steps Toward Relevance: An Interest-Centered Curriculum," by Ohme, in Section 8.

LEARNING ACTIVITIES

Articles in this section will assist you in identifying and understanding the various approaches to the selection, organization, and uses of knowledge in curriculum and instruction planning.

Other learning alternatives are suggested at the end of this section.

POSTASSESSMENT

After attempting the preassessment you may do one or more of the following:

1. Ask your instructor whether you are ready for a postassessment evaluation on knowledge and the curriculum. Most students will need further work on this curriculum base.
2. Read the articles on knowledge in this section and try to determine how the knowledge theories and research being discussed in each article should be considered in curriculum planning and teaching.
3. Choose additional activities and readings or films and videotapes from those listed at the end of this section.

4. Look for other films, books, or articles on knowledge that are in your library or media center.
5. Discuss the reading you have done and the films you have viewed with your fellow students. The key questions: How should the knowledge research and theories you've studied affect a school's curriculum? How should they be considered in planning for teaching?
6. When you are ready, ask your instructor for advice on a suitable postassessment for you for this topic. Satisfactory completion of number 5 under "Problems and Projects" at the end of this section might be one possibility. Or satisfactory written completion of the preassessment for this section, after completing other learning activities, might be a satisfactory postassessment. Consult your instructor about this. You can evaluate your ability to do either or both of these activities before seeing the instructor.

Structures In Learning

Jerome S. Bruner

Every subject has a structure, a rightness, a beauty. It is this structure that provides the underlying simplicity of things, and it is by learning its nature that we come to appreciate the intrinsic meaning of a subject.

Let me illustrate by reference to geography. Children in the fifth grade of a suburban school were about to study the geography of the Central states as part of a social studies unit. Previous units on the South-eastern states, taught by rote, had proved a bore. Could geography be taught as a rational discipline? Determined to find out, the teachers devised a unit in which students would have to figure out not only where things are located, but why they are there. This involves a sense of the structure of geography.

The children were given a map of the Central states in which only rivers, large bodies of water, agricultural products, and natural resources were shown. They were not allowed to consult their books. Their task was to find Chicago, "the largest city in the North Central states."

The argument got under way immediately. One child came up with the idea that Chicago must be on the junction of the three large lakes. No matter that at this point he did not know the names of the lakes—Huron, Superior, and Michigan—his theory was well reasoned. A big city produced a lot of products, and the easiest and most logical way to ship these products is by water.

But a second child rose immediately to the opposition. A big city needed lots of food, and he placed Chicago where there are corn and hogs—right in the middle of Iowa.

From *NEA Journal* LII, no. 3 (March 1963):26–27. Used by permission of the author and publisher.

A third child saw the issue more broadly—recognizing virtues in both previous arguments. He pointed out that large quantities of food can be grown in river valleys. Whether he had learned this from a previous social studies unit or from raising carrot seeds, we shall never know. If you had a river, he reasoned, you had not only food but transportation. He pointed to a spot on the map not far from St. Louis. "There is where Chicago ought to be." Would that graduate students would always do so well!

Not all the answers were so closely reasoned, though even the wild ones had about them a sense of the necessity involved in a city's location.

One argued, for example, that all American cities have skyscrapers, which require steel, so he placed Chicago in the middle of the Mesabi Range. At least he was thinking on his own, with a sense of the constraints imposed on the location of cities.

After forty-five minutes, the children were told they could pull down the "real" wall map (the one with names) and see where Chicago really is. After the map was down, each of the contending parties pointed out how close they had come to being right. Chicago had not been located. But the location of cities was no longer a matter of unthinking chance for this group of children.

What had the children learned? A way of thinking about geography, a way of dealing with its raw data. They had learned that there is some relationship between the requirements of living and man's habitat. If that is all they got out of their geography lesson, that is plenty. Did they remember which is Lake Huron? Lake Superior? Lake Michigan? Do you?

Teachers have asked me about "the new curricula" as though they were some special magic potion. They are nothing of the sort. The new curricula, like our little exercise in geography, are based on the fact that knowledge has an internal connectedness, a meaningfulness, and that for facts to be appreciated and understood and remembered, they must be fitted into that internal meaningful context.

The set of prime numbers is not some arbitrary nonsense. What can be said about quantities that cannot be arranged into multiple columns and rows? Discussing that will get you on to the structure of primes and factorability.

It often takes the deepest minds to discern the simplest structure in knowledge. For this reason if for no other, the great scholar and the great scientist and the greatly compassionate man are needed in the building of new curricula.

There is one other point. Our geographical example made much of discovery. What difference does discovery make in the learning of the young? First, let it be clear what the act of discovery entails. It is only rarely on the frontier of knowledge that new facts are "discovered" in the sense of being encountered, as Newton suggested, as "islands of truth in an uncharted sea of ignorance." Discovery, whether by a schoolboy going it on his own or by a scientist, is most often a matter of rearranging or transforming evidence in such a way that one is now enabled to go beyond the evidence to new insights. Discovery involves the finding of the right structure, the meaningfulness.

Consider now what benefits the child might derive from the experience of learning through his own discoveries. These benefits can be discussed in terms of increased intellectual potency, intrinsic rewards, useful learning techniques, and better memory processes.

For the child to develop *intellectual potency*, he must be encouraged to search out and find regularities and relationships in his environment. To do this, he needs to be armed with the expectancy that there is something for him to find and, once aroused by this expectancy, he must devise his own ways of searching and finding.

Emphasis on discovery in learning has the effect upon the learner of leading him to be a constructionist—to organize what he encounters in such a manner that he not only discovers regularity and relatedness, but also avoids the kind of information drift that fails to keep account of how the information will be used.

In speaking of *intrinsic motives* for learning (as opposed to extrinsic motives), it must be recognized that much of the problem in leading a child to effective cognitive activity is to free him from the immediate control of environmental punishments and rewards.

For example, studies show that children who seem to be early over-achievers in school are likely to be seekers after the "right way to do it" and that their capacity for transforming their learning into useful thought structures tends to be less than that of children merely achieving at levels predicted by intelligence tests.

The hypothesis drawn from these studies is that if a child is able to approach learning as a task of discovering something rather than "learning about it" he will tend to find a more personally meaningful reward in his own competency and self-achievement in the subject than he will find in the approval of others.

There are many ways of coming to the *techniques of injury*, or the heuristics of discovery. One of them is by careful study of the formalization of these techniques in logic, statistics, mathematics, and the like. If a child is going to pursue inquiry as an eventual way of life, particularly in the sciences, formal study is essential. Yet, whoever has taught kindergarten and the early primary grades (periods of intense inquiry) knows that an understanding of the formal aspect of inquiry is not sufficient or always possible.

Children appear to have a series of attitudes and activities they associate with inquiry. Rather than a formal approach to the relevance of variables in their search, they depend on their sense of what things among an ensemble of things "smell right" as being of the proper order of magnitude or scope of severity.

It is evident then that if children are to learn the working techniques of discovery, they must be afforded the opportunities of problem solving. The more they practice problem solving, the more likely they are to generalize what they learn into a style of inquiry that serves for any kind of task they may encounter. It is doubtful that anyone ever improves in the art and technique of inquiry by any other means than engaging in inquiry, or problem solving.

The first premise in a theory concerning the *improvement of memory processes* is that the principal problem of human memory is not storage, but retrieval. The premise may be inferred from the fact that recognition (i.e., recall with the aid of maximum prompts) is extraordinarily good in human beings—particularly in comparison to spontaneous recall when information must be recalled without external aids or prompts. The key to retrieval is organization.

There are myriad findings to indicate that any organization of information that reduces the collective complexity of material by imbedding it into a mental structure the child has constructed will make that material more accessible for retrieval. In sum, the child's very attitudes and activities that characterize "figuring out" or "discovering" things for himself also seem to have the effect of making material easier to remember.

If man's intellectual excellence is the most important among his perfections (as Maimonides, the great Hispanic-Judaic philosopher once said), then it is also the case that the most uniquely personal of all that man knows is that which he discovers for himself. What difference does it make when we encourage discovery in the young? It creates, as Maimonides would put it, a special and unique relation between knowledge possessed and the possessor.

Reducing the Behavior Gap

Mario D. Fantini
Gerald Weinstein

The acuteness of our present "crisis" with so-called disadvantaged learners is forcing educators to examine closely virtually everything they know about learning and teaching in an effort to provide more effective education for such children. This offers educators unusual opportunities to consider anew basic educational questions and to introduce needed innovation and reform which may benefit *all* learners.

We suggest, as a start, that a close look be given to an important goal of education—the encouragement of certain kinds of social behavior. We must all concede that there is a wide discrepancy between much of the behavior of individuals in society and what they have been taught in school. This behavior gap is wide enough to stimulate us to examine the few established channels in education for changing or affecting behavior.

Traditionally, these channels have been the subject matter per se of the school—the courses offered, the curriculum taught. An examination of these channels, however, confronts us with a startling realization: The objectives of the subject matter itself have become the ultimate aims of the school. These aims can satisfy only the more obvious objective of education—to provide the child with necessary academic skills. They cannot meet the need every child has for positive self-definition, for positive relationships with others, and for some control over what happens to him. What we require, therefore, is another channel which will lead to more consonance between education and the way people ought to behave in society.

In seeking greater consonance, we consider again our crisis clientele, the disadvantaged. It is they who are most acutely symptomatic of the problems confronting all learners. One of the most glaring deficiencies of their education is its lack of contact with them: "School is phony—it has nothing to do with life like we know it."

From *NEA Journal* LVII, no. 1 (January 1968):22–25. Used by permission of the author and publisher.

The person caught in the bind of attempting to make a difference with such students is the teacher. Most teachers and administrators who work with the disadvantaged ask, "How can we make contact with our children, make education more meaningful to them?" Hungry for answers, they flock to the many workshops and institutes recently made available by federal legislation, where they learn a great deal about the nature of the "culturally deprived child"—primarily in terms of *description*.

As one teacher explained, "I understand my children better now, but I still don't know what to do with them. I learned, for example, that one-third of my children probably come from broken homes and that this poses severe problems for the growing child. Now that I know this fact, what do I do to teach them better?"

The task now is to develop *prescriptions* that are functionally linked to these descriptions. The few rudimentary prescriptions that currently exist have not touched the core of the problem; they lack intrinsic relevance for many children and for the disadvantaged in particular. And it is relevance, the linking of what he learns to what he feels and cares about, that makes schooling meaningful to the child. We suggest that there are at least four levels in education on which relevance may be achieved:

1. Teaching procedures and learning styles should be matched. If disadvantaged children learn best in kinesthetic, concrete, inductive, and relatively nonverbal situations, their teachers should use methodology suited to this learning style. Thus, there would be a degree of relevance in whatever is being taught because of *how* it is being taught.
2. The material presented should either be within the learner's knowledge of his physical realm of experience or it should be easily connected with it. Relevance is achieved by making *what* is being taught germane to the child's knowledge and experience.
3. *What* is being taught and *how* it is being taught must not ignore the learner's *feelings* about his experiences. A teacher may plan to use a unit on city policemen because the learner "knows" them. If the child's experience with policemen has led him to fear them, however, learning may in fact be inhibited unless the teacher gives him a chance to express his real feelings and to think them through.
4. Teaching must not ignore the *concerns* of learners. Concerns are the deep-felt feelings and emotions, the persistent, persuasive anxieties and underlying uneasiness children have about themselves and their relationship to the world. Education gains relevance on this level if the teacher attempts to deal with the questions people most consistently ask themselves: "Who am I?" "What can I do about things?" "Who am I really connected to or concerned about?"

The most effective teaching utilizes all four areas of relevance. At present, educators are beginning to use the first two, but they must give more attention to levels three and four. It is this area of emotion, feeling, concern that is undernourished by the school in terms of its content.

The school is not helping to answer the spoken and unspoken questions that trouble all children: "Why do I feel the way I do?" "What made me do that?" "Do they think I'm any good?" Instead, the school asks children: "What do we mean by the Common Market?" "How are animals and people different?" Ignored in the process is one of the child's primary enigmas: "What does it have to do with *me*?" By directing themselves to supplying acceptable answers to this pervasive query, educators can make the connection between the child's basic emotions and feelings (affect) and his processing of information and developing of concepts from that information (cognition).

The relationship between cognition and affect cannot be too strongly stressed. Cognition appears to be a natural way of equipping the individual with the capability to deal with the basic drives that direct and control behavior. It should link those drives to his environment and provide him with the means to cope with the demands the environment makes. In other words, cognition should not only be functionally linked to affect; it should *serve* affect.

Although educators have hinted at such a relationship between affect and cognition, the functional linkage is seldom made. Too often, the school severely limits the relationship between the two with its very definition of *affect*. It considers affect only in terms of play, interests, classroom climate, readiness, teacher-pupil interaction, motivation, and the like, all of which it can utilize to induce the child to accept prescribed academic content.

Feelings are made to serve as basic hooks for linking outside content (curriculum) to inside natural dispositions. They are the tools used to get to the institutionalized cognitive content—the subject matter. In the standard educational process, cognitive development is equated with a "knowing about" a variety of academic subjects, rather than with an understanding of how these subjects may serve the student's needs. Too many instructional roads seem to lead to cognition as the end product.

Yet it is obvious that knowing something cognitively does not always result in behavior that follows on that knowing. This is because knowledge alone cannot influence total behavior. Moreover, all kinds of knowledge are not equally influential. The missing ingredient in this equation seems to be knowledge that is related to the affective or emotional world of the learner.

What most often prompts action, or behavior, is a feeling or emotion about something rather than knowledge per se. It may be that "knowing about" can prompt feeling, but it is feeling that generates behavior. *Unless knowledge relates to feeling, it is unlikely to affect behavior appreciably.* When education begins to make better use of this basic concept, we will have taken a giant step toward reducing the behavior gap—the discrepancy between how people behave and how they have been taught to behave.

It appears to us that the child's concerns, wants, interests, fears, anxieties, joys, and other emotions and reactions to the world contain in them seeds of intrinsic motivation and are legitimate content in their own right. Moreover, when we deal with this inner content, we tell the child, in effect, that he *does* know something. This is perhaps the most important factor in linking relevant content with self-concept. For when the school tells the child that the experience he brings with him—that is part of him, that *is* him—has nothing to do with the "worthwhile" knowledge and experience that the school intends to set before him, it is telling the child that he is worthless.

Every teacher is familiar with the marked increase in attentiveness when the class has embarked on a discussion of the problems the students are facing. This is because the students are relating what they are learning cognitively to their own concerns. We conclude, then, that *relevance becomes a matter of functionally linking extrinsic curriculum to these basic intrinsic concerns and feelings.*

One of our fundamental premises is that achieving curriculum relevance is largely a matter of allowing the intrinsic (affective) dimensions of learning to direct more of the extrinsic (cognitive) dimensions. This line of movement is crucial, but it is usually reversed, with the cognitive dictating what areas of affect should be included.

An illustration of this may be helpful. A science teacher decides that Johnny must learn the substance of matter, which is a cognitive task. The teacher may then ask himself, "What do I have to know about Johnny's concerns or feelings to help him learn about matter?" He would be attempting, then, to make Johnny's feelings facilitate the acquisition of this bit of knowledge.

On the other hand, if he is aware of the important connection to be made, he may start with: "I want to work with Johnny on his concerns and feelings, on the things that bother him. What in science can help him to cope better with them?" By approaching the material in this fashion, he would be starting with the affective; he would have selected a piece of cognition that can serve the affective. This is the sort of spiraling direction that we are suggesting.

Our observations force us to conclude that the school has virtually ignored the insistent demands of the child's feelings and instead assumes that if enough pressure is placed upon them, students will be motivated to adjust to an extrinsic body of content, the curriculum. The learner is asked to give up his inner content in favor of an outer content which too often bears little connection to him. This adjustment, although made, appears at best an exercise to be tolerated or a system to beat.

We are not suggesting that all the skills and subject matter which make up school curriculum be replaced or discarded. We *do* suggest that linking academic content to the affective drives of the child represents a more natural process, one that can increase learning ability as well as influence social behavior.

This in no way minimizes the role of cognition. On the contrary, cognition gains greater potency because of its instrumental relationship to the affective. Content so linked is less irrelevant or phony, for it is connected with the learner's concerns, the very foundation of his motivation and actions. Affect thus becomes the basic reality and gives to cognition real meaning.

It will clarify the relationship of skills and concepts curriculum to the programming of the affective realm if one visualizes a school with three interlocking tiers of content.

One tier contains the basic skills, information, and concepts that are generally agreed upon as essential building blocks for the intellectual development of the child. These include reading, computation, and writing skills, among others, as well as the basic information provided by such disciplines as social studies, science, language.

The second tier involves development of the learner's idiosyncratic interests and talents. This personal-discovery tier allows for individual creativity and exploration of interests.

The third tier consists of a group-inquiry curriculum dealing with social issues and problems (such as civil rights) that are related to the personal, and with common personal concerns. (We are *not* suggesting that the classroom become a place for solving individual emotional problems. When we speak of "personal" concerns, we do so only in terms of the threads of *common interest* that run through these issues.)

Inherent in this tier is the development of the individual's interpersonal relationships: identifying, articulating, and evaluating his feelings, concerns, and opinions; comparing and contrasting them with those of others in a group. Although the affective may be used in any of the tiers in terms of process, it is chiefly in this third tier that we see the affective used as fully developed content.

We are very much aware that what we suggest here is far from simple. To shift content emphasis from cognition to affect means that school people will have to search for new points of departure for subject matter approaches that have been hallowed by time and custom. But our swiftly changing society requires great flexibility and dynamism of its educational system. It requires that new channels be found, new ways be opened, to reach the deep-down sources that motivate the student to learn and are the primary factors in influencing his social behavior. If educators can meet these requirements, if they can link the student's feelings with what they hope to teach him, they will be making a good start in reducing the unacceptable gap between the way people behave and the way they have been taught to behave.

The Process of Education Reconsidered

Jerome S. Bruner

Ten years have passed since The Process of Education[1] was published—a decade of enormous change in the perspective and emphasis of educational reform. I am torn between beginning my account as an archaeologist reconstructing that period by its products, or beginning with a message of revolutionary import. I shall moderate both impulses and begin with a bit of archaeology and show how my excavations lead me to a certain revolutionary zeal.

PROLOGUE ON THE PAST

Let me reconstruct the period in which The Process of Education came into being. The year 1959 was a time of great concern over the intellectual aimlessness of our schools. Great strides had been made in many fields of knowledge, and

From "The Process of Education Reconsidered." In: Robert R. Leeper, editor. Dare to Care/Dare to Act. Washington, D.C.: Association for Supervison and Curriculum Development, 1971, pp. 19–30. Reprinted with permission of the Association for Supervision and Curriculum Development and Jerome S. Bruner. Copyright © 1972 by the Association for Supervision and Curriculum Development.
[1] Jerome S. Bruner. The Process of Education. Cambridge, Massachusetts: Harvard University Press, 1960. 97 pp.

these advances were not being reflected in what was taught in our schools. A huge gap had grown between what might be called the head and the tail of the academic procession. There was great fear, particularly that we were not producing enough scientists and engineers.

It was the period, you will recall, shortly after Sputnik. The great problem faced by some of my colleagues in Cambridge, Massachusetts, at the time was that modern physics and mathematics were not represented in the curriculum, yet many of the decisions that society had to make were premised on being able to understand modern science. Something had to be done to assure that the ordinary decision maker within the society would have a sound basis for decision. The task was to get started on the teaching of science and, later, other subjects. They were innocent days; but beware such judgments rendered in retrospect. At worst, the early period suffered an excess of rationalism.

The prevailing notion was that if you understood the structure of knowledge, that understanding would then permit you to go ahead on your own; you did not need to encounter everything in nature in order to know nature, but by understanding some deep principles, you could extrapolate to the particulars as needed. Knowing was a canny strategy whereby you could know a great deal about a lot of things while keeping very little in mind.

This view essentially opened the possibility that those who understood a field well—the practitioners of the field—could work with teachers to produce new curricula. For the first time in the modern age, the acme of scholarship, even in our great research institutes and universities, was to convert knowledge into pedagogy, to turn it back to aid the learning of the young. It was a brave idea and a noble one, for all its pitfalls. It is an idea that still bears close scrutiny, and we shall give it some later.

It was this point of view that emerged from the famous Woods Hole conference on improving education in science (the impetus and inspiration for *The Process of Education*). No curriculum project in the first five years after that was worth its salt unless it could sport a Nobel laureate or two on its letterhead!

The rational structuralism of Woods Hole had its internal counterpoise in intuitionism—the espousal of good guessing, of courage to make leaps, to go a long way on a little. It was mind at its best, being active, extrapolative, innovative, going from something firmly held to areas which were not so firmly known in order to have a basis for test.

Of course, everybody knew that good teachers always have encouraged such use of mind. But perhaps good teachers were being driven underground by the prevailing literalism. It is hard not to wonder, reading Plato's *Meno*, how it is that the naïve slave boy in the famous dialogue with Socrates turns out to be so enormously expert in geometry. Is it a put-on by Plato—to tease people into recognizing how far a learner can go if you provide the right opportunity to make guesses, if you structure the information for him to enable him to take off on his own? It is a wedding of rationalism and intuition, arranged by a canny teacher.

At Woods Hole and after there was also a great emphasis on active learning, poking into things yourself, an emphasis on active discovery rather than upon the passive consumption of knowledge. It too derived from the idea that making things one's own was an activity that would get things structured in one's own way rather than as in the book. Some enthusiasts ran away with the idea of the "discovery method," declaring that one should even discover the names of the constellations! It is a modest idea, but with profound consequences, some of which were not understood at the time—and we shall come back to it.

During the early sixties, in various projects, it was discovered again and again how difficult it was to get to the limit of children's competence when the teaching was good. It was Socrates and the slave boy constantly being replayed. No wonder then that we concluded that any subject could be taught in some honest form to any child at any stage in his development. This did not necessarily mean that it could be taught in its final form, but it did mean that basically there was a courteous translation that could reduce ideas to a form that young students could grasp. Not to provide such translation was discourteous to them. The pursuit of this ideal was probably the most important outcome of the great period of curriculum building in the sixties.

With all of this there went a spirit and attitude toward students. The learner was not one kind of person, the scientist or historian another kind. The schoolboy learning physics did so as a physicist rather than as a consumer of some facts wrapped in what came to be called at Woods Hole a "middle language." A middle language talks about the subject rather than talking the subject.

I remember hearing the following joke at the time, which illustrates how we wanted learners to approach a subject like physics—with humor, with gaiety, with abandon, taking the thing apart, putting it back together again.

A student at the University of Chicago was taking an examination in introductory physics. There is a question which reads, "You have a barometer. Your task is to find the height of such and such a building in central Chicago. How do you proceed?"

The student answers, "There are several ways of proceeding. One is to go to the top of the building, station a confederate below, hold the barometer over the edge with your handkerchief poised to signal and, as you drop the barometer, wave your handkerchief. Your confederate starts a stop watch at the signal, timing the fall of the barometer until it hits the ground. By the use of a simple correction for the friction of the atmosphere, the height of the building is easily figured by the duration of the fall.

"Unfortunately, this method requires destruction of the barometer and thus precludes a test of reliability. Therefore, a second method may be tried, although it is a bit more strenuous. Measure the length of the barometer, then lay it end over end over end as you ascend the stairway of the building to be measured. Then multiply the length of the barometer by the number of rotations of the barometer.

"Still another technique is available. Station a man of known height on top of the building, holding the barometer up at arm's length. Station a confederate true north of the building. Wait for Local Apparent Noon and determine the extreme limit of the shadow of the barometer to the nearest centimeter and the Zone Time for Local Apparent Noon that day. Determine the day of the year and the latitude of the building. Consult a nautical almanac for sun's elevation at Local Apparent Noon at that latitude. Assuming the building stands upright, you now have two angles and the length between them and the rest is simple geometry.

"While this is highly accurate, it may take somewhat longer than you have time for. It is suggested that the following procedure be used by those with limited time. Take the barometer to the building. Proceed to the basement where you will find a door marked 'Superintendent.' Push the doorbell. It will be answered by the superintendent. Say to him, 'I have a barometer here that is worth $12.75. I will give it to you if you will tell me the height of this building.' "

That is good science! It also embodies a proper respect for students. It was our hope that we could produce students like this—capable of intuition, wit, and lighthearted seriousness. Not a bad ideal.

I recall a dark day on Cape Cod, the day after the Woods Hole conference ended. It was raining. We, the Steering Committee, thought surely the whole enterprise had been wrongly conceived. We would end, we feared, by turning the Educational Establishment against us and science. Then *The Process of Education* was published. It was acclaimed. Acclaim is very hard to cope with if you have business in mind; for once something is acclaimed it can be ignored in a noble way. The acclaim from which we suffered was that each reader-teacher picked the part he liked best and proclaimed it was exactly what *he* was doing! But the period of being acclaimed into impotence passed as soon as new curricula began to appear.

Producing curriculum turned out to be not quite as we academics had thought! Something a bit strained would happen when one caused to work together a most gifted and experienced teacher and an equally gifted and experienced scientist, historian, or scholar. There was much to be learned on both sides and the process was slow and decisions had to be made about the level at which one wanted to pitch the effort—the college-bound, the "average," the slum kid?

There were aspects of the undertaking that we had not counted on—mostly after the production. One was the problem of bureaucracy in education, the subject of an entire yearbook recently published by the Association for Supervision and Curriculum Development[2]—the issue of adoption, of distribution of materials, and so forth. A second was an even deeper problem: the training of teachers to use curricula. Both of these problems remain unresolved—the first constrained by fiscal difficulties, the second by the genuinely puzzling questions of teacher recruitment, training, and supervision. I cannot pretend to competence in these areas.

Let me insert here a few words about the political uses to which *The Process of Education* has been put. The book has been translated into 21 languages. The first language into which it was translated was Russian, and I gather from Russian friends that it is a very good translation indeed and that it has had a large sale. Why did the Russians take the trouble? It soon became clear that they had a very good if surprising reason. This was the period of crucial debate between the Stalinists on the one side and the new reformers under Khrushchev on the other. The reformers were urging that it was not enough to present socialist realism. To interest the learner, one had to lead him to discover it in his own way. Moreover, the guarantee against dogmatism was intuition. Finally, the Russians were themselves rejecting easy ideas about readiness and they welcomed allies. They had discovered earlier that readiness was a product of middle class upbringing.

In Italy, ironically, the book was being used in a battle by the moderate Left, against doctrinaire Marxist educators on the one side and against traditionalists on the other who wanted to maintain a classical curriculum. Since school reform

[2] Vernon F. Haubrich, editor. *Freedom, Bureaucracy, & Schooling.* 1971 Yearbook. Washington, D.C.: Association for Supervision and Curriculum Development, 1971. 293 pp.

is close to the heart of Italian political debate, the Italian translation is very much treated as a political as well as pedagogical tract.

In Japan there is a distinction between the "wet" and the "dry." "Wet" refers to the traditionally Japanese; "dry" to Westernizing. The Japanese translation was used by adherents of the "dry" group to make the point that Western education did not simply mean the teaching of utilitarian subjects, that it also respected mind and intuition, that there were structures worthy of mastery whether by a "wet" or "dry" mind. The sale in Japan was enormous.

The Process of Education is available in Hebrew and in Arabic. When I asked Israelis why they had translated it they said, "Because it works." My Roumanian translator said the book was very much in the spirit of contemporary intellectual trends there. I shall be interested to know whether Husak's government has suppressed the translations into Czech and Slovak. And I am bemused that there is no French translation! What an extraordinary venture a book of this sort is. If I had ever doubted that education is a crucial arm of ideology, I would have been well taught by the foreign editions.

PRESENT AND FUTURE

So much for the archaeology. What I should like to do now is shift to other matters more concerned with present and future.

The movement of which *The Process of Education* was a part was based on a formula of faith: that learning was what students wanted to do, that they wanted to achieve an expertise in some particular subject matter. Their motivation was taken for granted. It also accepted the tacit assumption that everybody who came to these curricula in the schools already had been the beneficiary of the middle class hidden curricula that taught them analytic skills and launched them in the traditionally intellectual use of mind.

Failure to question these assumptions has, of course, caused much grief to all of us. Let me quote from the preface of a book I have just written, *The Relevance of Education*:

> This book is built around essays written between 1964 and 1970, years of deep and tumultuous change. They were disturbing years. They had an impact in their own right, amplified by my increasingly strong involvement during the period with very young human beings. These were my "subjects" in experiments and observations. The contrast between the exterior social turbulence and the human helplessness I was studying kept imposing itself.
>
> The period of these essays is the period of the elaboration of youth culture, with its concomitant revolt against "establishment" schooling. It extends from Berkeley to Columbia, through the Harvard bust and the Sorbonne riots, to the Prague spring and summer, and the beginnings of the long and cruel winter that followed. In our own universities, we have gone from the salad days of "new colleges" to the present "hard line" of so many faculties. The young began the period in political activism; then there was the sharp fire of a new extremism; now, in the early winter of 1971, it is a new disengagement.
>
> Through the turmoil and idealism of these years has run a theme of

"naturalness," of "spontaneity," of the immediacy of learning through direct encounter. A distrust of traditional ways has brought into question whether schools as such might not be part of the problem—rather than a solution to the problem of education. American educational reform in the early '60s was concerned principally with the reconstruction of curriculum. The ideal was clarity and self-direction of intellect in the use of modern knowledge.

There were brave efforts and successful ones in mathematics and physics, in chemistry and biology, and even in the behavioral sciences. The faltering of the humanists at this time was puzzling, though it later became clearer. A revision of the humanities involved too many explosive issues.

In the second half of the decade, the period of these essays, deeper doubts began to develop. Did revision of curriculum suffice, or was a more fundamental restructuring of the entire educational system in order? Plainly, the origins of the doubt go deep and far back into the changing culture and technology of our times. But our ruinous and cruel war in Vietnam led many who would have remained complacent to question our practices and priorities. How could a society be so enormously wealthy, yet so enormously and callously destructive, while professing idealism? How wage a war in the name of a generous way of life, while our own way of life included urban ghettos, a culture of poverty and racism.

We looked afresh at the appalling effects of poverty and racism on the lives of children, and the extent to which schools had become instruments of the evil forces in our society. Eloquent books like Jonathan Kozol's *Death at an Early Age*[3] began to appear.

It was the black community that first sought "free schools," freedom schools. They were to help black identity, to give a sense of control back to the community. Just as the civil rights movement provided models for social protest at large, so, too, the drive for free schools for the children of the black poor produced a counterpart response in the intellectual, middle-class community. The revolt against the system very quickly came to include the educational establishment. Generous-minded men like Ivan Illich and Paul Goodman, inveighing against the deadening bureaucratic hold of teachers and educational administrators, voiced a new romanticism: salvation by spontaneity, disestablish the established schools. It was a view that, as we know, took immediate root in the "in" youth culture.

But if romanticism was solace for some, despair was the order for others. By the spring of 1970, when Elizabeth Hall, one of the editors of *Psychology Today*, asked me what I thought about American education at the moment, all I could answer was that it had passed into a state of crisis. It had failed to respond to changing social needs, lagging behind rather than leading. My work on early education and social class, for example, had convinced me that the educational system was, in effect, our way of maintaining a class system—a group at the bottom. It crippled the capacity of children in the lowest socioeconomic quarter of the population to participate at full power in the society, and it did so early and effectively.

It is not surprising then that this little volume, arranged roughly in chronological order, should begin with an essay that bears the title, "The

[3] Jonathan Kozol. *Death at an Early Age: The Destruction of the Hearts and Minds of Negro Children in the Boston Public Schools*. Boston, Massachusetts: Houghton Mifflin Company, 1967. 240 pp.

Perfectibility of Intellect," vintage 1965, and end with one called "Poverty and Childhood," a product of 1970.[4]

And so a half-decade passed. By 1970 the concern was no longer to change schools from within by curriculum, but to refit them altogether to the needs of society, to change them as institutions. It is no longer reform but revolution that has come to challenge us. And it is not so plain what is the role of the academic in such an enterprise.

TO ACTIVATE THE LEARNER

What would one do now? What would be the pattern at a Woods Hole conference in 1971? It would not be in Woods Hole, in that once rural, coastal setting. More likely, we would gather in the heart of a great city. The task would center around the dispossession of the children of the poor and the alienation of the middle class child. In some crucial respect, the medium would surely be the message: the school, not the curriculum, or the society and not even the school. And in my view, through my perspective, the issues would have to do with how one gives back initiative and a sense of potency, how one activates to tempt one to want to learn again. When that is accomplished, then curriculum becomes an issue again—curriculum not as a subject but as an approach to learning and using knowledge.

The rest of what I have to say concerns these issues—of activating a learner, of giving him his full sense of intent and initiative.

Consider first getting people to want to learn something, how to make the learning enterprise sustained and compelling. In a recent article in the *Saturday Review*, I proposed that it is possible to conceive of a Monday-Wednesday-Friday curriculum covering the standard topics, and a Tuesday-Thursday and indeed Saturday way of doing things in which immediate and compelling concerns are given the central place—activism? Let them on Tuesdays and Thursdays prepare "briefs" in behalf of their views, make a case for things they care about. Let them prepare plans of action, whether they be on issues in the school, on the local scene, or whatever. What is important is to learn to bring all one's resources to bear on something that matters to you now.

These are the times for the migratory questions that wander on long after their answers are forgotten, just because they are great questions. And there must be more time for the expressive elements—the encounters, the hates, the loves, the feelings. All this need not be antic nor need it all be in the manner of presenting one's case. I have seen experiments using improvisational theatre, drama, film, and the like, to teach and to question history, projects in which one learns to construe events through different sets of eyes. To what an extraordinary extent do films and plays of the contemporary scene matter in this! Ionesco or Pirandello are not so much concerned with absurdity but with how not to be caught with the obvious. This is not something to be prescribed. But it can surely be explored: how it is we are perplexed by the texture of the society in which we live.

[4] Jerome S. Bruner. *The Relevance of Education.* Anita Gil, editor. New York: W. W. Norton & Company, Inc., 1971 © by Jerome S. Bruner.

An extraordinary, moving book called *Letter to a Teacher; Schoolboys of Barbiana*[5] is about a contemporary Tuscan hill town in Italy. The children there had failed so many times in so many ways in school that they had given up generation after generation—consigned to unskilled labor. A priest came to the parish. He started a school in which nobody was to fail, a school in which it was expected that everybody had to pass. It was everyone's responsibility to see that everybody in the class mastered the lesson before anybody could go on to the next lesson.

A community is a powerful force for effective learning. Students, when encouraged, are tremendously helpful to each other. They are like a cell, a revolutionary cell. It is the cell in which mutual learning and instruction can occur, a unit within a classroom with its own sense of compassion and responsibility for its members.

These were matters we did not do enough with at Woods Hole. We did not think about mutuality because we were stuck on the idea of curriculum—in spite of the fact that our laboratories and our very curriculum projects were set up rather like communes!

Inevitably, somebody will ask, "Well, how are you going to grade them?" You might also ask, "How in the world are you going to grade all of these distinguished colleagues who write collaborative articles among themselves and their graduate students?"

There is a group of high school girls in Concord, Massachusetts, who are tutoring in the local elementary school. Those who are acquainted with cross-age tutoring will know, as I discovered, the extent to which those who help are helped, that being a teacher makes one a better learner. But should it be such a surprise? Is this not what is meant by passing on the culture?

What we say of the peer group and the near-peer group holds for the different age levels within the society. For in some deep way, what is needed is the reestablishment of a "learning community" beyond formal school which, as now constituted, is far too isolating. This is not done just by removing the barriers between elementary and high school students or by establishing a lifetime relationship to one's college where one can return for sustenance and become part of a broader learning community again. Massachusetts Institute of Technology pronounced a few years ago that an engineer's education is obsolete after five years, so he must be brought back to bring him up to date. Let him come back, yes, but let the price of admission be that he discharge his obligation then to those who are just beginning—teacher, tutor, guide, other?

Finally I would like to explore, in the interest of relevance, whether we might not recapture something of the old notion of vocation, of ways of life, or—to use the expression of so many undergraduates today—of "life styles." I am impressed with contemporary concern for life styles. I have just finished a term as Master of Currier House, a Radcliffe-Harvard House, and I assure you of the genuineness of this concern. But I am appalled that it is rarely translated into what one *does* with a life style, the kind of vocation and livelihood in which we can express it.

Could it be that in our stratified and fragmented society, our students sim-

---

[5] *Letter to a Teacher; Schoolboys of Barbiana.* Translated by Nora Rossi and Tom Cole. New York: Random House, Inc., 1970.

ply do not know about local grocers and their styles, local doctors and theirs, local taxi drivers and theirs, local political activists and theirs? And don't forget the styles of local bookies, aspiring actresses, or unmarried mothers. No, I really believe that our young have become so isolated that they do *not* know the roles available in the society and the variety of styles in which they are played. I would urge that we find some way of connecting the diversity of the society to the phenomenon of school, to keep the latter from becoming so isolated and the former so suspicious.

Finally, let me add one last thing not directly connected with *The Process of Education*, but a problem of the first order today. One cannot ignore this problem in talking of education. We shall kill ourselves, as a society and as human beings, unless we direct our efforts to redressing the deep, deep wounds that we inflict on the poor, the outcast, those who somehow do not fit within our caste system—be they black, or dispossessed in any way. If there is one thing that has come out of our work with the very young, it is the extent to which "being out," not having a chance as an adult, or as a parent, very quickly reflects itself in loss of hope in the child. As early as the second or third year, a child begins to reflect this loss of hope.

When any group is robbed of its legitimate aspiration, its members will aspire desperately and by means that outrage the broader society, though the means are efforts to sustain or regain dignity. Inequity cannot be altered by education alone, another lesson we have learned in the past decade. The impact of poverty is usually transmitted through the school as well. Poverty cannot be counteracted by words unless there are also jobs and opportunities available to express society's confidence in what is possible after school.

There must be ways in which we can think honestly of reformulation of the institutions into which our schools, as one integral part, fit. Surely it requires that we redirect our resources, reorder our priorities, redefine our national effort, and come to terms with the fact that we have a deep and brutal racism in us—in all of us. We must learn how to cope with that. The young know this fact. They often despise our failure to talk about racism and our other difficulties. History may well side with them.

In the end, we must finally appreciate that education is not a neutral subject, nor is it an isolated subject. It is a deeply political issue in which we guarantee a future for someone; and, frequently, in guaranteeing a future for someone, we deal somebody else out. If I had my choice now, in terms of a curriculum project for the seventies, it would be to find the means whereby we could bring society back to its sense of values and priorities in life. I believe I would be quite satisfied to declare, if not a moratorium, then something of a de-emphasis on matters that have to do with the structure of history, the structure of physics, the nature of mathematical consistency, and deal with curriculum rather in the context of the problems that face us. We might better concern ourselves with how those problems can be solved, not just by practical action, but by putting knowledge, wherever we find it and in whatever form we find it, to work in these massive tasks. We might put vocation and intention back into the process of education, much more firmly than we had it there before.

A decade later, we realize that *The Process of Education* was the beginning of a revolution, and one cannot yet know how far it will go. Reform of curriculum is not enough. Reform of the school is probably not enough. The issue is one of man's capacity for creating a culture, society, and technology that not only feed him but keep him caring and belonging.

Conceptions of Knowledge: Their Significance for the Curriculum

Arno A. Bellack

In current debates about what should be taught in the schools, the "conventional wisdom" long honored in pedagogical circles about the nature of knowledge and the role of knowledge in the curriculum is being called into question. The enemy of conventional wisdom, Professor Galbraith (the originator of that felicitous term) tells us, is the march of events. The fatal blow comes when conventional ideas fail to deal with new conditions and problems to which obsolescence has made them clearly inapplicable. The march of events in the world at large that is placing new demands on the schools, and in the world of scholarship that is making available new knowledge in great quantities is forcing us to re-examine our ideas about the nature of knowledge and its place in the instructional program.

It is well to remind ourselves that the current debates about knowledge and the curriculum are not over the question of whether knowledge is relevant to the school's task. Although there are different views as to what knowledge should be taught and how it is to be taught, most educators would agree that knowledge is the stock in trade of the school. Few would deny that the fields of organized inquiry are significant aspects of our culture that the school is uniquely equipped to introduce to students. No other agency or institution in our society has the personnel or other resources to perform this function effectively. Unless students become acquainted with these important facets of the culture in school it is doubtful that they will learn about them elsewhere, at least not so well.

It is important to stress this at the outset, for today one frequently hears the view expressed that educationists responsible for planning the curriculum of the elementary and secondary schools have only recently, and belatedly, come to recognize that knowledge is a significant factor in teaching and in preparation for teaching. A brief glance at the historical development of the school curriculum should help to set the record straight on this score. Throughout our history, most elementary and secondary programs have been organized around the time-honored

From *The Nature of Knowledge: Implications for the Education of Teachers*, William Jenkins, ed. (Milwaukee: University of Wisconsin-Milwaukee, 1962), pp. 42–52. Used by permission of the author and publisher.

school subjects, even during the heyday of progressivism in the decades prior to World War II. The progressives too had a place for knowledge in their scheme of things: the curriculum was to be organized around personal and social problems, and the academic disciplines were to serve as resources in dealing with these problems. It was this central idea that attracted the sympathies of many educators who questioned the ability of traditional school to provide an effective way of preparing students to face the increasingly complex problems of modern living.

If then the fields of knowledge are no strangers to curriculum theory and practice, what is significantly different in contemporary efforts to redefine the role of knowledge in the curriculum? The activities and proposals of the projects in physics, chemistry, biology, mathematics, economics, geography, and English reveal certain common viewpoints and approaches.

1. Their aim is to introduce students to the universe of discourse, or more grandly, the ways of life, represented by the fields of scholarship. Students are to engage in activities patterned after those of the practicing physicist, chemist, or economist. Whereas formerly factual and descriptive content of the various fields was stressed, now the emphasis is on the basic concepts and conceptual relationships that scholars in the various fields use as intellectual tools to analyze and order their data.

2. Although most of the projects have developed programs for specific groups of students, particularly the college-bound, the view is widely held that similar approaches should be followed with all students. On this view, the disciplines are significant not only for the specialist, but for the average man as well. The aim is excellence in intellectual affairs not only for the academically talented, but for all students at levels commensurate with their ability.

3. Furthermore, these projects attach great importance to the participation of university scholars in continuing revision of the curriculum. Through such collaboration, schools are to keep their programs up to date with recent developments in university research.

The situation developing in the elementary and secondary schools thus begins to reflect, at least to some degree, the state of affairs in the universities with respect to the development and organization of knowledge, which Professor John Randall has described in this way:

> As reflected in the microcosm of the modern university, the world of knowledge has today become radically plural. It is a world of many different knowledges, pursued in varied ways to diverse ends. These many inquiries are normally carried on with little thought for their relation to each other. The student of John Donne's poetry, the student of the structure of the atom—each gives little enough attention to what the others are doing, and none at all to any total picture of anything. Each has his own goals, his own methods, his own language for talking about what he is doing and what he has discovered. Each seems happiest when left to his own devices, glad indeed if he can keep others from treading on his toes. Each is convinced that what he himself is doing is worthwhile. But none has too much respect for the others, though he is willing enough to tolerate them. They have all too little understanding of each other's pursuits—what they are try-

ing to do, how they are doing it, and what they really mean when they talk about it.[1]

The projects sponsored by the various curriculum commissions reflect this thoroughgoing diversity. Proposals for the teaching of biology, chemistry, and physics have, to the present time, been developed with little or no relationship to each other. The project in economics was unrelated to the other social sciences, although the Task Force recognized that these fields could also marshall cogent arguments for a place in the school program. In the field of English, three domains have been staked out: language, literature, and composition. Only in mathematics has there been a disposition to view the field as a whole, but this too is a reflection of developments within the field of mathematics at the highest levels of scholarship.

I emphasize this pluralism in the academic world not to deplore it, but to call attention to the problem that it presents for those who are concerned with the organization of the total curriculum. For there is not only the question of the structures of the individual disciplines, but also the question of the structure of the curriculum as a whole within which the fields of knowledge find their place. The problem can be very simply stated, if not easily solved: What general scheme of the curriculum can be developed so that autonomy of the parts does not result in anarchy in the program as a whole? This is one of two questions I propose to discuss briefly this morning.

The second question grows out of the proposal that students be introduced to the ways of thinking associated with the various disciplines in such fashion that they in fact become physicists, chemists, or economists. Professor Bruner puts it this way:

> What a scientist does at his desk or in his laboratory, what a literary critic does in reading a poem, are of the same order as what anybody else does when he is engaged in like activities—if he is to achieve understanding. The difference is in degree, not in kind. The schoolboy learning physics is a physicist.[2]

I take it this does not mean that the goal of general education is to train all students as specialists in mathematics, geography, history, or whatever other subjects they might study. Rather, the goal is to make available to students the intellectual and aesthetic resources of their culture in such a way that they become guides for intelligent action and help students create meaning and order out of the tangled world in which they find themselves. Professor Bestor, who scarcely qualifies as an advocate of education for life adjustment, has made this same point:

> The modern scientist or the modern scholar knows the delight of intellectual endeavor for its own sake, and he rightly resents the undervaluing of this motive. But when all is said and done he knows that the principal value to society of a man's cultivating the power of abstract thought is that he is thereby enabled to deal more effectively with the insistent problems

[1] John H. Randall, Jr., "The World to be Unified," in Lewis Leary, ed., *The Unity of Knowledge* (Garden City: Doubleday & Company, 1955), p. 63.
[2] Jerome Bruner, *The Process of Education* (Cambridge: Harvard University Press, 1960), p. 14.

of modern life. . . . The basic argument for the intellectual disciplines in the education is not that they lift a man's spirits above the world, but that they equip his mind to enter the world and perform its tasks.[3]

How is this widely accepted objective to be realized? Is the ability to relate what is learned in school to the world of human affairs to come as an inevitable by-product of the study of the disciplines, or must teachers give explicit attention to helping students see the relevance of such study for their own lives as individuals, citizens, and workers? This is the second issue I propose to discuss briefly.

KNOWLEDGE AND THE DESIGN OF THE CURRICULUM

When we look beyond the structures of the disciplines and ask about the structure of the curriculum within which the various fields of study take their places, we face a problem of the greatest complexity. What knowledge from the vast array of intellectual resources shall the schools teach? The accumulated and ever-growing knowledge in all fields has reached such proportions that comprehensive grasp of the total range of knowledge is out of the question for any one individual. The question raised by Spencer a hundred years ago, "What knowledge is of the most worth?" is even more relevant today than it was in his time. Indeed, it is an ever-renewed problem, one that apparently every generation has to solve over again for itself. Given the limited time and capacity of the school, what shall the schools teach to secure results that can be generalized beyond the immediate situation in which the learning takes place?

The progressives, taking their cue from Dewey, found their answer to this question in the "scientific method" (or the "method of intelligence" as it was frequently labeled) that was assumed to characterize all types of rational, intelligent activity in academic pursuits and in practical affairs as well. The problem-solving method came to be viewed as the basic ingredient in programs of general education.

But by no means is there agreement among scientists that there is a single all-encompassing set of procedures, even in the natural sciences, as assumed by those who talk about *the* scientific method. There seems to be little warrant for assuming that there is one over-arching method sufficiently flexible and inclusive to deal with problems in the various scientific fields, to say nothing of the arts, crafts, and applied areas. Indeed, as we have already noted, the intellectual world today is characterized by a plurality of methods and conceptual schemes developed by the disciplines to deal with problems within their individual spheres. Analysis of the various disciplines reveals a wide range of organization and intellectual methods associated with them. Instead of a unity of method or a single universe of discourse, we are confronted with a vast confederation of separate areas of study. Modes of thinking and analysis differ from field to field, and even from problem to problem within the same field.

The heterogeneous character of the resources that are a part of the culture is a fact of major significance for the curriculum builder. We would do well

[3] Arthur Bestor, *Educational Wastelands* (Urbana: University of Illinois Press, 1953), p. 15.

frankly to recognize this and make a place in our programs for the variety of organizations and logical orders that characterize the fields of knowledge on which we draw in building the curriculum. But *what* knowledge deserves a place in the curriculum? Let us consider two contrasting approaches to the curriculum that involve two conceptions of knowledge, both of which are significant for our purposes here.

But first we must take notice of the viewpoint recently expressed by a prominent Harvard historian, Oscar Handlin. Professor Handlin contends that the expansion of knowledge and the range of backgrounds and abilities of students now required to attend school make it futile to attempt to plan a program of common knowledge for all. Writing in the September, 1961, issue of *The Atlantic*, he argues that any effort "to define a body of knowledge that every educated man ought to have is futile and needless. By what criteria can we tell the boys and girls who enter high school next year to take French or Latin rather than German and Russian, Medieval rather than Oriental history, physics rather than chemistry? . . . The high school cannot endow its students with everything they ought to know. It can only equip them to get what they need as they come to recognize the need for it." And how is the school to go about doing this? "It ought to impart to its students the ability to communicate and to be communicated with, and it ought to introduce them to the quantitative techniques on which modern science and technology rest. If it succeeds in these tasks, it will give its graduates the equipment for future learning." Language and mathematics are thus to be required of all, with the rest of the curriculum tailor-made for each student on the basis of interests and ability.[4]

This viewpoint seems to me to be a counsel of despair that need not delay us long in our search for an answer to the question: What shall we teach? Without denying the importance of language and mathematics, other fields have equally legitimate claims to a place in the program of studies for all students.

The first approach I would like to have us examine briefly takes seriously the responsibility of the school to introduce students to the fundamental intellectual resources of their culture. These resources, communicated in meaningful fashion to succeeding generations, provide indispensable working capital in the management of human affairs and serve as the foundation from which continued progress is made. The supporters of this viewpoint are individuals and groups representing widely divergent backgrounds and philosophical outlooks. Nevertheless, there is remarkable unanimity among them when it comes to identifying the disciplines or broad groupings of disciplines that represent the basic cultural interests of our society. A few illustrations will make clear the nature of this approach.

Dr. Conant suggests that the curriculum in its general phases should include three major areas of study: (1) the humanities (art and literature); (2) the study of man (the social sciences), with history and philosophy the connecting links between these fields and the humanities; and (3) the natural sciences and mathematics.[5]

Professor Broudy contends that all students need knowledge that helps them

---

[4] Oscar Handlin, "Live Students and Dead Education," *The Atlantic*, September, 1961, pp. 32–33.
[5] James B. Conant, *Education in a Divided World* (Cambridge: Harvard University Press, 1948), chapters 5, 6, 7.

understand their relationships to the physical environment, the social environment and the environment of their own psychic self. His curriculum is therefore organized around three major areas: (1) the natural sciences (including mathematics); (2) the social sciences; and (3) living with the self or self-science (which includes literature, fine arts, and philosophy).[6]

The Council for Basic Education proposes a curriculum organized around five groupings with the constituent fields taught as separate subjects: (1) citizenship, history, geography; (2) composition and literature; (3) languages; (4) mathematics and science; (5) art, music, speech and philosophy.[7]

Sidney Hook outlines a program of studies that includes: (1) sciences and mathematics; (2) social sciences; (3) philosophy and logic; (4) language and literature; (5) art and music.[8]

Other illustrations might be cited; but these four, representing very different philosophical and educational orientations, are sufficient to show that there is substantial agreement regarding the disciplines and broad areas to be included in the program for all students: the natural sciences, mathematics, social sciences, and humanities. The primary differences among them have to do with the extent to which these areas of knowledge should be taught as separate fields or as broad areas of study.

The second approach views the world of ideas to which students are to be introduced from a different perspective, one concerned primarily with "the principal modes of intellectual activity." In making suggestions for the reform of general education in British secondary schools, Professor Peterson of Oxford University urges that educators cease thinking of general education in terms of "general knowledge":

> It is not a sign that a man lacks general education if he does not know the date of The Treaty of Utrecht, the latitude of Singapore, the formula for nitro-glycerine or the author of the Four Quartets. It does denote a lack of general education if he cares nothing for any of the arts, confuses a moral judgment with an aesthetic judgment, interprets the actions of Asian political leaders in terms of nineteenth century English parliamentarianism or believes that the existence of God has been scientifically disproved.[9]

He urges therefore that the British secondary schools devise programs of general education not in terms of wide general knowledge, but in terms of general development in the main modes of intellectual activity, of which he identifies four: the logical, the empirical, the moral, the aesthetic. These different modes of thought are associated with different uses of language. For example, the empirical mode has to do with statements about the world based on our experience of it. The moral and the aesthetic are concerned with statements of preferences, evaluations, and judgments of the good and the evil, the beautiful and the ugly, the

[6] Harry H. Broudy, Building a Philosophy of Education (New York: Prentice-Hall, Inc., 1954), chapter 7.
[7] James D. Koerner, ed., The Case for Basic Education (Boston: Little, Brown and Company, 1959).
[8] Sidney Hook, Education for the Modern Man (New York: The Dial Press, 1946). chapter 5.
[9] Oxford University Department of Education, Arts and Science Sides in the Sixth Form (Abingdon-Berkshire: The Abbey Press, 1960).

desirable and the undesirable. Any one discipline gives opportunity for the development of more than one mode of thought and each mode can be developed through more than one of the disciplines. For example, literature can contribute to the development of both moral and aesthetic judgment. Mathematics and philosophy both contribute to the development of the logical mode.

If students are to gain understanding of the nature of knowledge, the different modes of mental activity must be made explicit to them:

> They must have time and guidance in which to see that what is a proof in the Mathematics they pursue on Tuesday is not the same kind of thing as a proof in History, which follows on Wednesday; that the truth of George Eliot or Joseph Conrad is not the same thing as the truths of Mendel or Max Plank; and yet that there are similarities as well as differences.

Peterson accordingly suggests that in addition to giving attention to these varying modes of thought in the subject fields, the secondary program include a special course in which these ways of thinking are the object of study. One important aspect of such teaching has to do with ways in which these modes of thought are verified. Verification is particularly significant in that it is the guide to meaning of the various types of thought. For example, empirical statements are verified by tests conducted in terms of experience, whereas moral statements are verified by reference to criteria or principles of judgment.

The two complementary ways of viewing knowledge incorporated in these two curriculum approaches provide a fruitful basis for curriculum planning. In the first, emphasis is on the conceptual schemes and methods of inquiry associated with the disciplines and grouping of disciplines. In the second, attention is focused on modes of thought that transcend the boundaries of the individual fields. They thus represent two mutually reinforcing conceptions of knowledge that deserve consideration in curriculum building.

Professor Toulmin has coined two terms that might be helpful in clarifying what is meant here. He distinguishes between participant's language and onlooker's language.[10] Participant's language is the language used by members of a professional group or discipline as they carry on their work within these fields. Hence we talk today about the language of science, the language of psychology, the language of mathematics and even the language of education. Ralph Barton Perry once observed that you can tell the specialty of a man by the words he uses carefully and with precision. Participant's language has to do with the language systems that are the distinguishing characteristics of the various disciplined areas of study such as history, science, literature, mathematics, and the like.

Now if we want to examine or talk about the language we use in any one of these fields, we must use another level of discourse. We must, in Toulmin's terms, use onlooker's language. For example, Peterson is quoted above as saying that students need help in understanding that a proof in mathematics is not the same as a proof in science or that the "truth" of a scientist is not the same as the "truth" of the poet or novelist. To make these comparisons and contrasts we need a language system that enables us to look at these various areas of study

[10] S. Toulmin, *Philosophy of Science* (London: Hutchinson University Library, 1953), p. 13.

from the outside, as it were. The modes of thought identified by Peterson furnish us with language tools that are useful for this purpose. Hence their importance in teaching.

These two complementary conceptions of knowledge deserve consideration in curriculum building. Such planning would include:

1. A program of general education built around the structures and strategies of the four major areas of knowledge: the natural sciences, mathematics, the social sciences, and the humanities.
2. Explicit attention in the teaching of these fields to the various modes of thought and different uses of language incorporated in them.

In view of the significance of knowledge in our lives today, it seems reasonable to suggest that knowledge itself should become an object of study in the schools. At what points in their educational career students are able to carry on such study with understanding is an empirical question, certainly not answerable in the abstract. High schools might experiment with courses similar to the one suggested by Mr. Peterson for British schools. Already there are available in Britain excellent teaching materials prepared specifically for the kind of teaching here envisaged.[11]

One point implicit in the above proposal deserves special emphasis. I think it important that the context for curriculum planning be shifted from the individual disciplines, as is now the vogue, to the broad groupings of knowledge suggested above. I am not calling for indiscriminate scrambling of superficial knowledge. Indeed, at this point we would do well to suspend judgment as to when in the school program teaching should be organized around the individual disciplines, and when around the broad groupings of the disciplines. In all likelihood, different patterns of organization will be found to be appropriate for different levels of the school program. Dewey's notion of the "progressive organization of knowledge" might serve as a guiding conception in planning the sequence of the program through the elementary and secondary school years.

The significant point is that there is need for a broader context for curriculum planning than the separate disciplines, as is the case with most of the national projects now underway. Furthermore, the broad fields furnish a context within which we can consider fields of knowledge not now included in the programs of most schools, but which seem to have reasonable claims to a place in the curriculum. For example, in the social sciences, anthropology, political science, sociology, economics, and social psychology are given little or no attention at the present time. That these fields can make significant contributions in helping students understand the social and cultural changes now taking place around the world goes without saying.

In sum, scholars in the various disciplines must now be invited to join us in a search for new structures for teaching that avoid undue fragmentation of knowledge. The various fields must find their place in a pattern of studies that provides a substantial measure of coherence and relatedness for the program as a whole.

[11] See, for example, the following: E. R. Emmet, *The Use of Reason* (London: Longmans, Green and Company, Ltd., 1960); John Wilson, *Language and the Pursuit of Truth* (London: Cambridge University Press, 1958); R. W. Young, *Lines of Thought* (London: Oxford University Press, 1958).

Let us not underestimate the difficulties that we face in these efforts, for the tendencies in the academic world are almost all in the opposite direction. This fall, for example, Columbia University suspended one of its courses in Contemporary Civilization that had been taught for over thirty years as a social science offering. This course, as it was reported in the *New York Times*, was a "casualty of the trend in social sciences, especially economics, anthropology and sociology, having become so technical as to defy the attempt of 'translating technical language into ordinary discourse.' "[12] At the same time, there is growing recognition that new approaches must be found. Recently, Professor Zacharias of the M.I.T. Physics Project urged that we reconsider the entire pattern of science education from the elementary years on and commented, "You can't carve up a discipline there (in the elementary schools) the way we do in graduate school. A youngster has to see problems whole."[13]

RELATIONSHIPS OF KNOWLEDGE TO HUMAN AFFAIRS

That the schools ought to provide students with the means for intelligent action is not a new or controversial idea. When, however, it comes to deciding what to teach and how to teach to accomplish this goal, we find marked differences of opinion.

Is is sufficient in general education, for example, to have students learn how to behave like physicists, historians, or economists? I think not. For the economist as economist (to mention just one field) is in no position to prescribe courses of action regarding the host of public policy issues we face, and questions of public policy and decision loom large in general education. To be sure, economics does provide us with a body of theory that is essential in examining the probable consequences of alternative economic policies, and a good many of these analytical tools ought to become part of the intellectual equipment of all students. Economists are able to tell us what the probable consequences will be if the supply of money is increased, or if the interest rates are lowered; but they cannot as economists tell us whether or not we ought to take either of these two courses of action. Decision regarding these alternative courses of action involves weighing of values and technical economic analysis.

It is therefore clear that both values and economic theory come into play in deciding courses of action in economic affairs, and both must find their place in social studies teaching. Here the different modes of thought suggested by Peterson's approach come prominently into play. Technical economic analysis involves the empirical mode of thinking (i.e., it is concerned with matters of fact and theory), while considering alternative values involves the moral mode (i.e., it is concerned with criteria of what is desirable or undesirable). The teacher's job is to help students learn to make these necessary distinctions, so that they recognize when questions of fact and analysis are under consideration and when questions of value are at stake.[14] This would seem to hold as well for instruction

12 *New York Times*, July 9, 1961.
13 *Saturday Review*, October 21, 1961, p. 52.
14 See *Economic Education in the Schools*, Report of the National Task Force on Economic Education, 1961.

in fields of study other than economics, which I have used here for purposes of illustration.

Thus far we have been talking about problems associated with a single field. But problems in the world of human affairs do not come neatly labeled "historical," "economic," or "political." They come as decisions to be made, and force us to call upon all we know and make us wish we knew more. It was concern for broad cultural and moral questions that go beyond the boundaries of any one discipline that led the progressives to urge that students have the opportunity to deal with them in all their complexity. They proposed a new curriculum, one centered on the problems of youth and broad social issues, and drawing upon the academic disciplines as they become relevant to the problems under study. This idea became the hallmark of progressivism in curriculum building. It gained wide acceptance among educators and found expression in many influential statements of policy and opinion during the 1920's–40's. Attempted applications of this viewpoint were made in courses labeled "core," "common learnings," and the like.

Difficulties in this approach soon became apparent, not the least of which was the students' lack of first-hand acquaintance with the disciplines that were the source of the concepts and ideas essential to structuring problems under study. Without adequate understanding of the various fields of knowledge, students had no way of knowing which fields were relevant to problems of concern to them. As a matter of fact, without knowledge of the organized fields, it was difficult for them to ask the kinds of questions that the various disciplines could help them answer.

And yet, one feels that giving students an opportunity to grapple with broad social and cultural problems was basically a promising innovation. At the same time one is forced to recognize that problem solving on such a broad base cannot be pursued successfully without growing understanding of the fields of knowledge on which the problem solver must draw.

Recognizing then (1) the value in systematic study of the fields of knowledge and (2) the importance of developing competence in dealing with problems and issues that are broader than those of any one field, the question arises why opportunities for both types of activities should not be included in the program for all students. One might envision a general education program that would include basic instruction in the major fields defined earlier in this paper (the natural sciences, physical sciences, mathematics, and the humanities) together with a coordinating seminar in which students dealt with problems "in the round" and in which special effort is made to show the intimate relationships between the fields of study as concepts from these fields are brought to bear on these problems. Such a seminar would also furnish excellent opportunities to help students become aware of the different modes of thought or various types of language usage involved in dealing with problematic situations and the necessity for making clear distinctions among them.

Toward a Mankind Curriculum: From Kindergarten through Twelfth Grade

Frederick O. Gearing

The schools appear ready, and all the necessary tools are at hand to have the social studies curriculum deal with, not men, but Man, from kindergarten through the twelfth grade. The condition of the nation and world requires it. The psychological comfort of concerned and puzzled students requires it. Education, in the oldest and least complicated sense of the word, requires it. So let's get on with it.

The essential content of a "mankind curriculum" is an empirical fact: All men are Man, members of the single species, *Homo sapiens*. That fact was *discovered*, bear in mind, through hard empirical work, and not so long ago. A mankind curriculum involves a concerted study throughout the grades of the nature of Man.

A mankind curriculum invites students at all grade levels to take frequent looks far afield at the culturally strange and alien lives of people remote in time or place. But note well: The main purpose in doing this is to help the student gain deeper understanding of himself, of his own human nature, thereby enabling him to relate with comfort and a degree of empathy to a heterogeneous nation and world.

In making a mankind curriculum, schools are ill-advised to start from scratch or from only a general framework. Rather, a baseline is required such as can be provided by a fully embodied existing mankind course (or several such courses) to serve as a firm foundation on which to build further curriculum. The reasons are obvious: Preparing a good curriculum from scratch is very costly, but once the teaching of a well-developed course is under way, modifying and extending it is not too expensive. Good curriculum making in this particular realm also requires special substantive knowledge that is in short supply, but modification and extension can safely proceed with less special advice because a truly good mankind course is itself an education for the teachers and other curriculum makers.

Happily, two such courses, both excellent foundations from which a mankind curriculum can grow, now exist. These are "Man: A Course of Study" (a yearlong course appropriate for the upper elementary grades), developed with National Science Foundation support by the Education Development Center of Cambridge, Massachusetts, and available on a nonprofit basis from the Education Development Center directly; and "Patterns in Human History" (a semester

From *Today's Education* LIX, no. 3 (March 1970):28–30. Used by permission of the author and publisher.

course designed for grades 9 and 10, but probably usable in grades 7 through 12), developed with National Science Foundation support by the Anthropology Curriculum Study Project in Chicago (a program of the American Anthropological Association), which will be available from the Macmillan Company by early 1971. Each can, in its way, provide the solid foundation from which schools can make a mankind curriculum.

A mankind curriculum views the lives of many men, remote in time and place and close at hand. Men are thus seen in the full sweep of the total human career (over 99 percent of which was passed in the fully human condition we are today pleased to call "primitive"). All these men, at home and afield, variously express some selected aspect of the wide range of their shared capacities. Thus, a mankind curriculum persistently asks: What is human about all humans? How do any peoples, whoever, wherever, whenever they are, uniquely express that common humanity? And also: How does any society abuse and thwart its own humanness or that of its neighbors?

At bottom, this curriculum provides the student with a grand exercise in the art of comparison. By looking at the life of a people, familiar or strange, and by comparing sameness and difference, he can come to see himself more clearly. He sees differences and begins to sense his own uniqueness. At the same time he can through effort recognize sameness by vicariously entering into their experiences. Finding the underlying common humanity will prove to be most difficult when the cultural differences are greatest, but success under these circumstances has the greatest positive effect on the student's expanding self. By looking "out" and comparing, the student is better able to see "in."

One cannot teach a mankind curriculum didactically, but only through individualized classroom simulation of discovery. Each student must see "out there" himself, and so must his teacher. This requires rich data presented in several media. It requires much interchange between student and student, and teacher and student. It requires well-conceived and judiciously posed questions. In short, it requires individual inquiry.

Robert Redfield once said:

> He who goes to live with an exotic people often begins, as does many a common viewer of primitive art, with a first impression that these people are opaque, not to be understood, somehow not me at all but something quite different. The usual outcome of persisting effort to understand is so to alter this first impression as to make the exotic people seem almost like the outsider's friends back home. One of the best of the ethnological students of West African peoples has confessed that when he began to study a certain people there about whom he is now the leading authority, he thought of them as hardly human. They have now become human to him, quite human. In coming to understand an alien way of life, as in coming to understand an alien art, the course of personal experience is essentially the same: One looks first at an incomprehensible other; one comes to see that other as one's self in another guise.

Or as a kindergartner, poor and black, said during a study of an American Indian group: "Do them Indian boys cuss like me when somebody's made them real mad?" In asking that question, this kindergartner was in his own way asking:

What is human about all us humans? For openers, try topping his concrete and wise query.

"Man: A Course of Study" brings into sharp focus the question: What is human about humans? It guides student inquiry largely by means of a wide-ranging and unhurried look at one small human community very different from the student's own—that of the Netsilik Eskimo. Unnarrated film with natural sound is the main means of conveying their way of life to the students. Readings adapted from ethnographic sources support the film.

The course opens by examining a series of animals—salmon, gulls, baboons —then moves to the examination of Eskimo life. The key ideas are the nature of animal adaptation (through natural selection) and the nature of human adaptation (through culture, made possible by language). Thus: Man is a profoundly unique animal in that he talks, therefore creates technologies, organizations, ideologies, in short, cultures and therefore may adapt to virtually all environments, including the very harsh one of the Netsilik. The data throughout are unusually rich, evocative, inherently engaging, contained in a wide variety of wisely selected media, including strategy "games" (a caribou hunt, a seal hunt) that seek to help the student get inside the "calculating head" of the Eskimo hunter as he pursues these life-and-death subsistence activities.

"I wouldn't want to be an Eskimo, but if I were, I think I'd be happy. My Eskimo parents would keep me warm," said a fifth grade girl. She had certainly vicariously shared the experience of her Eskimo counterpart, had seen difference, but had also come to recognize the underlying sameness, not romantically, but quite realistically. Probably she has never said, "All men are Man," or even "Eskimos are Man." But she experienced that fact. And as a result, she is not quite the same girl she was before.

"Patterns in Human History" also considers the question: What is human about humans? But whereas "Man: A Course of Study" treats one human community extensively, this course looks analytically at an array of human communities, both familiar and strange, selected for their contrasts in size and form.

"Patterns in Human History" begins with the immediate experience of the students and on that basis helps them develop a working command of the concept of role, and this, in turn, provides the main analytic tool through which students trace the human career and compare the diversity of human communities. The course then looks at the overall shape of the long human career, the major turning points in that career, and the contemporary diversity of human communities seen as three very general types—tribal, peasant, urban. Finally, the course turns to the contemporary problem of "economic development" viewed from the perspective of the village peasant. Course data are quite rich and presented in a variety of media, although in the interests of economy, there are no motion pictures.

"Man: A Course of Study" and "Patterns in Human History," to serve as models and foundations, should exist, as such, in selected grades. These courses provide fresh perspective for social studies materials already in the schools, as well as new integration of otherwise disparate studies or courses. Whenever it wishes to do so, a teaching staff can reorient almost any existing social studies course to the mankind perspective.

To my knowledge, no mankind course exists for the primary grades, nor does the need for an ambitiously organized "course" appear to be pressing. Rather, in these grades, schools are well advised to indulge the young child's special capacity to appreciate the wonder of the human universe, especially as that wonder is conveyed by folk song and dance, folk tales and myths, and good pictures. Such indulgence is already a mankind curriculum.

These very young children have several assets that most of them will soon lose. They are beautifully naïve and hence are usually willing to accept a rain dance, for example, as a pretty good idea and to enjoy the song and dance and color directly. They are not much concerned about lineal time and space; thus they are usually able to enjoy a remote people's folktale as if those people existed with them in some timeless and spaceless universe.

In the great majority of primary settings, more than this is possible, of course. To guide the planning of more structured courses, the curriculum maker may find it helpful to ask himself three questions that were formulated by a group of social scientists who addressed themselves to the matter.

The three questions are in sequence:

1. What aspects of human behavior especially puzzle and preoccupy many children during these years? Rules fall in that category simply because, in coming to school for the first time, young children run into a host of new rules—in the classroom and on the playground—and they do so at a time when many of them are in the midst of moving from the idea of rules as simply existing to the realization that they are man-made.

2. Given this preoccupation, what studies of *animal* behavior might help the child, through comparison, to "see" that it is rules, rules in general, that puzzle him? For example, rules of a sort and their enforcement underlie the squabbles of white rats in a cage, the pecking order of fowl, the dominance hierarchy in a baboon troop. Materials on all of these kinds of behavior are available.

3. What studies of *human* behavior in some small, culturally strange community would, through comparison, help the child to see the particular nature of the rules that puzzle him and would help him to recognize the man-made nature of rules in general? One should not look for explicit treatment of rules, of course, but rather for storylike materials in which rules are paraded, acted out. Appropriate narrative stories, films, and so on, are available in vast quantities.

(The approach used for exploring rules will also work in dealing with other topics that preoccupy young children. To cite only one of many such topics, infant dependency puzzles youngsters, who have just left it or are still struggling to leave it. Studying infant dependence in the animal world and in culturally strange communities will help them understand.)

The current wave of ethnic studies is one evidence that the schools are moving toward a mankind curriculum. This wave has already produced one happy result. It has caused us to recognize that the traditional social studies course was itself an ethnic study and that through the grades all the traditional social studies were fundamentally one grand ethnic study treating, with only trivial interruption, a rather small sector of this one society.

That approach to social studies was embarrassingly parochial and invidious. We can hardly expect that the emerging ethnic studies will be less so. An array of competing parochialisms, while no doubt better than one reigning parochialism, is hardly good enough. But a mankind curriculum—a concerted study that views any human experience as one expression of the common potentials of the single species, *Homo sapiens*, can transform any ethnic study, traditional or new. Probably, a mankind curriculum is the only context in which the emerging variety of ethnic studies can thrive, as they must. Happily, all men are, in fact Man.

A Schoolman's Guide to Marshall McLuhan

John M. Culkin, S.J.

Education, a seven-year-old assures me, is "how kids learn stuff." Few definitions are as satisfying. It includes all that is essential—a who, a what, and a process. It excludes all the people, places, and things which are only sometimes involved in learning. The economy and accuracy of the definition, however, are more useful in locating the problem than in solving it. We know little enough about *kids*, less about *learning*, and considerably more than we would like to know about *stuff*.

In addition, the whole process of formal schooling is now wrapped inside an environment of speeded-up technological change which is constantly influencing kids and learning and stuff. The jet-speed of this technological revolution, especially in the area of communications, has left us with more reactions to it than reflections about it. Meanwhile back at the school, the student, whose psyche is being programmed for tempo, information, and relevance by his electronic environment, is still being processed in classrooms operating on the postulates of another day. The cold war existing between these two worlds is upsetting for both the student and the schools. One thing is certain: It is hardly a time for educators to plan with nostalgia, timidity, or old formulas. Enter Marshall McLuhan.

He enters from the North, from the University of Toronto where he teaches English and is director of the Center for Culture and Technology. He enters with the reputation as "the oracle of the electric age" and as "the most provocative and controversial writer of this generation." More importantly for the schools, he enters as a man with fresh eyes, with new ways of looking at old problems. He is a man who gets his ideas first and judges them later. Most of these ideas are summed up in his book, *Understanding Media*. His critics tried him for not delivering these insights in their most lucid and practical form. It isn't always cricket, however, to ask the same man to crush the grapes and serve the wine. Not all of McLu is nu or tru, but then again neither is *all* of anybody else. This article is

From *Saturday Review* L, no. 11 (March 18, 1967):51–53, 70–72. Used by permission of the author and publisher. Copyright 1967 Saturday Review, Inc.

an attempt to select and order those elements of McLuhanism which are most relevant to the schools and to provide the schoolman with some new ways of thinking about the schools.

McLuhan's promise is modest enough: "All I have to offer is an enterprise of investigation into a world that's quite unusual and quite unlike any previous world and for which no models of perception will serve." This unexplored world happens to be the present. McLuhan feels that very few men look at the present with a present eye, that they tend to miss the present by translating it into the past, seeing it through a rearview mirror. The unnoticed fact of our present is the electronic environment created by the new communications media. It is as pervasive as the air we breathe (and some would add that it is just as polluted), yet its full import eludes the judgments of commonsense or content-oriented perception. The environments set up by different media are not just containers for people; they are processes which shape people. Such influence is deterministic only if ignored. There is no inevitability as long as there is a willingness to contemplate what is happening.

Theorists can keep reality at arm's length for long periods of time. Teachers and administrators can't. They are closeted with reality all day long. In many instances they are co-prisoners with electronic-age students in the old pencil box cell. And it is the best teachers and the best students who are in the most trouble because they are challenging the system constantly. It is the system which has to come under scrutiny. Teachers and students can say, in the words of the Late Late Show, "Baby, this thing is bigger than both of us." It won't be ameliorated by a few dashes of good will or a little more hard work. It is a question of understanding these new kids and these new media and of getting the schools to deal with the new electronic environment. It's not easy. And the defenders of the old may prove to be the ones least able to defend and preserve the values of the old.

For some people, analysis of these newer technologies automatically implies approbation of them. Their world is so full of *shoulds* that it is hard to squeeze in an *is*. McLuhan suggests a more positive line of exploration:

> At the moment, it is important that we understand cause and process. The aim is to develop an awareness about print and the newer technologies of communication so that we can orchestrate them, minimize their mutual frustrations and clashes, and get the best out of each in the educational process. The present conflict leads to elimination of the motive to learn and to diminution of interest in all previous achievement: It leads to loss of the sense of relevance. Without an understanding of media grammars, we cannot hope to achieve a contemporary awareness of the world in which we live.

We have been told that it is the property of true genius to disturb all settled ideas. McLuhan is disturbing in both his medium and his message. His ideas challenge the normal way in which people perceive reality. They can create a very deep and personal threat since they touch on everything in a person's experience. They are just as threatening to the establishment whose way of life is predicated on the postulates he is questioning. The establishment has no history of organizing parades to greet its disturbers.

His medium is perhaps more disturbing than his message. From his earliest work he has described his enterprise as "explorations in communication." The word he uses most frequently today is "probe." His books demand a high degree of involvement from the reader. They are poetic and intuitive rather than logical and analytic. Structurally, his unit is the sentence. Most of them are topic sentences—which are left undeveloped. The style is oral and breathless and frequently obscure. It's a different kind of medium.

"The medium is the message," announced McLuhan a dozen years ago in a cryptic and uncompromising aphorism whose meaning is still being explored. The title of his latest book, an illustrated popular paperback treatment of his theories, playfully proclaims that *The Medium Is the Massage*—a title calculated to drive typesetters and critics to hashish and beyond. The original dictum can be looked at in four ways, the third of which includes a massage of importance.

The first meaning would be better communicated orally—"The *medium* is the message." The *medium* is the thing to study. The *medium* is the thing you're missing. Everybody's hooked on content; pay attention to form, structure, framework, *medium*. The play's the thing. The medium's the thing. McLuhan makes the truth stand on its head to attract attention. Why the medium is worthy of attention derives from its other three meanings.

Meaning number two stresses the relation of the medium to the content. The form of communication not only alters the content, but each form also has preferences for certain kinds of messages. Content always exists in some form and is, therefore, to some degree governed by the dynamics of that form. If you don't know the medium, you don't know the message. The insight is neatly summed up by Dr. Edmund Carpenter: "English is a mass medium. All languages are mass media. The new mass media—film, radio, TV—are new languages, their grammars as yet unknown. Each codifies reality differently; each conceals a unique metaphysics. Linguists tell us it's possible to say anything in any language if you use enough words or images, but there's rarely time; the natural course is for a culture to exploit its media biases. . . ."

It is always content-in-form which is mediated. In this sense, the medium is co-message. The third meaning for the M-M formula emphasizes the relation of the medium to the individual psyche. The medium alters the perceptual habits of its users. Independent of the content, the medium itself gets through. Pre-literate, literate, and post-literate cultures see the world through different-colored glasses. In the process of delivering content the medium also works over the sensorium of the consumer. To get this subtle insight across, McLuhan punned on message and came up with massage. The switch is intended to draw attention to the fact that a medium is not something neutral—it does something to people. It takes hold of them, it jostles them, it bumps them around, it massages them. It opens and closes windows in their sensorium. Proof? Look out the window at the TV generation. They are rediscovering texture, movement, color, and sound as they retribalize the race. TV is a real grabber; it really massages those lazy, unused senses.

The fourth meaning underscores the relation of the medium to society. Whitehead said, "The major advances in civilization are processes that all but wreck the societies in which they occur." The media massage the society as well as the individual. The results pass unnoticed for long periods of time because people tend to view the new as just a little bit more of the old. Whitehead again:

"The greatest invention of the nineteenth century was the invention of the method of invention. A new method entered into life. In order to understand our epoch, we can neglect all details of change, such as railways, telegraphs, radios, spinning machines, synthetic dyes. We must concentrate on the method in itself: That is the real novelty which has broken up the foundations of the old civilization." Understanding the medium or process involved is the key to control.

The media shape both content and consumer and do so practically undetected. We recall the story of the Russian worker whose wheelbarrow was searched every day as he left the factory grounds. He was, of course, stealing wheelbarrows. When your medium is your message and they're only investigating content, you can get away with a lot of things—like wheelbarrows, for instance. It's not the picture but the frame. Not the contents but the box. The blank page is not neutral; nor is the classroom.

McLuhan's writings abound with aphorisms, insights, for-instances, and irrelevancies which float loosely around recurring themes. They provide the raw materials of a do-it-yourself kit for tidier types who prefer to do their exploring with clearer charts. What follows is one man's McLuhan served up in barbarously brief form. Five postulates, spanning nearly 4,000 years, will serve as the fingers in this endeavor to grasp McLuhan:

1) 1967 B.C.—*All the senses get into the act.* A conveniently symmetrical year for a thesis which is partially cyclic. It gets us back to man before the Phoenician alphabet. We know from our contemporary ancestors in the jungles of New Guinea and the wastes of the Arctic that preliterate man lives in an all-at-once sense world. The reality which bombards him from all directions is picked up with the omni-directional antennae of sight, hearing, touch, smell, and taste. Films such as *The Hunters* and *Nanook of the North* depict primitive men tracking game with an across-the-board sensitivity which mystifies Western, literate man. We mystify them too. And it is this cross-mystification which makes intercultural abrasions so worthwhile.

Most people presume that their way of perceiving the world is *the* way of perceiving the world. If they hang around with people like themselves, their mode of perception may never be challenged. It is at the poles (literally and figuratively) that the violent contrasts illumine our own unarticulated perceptual prejudices. Toward the North Pole, for example, live Eskimos. A typical Eskimo family consists of a father, a mother, two children, and an anthropologist. When the anthropologist goes into the igloo to study Eskimos, he learns a lot about himself. Eskimos see pictures and maps equally well from all angles. They can draw equally well on top of a table or underneath it. They have phenomenal memories. They travel without visual bearings in their white-on-white world and can sketch cartographically accurate maps of shifting shorelines. They have forty or fifty words for what we call "snow." They live in a world without linearity, a world of acoustic space. They are Eskimos. Their natural way of perceiving the world is different from our natural way of perceiving the world.

Each culture develops its own balance of the senses in response to the demands of its environment. The most generalized formulation of the theory would maintain that the individual's modes of cognition and perception are influenced by the culture he is in, the language he speaks, and the media to which he is exposed. Each culture, as it were, provides its constituents with a custom-made set of goggles. The differences in perception are a question of degree. Some cultures are close enough to each other in perceptual patterns so that the differences pass unnoticed. Other cultural groups, such as the Eskimo and the American teen-ager, are far enough away from us to provide esthetic distance.

2) *Art imitates life.* In *The Silent Language* Edward T. Hall offers the thesis that all art and technology is an extension of some physical or psychic element of man. Today man has developed extensions for practically everything he used to do with his body: stone axe for hand, wheel for foot, glasses for eyes, radio for voice and ears. Money is a way of storing energy. This externalizing of individual, specialized functions is now, by definition, at its most advanced stage. Through the electronic media of telegraph, telephone, radio, and television, man has now equipped his world with a nervous system similar to the one within his own body. President Kennedy is shot and the world instantaneously reels from the impact of the bullets. Space and time dissolve under electronic conditions. Current concern for the United Nations, the Common Market, ecumenism, reflects this organic thrust toward the new convergence and unity which is "blowing in the wind." Now in the electric age, our extended faculties and senses constitute a single instantaneous and coexistent field of experience. It's all-at-once. It's shared-by-all. McLuhan calls the world "a global village."

3) *Life imitates art.* We shape our tools and thereafter they shape us. These extensions of our senses begin to interact with our senses. These media become a massage. The new change in the environment creates a new balance among the senses. No sense operates in isolation. The full sensorium seeks fulfillment in almost every sense experience. And since there is a limited quantum of energy available for any sensory experience, the sense-ratio will differ for different media.

The nature of the sensory effect will be determined by the medium used. McLuhan divides the media according to the quality or definition of their physical signal. The content is not relevant in this kind of analysis. The same picture from the same camera can appear as a glossy photograph or as a newspaper wirephoto. The photograph is well-defined, of excellent pictorial quality, hi-fi within its own medium. McLuhan calls this kind of medium "hot." The newspaper photo is grainy, made up of little dots, low definition. McLuhan calls this kind of medium "cool." Film is hot; televison is cool. Radio is hot; telephone is cool. The cool medium or person invites participation and involvement. It leaves room for the response of the consumer. A lecture is hot; all the work is done. A seminar is cool; it gets everyone into the game. Whether all the connections are causal may be debated, but it's interesting that the kids of the cool TV generation want to be so involved and so much a part of what's happening.

4) *We shaped the alphabet and it shaped us.* In keeping with the McLuhan postuate that "the medium is the message," a literate culture should be more than mildly eager to know what books do to people. Everyone is familiar enough with all the enrichment to living mediated through fine books to allow us to pass on to the subtler effects which might be attributed to the print medium, independent of the content involved. Whether one uses the medium to say that *God is dead* or that *God is love* (--- -- ----), the structure of the medium itself remains unchanged. Nine little black marks with no intrinsic meaning of their own are

strung along a line with spaces left after the third and fifth marks. It is this stripping away of meaning which allows us to X-ray the form itself.

As an example, while lecturing to a large audience in a modern hotel in Chicago, a distinguished professor is bitten in the leg by a cobra. The whole experience takes three seconds. He is affected through the touch of the reptile, the gasp of the crowd, the swimming sights before his eyes. His memory, imagination, and emotions come into emergency action. A lot of things happen in three seconds. Two weeks later he is fully recovered and wants to write up the experience in a letter to a colleague. To communicate this experience through print means that it must first be broken down into parts and then mediated, eyedropper fashion, one thing at a time, in an abstract, linear, fragmented, sequential way. That is the essential structure of print. And once a culture uses such a medium for a few centuries, it begins to perceive the world in a one-thing-at-a-time, abstract, linear, fragmented, sequential way. And it shapes its organizations and schools according to the same premises. The form of print has become the form of thought. The medium has become the message.

For centuries now, according to McLuhan, the straight line has been the hidden metaphor of literate man. It was unconsciously but inexorably used as the measure of things. It went unnoticed, unquestioned. It was presumed as natural and universal. It is neither. Like everything else it is good for the things it is good for. To say that it is not everything is not to say that it is nothing. The electronic media have broken the monopoly of print; they have altered our sensory profiles by heightening our awareness of aural, tactile, and kinetic values.

5) 1967 A.D.—*All the senses want to get into the act.* Print repressed most senselife in favor of the visual. The end of print's monopoly also marks the end of a visual monopoly. As the early warning system of art and popular culture indicates, all the senses want to get into the act. Some of the excesses in the current excursions into aural, oral, tactile, and kinetic experience may in fact be directly responsive to the sensory deprivation of the print culture. Nature abhors a vacuum. No one glories in the sight of kids totally out of control in reaction to the Beatles. Some say, "What are the Beatles doing to these kids?" Others say, "What have we done to these kids?" All the data isn't in on what it means to be a balanced human being.

Kids are what the game is all about. Given an honest game with enough equipment to go around, it is the mental, emotional, and volitional capacity of the student which most determines the outcome. The whole complicated system of formal education is in business to get through to kids, to motivate kids, to help kids learn stuff. Schools are not in business to label kids, to grade them for the job market or to babysit. They are there to communicate with them.

Communication is a funny business. There isn't as much of it going on as most people think. Many feel that it consists in saying things in the presence of others. No so. It consists not in saying things but in having things heard. Beautiful English speeches delivered to monolingual Arabs are not beautiful speeches. You have to speak the language of the audience—of the *whom* in the "who-says-what-to-whom" communications diagram. Sometimes the language is lexical (Chinese, Japanese, Portuguese), sometimes it is regional or personal (125th Street-ese, Holden Caulfield-ese, anybody-ese). It has little to do with words and much to do with understanding the audience. The word for good communication is "Whom-ese"—the language of the audience, of the "whom."

All good communicators use Whom-ese. The best writers, film-makers, advertising men, lovers, preachers, and teachers all have the knack for thinking about the hopes, fears, and capacity of the other person and of being able to translate their communication into terms which are *relevant* for that person. Whitehead called "inert ideas" the bane of education. Relevance, however, is one of those subjective words. It doesn't pertain to the object in itself but to the object as perceived by someone. The school may decide that history is *important for* the student, but the role of the teacher is to make history *relevant to* the student.

If *what* has to be tailored to the *whom*, the teacher has to be constantly engaged in audience research. It's not a question of keeping up with the latest slang or of selling out to the current mores of the kids. Neither of these tactics helps either learning or kids. But it is a question of knowing what values are strong in their world, of understanding the obstacles to communication, of sensing their style of life. Communication doesn't have to end there, but it can start nowhere else. If they are tuned in to FM and you are broadcasting on AM, there's no communication. Communication forces you to pay a lot of attention to other people.

McLuhan has been paying a great deal of attention to modern kids. Of necessity they live in the present since they have no theories to diffract or reflect what is happening. They are also the first generation to be born into a world in which there was always television. McLuhan finds them a great deal different from their counterparts at the turn of the century when the electric age was just getting up steam.

A lot of things have happened since 1900 and most of them plug into walls. Today's six-year-old has already learned a lot of stuff by the time he shows up for the first day of school. Soon after his umbilical cord was cut he was planted in front of a TV set "to keep him quiet." He liked it enough there to stay for some 3,000 to 4,000 hours before he started the first grade. By the time he graduates from high school he has clocked 15,000 hours of TV time and 10,800 hours of school time. He lives in a world which bombards him from all sides with information from radios, films, telephones, magazines, recordings, and people. He learns more things from the windows of cars, trains, and even planes. Through travel and communications he has experienced war in Vietnam, the wide world of sports, the civil rights movement, the death of a President, thousands of commercials, a walk in space, a thousand innocuous shows, and, one may hope, plenty of Captain Kangaroo.

This is all merely descriptive, an effort to lay out what *is*, not what should be. Today's student can hardly be described by any of the old educational analogies comparing him to an empty bucket or a blank page. He comes to the information machine called school and he is already brimming over with information. As he grows his standards for relevance are determined more by what he receives outside the school than what he receives inside. A recent Canadian film tells the story of a bright, articulate middle class teen-ager who leaves school because there's "no reason to stay." He daydreams about Vietnam while his teacher drones on about the four reasons for the spread of Christianity and the five points such information is worth on the exam. Only the need for a diploma was holding him in school; learning wasn't, and he left. He decided the union ticket wasn't worth the gaff. He left. Some call him a dropout. Some call him a pushout.

The kids have one foot on the dock and one foot on the ferryboat. Living in two centuries makes for that kind of tension. The gap between the classroom and the outside world and the gap between the generations is wider than it has ever been. Those tedious people who quote Socrates on the conduct of the young are trying vainly to reassure themselves that this is just the perennial problem of communication between generations. 'Tain't so. "Today's child is growing up absurd, because he lives in two worlds, and neither of them inclines him to grow up." Says McLuhan in *The Medium is the Message*. "Growing up—that is our new work, and it is *total*. Mere instruction will not suffice."

Learning is something that people do for themselves. People, places, and things can facilitate or impede learning; they can't make it happen without some cooperation from the learner. The learner these days comes to school with a vast reservoir of vicarious experiences and loosely related facts; he wants to use all his senses in his learning as an active agent in the process of discovery; he knows that all the answers aren't in. The new learner is the result of the new media, says McLuhan. And a new learner calls for a new kind of learning.

Leo Irrera said, "If God had anticipated the eventual structure of the school system, surely he would have shaped man differently." Kids are being tailored to fit the Procrustean forms of schedules, classrooms, memorizing, testing, etc., which are frequently relics from an obsolete approach to learning. It is the total environment which contains the philosophy of education, not the title page in the school catalogue. And it is the total environment which is invincible because it is invisible to most people. They tend to move things around within the old boxes or to build new and cleaner boxes. They should be asking whether or not there should be a box in the first place.

The new learner, who is the product of the all-at-once electronic environment, often feels out of it in a linear, one-thing-at-a-time school environment. The total environment is now the great teacher; the student has competence models against which to measure the effectiveness of his teachers. Nuclear students in linear schools make for some tense times in education. Students with well developed interests in science, the arts and humanities, or current events need assistance to suit their pace, not that of the state syllabus. The straight line theory of development and the uniformity of performance which it so frequently encourages just don't fit many needs of the new learner. Interestingly, the one thing which most of the current educational innovations share is their break with linear or print-oriented patterns: team teaching, nongraded schools, audio-lingual language training, multi-media learning situations, seminars, student research at all levels of education, individualized learning, and the whole shift of responsibility for learning from the teacher to the student. Needless to say, these are not as widespread as they should be, nor were they brought about through any conscious attention to the premises put forward by McLuhan. Like the print-oriented and linear mentality they now modify, these premises were plagiarized from the atmosphere. McLuhan's value is in the power he gives us to predict and control these changes.

There is too much stuff to learn today. McLuhan calls it an age of "information overload." And the information levels outside the classroom are now higher than those in the classroom. Schools used to have a virtual monopoly on information; now they are part-time competitors in the electronic informational surround. And all human knowledge is expanding at computer speed.

Every choice involves a rejection. If we can't do everything, what priorities will govern our educational policies? "The medium is the message" may not be bad for openers. We can no longer teach kids all about a subject; we can teach them what a subject is all about. We have to introduce them to the form, structure, gestalt, grammar, and process of the knowledge involved. What does a math man do when a math man does do math? This approach to the formal element of a discipline can provide a channel of communication between specialists. Its focus is not on content or detail but on the postulates, ground rules, frames of reference, and premises of each discipline. It stresses the modes of cognition and perception proper to each field. Most failures in communication are based on disagreement about items which are only corollaries of a larger thesis. It happens between disciplines, individuals, media, and cultures.

The arts play a new role in education because they are explorations in perception. Formerly conceived as a curricular luxury item, they now become a dynamic way of tuning up the sensorium and of providing fresh ways of looking at familiar things. When exploration and discovery become the themes, the old lines between art and science begin to fade. We have to guide students to becoming their own data processors to operate through pattern recognition. The media themselves serve as both aids to learning and as proper objects of study in this search for an all-media literacy. Current interest in film criticism will expand to include all art and communication forms.

And since the knowledge explosion has blown out the walls between subjects, there will be a continued move toward interdisciplinary swapping and understanding. Many of the categorical walls between things are artifacts left over from the packaging days of print. The specialist's life will be even lonelier as we move further from the Gutenberg era. The trends are all toward wholeness and convergence.

These things aren't true just because Marshall McLuhan says they are. They work. They explain problems in education that nobody else is laying a glove on. When presented clearly and with all the necessary examples and footnotes added, they have proven to be a liberating force for hundreds of teachers who were living through the tension of this cultural fission without realizing that the causes for the tension lay outside themselves. McLuhan's relevance for education demands the work of teams of simultaneous translators and researchers who can both shape and substantiate the insights which are scattered through his work. McLuhan didn't invent electricity or put kids in front of TV sets; he is merely trying to describe what's happening out there so that it can be dealt with intelligently. When someone warns you of an oncoming truck, it's frightfully impolite to accuse him of driving the thing. McLuhan can help kids to learn stuff better.

SECTION 4 ADDITIONAL LEARNING ACTIVITIES

Problems and Projects

1. Prepare a lesson plan in your field of teaching in which you use "discovery learning" as the method of teaching. Review Bruner's article ("Structures in Learning") for assistance in preparing the plan. For further help, read Jerome Bruner, *The Process of Education*, pp. 1–34.
2. Prepare a lesson plan in which you use the methods suggested by Bruner in his article "The Process of Education Reconsidered."
3. Prepare a teaching plan in which you try to use the "four areas of relevance" presented by Fantini and Weinstein in their article "Reducing the Behavior Gap."
4. If possible, use one of the plans you've prepared in numbers 1, 2, or 3 in actually teaching a class.
5. Continue to develop a "case problem" about one school you know well. Describe the curricula and teaching in that school as it may be related to knowledge theories. Does it use discovery learning, the structure of the disciplines, the problems approach? (See article by Bellack, as well as Bruner's "The Process of Education Reconsidered.")

Films

Knowing to Learn. 16mm, black and white, 58 mins. Looks at the revolution in education, the effects of electronics and computer technology on teaching. Distributed by McGraw-Hill text films, 330 W. 42nd Street, New York, New York 10036.

Books to Review

Ausubel, D. P. *Educational Psychology: A Cognitive View.* New York: Holt, Rinehart and Winston, 1968.

Block, James H., ed. *Mastery Learning: Theory and Practice.* New York: Holt, Rinehart and Winston, 1971.

Bloom, B. S.; Engelhart, M. D.; Furst, E. J.; Hill, W. H., and Krathwohl, D. R., eds. *Taxonomy of Educational Objectives: Handbook I: Cognitive Domain.* New York: David McKay Company, 1956.

Booth, Wayne C., ed. *The Knowledge Worth Having.* Chicago: University of Chicago Press, 1967.

Bruner, Jerome. *The Process of Education.* Cambridge, Massachusetts: Harvard University Press, 1961.

————. *The Relevance of Education.* New York: W. W. Norton and Company, 1971.

————. *Toward a Theory of Instruction.* Cambridge, Massachusetts: Harvard University Press, 1966.

Cooney, T. J., and Henderson, K. B. "A Model for Organizing Knowledge," *Educational Theory* 21 (Winter 1971):50–58.

Dewey, John. *Experience and Education.* New York: Macmillan Co., 1938.

Fabun, Don. *Communications: The Transfer of Meaning.* Beverly Hills, California: Glencoe Press, 1968.

Furth, Hans G. *Piaget and Knowledge.* Englewood Cliffs, New Jersey: Prentice-Hall, 1969.

Gowin, D. Bob. "The Structure of Knowledge," *Educational Theory* 20 (Fall 1970):319–328.

Havenstein, A. Dean. *Curriculum Planning for Behavioral Development.* Worthington, Ohio: Charles A. Jones Publishing Company, 1972.

Hudgins, Bryce. *The Instructional Process.* Chicago: Rand McNally and Company, 1971.

Krothwohl, D. R., Bloom, B. S., and Masia, B. B. *Taxonomy of Educational Objectives. Handbook II: Affective Domain.* New York: David McKay Company, 1974.

McLuhan, M. *The Medium is the Message.* New York: Random House, 2nd edition, 1967.

Martorella, Peter H. *Concept Learning-Designs for Instruction.* Scranton: Intext Educational Publishers, 1972.

Parker, J. Cecil, and Rubin, Louis. *Process As Content: Curriculum Design and the Application of Knowledge.* Chicago: Rand McNally and Company, 1966.

Smith, B. Othanel, Cohen, S. B., and Pearl, Arthur. *Teachers for the Real World.* Washington, D.C.: American Association of Colleges for Teacher Education, 1969, chapters 4, 5, 9 and 10.

Taba, Hilda. *Curriculum Development: Theory and Practice.* New York: Harcourt, Brace and World, 1962, chapter 11.

Vandenberg, Donald, ed. *Theory of Knowledge and Problems of Education.* Urbana: University of Illinois Press, 1969.

Curriculum Criteria

PREREQUISITES

Reading and study of the Introduction and Sections 1, 2, 3, and 4 of this book.

RATIONALE

In considering the rationale for our study of curriculum criteria, we must examine the definition of *criterion*; the significance of objectives; behavioral objectives; performance competency; and various lists of criteria or approaches to this topic that may be useful to us.

Criterion—Definition

A criterion is a standard on which a decision or judgment can be based; it is a basis for discrimination. Curriculum criteria are guidelines or standards on which curriculum and instruction decisions can be made.

If you have read this far in this book you should now have some understanding of the significance of social forces, human development, the nature of learning, and the nature of knowledge in planning a curriculum. It is necessary that all four of these bases be considered in any adequate curriculum planning. A major goal of this section is to emphasize that the curriculum maker should consider all of the four bases presented in Sections 1 to 4 as curriculum criteria: they should be used together as guidelines for curriculum and instruction decisions.

A knowledge of social forces and human development represent two ways of approaching the task of understanding the learner and his needs. Learning theories suggest that there are different ways of learning that may be superior in different circumstances, for different learning tasks, or for different learners. Knowledge theories indicate that learners have a personal organization of knowledge that may be different from the structure of the disciplines, and that both should be considered by the curriculum planner or teacher.

As you grow in knowledge and understanding of the bases of curriculum-decisions studied so far, try to use them together. Theories of human development, theories of learning, theories about the individual in society, and theories about the nature of knowledge each describe only a portion of the learner's setting, nature, and action. But used together they constitute multiple curriculum criteria to aid the teacher and curriculum maker in planning and evaluating.

Objectives of a Curriculum Plan or Teaching Plan

The purposes of a curriculum or teaching plan are the most important curriculum criteria. They should provide the first guidelines for determining the learning experiences to be included in the curriculum. Unfortunately, schools commonly lack a comprehensive and reasonably consistent set of objectives on which to base curriculum decisions, and teachers often fail to use a set of objectives to guide their planning for teaching.

Without having a set of objectives clearly in view, teachers and curriculum planners cannot make sound professional judgments. They cannot use their knowledge of the curriculum bases to make choices of content, materials, or procedures that will further student learning toward intended ends. To choose among curriculum alternatives or instructional strategies, the educator must know the goals he is seeking and the curriculum bases on which he may make his choices. Otherwise, his selections will be little more than random; they cannot be termed professional in the light of today's knowledge of cultural and social forces, human development and learning, and knowledge and cognition.

Learners should be clearly aware of the objectives being sought by teachers and by the curriculum they are experiencing. In the process of instruction, learners should share in defining the objectives. While the objectives the teacher uses to guide his planning and those sought by the learners need not be identical, there should be much overlapping. The teacher's and learners' goals for a learning experience certainly must be understood by both the teacher and the learners, and they must be compatible or they are not likely to be achieved. This sharing of objectives by teachers, curriculum planners, and learners can only be achieved by student-teacher planning. In the article "Who Should Plan the Curriculum," Hass states that the student is the "major untapped resource in curriculum planning."

Broad, general goals are needed in planning the objectives of a program of education and for teaching it. Such objectives can then be used to define the need for various courses, activities, and experiences in the community. The writer has found it useful to think of the broad, general goals as necessarily including goals in four areas; education for citizenship, vocation, self-realization, and critical thinking. These four goals can be placed in two broad areas, both of which should always be considered in curriculum planning: the goals that relate to the society and its values; the goals that relate to the individual learner and his talents, needs, interests and abilities in a changing society.

The four bases of the curriculum should be considered in selecting goals and in seeking their attainment.

Every faculty and each teacher should consider the objectives that are pertinent for learners with whom they work. Objectives *in a particular setting* are related to the social forces, values, and needs of that community, the needs for individual development revealed by study of *particular learners*, and the significance of knowledge for interpretive use both in the local and larger society.

Behavioral Objectives and Performance Goals

No topic has received more attention in the field of curriculum and instruction since 1968 than behavioral objectives. The pros and cons of behavioral objectives are presented in this section (see articles by Gagné and Kneller). The discussion of behavioral objectives has served an important function in the curriculum field by calling attention to the need for objectives that are clearly and publicly stated and by emphasizing the need to use objectives in guiding, planning, activities, and evaluation of outcomes of instruction.

Performance goals refer to learning in which performance competencies are the outcomes sought. When performance competencies are the goals of learning, curriculum planning must focus on the development of the knowledge, skills, and experiences that are needed by the learner if he is to be able to analyze, organize, implement, and evaluate his performance in some aspect of a role. Inferences about success in learning are then made from total performance rather than from small specific behaviors.

Performance goals are specified in advance, and to be successful in learning, the learner must be able to perform the essential tasks and behaviors related to the goals. As stated in the introduction, the purpose of this book is to help you to achieve skill in many of the performance competencies you need in curriculum planning and teaching.

Lists of Curriculum Criteria

The planned objectives are among the most significant criteria for developing and evaluating any curriculum plan. This is true regardless of what the objectives are or how they are stated. The four bases of the curriculum should also be used as curriculum criteria in curriculum and instruction planning.

Other criteria are often suggested. Among those most frequently suggested are *individual differences, continuity, balance, flexibility, cooperative planning, student-teacher planning, teaching of values, systematic planning, self-understanding,* and *problem-solving.* The importance of most or all of these criteria can be derived from the bases of the curriculum. For instance, understanding of social forces, human development, learning theories, and knowledge theories supports the need to provide for individual differences in planning the curriculum.

Articles by Fantini, Nash and Harris; Wiles; Ianni; Hounshell and West, and Hass in this section each present different curriculum criteria to be emphasized, depending on the writer's particular area of curriculum concern.

This variety of emphases should suggest to you that you need to develop your own set of criteria for use in planning for curriculum and teaching. Your criteria should reflect your own thinking as well as the particular subject or area of the curriculum with which you are concerned.

OBJECTIVES

Your objectives in studying curriculum criteria should be as follows:

1. To be able to use the four bases of the curriculum *together* as guidelines for curriculum and instruction planning and decision-making.
2. To be able to analyze and describe the ways in which some of the contemporary curriculum theorists utilize social forces, community factors, student factors, human development factors, learning theory, and knowledge theory in their curriculum planning.
3. To be able to develop a set of criteria appropriate for particular curriculum planning tasks from a knowledge of objectives; social forces; human development, learning and knowledge theories; and other criteria such as individual differences, balance, continuity, or flexibility.
4. To be able to describe and evaluate a curriculum plan in terms of your selected set of curriculum criteria.
5. To be able to suggest improvements in a curriculum plan in terms of your selected set of curriculum criteria.

PREASSESSMENT

The purpose of the preassessment is to enable you to determine whether you already possess the performance competencies in curriculum planning that are listed under Objectives, above.

1. Select several objectives, social forces and community factors and at least one theory each from the areas of human development, learning theory, and knowledge theory and tell how you would use them together in curriculum planning or the planning of teaching.
2. Prepare a list of curriculum criteria for the curriculum and instruction planning areas with which you are most concerned. Defend your list for adequacy and appropriateness.
3. Select any curriculum plan of your choice, at any school level, and describe and analyze it in terms of your list of curriculum criteria.
4. Suggest improvements or changes in the curriculum plan as a result of your analysis in number 3.

From your study of earlier sections of this book, you already know that curriculum plans frequently are not based on an adequate set of criteria. Therefore, suggest improvements in the plan on the basis of your curriculum criteria.

You have also undoubtedly noted that often when a curriculum plan makes good use of one of the bases, such as human development, the other curriculum bases are not considered or are not adequately considered. When you recognize this in a curriculum plan, suggest possible improvements in the plan, derived from the curriculum bases and criteria not utilized in the planning.

You might choose to analyze the following curriculum plans in answering numbers 3 and 4 of the preassessment:

1. "Team Teaching in Canton's Model School," by Measel and Fincher, in Section 6.

2. "The John Dewey High School Adventure," by Levine, in Section 8.
3. "Bronx Community College Faces Change," by Donovan, in Section 9.

LEARNING ACTIVITIES

Articles in this section will assist you in understanding types and functions of objectives in curriculum planning. Also, a number of the articles will help you prepare your own list of criteria.

Other learning alternatives are suggested at the end of this section.

POSTASSESSMENT

After attempting the preassessment you may do one or more of the following:

1. Ask your instructor if you are ready for a postassessment evaluation on curriculum criteria. Most students will need further work on this topic.
2. Read the articles on curriculum criteria in this section and try to determine how the criteria being discussed in each article should be considered in curriculum planning and teaching.
3. Choose additional activities and readings or films and videotapes from those listed at the end of this section.
4. Look for other films, books, or articles on curriculum criteria that are in your library or media center.
5. Discuss the reading you have done and the films you have viewed with your fellow students. The key questions: How should the curriculum criteria you've studied affect a school's curriculum? How should they be considered in planning for teaching?
6. When you are ready, ask your instructor for advice on a suitable postassessment for you for this topic. Satisfactory completion of numbers 1, 2, or 10 under Problems and Projects at the end of this section might be one possibility. Or satisfactory written completion of the preassessment for this section, after completing other learning activities, might be a satisfactory postassessment. Consult your instructor about this. You can evaluate your ability to do either or both of these activities before seeing the instructor.

The Central Purpose of American Education

Educational Policies Commission

In any democracy, education is closely bound to the wishes of the people, but the strength of this bond in America has been unique. The American people have traditionally regarded education as a means for improving themselves and their society. Whenever an objective has been judged desirable for the individual or the society, it has tended to be accepted as a valid concern of the school. The American commitment to the free society—to individual dignity, to personal liberty, to equality of opportunity—has set the frame in which the American school grew. The basic American value, respect for the individual, has led to one of the major charges which the American people have placed on their schools: to foster that development of individual capacities which will enable each human being to become the best person he is capable of becoming.

The schools have been designed also to serve society's needs. The political order depends on responsible participation of individual citizens; hence the schools have been concerned with good citizenship. The economic order depends on ability and willingness to work; hence the schools have taught vocational skills. The general morality depends on choices made by individuals; hence the schools have cultivated moral habits and upright character.

Educational authorities have tended to share and support these broad concepts of educational purposes. Two of the best-known definitions of purposes were formulated by educators in 1918 and 1938. The first definition, by the Commission on the Reorganization of Secondary Education, proposed for the school a set of seven cardinal objectives; health, command of fundamental processes, worthy home membership, vocational competence, effective citizenship, worthy use of leisure, and ethical character. The second definition, by the Educational Policies Commission, developed a number of objectives under four headings: self-realization, human relationship, economic efficiency, and civic responsibility.

The American school must be concerned with all these objectives if it is to serve all of American life. That these are desirable objectives is clear. Yet they place before the school a problem of immense scope, for neither the schools nor the pupils have the time or energy to engage in all the activities which will fully achieve all these goals. Choices among possible activities are inevitable and are constantly being made in and for every school. But there is no consensus regarding a basis for making these choices. The need, therefore, is for a principle which will enable the school to identify its necessary and appropriate contributions to individual development and the needs of society.

From *NEA Journal* L, no. 6 (September 1961):13–16. Used by permission of the publisher.

Furthermore, education does not cease when the pupil leaves the school. No school fully achieves any pupil's goals in the relatively short time he spends in the classroom. The school seeks rather to equip the pupil to achieve them for himself. Thus the search for a definition of the school's necessary contribution entails an understanding of the ways individuals and societies choose and achieve their goals. Because the school must serve both individuals and the society at large in achieving their goals, and because the principal goal of the American society remains freedom, the requirements of freedom set the frame within which the school can discover the central focus of its own efforts.

FREEDOM OF THE MIND

The freedom which exalts the individual, and by which the worth of the society is judged, has many dimensions. It means freedom from undue governmental restraints; it means equality in political participation. It means the right to earn and own property and decide its disposition. It means equal access to just processes of law. It means the right to worship according to one's conscience.

Institutional safeguards are a necessary condition for freedom. They are not, however, sufficient to make men free. Freedom requires that citizens act responsibly in all ways. It cannot be preserved in a society whose citizens do not value freedom. Thus belief in freedom is essential to maintenance of freedom. The basis of this belief cannot be laid by mere indoctrination in principles of freedom. The ability to recite the values of a free society does not guarantee commitment to those values. Active belief in those values depends on awareness of them and of their role in life. The person who best supports these values is one who has examined them, who understands their function in his life and in the society at large, and who accepts them as worthy of his own support. For such a person these values are consciously held and consciously approved.

The conditions necessary for freedom include the social institutions which protect freedom and the personal commitment which gives it force. Both of these conditions rest on one condition within the individuals who compose a free society. This is freedom of the mind.

Freedom of the mind is a condition which each individual must develop for himself. In this sense, no man is born free. A free society has the obligation to create circumstances in which all individuals may have opportunity and encouragement to attain freedom of the mind. If this goal is to be achieved, its requirements must be specified.

To be free, a man must be capable of basing his choices and actions on understandings which he himself achieves and on values which he examines for himself. He must be aware of the bases on which he accepts propositions as true. He must understand the values by which he lives, the assumptions on which they rest, and the consequences to which they lead. He must recognize that others may have different values. He must be capable of analyzing the situation in which he finds himself and of developing solutions to the problems before him. He must be able to perceive and understand the events of his life and time and the forces that influence and shape those events. He must recognize and accept the practical limitations which time and circumstance place on his choices. The free man, in short, has a rational grasp of himself, his surroundings, and the relation between them.

He has the freedom to think and choose, and that freedom must have its roots in conditions both within and around the individual. Society's dual role is to guarantee the necessary environment and to develop the necessary individual strength. That individual strength springs from a thinking, aware mind, a mind that possesses the capacity to achieve aesthetic sensitivity and moral responsibility, an enlightened mind. These qualities occur in wide diversity of patterns in different individuals. It is the contention of this essay that central to all of them, nurturing them and being nurtured by them, are man's rational powers.

THE CENTRAL ROLE OF THE RATIONAL POWERS

The cultivated powers of the free mind have always been basic in achieving freedom. The powers of the free mind are many. In addition to the rational powers, there are those which relate to the aesthetic, the moral, and the religious. There is a unique, central role for the rational powers of an individual, however, for upon them depends his ability to achieve his personal goals and to fulfill his obligations to society.

These powers involve the processes of recalling and imagining, classifying and generalizing, comparing and evaluating, analyzing and synthesizing, and deducing and inferring. These processes enable one to apply logic and the available evidence to his ideas, attitudes, and actions, and to pursue better whatever goals he may have.

This is not to say that the rational powers are all of life or all of the mind, but they are the essence of the ability to think. A thinking person is aware that all persons, himself included, are both rational and non-rational, that each person perceives events through the screen of his own personality, and that he must take account of his personality in evaluating his perceptions. The rational processes, moreover, make intelligent choices possible. Through them a person can become aware of the bases of choice in his values and of the circumstances of choice in his environment. Thus they are broadly applicable in life, and they provide a solid basis for competence in all the areas with which the school has traditionally been concerned.

The traditionally accepted obligation of the school to teach the *fundamental processes*—an obligation stressed in the 1918 and 1938 statements of educational purposes—is obviously directed toward the development of the ability to think. Each of the school's other traditional objectives can be better achieved as pupils develop this ability and learn to apply it to all the problems that face them.

Health, for example, depends upon a reasoned awareness of the value of mental and physical fitness and of the means by which it may be developed and maintained. Fitness is not merely a function of living and acting; it requires that the individual understand the connection among health, nutrition, activity, and environment, and that he take action to improve his mental and physical condition.

Worthy home membership in the modern age demands substantial knowledge of the role that the home and community play in human development. The person who understands the bases of his own judgments recognizes the home as the source from which most individuals develop most of the standards and values they apply in their lives. He is intelligently aware of the role of emotion in his own life and in the lives of others. His knowledge of the importance of the home environment in the formation of personality enables him to make reasoned judgments about his domestic behavior.

More than ever before, and for an ever-increasing proportion of the population, *vocational competence* requires developed rational capacities. The march of technology and science in the modern society progressively eliminates the positions open to low-level talents. The man able to use only his hands is at a growing disadvantage as compared with the man who can also use his head. Today even the simplest use of hands is coming to require the simultaneous employment of the mind.

Effective citizenship is impossible without the ability to think. The good citizen, the one who contributes effectively and responsibly to the management of the public business in a free society, can fill his role only if he is aware of the values of his society. Moreover, the course of events in modern life is such that many of the factors which influence an individual's civic life are increasingly remote from him. His own first-hand experience is no longer an adequate basis for judgment. He must have in addition the intellectual means to study events, to relate his values to them, and to make wise decisions as to his own actions. He must also be skilled in the processes of communication and must understand both the potentialities and the limitations of communication among individuals and groups.

The *worthy use of leisure* is related to the individual's knowledge, understanding, and capacity to choose, from among all the activities to which his time can be devoted, those which contribute to the achievement of his purposes and to the satisfaction of his needs. On these bases, the individual can become aware of the external pressures which compete for his attention, moderate the influence of these pressures, and make wise choices for himself. His recreation, ranging from hobbies to sports to intellectual activity pursued for its own sake, can conform to his own concepts of constructive use of time.

The development of *ethical character* depends upon commitment to values; it depends also upon the ability to reason sensitively and responsibly with respect to those values in specific situations. Character is misunderstood if thought of as mere conformity to standards imposed by external authority. In a free society, ethics, morality, and character have meaning to the extent that they represent affirmative, thoughtful choices by individuals. The ability to make these choices depends on awareness of values and of their role in life. The home and the church begin to shape the child's values long before he goes to school. And a person who grows up in the American society inevitably acquires many values from his daily pattern of living. American children at the age of six, for example, usually have a firm commitment to the concept of fair play. This is a value which relates directly to such broad democratic concepts as justice and human worth and dignity. But the extension of this commitment to these broader democratic values will not occur unless the child becomes aware of its implications for his own behavior, and this awareness demands the ability to think.

A person who understands and appreciates his own values is most likely to act on them. He learns that his values are of great moment for himself, and he can look objectively and sympathetically at the values held by others. Thus, by critical thinking, he can deepen his respect for the importance of values and strengthen his sense of responsibility.

The man who seeks to understand himself understands also that other human beings have much in common with him. His understanding of the possibilities which exist within a human being strengthens his concept of the respect due every man. He recognizes the web which relates him to other men and perceives the necessity for responsible behavior. The person whose rational powers are not well developed can, at best, learn habitual responses and ways of conforming which may insure that he is not a detriment to his society. But, lacking the insight that he might have achieved, his capacity to contribute will inevitably be less than it might have become.

Development of the ability to reason can lead also to dedication to the values which inhere in rationality: commitment to honesty, accuracy, and personal reliability; respect for the intellect and for the intellectual life; devotion to the expansion of knowledge. A man who thinks can understand the importance of his ability. He is likely to value the rational potentials of mankind as essential to a worthy life.

Thus the rational powers are central to all the other qualities of the human spirit. These powers flourish in a humane and morally responsible context and contribute to the entire personality. The rational powers are to the entire human spirit as the hub is to the wheel.

These powers are indispensable to a full and worthy life. The person in whom—for whatever reason—they are not well developed is increasingly handicapped in modern society. He may be able to satisfy minimal social standards, but he will inevitably lack his full measure of dignity because his incapacity limits his stature to less than he might otherwise attain. Only to the extent that an individual can realize his potentials, especially the development of his ability to think, can he fully achieve for himself the dignity that goes with freedom.

A person with developed rational powers has the means to be aware of all facets of his existence. In this sense he can live to the fullest. He can escape captivity to his emotions and irrational states. He can enrich his emotional life and direct it toward ever higher standards of taste and enjoyment. He can enjoy the political and economic freedoms of the democratic society. He can free himself from the bondage of ignorance and unawareness. He can make of himself a free man.

THE CHANGES IN MAN'S UNDERSTANDING AND POWER

The foregoing analysis of human freedom and review of the central role of the rational powers in enabling a person to achieve his own goals demonstrate the critical importance of developing those powers. Their importance is also demonstrated by an analysis of the great changes in the world.

Many profound changes are occurring in the world today, but there is a fundamental force contributing to all of them. That force is the expanding role accorded in modern life to the rational powers of man. By using these powers to increase his knowledge, man is attempting to solve the riddles of life, space, and time which have long intrigued him. By using these powers to develop sources of new energy and means of communication, he is moving into interplanetary space. By using these powers to make a smaller world and larger weapons, he is creating new needs for international organization and understanding. By using these powers to alleviate disease and poverty, he is lowering death rates and expanding populations. By using these powers to create and use a new technology, he is achieving undreamed affluence, so that in some societies distribution has become a greater problem than production.

While man is using the powers of his mind to solve old riddles, he is creating new ones. Basic assumptions upon which mankind has long operated are being challenged or demolished. The age-old resignation to poverty and inferior status for the masses of humanity is being replaced by a drive for a life of dignity for all. Yet, just as man achieves a higher hope for all mankind, he sees also the opening of a grim age in which expansion of the power to create is matched by a perhaps greater enlargement of the power to destroy.

As man sees his power expand, he is coming to realize that the common sense which he accumulates from his own experience is not a sufficient guide to the understanding of the events in his own life or of the nature of the physical world. And, with combined uneasiness and exultation, he senses that his whole way of looking at life may be challenged in a time when men are returning from space.

Through the ages, man has accepted many kinds of propositions as truth, or at least as bases sufficient for action. Some propositions have been accepted on grounds of superstition; some on grounds of decree, dogma, or custom; some on humanistic, aesthetic, or religious grounds; some on common sense. Today, the role of knowledge derived from rational inquiry is growing. For this there are several reasons.

In the first place, knowledge so derived has proved to be man's most efficient weapon for achieving power over his environment. It prevails because it works.

More than effectiveness, however, is involved. There is high credibility in a proposition which can be arrived at or tested by persons other than those who advance it. Modesty, too, is inherent in rational inquiry, for it is an attempt to free explanations of phenomena and events from subjective preference and human authority, and to subject such explanations to validation through experience. Einstein's concept of the curvature of space cannot be demonstrated to the naked eye and may offend common sense; but persons who cannot apply the mathematics necessary to comprehend the concept can still accept it. They do this, not on Einstein's authority, but on their awareness that he used rational methods to achieve it and that those who possess the ability and facilities have tested its rational consistency and empirical validity.

In recent decades, man has greatly accelerated his systematic efforts to gain insight through rational inquiry. In the physical and biological sciences and in mathematics, where he has most successfully applied these methods, he has in a short time accumulated a vast fund of knowledge so reliable as to give him power he has never before had to understand, to predict, and to act. That is why attempts are constantly being made to apply these methods to additional areas of learning and human behavior.

The rapid increase in man's ability to understand and change the world and himself has resulted from increased application of his powers of thought. These powers have proved to be his most potent resource, and, as such, the likely key to his future.

THE CENTRAL PURPOSE OF THE SCHOOL

The rational powers of the human mind have always been basic in establishing and preserving freedom. In furthering personal and social effectiveness they are becoming more important than ever. They are central to individual dignity, human progress, and national survival.

The individual with developed rational powers can share deeply in the freedoms his society offers and can contribute most to the preservation of those freedoms. At the same time he will have the best chance of understanding and contributing to the great events of his time. And the society which best develops the rational potentials of its people, along with their intuitive and aesthetic capabilities, will have the best chance of flourishing in the future. To help every person develop those powers is therefore a profoundly important objective and one which increases in importance with the passage of time. By pursuing this objective, the school can enhance spiritual and aesthetic values and the other cardinal purposes which it has traditionally served and must continue to serve.

The purpose which runs through and strengthens all other educational purposes—the common thread of education—is the development of the ability to think. This is the central purpose to which the school must be oriented if it is to accomplish either its traditional tasks or those newly accentuated by recent changes in the world. To say that it is central is not to say that it is the sole purpose or in all circumstances the most important purpose, but that it must be a pervasive concern in the work of the school. Many agencies contribute to achieving educational objectives, but this particular objective will not be generally attained unless the school focuses on it. In this context, therefore, the development of every student's rational powers must be recognized as centrally important.

The Rediscovery of Purpose in Education

Harold G. Shane

Something seemed to go awry with the once-sustaining purposes of U.S. education in the years between 1920 and 1970. By the late 1960's there was even the gloomy prospect that our instructional landscape might be on the way to becoming a littered ideological junkyard.

Harold G. Shane, "The Rediscovery of Purpose in Education." *Educational Leadership* 28 (6):581–84; March 1971. Reprinted with permission of the Association for Supervision and Curriculum Development and Harold G. Shane. Copyright © 1971 by the Association for Supervision and Curriculum Development.

As we entered the 1970's there undoubtedly were more than a few Americans who uneasily speculated, and not without some reason, that we were moving into a confused, "Twilight of the Goals" interval which foreshadowed a social and educational Armageddon that was likely to occur in the next decade or two.

THE REDISCOVERY OF BASIC PURPOSE

Because of contemporary educational problems too well known to need recounting, it is suggested here with a sense of urgency that the need for a rediscovery of educational purpose is becoming frighteningly obvious. After 10,000 years we appear to have come full circle and once again need to rediscover the purpose of primitive man's education—human survival in the face of a dangerous, implacable environment.

From a life-and-death battle with a hostile nature early in our history we have cycled back to a point at which we face an analogous struggle to protect ourselves from an environment—a *biosphere* to use fashionable terminology—which has been made dangerous for man by man. Among the present, clear dangers are our propensity for overbreeding, our ingenuity in devising deadly weapons, the careless release of poisonous technological wastes, and the thoughtlessly accumulated mountains of "indisposable" trash which crowd our living space.

It is simple to propose that learning to survive has become a new central goal of education; it is decidedly less simple to conjecture about how to go about approaching such an objective.

ATTAINING NEW "SURVIVAL BEHAVIORS"

At least two paths of action present themselves if we accept the concept that survival in a meaningful world is an immediate goal for education. One of these is a reinterpretation of what *constitutes* "survival behaviors." The other is an educational reformation which will not only permit but which will begin to *ensure* that children and youth in our schools put together valid "behavioral survival kits." Such kits will help them not only to make it into the next century but, in the process, to begin to recast the world so that it promises to remain a nutritive bioenvironment suitable for mankind to inhabit. Let us look first at survival behavior.

From earliest times, the notion of survival was associated with attaining and staying at the apex of a socioeconomic pyramid. At least until the 19th century, about 15 percent of Western Europe's population—aristocrats, soldiers, ecclesiastics, scholars—was supported by the laborers, agrarians, and artisans making up the other 85 percent. Man fought like Duke William at Hastings to get to the top of the pile and schemed like King John at Runnymede to stay there. Indeed, through the ages, history has defined the one who survives as "successful" and has bestowed its worldly favors on those caesars who proved to have the highest "survival quotients" in life's arenas!

In the past century, however, science, technology, and democracy have combined to invert the human pyramid. Today in the United States, no more than 7 percent of the population is needed on our mechanized farms to produce food for the remaining 93 percent. Theoretically, one-third of our adults, by 1985, would not even need to be productive workers. The remaining two-thirds of the U.S. population doubtless could meet not only their own material needs but those of tens of millions of others who would produce nothing. This is a projection of a repugnant possibility, however, and not a prophecy!

Despite the reversal of our human pyramid, a 50,000-year interval of deep-rooted survival behavior is not quickly forgotten. For the most part, society and its schools have both failed to teach and failed to understand that man is becoming more capable of surviving by living *with* his fellows rather than by living *on* his fellows. Conjecture clearly suggests that there is not only "room at the *top*" but room *everywhere* for self-realization and for a better life for all in the inverted social pyramid of the present century *if we can discipline ourselves to make the needed "survival decisions."* To put it bluntly, a 180° reversal is needed in the traditional concept of "get-ahead behavior" that man has learned to accept during the past 500 centuries. We now need to learn how to stop behaving like troglodytes in trousers and take the steps that lead from being the scattered members of insecure tribes to becoming a secure mankind.

NEW PURPOSE AS A SOURCE OF DIRECTION FOR EDUCATIONAL CHANGE

Educational reforms of a sweeping and significant nature rarely have come about through the action of the schools in and of themselves. Educational practice tends to reflect what a majority or at least a plurality of society chooses to support in the classroom. Under such circumstances it seems reasonable to argue that *society itself must make itself accountable* for changes that are needed in the fabric of teaching and learning in order to bring us closer to a new central purpose for education.

Below is a sample of the kind of neglected or minimized learnings that a society interested in the survival and in the physical and psychological health of the children and youth should mandate that its schools recognize:

1. That we need to begin to lead less wasteful, extravagant lives, to do with less, and to rediscover enjoyment in simpler activities, objects, and pleasures so that our posterity will not live a marginal existence in a world stripped half-naked of its inheritance.
2. That the despoliation of our forests and the pillage of our pure air and clean water shall cease along with the poorly managed exploitation of fuels, fertile soils, and metals. Such abuses must be terminated by group consensus and by the legislation to which it leads.
3. That no one has the right to befoul or poison the earth with chemicals or radioactive wastes or poorly removed sewage and garbage.
4. That unless we exercise prudence and personal responsibility, we will suffer badly from the malignant consequences of changes that affect man's relationships with his environment, as in faulty city planning, random dam building, or unwise land use.
5. That there is a need to understand the immediate danger of irresponsible and

uncontrolled human breeding as the world's population builds up toward the 4,000,000,000 mark.

6. That the folly of conflict is becoming more and more incongruous in a world grown capable of self-destruction.

7. That mass media need to become more positive agents for reinforcing the educational guidance of the young, for producing less misleading advertising, for more thoughtful and less strident news, and for a more accurate and dignified portrayal of life in the global village.

8. That we must learn to be more personally responsible for the participation and earned support that are needed to ensure an increase in the number of able, dedicated public servants in elective and appointive governmental offices.

THE DEEPER MEANING OF "RELEVANCE"

What we mean by "relevance" in education is implicit in the previous eight points. "Relevance" is more than teaching subject matter and providing experiences that the young say they find immediately meaningful, more interesting, and more useful to them. A relevant education, an education for survival, is one which introduces children and youth to participation in the tasks that they and adults confront together in the real world of the 1970's.

Furthermore, if we are to make rapid progress toward the successful attainment of a new central purpose for education, society must not only encourage but *require* that the schools work to produce a generation of hardheaded young people committed to survival yet remembering the meaning of compassion; persons who have been taught the *Realpolitik* of life with honesty but who are nonetheless untainted by cynicism because they believe that it is not yet too late to cope with man's threat to himself.

THE FIRST STEP IN REFORMATION

Making a beginning in reform is not up to "society" as an abstract entity but to each of us as the individuals who make up society. It is through a new sense of imprescriptible personal responsibility that we can dispel the threatening twilight that recently has shadowed our goals.

In the process of creating a more benign environment, some of our sensate pleasures and much of our conspicuous consumption must diminish. Also, today's thoughtless waste of human and material resources must first be decreased and then ended as quickly as possible. In the process, our lives will perforce become not only simpler and less hedonistic; they will become more people-centered and less thing-centered. This necessary redirection can bring us far more gain than loss. The satisfactions of 40 or 50 years ago were not necessarily less warm or less desirable because feet, bicycles, or street cars transported an older generation to shops, schools, or theatres!

Furthermore, the short and long range changes that an endangered world requires for its future well-being should also involve fewer tensions, less erosive competition, and a clearer, more relaxing perspective with regard to what is most worth doing and most worth having.

A CONCLUDING CONJECTURE

Assuming we do avoid extinction, there would seem to be two levels or kinds of survival for man: as a biological *species* and as *humans*. The eight survival learnings itemized here should help to ensure that the species is around for some time to come. If nothing else, sheer panic seems likely soon to motivate us to diminish the interrelated problems of ecology, of hunger, of waste, and of conflict.

To survive in a truly *human* context rather than a merely biological one is something else! Here we come to a more subtle aspect of a "survival kit" for young learners. Our rediscovery of purpose and of personal responsibility for the social and educational reforms that are prerequisite to physical survival is but one side of the coin.

There is the concomitant task of helping the young of each generation to discover for themselves a moral, aesthetic, intellectual, and scientific heritage that they see cause for making a part of themselves. Does it not then seem reasonable that our success in guiding this freshening, continuing rediscovery by the young of *what makes us human* is what gives the real meaning to "education for survival"?

And may one not rightly conjecture that as a society-of-the-individually-responsible accepts this task, it simultaneously could become its own best hope for survival through the rediscovery of sustaining purpose in education?

Behavioral Objectives? Yes!

Robert M. Gagné

Few people who are professionally concerned with education in the United States are unacquainted with "behavioral objectives." Knowledge of this term and its meaning has become widespread. It is therefore timely to pose a question which inquires about the need for behavioral objectives, the possible uses they may have, and the educational functions that may be conceived for them.

NATURE OF INSTRUCTIONAL OBJECTIVES

The statement of a behavioral objective is intended to communicate (to a specified recipient or group of recipients) the outcome of some unit of instruc-

Robert M. Gagné. "Behavioral Objectives? Yes!" *Educational Leadership* 29(5):304–306; February 1972. Reprinted with permission of the Association for Supervision and Curriculum Development and Robert M. Gagné. Copyright © 1972 by The Association for Supervision and Curriculum Development.

tion. One assumes that the general purpose of instruction is learning on the part of the student. It is natural enough, therefore, that one should attempt to identify the outcome of learning as something the student is able to do following instruction which he was unable to do before instruction. When one is able to express the effects of instruction in this way, by describing observable performances of the learner, the clarity of objective statements is at a maximum. As a consequence, the reliability of communication of instructional objectives also reaches its highest level.

To some teachers and educational scholars, it appears at least equally natural to try to identify the outcomes of learning in terms of what capability the learner has gained as a result of instruction, rather than in terms of the performance he is able to do. We therefore frequently encounter such terms as "knowledge," "understanding," "appreciation," and others of this sort which seem to have the purpose of identifying learned capabilities or dispositions. Mager (1962) and a number of other writers have pointed out the ambiguity of these terms, and the unreliability of communications in which they are used.

Actually, I am inclined to argue that a complete statement of an instructional objective, designed to serve all of its communicative purposes, needs to contain an identification of *both* the type of capability acquired as a result of learning, and also the specific performance by means of which this capability can be confirmed (cf. Gagné, 1971a). Examples can readily be given to show that perfectly good "behavioral" verbs (such as "types," as in "types a letter") are also subject to more than one interpretation. For example, has the individual learned to "copy" a letter, or to "compose" a letter? The fact that no one would disagree that these two activities are somehow different, even though both are describable by the behavior of "typing," clearly indicates the need for descriptions of what has been learned which include more than observable human actions. Complete instructional objectives need to identify the capability learned, as well as the performance which such a capability makes possible.

The implications of this view are not trivial. If in fact such terms as "knowledge" and "understanding" are ambiguous, then we must either redefine them, or propose some new terms to describe learned capabilities which can be more precisely defined. My suggestion has been to take the latter course, and I have proposed that the five major categories representing "what is learned" are motor skills, verbal information, intellectual skills, cognitive strategies, and attitudes (Gagné, 1971b). Completing the example used previously, the statement of the objective would be "Given a set of handwritten notes, *generates* (implies the intellectual skill which is to be learned) a letter *by typing* (identifies the specific action used)."

The alternatives to such "behavioral" statements have many defects, as Mager (1962) and other writers have emphasized. However they may be expanded or embellished, statements describing the *content* of instructional presentations invariably fail to provide the needed communications. The fact that a textbook, or a film, or a talk by a teacher, presents "the concept of the family" is an inadequate communication of the intended learning outcome, and cannot be made adequate simply by adding more detail. The critical missing elements in any such descriptions of instruction are the related ideas of (a) what the student will have learned from instruction, and (b) what class of performances he will then be able to exhibit.

USES OF BEHAVIORAL OBJECTIVES BY SCHOOLS

Statements describing instructional objectives have the primary purpose of *communicating*. Assuming that education has the form of an organized system, communication of its intended and actual outcomes is necessary, among and between the designers of instructional materials, the planners of courses and programs, the teachers, the students, and the parents. In order for the process of education to serve the purpose of learning, communications of these various sorts must take place. When any of them is omitted, education becomes to a diminished degree a systematic enterprise having the purpose of accomplishing certain societal goals pertaining to "the educated adult." There may be those who would argue that education should not serve such goals. Obviously, I disagree, but cannot here devote space to my reasons.

Some of the most important ways in which the various communications about objectives may be used by schools are indicated by the following brief outlines:

1. *The instructional designer to the course planner.* This set of communications enables the person who is planning a course with predetermined goals to select materials which can accomplish the desired outcomes. For example, if a course in junior high science has the goal of "teaching students to think scientifically," the planner will be seeking a set of materials which emphasize the learning of intellectual skills and cognitive strategies, having objectives such as "generates and tests hypotheses relating plant growth to environmental variables."

In contrast, if the goals of such a course are "to convey a scientific view of the earth's ecology," the curriculum planner will likely seek materials devoted to the learning of organized information, exhibited by such objectives as "describes how the content of carbon dioxide in the air affects the supply of underground water."

2. *The designer or planner to the teacher.* Communications of objectives to the teacher enable the latter to choose appropriate ways of delivering instruction, and also ways of assessing its effectiveness. As an example, a teacher of foreign language who adopts the objective, "pronounces French words containing the uvular 'r,'" is able (or should be able) to select a form of instruction providing practice in pronunciation of French words containing "r," and to reject as inappropriate for this objective a lecture on "the use of the uvular 'r' in French words."

Additionally, this communication of an objective makes apparent to the teacher how the outcome of instruction must be assessed. In this case, the choice would need to be the observation of oral pronunciation of French words by the student, and could not be, for instance, a multiple-choice test containing questions such as "which of the following French words has a uvular 'r'?"

3. *The teacher to the student.* There are many instructional situations in which the learning outcome expected is quite apparent to the student, because of his experience with similar instruction. For example, if the course is mathematics, and the topic changes from the addition of fractions to the multiplication of fractions, it is highly likely that the naming of the topic will itself be sufficient to imply the objective.

However, there are also many situations in which the objective may not be at all apparent. A topic on "Ohm's Law," for example, may not make apparent by its title whether the student is expected to recognize Ohm's Law, to state it, to substitute values in it, or to apply it to some electric circuits. It is reasonable to suppose that a student who knows what the objective is will be able to approach the task of learning with an advantage over one who does not.

4. *The teacher or principal to the parent.* It is indeed somewhat surprising that parents have stood still for "grades" for such a long period of time, considering the deplorably small amount of information they convey. If the trend toward "accountability" continues, grades will have to go. Teachers cannot be held accountable for A's, B's, and C's—in fact, grades are inimical to any system of accountability. It seems likely, therefore, that the basis for accountability will be the instructional objective. Since this must express a learning outcome, it must presumably be expressed in behavioral terms. Several different forms of accountability systems appear to be feasible; objectives would seem to be necessary for any or all of them.

These appear to be the major communication functions which schools need to carry out if they are engaged in systematically promoting learning. Each of these instances of communication requires accurate and reliable statements of the *outcomes of learning*, if it is to be effective. Such outcomes may be described, accurately and reliably, by means of statements which identify (a) the capability to be learned, and (b) the class of performances by means of which the capability is exhibited. There appears to me to be no alternative to the use of "behavioral objectives," defined as in the previous sentence, to perform these essential functions of communication.

REFERENCES

Gagné, R. M. "Defining Objectives for Six Varieties of Learning." Washington, D.C.: American Educational Research Association, 1971a. (Cassette tape.)

Gagné, R. M. "Instruction Based on Research in Learning." *Engineering Education* 61: 519–23; 1971b.

Mager, R. F. *Preparing Instructional Objectives.* Belmont, California: Fearon Publishers, Inc., 1962.

Behavioral Objectives? No!

George F. Kneller

The use of behavioral objectives in instruction is characteristic of a culture which sets a high value on efficiency and productivity. Such a culture seeks to measure accomplishment in standard units. Theoretical justification for behavioral objectives comes from behavioral psychology (Kendler, 1959, p. 179). This type of psychology defines learning as behavior that is changed in conformity with predicted, measurable outcomes and with little or no measurable "waste."

Teacher education institutions that advocate the use of behavioral objectives transmit methods of instruction that are standardized, empirically tested, and aim at measurable results. Such methods work best in school systems that are highly sensitive to the economic and behavioral determinants of educational practice.

ANALYSIS

This approach to instruction rests on assumptions about human behavior that are reductionist, deterministic, and physicalist. It is opposed to the view that learning is self-directed, unstructured, and in large part unpredictable.

Advocates of the behavioral approach deny these two points (Popham, 1968; Block, 1971). Behavior, they say, covers a wide range of experience, including creativity, imagination, even serendipity. Nor need objectives be fixed; they can be modified, adjusted to individuals, even abandoned in favor of others (Baker, 1968; Block, 1971, p. 291). But if so, if the terms "behavior" and "objectives" can be made to mean many different things, what things could they not mean? If a term is to have a clear-cut meaning, we must at least be able to define its contradictory.[1]

Many advocates now speak of "instructional" rather than "behavioral" objectives (Mager, 1962). Nevertheless, one's notion of instruction depends on assumptions about the nature of the mind and of the persons involved in the

George F. Kneller. "Behavioral Objectives? No!" *Educational Leadership* 29(5):397–400; February 1972. Reprinted with permission of the Association for Supervision and Curriculum Development and George F. Kneller. Copyright © 1972 by the Association for Supervision and Curriculum Development.
[1] The meaning of "behavior" becomes more complicated still when, in relation to learning, it is stratified according to dispositions. Learning defined as changed behavior then includes changes in *dispositions* to behave. See: James E. McClellan. "B. F. Skinner's Philosophy of Human Nature." *Studies in Philosophy and Education* 4: 307–32; 1966; and L. B. Daniels. "Behavior Strata and Learning." *Educational Theory* 20 (4): 377–86; Fall 1970. A satisfactory theory of human behavior has yet to be proposed.

instructional process (Noddings, 1971, p. 40). The new term may imply a more modest approach to instruction and force us to concentrate on matters more central to education. Yet learning still is conceived as a series of measurable responses to carefully prearranged stimuli (Steg, 1971). The sameness of individuals is judged to matter more than their differences; schooling is systems-oriented; adjustment to the curriculum is presupposed; replication is prized; and computer-assisted instruction is cordially welcomed (Broudy, 1970, p. 49; Dreyfus, 1967, pp. 13–33).

It is claimed that, using behavioral objectives, a teacher can teach an entire class and cater to individual differences as well (Block, 1971). He can do so, it is said, either by adapting predetermined objectives to individuals or by composing a special set of objectives for each member of the class. However, this proud claim entails that the teacher must (a) handle a staggering number of objectives,[2] (b) accept a scientific theory of human behavior which tends to exclude individualized (idiosyncratic) learning, and (c) act on the false assumption that learning, knowing, and behaving are the same process.

As regards (c), not only are there many kinds of learning, pacing being only one of them, there are also many kinds of knowing and behaving. These processes, psychologically speaking, are separate and distinct. The subject is too complex to be argued here, but this much may be said: Learning leads to no particular behavior. It is impossible to coordinate learning or knowing with behaving, because there is no theory which interrelates these phenomena, and consequently there is no way of understanding how their putative instances might be brought into relation in actual practice (Deese, 1969, 516–17). To use behavioral objectives in individualized instruction is to overlook the essential differences between individual learning, knowing, and behaving.

Behavioral objectivists are apt to be scornful of teachers who refuse to adopt clearly specified goals. This refusal, we are told, is partly responsible for the "present failure" of American education (Popham, 1968). I do not see how this could be shown to be the case. I am still less impressed by the claim that if we adopted behavioral objectives, we would solve most of our instructional problems.

All depends on what one considers good teaching and learning to be. Teachers might be held more "strictly" accountable, learning might be evaluated more "reliably," and parents might perceive their children's achievements more "accurately"—but only if teaching and learning are drastically circumscribed. Here is the heart of the matter. Undoubtedly, the process of education can be more tightly controlled, most simply by giving everyone less freedom of choice. This suits the behavioral objectivist, because his philosophy is one of control, but it does not suit educators of other persuasions.

---

[2] Behavioral objectivists maintain that the number of objectives for a single course could run as high as two thousand, if the teacher sought to cover everything. If there were 30 students in a class, the number of individual objectives would amount to as many as sixty thousand. The high school teacher of 150 students would be handling millions of objectives—conceivably. Given the behaviorists' claim that behavior includes everything that can occur in a learning situation, these figures are plausible enough. Block (1971, p. 292) correctly observes that the computer has a tremendous capacity to tailor-make programs. Item banks could be constructed and stored. Yet this of course would require that the teacher specify goals in appropriate computer terms.

SPECULATION

Under what circumstances may schools be said to "need" behavioral objectives? For one thing, such objectives can be used to define and measure accomplishment in those basic intellectual abilities that all students need if they are to pass successfully from one learning experience to another. Failure by a student to acquire a basic skill may, if uncorrected, hinder all his future learning and so his whole attitude toward education. The young man who desires to be a master mechanic must first acquire the skills of an apprentice, and then of a journeyman. He cannot acquire them unless he can read, write, and compute. A long history of painful, unsuccessful learning experiences can severely damage a student's self-concept, his personality development, and his entire life style (Block, 1971, pp. 297–98).

That many of our youth are damaged in this way, especially in the elementary school, is distressingly obvious. The school has a clear responsibility to ensure that *all* students succeed in learning basic skills. In order to meet this responsibility, the school must possess a schedule of clearly specified objectives for all students to achieve, together with adequate instruments for measuring what is achieved. Every student must know concretely and specifically what he is accomplishing relative to (a) what may reasonably be expected of him, and (b) what his peers are achieving.

"SPECIFIED" OBJECTIVES

The objectives I suggest are "specified" rather than "behavioral." They are chosen, or specified, by the school according to its own philosophy of education, and they are specified only for certain subject matter which the school considers basic.[3] Certain specific content (or skills) could be required of all students at certain levels, and the students could be tested on how well they had acquired it. It would be the sort of content on which it is fairly easy to test in accordance with minimum standards of achievement.

Yet at another level, a level at which standardization is difficult, impossible, or undesirable, the individual teacher should specify objectives, to be achieved by either the individual student or groups of students, in accordance with (a) a theory of knowledge and value adopted by the teacher himself, and (b) the talents and choices of the student. Take two subjects where rigorous evaluation is quite impossible, art and music. The teacher might perhaps stipulate that a certain number and kind of songs be learned, that at least one song be composed, and that a symphony be analyzed. He might also stipulate that a number of drawings be made, and that one essay be written on a painting and another on an art movement such as dadaism or impressionism. In teaching these and other

---

[3] I agree with Maccia (1962) and Steg (1971) that although some learning goals can be specified, we should give wide play to the discovery impulse in learning. Much knowledge may be set out for the student to acquire. Yet the teacher must also open the gates for students both to acquire knowledge that interests them personally and to inquire beyond the knowledge we now have.

subjects, the teacher should be guided by a defensible philosophy and psychology of learning and instruction.[4]

Ultimately, however, it is not the schools but the teachers who must decide what objectives should be specified, and they must do so as individuals, taking their students into consideration. They must therefore acquire the knowledge and skills that are needed to specify educational objectives and evaluate the results obtained. Behavioral objectivists can help by providing models to spur investigation. Yet if these models are adopted uncritically by the rank and file of teachers, education will decline into an inauthentic and spiritless conditioning.

For, properly conceived, education is a dialogue between persons in the community of the school, a dialogue in which the teacher encourages the student to enter into acts of learning that fulfill him personally. This is education at its finest, and the program of the behavioral objectivist has very little place in it.

REFERENCES

BAKER, EVA. *Defining Content for Objectives.* Los Angeles: Vincet Associates, 1968.

BLOCK, JAMES H. "Criterion-Referenced Measurements: Potential." *School Review* 79 (2):289–98; February 1971.

BROUDY, HARRY S. "Can Research Escape the Dogma of Behavioral Objectives?" *School Review* 79 (1):43–56; November 1970.

DANIELS, L. B. "Behavior Strata and Learning." *Educational Theory* 20 (4): 377–85; Fall 1970.

DEESE, JAMES. "Behavior and Fact." *American Psychologist* 25 (5):515–22; May 1969.

DREYFUS, H. I. "Why Computers Must Have Bodies To Be Intelligent." *Review of Metaphysics* 21 (1):13–33; September 1967.

EBEL, ROBERT L. "Behavioral Objectives: A Close Look." *Phi Delta Kappan* 52 (3): 171–73; November 1970.

EISNER, E. W. "Educational Objectives: Help or Hindrance?" *School Review* 75 (3):250–66; Autumn 1967.

EISNER, E. W. *Instructional and Expressive Objectives: Their Formulation and Use in Curriculum.* AERA Monograph Series. Chicago: Rand McNally & Company, 1969.

KENDLER, HOWARD H. "Teaching Machines and Physchological Theory." In: Eugene Gallanter, editor. *Automated Teaching.* New York: John Wiley & Sons, Inc., 1959.

MACCIA, ELIZABETH S. "Epistemological Considerations in Relation to the Use of Teaching Machines." *Educational Theory* 12 (4):234ff.; October 1962.

MAGER, ROBERT F. *Preparing Instructional Objectives.* Belmont, California: Fearon Publishers, Inc., 1962.

[4] On learning goals and knowledge considerations, see Maccia (1962) and Steg (1971). Maccia shows that knowledge is an open system, and Steg warns against using objectives as anything more than a means for focusing purposes: "They must never become the overriding concern of education." Although both writers deal primarily with teaching machines, they are concerned with means by which students can create knowledge (and values, for that matter) instead of simply absorbing it. Learning, says Steg, is "the possibility of going outside a frame of activity" (p. 49). "We must consider logical goodness," says Maccia, "in relation to [new] knowing as well as in relation to knowledge" (p. 238).

NODDINGS, NELLIE L. "Beyond Behavioral Objectives: Seeing the Whole Picture." *Focus on Learning* 1 (1):35–41; Spring 1971.

NYBERG, DAVID. *Tough and Tender Learning.* Palo Alto, California: National Press Books, 1971. p. 68.

POPHAM, W. JAMES. "Probing the Validity of Arguments Against Behavioral Goals." Symposium presentation, AERA meeting, Chicago, February 1968.

STEG, D. R. "The Limitations of Learning Machines and Some Aspects of Learning." *Focus on Learning* 1 (1):43–51; Spring 1971.

Seeking Balance in the Curriculum

Kimball Wiles

In the controversy over education since Sputnik was placed in orbit, many persons have made a plea for balance. Some have asked for more math and science. Some have insisted that we continue to devote the same proportion of school time to the social studies and the humanities that we did before Sputnik. One professional association has designated the study of balance in the curriculum as a major emphasis in its national program.

Demands for balance are not new. Whenever people ask for a new emphasis in the curriculum or argue to maintain the present status, the plea for balance is a typical appeal to reason.

Some ask for even distribution of time among science, math, art, music, English and history.

Some ask that more attention be given to the cultures of the Far East, Africa and Latin America.

Some ask for more study which will enable pupils to develop ways of solving social problems.

Some ask for inclusion of more information about local community.

Some ask for more attention to problems of social adjustment.

Some ask that a variety in social points of view be represented in the curriculum and instructional materials.

Some ask for more time for TV teaching.

Some ask that pupils be made more anxious and concerned about failure.

Some ask that pupils be helped to be more secure so that they will be free to venture.

Some ask for a greater amount of creative activity.

Some ask for more teaching of common values.

Some ask for more stress of the fundamental skills.

What is the balance sought? How can it be attained?

From *Childhood Education* XXXVI, no. 2 (October 1959):69–73. Reprinted by permission of the Association for Childhood Education International, 3615 Wisconsin Avenue, N.W., Washington, D.C.

ATTEMPTS TO ATTAIN BALANCE

Balance in the curriculum has been sought in various ways. Some school systems follow a curriculum pattern designed by scholars, in which all youngsters are brought into contact with the facts, concepts and generalizations it is assumed all students should know.

Some schools attempt to develop balance by assigning portions of days to designated subjects—fifteen minutes for spelling, twenty minutes for reading, twenty minutes for arithmetic, and so on. Certain assumptions are made about desirable balance in amounts of time provided for different activities.

Some schools try to obtain balance by having a classroom teacher plus some special teachers who come in to teach music, art, physical education and things the administrators think the classroom teacher cannot or does not teach well.

Other schools seek to achieve balance by maintaining self-contained classrooms in which the teacher knows all the activities in which youngsters engage. It is assumed the teacher has some criterion by which he can tell if there is a balance.

Some systems appoint supervisors to guide teachers toward more balance than they are providing. It is assumed the supervisors have a gauge by which they can determine proper balance.

PROBLEMS IN SECURING BALANCE

From the point of view of recent developments in research, seeking balance through division and allocation of content or administrative procedure has little chance for success. The research on perception (Kelley's report in *Education for What Is Real* or the research of McClellan and others at the University of Chicago) indicates that *people perceive differently, in terms of their purposes, their needs, and their background.* Acceptance of this evidence leads to the proposition that a curriculum provided by a school is not the same for any two people going through it and that a balanced curriculum for the individual cannot be achieved by attempting to give everybody the same thing.

Difference in maturation rates makes it difficult to provide balance for the individual. American education is organized around homogeneous grouping by age. But the evidence being provided about maturation rates reveals that some nine-year-olds are as large as the average seventeen-year-old and some seventeen-year-olds are as small as the average nine-year-old. Willard Olson's studies show that *people grow at different rates and mature at different ages.* When teachers talk about developmental tasks as though they occur for all eleven-year-olds at the same time, they are not supported by research. When balance is sought by establishing a curriculum structure ahead of time, it is gained for one youngster and hindered for another.

Further, *learning rates differ.* If schools do a good job, the longer youngsters are in school, the greater the difference in range of achievement at a given grade level. It seems rather hopeless to look at balance as something that can be prestructured by organizing concepts and activities into scope and sequence for given grades without consideration of a specific individual or class.

Add to differences in rates of maturation and learning variation in the purpose and the problems that children have, and the pre-structuring approach appears even less productive. Statements like Daniel Prescott's "Persistent emotional problems decrease the range of facts that are significant for the individual" illuminate the task of attempting to achieve balance by organizing content.

BALANCE FOR THE INDIVIDUAL

What alternative is left? How can balance be obtained? *Balance must be sought for the individual.* It is the assumption of the writer that each faculty must decide upon the types of growth it wants to develop and must use the program of activities to promote these growths in each child. Curriculum balance is determined by the extent to which a child's experiences promote *in a satisfactory manner* all of the growths the faculty deems important.

In arriving at the decision concerning desired growth, community groups, such as advisory groups or homeroom parent groups, should be brought in on the thinking. If not, lack of communication or lack of agreement may separate the school and homes, jeopardizing both support for the program and balance in the program.

Continuous evaluation and planning are necessary if balance is to be obtained. Evidence must be collected concerning the amount and kinds of growth being produced and the program for individuals revised in terms of the data secured.

The program that is balanced for one pupil may not be for another. The staff or the individual teacher must revise the schedule, method or activity when the evaluation reveals that classes or individuals are not making some of the growths sought. *Judgments must be made continuously by parents and teachers as to whether the present balance of pupil growth is satisfactory.* The basis for determining satisfactory balance should be the personal and social needs and purposes of the individual.

To maintain balance in the curriculum means that the teacher must be experimental to the extent that he will change his procedures when the evidence indicates he is ineffective. Each school needs a curriculum committee responsible for continuous evaluation of the program and recommendation of needed changes to the faculty.

THE METHOD IN OPERATION

How does this formula work in a school? Let's examine the operation of one school.

This school, faculty and parents, agreed on the types of growth desired. They said they wanted continuous growth of pupils in eight areas. Note the use of *continuous.* They do not expect all students to achieve given levels at any grade but want *uninterrupted progress* for all pupils in all of the types of growth desired.

First, they want continuous improvement in mental and physical health. A six-year-old observed students leaving the school at the end of the day. He looked at his mother and said, "This is a happy school, isn't it?" Even a six-year-old could see the youngsters as they came out of the school were happy. If the learning environment is to produce mental health, the people who go there must enjoy it and be happy.

In the kindergarten the five-year-olds go to the teacher when they are troubled, tug on her skirt and say, "lap." She sits down and holds them until they are ready to get down and face the world again. She gives them confidence of their worth. Evidence of her contribution is illustrated in the following incident. Joe, a five-year-old in Miss Jones' class, was being disciplined by his mother. She said, "If you don't behave, people won't like you." The little boy replied, "You know, Mother, no matter what Joe does, two people will like him. God and Miss Jones."

It is hoped all children will develop this sense of worth and acceptance.

Second, they want continuous growth in the fundamental skills. The official testing program is designed to sample growth in reading and arithmetic at the end of the second, fourth and sixth grades, and this is supplemented by each teacher's collecting evidence of progress.

At the beginning of the year the fifth-grade teacher asked each youngster to put into a Manila folder samples of all the work during the year of which he was proud. During January she asked each youngster to go through his folder and make a list of the ten most important things on which to work during the second semester. One boy, who read at the eighth-grade level and did arithmetic at the third-grade level, put as Number 1 on his list, "Work on my 8 tables." He did not have to be told to do it. He was using the evidence to make decisions about his status and desirable next steps. In a good intellectual climate, growth in fundamental skills is an individual matter in which pupils move ahead at their own best rate.

Third, they want continuous growth in the development of a set of values. The kindergarten teacher has the kind of relationship with children that enables them to discuss their problems with her. Even some youngsters in the first and second grades come back to talk with her. One little girl went to her and crawled upon her knee and said, "What happens if lightning strikes you?" The teacher said, "It may kill you." The little girl said, "What happens if you die?" The teacher said, "Different people believe different things." The little girl said, "Do you go to heaven?" The teacher knew that this little girl's parents did not believe in heaven or hell and she said, "Some people think so." The little girl said, "Is heaven near the sun?" The teacher said, "Some people think it is." The little girl said, "Is it warm there?" The teacher said, "If it's near the sun, it would be." The little girl said, "Then I want to go there." Each person chooses his own counselor, and the essence of guidance is creating the kind of situation where people can analyze their values with people they trust. The school recognizes this phenomenon and seeks to keep the type of flexible organization which facilitates its operation.

Fourth, they want continuous growth in creative ability. Great emphasis is placed on seeking solutions to problems and on expression of feelings and perceptions. When the second-grade teacher asked her class to draw a picture of their family, one girl drew a picture of five fish. In the center was a great big fish and in the corners were four little fish. It would have been very easy to look at this picture and assume that the big fish in the center was the little girl. When the teacher asked her to explain the picture, the little girl said, "The big fish in the center is my big brother and all the rest of us are out on the edges." The picture was drawn at the height of the football season and her brother was the fullback.

When teachers give youngsters a chance to express themselves creatively, not only do they develop a skill that will be important the rest of their lives, they reveal to teachers the learnings that they are doing in such a way that teachers can know how to relate to them. Teachers in this school examine their methods and the activities they provide to see if they are encouraging creativity.

Fifth, they want continuous growth in skill in making independent and intelligent decisions. The fifth-grade teacher described previously asked each child as he went back through his folder to decide, "What are the ten most important things for you to do?" Each was asked to analyze himself to determine his strengths and his weaknesses and to say, "These are the important next steps to take." By this process, the staff hopes the school will develop mature, self-directing people.

Sixth, they want continuous growth in skill in democratic group participation. From kindergarten to the sixth year, teacher-pupil planning and teacher-pupil evaluation occur daily. Teachers try to foster this growth by the way they work. Group work and committee work are a part of every class. When John Lovell, of Auburn Polytechnic Institute, studied the way teachers develop group participation skill in this school, he found that at every level the way the teacher operated with his class was reflected in the way the committee chairmen behaved with student groups. People learn as much about group participation by the way the teacher operates as by anything they read or hear.

Seventh, they want continuous growth in individual interests and skill in following individual interests. When a boy from the north moved to Florida, the thing he became most interested in was poisonous snakes. He went to his third-grade teacher and said, "I want to read about moccasins, rattlers, and coral snakes." She didn't say, "That's not in the third-grade curriculum; that's in tenth-grade biology—you'll get it there." She didn't say, "We don't have any instructional materials in the third grade which will permit you to read about poisonous snakes. We didn't buy any last year." She said, "Let's go to the school library and see if the librarian can help us find something." Because this teacher was willing to let this boy follow an individual interest for a portion of the day, his reading ability jumped from the third grade to the sixth grade in one year.

A fourth-grade boy was much interested in writing. He went on Saturday mornings to meet his fourth-grade teacher and began writing a book. It was never published, but the teacher took his time to work with a youngster on the pursuit of an individual interest.

Eighth, they want continuous growth in acquisition of an understanding of our cultural heritage. Experiences which acquaint pupils with social studies, language and literature are a part of the program; and administration of standardized tests at regular intervals throughout the elementary program determines whether or not classes and individual pupils are meeting expectations for pupils of their age and grade. The achievement of others assists in the interpretation of progress but is not a pattern or profile to seek.

Each teacher in this school believes these eight types of growth are important. He uses them as criteria to judge the curriculum of each pupil. He checks each youngster's progress and the things that he does by them. *He brings pupils and parents into decision-making situations at which it is decided if types and amounts of growth are in proper balance.* Teachers cannot make these judgments alone and be assured of validity. The purposes and concerns of those involved must enter the decision as to whether rates of growth in the areas are in balance.

Each teacher attempts to achieve balance by planning with the parents. Both share evidence that they have of growth or lack of growth in any of the eight areas and decide how they can supplement each other to bring a youngster up in an area where he may not be progressing as satisfactorily as they hope.

Not all faculties would establish the same types of growth as important. Differing values and community pressures might lead to the establishment of a different set of desirable outcomes. The formula that looks most promising is:

clear definition of the types of pupil growth sought

continuous collection of evidence concerning pupil growth in the specified areas

revision of the individual student's program when he is not making satisfactory progress in all areas

continuous study of the total program to discover ways of providing flexibility which permits greater adaptation of program to individual needs.

Options for Students, Parents, and Teachers: Public Schools of Choice

Mario Fantini

Samuel Nash

Donald Harris

The art of governance in a free society rests with citizen decision making. The more informed the citizen, the more capable he is of making decisions. The more options he has, the more chance he has of making a selection which is self-satisfying.

Transferring this notion to schools, the citizen as consumer should be able to decide on the kind of school his child should attend or the kind of educational environment he would like his children to have. This type of decision making would be school governance in its purest form. Making every parent the decision maker for his family's education is a significant stage beyond electing representatives to decide what kind of education makes the most sense for the majority in the locality. This is what we now have through our representative form of school governance, that is, through electing local school boards. In any majority-rule approach, significant numbers of citizens must accept majority rule in the kind of education their children receive. Therefore, diversity in education is severely restricted. Public schools then become social institutions which foster uniformity rather than diversity. Citizens who want other options must turn to private schools, if they can afford them. The private-school option is not available to many low-income citizens.

The trick is to get the *public schools* to respond to both diversity and individual rights in school decision making. However, in addition to governance, both *substance* and *personnel* are essential pillars which must be altered if genuine reform is to take place in American education. We therefore need to examine the implications of these two areas in a pattern which maximizes choice for the consumer.

A system of choice maximizes variation in both the substance and personnel of education. For example, consumers who select a school program based on a Montessori model will have important substantive differences from those who select a classical school. Choice does legitimize new programs, each of which carries with it new curriculum and new personnel.

Certainly, professionals who are attracted to a Summerhill-like school are different from those who prefer a classical school environment.

From *Phi Delta Kappan* LII, no. 9 (May 1971):541–543. Used by permission of the authors and publisher.

The point is that a public school system that maximizes consumer choice legitimizes new as well as old educational approaches to common objectives. The new educational approach will be made operational by public consent. Moreover, educators will also be able to choose from among these educational alternatives, possibly enhancing their sense of professional satisfaction.

This choice model, therefore, tends to minimize conflict among interest groups because each individual is making direct decisions in educational affairs. Furthermore, as a supply and demand model, the choice system has a self-revitalizing capability. As the options prove successful, they will increase in popularity, thereby increasing the flow of successful programs into the public schools and generating a renewal process for public education.

Under the present system, new programs are introduced into the public schools largely through professional channels, with parents, students, and teachers having little say. However, parents, students, and teachers can actually veto any new program. Some programs, such as sex education, become controversial, especially if they are superimposed by the administration.

School systems are currently structured to present only one model or pattern of education to a student and his parents. If economic factors or religious beliefs preclude nonpublic schools as an alternative, the parent and student have no choice but to submit to the kind and quality of public education in their community. With the exception that one or two schools may be viewed as "better" or "worse" by parents and students (generally because of "better teachers" or because "more" graduates go to college or because the school is in a "good neighborhood"), the way materials are presented and "school work" is done is essentially the same in all schools on the same level. It should be possible to develop within one school or cluster of schools within a neighborhood, district, or system several different models that would offer real choices to all those involved in the educative process.

A school district might offer seven different options in its elementary schools:

Option one: The concept and programs of the school are traditional. The school is graded and emphasizes the learning of basic skills—reading, writing, numbers, etc.—by cognition. The basic learning unit is the classroom, which functions with one or two teachers instructing and directing students at their various learning tasks. Students are encouraged to adjust to the school and its operational style rather than vice versa. Students with recognized learning problems are referred to a variety of remedial and school-support programs. The educational and fiscal policy for this school is determined entirely by the central board of education.

Option two: This school is nontraditional and nongraded. In many ways it is very much like the British primary schools and the Leicestershire system. There are many constructional and manipulative materials in each area where students work and learn. The teacher acts as a facilitator—one who assists and guides rather than directs or instructs. Most student activity is in the form of different specialized learning projects done individually and in small groups rather than in the traditional form where all students do the same thing at the same time. Many of the learning experiences and activities take place outside of the school building.

Option three: This school emphasizes learning by the vocational processes—

doing and experiencing. The school defines its role as diagnostic and prescriptive. When the learner's talents are identified, the school prescribes whatever experiences are necessary to develop and enhance them. This school encourages many styles of learning and teaching. Students may achieve through demonstration and manipulation of real objects, as well as through verbal, written, or abstractive performances. All activity is specifically related to the work world.

Option four: This school is more technically oriented than the others in the district. It utilizes computers to help diagnose individual needs and abilities. Computer-assisted instruction based on the diagnosis is subsequently provided both individually and in groups. The library is stocked with tape-recording banks and "talking," "listening," and manipulative carrels that students can operate on their own. In addition, there are Nova-type video-retrieval systems in which students and teachers can concentrate on specific problem areas. This school also has closed-circuit television facilities.

Option five: This school is a total community school. It operates on a 12- to 14-hour basis at least six days a week throughout the year. It provides educational and other services for children as well as adults. Late afternoon activities are provided for children from the neighborhood, and evening classes and activities are provided for adults. Services such as health care, legal aid, and employment are available within the school facility. Paraprofessionals or community teachers are used in every phase of the regular school program. This school is governed by a community board which approves or hires the two chief administrators and is in charge of all other activities in the building. The school functions as a center for the educational needs of all people in the neighborhood and community.

Option six: This school is in fact a Montessori school. Students move at their own pace and are largely self-directed. The learning areas are rich with materials and specialized learning instruments from which the students can select and choose as they wish. Although the teacher operates within a specific and defined methodology, he remains very much in the background, guiding students rather than directing them. Special emphasis is placed on the development of the five senses.

Option seven: The seventh is a multicultural school that has four or five ethnic groups equally represented in the student body. Students spend part of each day in racially heterogeneous learning groups. In another part of the day, all students and teachers of the same ethnic background meet together. In these classes they learn their own culture, language, customs, history, and heritage. Several times each week one ethnic group shares with the others some event or aspect of its cultural heritage that is important and educational. This school views diversity as a value. Its curriculum combines the affective and cognitive domains and is humanistically oriented. Much time is spent on questions of identity, connectedness, powerlessness, and interpersonal relationships. The school is run by a policy board made up of equal numbers of parents and teachers and is only tangentially responsible to a central board of education.

Distinctive educational options can exist within any single neighborhood or regional public school. The principle of providing parents, teachers, and students with a choice from among various educational alternatives is feasible at the individual school. In fact, this may be the most realistic and pervasive approach, at first. For example, in early childhood a single school might offer as options: 1) a Montessori program, 2) an established kindergarten program, 3) a British infant school program, and 4) a Bereiter-Engleman program. Again, parents, teachers, and students will have to "understand fully" each program and be free to choose from among them.

Some may ask whether a Nazi school or a school for blacks that advanced the notion that all white people were blonde-haired, blue-eyed devils and pigs could exist within the framework of a public system of choice. Plainly, no. Our concept speaks to openness; it values diversity; it is nonexclusive; it embraces human growth and development and is unswerving in its recognition of individual worth. Within these bounds, however, is an infinite spectrum of alternative possibilities in creating new educational and learning forms.

Although we have suggested several different ways in which schools might be structured under a public schools of choice system, it should be clear that there are many other possibilities. The flexibility of the concept lends itself to a whole range of options without forcing people to accept any one option they are not attracted to. The choice educational system starts where the public school system and the clients are and develops from that point. For example, we have described above what could be developed within a school district. The same variety of offerings, teaching styles, and learning environments could be presented within one school facility. This would permit the bulk of parents and students in our hypothetical district to continue with educational programs and activities just as they have been, but those who wanted to try different options could do so. There could be six or seven choices in the educational supply of options from which parents and students could choose.

Another application of the public schools of choice system could be implemented on the high school level in a moderate-size city.

Distinctive high school models could be integrated into the public system, providing parents and students with choices about learning style, environment, and orientation that best met the individual needs of the learner and teacher. For example, there could be a standard or traditional high school; a university experimental high school that is a learning center for students, teachers, and those who train teachers; a classical school that emphasizes languages, learning, and rigid disciplines (Boys Latin in Boston is an example); a vocational-technical complex; a high school that emphasizes independent work and personal development, where students and teachers share a joint responsibility for the program; a high school (or student-run high school supplementary program) that in some way addresses itself to the special concerns of particular students—where perhaps black students could work out questions of identity, power, and self-determination on their own terms in their own style; and, finally, a high-school-without-walls concept, such as in Philadelphia, where students utilize the resources and institutions of the city and community as learning environments.

These alternatives, and others, are not unrealistic or significantly beyond the reach of a city school system that is concerned with the quality of its public education. Although many of these ideas have been tried in isolation, they have not been incorporated into a public education system. When they are, we will have entered a new era of public education.

We have learned from our early experience with participation that the mood among the major parties of interest is tense. The lessons from our experiences with reform can be summarized as follows. A good reform proposal:

1. demonstrates adherence to a comprehensive set of educational objectives—not just particular ones. Proposals cannot, for example, emphasize only emotional growth at the expense of intellectual development. The converse is also true. Comprehensive educational objectives deal with careers, citizenship, talent development, intellectual and emotional growth, problem solving, critical thinking, and the like.
2. does not substantially increase the per student expenditure from that of established programs. To advance an idea which doubles or triples the budget will at best place the proposal in the ideal-but-not-practical category. Further, an important factor for reformers to bear in mind is that the new arena will deal with wiser use of *old* money, not the quest for more money.
3. does not advocate any form of exclusivity—racial, religious, or economic. Solutions cannot deny equal access to any particular individual or groups.
4. is not superimposed by a small group which is trying to do something for or to others.
5. respects the rights of all concerned parties and must apply to everyone—it cannot appear to serve the interests of one group only. Thus, for instance, if decentralization plans of urban school systems are interpreted to serve only minority communities, then the majority community may very well oppose such efforts. Similarly, if plans appear to favor professionals, then the community may be in opposition.
6. does not claim a single, across-the-board, model answer—is not a blanket panacea to the educational problem. Attempts at *uniform* solutions are almost never successful.
7. advocates a process of change which is democratic and maximizes *individual* decision making. Participation by the individual in the decisions which affect his life is basic to comprehensive support.

These seven ground rules should be borne in mind, whatever options we offer, but, above all, we must offer options, through public schools of choice.

Technology and Culture in Education

Francis A. J. Ianni

The renaissance in American education, which dates from shortly after World War II, has been characterized by vigorous innovation in the curriculum and the infusion of a variety of new techniques and materials in the schools. Sparked largely by forces outside the schools, dissatisfaction with the status quo led to a wave of curriculum reforms, new administrative arrangements, and the development of a vast new technology which, whether one applauds or laments the outcomes, must be credited with giving a new look to education. It is not the same establishment it used to be.

First, scholars and scientists went into the classroom and created, tested, and revised materials that contain the best knowledge available today. Now, growing largely out of this restiveness over the curriculum and out of advances in electronic technology, the computer and its associated technology promise or threaten to shape yet another series of dramatic changes in education. New approaches to teaching and to the preparation of teachers have begun to appear both within and without the educational establishment. Finally, new administrative arrangements such as the ungraded school, the educational plaza, and flexible scheduling programs suggest major changes in the environment within which education will develop.

Each of these developments, however, has come about largely in isolation from the others, and often there is little or no relationship between a new piece of curriculum or technology and the administrative arrangements necessary to see it into place in the schools. A classic example is what happened to the so-called "teaching machine." The teaching machine, a programed learning device, was a resounding failure in this country because the educational system simply was not ready for it either in terms of deciding what to put into the machine or devising some means of using what came out of it. Consequently, when one encyclopedia publisher began selling teaching machines door to door long before either the machine or the educational community was ready, the bubble burst and another promising educational innovation was a failure.

THE SCHOOL AS SOCIAL SYSTEM

This separatism within the educational system is, however, unrealistic when one looks at the operation of the system. Schools are not random associations of teachers, students, and administrators but are, rather, well-ordered systems with

From *The Bulletin of the National Association of Secondary School Principals* LIV, no. 343 (February 1970):1–8. Used by permission of the author and publisher.

a well-defined institutional structure and a normative system. Schools themselves are part of a well-articulated institution which has an existence apart from all others. As in any organic structure, all of the parts must be understood before any of the parts can be systematically developed. The school consists of four major domains—the students or learners, the instructors or teachers, the materials taught or the curriculum, and the administrative and cultural environment within which all of this takes place. If we consider all the spatio-temporal arrangements within the school, "the administrative climate," the ways in which teachers and pupils are deployed, the traditions, customs and folklore of that school which make it different from others, we are looking at the school as a social system, and it becomes amenable to the same kinds of structural analysis as any other social system. And, of course, the school itself must be considered as part of other cultural, administrative, and social systems. Now, it is apparent, new functions and new devices seem destined to alter the workings of this school "system."

WIDE ACCEPTANCE OF INNOVATION

Hardly a day passes without the unveiling of some new device or development which says that education and schooling as we know them are a part of the present which will soon become past and in every sense outdated. Neither idle dreams nor prototype probabilities, many of these advances are already in place. Computer-aided learning, the current front runner in the new educational technology, is already in use throughout the country, and new and increasingly sophisticated electronic learning aids are beginning to appear. While most of the attention has focused on the new hardware of education, on the computer and other marvels of the electronic age, the real basis for these changes and the principal hope for the future is in the development of four ideas which have liberated and liberalized our attitude toward innovation and experimentation:

(1) the realization that we have scarcely scratched the surface of man's ability to learn
(2) the insistence on the importance of individual differences in learning ability and the resulting primacy of individualized instruction
(3) the quiet but consistent growth of the concept of diagnostic teaching to complement individualized instruction, and
(4) a new value orientation which demands quality as a companion for equality of opportunity in education.

Each of these ideas has been far more powerful in producing the climate for change than any computer. In my judgment each will do far more to ensure that change has design and direction and that innovation is purposeful than will any of the revolutionary pieces of hardware.

Realizing that individualization of learning and a strong injection of quality are in the future of educational improvement programs, many schools are beginning to go down the long road which leads to new and improved educational systems. But, as in any journey into new areas, there are hazards and problems along the way.

It has now become the vogue to begin every discussion of educational programs by asking, "What are the behavioral objectives for this program?" This rationalization of the process of educational planning is a welcome movement forward from the old days of random trial of new ideas and techniques. But, because we are so new at it, we have yet to learn where to look for objectives and, more important, to understand that goals—the best education for every child, for example—are not the same as objectives since it is impossible to measure progress toward the realization of such all-encompassing values. Nowhere is this confusion more obvious than in the area of educational technology. The computer as an aid to learning has been around long enough that we should have accumulated a large bank of carefully researched evidence that the computer can, in fact, make for major advances in how we teach and learn. Such evidence is yet to appear. Some bits of evidence, yes; but not evidence which in amount or quality is decisive.

The reason why modern technology has been able to send rockets to the moon but seems unable as yet to teach children to read are associated with our failure to understand the cultural nature of learning or to apply technology effectively to learning behavior. In the first instance we have so far ignored the overwhelming evidence that learning is more than situational; it is in fact heavily conditioned by the culture within which it develops. If we rule out, for the moment, the many correlational studies of intelligence and family background or child-rearing practices and personality, little systematic study appears to have been given to the child-rearing antecedents of cognitive behavior and even less to the development of teaching strategies based upon such knowledge. Yet, if we consider learning as essentially an exploration of alternatives and if one of the functions of teaching is the economizing of random activity in choice-making, then teaching strategies must take into account the fact that the propensity to explore is heavily conditioned by the cultural context within which it takes place. That is to say, every culture or subculture produces predisposing factors which develop or inhibit the child's drive to explore and to consider alternatives. An adequate pedagogy, then, must understand these factors and develop an instructional system which builds upon or vitiates the predisposing factors.

INSTRUCTION AS SYSTEM

The present mode of so-called diagnostic teaching illustrates the point. This teaching strategy, which places strong emphasis on individualized instruction, posits certain optimal conditions for instruction: (a) the teacher operates within a system which identifies and exploits the antecedent experiences which predispose a child to learn; (b) the information to be transmitted is carefully structured for optimal comprehension and presented in a properly programed sequence; and (c) the system provides for appropriate uses of rewards and punishments. The cultural context is a critical, though largely overlooked, factor in the operation of this strategy. Obviously, such elements as the degree of intellectual stimulation the child receives from his family, the value his society places upon learning, and the richness of his cultural environment will influence his predisposition to learn. But the structure of knowledge and the mode of presentation are equally dependent on cultural factors. We see, for example, the difference in instructional modes between our own and primitive societies. We teach the young by telling about an action—abstracting out of context; they instruct by showing the action itself. Finally, the cultural differentiation of rewards and punishments, both intra-culturally and cross-culturally, operates constantly even though many of us may not recognize it as such.

Just as damaging, however, has been our failure to view educational technology as the product of rather than the revolutionizing force behind changes in teaching/learning processes. For all of our talk about a systems approach in education, we continue to search for that single revolutionary device or technique which will make it possible to teach all children to read quickly, think efficiently, and study painlessly. We scurry around trying to adapt this piece of industrial hardware or that academically developed strategy of instruction to use in education without ever actually looking at the systematic relations which make education work. Education has rarely been examined in this systematic fashion, particularly by educators. In fact, while there have been some studies on social climate in the schools, most research has concentrated on the learner as part of that system, and, in recent years, on what is taught in that system. Little attention has been given to the total organizational structure of education viewed as a system and even less to an analysis of that structure as a device for administrative or management training. What is necessary here—and I consider it urgently necessary—is that just such a theoretical framework must be employed if we are to understand and manage educational affairs as a system. Let's accept this proposition and then move speedily to develop the technology to make it work.

Each of the behavioral sciences has now adopted a systems approach which looks at behavior as part of a relational pattern of elements rather than as a series of discrete acts. Whether it is the structural analysis of a kinship system or of a behavioral gestalt, or of a social system, the same intellectual methodology is applied. Elements in constant dynamic relationship cannot be fully understood in isolation from that interaction because constancy is an illusion when human behavior is properly seen as a series of interactions. Applied to education, the systems approach suggests an analysis of a total system of related organization, behaviors, and outcomes rather than the separate analyses of curriculum, administration, and teaching. In part this new approach derives from the practical experience of educators who have seen the failure of piecemeal attempts to improve education and have come to appreciate the relational interdependence of the educational system. The very promising curriculum revolution of the 1950's and the 1960's was far less successful than it might have been because it had as its motive and its mode the improvement of education through the improvement of one component—and only one component—of the system: the curriculum. There is now ample evidence that modifying the curriculum is a necessary but, by itself, an insufficient step in school improvement. There must be concomitant changes in the rest of the system if true and lasting improvement is to result.

TECHNOLOGY NO SAVIOR

The current stance of educational technology assumes that the machine has come to rescue a moribund educational system from its own excesses, and that little that has gone before will be of any value in the educational future. While many a harassed and weary teacher or administrator would welcome the rescue, I can report that the cavalry is not just over the horizon. In the first place, the frequent assertion that the machines are already in hand but that the educational materials to go into the machine are not ready and are thus responsible for inaction just is not so. It is more accurate to say that neither the state of development of the machines nor the state of the art of the materials is presently at a level which permits any confidence in the supremacy of the machine.

Make no mistake, however: the computer is an important tool in learning, and it will produce major changes in how we teach and learn, even though some important aspects of learning seem immune to computerization. There are three major modes or patterns in the teaching-learning sequence. The first of these is the technique by which we store up simple or complex facts—we memorize. The second mode I call the "question and answer" system where the learner quizzes the teacher or the teacher the learner, in either case the motivation being a request for a specific piece of information. Most questions deal with facts again but this technique differs from the previous one primarily in that it creates an interface between the learner and some other active source of information. Finally, there is the mode in which there is continuous interplay of minds and emotions and in which the development of values, style, individuality, and the ability to ask new questions is the hoped-for end result.

Electronic devices are already in hand which can operate on the simple presentation-of-facts level far more efficiently than any teacher can or should. In fact, in order to compete with the machine, we would probably have to move to a one-to-one ratio of teachers to students. The state of the art in computer-aided learning is now such that there is no question that machine systems can be developed for mode two—the "question and answer" technique—which, again, will provide far more opportunity for realizing the student's learning potential than any teacher can offer. What mere mortal can match the storage, synthesizing, and accuracy of an electronic memory device? But when one moves from information to values and creativity and from the one-to-one interface to free-ranging discussion where every student and teacher has the stimulation and innovative ability of every other individual in that group, no machine now extant or planned can replace unique individuals. I conclude therefore that no educational system can operate without a well educated teacher. The machine can be a boon because it will both get the teacher out of the way of the student's quest for knowledge and, at the same time, free him for the role we have always demanded of him but never allowed; that is, a specialist and diagnostician who identifies individual problem areas and works to overcome them.

Educational technology can make a difference, and an important one, in shaping and molding the educational future. But no matter how sophisticated the device or how potent the programing, a technology which does not grow out of a careful analysis of the educational system and an awareness of how children learn will only make this revolution the most expensive failure yet. The imperatives for a successful educational technology are clear: *understanding the psychocultural system of learning* and *developing both software and hardware out of an understanding of this system*, resisting every temptation to move ahead merely by imposing existing or newly-invented devices and techniques on this system. Failure to adhere to these imperatives explains, in most cases, technology's present inability to make any dramatic change in education. Continuing to ignore them will once again produce change but not growth.

Trends in the Teaching of Science

Paul B. Hounshell

Edwin L. West, Jr.

Fostered by the technological revolution of the sixties, increased monetary support, the knowledge explosion, and new curriculum studies, science education is at the forefront of educational change in the United States. An overview of several trends now emerging as a result of these forces is presented here. There will be overlapping and interrelationships, but all these changes are significant.

Emphasis on the "why" of science. In years past, the focus of education was on facts, but it has become evident that knowledge of vast reservoirs of facts, while beneficial, is not necessary. Particularly is this true since today's "facts" in science may be tomorrow's falsehoods, and since past and current knowledge may now be stored in an electronic brain. The trend today is to utilize man's capabilities as a thinker and to encourage him to seek the answers to the "why" behind the "what." In other words, science should be taught as an intellectual pursuit. The student thus learns how to think as a scientist, the ways and approaches of a scientist, and the attitudes of a scientist. Through carry-over to other subject areas, this trend could affect the total curriculum of each pupil.

The most important aspect of this trend, however, is that through the search for explanation of phenomena, learning becomes a process of self-directed self-discovery. Educating the learner to seek explanation of his environment enhances and perpetuates continuous learning.

Greater student involvement in the teaching-learning act. Unless the student understands and engages in learning activities similar to those of a scientist, he will not, in all probability, come to "know" science, to think scientifically, and to acquire the attitudes, skills, and competencies which are to be desired in contemporary man. The student who is involved in determining "why" is engaged in the process of scientific inquiry; he will learn to devise, improvise, and utilize in the same manner as a scientist. He learns as a scientist learns: from first-hand experiences.

As the student becomes involved in the teaching-learning processes, he also begins to experience success, which fosters a desire for further learning and involvement, and enhances his feelings about himself.

Emphasis on problem solving rather than problem doing. Although the virtues of problem solving have long been extolled by science educators, what actually has

From *The High School Journal* LIII, no. 4 (January 1970):207–216. Used by permission of the authors and publisher.

taken place has often been problem *doing*—that is, cookbook science with experiments which follow step-by-step instructions and, if done correctly, lead to prepackaged solutions. True problem solving, as emphasized in the current trend, involves an open-ended investigation, one in which the solution of one problem leads to the creation of additional ones. The problem is approached in a variety of ways, utilizing numerous resources and many texts.

Utilization of a multiplicity of learning materials. Funds made available through the Elementary and Secondary Education Acts for purchasing learning aids and materials have enabled educators to take steps toward making learning more lifelike. The timing of this act could not have been more appropriate in light of the impact on youth of such media as television, movies, magazines, billboards, and music. With the multiplicity of new materials, teachers have been able to make learning relevant as well as appealing to various senses and approaches. This utilization of a variety of aids facilitates the processes of true problem solving, for it allows the learner to go to many sources in search for solutions to problems.

Emphasis on individualized instruction. Like "problem solving," the phrase "individualizing instruction" has been in the educator's vocabulary for years, but until the current reformation it has been more dream than reality. The changes which have facilitated the individualization of instruction are not only instructional (independent study programs, nongraded or continuous progress programs, programed learning, modular scheduling), but also electronic (tape recorders, copy machines, microfilm readers, computers, projectors, etc.) and architectural (flexible structures, changeable as needs dictate; better planned and equipped laboratories and classroom space).

Changes in length of class periods, scheduling on the basis of purpose and need, pupil programs based on maturation, interest, and achievement, varied instructional tools, and new physical arrangements will not, in themselves, bring about individualization of instruction, but they provide teachers an opportunity to individualize. Such changes give teachers the freedom to organize their teaching for individuals and small groups rather than continually working with large groups, and to utilize a problem solving approach allowing for greater involvement of students in the teaching-learning act. In so doing, teachers will be providing greater opportunities for students to experience success and to develop adequate self-concepts.

STRUCTURE OF SCIENCE

Emphasis on the structure of science. Emphasis on the "structure" of a discipline—those fundamental, underlying concepts or principles which tie or hold the discipline together—has had a profound effect on curriculum development in science. Most of the new science curriculum studies have gone through the ordeal and process of identifying the basic structure of their respective disciplines.

This emphasis has been increasingly evident since the publication in 1962 of *The Process of Education.* In that book, Jerome Bruner suggested that teaching the structure of a discipline (a) makes the discipline more understandable and comprehensible; (b) allows for greater comprehension of detail; (c) fosters transfer of learning; and (d) facilitates narrowing the gap between advanced and elementary knowledge.

It could be stated, then, that emphasis on understanding the structure of a discipline encourages a pupil to develop a way of looking at, or thinking about, a subject. It encourages him to look for relationships in other science areas, and thus he learns to examine a discipline in the same manner as a scientist.

Emphasis on open-ended evaluations. Typically, pupil progress has in the past been evaluated through quizzes or tests. Because of such factors as lack of time, large pupil-teacher ratios, and teacher background and experience, these were often factually oriented. Now there is a movement toward evaluation in which all pupils are not expected to have the same answer, which is dependent on each child's abilities, and which is of a problem solving nature.

This trend was influenced by the work of perceptual psychologists Maslow, Combs, Rogers, and others, who stressed the effect that failure or success has on the self-concept of pupils. A poorly constructed objective test leads to the development of negative attitudes toward learning and school. An open-ended type of evaluation makes allowance for individual differences, backgrounds, perceptions, and at the same time includes questions which foster problem solving or application type evaluations. For example, instead of "Draw and label a typical cell," the teacher may instruct the students, "Compare the organization or structure of the cell to the structure or organization of society in the United States." This requires that the pupil possess knowledge of the cell and its working, but it also requires application and transfer of knowledge, and allows for individual differences and abilities among students. Students will be learning to think critically while engaging in an evaluation exercise.

If the emphasis in teaching is on seeking the "why" of science, involvement of students in the learning act, problem solving, and individualizing of instruction, then evaluations must be of the same nature.

Emphasis on self-concept development. All students possess feelings about themselves as persons and as learners. The importance of facilitating the development of an adequate self-concept has become increasingly apparent to educators. If the student cannot accept himself as a person and learner, he will learn little.

If a science classroom lends itself to student involvement, pupil performed laboratory work which is characterized by a variety of experiments utilizing varying abilities and interests, and individual pupil assignments in lifelike situations, students will, in all probability, experience success in learning. This, in turn, will foster feelings of adequacy on the part of the learner.

DEVELOPMENT OF VALUES

Emphasis on development of values. Louis E. Raths and his associates, in *Values and Teaching*, state that there are too many children in schools who do not learn as well as they might because they are unclear about what they value. In many instances, this may be due to conflicts between the values of the home and those of the school.

This does not mean that teachers should give "moral" lessons or force their value structures on students. The meaning for teachers is outlined in the 1962 ASCD yearbook, *Perceiving, Behaving, Becoming—A New Focus for Education:*

"In general, this means that we must find ways of creating school and classroom atmosphere which facilitates the process of exploration and discovery of personal meaning—where there can be a freeing, expanding, and changing of perception. Students need to have many choices; when they discover something of interest, they need to have plenty of time to work at it. Self-selection in an environment rich in materials, where students sense that how they feel and what they think are important, can be extremely effective in helping students to become more fully functioning. Through acceptance and trust, particularly, teachers play a strategic role in this learning process."

For science teachers, this indicates the provision of a classroom atmosphere which allows for flexibility, freedom to experiment, to follow discovered science interests, with sufficient time and variety in materials to enable students to become involved in relevant learning situations to the extent that they discover who they are and what is important. There must be acceptance and trust by the teacher of each pupil, or the whole process will be fruitless.

The development of values is closely interwoven with the other trends cited above. If all are implemented, each will facilitate the success of the other.

Who Should Plan the Curriculum?

Glen Hass

In this time of rapid change and increasing attention to education it is important that professional educators and others take a fresh look at the question, "Who Should Plan the Curriculum?" Recent developments suggest that some new answers to this central question are in order.

Today, the educated man is the central resource of society. The supply of such men and women available to each nation is the real measure of its economic, political and military potential. We are now undergoing the educational revolution because educated people are the capital of industrial society. Every chemist, every doctor, every engineer creates opportunity and need for more men who can apply knowledge and concepts.

In addition, change is so rapid in our innovating, industrial society, that today's education is unsuited for tomorrow's world and is as outmoded as the Model T for the world of 20 years from tomorrow—the world whose leaders are now in the classrooms of America.

From *Educational Leadership* XIX, no. 1 (October 1961):2–4 and 39. Used by permission of the publisher.

THE CURRICULUM WE NEED

Today's curriculum planners should study conditions and trends in contemporary society and probable conditions and requirements for democratic living in the last half of this century. It may be we are planning to educate children for a society that does not now exist. Education for the immediate future in our rapidly changing society is almost useless unless it prepares learners to meet problems that are new and that neither they nor anyone else has ever encountered before.

The planners will almost certainly find that we need a curriculum which emphasizes the central concepts of the disciplines, concepts that explain phenomena in terms of their future state and direction. The increase in knowledge is becoming unteachable without emphasis on the rules for discovering the nature of the discipline.

The curriculum planners will learn that the school which faces toward the future world must teach innovation, problem solving, a love of learning; its students must acquire the tools of analysis, expression and understanding. They will surely find that learners must be prepared for work that does not yet exist. They will see that our democracy will have numerous increasingly complex tasks as buyers, voters, legislators and cooperative planners.

It is apparent that the curriculum planning which will be needed involves an interrelationship of factors that go beyond the scope of any single discipline or profession.

In America, all interested citizens, parents, learners and scholars from all of the disciplines must work with teachers, principals and supervisors in the planning. This planning should go on throughout America on a local, state and national basis. A democratic society cannot permit uniformity and centralization. The onrushing future requires many different autonomous, competing efforts to cope with its problems.

In the past the columns of *Educational Leadership* have contained many statements that laymen should work with professional educators in planning the curriculum. We have, however, given inadequate attention to the particular role of each type of planner in the planning process. Lacking adequate role definition we may have often, as professionals, over-emphasized our mission to instruct the public, and may have been undersensitive to, or intolerant of, suggestion and dissent. Let us try to define the particular role of each group in the planning.

ROLE OF THE SCHOLAR

In this period when the front line of our defense has moved from the trenches, to the factory, to the classroom, it is fortunate that professional educators are learning again how to communicate with the scholars and research workers in the various disciplines. It is doubly fortunate that scholars in other disciplines are showing renewed interest in the public school curriculum and are frequently now working with professional educators in curriculum planning.

What is the particular role in curriculum planning of the scholar from a discipline other than education? There are at least two ways in which he can help. He can often give crucial advice regarding *what* should be taught; and he can often suggest *means of implementing* curriculum decisions.

For instance, scholars in biology, mathematics, and physics are now working with teachers and other curriculum workers in determining what should be taught. These planners found that the textbooks in use contained almost none of the modern concepts, although greater change in knowledge has occurred in the past 50 years than in the preceding 500. They have also learned that much of the grade placement of the material seemed to be wrong and that greater emphasis was needed on unifying concepts so that the total number of basic ideas to be taught might be reduced.

The sociologist can give particular assistance in determining the means by which the goals of education may be achieved and in identifying the essential values and behavior patterns which must be taught as society changes. Of greatest importance, perhaps, is the fact that the sociologist can aid the educator in understanding the nature of the society in which his students will live in the future. Together they can devise an educational program to prepare for it.

The anthropologist can throw light on the reasons for the development of various aspects of the culture. He can help the school to plan to counterbalance current pressures for conformity and to attach greater emphasis to creativity and critical judgment. He can help in planning to develop in each student an understanding of his powers and limitations for creating and modifying society.

The scholars from all disciplines can aid in curriculum planning by identifying the central concepts and rules for discovering the nature of the discipline. In the terms in which they are now represented many of the disciplines are increasingly unteachable. We need a philosophical synthesis, appropriate to our world and to the learners, that can be taught—and only the scholar working alongside the educator can achieve this.

ROLE OF PARENTS AND OTHER CITIZENS

In the long run, we can only build the curriculum and use the teaching methods which the active school public will accept. We must work with the public and have orderly patterns for its participation. People need to be involved in the process of planning and curriculum in order to change their beliefs, attitudes and behavior regarding it.

It is a matter of crucial importance that many school systems invent structural devices to bring about a sharing of thinking about the curriculum by the lay citizens of the community and the professional staff members.

Staff members must learn to work with citizens; citizens must take part but not take over. This should begin at the level of the parent planning with the teacher about the needs of his child and should move from there to the citizens' advisory council and the curriculum committee. The profession, in each community, is responsible for establishing these channels.

ROLE OF THE STUDENT

The student is the major untapped resource in curriculum planning. Students are in the best position to explain many of the advantages and deficiencies of the present curriculum. Their ideas and reactions are of very great importance. Learning is significantly improved by putting greater responsibility on the student.

Too little use is made of teacher-pupil planning. The understanding and skills of planning are among the most important outcomes of education in our society. Perhaps more teachers would plan with their students if they realized that student-teacher planning has at least six aspects:

1. What is to be studied?
2. Why are we having this learning activity?
3. How shall we go about it?
4. Where do we do what needs to be done?
5. When do we do it?
6. Who will do each part of the job?

While student participation in the choice of topics may be possible only in certain subjects, there is no reason why extensive use of the other aspects of teacher-student planning should not be used in all subjects.

ROLE OF THE EDUCATOR

The role of the professional educator is one of growing stature and is one that will continue to grow as he works with the scholars and other members of the community.

It is the job of the professional educators to provide structure for planning with others, to inform, to offer recommendations, to bring together contributions from all sources, and to work out a recommended plan of action for curriculum change. In the analysis of the curriculum which is planned, the professional educator must be certain that it takes account of the nature of the learner and of the society of which he is a part. The part of the professional educator's role is not new but it will have increasing importance as he works and plans with others who are not so likely to give adequate attention to these bases for curriculum decisions.

The professional educator must be alerted to the necessity for relating schools to the surrounding political, economic and social forces so that the means and goals of education harmonize with the lives of men in particular circumstances. He should seek the unifying norms as he works with others in curriculum planning.

Frequently educators need to take a stand for what they believe, sharing what they know and feel. The public relies on the vision and courage of educators to present recommendations for curriculum improvement. Such recommendations should be related to a sense of purpose, the ability to think and analyze and a proper respect for the requirements of human response. The educator, in recommending, must carefully avoid the appearance that the curriculum is solely the professional's business. Experience over time in working together will help to solve this problem.

A most important part of the teacher's role is to communicate to students his own valuing of learning. Teachers motivate young people by their own motivations. Learners learn to like to learn from teachers who exhibit the intellectual accomplishment of regularly acquiring and acting on new knowledge.

Finally, the professional educator must evaluate and interrelate the contributions from other disciplines and evolve a curriculum plan for the approval of the curriculum committee or council and the school board.

MOVING AHEAD

If it is recognized that all public policy in education is the product of professional-lay interaction, then the main roadblocks to progress can be removed. The increasing communication between scholars in various disciplines and professional educators is a valuable step forward. A next step is to make greater use of that largely untapped resource—student contributions to curriculum planning. In each community professional educators should move to establish the structural devices needed so that scholars, citizens, students and professional educators may plan the curriculum needed for the 1970's. It will be particularly helpful if the persons are recognized and utilized. Because of the importance of education in today's world, each should be enabled to make his particular contribution to curriculum planning.

Who should plan the curriculum? Everyone interested in the future of America; everyone concerned for the quality of education being experienced by the leaders of the future who are now in our classrooms. . . .

SECTION 5 ADDITIONAL LEARNING ACTIVITIES

Problems and Projects
1. In this section Fantini, Nash, and Harris discuss the need for "public schools of choice," or alternative schools. They caution that a good reform proposal does not claim a "single, across the board, model answer." Provision for individual differences is the curriculum criterion of central concern in proposals for schools and curricula of this kind. Keeping these ideas in mind, you may learn much about curriculum planning by visiting free schools, alternative schools, or other similar programs that exist in your area. Examine one of these programs in terms of objectives of education, curriculum bases, and curriculum criteria.
2. Many interesting proposals have been made in recent years that are critical of public school curricula and that describe the needs of particular groups of learners. Read one of the following books and examine the proposals it makes in terms of objectives, bases, and criteria presented in this book. Your instructor might permit you to do this as your postassessment for this topic.

Dennison, George. *The Lives of Children*. New York: Random House, 1969.
Gross, Ronald, and Osterman, Paul. *High School*. New York: Simon and Schuster, 1971.
Holt, John. *Freedom and Beyond*. New York: E. P. Dutton and Company, 1972.
Illich, Ivan. *Deschooling Society*. New York: Harper and Row, Publishers, 1970.
Kohl, Herbert. *Thirty-Six Children*. New York: Signet Books, 1968.
Kozol, Jonathan. *Death at an Early Age*. New York: Houghton Mifflin Company, 1967.
Leonard, George B. *Education and Ecstasy*. New York: Delacorte Press, 1968.
Silberman, Charles E. *Crisis in the Classroom*. New York: Random House, 1970.
Woock, Roger R., ed. *Education and the Urban Crisis*. Scranton, Pennsylvania, 1970.

3. The rationale for this section states that broad, general goals are needed to guide curriculum planning and teaching. The writer of the rationale states that he uses goals in four areas for such planning: education for citizenship, vocation, self-realization, and critical thinking. Do you agree with this statement of broad goals? Try to construct your own list of general goals for education. Compare your list with the suggestions made in "The Central Purpose of American Education" in this section. Consider your list in terms of the criterion "balance" presented in the article "Seeking Balance in the Curriculum."
4. Most curriculum leaders consider "cooperative planning" to be a curriculum criterion of major importance. The article "Who Should Plan the Curriculum?" defines who should be included in cooperative planning and the special role of each group of planners. Who do you think should be included in curriculum planning and the planning of teaching? What role do you suggest for each planner? Do you agree or disagree with the statement, "The student is the major untapped resource in curriculum planning"?
5. Turn to the Introduction and review the discussion of the definitions of *curriculum* and *instruction*. Then look for definitions of these terms in other books. It is suggested you see:

A. J. Lewis and Alice Miel, *Supervision for Improved Instruction*. Belmont, California: Wadsworth Publishing Co., pages 24–32.

J. Galen Saylor and William M. Alexander, *Curriculum Planning for Modern Schools*. New York: Holt, Rinehart, and Winston, Inc., 1966, pages 5–6.

Compare the definitions in these books with those in the Introduction. How do the definitions of *curriculum* and *instruction* that you adopt affect your planning of curricula? Try to write the definitions of these terms as you see them. Compare your definitions with those of other persons.

6. Continuity is one of the important curriculum criteria. Read "Curriculum and Instructional Practices for Continuous Learner Progress," by Glen Hass, published by the Florida Educational Research and Development Council for Project Ideals. (Write FERDC, College of Education, University of Florida, Gainesville, Florida: price, $2.00.) This publication summarizes research regarding graded versus non-graded schools, individualizing instruction, continuity in learning, and exemplary practices in these areas.

7. Read about *individually prescribed instruction* (IPI) in Section 6. Articles by Yetter and Tillman present both favorable and unfavorable views regarding this new childhood education trend. In the article by Tillman ("Do Schools Need IPI? No!"), a contrasting plan for childhood education fostered by Marion Nesbitt is described briefly.

What is the basis of *continuity* in the IPI curriculum? Is it human development, learning, knowledge, or social forces?

To decide, you may need to read from additional sources. Read more about IPI in *Programed Instruction*, pages 217–253 (this is the 66th Yearbook of the National Society for the Study of Education, Part II. Chicago, Illinois: University of Chicago Press, 1967).

Read more about the curriculum described by Marion Nesbitt in her book *A Public School for Tomorrow* (New York: Dell Publishing Co., 1967).

8. What is the basis for providing for *individual differences* in the two curricula in number 7? In IPI do the curriculum planners focus on differences in human development between learners, differences in the knowledge or skills being studied, differences in styles of learning, or differences in learners resulting from social forces? After deciding this, can you suggest improvements for making provisions for *individual differences* in the IPI program? Discuss this with others.

9. What is a *balanced curriculum*? Discuss this with others. Do you agree with Kimball Wiles' ideas about balance in his article in this section? Examine the article by Bellack and the two articles by Bruner in Section 4. How do you think these two educators would determine whether a curriculum is balanced? What is the relationship of the four bases of the curriculum to the concept of a balanced curriculum? How did Bruner's ideas about balance change between 1963 (see "Structures in Learning") and 1971 ("The Process of Education Reconsidered")?

10. Continue to develop a case problem about one school you know well. Describe the curricula and teaching in that school as they may be related to curriculum criteria such as individual differences, student-teacher planning, continuity, and balance.

Filmstrips

Educational Objectives: An Instructional Program. Series of 18 filmstrips and audio tapes. Titles include *Educational Objectives, Systematic Decision-Making, Defining Content for Objectives, Identifying Affective Objectives, Knowledge of*

Results. While there is some overlap, the 18 programs deal with the following topics: (1) instructional objectives (2) instructional sequences, and (3) evaluation in a criterion-referenced context. Distributed by Vimcet Associates, P. O. Box 24714, Los Angeles, California 90024.

Audio Tapes

How Can the American Educational System Best Meet the Needs of Our Society? 1 hour audio tape. Discusses how the needs of youth and the needs of society can be fulfilled by the American School System. Distributed by National Tape Repository, University of Colorado, Boulder, Colorado 80302.

Films

Promises to Keep, 16mm., color, 28 mins., 1969. Examines several federal projects in inner city schools in Philadelphia, Miami, and San Diego that were attempting to raise the level of education received by the children. Discusses problems facing inner-city schools. Distributed by Motion Picture Productions of Texas, Inc., 1101 Nueces, Austin, Texas 78701.

Make a Mighty Reach. 16mm., 45 min., color. Deals with school improvement through innovation. Emphasizes that new ideas in education must be aimed at making learning easier and more efficient. A number of different schools are featured in the film. Distributed by Institute for Development of Educational Activities, P. O. Box 446, Melbourne, Florida 32901.

Books to Review

Bloom, Benjamin, ed. *Taxonomy of Educational Objectives: The Classification of Educational Goals, Handbook I: Cognitive Domain.* New York: David McKay Company, 1956.

Broudy, Harry; Smith, B. Othanel; and Burnett, Joe R. *Democracy and Excellence in American Secondary Education.* Chicago: Rand McNally and Company, 1964.

Brown, Bob Burton. *The Experimental Mind in Education.* New York: Harper and Row, Publishers, 1968.

Buswell, David, and Rappaport, Donald, eds. *Planned Change in Education: A Systems Approach.* New York: Harcourt Brace Jovanovich, 1971.

Crary, Ryland. *Humanizing the School: Curriculum Development and Theory.* New York: Alfred A. Knopf, 1969.

Doll, Ronald C. *Curriculum Improvement: Decision-Making and Process,* 2d ed., Boston: Allyn and Bacon, 1970.

Kibler, Robert; Barker, Larry; and Miles, David. *Behavioral Objectives and Instruction.* Boston: Allyn and Bacon, 1970.

Krathwohl, David; Bloom, Benjamin; and Masia, Bertram. *Taxonomy of Educational Objectives: The Classification of Educational Goals, Handbook II: Affective Domain.* New York: David McKay Company, 1956.

Leeper, Robert R., ed. *Curricular Concerns in a Revolutionary Era: Readings From Educational Leadership.* Washington, D.C.: Association for Supervision and Curriculum Development, 1971.

Popham, W. James. *The Teacher-Empiricist: A Curriculum and Instruction Supplement.* Los Angeles: Aegeus Publishing Company, 1965.

Taba, Hilda. *Curriculum Development: Theory and Practice.* New York: Harcourt, Brace and World, 1962.

Wilson, L. Craig. *The Open Access Curriculum.* Boston: Allyn and Bacon, 1971.

PART TWO

The Curriculum

Childhood Education

PREREQUISITES

1. Reading and studying of the Introduction and Sections 1 through 5 of this book.
2. The development of, and ability to use, a set of curriculum criteria to describe and evaluate a curriculum plan. You must be able to use this set of criteria in order to critically analyze and make curriculum and teaching decisions regarding programs and trends and teaching practices described in this section.

RATIONALE

All curriculum planners and teachers should be acquainted with the goals and trends in education at all levels, regardless of the level of the program of education at which they plan to work. For instance, you should know about goals and trends in childhood education whether you plan to work at this level or not. You will be able to be a better curriculum planner or teacher at one of the other levels if you have this information. This view is based on such curriculum criteria as continuity in learning, balance in the curriculum, and provision for individual differences.

This section is now called "Childhood Education" rather than "Preschool and Elementary School." In keeping with the definition of *curriculum* presented in the Introduction, the focus will be on programs of education rather than exclusively on school programs.

The graded elementary school was established in the nineteenth century when there was little knowledge of the nature and extent of individual differences. It was developed in conformity with the then prevalent ideas of child development and education. It was conceived in the faith that all men are created equal and that individual differences in education are undesirable.

The elementary school often has the most intense impact of any school in the educational system; the year the child spends in first grade is one-sixth of his entire life to that point. Therefore, the lack of adequate provision for individual differences frequently can result in intense feelings of failure and rejection as well as retardation or elimination from school for some children. Failure to achieve in any of the essential functions at the elementary school level can exact a high price at other levels where the resulting deficiency can hardly be overcome.

A major problem for the elementary school is to establish effective contact with each child. Provision for individual differences, and flexibility and continuity in learning thus are curriculum criteria of major significance.

There is a nationwide thrust toward early childhood education that may become one of the significant educational trends of the 1970s. It is estimated that nearly forty percent of all three- to five-year-old children are now enrolled in programs of education. This boom is due to social forces such as the women's liberation campaign for day-care centers, the federal government's programs for assisting educationally deprived children, and feelings of many members of the middle class that competition for college admission will continue to be intense and that their children need a head start in learning. It is also due to human development and learning theories that emphasize the need for early stimulation and encouragement of curiosity in infants and young children if their intellectual potential is to be developed. Several articles in this section explain and develop the idea that the human mind and personality are formed in large part by nursery school age. This idea is being translated into educational practice. The importance of the parent is emphasized, and many of the programs of early childhood education focus as much on the parents as the children.

As early childhood education continues to grow, sending better prepared children into the existing elementary schools, the schools will almost certainly come under fierce pressures for change. And as the importance of "child advocacy programs" gains recognition (See "Components of a Child Advocacy Program," by Ward, in this section) more community programs of childhood education and family education enterprises are likely to develop (in contrast to programs of childhood education largely confined to schools). What is needed now is a focus on: (1) the needs of children and how they may be met, and (2) planning for the curriculum changes that must be made at the childhood education level when many children (but not all) bring two, three, or even four years of carefully planned experiences to the primary school.

Traditionally, parents have been told to bring their children to the elementary school door and then to leave. But the increasing emphasis on the importance of the parents in early mental development suggests that the parents should have a much more active role in programs of education. This emphasizes the need for our new definition of *curriculum*. It also implies the need for changes in childhood education, in the roles of childhood education teachers, and in teacher education programs for teachers of this age group.

What should be the *objectives* of programs of childhood education (ages two through eleven or twelve)? Many goals might be suggested; some are derived from social forces, some from human development and learning theories, and some from theories about knowledge and cognition. The list would surely include many of the following *objectives*:

1. Helping learners to develop feelings of trust
2. Developing autonomy and initiative
3. Introducing structure and organization without stopping self-expression and creativity
4. Providing social activities in large groups, small groups, and individually
5. Providing adequate and appropriate physical and health education
6. Teaching the fundamental skills of communication and computation
7. Establishing a desire to learn and an appreciation for education by teaching under conditions that enhance interest and curiosity
8. Developing interests in many areas by exposure to many fields of knowledge and experience
9. Developing feelings of self-worth and security by providing varied experiences on which each child can base and build his success
10. Providing many opportunities for achievement for each child
11. Developing appreciation for the worth and differences of others
12. Developing the processes of conceptualizing, problem-solving, self-direction, and creating.

What additions or changes would you propose for this list?

In order to attain goals like these in programs of childhood education, many innovations are being proposed and tried. The following list of *innovations and trends* in childhood education includes references to pertinent articles. All the articles except numbers 8 and 12 are reprinted in this section.

1. Nongraded schools ("The Nongraded School: An Overview")
2. Team teaching ("Team Teaching in Canton's Model School")
3. Differentiated staffing ("Team Teaching in Canton's Model School")
4. Cross-age grouping ("Team Teaching in Canton's Model School")
5. British primary school program ("English and American Primary Schools")
6. Early stimulation of young children ("Why Programs for Young Children?")
7. Headstart programs ("Early Childhood Education: For What Goals?")
8. Schools without walls (See "High School with No Walls—It's a Happening in Philadelphia" in Section 8. The article includes a description of an elementary school for kindergarten through fourth grade with no walls).
9. Montessori methods ("Early Childhood Education: For What Goals?")
10. Child advocacy ("Components of a Child Advocacy Program")
11. Continuous learner progress ("Early Childhood Education"; "Influence on the Elementary School")
12. Mankind curricula and ethnic studies ("Toward a Mankind Curriculum: From Kindergarten through Twelfth Grade"—in Section 4)
13. Career education ("Occupational Preparation in the Elementary School")
14. Laboratory approach to teaching ("The Self-Selection Classroom"; "Laboratory Approach to Elementary Mathematics")
15. New ways of teaching reading ("Reading Instruction in the Elementary School")
16. Individualizing instruction—("Do Schools Need IPI? Yes!"; "Do Schools Need IPI? No!")

Will these innovations and trends, if adopted, provide needed changes in programs of childhood education? Will they provide improved implementation of the objectives of childhood education? Will they provide the means for new flexibility and continuity in these programs, as well as ways to establish effective contact with each child as an individual?

We must evaluate the innovations and trends in comparison with present programs. The consideration of (1) objectives, (2) the four bases of the curriculum, and (3) other curriculum criteria provide professional means for making these decisions.

OBJECTIVES

Your objectives in studying childhood education as part of the curriculum should be as follows:

1. To be familiar with the objectives, current innovations, and recent trends in childhood education.
2. To be able to explain the functions and goals of childhood education as part of the total curriculum.
3. To be able to use the objectives of childhood education, the curriculum bases, and other criteria in making curriculum and/or instruction decisions regarding present programs as well as regarding proposed innovations and trends.
4. To be able to suggest improvements in childhood education curriculum plans through the decisions made in number 3.

PREASSESSMENT

1. Identify each of the sixteen childhood education innovations and trends listed in the Rationale, and discuss their implications.
2. Evaluate each of the trends in terms of objectives, bases of curriculum and curriculum criteria such as individual differences, balance, and continuity.
3. Select any childhood education curriculum plan and describe and analyze it in terms of childhood education objectives, the four curriculum bases, other curriculum criteria, and innovations and trends at this level of education.
4. Suggest improvements or changes in the curriculum plan in number 3 in the light of your analysis.

In answering numbers 3 and 4 of the preassessment, you might choose to analyze the curriculum plans discussed in the following articles:

1. "Team Teaching in Canton's Model School," by Measel and Fincher, in this section.
2. "The Self-Selection Classroom," by Billings, in this section.

LEARNING ACTIVITIES

Articles in this section will help you to understand the purposes and functions of childhood education as an important part of the curriculum. They will also acquaint you with the problems, as well as the innovations and trends, of programs of childhood education.

Other learning alternatives are suggested at the end of this section.

POSTASSESSMENT

After attempting the preassessment you may do *one or more* of the following:

1. Ask your instructor whether you are ready for a postassessment evaluation on childhood education. Most students will need further work on this topic.
2. Read the articles on childhood education in this section and try to determine how the practices, trends, and innovations being discussed in each article should be considered in curriculum planning and teaching at the childhood education level.
3. Choose additional activities and readings or films and videotapes from those listed at the end of this section.
4. Look for other films, books, or articles on childhood education that are in your library or media center.
5. Discuss the reading you have done and the films you have viewed with your fellow students. The key question: How should the goals, practices, trends, and innovations you've studied affect curriculum planning at the childhood education level? How should they be considered in planning for teaching?
6. When you are ready, ask your instructor for advice on a suitable postassessment for you for this topic. Satisfactory completion of numbers 3 or 6 under Problems and Projects at the end of this section might be possibilities. Or satisfactory written completion of the preassessment for this section, after completing other learning activities, might be a satisfactory postassessment. Consult your instructor about this. You can evaluate your ability to do these postassessment activities before seeing the instructor.

Why Programs for Young Children?

James L. Hymes, Jr.

We say we want programs for young children, but why do we want them? What do we expect them to accomplish? What will the children gain from them? How will having such programs help all the rest of us? Narrow answers to these questions too often lead us to little efforts—and in the wrong directions.

Why nursery schools and kindergartens? Too quickly the answer comes: "To prepare children for the first grade." But if the children are in nursery schools or kindergartens, nursery school or kindergarten *is* the first grade. And the fourth or

From *Today's Education* LIX, no. 4 (April 1970):34–36. Used by permission of the author and publisher.
Adapted from "The Goals of Kindergarten Education," a chapter in *Kindergarten Education*, published by the American Association of Elementary-Kindergarten-Nursery Educators (1968. 72 pp. $2. Stock No. 281-08844).

fifth year of life is as worthy as the sixth year of life. There is no need for "prep" schools, no need for boot camps, certainly no need at this early stage in life to give up today for the sake of tomorrow.

"Preparing children for the first grade" is not a reason. First grade teachers have the same job every teacher faces: to work with the children who come, to work with them as they are. Each grouping has its children and each, its job to do. But preparation—breaking them in, getting them ready, softening them up —is not the job of any one grade. It's not the job of first grade to get them ready for second grade, not the job of kindergarten to get them ready for the first, not the job of nursery school to get them ready for kindergarten. This is a needless, dead-end, and even an indecent way of thinking about any year of life.

Why early childhood programs? Too quickly the answer comes: "To teach reading readiness." But if the program is worth its salt, it isn't teaching reading readiness—it is teaching reading! It is teaching as much reading as every individual child is ready for, and it is teaching that reading in ways appropriate for that child's development. It is teaching more than reading. It is teaching science—not science "readiness." And it is teaching mathematics and art and music and the social studies. It is teaching all the fields of human knowledge, as every school of general education must, in ways that will make these fields of knowledge important and real and meaningful and useful to its students.

To isolate one area of human experience—reading—and make it the kingpin is to turn the early childhood program away from general, humane, liberal arts education and to change these early years of life into narrow, limited, technical "trade schools" for young children. To distort this one area of human experience into some utterly artificial, pseudo area of knowledge, "reading readiness," is to open the door to insipid workbooks—anti-intellectual in their content, adult-dominated in their method, narrow and barren in their yield.

Learning to read is a continuous process. All children start on this process long before they come to kindergarten, long before they come to nursery school. The language the child speaks is a part of this process. The solid knowledge he has is a part of this process. The skills he develops in reading are a part of this process. The development of his powers of observation is a part of it, as are his careful listening, his attention to detail, and his interest in ideas.

No child ever learns to read in the first grade; he only learns his first-grade's worth. He learns more about reading (and more about science and mathematics and the humanities and the social studies) in the fourth grade and junior high and high school and college. No child starts life in nursery school or kindergarten, nor does his readiness start there. Each year—in its own way, functionally, appropriately—capitalizes on all the readiness the child has at the time so that he makes the greatest progress he can at the time—and always, if it is general education and not a trade school, in all the fields of human learning, not in one field, isolated and set apart.

Why nursery school or kindergarten? Too quickly the answer comes: "To socialize the child." Sadly this must frequently be translated to mean: to teach him the little ways that will make him easier to live with in first grade. A true, sound, healthy socialization is probably one of the greatest needs of the human race. If this were the actual goal, one could quarrel less with it, although one would have to stress the same truth that applies to reading: A four- or five-year-old can only learn a four- or five-year-old's worth. But there is no great new humane concern with the quality and satisfaction of our living together. Socialization means "first grade socialization": Raise your hand before talking and don't talk too loud, walk on your tiptoes and don't ever run, sit quietly in your seat and mind your own business.

Too often the worst of first grade—the living that is inappropriate for sixes —seeps down most quickly and is imposed on fives and fours: *Be obedient. Be conforming. Don't feel emotion and don't show it if you do. Follow the crowd and stay in line.* These are unworthy goals. If sixes really have to learn these rules to get along, they are frighteningly easy to learn. Clearly, neither nursery school nor kindergarten has to be given over to the likes of this.

But even a broader, more thoughtful concept of the kind of socialization humans need today is not in itself the reason for early programs. Productive, constructive socialization may be one of the goals—it cannot be the *only* goal. A good nursery or kindergarten program seeks to promote the maximum social development of each child. It equally seeks to promote his physical development, his intellectual development, his emotional maturity. It is not designed to deal with one separate slice of the human: the cognitive slice, the physical slice, the social slice. The good nursery or kindergarten recognizes the wholeness of human beings and the inevitable, inescapable integration in human behavior of all facets of the person: his knowledge, his feelings about himself and about others, his body, his brain, and his heart.

A good nursery or kindergarten is a school. Because it seeks to promote the child's maximum total development through the school's special province—learning—its job is the same as the job of all schools: to teach.

We have programs for young children because fours and fives are fully ready to learn if we will but have the wisdom and the sensitivity to adjust the ways of teaching to fit them. But no good school is concerned with learning for learning's sake. Nor are the liberal arts or the 3 R's or however one wants to categorize human knowledge ends in themselves. We work through learning; we work through knowledge. These are our particular approaches, but the goals of early childhood education—the ultimate reason why we use these approaches—are something more.

We teach the young child to live these early years of his life with more joy, with more meaning, with more purpose, with more satisfaction. We have these programs so that the individual youngster can function with more freedom and ease and zest—being true to himself, using his powers, being his best. Responsibility to the individual is a moral imperative of early childhood education. The joy that school brings to the child's life, the sense of fulfillment, is the prime standard by which to judge a program. This one basic goal sets the pace for the quality of the adult-child relationship, of child-to-child relationships, of space and materials, and of methods and content. If these relationships do not add up to a tingling sense of vigorous living within the youngster, a fundamental point has been lost, no matter what other gains may seem to show up on any tests.

But schools—nurseries and kindergartens—are not for the individual alone. Schools are society's insurance policy. We rely on them to ensure that our world will become an ever better place. As we seek to cultivate and nurture the best quality of the child's living *now*, at- this moment in his life, we must simultaneously seek to build those human qualities that will continue to make the child good for all of us to live with.

Although we cannot spell out all that we must treasure and nurture and rebuild in each new generation if our living together is to become mutually supportive rather than destructive, we can certainly agree on at least the start of a list of those humans whose qualities we prize: people who know and value freedom; those who have a heart and who are generous and caring in their relationships; knowing people, wise, informed, curious, in love with the wonder of the world and enchanted with solving its mysteries; people who are individualists, who are different, who are a joy to know and work and live with because of their special ways.

The second major goal from the standpoint of the rest of us—from the standpoint of society—is to have the child begin to breathe in the air of the best of human society, the healthiest form of human association that a teacher's finest dreams can devise.

A nursery or kindergarten is a child's little world, his first step out into the wider world. It is a school of general education where children learn their year's worth of all the forms of human knowledge, but they learn it in a setting and in a way and through relationships and to the end that they are moved a little toward those qualities of the human on which the good life itself depends.

Early Childhood Education: For What Goals?

Milton J. E. Senn, M.D.

There is today a cleavage between educators of young children who favor educational practices based on concepts of the child in relation to his *whole* emotional-cognitive development and those who favor practices aimed only at developing certain measurable skills defined as "intelligence."

In my opinion the sane perspectives on the hierarchy of values have been turned on end. We are now urged to believe that highly structured, mechanical, and rigid practices in teaching are superior to those that are flexible, child-experience oriented, and focused on human relationships. We are being led to expect both immediate and lasting results from programs aimed at speeding up the learning in the youngest minds. Emphasis on the intelligence quotient as the measure of achievement continues despite strong evidence that questions the validity of this practice.

From *Children* XVI, no. 1 (January–February 1969):8–13. Used by permission of the author. Condensed from the first Evangeline Burgess Memorial Lecture presented at Pacific Oaks College and Children's School, Pasadena, Calif., April 3, 1968.

Obviously the changing nature of societies forces a reconsideration of how to educate a new generation. The Russian launching of Sputnik in 1956 triggered a near phobia about making American minds equal, if not superior, to those of our cold war competitors. More recently the civil rights movement has moved us as never before to take stock of our human resources. Now there is a readiness to accept the long-held premise of persons in the field of child development that the beginnings of waste start in the early years, and research in the education of young children is proliferating.

We have had few great educational theorists in the United States other than G. Stanley Hall, John Dewey, and William James to lead the way. For the most part we have looked to foreign countries for basic theories about the nature of man, his attributes, and his needs and for concepts of how these are to be dealt with educationally—to such geniuses as Jean Jacques Rousseau, John Locke, Henry Pestalozzi, Friedrich Wilhelm Froebel, Maria Montessori, and of course Sigmund Freud. To this list has recently been added the contemporary Swiss epistemologist, Jean Piaget, who has had a profound influence on American psychologists and researchers in child development since the early 1950's.

PIAGET'S INFLUENCE

Piaget and his colleagues in Geneva are primarily recognized for the work they have done in the field of cognition, although Piaget has been mostly concerned with the nature of knowledge and with the structures and processes by which it is acquired. His discoveries that experiences in the first 5 years of life are vital and long lasting and that infantile sensory-motor coordinations are forerunners of the form and content of adult thought substantiate the theories of Freud. While Piaget is informed about Freudian theories and has long realized the importance of emotional processes in learning, he has said that time has limited his considerations to study of *intellectual development* and that he would leave to others the consideration of *feeling states* and their relationship to learning. However, few of his disciples in the field of experimental psychology have been inclined to integrate their research on cognition with research on personality development.

Piaget views the growth of the structures of knowing as proceeding over time, beginning in early infancy and ending in adolescence.[1] Not only is there a distinct beginning and ending in the schema he presents, but there are also certain *critical periods* along the way. Human intelligence (or knowing) begins with the phase of sensory-motor responsiveness. The infant is equipped by heredity and constitution with reflex patterns for reacting to touch, vision, sound, and kinesthesis; his behavior is shaped by external demands imposed by the environment; response to these demands goads his mental growth.

As he assimilates his experiences, the baby learns strategies for coping with both external and internal demands, and with time he organizes the information he has acquired into systems. By the end of his first year the child is able to construct a theory of the world that transcends direct sensory experience, as when he appreciates the existence of an object he cannot see and develops skill in searching

[1] Piaget, J. *Six psychological studies.* Random House, New York. 1967.

for the unseen. By the time he develops language, which is dependent on his sensory-motor functions, he is more manipulatable in thought and more susceptible to social correction. We say he is able to "internalize his actions," to use his mind and proceed from perception and manipulation to reflection.

The phases of intellectual development follow each other, not in strictly chronological fashion, but in a sequential and orderly manner from early infancy into early adolescence. Piaget believes that these phases may be accelerated to some extent by manipulating the environment but that such manipulation will only be effective up to a certain point. The environment *is* important but only as a child is able to pay attention to it, and this ability depends on the degree of assimilation which has taken place. However, the greater the *variety* of experiences a child copes with, the greater becomes his ability to cope.

Piaget never points to any practical implications of his work. Aware of what some of his followers are doing in the application of his studies to the education of young children, he has issued a timely warning by inquiring, "What is learning for—to know a certain *number* of things, or to be capable of creating or inventing new things?"

There continues to be much unclarity in the minds of many of Piaget's adherents about the meaning of the term "cognition." Piaget himself, pointing out that his theories are unfinished, continues to change his emphasis, concepts, and terminology.

Cognitive psychologists interested in infant behavior and learning have also found encouragement in the research of other scientists who have studied babies reared in different environments. René Spitz and others, for example, have reported harmful effects of impersonal care and understimulation suffered by babies reared in foundling hospitals.[2] Although the emphasis in such research was at first on affect deprivation, later investigators have reported damage to cognitive functions as well.[3]

EARLY STIMULATION

For the past several years there has been a burgeoning of investigation into the physiological, psychosocial, and intellectual deficiencies resulting from understimulation and of efforts to prevent and ameliorate deficiencies by sensory stimulation. Studies of sense organ stimulation in newborn infants have had special appeal to investigators. Often this research has resembled the experiments conducted in Russia for over a decade, in Moscow under A. S. Louria and in Leningrad under the Pavlovian-trained pediatrician Nicholas Krasnagorski. The American investigators, like the Russian, have found that a baby not only changes his physiological reflex responses after sensory stimulation, but that he learns to change his behavior if he feels rewarded by the process of stimulation. For

[2] Spitz, R. A. Hospitalism: an inquiry into the genesis of psychiatric conditions in early childhood. In *The psychoanalytic study of the child*. Vol. I. International Universities Press, New York. 1945.
[3] Goldfarb, W. Emotional and intellectual consequences of psychologic deprivation in infancy: a re-evaluation. In *Psychopathology of childhood*. Grune & Stratton, New York. 1955.

example, newborn babies learn how to change their rate of sucking and how to move a mobile with their toes when pleasurably stimulated by sight and sound. The inference from such findings is that babies can learn more than we realize if they are taught by techniques that stimulate the nervous system.

The Russians believe that through conditioning they can overcome the ill effects of prematurity very early in infancy. While this theory has never been validated elsewhere, many American cognitive psychologists believe that through early stimulation of the central nervous system of normal babies, they may speed up their intellectual development so that by the time the children are 4 years old they will be greatly beyond the normally expected level. Since it is commonly believed that by age 4 a child has attained half of his final intellectual capability, the race seems to be on not only to have American children attain their full intellectual potential before adolescence, but to keep it increasing to a higher degree than is normally attained.

Some cognitive psychologists believe that future generations can reach 30 IQ points ahead of the present generation through better management of their early environment, beginning in infancy. Yet the definition of intelligence remains unclear. Moreover, there is no agreement on the details of *how* and *when* to manipulate the environment.

In reviews of the research on stimulation of infants, one rarely finds words of warning or descriptions of any harmful effects of early stimulation. But the research of Burton L. White of Harvard points in that direction.[4] In studying institutionalized infants, he found what Spitz and others had described: delays in motor response due to lack of visual stimulation. In attempts to find ways of preventing such deficiencies, White studied a group of 6-day-old normal babies in a hospital. He saw that they got more physical handling, more opportunity to look around, and more bright objects to see than is usual. He found that this special stimulation upset the babies; they cried a lot and paid less attention to their surroundings. However, when he provided similar ministrations to babies 2½ months old, favorable responses resulted; these babies smiled at objects, vocalized, and seemed happier than unstimulated controls. Thus, the timing and amount of external stimulation are important.

The Russians report that although a newborn baby may be helped to mature more rapidly by conditioning, all newborns do not respond favorably to such treatment. This is because there is a basic difference in equipment in each individual, which makes the *timing* of the conditioning important. As one would surmise, the more mature babies respond more favorably than the less mature. Nevertheless, in Russia all normal newborns in hospital nurseries are stimulated visually and aurally; "teachers" sing to them at prescribed times each day, dangle colored rings before their eyes, and shake a tambourine next to their ears.

John L. Fuller, senior staff scientist at the Jackson Laboratory in Bar Harbor, Me., has also substantiated the theory that timing and quality of stimulation are important. Experimenting with dogs, he discovered that animals that had been isolated and deprived of sensory stimulation from birth could be helped to overcome their deficits only if the changes in their environment were made gradually

---

[4] White, B. L.; Held, R. Plasticity of sensory-motor development in the young infant. In *The causes of behavior: readings in child development and educational psychology.* Allyn & Bacon, New York. 1966.

and in a way that permitted their sensory-motor capacities to adapt slowly. When the transition from the depriving to the stimulating environment was made too rapidly, the adaptive mechanisms were overstrained and the dogs became especially fearful.[5]

Fuller described another important aspect of appropriate stimulation when he reported that only when the stimulated animals' stress was reduced by stroking and handling were they able to make any contact with other objects, whether toys or humans, without irrational fear. These observations tend to verify the conviction of many teachers that contact with humans is more important than stimulation from impersonal objects and that human relationships are the primary factors in helping children to learn.

Other psychologists have found that children who have been deprived and are abruptly exposed to new stimulating experiences do not learn readily, because they become excited and have less control over their impulses than usual.

Another researcher speaks to the question of appropriate quality of stimulation when he describes his longitudinal studies on infants from 4 months to 4 years of age. Measuring how much babies in the first year of life perceive and understand of their environment, Jerome Kagan of Harvard University observed differences between babies from different socioeconomic backgrounds. The *distinctiveness* of the stimulation, more than the *amount* of stimulation, marked the difference between children from middle and lower socioeconomic groups. Kagan has concluded that learning should be fostered in infancy through a *distinctive* (not yet clearly defined) stimulation provided by parents and that all parents need education about this process. He also believes that the classroom environment for children must be designed to fit the child's needs, and that these needs vary according to the child's early rearing.[6] Thus, inappropriate stimulation, as well as overstimulation, may be as disastrous for children as understimulation.

PRESCHOOL PROGRAMS

Awareness of the great difference in learning between slum children and those reared in more affluent circumstances led to the founding of Project Headstart in 1965. Unfortunately, it was begun as a crash program, without sufficient time to recruit well-trained, experienced teachers. Many of those who accepted teaching and administrative roles received only short periods of training before they began to work. Often they did not know the characteristics of children aged 3 to 5 years of any racial or socioeconomic background, nor how to fashion appropriate learning opportunities, and they were unprepared for the upsurge of their own feelings in dealing with the children brought to them. Therefore, many of the Headstart classes have failed to give children enough of the kinds of experience they most needed.

This is not to say that gains have not resulted from Headstart. Although the greatest gains may come from the early recognition of disease and the correction of physical defects in children who otherwise would not have received any medical care, children may also have gained educationally by becoming better informed

[5] Fuller, J. L. Experimental deprivation and later behavior. *Science*, December 29, 1967.

[6] Kagan, J.; Lewis, M. Studies of attention in the human infant. *Merrill-Palmer Quarterly*, April 1965.

about themselves, their neighborhoods, and the world around them. Too frequently, however, Headstart programs have failed to teach children what they were ready for, such as a better use of language for communication. On the other hand, in a few sophisticated urban communities, the Headstart program has become a pawn in the struggle between advocates of differing methods of early childhood education.

Some critics of the standard, play-oriented nursery school approach have recommended more structured and didactic methods of teaching, not only for Headstart but for all early childhood education. A program originated by Siegfried Engelmann and Carl Bereiter at the University of Illinois concentrates on teaching children certain special *items* which these experimenters believe every child must know when he enters first grade. The program has three distinctive characteristics: (1) a high ratio of teachers to students, (2) reliance on drill, and (3) learning by rote. Children are made to repeat after the teacher the names of objects, numbers, and descriptions of various items held in front of them. No deviation of response is permitted; there is always only one right answer. The children are asked to answer in unison as well as individually. There is little tolerance or time for an original idea or an association spontaneously expressed. The conditions are conducive neither to curiosity nor to learning the connections between the things recited and things experienced.

This method of teaching will be remembered by many older persons as the kind they experienced in school. However, it differs in one respect in that the young pupils are not expected to sit impassively with hands folded. The children are encouraged to recite as a group with simultaneous loud clapping of hands and other rhythmic movements.

In watching any of these classes, one is impressed with the seriousness of the work at hand. The emphasis in learning is on work, not play, and on making everything count as if time needed to be conserved. Disapproval of mistakes is expressed not only in strong words but occasionally by slapping a child's hands, as if to emphasize that a person must feel guilty when he makes mistakes and that errors are similar to misbehavior in being punishable.

It is not easy to determine the effects of this kind of teaching on children. Engelmann and Bereiter have been pleased that their children learned to speak in sentences, progressed in arithmetic, reading, and spelling, and in general increased their IQ levels.[7] There are reports that the children have made gains in psycholinguistic ability. There are also reports that the children are very often tense and frightened and respond automatically. Some child development specialists doubt whether the results of rote learning will carry over into the later years of schooling and suggest that the children may even develop a fear of and distaste for school.

The question arises as to whether children taught by these methods have really learned to think, to reason, and to conceptualize, or merely to parrot unquestioningly whatever they are told by authoritarian teachers.

In an experiment at the University of Florida, mothers of very young babies are being taught in well-baby clinics how to use toys so that their children will learn concepts of size, relationships, and color. This program is similar to one

---

[7] Bereiter, C.; Engelmann, S. *Teaching disadvantaged children in the preschool.* Prentice-Hall, Englewood Cliffs, N.J. 1966.

in Russia wherein mothers are taught how to play with their children and to use toys recommended by the polyclinic staff. The Florida experimenters, like the Russian, emphasize attention to small muscle movements, exercises, and body massage as ways of producing kinesthetic stimulation and fostering mental development. Here again, the emphasis seems to be on how to get the children to learn *more* and to develop various *skills* without any attempt to foster their creativity or individuality.

Teaching the use of toys in such a didactic manner resembles the methods of Montessori. This Italian physician-educationist worked with slum children 3 to 7 years of age in a day-care center in Rome in the early part of this century. She invented educational toys and used them in didactic teaching to help children develop their intelligence. She also sought to inculcate discipline and good habits of study. But in contrast to some present-day American educators, she was also concerned with the cultivation of independence and curiosity as well as persistence in learning.

The Montessori system never really got started in the United States until about 10 years ago, when it suddenly spread across the country. However, there have been so much unorthodoxy and deviation from the original methods that it is rare to find two Montessori nursery schools in which the methods are applied alike. The revisionists have tended to favor modification in the use of the equipment, flexibility in programming, and more free play.

What the long-term effects of these various techniques will be remains unclear. Those researchers who are providing more stimulation to children have not demonstrated that sensory stimulation enhances the use and understanding of symbols, which are necessary for the development of a sense of meaning. Those who use teaching machines acknowledge that unless wisely used such products of educational technology could destroy initiative and individuality, "making all men alike and not necessarily alike in nice ways."

Barbara Biber of the Bank Street College of Education has pointed out that "the method, through its effects on attitude and therefore on motivation, becomes a secondary determinant of how far the original learning goal will be realized."[8]

DEFINING GOALS

Program planners today in discussing appropriate goals for early childhood education show little understanding of the difference between intelligence and intellect and to which of these qualities educational efforts should be directed.

The historian, Richard Hofstadter of Columbia University, however, has given much thought to the differences between intelligence and intellect. "Intelligence," he says, "is an excellence of mind that is employed in a fairly narrow. immediate, and predictable range. Intellect on the other hand is the critical, creative, and contemplative side of mind. Whereas *intelligence* seeks to grasp, manipulate, reorder, adjust, *intellect* evaluates and looks for the meanings of situations as a whole. It implies a special sense of the ultimate value and the

[8] Biber, B. A learning-teaching paradigm integrating intellectual and affective processes. In *Behavioral science frontiers in education.* John Wiley & Sons, New York. 1967.

act of comprehension. Socrates struck its essence when he said that the unexamined life is not worth living."[9]

In assessing the effects of programs, emphasis too often has been on measuring cognitive development or other learning on the basis of changes in IQ scores. Many of the new teaching techniques do seem to bring about significant increases in IQ scores. Others, however, do not effect gains as measured by tests, yet do help disadvantaged children develop skills they would not otherwise have. This discrepancy between test results and achievement has led clinical psychologists to reappraise the standard tests of intelligence, and to attempt to design substitutes that take into consideration the tested child's cultural heritage and areas of deprivation and that can detect gains in ability to learn as well as changes in IQ.

Martin Deutsch of the Institute of Developmental Studies, New York City, in discussing the relevance of intelligence testing to work with socially deprived children, warns that the current faith in test results tends to overshadow another worthwhile source of evaluation—reports of individual teachers. He points out that teachers stimulate curiosity and initiative in children, two characteristics that the usual testing in schools does not measure.

In early childhood education, as in all child care and rearing, we should be concerned with the "whole child," the total self, not just the development of certain mental characteristics or the learning of skills. The conception of the whole child need not be as generalized, vague, or overflowing with inspirational platitudes as some people have made it. The "whole child" represents a composite organism, the physical, emotional, and social self that learns through a variety of processes, cognitive learning being only one important component and one which also involves feelings and emotions.

When I say I believe in helping children experience joy and happiness in learning, I do not mean protecting them artificially against the crises of life or from all experiences of fear, anxiety, and unhappiness. When I say I want children to feel free to ask questions, to explore, to experiment, to be spontaneous, I am not advocating license in a classroom that is unsupervised or led by a teacher who is incompetent or irresponsible. I expect teachers to be informed about appropriate curricular materials, but also to know how to incite the deep interest of children through their teaching skill and their relationship with pupils, without resorting to pedagogical tricks. I expect educational programs to help children find themselves as individuals—learners, thinkers, doers, persons with feelings, increasing clarity as to their identities, and appropriate roles in life. Such programs can be based on sound experimental studies of learning and teaching and the results evaluated by rigorous methods that go beyond the measurement of changes in IQ.

Herbert J. Muller puts it this way: "What is needed, under any name, is the view of the biological whole man, a view in which we can make out the full value of the rational, but also the necessity of the nonrational—feeling, sentiment, desire. The activities of the higher motor centers, known as the exercise of reason, are the most advanced point in man's development, the finest means of adaptation; but they do not by themselves actually run man. They belong

[9] Hofstadter, R. *Anti-intellectualism in American life.* Vintage Books, New York. 1966.

to a nervous system, which, in turn, is subordinate to the system of needs and purposes that is the whole organism."[10]

It seems to me that, at the very least, our goal should be the enhancement of all those factors that inevitably interact and foster the appropriate development of all parts of a child as he moves from infancy to childhood, then to adolescence and to adulthood. This will include the environmental, emotional, social, psychological influences as well as the cognitive and all other elements involved in learning. Above all we should avoid the myopia of fragmentation wherein understanding of the whole organism is obscured by focus on a part.

Children do need to learn how to adapt to a rapidly changing world, but a speedup in their learning, in skill proficiency, does not guarantee ability to cope with life at any tempo. Too frequently today the emphasis is on speed, on hastening learning. Children are denied time to reflect, to cogitate, to dream. I believe this denial hinders the development of the intellect as distinguished from development of intelligence.

By concentrating on intelligence and discouraging intellect, current educational methods may lead to the unexamined life deplored by Socrates. Yet without the ability to examine life, the individual is impoverished and society is deprived; it could be that without the ability and the will to examine life we may stop living.

What goals are we striving for in education and child rearing? My personal hope is that our passion for mass education will be founded primarily on belief in the desirability of developing the mind, and on a pride in learning and culture for their own sakes, rather than on political or economic benefits; and having set that goal, that we will implement it by doing whatever is necessary, so that we may finally realize the kind of education we have idealized in words for over 200 years.

[10] Muller, H. J. *Science and criticism.* Yale University Press, New Haven, Conn. 1964.

Early Childhood Education: Influence on the Elementary School

Helen Heffernan

The policy of making the kindergarten an integral part of the elementary school is gradually gaining nationwide acceptance. A mountain of evidence has accumulated to prove the importance of the early years of life for all kinds of learning—cognitive, affective, and psychomotor. Benjamin Bloom's statement that

From *Today's Education* LIX, no. 4 (April 1970):41–42. Used by permission of the author and publisher.

"about 17 percent of growth [in educational achievement] takes place between ages 4 and 6" has been reinforced by recent experience and further experiments in the educability of young children. No defensible doubt can remain today about the responsibility of society to exploit fully the young child's capacity to learn.

The decade ahead should witness great progress on how each child's general learning pattern can best be developed, what curricular experiences are most conducive to further learning, and who can participate most effectively in the young child's adventures in learning.

Although the social trend is toward adding a year or more of schooling prior to the traditional first grade, a less publicized but equally significant trend is toward recognition of the important role of parents, the home, and the community in the education of young children. If home-community language is deficient, the child comes to school seriously handicapped. If the parents have not introduced the young child to some of the complexities of his social environment and some of the wonders of his natural environment, he comes to school lacking the basic concepts essential to make reading meaningful. If parents have not read to a child or told him stories, have not sung to him, or encouraged him to participate in household activities, he comes to school lacking many of the skills of his more fortunate age mates.

Any examination of the organization of the educational program because of the added year or years is superficial if it does not include plans to provide opportunity for parents and prospective parents to learn about child-rearing practices conducive to optimal development and about their appropriate roles as the first teachers of their children. Part of the nursery school, kindergarten, or primary teacher's time might well be assigned to helping parents learn to become full partners with the school in the education of their children.

The extension of education downward confronts the school with the necessity of providing continuity and progression in the educational program. Children need to recognize an orderly sequence of experiences in which each new experience builds on previous ones and enriches and enhances their lives. All education of children should include this feeling of progression—a dynamic forward movement toward new goals. Progression involves the excitement of living through achievement in learning and through meeting new challenges that the child is capable of dealing with successfully after a reasonable expenditure of time and effort.

To provide for continuity, those entrusted with making policy decisions for a school system or for other programs should reconsider their goals for the education of children. Various age spans that seem appropriate for the particular school system may be defined. Ages five to eight, ages three or four to eight may be right for programs beginning at the specific lower ages. Other programs may include an age span from birth through age eight, particularly in communities where coordination of health, social welfare, and education services has been achieved or is feasible. Considering the entire life period to adolescence as a unit, other communities may wish no artificial divisions into early and later childhood education.

Each year is important in the life of a human being. The year the child is actually living is the most important one for him. School should provide the opportunity for him to live that particular year to the fullest. If the school provides a richly stimulating environment in terms of the child's developmental needs and encourages his free exploration of the environment with the guidance of thoroughly qualified teachers, then he will make progress in every behavior for which he is ready. This is true not only for the year (or years) of education added at early levels; but for the years that follow.

A year spent in a well-designed nursery or kindergarten program will produce development that should make subsequent learning easier for the child and reduce the pressure and tension that lead to school failure. The goals the school system sets and teacher guidance that leads to their realization will produce measurable results. The kindergarten year is marked for many children by improved physical and mental health, increased emotional control, improved psychomotor skills, self-identification, ability to work and play with other children, ability to follow a regular pattern of activities, increased fluency and facility in the use of language, increased understanding of the physical and social environment, and ability to use a wide variety of materials and equipment.

What changes, then, should the addition of the kindergarten year make in the elementary school curriculum? For each year of the child's education the goals are essentially the same. Schools strive to help each child to—

Protect, maintain, and improve his physical and mental health and his social and emotional adjustment.
Increase his ability to get along successfully with other people.
Expand his understanding of his natural and scientific environment.
Increase his skills of effective communication.
Increase his ability to use mathematical concepts, symbols, and processes.
Expand his knowledge and appreciation of the arts—music, art, literature, drama, the dance.
Expand his ability and desire to express himself creatively.

Each year the teacher will work with each child to enable him to achieve a full year's growth in regard to these goals. He will recognize and treat each child as a unique person. He will not compare one child's achievement with that of any other. He will not judge the child in terms of academic goals that are unrealistic for him. He will not be made a victim of so-called grade standards that ignore what is now well known about individual variation.

Whenever the school makes basic organizational changes, such as the addition, in this instance, of the kindergarten year, every elementary teacher should participate in an analysis and discussion of what the change means to the present structure.

Teachers will find that the broad objectives are identical at all levels of childhood but the means to achieve these ends are determined by the maturity of the children as they progress year after year through the educational program. The major difference lies in equipment and materials used. Charts based on the children's firsthand experiences may be highly satisfactory for the six-year-old, while delightful little books on life in different communities in the world reveal new horizons for the eight-year-old, and a wide range of reading materials on primitive life proves intriguing to the ten-year-old. A map of the neighborhood

showing the home of each five-year-old introduces a new concept of spatial relations. Eight-year-olds find that making a map of their own community is
fascinating, while the 11-year-olds need an excellent world map on which to
locate the current events in the increasingly complex world in which each is eager
to find his place.

The teacher will decide that steady progression in music experiences is highly
desirable and that each year should mean additions to the children's repertoire
of songs they can sing and music they can appreciate and enjoy. Similarly, as
children mature, the teacher will supplement or replace the art materials they
have been using with more sophisticated material. The goal, however, remains
the same at each level—to release the creativity of children.

Although many materials used in school have a wide appeal to children of all
ages, teachers may decide that continuity and progression will result from some
agreement within the school or school system concerning *when* to use certain
stories, poems, songs, pictures, science experiences, social studies activities, or
study trips. Such an agreement on materials and experiences that seem particularly suitable for each level of development leaves some material fresh for each
group as they proceed through the school. The richness of resources in all these
activities is almost limitless, and so every child can be stimulated by new and
delightful materials at each age level. These are the kinds of agreements conducive to good human relations among any group of adults responsible for the
education of the children of a community.

The addition of a year or two to the education of children calls for a reexamination of the elementary school because every year will be affected. To
many, modifying practice is painful, but a new organization is a challenge to
question our curriculum, the effectiveness of our methods, the influence of our
human relations. The advent of the kindergarten could well be the occasion to
initiate long-needed change and to cultivate a sensitive awareness of every child,
his home, his neighborhood, his unmet needs.

Components of a Child Advocacy Program

Spencer A. Ward

In the United States of America it is estimated that of persons under 17
years old there are:

5 million who suffer from malnutrition (which interferes with their physical and
mental growth).

From *Children Today* I, no. 2 (March–April 1972):38–40. Used by permission of the
author and publisher.

8 million who drop out of school each year (and are poorly prepared for the increasingly complex jobs available).

1 million who are involved in a court process due to delinquency.

5 million who have moderate to severe mental health problems, and 700,000 who receive some care from mental health facilities.

We have heard these figures so often that many of us have learned to ignore them. Child advocacy is a concept and process designed to make them real and to give us, at a local and national level, a structure to begin to deal with the problems.

The concept was discussed in the 1970 report of the Joint Commission on Mental Health of Children. Composed of a 55-member board of experts representing the fields of health and mental health, education, welfare, law, religion, politics and labor, the Commission was created by act of Congress to carry out a "program of research into and study of our resources, methods, and practices for diagnosing or preventing emotional illness in children and of treating, caring for, and rehabilitating children with emotional illnesses." Its report emphasized the fact that significant numbers of children are not receiving the care they need and pointed out that the responsibility for providing this care lies with the family. The nation as a whole, it observed, has not accepted its responsibility for making the necessary supports and resources available to families who need them. It outlined specific needs for more effective children's services and recommended a system of advocacy with neighborhood, area, state and federal level child advocacy councils made up of professionals and other concerned citizens. These councils would be "concerned with planning, facilitating and coordinating services and with insuring these services to children, youth and their families."

Child advocacy is most frequently referred to in terms of this system of councils. I would like to discuss advocacy in terms of the organization of such a system of councils, the systematic determination of the needs of children and their families, and the long-range, coordinated program of research needed to determine the best methods for providing specific services.

The needs of the nation's children are many and complex. Families and the community institutions providing children's services are dedicated to their tasks, and there is no reason to expect that another program can provide the required support unless it includes major increases in expenditures in the area as well as new methods of planning and cooperation. I am proposing that we think of child advocacy in terms of the following six components, each of which requires carefully planned and coordinated research.

1. *Processes for accurately defining the needs of children in the community.*

This involves community-level surveys and tabulation of data from such institutions as schools. Nothing can be done effectively to meet the unmet needs of children until we have a clear picture of the extent and causes of the problems. This information is usually best collected at a community level, since the causes and possible solutions of problems such as malnutrition will vary from one community to the next. It is also probably true that each community should gather its own data if the data are to have the personal impact and relevance needed to stimulate action.

2. *Methods to develop and support family and community responsibility for insuring children's services.*

It is expected that the community will organize itself to act to determine needs and to provide or obtain needed services. Such organization would include a community council. There is need to study methods of choosing councils and ways to provide responsibility most effectively to councils while still making optimal use of trained staff and expert resources. We can learn much about effective, ineffective and defeating methods in this area by studying the past efforts of Head Start and other community-based programs.

3. *Determination of the tasks of child advocates in the community.*

This involves defining the tasks of local residents as volunteer or paid child advocacy staff to help the community determine the needs of children and to act effectively in obtaining services to meet them.

4. *Determination of the most effective methods of providing care.*

Much money has been spent in this century in efforts to meet the needs of children and their families, but when any community wishes to act to provide services, it usually must start out on its own, without any data on what works best in its type of community. It would appear that one responsibility of a federal child advocacy program is to pull together findings from the many methods previously tried and studied and to make the data available to states and communities.

5. *Determination of the responsibilities for provision of defined services by each institution—family, school, welfare, courts, etc.—and the means whereby these institutions can cooperate.*

Often a need goes unmet because no person or agency accepts meeting it as their task, or because several agencies take partial responsibility and so interfere with each other's work. Equally familiar to many of us is the situation in which several different agencies are working with the same family, but where no one person is looking at the total picture or conducting—with the family—the total planning that is needed. Related to this issue is the fact that communities often find that agencies need to make significant changes in their programs in order to apply their funds most effectively to meet existing needs. Families and advocates then must work with agencies to produce the needed changes.

6. *Determination of the most effective system of advocacy councils at local, state and federal levels to support the community in its efforts.*

We know that in many communities there is a sense of helplessness to change things. This sense of helplessness, combined with the fact that they are rarely expected to express their wishes, leads to the present situation in which many people—suburban and urban, middle class and poor—tend to ignore children's problems. If families and communities are to accept their responsibility for their children, there must be some system whereby the needs at the local level can be communicated to state and federal agencies, which can provide the energy and support needed to attain the desired goals. Without this source of power, the family and community will continue to feel powerless and perhaps ignore the resources available.

FAMILY AND COMMUNITY RESPONSIBILITY

Family and community responsibility is the central concept in the components discussed. There was a time in the development of our nation when communities were small enough and life simple enough for them to provide the social pressure and support needed for families to carry out the difficult tasks of being parents. The natural support in terms of family and friends has diminished as our cities have grown larger and our population more mobile.

If we, as a nation, expect parents and communities to take their appropriate responsibility for providing for their children, we must make that expectation clear. The courts, schools, and other institutions can no longer ignore cases where parents do not provide for children's needs. The nation must expect that parents will feed and clothe their children, get them to school, provide appropriate limits on their behavior, and so on.

However, there will be times when families cannot carry out their responsibilities alone—when they have children whose needs are such (because of physical or psychological disabilities, for example) that they could not be expected to meet them. At other times, families may be prevented from fulfilling responsibilities by a lack of knowledge, skill or other resource. In these cases it is the responsibility of parents to obtain needed services from the community. It is also the responsibility of the community and the nation to make available to parents resources which can be freely utilized at such times. Without this kind of support, families and children tend to give up, leaving all the responsibility with the community and the state.

EVALUATION

One of the universal problems in this area is that much evaluation has been so poorly done that when a project is completed we rarely have reliable information on its outcome. If the child advocacy concept is to serve its intended purpose, some central organization must accept responsibility for evaluating pilot efforts and providing needed information to local communities.

There are a number of pilot projects currently supported by the Federal Government which are labeled as child advocacy. It seems important at this point to be clear that these projects are not set up to test the concept of child advocacy. They are, rather, logical extensions of past efforts in the area to perfect further one or more of the six components of an advocacy program.

FINALLY

The report of the Joint Commission and the report of the 1970 White House Conference remind us emphatically of the unmet needs of children. Our children are our greatest resource. If current problems of drug abuse, alcoholism, mental illness, unemployment, etc. are to be effectively dealt with, we must take seriously the needs of today's children. Over the last 30 years we have witnessed two very effective, major national efforts leading to the development of nuclear weapons and the space program. Each of these has required large expenditures of money, involvement of some of the nation's greatest thinkers and, most importantly, a coordinated, systematically planned and implemented research and development effort.

On the basis of our past experience, we cannot expect to effect lasting change without such a serious commitment. We could determine, for example, that by 1982 our nation will be one where each child receives the care and education he needs to become a healthy and productive member of society. In 10 years the world balance of power and our continued freedom may well be determined by the commitment this nation, and each one of us, makes to our children now.

The Nongraded School: An Overview

Robert H. Anderson

Few topics on the current scene are of greater interest to elementary school teachers and administrators than the nongraded school. The subject of a rapidly expanding literature, nongradedness has probably received more attention over the past decade in national, state, and regional meetings than any other aspect of school organization, and DESP's mailbox is constantly full of inquiries about it. Yet, for all the publicity it has received, nongradedness apparently remains a somewhat nebulous, even confusing, concept. It is therefore both timely and fortunate that DESP has reserved two issues of *The National Elementary Principal* for a thorough examination of the nongraded plan.

NONGRADEDNESS DEFINED

One reason for the uncertainty that surrounds the concept of nongradedness is that its vocabulary is both imprecise in meaning and negativistic in tone. "Nongradedness" is a clumsy and unsuitable term, since it refers primarily to what it is *not* rather than to what it *is*. Furthermore, the label "nongraded" has often been applied to programs which have made only very limited departures from conventional gradedness (for example, only the reading program has been rendered more flexible), or are merely a version of homogeneous grouping or even departmentalization. Often, too, visitors to so-called nongraded classes discover that terms such as "first grade" and "third grade" are still in common use and pupils may still be confronted by conventional A-B-C-D-F report cards, as well as the administrative machinery of promotion and nonpromotion. In the absence of agreement concerning its meaning, and because of the carelessness with which it is used, "nongradedness" is therefore a term for which the profession desperately needs alternatives. For the moment, however, we must struggle along with it as best we can.

Nongradedness refers to at least two dimensions of the school and its

From *The National Elementary Principal* XLVII, no. 2 (November 1967):16–20. Copyright © 1967, National Association of Elementary School Principals. All rights reserved. Used by permission of the author and publisher.

atmosphere: 1) the philosophy (or, if you will, the value system) that guides the behavior of the school staff toward the pupils, and 2) the administrative-organizational machinery and procedures whereby the life of the pupils and teachers is regulated and facilitated. It is, in short, both an operational mechanism and a theoretical proposition. It is not a new staffing pattern, as is team teaching. It is not a technological innovation, as is educational television. It is not, as such, a component of the curriculum reform movement, though it may very well be the chief inspiration behind curriculum reform. Rather, it is a concept of what is right and a plan for implementation of that concept.

Many definitions have been offered, and for the most part they differ in the elegance and the comprehensiveness with which their authors have stated them, rather than in conceptual meaning. Without exception, the emphasis is upon individualizing instruction and upon developing each individual up to his full potential for physical, social, intellectual, and civic accomplishment. Without exception, too, there is reference to the fact that provision should be made for both differentiated *rates* of pupil progress and variations in the *kinds* of *programs* offered to this child and that. Many, though not all, refer to the need for more suitable forms of evaluating and reporting pupil progress, and most make some reference to the various *means* for individualizing instruction via pupil group, independent study, and other procedural arrangements. The titles of nongraded programs vary, many using phrases like "Continuous Progress Plan" or "Continuous Growth Plan," but others simply referring to the name of the school or city in a phrase such as "The Middletown Project."

Although most publications on nongradedness and an overwhelming number of pilot programs are at the early elementary level, the movement is in fact inclusive of all school levels from nursery schools through the university. The writings in this field are primarily in the form of magazine articles and pamphlets published by local school systems, although there are now a number of complete volumes dedicated to this topic. Several of those most recently published are in effect case histories of certain specific programs.

John I. Goodlad, in one of the three major volumes[1] produced by the NEA Project on Instruction, points out that there are several different models of school organization, or variants thereof, to be found in American schools today. One of these is the graded pattern which, we fervently hope, is rapidly disappearing from the American scene. Gradedness grows out of an assumption that schools are intended to cover and to inculcate in the pupils a specific body of subject matter which is carefully laid out in the successive grades and closely identified with those grades. In this model, the fact that children differ from each other is viewed primarily as an explanation for the differences in children's actual performances, and not as a basis for planning the program. Pupils who make slow progress are adjusted to the system by means chiefly of nonpromotion.

In the learner-centered, nongraded model which Goodlad then describes, the following assumptions are made:

School function: Schools are learner-centered—designed to develop the learner as an individual and as a member of society.

[1] Goodlad, John I. *Planning and Organizing for Teaching.* National Education Association, Project on the Instructional Program of the Public Schools. Washington, D.C.: the Association, 1963. pp. 54–57, 65–68.

Means of fulfilling function: Focus should be on ways of knowing and thinking. Emphasis is on the individual.

Organizational structure: Graded structure is either ignored as meaningless or replaced with a nongraded plan. Grouping patterns are flexible. Individual differences tend to be accounted for through intraclass provisions rather than interclass provisions.

Individual differences: Differences in many aspects of development are recognized and used in planning highly individualized programs.

Pupil progress: Provision is made for both differentiated rates of progress and variations in kinds of program, according to individual needs and abilities.

Nongradedness should not be confused with departmentalization, self-contained classrooms, or cooperative teaching plans. The latter three arrangements represent the major alternatives in horizontal school organization (i.e., the way the progress of children is regulated over a period of years). Every school must commit itself to both a vertical and a horizontal plan, and therefore if one believes in nongradedness he can, if he chooses, combine it with team teaching or with the self-contained classroom pattern, or (as in the Dual Progress Plan) with a form of departmentalization.

There is increasing reason to believe, as I do strongly, that nongradedness is both easier to develop and more effective in practice in schools that abandon the self-contained classroom arrangement in favor of its horizontal alternatives, especially cooperative teaching. It appears to be considerably more difficult for any one teacher by himself to carry on an appropriately flexible program for his class than it is for a group of teachers who share a larger number of pupils. However, having made this strategic suggestion let us return to our attempt at definition of a nongraded program.

In a full-fledged nongraded program, all of the following statements would be justified:

1. Suitable provision is being made, in all aspects of the curriculum, for each unique child.
   a. This implies flexible grouping and subgrouping of pupils.
   b. It implies an adaptable, flexible curriculum.
   c. It implies a great range of materials and instructional approaches.
2. The successive learning experiences of each boy and girl will be, to the greatest possible extent, pertinent and appropriate to his needs at that moment. Easier said than done, of course, but this—*not* teacher convenience or administrative convenience—is the creed that guides our professional decisions!
3. Each child is constantly under just the right amount of pressure—not too much, as in the graded school for slow learners, nor too little, as in the graded school for talented learners. Again, easier said than done—but we strive to do it!
4. Success, with appropriate rewards, is assured for all kinds of learners so long as they attend to their tasks with reasonable diligence and effort. Such success spurs the child to a conviction of his own worth, and to further achievement.
   a. Failure and frustration occasionally? Yes, but not nearly as much as faces the below-average child in the graded school!
   b. Over-confidence and complacence occasionally? If so, the system isn't working right.

5. Absent are grade labels (1st grade, 6th grade, etc.) and the related machinery of promotion-and-failure.
6. There is a reporting system consistent with the philosophy that says each child is a unique and precious individual. Teachers abolish the ridiculous and cynical system of A-B-C-D-F report cards.
7. There is more sophisticated curriculum planning, evaluation and record-keeping on the part of teachers than one finds in schools still loyal to graded practices.

Admittedly an element of propaganda seems to color the foregoing statements, but it seems reasonable to link some of the hoped-for qualities of the school atmosphere with the mechanism itself so long as our intent is to define the idea at its best.

One further dimension of the nongraded concept requires explanation before we proceed to a discussion of nongradedness in practice. One of the characteristics of the graded school, especially in this century in urban schools, has been the separation of children into classes by age. Granted that there is nonetheless a spread of two or more years within each class because some children progress more rapidly (for example, via double-promotion) or more slowly (via nonpromotion), the typical graded class is composed mostly of children who are approximately the same age.

In a nongraded school, it is possible to continue this practice although there is increasing reason to believe that heterogeneous, multi-aged class groups may be preferable. It is argued that children require regular social and intellectual contacts, not only with other pupils of like mind, talent, and experience, but also with pupils of differing backgrounds and predispositions. This implies that a nongraded class (or, preferably, team) of children spanning several years would be preferable to a class or team of youngsters all about the same age. Deliberate heterogeneity, therefore, is recommended as the broad criterion for establishing pupil groups. Subgroups within the total pupil membership, for example a reading group, may of course be homogeneous.

NONGRADEDNESS: A RECENT HISTORY

Nongradedness is by no means a new idea in American education. Even before 1900 the rigidity and the psychological invalidity of the graded school were under attack from various educators here and abroad, and numerous efforts were made to introduce more humane and appropriate practices into the schools. It is possible to trace a steady, though distressingly slow, erosion of the literally graded school throughout the first half of the 20th century, with such devices as "social promotion" or equivalent practices blunting the worst features of gradedness even though some of its outward forms remained. More recently, the profession's protests against gradedness have increased to the point where Francis Keppel, in 1966, proclaimed nongradedness to be the fastest-moving innovation on the elementary school scene.

At the same time, Keppel and others took note of the somewhat sorry state of the research and literature, and the need to link nongradedness with other reforms such as curriculum revision, the reorganization and retraining of personnel, and the like.

At the present time, indications from the federal government and from NEA and other sources suggest that about one school system in every four is known to be engaged in a serious effort to develop nongraded practices in one or more schools. Probably an even larger number of schools have been moving without fanfare in the direction away from gradedness, and it is interesting to speculate upon the percentage of classrooms in America within which there is not yet any appreciable sign of rigid and unrelenting gradedness giving way. Let us hope that the percentage is small indeed!

We have, then, at least four arrangements in American elementary schools today: 1) uncompromising gradedness; 2) nominal but eroding gradedness (perhaps this is the prevailing arrangement); 3) nominal nongradedness, but within which one finds disappointing evidence of gradedness still in the atmosphere; and 4) nongradedness which is, in large measure, faithful to the definition offered in the preceding section. Though the latter group may at present be small, our hope is that this will soon constitute the majority.

RESEARCH ON NONGRADEDNESS

Partly because the concept itself is difficult to define and is subject to various interpretations, partly because the "educational research community" (to use Keppel's phrase) has not yet developed appropriate research technology, and partly because excellent examples of nongradedness are all too few, there is as yet very little research evidence on which the profession can base its decisions. Further difficulty results from the tendency of researchers to rely heavily upon inappropriate research designs. Goodlad[2] has discussed this problem in some detail, along with commentary on specific studies published up to 1962. Unfortunately, most of the studies published since that date are marred by the same design problems, and it may be some years before more appropriate research studies become available.

A common problem in research using the "control-group-vs.-experimental-group" design is that the researchers fail to indicate the specific, functional ways in which the two groups actually differ from each other. Presumably, the control (graded) group is being treated in ways that differ significantly from the definition of nongradedness as applied to the experimental group. Presumably, too, the experimental group is being treated according to the definition. However, one reads many research reports in vain for this type of information. Sometimes, in fact, one discovers information that tends to deny the project's validity.

A case in point is an article published in 1965 regarding a project in Los Angeles County.[3] In the article, there is no description of the ungraded primary organization reportedly being used in twenty schools. Within the text, however, there are comments from which the reader can deduce that the so-called ungraded plan was mostly a system of homogeneous grouping. Several other comments suggest that the ungraded plan was not given sufficient administrative support (for

[2] See Goodlad, John I., and Anderson, Robert H. *The Nongraded Elementary School.* Revised edition. New York: Harcourt, Brace and World, 1963. pp. 213–19.
[3] Hopkins, Kenneth D.; Oldridge, O. A.; and Williamson, Malcolm L. "An Empirical Comparison of Pupil Achievement and Other Variables in Graded and Ungraded Classes." *American Educational Research Journal* 2:207–15; November 1965.

example, in instructional materials, or curriculum work). There is, further, no reference to differential procedures for inducting the primary pupils into 4th grade. The reader is therefore left to wonder whether there were any real differences, either operational or psychological.

Virtually the same question arises in connection with a study reported by Williams.[4] Although information is furnished to show certain administrative differences between the experimental and control groups (for example, use of grade labels and nonpromotion policy), there are statements which suggest that teachers in the so-called graded schools in fact made virtually the same adjustments to the individual differences in their classes as, supposedly (though no evidence is furnished), did the teachers of the so-called nongraded schools. A fascinating reference is made to the fact that the nongraded classes averaged 45 pupils per teacher, whereas the graded classes averaged 27! It seems doubtful that a better understanding of nongradedness can be gained by studies of this sort, whatever their conclusions.

A different sort of problem arises in connection with a 1966 report from Naperville, Illinois.[5] The article describes the difficulties encountered when the parents of four boys, all capable of completing the primary unit in two years, preferred that they not be accelerated (as were 25 others), and therefore "withdrew" their sons from the program. Apparently, too, there is relatively rigid graded structure (as perhaps in the Los Angeles County program) from 4th through 12th grades, and no opportunity within the primary school program for the brighter youngsters to engage in 4th grade-level work. One suspects that the limitations under which the program operates are both self-imposed and artificial.

David Lewin[6] makes the altogether reasonable plea that educators should report the weaknesses as well as the strengths of nongradedness if and when they appear. He then proceeds to examine what he as a supervisor in New York City perceives as problems: better teachers, supported by assistants, are needed; available materials and techniques for individualizing instruction are inadequate; nongrading requires heavy reliance on programed material; costs (for example, in guidance services) are greater; teachers need more conference and planning time; new systems of reporting progress must be developed; testing programs must be revised; administrators must work harder. While his concluding statement that perhaps the goal of greater individualization may also be achievable in graded classes is not supported by argument, Lewin has contributed a great deal by revealing the tough problems that exist in many of our schools. Obviously, as he and many of the other authors are saying, excellent education is not just a question of overhauling our organizational machinery.

In fact, if research and experience tell us anything, it is that the basic problems in improving instruction can be resolved only by a "package approach" in which nongradedness is merely one major component. To quote Calvin Gross: "Nongradedness takes its place among the other promising components of what I like to call 'the innovative package'; team teaching, flexible space, and hierarchies

[4] Williams, Wilmajean. "Academic Achievement in a Graded School and in a Non-Graded School." *Elementary School Journal* 67:135–39; December 1966.

[5] Barnickle, Donald W., and Lindberg, Ruth T. "The Unwilling Accelerate—A Problem of the Nongraded School." *Elementary School Journal* 67:84–87; November 1966.

[6] Lewin, David. "Go Slow on Non-Grading." *Elementary School Journal* 67:131–34; December 1966.

of teaching personnel backed up by mechanical and electronic instructional systems and devices. This mosaic of mutually reinforcing concepts and arrangements has demonstrated greater potential potency for individualizing instruction than any other design conceived so far."[7]

FURTHER COMMENTS AND REACTIONS*

Several writers have listed reasons why some observers do not consider the nongraded school as desirable. Alleged weaknesses are shown in the left hand column. In the right hand column, I offer my comment in response:

Allegation	*Comment*
1. Nongradedness leads to soft pedagogy; it lacks fixed standards and requirements.	1. This is probably true in the early stages, but as we grow more skilled in curriculum development, appropriate standards for each type of child are likely to emerge. Nongradedness may, indeed, lead us away from soft pedagogy by enabling all youngsters to master what they study.
2. It places an impossible burden on the teacher.	2. Quite true, especially if we persist in having self-contained classrooms! The burden will lift as we find ways of sharing teaching responsibilities.
3. It replaces grade requirements by reading levels.	3. Only in the primitive stages and where nongradedness is not well understood.
4. It results in a lack of information on pupil progress to parents.	4. Only when the teachers are lazy, foolish, or incompetent in their reporting.
5. It is difficult to put into practice, because teachers are inadequately and insufficiently prepared.	5. True. Therefore, let's start a revolution in teacher education!
6. It does not have minimal standards for all children.	6. It is better to have standards for *each child*, is it not?
7. Its curriculum sequence tends to lack specificity and order.	7. Again, if true it may be just as well! What we need, it must be admitted, is a far more adequate curriculum. The graded curriculum is scarcely the ideal.

[7] Gross, Calvin, in the Foreword to *How to Organize a Non-Graded School*, by Howard, Eugene R., and Bardwell, Roger W. Englewood Cliffs, New Jersey: Prentice-Hall, 1966. p. 4.
* This section is adapted from pp. 61–63 of Robert H. Anderson, *Teaching in a World of Change*. (New York: Harcourt, Brace & World, Inc.) 1966.

8. It is only an improved means to an unimproved end.

8. This sounds like double-talk, but if the end is individual fulfillment then nongradedness is a better way to get there.

9. It does not guarantee that improved teaching will result.

9. No organization provides such a guarantee. To improve teaching is a very difficult task.

10. It suffers from widespread use and even abuse of the term "nongraded."

10. Amen!

11. There is some difficulty in aligning graded with nongraded schools (for example, a primary unit and a graded intermediate program).

11. This is true only if the graded unit continues to deal with youngsters in an inappropriate way. And even so, it is no problem for the children; the annoyance is only to the grade-minded teachers.

12. Teachers and parents are so conditioned to the graded structure that they continue "grademindedness."

12. Yes, but over time this is a disease that can be cured.

13. Extensive records must be kept for each child.

13. Some teachers may regard this as a disadvantage but they are wrong!

14. Planning new methods of reporting to parents demands much time and work from the already heavily burdened faculty.

14. Very true. Administration must make better provision for supporting services (for example, substitute teacher help) and for retraining teachers in the technology of reporting.

As one considers the complaints that are raised against nongraded plans, he notes that often the critic displays an ingenuous faith in organizational structure as panacea. Would that it were so easy! If all it took to modernize and improve school offerings was an edict to abolish the graded plan, we could all have been in Educational Heaven long ago!

But organizational reform is only a part of the job that must be done. Given the will, we could do it easily and quickly. Then at last we could turn our energies to the really crucial tasks of reform, namely the renovation and redevelopment of curriculum. Judging by their relative detachment from the school reorganization movement thus far, the curriculum people themselves seem not yet to have appreciated this fact; and it may be that nongradedness will ultimately be appreciated because of the curriculum work that it forced educators to do.

WHAT, THEN, SHOULD WE DO?

In this article I have tried to show that nongradedness is not merely an organizational gimmick but rather a framework within which educators try to express and accomplish what they consider essential to each child's development.

I have acknowledged that the idea is as yet underdeveloped, and have endorsed the notion that it offers greatest promise when developed in conjunction with such arrangements as team teaching, multi-age pupil grouping, and technological innovations. Note also that extensive curriculum work and teacher education activities must both precede and accompany nongradedness, along with such important work as the revision of evaluation and reporting procedures.[8] In short, if the idea of nongradedness is to flourish as it deserves, and if children are indeed to be served according to our profession's earnest intentions, our schools and teacher training institutions must literally overhaul themselves. Are we prepared to go this far?

[8] See the May 1966 issue of *The National Elementary Principal*.

Do Schools Need IPI? Yes!

Clyde C. Yetter

Educators and parents across the country seem to agree that a system of individualized instruction is much needed in our schools today. This has been evident to any parent who has raised more than one child and to every teacher who has stood in front of a class. The big question has always been: "How do you do it?"

BACKGROUND

Individually Prescribed Instruction (IPI) represents one approach to individualization for children. The original developmental effort of the IPI system took place at the Learning Research and Development Center of the University of Pittsburgh. Field testing, field development, and dissemination have been conducted by Research for Better Schools, Inc. (RBS), located in Philadelphia. IPI has been carefully engineered with quality control during installation. Teachers and children have had a lot to do with its development. Robert G. Scanlon of RBS says[1]:

> IPI is not a new set of ideas but a reexamination and re-assembly of many curriculum developments. IPI is a vehicle that allows the teacher to

Clyde C. Yetter. "Do Schools Need IPI? Yes!" *Educational Leadership* 29(6):491–94; March 1972. Reprinted with permission of the Association for Supervision and Curriculum Development and Clyde C. Yetter. Copyright © 1972 by the Association for Supervision and Curriculum Development.
[1] Robert G. Scanlon. "The Expansion of an Innovation." *Audiovisual Instruction* 13 (9): 946–48; November 1968.

monitor each child's progress but more important it allows each child to monitor his own behavior in a particular subject.

IPI is a systematic approach to learning. Scanlon points out:

It is based on a set of specified objectives correlated with diagnostic instruments, curriculum materials, teaching techniques, and management capabilities. The objectives of the system are:

1. To permit student mastery of instructional content at individual learning rates
2. To ensure active student involvement in the learning process
3. To encourage student involvement in learning through self-directed and self-initiated activities
4. To encourage student evaluation of progress toward mastery
5. To provide instructional materials and techniques based on individual needs and styles.[2]

IPI is currently being used in over 300 elementary schools, with 85,000 students in the program. Feedback from these schools has expressed many advantages for the students, teachers, and parents. Let us look at IPI from a visitor's viewpoint.

SCHOOL VISIT

Upon entering the school, I was informed by the secretary that the principal was not in his office. She explained that he was in the conference room with four teachers, having their twice-weekly conference relating to individual students. We were invited to sit in on the session.

It became evident to me immediately that the conferees seemed genuinely interested in their discussion of individual student problems. The principal had reviewed the progress of each student in the teachers' classes. He pointed out that some of the students had not gained in achievement within the past week. Plans were made to improve the progress of each student. The principal reminded each teacher that progress would be reviewed again the next week. The teachers seemed to show that the old possessiveness complex that "these are my 30 kids and you tend your own 'store'" had fallen by the way.

The principal was politely active in the conference, showing that he was interested in the progress each student was making. He wanted to get to know about his own school problems and progress and made it plain that if he is to be held accountable for his school's progress, knowledge about the curriculum is necessary. Obviously he preferred to spend his time making instructional decisions instead of taking care of bus schedules and collecting milk money.

A sixth grade student came to the conference room to give me a short orientation upon what to look for during a visit to the classroom. During this time and later, in conversations with students in the hallway going from their classrooms to the material center or vice versa, I found their views intriguing.

[2] Robert G. Scanlon and Mary V. Brown. "Individualizing Instruction." *Planned Change in Education.* New York: Harcourt Brace Jovanovich, Inc., 1971.

One fifth grade boy said: "I like IPI because it really puts your brain to work to get smarter." A fifth grade girl said: "You don't have any homework. You don't do work you already know." Another said: "I like IPI because I can go as fast as my brain can go." A sixth grade boy said: "The only thing I don't like is waiting for a prescription, because while you are waiting you lose time to work." A fourth grade girl said: "One thing I don't like about IPI mathematics is that if you don't know something, in the other mathematics I could go on but in this mathematics I wait to learn it." A fifth grade boy said: "I like everything about IPI, so I don't have nothing to say."

Walking from classroom to classroom, noticing the freedom in the halls, I took the opportunity to ask a second grade student just where he was going. He remarked: "I've just been to the material room to pick up my post-test and I hope you won't talk to me too long, because I'm in a hurry to return to my classroom and take this test."

When I entered Mrs. Davis' classroom, the partition to the next room had been rolled back and an IPI mathematics class was in progress. It was interesting to note the work of the teacher's aide. Mrs. Davis said that "The aide's most important function is the scoring, recording, and filing of students' test and skill sheets; but aides do interact with students and are often asked to take further responsibilities within the classroom."

Mrs. Davis spoke of a recent IPI Teachers' Conference and related statements that were made by the teachers in their summarization of the changing role. She is no longer a dispenser of information but a diagnostician of learning problems. Furthermore, a shift of responsibility from the teacher to the student, with the teacher being more responsive to students' needs, is obvious. For IPI to be effective, more communication and cooperation among teachers and administration are needed. Teachers are less active and more re-active to students.

The teachers pointed out that parents at first were somewhat confused, especially with the grading system. One parent remarked that she was astounded when her third grade boy came home with an F3 for his mathematics grade. She said her son was quick to inform her that this grade was good; it meant that he was really doing what she knew as fourth grade mathematics; that he was on level F, unit 3, of the mathematics curriculum. And the parent remarked that she was pleased with the system because there was so little, if any, homework required, and the interest in attending school was most gratifying. Still another parent remarked that her children seemed to have a greater interest in what they were learning.

In summary, individual differences do exist. Most teachers want review materials and management techniques to help meet their differences. IPI is a step toward the superior classroom, because the system includes material that can be used independently, allowing each child to learn at his own rate and realize success. The technology, training program, and management technique give the teacher tools for assessment, mastery measurement, and specified management techniques. One of the best features of IPI is the assumption that it is never completed; and with the feedback mechanism, it can constantly be renewed.

IPI is one system that can meet the needs of our exciting changing world; if for no other reason, it has helped change the attitude and interest of many students in learning to learn. Furthermore IPI brings a new instructional technology and classroom management to the teachers of America.

REFERENCES

BECKER, JAMES W. "Incorporating the Products of Educational Development into Practice." *Journal of Research and Development in Education* 3 (2):81–103; Winter 1970.

BOLVIN, J. O. and GLASER, ROBERT. "Developmental Aspects of Individual Pre-scribed Instruction." *Audiovisual Instruction* 13 (8):828–31; October 1968.

GLASER, ROBERT. "Adapting the Elementary School Curriculum to Individual Per-formance." Address delivered at the 1967 Invitational Conference on Testing Problems on October 28, 1967, in New York City, under the auspices of the Educational Testing Service, Princeton, New Jersey. Reprint 26, Learning Re-search and Development Center, University of Pittsburgh, 1967.

LINDVALL, C. M. and BOLVIN, J. O. "Programmed Instruction in the Schools: An Application of Programming Principles in Individually Prescribed Instruc-tion." *Programmed Instruction.* Sixty-sixth Yearbook of the National Society for the Study of Education. Part 2. Chicago: University of Chicago Press, 1967. pp. 217–54. Reprint 16, Learning Research and Development Center, Uni-versity of Pittsburgh, 1967.

LINDVALL, C. M. and COX, R. C. "The Role of Evaluation in Programs for In-dividualized Instruction." *Educational Evaluation: New Roles, New Means.* Sixty-eighth Yearbook of the National Society for the Study of Education. Chicago: University of Chicago Press, 1969.

SCANLON, ROBERT G. "The Expansion of an Innovation." *Audiovisual Instruction* 13 (9):946–48; November 1968.

SCANLON, ROBERT G. and BROWN, MARY V. "In-service Education for Individual-ized Instruction." *Educational Technology* 10 (2):62–64; February 1970.

Do Schools Need IPI? No!

Rodney Tillman

In December 1967, two publications arrived in the same mail delivery. One, *Education U.S.A.*, featured as its lead article a description of the Individually Prescribed Instruction (IPI) program under way in the Oakleaf Elementary School. It was described as "the nation's first successful operation of individualized instruction on a systematic, step-by-step basis throughout an entire school pro-gram." An explanation of the difference between this program and today's regular school is reported as:

Rodney Tillman. "Do Schools Need IPI? No!" *Educational Leadership* 29(6):495–98; March 1972. Reprinted with permission of the Association for Supervision and Curriculum Development and Rodney Tillman. Copyright © 1972 by the Association for Supervision and Curriculum Development.

Pupils are working on their own. The second and third grade reading class of 63 pupils, for example, is using a learning center and two adjoining rooms. Two teachers and the school librarian act as coordinators and tutors as the pupils proceed with the various materials prepared by the school's teachers and IPI's developer, the Learning Research and Development Center at the U. of Pittsburgh. Each pupil sets his own pace. He is listening to records and completing workbooks. When he has completed a unit of work, he is tested, the test is corrected immediately, and if he gets a grade of 85% or better he moves on. If not, the teacher offers a series of alternative activities to correct the weakness, including special individual tutoring. There are no textbooks. There is virtually no lecturing by the teacher to the class as a whole. Instead, she is busy observing the child's progress, evaluating his tests, writing prescriptions, and instructing individually or in small groups of pupils who need help.[1]

I was pondering the underlying assumptions of the IPI approach reported, as I continued opening the mail, which also included the 1967 revision of *A Public School for Tomorrow* by Marion Nesbitt. There I read:

The elementary school based in humanism which is now emerging from the post-*Sputnik* years and hopefully will flourish, will first of all be characterized as a good place for children to live and learn and grow, a place that is warm and accepting of human hopes and human frailties, a place where learning is stimulating and challenging, recognizing that facts are for the illumination of ideas, a place where there are values and ideals toward which one strives, a place where one always holds out hope, knowing that to despair of a child is to make him desperate.

The school staff will devote time and energy to creating an environment in which search, inquiry, and thinking can take their place as truly fundamental concepts from which broad realms of knowledge are developed. In this process, discussion of ideas will be emphasized. Question-and-answer learning will become secondary since such an approach must of necessity narrow the curriculum to a limited number of facts. When mainly right answers are rewarded, it is sometimes disastrous for a child to make a mistake. On the other hand, discussion is a dynamic verbal process whereby insights are exchanged, issues are clarified and problems are solved. At its best, discussion is a process by which the human spirit is lifted and refreshed as minds touch each other and allow themselves to be influenced for the better.[2]

"WHERE STUDENTS ARE"

I found these two descriptions both encouraging and disturbing. General acceptance of the idea that we need to recognize individual differences and "take students where they are" is encouraging. It was disturbing to me that the approaches to dealing with individual differences seemed to be based on such differing beliefs about learning, teachers, and the learning process. It is my belief

[1] "Experiment Remaking Face of Education." *Education U.S.A.*, December 11, 1967.
[2] Marion Nesbitt. *A Public School for Tomorrow*. New York: Dell Publishing Company, 1967. p. 150. © 1953 Harper & Brothers.

that schools need instructional programs based upon the model as described by Nesbitt, not the IPI model.

First, I would question that schools (in general) "need" any program which is still ephemeral and practically impossible to describe. It is impossible to describe the "up-to-date" operation of the IPI model. In October 1971, William W. Cooley, Co-director of the Learning Research and Development Center, University of Pittsburgh, gave—to deans of schools and colleges of education attending a seminar at the IBM center at Endicott, New York—the reprints, "The Computer and Individualized Instruction"[3] and "Computer Assistance for Individualized Education,"[4] papers which describe IPI. Cooley commented: "I no longer believe a lot of what is said there" and "Look at this as a Model T." He identified with IPI two kinds of activities—highly structured and exploratory. He indicated that there is a need for much more work in the "exploratory component—open-ended questions." Including open-ended questions undoubtedly will improve the actual operation of the IPI program in the schools. However, it is my opinion that many of the schools now operating an IPI program are doing so with a "pre-Model T" version. Also, from a practical standpoint, it would be impossible, in a large number of schools, to initiate versions beyond the "Model T," as these latter versions require considerable expenditures for initial computer installation and for maintenance. I do not believe a school district should make a commitment which binds it to an unproven approach.

It is not, however, this practical operating principle, nor the financial consideration necessary for a truly effective implementation of IPI, that leads me to oppose this approach for schools. It is the underlying beliefs associated with the IPI approach. The expectations of teachers and learners and the views regarding learning held by the designers of IPI lead me to my position regarding this approach. These views and expectations have remained essentially the same regardless of the manner of delivery of the program (computer or non-computer).

The actual name of the program leaves me with concern. Usually we associate prescriptions with sickness, and while it may be helpful to "prescribe" for those unable to function in a normal manner, the prescription approach for all children leaves much to be desired. With students, as with all people, there is need for the learner to be involved in determining that which is to be learned. Even though recent modifications of the IPI program have increased opportunities for students to make choices, their involvement still falls far short of desirable cooperative procedures in learning—procedures which were in force in many schools in the pre-Sputnik years.

From the early reports in *Education U.S.A.* to more recent descriptions, the main functions of the teacher in IPI have remained: (a) writing prescriptions for courses of study; (b) diagnosing student difficulties; and (c) tutoring individuals and small groups of students.[5] These I cannot accept as the main functions of teachers. To designate these as their main functions is inconsistent with the body of research regarding teaching functions which has been produced in the past decade. Gertrude M. Lewis states that a reader of the research studies

[3] William W. Cooley and Robert Glaser. "The Computer and Individualized Instruction." *Science* 166:574–82; October 31, 1969.
[4] William W. Cooley. "Computer Assistance for Individualized Education." *Journal of Educational Data Processing* 7:18–28; 1970.
[5] Cooley and Glaser, op. cit., p. 579.

relative to the teaching act is "impressed with the agreement in their findings, particularly as related to teacher-student participation, teaching and the self-image of children, liking for school and general friendliness, and achievement."[6] Some observers have reported that teachers find it hard to accept a secondary role for themselves as is necessary in the IPI program. Some have also equated the teacher's role in an IPI program to his role in a "child-centered" program.[7]

In my opinion, these factors are not equivalent. The IPI program is essentially based on a "what they should be taught" approach, while a child-centered approach is based on "observations of how children learn." In one, success comes from the teacher's skill in following the program. In the other, success comes from his professional observations of the student and the creative use of time, space, and available resources to enable the fullest development of the learner's potentials.

HANG-UPS OF IPI

Within the model itself, there are three other factors which I consider "hang-ups" of IPI. These are: (a) the strong emphasis on sequence; (b) the validity placed on diagnostic tests; (c) the determination of 85 percent correct responses as a major criterion for determining success. There is much experience, research, and expert opinion to refute heavy reliance on any of these as "near absolutes."

The debate regarding sequence has been around for many years. For many students, carefully sequenced learning has been successful; however, most of us know of many exceptions. A thoughtful discussion of this topic is found in Alice Miel's statement, *Sequence in Learning—Fact or Fiction.*[8]

I favor the position that sequence resides within the student and that the teacher's role is to provide a wide range of learning opportunities which will enable the student to become successful. Many desirable learning opportunities cannot be prestructured into a carefully controlled sequence. I find it difficult to accept the IPI approach as individualized when it equates individualization to a variable pacing arrangement.

Regardless of the quality of the program and the manner delivered—workbook, work-sheet, or computer—flexible timing is only one of the many factors necessary in individualizing instruction. I believe that associated with sequence and learning is the factor of motivation. The degree of student motivation, and other differences, may require students to undertake varied sequences to achieve similar learning goals.

Tests and the belief that accurately stated objectives may be tested have a higher priority in the IPI program than is deserved in a good educational program. There is ample evidence around that programs based on predetermined tests are not in the best interests of learners. It is this belief which has resulted

[6] Gertrude M. Lewis. *The Evaluation of Teaching.* Washington, D.C.: American Association of Elementary-Kindergarten-Nursery Educators, National Education Association, 1966. p. 19.
[7] Carl C. Fehrle. "A Look at IPI." *Educational Leadership* 28 (5):480–83; February 1971.
[8] Alice Miel. *Sequence in Learning—Fact or Fiction.* Washington, D.C.: American Association of Elementary-Kindergarten-Nursery Educators, National Education Association, 1966.

in modifications of the originally announced procedures associated with the National Assessment movement.

Rationale for the acceptance of a grade of 85 percent as the criterion for movement to the next unit of work is unclear to me. It seems to me that there are certain units, such as driver education and safety, in which the responses must be above that fixed percentage, while in some others almost any level of achievement might be acceptable. The arbitrary nature of a specific percentage for all students and all units of work I find unacceptable.

In conclusion, I consider the IPI approach short in stressing many of the most valuable skills needed for successful living in the years ahead—skills of discussion and skills in interpersonal relationships. Schools need approaches which make them more humane and open institutions. Implementation of the eleven characteristics for moving in this direction outlined in *To Nurture Humaneness* provides a workable direction for all schools.[9]

While some persons see the IPI program as aimed in the direction of "humaneness and openness," I consider its implementation a step in the opposite direction for many schools. For more than 50 years, many recognized leaders in education have worked to move learning opportunities provided in our schools from "rigid, passive, rote, and narrow" to "open and humane." We must not be diverted from this goal by programs which, though wearing the technological dress of the 1970's, continue to place high value on learning opportunities basically "rigid, passive, rote, and narrow."

[9] Mary-Margaret Scobey and Grace Graham, editors. *To Nurture Humaneness: Commitment for the 70's.* 1970 ASCD Yearbook. Washington, D.C.: Association for Supervision and Curriculum Development, 1970. pp. 223–30.

English and American Primary Schools

Vincent R. Rogers

Ideas that American educators have been talking about for a long, long time are being put to practice in a large percentage of English primary schools. Education for life, basing instructional activities on the interests and problems of children, integration of subject matter, emphasis on *learning* rather than *teaching* and on *process* rather than *product*, development of independence and responsibility in children, concern for the creative aspects of learning—all of these are standard phrases in the lexicon of American education. But in England they are more than phrases. They are being brought to life daily in the primary classrooms which I visited during my stay in England as a Fulbright scholar in 1966.

From *Phi Delta Kappan* LI, no. 2 (October 1969):71–75. Used by permission of the author and publisher.

When I made known my desire to get inside some schools, my English friends and advisers guided me initially to Oxfordshire, where I visited the Bampton, Brize-Norton, and Tower Hill primary schools. I have never been quite the same since. Seventy-two schools later I still found myself wondering if what I saw was real, if such schools and teachers do exist. Four cartons of notes taken on 3 × 5 cards give material support to my impression that these schools do indeed exist, and that they are becoming increasingly influential not only in England but in other countries as well.

I must note here that only about 25 percent of England's primary schools fit the model described in the following paragraphs. Perhaps 40 percent can be described as quite traditional, while another third or so are in various stages of transition. Nevertheless, 25 percent is a significant number of schools when one looks at the size of the total educational enterprise in England, and even more significant is the obvious movement toward this new kind of education among schools which cannot as yet be included among the exciting and innovative 25 percent.

What is there that is so unusual about these schools? To begin with, it seems as if the new English primary school is committed to the notion that children should live more fully and more richly *now*, rather than at some ill-defined time in the distant future. Education, then, is not preparation for life; education *is* life, with all of its excitement, challenge, and possibilities. This is happening here and now in perhaps 20 to 30 percent of the primary schools in England.

English teachers and headmasters conceive of the curriculum as a series of starting or jumping-off places. An idea, a question, an observation—child's or teacher's—acts as a stone thrown into the middle of a quiet pond. The ripples begin, one idea leads to another, and a study is under way. In contrast, American educators seem far more concerned from a curricular point of view with identifying and then covering a series of ideas, concepts, generalizations, or skills that (theoretically) form the backbone of the curriculum in any area. We shall discuss this in greater detail later. However, it seems worth mentioning that there appears to be very little subject matter that is perceived of as "basic" and "essential" in the eyes of the English teacher or headmaster. The curriculum emerges through the mutual interests and explorations of children and their teachers, working together occasionally in large groups, sometimes in small groups, and often as individuals.

Another characteristic of the emerging British primary school, and one that is closely related to the preceding point, has to do with the eagerness of teachers to cut across disciplinary lines in their handling of any study that may evolve in their classrooms. Art, music, history, poetry—all are brought to bear on a given problem or topic, and it is often difficult to tell whether children are studying history or geography, art or science. This, of course, tends to give a wholeness to learning that must be lacking in more compartmentalized curricula, and it helps support and build the image of the school as a place where lifelike questions are investigated as opposed to questions that are narrowly academic.

A fourth observation is that the English teacher is concerned with *learning* as opposed to teaching. Rarely will one find such a teacher standing in front of the room teaching a "class" lesson. Rather, the teacher is largely a stage-setter, a stimulator, who encourages and guides but who does not direct. It is often difficult to find the teacher when one first walks into a typical classroom, since she is likely to be working with a child here and a child there, moving around the room and among the children.

Having said all of this, a fifth conclusion is inescapable: The English teacher accepts the significance of *process* over *product* in the education of the child. There seems little doubt that English teachers are greatly concerned with *how* a child learns, the kinds of questions he asks, and the ways in which he goes about resolving them. Over the long haul, English teachers believe these learning "strategies" will prove to be infinitely more valuable than the subject matter.

Similarly, English teachers seem greatly concerned about the development of independence and responsibility in children—often to a far greater extent than American teachers. In the best of English primary schools, a degree of individual freedom, flexibility, and responsibility exists in a way that is virtually unknown in most American elementary schools. Teachers do not hang over their children, supervise them in every conceivable activity, watch them on the playground, in the halls, in the buses, and in the washrooms. All of this is done, of course, in a calculated way, recognizing that such qualities as independence and reliability need to be "practiced" as well as spoken about.

Finally, one might say that the teachers in the kinds of schools I visited seem to care deeply, perhaps passionately, about *children*. Children are to be taken seriously, not laughed at or ridiculed in the staff room. Children are to be watched; children are to be listened to; children are to learn from; children are the essential ingredient in the teaching-learning process; children make one's job exciting, challenging, and truly professional. This point cannot possibly be exaggerated. It is, in fact, the day-to-day practical implementation of the intellectual rationale for a very real revolution in education.

As one reads about these exciting developments in English schools, one cannot help but wonder why such ideas have never really caught on here on the scale they have in England. There is, of course, much talk about creativity, the needs of children, and the importance of the student taking responsibility for his own learning. Indeed, bits and pieces of the educational processes described in the preceding pages do exist all over America. It is, rather, the complete expression of, and commitment to, a set of educational ideals that seems to be missing in this country.

Let us examine some possible reasons for American reluctance to move in similar directions. One must say at the beginning of such an analysis that a number of American teachers, writers, and teachers-turned-writers are passionately involved in a movement to bring a looser, more relevant, more child-centered and experience-based kind of education to American children. One thinks immediately of Jonathan Kozol, Herbert Kohl, James Herndon, and John Holt as examples of the turned-on, deeply concerned teacher who, on the basis of his experiences in classrooms, has something to say about American education. In addition, journalists like Joseph Featherstone and Charles Silberman are also joining the crusade, and even as influential a group as the Educational Development Center in Cambridge, Massachusetts (the base for Jerome Bruner's curricular operations) has recently hired an Englishman or two to help plan the center's various projects.

Because of the pressures brought to bear by this new breed of educational critic, changes are being made in some public schools, and a few private schools have been founded here and there that are more completely faithful to the educational point of view described in this article. Nevertheless, and in all fairness, it must be said that these disparate efforts are hardly an organized, well-directed, and advancing movement.

Perhaps one reason for American failure to move more rapidly in this direction can be traced to the curricular and methodological impact of the launching of the Russian Sputnik in 1957. The event was perceived as an educational humiliation, and the curricular developments that followed it during the next decade all gave a push to a kind of education that was vastly different from the movement that was already under way in England.

It is no news to American or English educators that the search for "structure," for "basic concepts and generalizations" in mathematics, science, social studies, literature, and other fields, has dominated curricular activity in the U.S. during the years following Sputnick. This has led, quite logically, to an emphasis upon separate subjects rather than upon the integration or wholeness of the curriculum; it has led to further support for a traditional educational disease which we will call "the covering syndrome," i.e., one must deal with certain "basic" ideas, topics, or problems, or else one is clearly derelict in one's duty; therefore, one must avoid those diversions, those side-tracking situations that often lead to relevant and exciting learning, even though they do interfere with "coverage."

In an attempt to be as faithful as possible to what we perceive of as the "work-ways" or methods of the various disciplines, American educators have spent a great deal of time and energy in organizing the new curricula so that children will not merely memorize and repeat concepts and generalizations as they memorized and repeated the much despised "facts" of the old. Therefore we talk a great deal about inquiry and discovery approaches to learning. However, a careful examination of the materials and methods that comprise many of the new curriculum projects and packages reveals (with some exceptions) that the kinds of questions raised, the problems studied, the discoveries or generalizations arrived at are rarely the children's. We try valiantly; we smile, entreat, and cajole. Some of the kids are caught up in it some of the time—perhaps an unusually challenging topic catches their fancy or perhaps an unusually dynamic teacher draws them out through the force of his personality. More often than not, however, we end up with something Vincent Glennon has described as "sneaky telling." We know where we're going; we know what the questions should be, what the "big ideas" are, and the conclusions one should come away with, if the teacher's manual is followed.

Perhaps, in the final analysis, this is the best way to teach. Perhaps we cannot afford the luxury of exploring children's questions in whichever direction they may take us. Certainly there is little evidence which demonstrates empirically that the less-structured, more child-centered English teacher is producing a "better product" than is the tighter, more discipline-centered American teacher. At the moment, the best evidence I can offer is simply watching children at work and at play over extended periods of time in schools. If their reactions, their activity, their art, music, and poetry, their attitudes toward teachers and toward school are valid criteria, then we have a great deal to learn from the English.

Perhaps another reason for our reluctance to move in the same direction as the English is our comparative affluence, which enables us to develop and pay for mechanical panaceas, with whatever educational hardware happens to catch our fancy. In both countries "to individualize" is thought of as a good thing. Increasing numbers of conferences and workshops are devoted to this theme in America, yet American teachers seem not to have learned the lesson that is grasped so well by many English primary teachers: One individualizes, as Philip Jackson* put it, by

> . . . injecting humor into a lesson when a student seems to need it, and quickly becoming serious when he is ready to settle down to work; it means thinking of examples that are uniquely relevant to the student's previous experience and offering them at just the right time; it means feeling concerned over whether or not a student is progressing, and communicating that concern in a way that will be helpful; it means offering appropriate praise . . . because the student's performance is deserving of human admiration; it means in short, responding as an individual to an individual.

This conception is much, much more than allowing for differences in speed when moving through some particular "program"; it is more than telling us automatically, if politely, that "you are wrong, please turn to page 15 for another explanation."

In other words, one individualizes by watching and listening to children. Mechanical aids are useful, but there is no substitute for the conception of individualization expressed so ably by Jackson in the preceding paragraph. Many American teachers have been seduced by the promise of technology; their less affluent English counterparts know that individualization will come to their children only if they make a concerted effort to bring it about under classroom conditions that are not likely to change radically soon. So they collect, construct, beg, borrow, and, I suspect, steal materials of all kinds to provide the kind of learning environment they know is good—and they often do so for classes of 40 children or more. Most English teachers are willing to agree with Mort Sahl that "the future lies ahead." They are not banking on an educational promised land that may lie just around the corner. They are addressing themselves to solving the individualization problem in terms of their own intelligence and energy—now.

A third invidious comparison one is forced to make with American elementary schools when he visits an English primary school is in the area of aesthetics. Aesthetics—art, music, movement—is in a dismal state in American schools as compared with their English counterparts. Even for our very young children, many schools have music and art teachers who conduct 20-minute, weekly lessons that become the art or music program. Aesthetic activities generally take a back seat to the more academic components of the curriculum.

Perhaps this is a problem inherent in American culture rather than a school problem. These things are considered effete; they are not valued in the same way that reading and mathematics are. It would be rare, indeed, to see an American teacher seriously encourage children to use their bodies as a mode of expression. It would be even more rare to find the teacher herself joining the children and participating in the creation of a dance pattern. (Perhaps a new generation of teachers, reared on the less inhibited use of their bodies that has developed with the universal acceptance of "rock," will see possibilities in movement that their predecessors did not.)

*P. W. Jackson, *The Teacher and the Machine: Observations on the Impact of Educational Technology* (Mimeographed, University of Chicago, 1966).

In my judgment, aesthetics plays an infinitely more important role in the education of English children than in that of American children, and the hesitancy of American teachers to utilize these means of reaching children is a major difference between primary education in England and in the U.S.

Another curious factor that gets in the way of American movement toward a more free and less-structured school may lie in our dichotomous treatment of kindergarten and primary children. In England, children are treated as individuals from the moment they enter school at the age of five until they leave the primary school. Teachers of "reception classes" (five-year-olds) move children into reading, for example, if the child seems ready to read. Similarly, a six-year-old child in an English primary school is not pushed, hounded, and bullied, ready or not, into reading when he reaches that magical age. In other words, we have created a very unreal and unwise division between what learning ought to be for five-year-olds and what it ought to be for sixes. One might call this the kindergarten-primary grade dilemma. We usually find a far greater degree of freedom child-centeredness, looseness, or lack of structure in our kindergartens than we find at any other level in the elementary school. Many American children begin their education enjoying learning, being happy in school, and contented with themselves. For many of these children, however, first grade becomes a cruel awakening. No more time now for learning as fun; now we must "work"; now we must put away dress-up clothes, blocks, and spur-of-the-moment curricular explorations.

In a good English primary school, this dichotomy does not exist. A child comes to school initially to learn, and to learn at his own pace. This point of view is carried continuously through the primary years.

Finally, we might mention one other factor that may play a role in discouraging the adoption on a large scale of the sort of primary school we have been describing in these pages. I refer to the relative freedom that English teachers and headmasters have to develop the kinds of educational programs that they, as professionals, deem right—with minimum concern for outside pressure groups. Conversely, American teachers and principals are subject to tremendous pressures from the community, and no state-suported school can casually ignore them. This means that some changes will be easier to bring about than others; that what the lay public conceives of as "good" education may be adopted in the schools more readily than other changes. At this point, the American public seems to see "good" education as a hard-driving, highly competitive academic race, and educational innovations fitting that image stand a better chance of acceptance than do other innovations.

In England, which has traditionally had an exceedingly competitive education system, the movement toward drastic change in the education of young children originated and was carried out largely by professionals and often *against* the wishes of parents. This is not to say that English teachers and headmasters can do as they please. It does mean, however, that they are more independent of, and more protected from, outside pressures of all kinds than American educators. Vulnerability to public pressures probably causes American school people to be reluctant to adopt a child-centered approach to teaching.

Having examined and compared English and American primary school programs, I turn now to criticism. This will be difficult, since I have not attempted to hide my considerable admiration for what I see happening in the modern English primary school. Nevertheless, what seems good can no doubt become better, and perhaps some of the following questions may serve to further that purpose.

The first point is really not a criticism of classroom practices at all. Rather, it is a plea for some form of systematic evaluation of the achievements of the schools described in these pages. Those of us fortunate enough to have visited good English primary schools recognize almost intuitively that what we are seeing is mostly right, mostly effective, mostly sound. On the other hand, many educators have a way of asking questions that cannot be adequately answered by referring to one's personal observations. How, in fact, do children in such schools perform on various objective measures when compared to children who have had quite a different sort of school experience? Obviously, academic achievement is not the basic goal of such schools, but since it is not, what effects do these schools have on children's attitudes toward school, teachers, and peers? How does this experience affect their approach to learning, the problem solving strategies they adopt, their persistence, their curiosity?

A more direct criticism is exemplified, perhaps, by a description of an afternoon spent in what was, in many ways, a fascinating primary school in rural Leicestershire. During the entire afternoon the children were free to carry out projects that were of interest to them. There was a great deal of arts and crafts activity—carpentry, weaving, block printing, etc. The children were obviously well-behaved, busy, and interested in their work. Yet I couldn't help but feel that this happy, involved group of children were somehow existing in the middle of what we all know to be a terribly complex, rapidly changing world—divorced from its reality, protected from its problems, and uninvolved in its conflicts and dilemmas.

Somehow, the "real" world that children explore in such schools is often a rather limited version of reality. It is a real world of fields, streams, trees, rocks, stones, flowers, birds, and insects, if it is a country school. If it is a city school, it is a real world of traffic patterns, nearby shops, local museums and libraries, parks and gardens. The "real world" is often conceived of as that world which is nearby, and more precisely, that world which can be seen, felt, smelled, touched, or listened to.

One might suggest, then, that there are, after all, limits to how far one can go with personal, concrete experience as the essential teaching technique. Children can study only a small part of the world by direct observation and experience, and one must question the hours that are spent in making, building, and physically "doing" that could, conceivably, be used in other ways as well. One wonders, for example, if in studying the wool industry the process of making wool does not get treated all out of proportion to some of the related economic, social, and political problems that might be implied in such a study—granting, of course, that much of this "activity" would be intellectual rather than physical, vicarious more than direct.

If one largely limits the objects of one's study to those found only in the local environment, it is difficult to see how the school can play a significant role in helping children understand the broader world in which they live. Conflict exists about Rhodesia and about the immigrants who have recently settled in sections of English cities such as Wolverhampton and Bradford. These problems are important to all English people. The fact that they do not lend themselves to direct or "concrete" experience does not render them any less important.

The real world of social conflict exists, and no school, no teacher, no syllabus will ever completely isolate children from it. Yet the schools' responsibility would seem to include some attempts at increasing children's awareness of the inadequacies and inequalities that exist in both their local and their wider environments. Failing this, children will, of course, muddle through, picking up ideas and attitudes wherever they find them and becoming more and more aware (perhaps through harsh personal experience) of the conflict that exists between the school world and the world of social reality.

Similarly, one might question the degree of curricular egalitarianism that exists in the emerging British primary school. Obviously, only the simplest of societies can hope to teach its children "all they need to know." Therefore, it has become increasingly important to ask, what knowledge is of the most worth to our society at this particular moment in time? Which ideas will help the non-specialist citizen to understand the world in which he lives? Which ideas are fundamental enough to have transfer value? Which ideas will help one to better understand a unique phenomenon that has not been formally studied before?

My English colleagues will immediately argue that only the *child* can know what knowledge, what information, what understanding, is important and necessary to him. Identifying significant ideas seems to smack of pre-digested academic luncheons that have little relevance to children's interests or needs. I would also agree. I would indeed argue further that this appears to be the major weakness in many of the American curriculum projects which were developed during the Brunnerian revolution of the 60's.

However, this does not negate the argument that there are some things worth knowing, that some ideas help to order and explain our lives and the lives of others while other ideas do not. It seems to me that the great weakness one observes in both English and American schools is the lack of knowledge about and understanding of such ideas among *teachers*.

It would be foolish indeed to suggest that a discipline like anthropology has developed no ideas that are really worth teaching to children, no concepts that help order, classify, and explain the social world in which we find ourselves. The real value, the ultimate utility of such ideas, however, lies *not* in the creation of prepackaged "teacher-proof" curricula; rather, it is the classroom teacher who must grasp them and utilize them at the appropriate moment. In other words, "structure" belongs in the minds of teachers.

One might mention other arguments, other "weaknesses"; these, however, seem to me to be among the most fruitful to discuss and perhaps are among the questions most likely to be raised by American educators.

Occupational Preparation in the Elementary School

Walter N. Gantt

At Congressional hearings in 1968 on amendments to the Vocational Education Act of 1963, significant testimony was given. One witness stated that it was economically and socially sound to give attention to the growing number of students who do not "fit the system" or are "failed" and leave school. Something, he held, should be done early in the educational lives of students to protect them from the events that keep many of them from achieving acceptable social goals.[1] He was expressing the widespread concern about those students who, yearly, merge into the pool of the occupationally unfit—those who lack skills which render them employable.

Within the context of the total school curriculum, occupational preparation, or vocational aspects of education, may be defined as planned experiences "designed to prepare the learner to enter the world of work successfully or to maintain himself as a productive worker throughout an ever-changing occupational life."[2] The strategies used by the school to provide opportunities for needed experiences at the elementary level may have a significant impact upon the pool of unemployed, underemployed, or dissatisfied workers.

The role of the elementary school in preparing pupils for the world of work is described in the following passage:

> What is needed now is a developmental system of education. Such a system introduces in the elementary grades awareness of the relationships which exist between schooling and work. . . . In the main the elementary school role is diagnostic and prescriptive. It provides whatever experiences a child may need to make learning real through a continuing examination of how man uses work for self-support, how major occupations employ knowledge, and how productivity is related to a variety of abilities. A major objective of elementary education is to discover the talents of each child and demonstrate their relationship to the work world.[3]

Walter N. Gantt. "Occupational Preparation in the Elementary School." *Educational Leadership* 28(4):359–63; January 1971. Reprinted with permission of the Association for Supervision and Curriculum Development and Walter N. Gantt. Copyright © 1971 by the Association for Supervision and Curriculum Development.

[1] National Committee on Employment of Youth. *A Guide to the Development of Vocational Education Programs and Services for the Disadvantaged.* U.S. Department of Health, Education, and Welfare. Washington, D.C.: Superintendent of Documents, U.S. Government Printing Office, 1969. p. 5.

[2] Gerald B. Leighbody. "Vocational Education." *New Curriculum Developments.* Report of ASCD's Commission on Current Curriculum Developments. Washington, D.C.: Association for Supervision and Curriculum Development, 1965. p. 79.

[3] National Committee on Employment of Youth, *op. cit.*, p. 22.

A review of the current literature uncovers a number of plans and suggestions for enabling the elementary school to achieve this objective. These current beliefs and practices have been reviewed and are organized under the previously mentioned learning experiences in the sections which follow. Evaluative comments in the form of recommendations are then indicated.

HOW MAN USES WORK FOR SELF-SUPPORT

Many different programs resulting from independent efforts and lacking coordination are being tried out and reported. Those with desirable components are readily identified, yet all offer problems of choice to supervisors and teachers who seek a place for them in an already overcrowded curriculum. Decisions must be made about what substitutions, modifications, or additions are feasible.

In general, there are two ways that occupational information is provided. One is to treat work as one of the recurring themes, or generalizations, in selected units centered around activities of people at various locations in time and space. A second method is discussed in the section which follows.

Current Beliefs and Practices

1. Michaelis[4] cites the following work-related theme which is incorporated in units at various levels of instruction: "The work of society is done through groups formed to achieve common goals." This idea may be introduced in kindergarten and expanded in each subsequent grade. For example: Kindergarten—Local Environment Studies Unit includes The Service Station, The Airport, The Store; Grade 1—Family, School and Community Life Unit includes Family at Work, Neighbors at Work, Community Workers; Grade 2—Community Studies Unit includes Workers Around the World; Grade 3—Metropolitan Communities includes opportunities to develop this idea in relation to government workers. Similar opportunities are suggested in the units prescribed for Grades 4, 5, and 6.[5]

2. Some schools allow the teacher more choice in the development of units. Themes are identified which are the center of course activities. The work-related theme "Man seeks to satisfy his changing needs and desires through work and invention"[6] can be implemented in a series of current units and broadly based curriculum experiences.

HOW MAJOR OCCUPATIONS EMPLOY KNOWLEDGE

Teachers tend to be influenced by their own experiential backgrounds in selecting content for presentation to their students. Their own work history is often limited and little or no information is provided in programs preparing teachers for elementary education.

Small wonder, then, that teachers lack consistent treatment of this topic. There is great need to correct this neglect, and to provide a motivational thrust

---

[4] John U. Michaelis. *Social Studies for Children in a Democracy*. Fourth edition. Englewood Cliffs, New Jersey: Prentice-Hall, Inc., 1968. p. 121.

[5] New York City Board of Education. *Curriculum and Materials*. New York: The Board, 1965.

[6] Baltimore City Public Schools. *A Guide to Elementary Education*. Baltimore: Bureau of Publications, 1967. p. 247.

for students who must note extended work options and must recognize direct relationships between competencies which they develop in school and those needed in various occupations. A more direct method of curriculum organization is therefore being investigated. This method stresses the study of occupations and the exploration of work skills as distinct areas of inquiry. Although job obsolescence is an important consideration, it is even more vital for children to ascertain interests and to assess their own potentialities. Topics studied include the importance of the task to society, salary, working conditions, training needed, duties, and relevant educational experiences. Provisions for obtaining these experiences in language, mathematics, science, personal development, and human relations skills are made.

Current Beliefs and Practices

1. A finding of a study which is a part of the *Occupational Information Project* in the Atlanta, Georgia, Public Schools gives reason for reflection. Only ten percent of students interviewed mentioned an education occupation in response to the question, "What kinds of work have you seen people doing?"[7] This clearly shows the need for instilling a heightened awareness of the world of work as a primary objective of the elementary school.

Devised for children in grades three through eight, the project employs television, printed materials, and tapes to help them gain knowledge of themselves and facts about occupations. It is believed that pupils will be motivated to complete high school and seek needed vocational training afterward or vocational training in the event they leave earlier.

2. The New Jersey State Department of Education operates a *Technology for Children Project*. It is a grade-by-grade curriculum which utilizes work-oriented activities. These provide a center for the development of skills in mathematics, science, language arts, and social studies. As they work upon various preplanned episodes, such as preparing a newspaper or producing a television program, children use tools and machines, perform jobs which challenge their interests, and assume responsibility for learning relevant academic tasks.[8]

3. *You and Work* is a representative instructional system. It is a sequence of individualized learning experiences which utilize self-instructional, self-pacing devices (films, slides, and programmed response units). Content, related to five major job families, is categorized as white collar, manual, farm, armed forces, and services. There are 13 subsystems in all. The purpose of the program is informational. It "is based on the premise that (elementary) children should be provided with some orientation to the meaning of work and its importance to them and society (even though they) are not ready to make a definite vocational choice."[9]

4. Another approach is to provide children with occupational information about clusters of jobs in selected industries such as television, home construction,

[7] Occupational Information Materials Project. "Children Talk About Work—An Analysis of Interviews with Children." Atlanta: Atlanta Public Schools. (Mimeographed.) Not dated.

[8] Technology for Children Project. "Questions and Answers." Trenton: New Jersey State Department of Education. (Mimeographed.) Not dated.

[9] Gerald Diminico. "You and Work—An Instructional System for Children in Elementary Schools." *American Vocational Journal*, December 1969. p. 22.

a toy factory, and a hospital.[10] As a stimulus for attending school and putting forth effort, youngsters are pictured in simulated activities as they are photographed in adult job situations. Job information in verse accompanies each photograph.

HOW PRODUCTIVITY RELATES TO A VARIETY OF ABILITIES

Another crucial task of the elementary school is to instill an attitude of respect and appreciation for people whose work contributes to the effective functioning and well-being of society. Needed is the feeling that there is dignity and honor asociated with serviceable activity and for the individual who performs it. This attitude is one that is difficult to implement in a society which glorifies leisure, distributes its rewards sparingly, and grudgingly compensates those who provide essentials. We have also neglected the fostering of self-esteem and the nurturing of talents which lie dormant in barren environments. A consciousness of this added responsibility of the school emerges as it girds itself to meet the vocational needs of children with social, economic, emotional, physical, and cultural handicaps.

Current Beliefs and Practices
1. The development of programs which are responsive to varying abilities must be affected by this observation:

> People learn differently. Some do best with the written word as the main learning process; others by handling tools and materials; others by making charts and graphs and using other graphic arts media; still others, through film making and drama. Any of these means or others might be used to teach any subject, depending upon the pupil's learning style.[11]

Bearing this in mind, it is apparent that no one program will suffice.

2. Opportunities are provided for visits to various work centers: food processing, water purification, sanitation, newspaper, and television. Community adults are also invited to the classroom to discuss their occupation. The emphasis is upon the workers: the skills and knowledges which they need; positive feelings about their importance; and what the school can do to help.

3. Aptitudes and strengths noted as classroom tasks are performed are identified and communicated to the student by the teacher. Real situations are provided in which individual responses may be tested, diagnosed, and developed. Limitations are more readily accepted when counterbalanced by an awareness of assets. Such understandings assist the child in making tentative decisions about the future.

4. Increasing importance is being attached to the role of the elementary school in discovering the hang-ups of the disadvantaged pupil and the social, economic, and psychological barriers to the realization of his potential. More important, the child must be given help in overcoming these barriers. In this respect, the position of the elementary counselor assumes significance. He acts

[10] Jean and Ned Wilkinson. *Come to Work with Us Series*. Milwaukee: Sextant Systems, Inc., 1970.
[11] Marvin Feldman. "Vocational Education in a New Comprehensive System." *Today's Education* 58:47; November 1969.

as a liaison between the child and the school and also relates closely to his home situation. The counselor can also draw upon an array of community resources for special cases: medical and dental services; case work, testing, and psychiatric services; day care or baby sitters; legal services for dealing with police and related problems; and loan and welfare services.[12] Resources of this type must be utilized in helping some pupils establish necessary psychological supports as they approach adult responsibilities.

RECOMMENDATIONS AND CONCLUSIONS

Function of the elementary school. The function of the elementary school is not to achieve closure in occupational identification and selection. Rather, it is to provide many situations in which the individual may develop his potentialities, deepen his interests, and increase his motivation to learn. As he recognizes the operation of school-related skills within various vocational hierarchies, he will gradually identify degrees of fitness with his own inclinations and proficiencies.

Most important is the effect upon attitude—the fostering of aspirations through helping the individual to become knowledgeable of his inner resources which make possible the satisfaction of his immediate wants and, at the same time, suggest future contributions.

Curriculum provisions. Essentially, occupational preparation should be a conscious force in the curriculum from the time the child enters school. The classroom teacher is primarily responsible for arranging conditions which develop attitudes, appreciations, knowledges, and strengthen the self. Some curriculum objectives may be achieved within the group setting. Work orientation may be one of many themes which permeate the class settings with children whose academic goals are long range. These activities are within the province of the regular teacher.

An appraisal of other children may reveal that vocational involvement is more imminent due to academic limitations or socioeconomic factors which impinge upon their range of educational options. For them, classroom activities must be more immediately applicable to the world outside. Still others have special skills which should be developed early and continuously. More direct instruction in occupations and technical skills will be required for them. Flexible arrangements are necessary to assure that none will be placed in compartments which limit growth possibilities. No path which will lead to a realistic occupational decision by the student should be blocked. Finally, there are those with personal and emotional problems which must be adjusted. Personnel with special training—industrial arts, social work, counseling, psychological testing, and others —are needed to reinforce and supplement the efforts of the classroom teacher by providing individual attention in such instances.

Importance of the teacher. The teacher, by his example, is in an excellent position to establish a model of personal fulfillment and service by the way he reacts to the child. As described in captions under pictures of one teacher obviously enjoying her job:

"Happiness is my happy teacher—

---

[12] National Committee on Employment of Youth, *op. cit.*, p. 15.

> She is doing the work she wants to do—
> Teaching ME—
> and my friends."[13]

Happiness begins for many children as they are revealed to themselves by an accepting teacher. This is an indispensable first step in establishing meaningful interpersonal relationships so important for future vocational success.

[13] Occupational Information Materials Project. *Happiness Is—My Teacher at Work.* Atlanta: Atlanta Public Schools, 1969.

The Laboratory Approach to Elementary Mathematics

Edwina Deans

Elementary teachers are finding the laboratory approach an effective means of individualizing the teaching of mathematics. The approach is useful in motivating children to learn, in providing them with more than one way of learning the same material, and in fitting methods to the child's learning style.

The laboratory approach exposes children to a wide range of manipulative, concrete materials and practical activities from which they can abstract mathematical ideas. Each child has the opportunity to learn individually—at his own rate—and to work with a buddy (or a small group) as he explores and discovers mathematical relationships. Both teachers and students experience delight in an approach that emphasizes individual learning—in settings that foster discovery and lead children to experience math that not only makes sense to them but is fun to learn.

An elementary school mathematics laboratory doesn't have to be an all or none affair. It may start with a few well-chosen materials arranged on a table and shelves in a corner of the classroom.

Of course, it would be highly desirable to have a special laboratory room with its own mathematics equipment—and ample storage space where materials can be categorized, labeled, and made accessible to teachers and students. Such a room should have lots of open space, with furniture (mainly tables and chairs) that can be easily moved about. However limited or extensive the lab may be, it should be operated with the full cooperation of the school's library resource center, thus ensuring that films, filmstrips, tapes, and supplementary books and reference materials will be readily available.

From *Today's Education* LX, no. 2 (February 1971):20–22. Used by permission of the author and publisher.

The teacher who sets up a mathematics laboratory has at least three general types of materials in mind. The first type is largely motivational and encourages children to learn mathematics. The second type provides horizontal enrichment of the basic program for each child at his level. The third type offers vertical enrichment of the kind that enables the child to work on extensions of topics included in the program and on selected topics outside the program.

Games, mathematical puzzles, and tricks are examples of the motivational type of material. Some games require children to build number sentences and equations (Tuf, Equations) while others provide practice in operations with whole numbers and fractions (Number Bingo, Orbiting the Earth). Examples of mathematical puzzles include the Tower of Hanoi (or pyramid puzzle); the Chinese shuttle (or strip puzzle); and Tangram puzzles, in which two or more pieces are fitted together to form a square, triangle, or hexagon. Puzzle games (Twenty-One, Nim) fascinate young and old alike.

Shortcuts for adding and multiplying, schemes for finding a person's age and the month in which he was born or for telling the number a person is thinking of, and the arrangement of numbers in magic squares may look like tricks to the observer. However, with the use of cue cards which take children through a sequence of activities, a student may discover the rules and principles on which puzzles and tricks of this sort are based. Logical thought, practice on number facts, and discovery of mathematical principles and relationships are highly desirable concomitant values to the major purpose of stimulating and maintaining children's interest in learning mathematics.

Horizontal enrichment materials supplement the program by providing concrete experiences when a new topic is introduced. Their function is to extend the development of a concept, or to offer a different way of approaching a topic.

Two examples of horizontal enrichments for young children are attribute blocks or similar materials varying in size, color, and shape which are used in working with sets, and the Piaget-type activities which guide children to form concepts of conservation of number and counting, of order and reversibility. These are essential prerequisites to learning the facts of the operations.

For slightly older children in the elementary school, materials already in use by some teachers could qualify: rods, beads, and blocks based on a standard unit (Cuisenaire rods, Dienes blocks), counting frames, hundred boards, place value materials, flannel boards, and cutouts—for work with whole numbers, fractions, geometry, and problem solving—as well as a magnetized section of the chalkboard with a supply of magnetic discs and other shapes to use on it.

The teacher should select horizontal enrichment materials to help individual pupils overcome specific difficulties and to reteach topics that are preventing them from making progress in mathematics. This implies starting each pupil at his level of understanding. It also implies diagnosis to uncover gaps in his learning, and remediation through experiences with materials that will help close those gaps.

Assigning a pupil a lot of drill work of the same type that has already given him difficulty is not the answer to his problem. What he really needs is an opportunity to learn by means of a new approach with different materials. And most of all he needs sustained encouragement that will stimulate him to keep working at a task that he feels he can do and wants to do.

These children must also have experience with materials of the motivational type and much experience with a variety of horizontal enrichment materials described earlier. How dull it would be for a child to spend all of his laboratory time in phases of mathematics with which he already feels defeated!

Vertical enrichment consists of providing open-ended, ungraded materials that encourage the child to go as far as his ability and interest enable him to go with a specific topic. These materials are often developed around areas of mathematics that teachers feel receive skimpy treatment in the regular program and that therefore make it difficult for able students to explore their special interests.

For example, to enhance the study of geometry, the laboratory contains such materials as geoboards (nailboards), rubber bands for enclosing geometric shapes, cards or work sheets to guide the pupil in individualized learning, and dot paper simulating the geoboards so that he has a permanent record of his discoveries.

Mirror cards and unbreakable mirrors can stimulate a study of mirror reflections and learning about lines of symmetry. Units developed from current space exploration and sports events, from weather conditions, and other environmental happenings in the news—or units combining either mathematics and science or mathematics and social studies—may bring new insights in mathematics and its relationship to other fields.

Other types of material for vertical enrichment include the Shoe Box Kits developed under the direction of Robert B. Davis of Syracuse University, director of the Madison Project, which was partially sponsored by the U.S. Office of Education, and learning packages and sets of activity cards which are now available on a number of mathematical topics.

Of course, some materials, such as activity cards, serve more than one purpose. They may either be purchased or prepared by teacher and pupils. For example, the following activities require a sheet of one-inch squared paper, pencil, scissors, and ruler.

Card 1: Place your foot on the paper and trace around it. Cut out the pattern. Determine the number of whole, one-inch squares in your pattern. Put all the pieces of squares together and find out *about* how many whole squares they will make. Write up what you did and how you found your answer.

Card 2: Use your ruler to measure your foot pattern the long way to the nearest inch. This is your foot length. Use your foot length to measure five things in the room. Then use your ruler to measure the same five things, and write up your findings.

If funds for the laboratory are limited, homemade games for providing practice in computation are often highly satisfactory substitutes for commercial products. For example, a simple miniature tenpins game can be made from 10 spring-type clothespins, a small sponge ball, and a runner marked to show starting line at one end and circles at the other arranged to indicate placement of the pins.

A game resembling a commercially produced one can be made from an egg carton. First, write the numerals from 1 through 12 in the partitions of the carton. Use colored, see-through discs to cover the numerals.

A child throws two dice and then covers either a single numeral in the egg carton that represents the sum of the throw or any two numbers that add up to the sum. He continues until he can no longer cover any of the remaining numerals or until all numerals are covered. (The latter rarely happens.)

The player finds his score by adding the numbers which he has been unable to cover. Since a low score is desirable in this game, each child tries to figure out the strategy of covering numbers that will enable him to get the lowest possible score.

Children enjoy collecting materials for the laboratory, and they are often able to assist in categorizing and classifying them for later use. One day they might concentrate on bringing in materials to use as counters: buttons, acorn caps, bottle tops, small stones, and large seeds. Another day they might bring containers made in various geometric shapes—cube, cylinder, and the like. Children also enjoy collecting pictures that illustrate number facts; maps to use in determining distances; and cloth scraps and wallpaper patterns with repeating designs for use with mirror work.

Pupils receive further experience by classifying materials. For example, they can sort buttons according to the number of holes (0, 2, 4), according to size (small, medium, large), or according to color. Thus, a button collection serves as a satisfactory substitute for attribute blocks.

Once they actively participate in setting up a laboratory, pupils begin to view their surroundings with a mathematical eye. The paper in daddy's adding machine is a natural material for making number lines; mother's kitchen equipment may be useful for the measurement display; throwaways around the house (boxes, cartons, blocks, old clocks) are also useful.

A listening center serves many purposes in the mathematics laboratory. A teacher may prepare practice tapes following diagnosis of the facts a pupil needs to practice. On the basis of written and oral interview testing, each child would have his own grid table of addition or multiplication. (The facts he already knows are blocked out immediately, and his practice tape is made of the remaining facts.)

The same tables can be used for subtraction and division. To make the tape, read each fact onto the tape—allowing sufficient time after each item for the child to respond orally or in writing. This becomes the child's own tape; he may listen to it as often as necessary. As a pupil works on his practice tape and sees the task becoming smaller and less formidable, he is encouraged to keep working for accurate responses until all facts are blocked out.

Tapes may also help children with reading disabilities which interfere with their success in mathematics. Instructions for work sheets and activity cards may be put on tape, until the child develops better reading skills.

Classroom teachers can use a special laboratory room in different ways. Part of the class may have a laboratory period, while the regular teacher works with the rest of the children.

Good students who finish assignments and have time to spare may find greater challenge from laboratory offerings than most classrooms are able to provide. Under no circumstances, however, should the laboratory be reserved only for children who finish assigned work early. Weaker students are stimulated to greater effort as they become successful with individualized activities in the laboratory and begin to grasp some idea of the scope of mathematics.

How to evaluate individual laboratory procedures and results is a persistent problem that challenges the regular classroom teacher and the laboratory teacher alike.

One teacher uses a weekly period when half the class is out of the room for checking the children's progress and for planning future laboratory activities. Some teachers use a file folder for each child with record sheets for checking off work accomplished (games played, or units, work sheets, and activity cards completed). These are checked by the teacher and pupil, as they plan together for the child's needs.

A diary-type record in which the child describes his project, and what he learned from it, is a good self-evaluation device. The possibilities for integrating mathematics with the language arts program are apparent in this approach, for the child must organize his thoughts, plan his work, and express his ideas in sentence form.

Certainly, some aspects of a laboratory approach are feasible for any teacher. As he becomes more comfortable with the approach he has chosen, he may wish to include more mathematics topics, devote more time to them, or even to expand the program to include subjects other than mathematics.

Reading Instruction in the Elementary School

Nila Banton Smith

Reading is so much a part of the fabric of American life that it changes with crucial epochs in our history. Certainly we are now in the midst of such an epoch, and, as usual, reading instruction reflects our progress, our concerns, our intuitions.

Some of today's deepest concerns grow out of the desire on the part of all Americans to realize their personal identity and out of their demand for a fair share of this country's blessings.

Some milestone education legislation has resulted from this desire and demand. We have placed emphasis on teaching illiterate youth and adults to read; made grants for research in reading; provided books and supplies to some schools; and, in some cases, equipped and staffed reading clinics. All these measures are contributing to reading improvement and probably will do so increasingly in the future.

At all levels, experimental programs are under way for teaching reading to the disadvantaged, and reading materials and procedures are being developed for the disadvantaged. We are also searching vigorously for the best ways to teach reading to children of different language groups—the Puerto Ricans and Mexican-Americans, the Japanese.

A working relationship between teachers and parents is important in teaching

From *Today's Education* LIX no. 1 (January 1970):42–43, 69–71. Used by permission of the author and publisher.

disadvantaged students. Several studies made in depressed areas have shown that when teachers work closely with parents, reading improves. Though we still have a lot to accomplish in school-community relationships, some school systems are doing interesting things in this area.

Public education for increasing numbers of preschoolers is another outgrowth of society's rising concern that each child should be given the opportunity to reach his potential. This development should have a salutary effect on reading instruction at the elementary level. Now that the government has set the pattern for programs of the Head Start variety for young children, all public school systems may have nursery schools by 1980.

Along with this movement, a new philosophy regarding the education of young children has arisen. The philosophy is dramatized in Maya Pines' book, *Revolution in Learning,* in which she says, "From birth to six, children can learn more—and more rapidly—than at any other time in their lives. . . . We are wasting the capacities of millions of children by failing to stimulate them intellectually during their earliest years." Many other educators agree with Pines' advocacy of giving young children more work in skill and content. [See "How and What To Teach the Very Young Child," NEA JOURNAL, February 1968.]

As far as reading is concerned, this philosophy is revolutionary indeed. For half a century, beginning reading instruction has been the private domain of the first grade teacher who has accepted the traditional view that children must have reached the magic age of six before it is safe to teach them to read.

Early instruction in reading was considered harmful to the young child's eyes and likely to develop in him a distaste for reading or to cause emotional difficulties. Several recent studies indicate that these ill effects do not ensue. Neil Harvey, for instance, conducted a highly structured and coordinated television teaching program with three-year-olds. At the outset and at the end of the experiment both a control and an experimental group were tested. Members of the latter group made a substantial achievement in reading, had enjoyed their reading activities, and displayed no negative learning effects.

Many educators do not yet support the movement to teach young children to read. They await more extensive long-term research that will tell whether children show an academic advantage in middle or upper grades because of having learned to read in their early years. The idea is nevertheless beginning to receive a certain degree of professional respectability. If it has the promise that many people think it has, this movement should help to rev up reading instruction.

Revolutionary advances in biochemistry also promise exciting things for education. Scientists are now conducting experiments in the use of drugs to increase learning ability and to improve memory.

By feeding a drug called *Cylert* to rats, Nicholas Plotnikoff of Abbott Laboratories in Chicago increased their performance capacity in learning tests up to five times that of untreated rats. James McGaugh at the University of California at Irvine also has experimented in giving memory-enhancing drugs to mice. He found that treated mice remembered how to get out of a maze better than untreated mice. [See "Learning and Memory" by James L. McGaugh in the April 1968 JOURNAL and "Frontiers of Medicine" by Donald G. Cooley, TODAY'S EDUCATION, December 1968.] G. Ungar of Baylor University College of Medicine in Houston experimented with memory transfer by injection. He took brain matter from trained rats and injected it into untrained mice, and contends that the results prove that learning can be transferred. [See "Chemical Transfer of Learning?" an interview with Dr. Ungar, February 1969 issue of TODAY'S EDUCATION.]

Possibly in the future, in certain cases where learning is slow or memory is weak, the remedial reading student will be able to improve his ability by taking a pill rather than by spending long dreary hours drilling on phonics.

As David Krech says: "Both the biochemist and the teacher of the future will combine their skills and insights for the educational and intellectual development of the child. Tommy needs a bit more of an immediate memory stimulator; Jack could do with a chemical attention-span stretcher; Rachel needs an anticholinesterase to slow down her mental processes; Joan, some puromycin—she remembers too many details, and gets lost.

"To be sure, all our data thus far come from the brains of goldfish and rodents. But is anyone so certain that the chemistry of the brain of a rat (which, after all, is a fairly complex mammal) is so different from that of a human being that he dare neglect this challenge—or even gamble—when the stakes are so high?"

New administrative arrangements for grouping and individualization hold forth still another way of revving up reading instruction. For many years the traditional three-group plan stood as an invincible bulwark in American schools. During the last few years, however, a quiet revolution in forms of grouping has been taking place. In fact one might say we have been "groping for grouping."

We have the multigrade plan, the intergrade plan, the Joplin plan, the ungraded plan, and the flexible scheduling plan, as well as individualized instruction in reading. All these are steps toward meeting individual needs, and teachers should be encouraged to experiment with them. But these experimental forms of classroom organization have not attained unequivocal results from which we can make wide generalizations about improvement in reading. In other words, when educators adopt one of these new administrative arrangements, they cannot depend upon that arrangement, alone, to take care of all their reading problems. The arrangement may help, but the quality of instruction is a much more important factor than classroom organization in improving reading.

The next administrative arrangement, one that is already appearing here and there, may be the grouping of instructional personnel rather than the grouping of children. Perhaps for some 200 elementary children, a future school will have an instructional group of personnel consisting of a specialist in science and math, one in social studies, and certainly one in reading. Then there may be four or five paraprofessionals representing different subject areas, and four or five aides. There may also be such other specialists as a computer technician and programmer in a computer support center.

Each day this *instructional group* of personnel will arrange for teaching or supervising the independent study of pupils who will work individually or in groups according to their particular needs. Such an arrangement should contribute much more to improving reading instruction than would adoption of a formally designed pattern of grouping children. I hope that many administrators will experiment with plans of this type.

The reading explosion of the sixties is responsible for an outcropping of many new approaches to beginning reading. We have the Initial Teaching Alphabet, linguistic reading materials, programmed instruction, Words in Color, and several other new approaches.

What about the future of these methods and materials that have burst upon us? Some of them may be with us for two or three decades, but integrated within new frameworks. Some may remain much as they are and be provided to teachers along with several other sets of material. Under such conditions, the teacher may choose those methods best suited to the individual child's style of learning. Other so-called new methods may disappear entirely only to return fifty or a hundred years later in new guises.

In my research, I have found that there are such things as historical cycles in reading. No doubt some approaches undreamed of at present will have appeared by 1980 and will have begun their cycle of modification, integration, or obsolescence, as the case may be.

As for the effect of these new approaches on reading instruction, you will recall that the First Grade Reading Studies sponsored by the U.S. Office of Education suggested that the teacher, rather than the method, was the most important factor in getting results. Several other studies have yielded the same conclusion.

Since there will never be any single best technique for teaching reading, one should try them all. Teachers have different styles of teaching; children have different styles of learning. Some teachers may succeed with one method; some children with another. There is no blanket cure-all.

On the positive side, we can say that all these new approaches are enriching our knowledge of teaching reading. It is encouraging to know that so many people are trying to find better ways to teach reading. I hope the search continues.

We come now to the revolution that overshadows all others—the technological revolution. Many people are predicting that all learning in the future will be administered by computers, TV, and other automated devices, and that books as we know them will become obsolete. Companies hoping to make a fortune in school hardware have widely bought out publishers of school textbooks. However, during the last year or two, these companies have shown strong signs of continued interest in publishing software. I think they have come to realize that there is a definite place for software, as well as hardware, in teaching reading.

As for hardware, the computer looms up as the most favored electronic device for improving reading instruction, and extravagant results are claimed for it. At all levels, including first grade, this device is under experimentation in teaching reading.

I have some comments to make about the future of computers in reading instruction. Let us begin by considering what a computer can do and what teachers will need to do. The computer can drill children in recognizing whole words, in learning phonetic elements, and perhaps in working with word structure. It can give a lot of practice in following directions. It can check literal comprehension with set answers.

One of our most urgent objectives is to teach students to think; hence, in all of our teaching of reading the emphasis should be on interpretation and on critical and creative reading. I can't see how a computer can develop these kinds of thinking processes. The computer may offer a child three answers from which he is to choose one. Thus, the child is confined to an answer resulting from someone else's thinking rather than doing his own thinking and coming up with his own answer. The computer may build a background designed to stimulate the student to ask a certain question or to make some other kind of specific response, but it can't guarantee the exact response that the student will make.

Perhaps at some time in the future computers will be able to enter into conversation with individuals, but it is difficult for me to see how they can ever participate in Socratic dialogue designed to stimulate students in thinking, discussing, comparing, analyzing, evaluating. You can't program thinking! We will always need astute teachers to stir up creative and reflective thought about reading content.

And what about children who do not learn to read with the computer? Certainly not *all* children are going to learn by computerized instruction any more than they all learn to read by any one method at present. Teachers will need to know how to conduct remedial work with these children.

Personally, I think the most important contribution computers will offer in reading instruction may lie in the diagnostic area. The computer will store vast banks of information about each child—specifics in regard to skill elements that he does or does not possess, and the stage of his development in each. It will also give objective evidence about the child's continuous progress in these elements. With this great accumulation of diagnostic data, the teacher will know *where* to take hold in improving each pupil's reading ability; but he will also need to know *how* to treat the weaknesses revealed by the computer.

In conclusion, I should like to suggest a common denominator for all the revolutions I have mentioned, that of humanness: human empathy, human understanding, human consideration, human kindness.

This coming age will need more humanness than has ever before been needed. We will have to cultivate it in working with the disadvantaged, in working with their parents, in working with other personnel in the school system, in meeting and talking with militant groups of many types.

As the use of technological hardware expands, so will the vital need for a strong emphasis on humanness. We must learn how machines and human beings can live together. But we must remember that machines cannot develop moral, social, and educational values. These will be developed, from now to eternity, solely through the association of human beings with other human beings.

The Self-Selection Classroom

Zilpha W. Billings

Are you in a rut? Has the sparkle and excitement of teaching dulled to a routine? Do you suddenly get the feeling that you've taught the same thing to the same students before?

If these questions make you nod your head—read on.

You're never too old or too young to join the swelling ranks of educators who are experimenting with a way of learning for children called the *Self-Selection Classroom*. This is an individual approach to learning—promising some exciting, unexpected and hopeful answers to the problem of education for the space age.

Modern technological advances are demanding that education prepare individuals who are flexible, capable of using the best of the old and of adapting to the challenge of the new, who are confident of their ability to meet problems and solve them, and who realize that to continue to progress one must continually pioneer. Yet, very little has been done about helping teachers decide *how* to do this.

That's why I would like to share with you in this article my personal quest to develop a learning environment for children that would help them to become more independent learners.

HOW MY SEARCH BEGAN

I started my career as a very self-satisfied high school French and English teacher. Having a desire to teach ever since I can remember, I had a vision of becoming, in time, one of the great language teachers!

My focus of interest in education changed with marriage and raising a family. Problems which my children encountered in school started some thoughtful questioning.

As I did much substitute teaching and heard teacher talk in many different schools, I realized it was often centered around problem children—the slow child, the lazy child, the daydreamer, the underachiever, the emotionally disturbed child.

Were our methods of teaching a part of these children's problems?

Due to the teacher shortage, I took over a fourth grade classroom and ran head-on into the problem children I had heard about in the teacher's lounge. Most fourth graders were so innocently eager to learn, so stimulating—all, that is, except a few. These few started more thoughts going round and round. Why,

From *Keeping Up with Elementary Education* (Washington, D.C.: American Association of Elementary-Kindergarten-Nursery Educators of the National Education Association), Spring, 1970, pp. 9–12. Used by permission of the author and publisher.

at the age of nine, had some children turned off school, tuned out teachers, become failures before they'd finished elementary school?

As I continued to teach in many school systems through the years the problem children who could not, or would not, learn became an increasing concern. Questions about methods and materials often ran unanswered through my mind.

Who decided that children learn effectively from the same textbook?
Does every child have to do the same subject at the same time?
Is learning acquired best in a silent classroom?
Why do children move in lines from one place to another?
Can children be trusted to play a more important role in their own education?
How do five-year-olds know so much before they've ever been to school?
How can children develop honesty and responsibility without a place to practice it?
What is a child's self-concept in the "slow" group?

When I questioned children about their turned off, tuned out attitudes on school, they had such reactions as, "afraid of being wrong," "afraid of being laughed at," "afraid of seeming dumb," "afraid of teachers," and "angry at not being trusted."

Were there teaching methods that could enable all children to develop a positive self-image?

Did the classroom situation build all children's self-confidence and self-esteem.

At this state in my questioning I was teaching a sixth grade at Flynn School in Burlington, Vermont, under a fine principal who believed that teachers often had better ideas than the textbook manual and encouraged and supported them in being creative. (There seems to be a direct relationship between a teacher's willingness and ability to make a dramatic change and a principal's confidence and supportive attitude toward her.) It was in this atmosphere that ideas for developing what I later called the Self-Selection Laboratory grew and grew.

As the classroom gradually changed from emphasis on teacher to emphasis on pupil, it was exciting and amazing to see changes in pupils' attitudes toward themselves, each other, and me. It seemed a big step to me when pupils were freed to select which story they'd read first in a basal reader. It was an even bigger step when they could select which story they would not read in the text. The step to individualized reading was easier as it became evident that boys and girls wanted to read about living—not stories with unreal endings.

I had experienced the satisfying, exciting results of offering to children the opportunity to learn without the pressure to do so at a teacher-set time. So, when the call came from the school administration, "Put ideas into action," I was ready!

I drafted my challenges and questions into a *Proposal for Organization of a Self-Selection Laboratory To Be Used by Zilpha Billings in the Sixth Grade at Flynn School, Year 1966–1967.* After the superintendent had approved it, I presented it at a public meeting to the school commissioners who also approved it. I was off!

THE FIRST EXPERIMENTAL YEAR

The year began with a completely heterogeneous group of forty sixth graders and a teacher aide. Meetings with parents of the students were arranged early in the school year to explain the Self-Selection concept and how it differed in use of materials and in philosophy of learning. Reaction was extremely favorable. When parents understood that the student's choices were not in the area of whether to work or not, but rather what subject he'd work in at what time and with what materials, with the goals of self-motivation and development of good study habits, they felt safe to let their children try.

Meetings were held with the staff of the school to explain the Self-Selection goals and to ask for their appraisal as the year went on.

Any program which is moving from the safe usual pattern to pioneer in relatively new and unknown areas creates anxiety and fear—fear of failure, fear of what others will think and say. Self-Selection was no exception, but the positive attitudes, concern, and understanding given by all the staff and my teacher aide made this first year a relaxed, fulfilling one.

At orientation workshop as school started, the students and I planned together to develop an understanding of the privileges, responsibilities, and duties each member must assume. We discussed the role of the teacher as the catalyst, resource person, guide, and friend and the student's role as a unique individual with his special strengths, needs, goals, and purposes.

Instruction in the proper use of all media in the classroom was undertaken. Students were helped to acquire procedures for evaluating their own learnings and identifying their own needs.

Curriculum guide lines, established by the teacher, for the areas were presented to each child to help him establish his goals. Because of the wide diversity in students' abilities, care was taken to establish meaningful guide lines within which all children could meet degrees of success each day.

The curriculum was divided into four areas to facilitate maximum use of all materials.

Language Arts—oral and written communication
Mathematics—the whole broad spectrum of this science
Science—man's place in sciences
Social Studies—a problem approach to man and his world

The materials for all curriculum areas were collected with totally individualized teaching in mind. Consequently, materials covered as wide a range of reading levels as possible, starting with a low fourth and advancing in some cases to college level.

I also prepared a short, concise summary of minimum achievements in each area to help the student find out where he presently was and where he hopefully might want to go. Thus, a student who might be working on fractions in the math area had the following routes he might take: (a) any one of as many math books as I could obtain with a teacher's edition for self correcting; (b) a game dealing with fractions; (c) an electric fraction board; (d) matching equivalent fraction line; (e) solving teacher-prepared, real-life problems dealing with fractions; (f) constructing and putting up a teaching fraction bulletin board; (g) discovering with manipulative fraction pieces; (h) working in a programmed prepared kit on fractions; (i) working through a visual package of transparencies on fractions; (j) making and solving his own fraction problems; (k) selecting a peer to teach or to be taught by; (l) listening to a tape while watching a filmstrip on fractions; (m) working on a page from a teacher-prepared, programmed math kit. This example typifies our attempt to have many different media for doing the same thing successfully so that each child could find a way which worked best for him.

The room was organized by portable room dividers into four flexible areas: Mathematics, Science, Language Arts, and Social Studies. Within each area the essential materials were kept.

Tables and stacking chairs replaced desks to facilitate free flow in the classroom. This arrangement created an opportunity for independent Self-Selection activities according to the development, needs, and interests of the individual or the group.

Pupils preplanned their day within varying blocks of time according to the evaluation of their needs and interests. Various methods of testing for evaluating were used, such as built-in tests of various programmed material, unit tests, teacher-made tests, pupil-made tests, and standard tests. The evaluative result was arrived at through a flexible arrangement, sometimes by the teacher alone, sometimes by the pupil alone, sometimes together.

The pupils selected the area they worked in, the materials they used there, and the length of time they stayed before moving on to another area. They chose from a wide variety of media the one best suited to meet their needs at the time. Each student worked through his preplanned schedule until he encountered difficulty, then requested assistance. As pupils gradually began to comprehend the actual degree of their involvement in the classroom, changes in the original planning occurred.

TEACHERS' APPRAISAL AND INVOLVEMENT

The interest and response of fellow teachers were rewarding, and by the end of the first year Self-Selection was being tried at several levels. As the second year continued, more and more teachers were experimenting with various methods of adaptation.

Teachers who selected to change were both experienced teachers and new teachers, ranging from kindergarten through grade six. The approaches they chose to move into Self-Selection varied with the experience and daring of the individual.

Interested teachers began to collect curriculum material for one area at a time. Since only regular budget money was available for this project, teachers became very creative in finding many ways to reach the same end. They poured through trade catalogues to find more materials to meet children's diverse needs. Books and existing materials were divided among many classrooms. In individualized teaching, materials for no more than six or eight pupils at a time were ever needed in an area. Thus many programmed kits could be equally divided among two or three rooms.

Teachers began to assemble a variety of work sheets from as many sources as possible to set up their own programmed kits. Some worksheets were made into transparencies to use on an overhead projector or at a child's seat; others were covered with X-ray film or laminating film to be written on directly and then erased. Each kit, when prepared, provided many levels of non-consumable, sequential-skill-development practice sets to fit the needs of all children in the class.

When enough materials were collected in the area a teacher felt most comfortable in, the change was talked over with the students and Self-Selection began. When a small beginning had occurred, the evolvement into total Self-Selection seemed inevitable, for it was rewarding to see busy, happy children working in a challenging, responsible manner.

TEACHER ASSISTANCE TEAM (T.A.T.) PROJECT

Two years ago the T. A. T. Project was developed with myself as director and my teacher aide as assistant to the director, with the express purpose of helping all teachers at Flynn develop the Self-Selection method as rapidly as they are able. There is no pressure of a time limit for change but various inducements and positive support are offered. This atmosphere seems to encourage effective and rather rapid change. A vital aspect of this success is the principal's commitment to the involvement in the total program. The staff deliberately works to create a climate where each one has a feeling of self-worth, where the opportunity for some success every day for all minimizes the fear of failure, where everyone has privileges and responsibilities which makes a unified working team.

At the present time all teachers are involved in varying degree in Self-Selection, from the beginning teacher who is experimenting in one curriculum area, to the teacher who has become a master in the field of Self-Selection.

For the second year Flynn School is a demonstration school for the state of Vermont. Last year a total of 371 educators and other interested people visited the school. They came from neighboring states and Canada, as well as from Vermont. This year promises to be equally busy. It is rewarding to see that more and more people are searching for better ways to meet the needs of our young people.

THE ROLE OF PARENTS

Parents have been actively involved in the total development of the program for the last two years. Their interest, understanding, and support were actively solicited last year at a weekly, morning meeting when Self-Selection was explained, a tour of classrooms was taken, and sincere, honest answers were given to questions. We are seeking the best education possible for our children, realizing that we do not have all the answers but that in working together we are making improvement.

The secret of Self-Selection is daring to continually employ self-assessment. In our changing world education must never become static.

SELF-SELECTION CLASSROOMS HAVE COMMON VALUES

As I move from classroom to classroom where Self-Selection is being used, I see many common values which I believe are important to children as they seek new knowledge and skills. Let me share these with you in closing.

Atmosphere is relaxed and happy. Visitors frequently comment on the relative quietness of the room. Thirty or more youngsters working independently, communicating their own ideas freely, do so with the low busy hum of a well-organized bee-hive. This analogy is appropriate as the teacher uses the "hum" level as a barometer to measure productive activity.

In the words of a child, "In this school, you can look forward to an adventure every day. I've never really despised school but I can't say I've ever really looked forward to going until Self-Selection. On the way to school, instead of thinking about the lesson we'll be getting or what I'll do at recess, I think about what *I'll* do when I get to class, and I really look forward to coming."

Instructional grouping is flexible. Teachers vary their instructional approach according to their own special concerns and the needs and abilities of their students. Large group instruction and participation occur when they prove to be more effective than individual instruction. Grouping in Self-Selection may be teacher or student initiated to meet a particular goal. No permanent grouping occurs as each child works at his own rate and level, which changes rapidly from day to day and week to week.

Individualized reading is used. Individualized reading is used to help each child reach his potential. Mini-books, made by taking apart basal readers and color coding a paper cover for each story according to reading level, allow each child on any level to read a book the first day of school. Nothing else builds positive attitudes better than success.

Curriculum materials are carefully selected. As often as possible, materials are *self-directing* to let a student feel his own inner strength, *Self-correcting* to immediately reinforce correct work habits and to help him assess his need to ask for help.

Pupils organize their day. Children on the primary level work with a weekly schedule in planning their day. During a pupil-teacher conference reasonable goals are set for daily achievement. As the teacher and pupil plan and evaluate progress together, signals are worked out to help the student keep his goals in mind. (A red dot in front of a subject heading is such a warning signal.) A child must be helped to determine what he ought to learn. When a tendency to avoid an important area occurs consistently, the pupil will be helped to understand its value and encouraged to undertake it through an avenue of his own interests and concerns.

Intermediate-level children accept the responsibility of writing their own schedules each day. The teacher offers exactly as much help as each pupil needs in order for him to become proficient in this. The degree of his success in planning a good day is directly related to the degree of his responsible production.

Heterogeneous grouping is used. Each level is deliberately grouped heterogeneously according to chronological age to simulate a mini-world, where real-life problems arise and can be handled under the alert guidance of the teacher.

There is time for the individual. There is time in a day for a child to think new thoughts uninterruptedly, to envision unknown frontiers, to create in a style peculiarly his own, to question established ideas and facts, to decide who he is and what he is in his world.

Now, if you agree that:

1. all children can and want to learn,
2. all children can identify real purposes for learning,
3. all children can learn to identify their needs,
4. all children can be self-directing in their learning,
5. all children can learn to evaluate their own learning,

then *Self-Selection* may be for you.

SUMMARY

This Self-Selection classroom gives each child maximum opportunity to plan, pursue, and evaluate his own learnings within broad curriculum guide lines established by the teacher. This program recognizes that no two children learn the same thing in the same way, at the same time; that each child has his own self-concept; his own learning style, goal, and purposes; his own level of social and intellectual maturity.

Team Teaching in Canton's Model School

Wes Measel

Glen Fincher

Most of the attempts at team teaching are predicated upon a particular architectural design. When one mentions team teaching to the average practitioner, the immediate conceptualization is that of a new building with wide open spaces and movable walls, all leading to maximum freedom of movement. However, most of our students are still housed in buildings which were built long before the advantages of team teaching became known.

The major goal of Canton's Model Experimental Elementary School is to develop team teaching in a traditional egg-crate type school building. The 13

Wes Measel and Glen Fincher. "Team Teaching in Canton's Model School." *Educational Leadership* 29(6):520–22; March 1972. Reprinted with permission of the Association for Supervision and Curriculum Development and Wes Measel and Glen Fincher. Copyright © 1972 by the Association for Supervision and Curriculum Development.

teachers on the staff at the Experimental School were specifically selected and divided into three teams of teachers to work with approximately 360 children. Team A consists of six teachers for children two through seven years of age.

An Early Childhood Development Center was added in the second year of the project. This center has 15 two- and three-year-old children in the morning and 15 four-year-old children in the afternoon. In addition to this, Team A has all six- and seven-year-olds placed in four homogeneous homerooms with two sections of kindergarten in a separate room. There is some movement of kindergarten children to rooms with six- and seven-year-olds in some subjects. Team B consists of four teachers for the eight- and nine-year-olds, while Team C has three teachers for the ten- and eleven-year-olds. Each team has the additional help of two teacher aides and one full-time teacher intern. The interns are college students who lack only the student teaching experience and who receive a $4,000 salary.

Differentiated staffing is an integral part of the team situation. In the Canton Experimental School, each team is differentiated in that it has an executive teacher (team leader) who coordinates and is responsible for all team activities. It has a professional teacher who is highly qualified and experienced and who is responsible for supervising interns, student teachers, aides, and volunteers. It also has a provisional teacher who is a beginner or one with very little experience. This hierarchy is based on differences in the teachers' educational background, experience, administrative responsibility, and salary.

Much of the hoped-for success of the project rests on cross-age grouping. This type of organization is aimed at eliminating the highly superficial grade-level barriers in elementary school education. This in turn allows for a much greater instructional flexibility. Cross-age grouping, however, is only effective in an ungraded situation. The Experimental School is approximately ungraded in all curricular areas. The social studies curriculum consists almost entirely of teacher-made units, with MACOS (Man: A Course of Study) being used in Team C. SCIS (Science Curriculum Improvement Study) science activities and materials are used in all teams. All teams have switched to the Sullivan (McGraw-Hill) programmed reading series and use the Warner Organic Reading-Writing-Spelling Method as a supplementary program. Physical education consists of a rigorous teacher-devised program of perceptual and physiological growth and development and is a 20-minute daily program for all children.

TEAM PLANNING

In the traditionally designed school, as in the modern open-area schools, the most important and vital aspect of team teaching is team planning. At the Canton Experimental School, teams are required to meet a minimum of three 50-minute periods each week. These planning sessions are organized by the executive teacher and are scheduled for different purposes. One session might deal with problems of grouping in reading, or the development of learning centers. As a result of the planning session, children might be changed from one group to another, from one level to another, or from one teacher to another.

Other planning sessions are scheduled during which a teacher presents long and short range plans and behavioral objectives for the entire team in a curriculum area. In this respect, each team has subject matter specialists in the various areas of the curriculum (Figure 1). For example, each team has a subject matter specialist in social studies. These specialists meet together to plan or change the overall curriculum in this one subject for the entire school. Since each team of teachers is represented in each subject matter team, communication is greatly en-

Type of teacher	Team A	Team B	Team C
Executive teacher	Social studies	Science and math	Math and science
Professional teacher	Language arts	Social studies	Language arts
Provisional teacher	Science and math	Language arts	Social studies

FIGURE 1. *Subject Matter Specialties of Team Members*

hanced. Once presented, these plans are discussed and constructively critiqued by other team members and appropriate changes are made. Planning is the *heart* of the program and teachers receive stipends for additional time spent in team meetings.

Finally, there is an additional team called the Curriculum Coordinating Committee (comparable to the Instructional Improvement Committee in the Individually Guided Education [I/G/E] plan) which is comprised of executive teachers, the principal, and the project director. This group works in terms of the direction of the total project and deals with items of concern to all teams. The executive teachers relate the content of this group's meetings to the other team members.

STAFF DEVELOPMENT

Continuous in-service education is crucial to the success of any innovative project. The team teachers were involved in in-service education for seven weeks during each of two consecutive summers and participate in on-site methods instruction throughout the entire year.

During the first quarter (fall 1970), for example, the concentration was in the area of diagnosing reading disabilities. Experts from nearby colleges and universities are used for these on-site methods courses. Their role is first to teach teachers, then to demonstrate with pupils, to observe the staff teaching, and to evaluate each member of the staff in his performance of these activities. An example is the administration of a diagnostic test in auditory perception. Following this phase of in-service was the implementation of learning centers based on the diagnosed needs of the students.

Teachers in the project are expected to stay at Lathrop for at least two years before moving to another school in Canton where they will put into effect some of the ideas gained during their time at Lathrop. The concept of "satellite" schools is beginning to take form. Also, the idea has been generated of eliminating the building principal and creating a new type of elementary school administrative organization. This new organization will involve utilizing the staff and more specifically the executive teachers in new and unique ways. One variation is to release the strongest executive teacher for a period of time during both the morning and afternoon to look after the entire building. This, of course, would require the help of an executive secretary. It can be seen that in this way funds might be released to pay for various paid interns and teacher aides, making the project transportable to other buildings at little or no extra cost.

EVALUATING THE PROJECT

If this project is to serve as a model for Canton and other school systems, we must be able to demonstrate its effectiveness with hard data. Thus, evaluation is one of the most important components of the project. The major objectives include attempting to raise significantly the achievement levels with regard to ability level and to raise significantly pupils' self-image as well as their attitude toward school. We also want to determine the constancy of the IQ. A control group, matched with the experimental group with regard to achievement and socioeconomic factors, is employed in the experiment and has been used in all pre- and post-testing.

Results of the first year of the project show that our major aims were achieved in significantly raising the achievement and IQ levels of Lathrop children. Pupils' self-image and attitude toward school were also significantly raised. In all cases referred to, the differences were statistically significant in favor of the experimental group. All other phases of the project have been evaluated, such as effectiveness of in-service education, the process of team planning, and cross-age grouping. The teachers participate in project evaluation by completing various types of questionnaires as well as face-to-face evaluation carried out in personal conferences and small group discussions. Outside evaluators are being used for the largest part of evaluation, and extensive use is made of the computer in project evaluation. Data will also be made available, in cooperation with ESEA Title I personnel, that will enable cost accounting to the extent of cost-per-month of increment in the different variables measured.

In closely examining the entire project, it appears that the term "team teaching" is a misnomer. In reality, a team's effectiveness and efficiency are directly related to the quality of its planning sessions. Also, a crucial factor in team teaching is the evaluation of children by teams of teachers meeting together. Thus, team teaching really consists of team planning, the resulting teaching-learning episodes, and finally, team evaluation of pupil progress.

Teachers' comments thus far can be summarized in statements such as "I learn so much more now that I meet with other teachers rather than when I was in a self-contained room"; "Pupils' needs are being met so much better than ever before due to the team teaching and flexible grouping"; and "I have developed a need and desire to change old methods of organization and instruction, as well as a much keener sensitivity to the problems of other teachers." Thus the members' subjective evaluation indicates that from their point of reference the project is successful.

Finally, in viewing the entire project to date, it appears that the staff has developed instructional competencies that are truly indicative of a profession. The project, thus, might be conceived of as a model for developing teacher effectiveness.

SECTION 6   ADDITIONAL LEARNING ACTIVITIES

Problems and Projects

1. Read *Summerhill*, by A. S. Neil (New York: Hart Publishing Co., 1964). Which of the curriculum bases—human development, learning, knowledge, social forces—figures most prominently in the curriculum of this school? What are the school's objectives? Based on your knowledge of curriculum planning and teaching, what improvements would you suggest in the school's program of education? Another book about Summerhill is *Inside Summerhill*, by Joshua Popenoe (New York: Hart Publishing Co., 1970).

   An abbreviated description of the Summerhill program may be found in *Radical School Reform*, by Ronald and Beatrice Gross, published by Simon and Schuster, 1971 (pages 247–257).

   Summerhill is one of the world's best-known schools.

2. Read *The Amidon School*, by Carl F. Hansen, Prentice-Hall, Inc., 1962. Amidon is very different from Summerhill, but it is also well-known. Both schools have been considered excellent by some elementary school educators.

   Which of the curriculum bases figures most prominently in the curriculum of this school (human development, learning, knowledge, social forces)? What are the school's objectives? Do you consider them adequate? Based on your knowledge of curriculum planning and teaching, what improvements would you suggest in Amidon School's program of education?

3. Read *A Public School for Tomorrow*, by Marion Nesbitt, published by Dell Publishing Company, 1967. What are the objectives of the program of education in this elementary school? Are the four curriculum bases all considered and utilized adequately in the school's program of education? What trends presented in this section might be considered at this school in an effort to improve its program of education?

4. Using the four curriculum bases, objectives, and criteria such as provision for individual differences, evaluate the program of education described in "English and American Primary Schools." For additional information on the British primary schools, read:

   (1) "The Open Classroom: Protect It from Its Friends," by Marilyn Hapgood, *Saturday Review* LIV, no. 38 (September 18, 1971), 66–69, 75. What problems related to social forces and social setting does Marilyn Hapgood see in adopting the methods of the British primary schools in this country?

   (2) "The Case of the New English Primary Schools," Chapter 6 in *Crisis in the Classroom* by Charles E. Silberman (New York: Random House, 1970), pages 207–265. What curriculum bases—human development, learning, knowledge, or social forces—does Silberman identify as important in the British primary schools? Do you agree with Silberman?

5. Jane Elliott, a teacher at the Community Elementary School, Riceville, Iowa, made outstanding use of social forces in planning the curriculum for her class. She conducted an "unforgettable experiment in prejudice and self-delusion." To learn about what she did read the following:

   (1) "Brown Eyes—Blue Eyes," *Reader's Digest*, April, 1971, pages 61–65.

(2) William Peters, *A Class Divided*. New York: Doubleday and Co., 1971.

What creative suggestions can you make for relating current social forces and needs to the planning of the curriculum and teaching in an elementary school classroom?

6. If you have been developing a "case problem" regarding an elementary school in relation to Sections 1 through 5, continue to work on that case, examining the curriculum and teaching in the school in terms of the trends in childhood education presented in this section. How can the school's curriculum and teaching be improved by incorporating one or more of the trends? Justify incorporating one or more of the trends in terms of objectives, curriculum bases, and curriculum criteria.

Additional Articles Related to Trends and Innovation in Childhood Education

Brunner, Jean. "Follow-up on Follow Through," *Grade Teacher* 89:2 (October 1971), pp. 56–60.

Kahl, David H. "Independent Study at Madison," *Phi Delta Kappan* 53:2 (October 1971), pp. 113–114.

Klausmeier, Herbert J. "The Multi-Unit Elementary School and Individually Guided Education," *Phi Delta Kappan* 53:3 (November 1971), pp. 181–184.

McLoughlin, William P. "Continuous Pupil Progress in the Nongraded School: Hope or Hoax?" *Elementary School Journal* 71:2 (November 1970), pp. 90–96.

———. "Individualization of Instruction vs. Nongrading," *Phi Delta Kappan* 53:6 (February 1972), pp. 378–381.

———. "Open Education: Can British School Reform Work Here?" *Nation's Schools* 87:5 (May 1971), pp. 47–61.

Resnick, Henry S. "Promise of Change in North Dakota," *Saturday Review* 54:16 (April 17, 1971), pp. 67–69 and 79–80.

Shane, Harold G. "The 'Domino Effect' of Early Childhood Education on the Elementary School," *National Elementary Principal* 51:1 (September 1971), pp. 31–35.

———. "Storefront Schools," *Grade Teacher* 88:6 (February 1971), pp. 40–51 and 59.

———. "Teaching in a Do-Your-Own-Thing School," *Grade Teacher* 89:5 (January 1972), pp. 34–37.

Pamphlets Related to Research, Innovations and Trends in Childhood Education

The Florida Educational Research and Development Council recently published sixteen pamphlets which undertook to summarize research and promising practices in many areas of curriculum and instruction. These pamphlets are available for $2.00 each from FERDC, "Project Ideals," College of Education, University of Florida, Gainesville, Florida 32601. The following titles are related to childhood education:

1. "Communication Skills, Part I," by Ruthellen Crews and Maurice Ahrens (1971). Includes listening, oral languages, and non-verbal communication.
2. "Communication Skills, Part II," by Emaline Henrickson (1971). Includes eight "Approaches to Teaching Reading."

3. "Communication Skills, Part III," by Maurice Ahrens (1971). Includes handwriting, spelling, and composition.
4. "Curriculum and Instructional Practices for Continuous Learner Progress," by Glen Hass (1970). Includes research on graded versus non-graded school, individualizing instruction, independent study, programed instruction, grouping for instruction, reporting learner progress, pre-school education, and summer and after-school programs. Exemplary practices are also reported.
5. "Organization for Instruction," by William M. Alexander (1969). Includes research and exemplary practices for early elementary and middle school years.

Films

Charlie and the Golden Hamster: The Non-graded Elementary School, 16 mm, color, 113 mins. Approaches the concepts of non-gradedness through the eyes of Charlie, a student in a non-graded school. Distributed by Institute for Development of Educational Activities, P. O. Box 446, Melbourne, Florida 32901.

Team Teaching in the Elementary School, 22mm, color, 12 mins. Explains the purposes and methodology of team teaching at the elementary level by showing a teaching day at the elementary school in Cypress, Texas. Distributed by Institute for Development of Educational Activities (IDEA), P. O. Box 446, Melbourne, Florida 32901.

Filmstrips

How Pupils and Teachers Plan Together, black and white, 48 mins. Presents details of teacher-pupil planning in a number of representative school situations. Distributed by Wayne State University, A. V. Production Center, 680 Putnam, Detroit, Michigan 48202.

Books to Review

Bassett, G. W. *Innovation in Primary Education*. New York: Wiley-Interscience, 1970.

Blackie, John. *Inside the Primary School*. New York: Shocken Books, 1971.

Burns, Paul; Alexander, J. Eshill; and Davis, Arnold. *Language Arts Concepts for Elementary School Teachers*. Itasca, Illinois: F. E. Peacock Publishers, 1972.

Duffy, Gerald, and Sherman, George. *Systematic Reading Instruction*. New York: Harper & Row, Publishers, 1972.

Featherstone, Joseph. *Schools Where Children Learn*. New York: Liveright, 1971.

Hass, Glen; Cooper, Joyce; Wiles, Kimball; and Michalak, Dan. *Readings in Elementary Teaching*. Boston: Allyn and Bacon, 1971.

Howes, Virgil. *Individualizing Instruction in Reading and Social Studies: Selected Readings on Programs and Practices*. New York: The Macmillan Company, 1970.

————. *Individualizing Instruction in Science and Mathematics: Selected Readings on Programs, Practices, and Uses of Technology*. New York: The Macmillan Company, 1970.

Jarvis, Oscar, and Rice, Marion. *An Introduction to Teaching in the Elementary School*. Dubuque, Iowa: Wm. C. Brown Company, Publishers, 1972.

Johnston, A. Montgomery, and Burns, Paul C. *Research in Elementary School Curriculum*. Boston: Allyn and Bacon, 1970.

Joyce, William, and Banks, James. *Teaching the Language Arts to Culturally Different Children*. Reading, Massachusetts: Addison-Wesley Publishing Company, 1971.

Palardy, J. Michael, ed. *Elementary School Curriculum: An Anthology of Trends and Challenges*. New York: The Macmillan Company, 1971.

Piaget, Jean, and Inhelder, Bärbel. *The Psychology of the Child*. New York: Basic Books, 1969.

Ragan, William B., and Shepherd, Gene D. *Modern Elementary Curriculum*, 4th ed. New York: Holt, Rinehart and Winston, 1971.

Schuster, Albert H., and Ploghoft, Milton E. *The Emerging Elementary Curriculum: Methods and Procedures*. Columbus, Ohio: Charles E. Merrill Publishing Company, 1970.

Thomas, K. Murray, and Brubaker, Dale L. *Curriculum Patterns in Elementary Social Studies*. Belmont, California: Wadsworth Publishing Company, 1971.

Weber, Lillian. *The English Infant School and Informal Education*. Englewood Cliffs, New Jersey: Prentice-Hall, 1971.

Wright, Betty; Camp, Louie; Stosbog, William; and Fleming, Babette. *Elementary School Curriculum: Better Teaching Now*. New York: The Macmillan Company, 1971.

Sources of Pamphlets and Bulletins

A number of professional associations publish materials of interest to childhood education.

Association for Childhood Education International (ACEI), 3615 Wisconsin Avenue, N.W., Washington, D.C. 20016, is a particularly valuable source. The reader, by writing to ACEI, can obtain a list of publications he can order on a number of different topics. The "Portfolio" Series is especially recommended to the reader (see, for instance, "The Transitional Years: Middle School Portfolio") for informative articles relating to both Section 6 and Section 7 of this book.

The Department of Elementary School Principals, National Education Association, has published a number of important publications. One, *The Nongraded School*, was published in 1968. It is available at a single copy cost of two dollars from National Education Association, Washington, D.C.

The National Association of Elementary School Principals, successor to the Department of Elementary School Principals, also produces a number of publications on childhood education. *The National Elementary Principal* (the journal of the Association of Elementary Principals), along with special bulletins and pamphlets, should be reviewed for current trends and innovations in childhood education.

The Association for Supervision and Curriculum Development (ASCD) is another important source of information on childhood education. Various committees and commissions of ASCD have published papers, pamphlets, booklets, etc. Listings of these publications, along with titles of the yearbooks of ASCD, may be obtained by writing the Association for Supervision and Curriculum Development, 1201 Sixteenth St., N.W., Washington, D.C. 20036. See ASCD publications in your library.

The National Education Association (NEA) produces many written and audio-visual materials on childhood education. Write NEA, 1201 Sixteenth Street, N.W., Washington, D.C., to obtain a listing of those materials. *Today's Education* (*NEA Journal*) is a valuable source for current trends and issues in elementary and early childhood education.

Other Related Activities

The reader is urged to write directly to interesting elementary schools for further information about innovative programs and to visit nearby programs whenever possible. Many schools will furnish films, filmstrips, or slides upon request.

The United States Office of Education and state departments of education are other good sources of information on childhood education.

Journals to Review

Childhood Education
Children
Children Today
Educational Leadership
Merrill-Palmer Quarterly
Phi Delta Kappan
Saturday Review (Education)
Today's Education

Education for Transescents and Early Adolescents

PREREQUISITES

1. Reading and studying of the Introduction and Sections 1 through 5 of this book.
2. The development of, and ability to use, a set of curriculum criteria to describe and evaluate a curriculum plan. You must be able to use this set of criteria in order to critically analyze and make curriculum decisions regarding programs and trends and teaching practices described in this section.

RATIONALE

All curriculum planners and teachers should be acquainted with the goals and trends in education at all levels, regardless of the level of the program of education at which they plan to work. You should know about goals and trends in education for transescents and early adolescents whether you plan to work at this level or not. You will be able to be a better curriculum planner or teacher at one of the other levels if you have this information. This view is based on such curriculum criteria as continuity in learning, balance in the curriculum, and provision for individual differences.

Simply defined, a transescent is a person who is passing from childhood to early adolescence. According to Bruno Bettelheim, biological adolescence begins, on the average, at age thirteen for girls and at age fifteen for boys; but, of course, many perfectly normal children mature either earlier or later than the average. There is a four-year range within each sex group from the time that the first significant fraction of the group attains puberty to the time that the last member of that sex reaches it. Generally, by the time they are twenty, both boys and girls have reached full physical growth and biological maturity. But social, psychological, and cognitive maturation are usually not in step with physical maturation. Pressures in modern industrial society tend to force the social, psychological, and cognitive changes of this period on the young person ahead of the biological. In any event, individual differences among students are greater during adolescence than at other stages of life. Transescence and early adolescence, in our society, is a period from about age ten to age fifteen.

It is necessary to consider the human development, social forces, learning, and knowledge bases of the curriculum for guidance in planning teaching and programs of education that are appropriate for persons age ten to fifteen. It is especially appropriate to turn to the research and theories of human development (in Section 2) by Robert Havighurst and by Erik Erikson (in the article "A Healthy Personality for Every Child") and Jean Piaget (in the article "The Development of Intelligent Behavior: Jean Piaget") to see how each of them describes the transescent and early adolescent stage. From them we can identify cultural, psychological, cognitive, social, and sex aspects of this period.

Transescence and early adolescence are characterized by rapid physical growth, which is frequently uneven, with some parts of the body growing faster than others; thus both boys and girls may frequently be clumsy and awkward. Rapid growth uses up much physical energy, and early adolescents need plenty of food and sleep to maintain good health. On many occasions they may have excess energy that needs to be worked off in lively physical activity.

The physical changes that take place during this period are only part of the process of change that is occurring. The child who has looked to his family for care, affection, and guidance must begin to find independence if he is to meet the emotional problems of this period and of adulthood. The early adolescent must learn to make his own decisions and to accept their consequences. Parents and teachers are needed who try to overlook the youth's shortcomings and praise accomplishments; encourage independence without pushing too far; and give affection without seeking too much in return. In this section, Thornburg discusses the physical, intellectual, and social development of transescents and describes six maturational learning tasks of this age group.

What should be the *objectives* of programs of education for transescents and early adolescents (age 10–15)? Many goals might be suggested: some are derived from social forces, some from human development and learning theories, and some from theories of knowledge and cognition. The list would surely include many of the following *objectives*:

1. Helping the learners to seek solutions to experiences and problems of physical change.
   a. Provide help and guidance in finding suitable solutions.
   b. Aid in meeting developmental tasks.
   c. Provide teacher-centered guidance program.
2. Helping the learners to learn to deal with wider social experiences and new social arrangements.
   a. Provide experiences with a more varied group of peers.
   b. Provide experiences with new learning arrangements.
   c. Provide opportunity for early adolescent peer culture to develop its supportive functions for its members.

3. Providing opportunities to explore many areas of knowledge and skill to help determine potential interests.
   a. Provide experiences that create broad interests as a basis for considering personal, social, and vocational goals.
   b. Provide learners with opportunities to explore their own potentialities.
4. Providing for a transition between childhood education and education for middle adolescents.
   a. Helping grade school students to prepare for high school by combining features of both elementary school and senior high school.
5. Providing an atmosphere adjusted to the developmental level of learners.
   a. Studying each learner carefully and modifying crude classifications based on age and grade.
   b. Providing a setting where a psychologically mixed group can develop in a framework not dominated by any one subgroup.
6. Helping the learners to deal with value questions that arise because of their developing cognitive competence, their growing need for independence, and rapid changes in society.

Several articles in this section provide other lists of objectives, including the articles by Van Til; Thornburg; and Abramowitz and Macari.

A major issue in education for transescents and early adolescents is whether it is best provided in a junior high school, a middle school, or some other form of school organization. This issue is the subject of several articles in this section. Van Til ("Junior High School or Middle School?") discusses the social forces that led to the development of the junior high school in the early part of this century, as well as the social influences that led to the development of the middle school in the 1960s.

The wide range of differences among learners of this age level suggests that *only nongraded school arrangements can be adequate.* One nongraded middle school is described by McCarthy in this section. He believes that the ideal solution would be to group all grades, K-12, in one large building. Then an ungraded approach could function in a supportive setting. But today adequate curriculum planning requires that a program of education be planned on an even broader base, with much of the learning planned to occur in settings other than the school. The following list of *innovations and trends* in education for transescents and middle adolescents includes references to pertinent articles in this section.

1. Special interest courses ("Guidelines for the Middle Schools We Need Now")
2. Independent study ("Guidelines for the Middle Schools We Need Now")
3. Different provisions for boys and girls ("Learning and Maturation in Middle School Age Youth")
4. Team teaching ("A Nongraded Middle School")
5. Learning resource centers ("Guidelines for the Middle Schools We Need Now")
6. Exploratory program ("Guidelines for the Middle Schools We Need Now")
7. Flexible scheduling and grouping ("Guidelines for the Middle Schools We Need Now")
8. Cross-age grouping ("A Nongraded Middle School")
9. Value clarification ("Values Clarification in Junior High School"; "Learning and Maturation in Middle School Age Youth")

10. Interdisciplinary approach ("A Nongraded Middle School")
11. Middle school organization ("Guidelines for the Middle Schools We Need Now")
12. Nongraded school ("A Nongraded Middle School")
13. Critical assessment of the junior high school ("Junior High School or Middle School?")
14. State certification of middle school and junior high school teachers ("Guidelines for the Middle Schools We Need Now")
15. Individualized instruction ("Individualized Science for the Slow Learner")
16. Laboratory approach to teaching ("Individualized Science for the Slow Learner")
17. Continuous learner progress ("A Nongraded Middle School"; "Guidelines for the Middle Schools We Need Now")
18. Problems approach ("Our Eighth Graders Tackled Air Pollution")

Will these trends, if adopted, provide the changes needed in programs of education for learners of this age group?

We must evaluate innovations and trends in comparison with present programs. The consideration of (1) objectives, (2) the four bases of the curriculum, and (3) other curriculum criteria provide professional means for making these decisions.

OBJECTIVES

Your objectives in studying education for transescents and early adolescents as part of the curriculum should be as follows:

1. To be familiar with the objectives, current innovations, and recent trends in education at this level.
2. To be able to explain the functions and goals of education at this level as part of the total curriculum.
3. To be able to use objectives of education at this level, the curriculum bases, and other criteria in making curriculum and/or instruction decisions regarding present programs as well as regarding proposed innovations and trends.
4. To be able to suggest improvements in curriculum plans and instruction at this level through the decisions in number 3.

PREASSESSMENT

1. Identify at least fifteen of the innovations and trends listed in the Rationale above, and discuss their implications for this level of education.
2. Evaluate the trends in terms of objectives, bases of curriculum, and curriculum criteria such as balance, individual differences, and continuity.
3. Select any curriculum plan for education at this level and describe and analyze it in terms of objectives, the four curriculum bases, other curriculum criteria, and innovations and trends at this level of education.
4. Suggest improvements or changes in the curriculum plan in number 3 in the light of your analysis.

You might choose to analyze the curriculum plan described in "A Nongraded Middle School," by McCarthy, in this section, in answering numbers 3 and 4 of the preassessment.

LEARNING ACTIVITIES

Articles in this section will help you to understand the purposes and functions of education for transescents and early adolescents as an important part of the curriculum. They will also acquaint you with the problems, as well as the innovations and trends, of programs of education at this level.

Other learning alternatives are suggested at the end of this section.

POSTASSESSMENT

After attempting the preassessment you may do *one or more* of the following:

1. Ask your instructor whether you are ready for a postassessment evaluation on education for transescents and middle adolescents. Most students will need further work on this curriculum base.
2. Read the articles on education for transescents and middle adolescents in this section and try to determine how the goals, practices, trends, and innovations being discussed in each article should be considered in curriculum planning and teaching at this level.
3. Choose additional activities and readings or films and videotapes from those listed at the end of this section.
4. Look in your library or media center for other films, books, or articles on transescent and middle adolescent education.
5. Discuss the reading you have done and the films you have viewed with your fellow students. The key questions: How should the goals, practices, trends, and innovations you've studied affect a school's curriculum? How should they be considered in planning for teaching?
6. When you are ready, ask your instructor for advice on a suitable postassessment for you for this topic. Satisfactory completion of number 3, 4, 5, 7, or 9 under "Problems and Projects" at the end of this section might be one possibility. Or satisfactory written completion of the preassessment for this section, after completing other learning activities, might be a satisfactory postassessment. Consult your instructor about this. You can evaluate your ability to do these postassessment activities before seeing the instructor.

Junior High School or Middle School?

William Van Til

Will the junior high school form of school organization or the middle school form of school organization be used as the road ahead for the junior high or middle years? If we are to answer the question with any degree of rationality, we must examine the circumstances under which the junior high school came into being and the circumstances under which the middle school is currently developing. We must also look at the difficult and possibly unanswerable problem of the degree of success experienced or to be experienced by these forms of organization. Only then will we be in a position to make intelligent decisions rather than at the mercy of the shifting winds of education.

GENESIS OF THE JUNIOR HIGH SCHOOL

The junior high school in the United States of America is now more than 60 years old. Incidentally, it is the only part of the American school system which was created in the United States of America. We inherited higher education from Europe. We inherited the elementary or grammar school and the secondary or high school from European antecedents. But the junior high school was authentically made in America.

In the fall of 1909, Columbus, Ohio, established a three-year intermediate school calling its new institution a "junior high school." The following January, Berkeley, California, opened two three-year intermediate schools that introduced a program specifically intended to meet the needs of young adolescents. These were first called "introductory high schools." The name never caught on. The Ohio capital was the first city to use the name "junior high school." The idea of the junior high school spread quickly. By 1911–1912, Los Angeles, California; Grand Rapids, Michigan; Concord, New Hampshire; Evansville, Indiana, and several other communities organized junior high schools.

A chart of the growth of the separate junior high school looks like a successful salesman's dream of what a growth chart should be. By 1920, there were 367 separate junior high schools. By 1930, there were 1,842. By 1940, there were 2,372. By 1950, there were 3,227. By 1960, there were 4,996. By 1965–66, there were 7,920. For 1970 reliable figures are unavailable.

From *Contemporary Education* XL, no. 4 (April 1970):222–231. Used by permission of the author and publisher.

SOCIAL INFLUENCES

It is of the highest importance for us to recognize that the junior high school in America grew out of the times. Society is so much with us that we sometimes fail to recognize its influence when accounting for changes. Certainly the junior high school movement got under way in the early twentieth century because of changing forces in a changing society. *This point is important to keep in mind when we turn later to the forces which influenced the movement in the 1960's toward a middle school in place of the junior high school.*

Exactly how did the junior high school in America grow out of the times? As the nineteenth century became the twentieth, this country was at the "watershed of American history," as the historian, Henry Steele Commager, has put it. On the nineteenth century side of the watershed lay a country that was predominantly rural and agricultural. On the twentieth century side of the watershed was an urban industrial nation. So we had to have education in America for an increasingly urban or city population.

In 1907 alone, well over a million immigrants entered the United States. By 1910, one-third of the American people were either foreign-born or of foreign-born parentage. Some went west to farm. But the greater majority of the newcomers settled in the teeming cities of the Northeast and contributed their "cheap labor" to the building of an industrial nation. So we had to have education in America for effective citizenship for immigrants and their children if they were to become Americans.

In the prosperous times of the early twentieth century, many workers were needed. Children worked in addition to men and women. In 1910, almost one out of every five children between the ages of ten and fifteen was employed. So we had to have education to help children make some kind of transition from school into jobs at approximately what came to be called the junior high school years. Richard Stephens of Indiana State University has cogently pointed out that the junior high school movement emerged in large part from forces which "honored the values of social and economic efficiency" and which supported "practical education for vocational efficiency."[1]

Early twentieth-century America had many pressing social problems. In the new fast-growing cities, the individual family was less effective as the social, recreational, and educational center for family members' lives. More time was spent away from the family, both in gainful employment and in commercial recreation. People were faced with the problem of living and working together with those who were of different national, religious and racial backgrounds.

When depressions came along, armies of the unemployed burdened urban society. The new city residents, including former farmers and often illiterate immigrants, were almost wholly dependent on factories and wages. Labor increasingly conflicted with capital. So we had to have education to help young people deal with pressing social problems.

What has this social setting to do with the initiation and growth of the junior high school? Essentially this: the question had to be raised of what to do with a growing number of young people who had acquired elementary education but apparently were not going on to college to become the future min-

[1] W. Richard Stephens, *The Junior High School, A Product of Reform Values, 1890–1920* (School of Education, Indiana State University, Terre Haute), pp. 1–2.

isters, business executives, and other professionals. These young people were increasingly living in urban environments. So it was argued that they needed education to help them to live in the growing cities. These young people were also often of foreign birth or background. Yet, each of them was destined to be an American citizen. So, it was argued that citizenship education and social problems were important in whatever education was to be provided for them. They were a few years (indeed, they were often a few months) away from employment in industry. So, it was argued that they needed vocational education.

And yet, what were their learning experiences in the schools? In the early twentieth century, schools were predominantly formal and traditional. Many pupils understandably felt that school work had little or no relationship to their lives. They saw no connection between school learning and out-of-school experience and interests. The same academic diet day after day resulted in a loss of appetite for education. The average and below-average child in particular found the heavily academic character of the work tedious and difficult. Poor readers were severely and continuously handicapped, because the school program was based almost exclusively on the printed word.

Then, at the ninth grade level, the opening of the high school years, the content became still more academic. The methods became still more formal. Suddenly, the student was confronted with many teachers instructing him in the formal subjects that made up the senior high school program.

The result? The result was frequent failure. The outcome of failure was often withdrawal. But the very ones who dropped out were the ones who were least prepared to succeed in an increasingly complex and competitive society.

But academic standards came first and individual differences were subordinated, if not ignored. Consequently, many children became leftbacks. About one third of the school children of the early twentieth century were left back at some time during the few years they spent in school. About one out of every six children in any grade was a repeater at that grade.

So American educators became increasingly critical of conditions that gave rise to so many leftbacks and dropouts. Between 1907 and 1911 several educators and psychologists made major studies of these twin problems and the results of their studies became important justifications for the junior high school. The major studies showed a high percentage of dropouts beyond the fifth grade. Only a little more than one-third of the students entering public school ever reached ninth grade. Only slightly more than one in ten first graders stayed to complete high school.

Again, what has this to do with the rise of the junior high schools? The connection is that when proposals for a junior high school were advanced, many educators and citizens were ready to approve. They hoped to serve education better by reducing leftbacks and dropouts. *It was the failure of the schools which partly accounted for the new junior high school movement.*

PSYCHOLOGICAL INFLUENCES

Another major development contributed to the acceptance of the junior high school in the early twentieth century. There developed a new emphasis on the importance of adolescence and individuality. Particularly, G. Stanley Hall, a giant among early psychologists, called attention to the importance of the adolescent period. Until then, adolescence had been accepted generally as a period that called for no special consideration of school organization. It was regarded as just another time of life, not as a revolution for the individual. Now Hall's writing directed considerable attention to the adolescent period of life and suggested the need for a new approach to adolescence. Consequently, the idea of the new school, a separate school, a school employing different methods for adolescents seemed eminently sensible to many.

Similarly, psychological studies called attention to individual differences. Early twentieth century education had been based largely on the assumption that people were very much alike. The notion that all people of a given age were very much alike received a blow from the psychologists who had been measuring mentality. They found striking differences among individuals. Nowhere were individual differences greater than at the junior high school age. Such wide variations among seventh, eighth, and ninth graders apparently called for special recognition by educators.

So the idea of a new junior high school fitted in nicely with the ideas of the psychologists who were writing about adolescence and the experimenters who were dealing with individual differences.

REORGANIZATION INFLUENCES

In addition, during the late nineteenth century and the early twentieth century, there were many commissions of educators which talked about economy of time and earlier college entrance. Leadership in reorganization initially rested with college presidents and professors. But as time passed, educators who were well acquainted with secondary education, including public school superintendents and principals, carried more weight. Their chief concern as reorganizers was for an educational program suited to the needs of young people.

INSTITUTIONALIZATION OF THE JUNIOR HIGH SCHOOL

What are we saying about the social and psychological and reorganization forces which combined to bring about junior high schools in the United States of America in the early twentieth century? We are saying that certain powerful forces supported and supplemented each other. For one thing, the junior high school movement grew out of a time of urbanization, immigration, demands for young workers, and emerging social problems. Thus, the junior high school grew out of a period in which it was increasingly recognized that young people who were not college bound needed urban-o. :nted vocational education, citizenship education, and orientation to social problems. The junior high school grew out of a widespread recognition that too many were being left back and being dropped out, that the schools were failing. The junior high school also grew out of the emergence of a new interest in adolescence and a new recognition of the importance of individuality by the psychologists. Finally, the junior high school movement was pushed along by reorganization commissions which grew increasingly realistic about the best possible education for children of the junior high school years.

This was an enormously powerful combination of forces. When we add to it a whole series of expedient reasons, such as the need for new buildings following World War I, the reasons for the initiation and growth of junior high schools in America become increasingly clear.

As usual, scholars came along to summarize the purposes and role of the new institution. The two most famous were Thomas H. Briggs and Leonard V. Koos. Both published books in 1920.[2]

Thomas H. Briggs was a professor at Teachers College, Columbia University, a recognized educational leader, an extraordinarily well-informed person, and a man of sound scholarship. He wrote that the purposes of the junior high school were:

1. To continue, insofar as it may seem wise and possible, and in a gradually decreasing degree, common, integrating education;
2. To ascertain and reasonably to satisfy pupils' important immediate assured future needs;
3. To explore, by means of material in itself worthwhile, the interests, attitudes, and capacities of pupils;
4. To reveal to pupils, by materials otherwise justifiable, the possibilities in the major fields of learning;
5. To start each pupil on the career, which as a result of the exploratory courses, he, his parents, and the school are convinced is most likely to be of profit to him and the investing State.[3]

So the junior high school grew out of the times and out of the forces. But times and forces have a way of changing. And they did.

Specifically, by the 1930's certain social conditions had changed, thus affecting the junior high school program. Child labor had markedly declined through changes in technology, the force of public opinion, and the power of unionism and law. In prosperous times, child labor was not needed or wanted by an increasingly complex society. In depressed times, jobs were reserved for a pool of experienced but job-hunting workers. In both prosperity and depression, more education was needed for job holding. Consequently, more and more students remained at school through the junior high school years. The role of the junior high school became increasingly one of guidance concerning occupations, not specific occupational training. The responsibility of the junior high school for general education for young people grew, while responsibility for specialized training for potential dropouts decreased as young people stayed in school. Consequently, when Thomas Montgomery studied the status of junior high schools during the 1930's for his 1940 dissertation, he found a distinct decline of vocational training and a transfer of vocational choice making to the high school. He found a lessening of specialized training and a growth of general education. He found increasing retention of students.[4]

---

[2] Thomas H. Briggs, *The Junior High School* (Boston: Houghton Mifflin Company, 1920). Leonard V. Koos, *The Junior High School* (New York: Harcourt, Brace and Howe, 1920).
[3] Briggs, pp. 162–174.
[4] Thomas Sears Montgomery, "A Study of the Philosophy and Changing Practices in the Junior High School" (unpublished doctoral dissertation, University of Texas, 1940), pp. 56–57.

When William T. Gruhn and Harl R. Douglass wrote their celebrated book on the modern junior high, first published in 1947 and being once again revised today, they summarized the major jobs of the junior high school as integration, exploration, guidance, differentiation, socialization, and articulation.[5] You will note from this statement by Gruhn and Douglass that there is no mention of economy of time. Nor is there direct mention of retention of pupils. The vocational aspect of junior high school education had become exploration. Heavily stressed was guidance, individualization and integration.

In the 1960's when Gordon Vars and John Lounsbury and I developed our 1967 edition of *Modern Education for the Junior High School Years*, we felt that we could state two basic overall purposes of the junior high school today. These purposes were: first, to continue the common education needed by all citizens in the democracy (general education) and, second, to provide experiences especially suited to the diverse abilities, needs, and interests of widely varying individual young adolescents (education for diversity). Putting it even more specifically, these functions could be achieved if junior high schools adopted the following:

1. Continuing and extending the general education program of the elementary schools, including development of the basic skills.
2. Providing for a transition between the organizational approach of the elementary school and that of the senior high school.
3. Introducing new subject areas and additional specialization within basic areas.
4. Providing opportunities for students to discover and pursue their special interests and aptitudes.
5. Providing appropriate experiences to assist and guide the rapid physical development which is characteristic of early adolescence.
6. Providing experiences that will develop the social competence needed as students enter adolescence.
7. Providing experiences that will assist individuals and develop values in building a philosophy of life.
8. Providing ample opportunity for self-management and the development of leadership under supervision.[6]

SUCCESS AND FAILURES

So we turn to the difficult question of whether the junior high school was a success. As the decade of the sixties opened in which the middle school form of organization was to emerge to challenge junior high school organization, the junior high school in terms of numbers was a success. Separate junior high schools increased from 4,996 in 1960 to 7,920 in 1965–66.

Even more significant is the fact that what the scholars call "reorganized

[5] William T. Gruhn and Harl R. Douglass, *The Modern Junior High School* (New York: The Ronald Press Company, 1947), pp. 59–60. (See also 2nd ed., 1956, pp. 31–32.)
[6] William Van Til, Gordon F. Vars, John H. Lounsbury, *Modern Education for the Junior High School Years*, Second Edition (Indianapolis: The Bobbs-Merrill Company, Inc., 1967), p. 35.

schools" had overwhelmingly replaced the "regular form of organization" made up of the old eight-year elementary school and four-year high school. In 1920, 83 out of every 100 secondary school pupils were in four-year "regular" high schools. But by 1959, of every 100 secondary school pupils, only 18 were enrolled in a "regular" four-year high school following the eight-year elementary school. By 1959, 25 out of every 100 secondary pupils were on the register of a separate junior high school. Thirty-two out of every 100 were enrolled in a combined junior and senior high school. (Bear in mind that these latter are not included in tabulations of the number of separate junior high schools.) Twenty-five out of every 100 were enrolled in either three-year senior high schools or four-year senior high schools in a 6-2-4 organization.

The larger the system the more the 6-3-3 system was used. The *NEA Research Bulletin* points out that more than 75 percent of school systems of 25,000 or more pupils used the 6-3-3 organization in 1966.[7] So with respect to numbers, the "success" of the junior high school and the reorganization movement was overwhelming.

We must recognize that the question of the success of the junior high school aside from number is more controversial. Here is a balance sheet with respect to the success of the junior high school in America.

As to the pros, the junior high school movement has made many contributions to American education. It has made available to early adolescents special facilities and instructional areas such as industrial arts, laboratory science, and, to an increasing degree, typing. It has made possible richer libraries and instructional materials for use by seventh and eighth graders.

The junior high school movement has advanced materially efforts to take care of the retarded and the gifted. It has supplemented the development of a sound teacher-centered, counselor-supplemented guidance program. It has brought more men teachers and administrators into the school program below the ninth grade. It has furthered the development of the integrated, problem-centered teaching and the block-scheduling of time needed to facilitate such an approach to general education.

In the final analysis, however, the greatest contribution of the junior high school movement has not been a specific but a spirit, the spirit of experimentation it brought to secondary education. Reorganization meant opportunity to try things out in a new school which was less handicapped by precedent and tradition. Despite the dominance of the senior high school, the junior high school has been a testing ground for such new approaches as the core curriculum.

The con side of the balance sheet includes the continuing unfortunate tendency to mimic the senior high school. The ninth grade is hardly distinguishable from a senior high ninth grade. The dearth of teachers specifically trained for work with young adolescents imposes a real obstacle to practice. The inadequate, leftover facilities often provided for junior high schools handicap programs.

The absence of adequate standards, regulations, and policies at the local and state levels hinders the proper development of junior high school education. The lack of prestige accorded education at this level is damaging. The very name of this intermediate institution reflects its all-to-often subordinate position.

[7] "Grade Organization and Nongrading Programs," *NEA Research Bulletin*, 45 (December, 1967), p. 118.

EMERGENCE OF THE MIDDLE SCHOOL

We turn now to the 1960's in which the new middle school movement arose and the 1970's in which the middle school is developing.

Scarsdale, New York, a rich suburb, was one of the first to build facilities intentionally for the middle school. Large city systems planning to change in the 1960's included New York, New Haven, Boston, and Pittsburgh.

Like the junior high school, the middle school grew out of the times. Once again we find that certain forces combined to encourage growth of a new institution, this time the middle school. Whether these forces are as potent and compelling as those forces which brought about the junior high school movement remains to be seen.

SOCIAL INFLUENCES

A first force contributing to the middle school movement is the force of emphasis on the academic. The 1950's and the 1960's were a time of heavy emphasis on the academic aspect of education. The post-Sputnik concern for academic excellence and the mounting pressures for post-high school education and college entrance have served to renew the early junior high school concern for college preparation. Whether motivated by fear or by an intelligent analysis of the issues, this concern has resulted in greater emphasis on the academic aspects of both junior and senior high programs.

Some who emphasize the academic argue that college preparation can best be achieved in the four-year high school. Specialized courses in science, for example, have long been a feature of the upper secondary grades. Also, senior high school guidance counselors, whose recommendations count so heavily in college admission, have an added year to become familiar with students in a school embracing grades 9 through 12. Such views, though open to debate, have helped to develop the new movement for a division of the curriculum in terms of elementary, middle school and high school, whether a five-three-four division or four-four-four.

Another force which helps explain the development of middle schools is related to the segregation of schools. A good illustration is supplied by New York City. In 1965, the nation's largest school system announced its intention to shift from a six-three-three to a five-three-four division. This move was recorded in the press as an abandonment of the junior high school. In reality, it was motivated largely by the racial integration problem faced at that time in this complex metropolitan area. Civil rights leaders recognized that it is almost impossible to desegregate the elementary schools in extensive Negro areas because of de facto segregation in housing. However, civil rights leaders recognized that older children from such areas could travel to more distant schools. Therefore, in order to get youngsters out of all-Negro schools as early as possible, many civil rights leaders supported a four-four-four division with desegregation in both intermediate and high schools.

Obviously, New York City is not the only metropolis with extensive de facto segregated areas. Therefore, proposals for intermediate schools as a way of encouraging desegregation are heard in other cities of the United States as de facto segregation persists. On the other hand, the situation in the 1970's, both in New

York City and in other major metropolises, differs from the 1965 situation. Now, increasingly, black separatists are urging black control of schools in ghetto areas. The former drive in metropolitan areas for racially integrated schools has slowed down. One might reasonably hypothesize that to the extent that black separatism rather than integration prevails, the concept of the intermediate school will be less attractive to black leadership. If the concept of racial integration prevails, the intermediate school will be more attractive to Negro leadership.

PSYCHOLOGICAL INFLUENCES

Both the academic emphasis and the integration emphasis, while not necessarily mutually supportive, represent social forces supporting the development of middle schools. But still another force leading to an emphasis on middle schools stems from the psychologists, even as the early nineteenth-century emphasis on adolescents and individualization stemmed from psychologists in support of the junior high school. In the 1960's an argument from the findings of psychology was frequently heard in support of the middle school, especially in the books being produced. The argument came especially from psychologists and anthropologists who believed that young people today are maturing earlier, physically and psychologically and socially, than did their recent counterparts. It was urged that if today's sixth grader is much like yesterday's seventh grader, then today's sixth grader requires the specialization of both facilities and faculty that ought to be found in the junior high school. It was argued that the handwriting on the wall demonstrates earlier maturation, whether that maturation is traceable to an improved diet that brings on earlier physical maturation or to the mass media and social culture that promotes precocious sophistication. Some educators, therefore, advocate recognition of sixth-grader maturity by supporting the five-three-four plan and sometimes by even supporting the four-four-four plan.

For instance, the April, 1965 issue of the *Bulletin* of the National Association of Secondary School Principals supplies abundant ammunition for those who argue that earlier psychological maturation makes a middle school more desirable than a junior high school form of organization.[8] The Committee on Junior High School Education of the National Association of Secondary School Principals, an organization which has supported distinctive junior high school education over many years, asked whether today's junior high school student is a different person from his counterpart of 25 or even 10 years ago. The answer of the NASSP Committee on junior high school education was clearly "yes."[9] This answer supports many arguments of exponents of the middle school. For instance, Robert J. Havighurst, writing in the NASSP *Bulletin* points to generation differences: "When we look at adolescents from the sociological or psychological points of view, we find great differences both in the social situation and in the self concept of the present-day adolescent compared with his parents in their adolescence. From the base-line of the earlier generation, the adolescent of today is more precocious and more complex."[10]

[8] *Bulletin* of the National Association of Secondary School Principals (April, 1965).
[9] *Ibid.*, "Foreword," page unnumbered.
[10] *Ibid.*, Robert J. Havighurst, "Lost Innocence: Modern Junior High School Youth," pp. 2–3.

No book on the middle school today is complete without a substantial section reviewing the research which indicates earlier maturation of young people. Such research reports are capped by the authors with the argument that there is more homogeneity among fifth, sixth, seventh, and eighth-grade students than among seventh, eighth, and ninth-grade students.

REORGANIZATION INFLUENCES

An additional force supporting the movement toward a middle school takes the form of the viewpoint of many current educational reorganizers. Interestingly enough, their viewpoint is often quite different from that of the academic supporters of the middle school. From the point of view of the educational reorganizers, the great failure of the junior high school was that it was literally what the term implies, a *junior* high school rather than a school especially designed for the early adolescent age group involved. It is not that the reorganizers want a more academic education marked by stricter subject matter division and advanced content. Instead, what they sometimes support is education reminiscent of that viewpoint in the American junior high school movement which strongly stressed the core or the block of time and which resisted a high degree of subject separation. Consequently, the general criticisms advanced by the current reorganizers of the junior high school are that (1) the junior high school failed to achieve its purposes, (2) the junior high school developed into a cheap imitation of the senior high school, and (3) the ninth grade remained college-preparatory oriented.

The claim of the reorganizers is that greater curriculum experimentation may be undertaken because the middle school will not be bound by college-entrance requirements. The school may focus on the needs of 11–14 year olds and become "a school for growing up." It is their hope that in such a school educational guidance will be emphasized. The reorganizers are quite aware of the failure of junior high school certification in America and hope that instead a middle school certification will be developed which will result in teachers trained especially to work with this age group.

(One such reorganizer put it to me quite frankly in an informal conversation in which the writer solicited his ideas as to why the middle school was preferable to the junior high school. He said frankly that he thought both types of schools theoretically and ideally represented the same goals today. But he added that the only way to make progress today was to create the kind of excitement and atmosphere of experimentation which comes from the shaking up of organizational forms. Therefore, he commented he intended to support the middle school as the way of arousing the junior high school movement which had grown largely dormant over the years.)

The educational reorganizers are particularly critical of the programs in the ninth grade of junior high schools. They point to a great gap between the eighth grade content and approaches and ninth grade content and approaches. Many of them would be delighted to cede the ninth grade to the high school and thus avoid the continuing pressure of college-entrance requirements. A school freed from the burden of the ninth grade could be a unique school for later childhood and the onset of adolescence, they say.

THE ROAD AHEAD

Whether the middle school represents, as its proponents proclaim, the second major stage in reorganization of the middle or junior high school years or whether it represents an interesting development which may spread yet not dominate the program for those years is an open question. In part, it depends on how strong the forces now fostering middle school education prove to be. The representatives of forces currently supporting middle school education include the academics, the integrationists, the early maturity group among psychologists, and the educational reorganizers. They are somewhat uncomfortable bedfellows.

A genuine question is whether these forces have the same powerful influence as the forces which combined to create the junior high school—namely, the social forces growing out of urbanization, integration, and social problems; the forces supporting vocational education; the studies of dropouts and leftbacks and the recognition that education was failing; the discovery of adolescents and individualism; and the reports of commissions. In other words, *are the forces fostering the middle school as powerful as the forces which fostered the junior high school?*

Once again scholars are coming along to summarize the purposes and roles of the new institution. *Middle School* by Theodore Moss is an excellent example of such scholarly analysis. Moss says:

The overall goal of the middle school like any other unit of the school system, is to serve the needs of the students and society. As the elementary school is concerned with children, and the high school focuses on adolescents, the middle school is designed specifically to meet the needs of pre-adolescents. To this end, the middle school should foster:

1. The individual physical well-being of the student during late childhood and early adolescence. Health and physical education activities are designed which are unique to this period of rapid growth and dramatic bodily change.
2. Individual mental health through a continuous program of sex education aimed at understanding the many epochal changes taking place during the years 11–14.
3. Learning specifically geared to immature and maturing students in an atmosphere which challenges but does not pressure the individual. Such programs recognize that there are many different learning styles and that large numbers of this age group cannot tolerate huge doses of subject matter because of their rapid physical metamorphosis.
4. A continuous program of educational guidance based on the concept that guidance belongs in all classrooms, but utilizing specially-trained guidance counselors as resource personnel. Thus all middle school teachers should be "guidance oriented," working with specialists as members of a professional team. Vocational and career guidance (including college counseling) belong in the high school, not the middle school.
5. A curriculum that is part of continuous nursery through 12th grade program but that takes cognizance of the purposes listed above. Such a program provides for articulation with the elementary school and with the high school.
6. Activities related to the interests and needs of middle school students. These recreations are a natural outgrowth of classroom activities and take the form of special interest clubs and intramural sports. Elaborate

graduation ceremonies, evening dances, cheer leaders, and marching bands do not belong in the middle school.[11]

Again we come to the question of success. Is the proposed middle school a success? One might logically respond that it is too early to judge. Numerically, middle schools are on the increase, though they cannot remotely compete in number with the 7,920 separate junior high schools of 1965–66. (On January 26, 1970, the Director of the Division of the National Education Association wrote in response to an inquiry, "We have just checked with a staff member of the U.S. Office of Education and have been told that the 1965–66 figures on the total number of junior high schools are the latest. The study for 1967–68 is nearing completion but statistics will not be available until spring.")[12] Up-to-date hard data on the number of middle schools is also difficult to obtain.

During 1965–66, William A. Cuff contacted the 50 state education departments in an attempt at measuring the trend toward middle schools. He defined a middle school as containing grades six and seven but not going below fourth grade and not including the ninth grade. From this study, Cuff identified over 490 middle schools throughout the United States during the school year 1965–66. Of these schools, 55 percent were organized on a 5-3-4 basis; 30 percent were 4-4-4; 9 percent with 3-5-4 and the others indicated other patterns (5-2-5; 4-3-5; 3-4-5). Cuff found the largest number of middle schools in Texas, Ohio, Maine, New Jersey, Illinois, Oregon, and New York.[13]

The *NEA Research Bulletin* reported in December, 1967 that 3.3 percent of all school systems enrolling more than 300 pupils used the 5-3-4 type of organization in 1966; 1.1 percent used the 4-4-4. In other words, middle school organization amounted to 4.4 percent in school systems in 1966.[14]

The preface to *The Emergent Middle School*, dated March 1968, says, "A survey currently being conducted by the first-named author [William M. Alexander] has already identified some 1100 schools in the United States having this [middle school] grade organization."[15]

The more trenchant question as to success, however, relates, of course, to the educational success of the middle school. In this connection, it is clearly much too early to judge. The movement is still in the phase of competing ideas as to curriculum organization and clarification of functions and purposes.

If the junior high schools are replaced by middle schools, it may be because of the failure of supporters of the junior high school to build a distinctive institution. Listen for instance to the comments of middle school supporters, William Alexander and collaborators, who wrote in 1968 in *The Emergent Middle School*:

[11] Theodore C. Moss, *Middle School* (Boston: Houghton Mifflin Company, 1969), pp. 20–21.

[12] Letter January 26, 1970, to Cunningham Memorial Library, Indiana State University from Glen Robinson, Director, Research Division, NEA.

[13] William A. Cuff, "Middle Schools on the March," *Bulletin* of the National Association of Secondary School Principals (February, 1967), p. 82 as reported by Theodore C. Moss, *Middle School*.

[14] "Grade Organization . . . ," *NEA Research Bulletin* (see footnote 7).

[15] William M. Alexander and others, *The Emergent Middle School* (New York: Holt, Rinehart and Winston, Inc., 1968), p. v.

The 6-3-3 plan as it exists today does not seem to meet adequately the needs of the in-between-aged student. The upper elementary program tends to be patchwork of separate subjects, usually under the guise of the self-contained classroom, where the teacher is required to provide instruction in subject fields for which he may have had little preparation. It treats fifth- and sixth-grade youngsters in very much the same way it provides for the first grader. The junior high school is, in many ways, a mimic of the senior high school. Its program is fragmented and rigid. Its teachers and administrators too often feel they are there on a temporary basis and have received little or no training specifically designed for teaching at that level. The high school impinges on the program of the ninth grade because of the requirements of the Carnegie unit schedule.

The purposes of the 6-3-3 plan as viewed in the literature have been eclipsed by administrative efficacy. The group which suffers most by this inadequacy is the in-between-aged students. They have been forced to the background in the planning of the school program.

We view the 6-3-3 plan in modern education as an anachronism analogous to the horseless carriage in a time of focus on a race for space. It is time to change to an organization and a program designed to care for youngsters in the middle years, too, as well as the younger and older ones.[16]

In 1965, Paul Woodring wrote in *Saturday Review*, "It now appears that the 6-3-3 plan with the junior high school, is on the way out."[17]

Will these predictions come true? It depends on the power of the forces now fostering middle school organization. It depends on the power of the forces still supporting junior high school organization.

But it depends also on what supporters of junior high school education actually do in their own schools and in state and university relationships. The success or failures of junior high school teachers and administrators in developing a distinctive junior high school program of education will contribute to choosing the road ahead—junior high school or middle school. For new forms of organization grow out of the power of new forces. New forms of organization also grow out of the failures of old forces.

[16] *Ibid.*, p. 59.
[17] Paul Woodring, "The New Intermediate School," *Saturday Review* (October 16, 1965), p. 77.

Guidelines for the Middle Schools We Need Now

William M. Alexander
and a Seminar

This article presents some guidelines for middle school development. They represent, in the seminar's judgment, 12 essential components of a plan for middle school development. Closely interrelated as they are, each component needs specific attention in an educational plan that aims to achieve the organizational goals described in the introduction to this issue: 1) to provide a good program of schooling for children passing from childhood to adolescence; 2) to offer a significant alternative to past organizations that too frequently crystallized as hard-to-change, at times incompatible, elementary and secondary units; 3) to facilitate the continuous progress of learners from school entrance in early childhood to school exit in adolescence.

Several considerations have influenced the development of these guidelines. For one, we are anxious that the new middle schools represent genuine efforts to provide a demonstrably better school program for children of the in-between years. Further, this program should bring about greater continuity in the entire system of schooling. Hence the guidelines tend to present ideal, rather than current, practice. At the same time, we are also anxious that such guidelines be as fully implemented and thoroughly tested as possible. Accordingly, each section of the guidelines describes the goals of its component and suggests several characteristic features of plans for implementing these goals. To give readers further sources on both the goals and plans for their possible implementation, a brief, selected bibliography is included.

FOCUSING ON THE BETWEEN-AGER

Goals. The middle school program is focused on education of children during the transition from childhood to adolescence. The entire program is based on the study of the physical, intellectual, social, and emotional development of the "between-ager." Thus it facilitates frequent physical activity and helps students relearn to manage their bodies skillfully during a period of rapid change in body dimensions and general awkwardness.

From *National Elementary Principal* LI, no. 3 (November 1971):79–89. Copyright © 1971, National Association of Elementary School Principals, National Education Association. All rights reserved. Used by permission of the authors and publisher.

The members of the graduate seminar (ED 731) on curriculum change responsible for preparing these guidelines were William M. Alexander, seminar professor, Crystal Compton, Jorge Descamps, Nancy Weber, and Jon Wiles. Assistance was also given by Joyce Lawrence, graduate student, and Emmett L. Williams, faculty consultant.

The academic program is oriented to help transescents move away from dealing primarily with concrete operations into levels of abstraction and hypothesizing as well. The transescent is also helped in his social development by interacting constructively with both peers and adults. A change in the individual's perception of himself and, consequently, a quest for a satisfying concept of self require many opportunities for self-direction and self-evaluation. The school as a whole is permeated by an open and democratic atmosphere in order to help students achieve appropriate patterns of independence and develop workable valuing processes. The school bridges, rather than duplicates, the elementary and high schools.

Plans:

1. The entire school program offers many opportunities for movement, treating learners as preadolescents who need frequent change in physical activity, not as "little adults" who are to sit still all day.

2. Through a variety of approaches to learning—including problem solving, laboratory experiences, and independent study—each learner has the opportunity to deal with abstractions, develop and test ideas, and bring personal meaning into the world of concrete experiences.

3. Many social activities, such as school clubs, trips, get togethers, and picnics, are encouraged. Students help to work out their own rules and plans for these activities.

4. Learning tasks are individualized and academic competition deemphasized to provide maximum success experiences.

5. Cooperative planning between students and faculty and student participation in the routine tasks of the school help establish an atmosphere of togetherness, making adults closer and more approachable for the transescents.

6. Out-of-school activities, such as working, camping, scouting, and games, are considered to be curriculum related and are freely discussed and planned at school.

7. Community resources—people, institutions, organizations—of interest to the between-agers are utilized as fully as possible to break down walls between schools and community and to make the curriculum personal and real.

8. Gaming, role playing, and "what if?" activities are frequently used in discussions of school and community problems of interest to the students to sharpen issues, reveal alternatives, and assess value choices. Small groups created from home base, advisory, block of time, or other organizations are used for these learner-oriented discussions.

PLANNING FOR STUDENTS' INDIVIDUAL DEVELOPMENT

Goals. All of a middle schooler's experiences in school and out of school contribute to his development as a person. However, a cluster of essential experiences and arrangements to this end can be identified as having a primary, almost exclusive focus on individual development. The learner in transition from childhood to adolescence needs quite particular, direct attention to his personal development. In the middle school planned to meet these needs, each learner is encouraged and helped to achieve self-confidence and self-direction. His counseling and instruction are personalized rather than merely individualized, so that some group norm can be achieved.

Plans:

1. Through a home base, advisory, block of time, or other arrangement, each learner spends a substantial amount of time with one adult to whom he can and does turn, daily if possible, for information and assistance regarding his objectives, program, and progress in school; the advisor frequently works more than one year with the same advisees.

2. The advisor is enabled to refer each advisee as needed to a variety of special services: counseling, psychological, medical, social work, and academic, including other teachers.

3. The health and physical education program provides for each learner opportunities appropriate to his own physical development with regard to: a) understanding the physiological and related aspects of puberty; b) personal hygiene, physical exercise, diet, rest, and related health practices; c) recreation through intramural sports programs, individual and team games, social and folk dancing, and such carry-over activities as swimming, tennis, bowling, and golf; d) health services for systematic identification and follow-up of visual, hearing, dental, nutritional, and other difficulties.

4. Through exploratory courses, mini-courses, activities and other arrangements, each learner has the opportunity to explore a wide range of possible interests in the arts, in occupations in the community and elsewhere, in leisure-time group and individual activities, and in discussions of current developments and events. Each student participates daily in at least one, and usually more, of these activities.

5. Independent study arrangements include seminars growing out of the major knowledge areas; in-school and out-of-school investigations of an individual nature planned by the student and his advisor or any other teacher; substitutions for, or extensions of, regular group work in a knowledge area; and special courses taken at a nearby high school. Each advisor helps his advisees schedule these arrangements as their interests and learning skills indicate.

6. Special group instruction and individual instruction are arranged for students who have explored and wish extended study in the arts, foreign languages, prevocational areas, or other fields. This instruction is available in either the middle school or a nearby high school, using instructors from other levels as needed and available.

7. Teacher education and staff development programs include specific training that is relevant to the foregoing guidelines. Specifically, provisions are currently lacking and needed in the preparation of most teachers for tasks relating to advisement, exploratory activities, and independent study.

PROGRAMING THE SKILLS FOR CONTINUED LEARNING

Goals. Learning skills introduced in the early grades require further instruction in the middle grades, and additional skills are required. The further career of the child as a learner—a career that needs to be lifelong—may be virtually settled in the middle school years. If he enjoys learning, if he becomes skilled in its processes, then a lifelong pursuit may be assured. At this level of schooling, independent study may be one way of focusing on the development of self-directing learners who will be able to achieve their potential in an ever-changing society.

Skills for continued learning include communications skills, such as listening, viewing, and reading; thinking skills, such as questioning, remembering, comparing, contrasting, inferring, generalizing, hypothesizing, and predicting; study skills, such as reading directions carefully, locating information, using the dictionary, interpreting graphic materials, outlining, and summarizing; and critical thinking skills, such as recognizing propaganda techniques and separating facts from opinions.

Every instructional situation can be an opportunity to encourage the learner to become more self-directing and to help him to strive continually to develop his potential to the maximum. Programs for developing these skills are a part of the curriculum plan and include responsibilities for each faculty member.

Plans:

1. The middle school faculty determines which skills are to be emphasized in all learning situations and which in only certain situations. Thus it is decided where reading skills will be developed and where and on what bases special reading instruction is to be given. Decisions are reached, too, on the responsibility for direct instruction in such skills as listening, viewing, and using the library— whether the latter is to be done in all language arts classes, for example, or by the librarian in a special series of instruction, or by some combination approach.

2. Any middle school is certain to have a number of students who need special instruction in reading, math, study skills, and writing. Decisions may be required on the use of a laboratory approach. If such an approach is decided on, who directs it? When and for how long shall students needing specialized instruction go to the laboratory? Can programmed materials be used, and under what conditions?

3. Independent study may take any one of several forms: an in-depth study done in conjunction with, or in addition to, regular classwork in response to a student's own interest or need; unscheduled time to work in an open lab situation to develop a skill or to ferret out facts; or a special project in art, science, or home arts that students have identified as "just something we'd like to do."

4. Whatever their form, the independent study plans include: a) structuring the independent studies by helping students plan the use of their time and by setting limits; b) selecting and planning students' independent study according to criteria they have helped to develop; c) interpreting the program to parents; d) planning the facilities, materials, and services needed; e) planning content and activities, including library research, creative efforts, and field experience (such as working or doing research in the community); and f) planning and participating in the evaluation of the independent study program.

5. Preservice and inservice training of teachers is a prerequisite for the processes involved in developing thinking skills, group participation skills, interviewing techniques, and other learning skills.

PLANNING THE ORGANIZED KNOWLEDGE AREAS

Goals. Two important considerations help shape the middle school curriculum in the areas of organized knowledge. First, middle school youngsters are developing a strong sense of need to systematize and organize their physical and social worlds. During childhood, almost any successful learning experience is self-rewarding, but during transescence, it becomes increasingly important for the learner to see that ahievements represent real accomplishments—achievements that are recognized and rewarded in a more adult world. Second, the major scholarly disciplines represent man's effort to understand, explain, and control the physical and social environments in which he exists. The goals, then, of this curriculum component include identifying the big ideas and underlying principles of the major disciplines and thereafter providing every student success experiences in organizing and using the data and the methods appropriate to the areas of organized knowledge. The school subject areas of English, language arts, mathematics, science, and social studies can make important contributions to the intellectual development of the middle school pupil if they are approached at the learner's own level and rate and if system and order are emphasized, rather than sequence and coverage of set amounts of content.

Plans:

1. Through use of subject area planning teams, the major themes, concepts, and organizing centers of the subject are identified and articulated in an overview plan.

2. Through use of home base teacher and/or instructional level teams, individual variations are planned around a common concept or major organizing center. A variety of topics, assignments, and materials are used for individualization.

3. In selecting and organizing knowledge, the emphasis is on a small, manageable number of big ideas, rather than on scope, sequence, and numerous details. The aim is to foster an awareness of the system and order inherent in the subject area.

4. Students are given directed practice in the use of the materials and the ways of knowing that are appropriate to the subject. That is, students are taught to observe the raw data of the subject field and then to catalogue, organize, apply, make and check out generalizations, and reflect on the meaning of these activities to the individual and his society. Use of problem-solving approaches, active engagement, independent study, and small group projects is frequent.

5. Through use of interdisciplinary team planning, occasional cross-subject theme units are carried on to foster understanding of the applicability and interrelationships among the several learning areas.

6. A guiding principle for selecting themes, topics, and generalizations in the social studies areas is that the tone be generally one of affirmation. That is, the transescent learner needs a base of those things in his background and his society in which he can believe and have pride before moving into systematic criticism and analysis of those things that need change. Biographies, legends, and experiences that illuminate man's ideals and successes are frequently used.

7. Involvement of the learner in helping to set his own learning goals and practice in evaluating his own and his classmates' progress toward accepted goals are important features of the middle school program.

ORGANIZING LEARNERS FOR INSTRUCTION

Goals. In recent years, the emphasis in education has shifted from styles of teaching to styles of learning. The teacher is encouraged to be creative not only with his own part of the interaction process in which students learn but with the setting in which it occurs. At the middle school level, the important goal is the matching of students, teachers, and situations to facilitate the interaction process.

Organization for instruction is an individual school matter governed by goals, students, school personnel, and facilities of each school. Flexibility is a necessity if a learner's progress through the educational process is to be continuous and unbroken. The challenge is to utilize the teacher's intimate knowledge of the interests and needs of the individual transescent student, along with the teacher's abilities, the school spaces, and the time available, to work out effective plans for large and small groups, laboratory groups, tutorial instruction, and independent study.

Plans:

1. Assigning a student to a home base where he may have frequent and sustained advisement and encouragement from a teacher-counselor is a popular way to provide the teacher with a better knowledge of the student and to meet the transescent's needs. The teacher-counselor is usually one of the teachers on the team to which the student is assigned.

2. Organizing the middle school into interdisciplinary teams can promote cooperative planning. One plan for teaming has four teachers—math, science, social studies, and language arts—working with 100 or so students.

3. An analysis of the student population to assess the range of intellectual, social, emotional, and physical development aids the faculty in placing students on teams.

4. Placing students in multiage groups helps to individualize instruction. A student may move quickly in areas for which he shows more aptitude and more slowly in areas in which he encounters difficulty.

5. Teaming students and teachers permits the scheduling of learning experiences into large time blocks based on planned activities, with the team responsible for scheduling within their block. Schedules vary from day to day and from team to team. Each team schedules activities such as lunch, physical education, home arts, and music in coordination with the other teams.

6. Team planning time is scheduled during the day. This time block is devoted to planning instructional relationships and to pooling observations that help teachers know their students in greater depth.

7. Care is given in scheduling the school day to allow adequate opportunity for recreation breaks and for special activity groupings through an activity period, a half hour after lunch, or another arrangement.

8. Whether children are classified by grades, years, or teams, no individual is assigned to a groove in which he must inevitably remain from year to year. Exploratory courses and activities are generally open to students without regard to grade or year classification.

9. Access to all learning resource spaces (library, audiovisual area, or laboratory) is as immediate and open as the rights of all learners permit, with special provisions possible for after-hours use.

STAFFING THE MIDDLE SCHOOL

Goals. The functions that the middle school aims to serve determine the qualifications and categories of the personnel to be employed. Since the middle school focuses on the developmental tasks of the between-ager, the staff is expected to have personal attributes that facilitate this growth. Teachers who have a positive view of themselves, who are not overly protective of their dignity, and who have the emotional strength to live with the ups and downs of transescents are likely to be more successful in their work with this age group. These teachers are flexible and open to change; they can live with and admit their errors and get involved with student concerns; and they have a great deal of patience and a readiness to listen. They have respect for the dignity and worth of the individual and a personal commitment to a value system supportive of a democratic society. They also have the ability to interact constructively with others and can easily relate to transescents. They are approachable, responsive, and supportive as youngsters struggle with the problems peculiar to their stage of development. Most of all, these teachers are personally committed to the education of transescents.

Plans:

1. Several categories of personnel are necessary to accomplish the functions of the middle school.

a. *Subject specialists and team members* who, in addition to giving instruction in their specialty, can serve as resource persons for other staff members and can lead disciplinary and interdisciplinary teams. These persons also serve as home base teacher-counselors.

b. *Special areas specialists,* including competent reading specialists and professionally qualified art, music, foreign language, home arts, and physical education resource teachers. These specialists belong on the staff of a good middle school; they cooperate with the teaching teams and may work as home base teachers.

c. *Specialized staff,* including learning resources personnel who help faculty and students retrieve information and provide ample resources for learning; guidance people who help staff members in their teacher-counselor role and in working with students; measurement and evaluation specialists who concentrate on the well-rounded development of the child.

d. *Administrative staff and supportive services* who provide leadership in improving the instructional program by providing services for students and teachers, and who facilitate the work of the instructional staff by managing the business, financial, and housekeeping aspects of the organization.

2. Until preservice programs for middle school teachers are generally available, a realistic approach for most schools is to employ a staff representing both elementary and junior high preparation and experience. Whenever feasible, arrangements are made that combine teachers from elementary and secondary backgrounds for cooperative planning.

3. The newly organized middle school seeks volunteers from all existing schools in the school district rather than automatic transfers from the predecessor schools.

4. Since no one set of teacher characteristics or teaching behaviors can be identified as "best" for all instructional purposes, it is desirable to staff the middle school with a variety of personality types who possess different teaching styles and different experiential backgrounds.

5. The use of student teachers, teaching interns, and paraprofessionals (including teacher aides, clerical aides, and technicians) enhances the instructional program.

PLANNING AND USING SCHOOL FACILITIES

Goals. Whether middle school youngsters are to be blessed with a brand new school or housed in a traditional building, a major goal of the plant is to provide for maximum flexibility whereby space is adaptable to the multidimensional, interdisciplinary program of learning. The ideal is a stimulating environment that challenges transescents to develop and fully use their five senses as they set about establishing a system of interrelationships with one another and with their environment. A contrast of colors, textures, and light, as well as a balance in spatial dimensions, relief and solid structures, and auditory effects, can make the school aesthetically satisfying. That middle schoolers like their school and find it a pleasant place to work and play in is a goal worthy of carefully planned efforts.

Plans:

1. Through representative and cooperative planning, teachers and students can contribute ideas for a new building or for renovations of the old. A teacher who has experienced, along with students, the frustration of insufficient storage space for an important but unfinished project can be persuasive when priorities are established.

2. Each aspect of the facility is evaluated for congruence with middle school beliefs. For instance, it would be difficult to justify enough seating space for interschool athletics in a school that professed to deemphasize competitive sports.

3. In recognition of middle schoolers' need for personal development, large open spaces conducive to social interaction are provided, as well as small private areas for pupil-teacher conferences and counseling. Furniture is arranged to encourage small group interaction.

4. Anticipating a team approach to instruction, multiaged groups of transescents are housed in a quad or pod arrangement in order for the students to identify with a smaller group.

5. Staff members have ample storage, work, and meeting space within their pod, quad, or designated area. The interdisciplinary team approach encourages frequent cooperative planning, and members want to be in close proximity to one another.

6. Students have access to systematized storage areas for learning resources, independent and paired work projects, and in-process endeavors of small and large groups. Opportunities abound in these areas for shared responsibilities in organizing, categorizing, and maintaining materials.

7. Multipurpose areas invite and encourage student participation in creative enterprise, as well as in the world of work. Easy access to these areas encourages experimentation while allowing for depth.

8. Extensive use of the out-of-doors can be an exciting way to implement middle school beliefs and values. Awareness of, and concern for, ecology take on a new meaning for the active transescent as he interacts with the environment beyond the walls of the school.

9. As students and staff spend time in the middle school, they become sensitized to the strengths and weaknesses of their school plant. A periodic charting and recording by a student-faculty committee might look carefully at the use of space within the building: How many students use this area in a week? Has this arrangement ever been changed? How might this area better serve our needs? What really goes on in that space? In addition to learning techniques of data

collection, students are involved in important decision-making processes and designing creative alternatives.

10. A school plant is developed to serve society's learners. In that spirit, middle schoolers can use their school many more hours each day than is the current practice. Resource people from the community and parents who work are often available at night. They provide an excellent opportunity for middle school students to experience authentic relationships with a variety of people—peers and adults!

SECURING COMMUNITY COOPERATION

Goals. Four groups with important abilities and responsibilities play significant roles in the process of developing and implementing a good middle school program: a) students, b) parents, c) citizens of the community at large, and d) the professional staff. The only way to ensure the participation of all concerned groups is to develop an informative community relations program. Involvement, consultation, and continuing dialogue are the necessary components of this program.

Plans:

1. Prior to the opening of the middle school, the professional staff, parents, and selected laymen from the community undertake a year-long study of the concepts important to the development of a good middle school program.

2. During the year-long study, the participants develop relevant documents or gather pertinent data, such as a philosophy, guidelines for selecting the staff, data obtained from an analysis of population, and feedback information from pupils who have gone through other schools in previous years. Participants in this phase of the study might be students presently and previously enrolled, parents, selected laymen, and the professional staff.

3. The planning groups arrive at basic commitments about staffing, organizing the school, and curriculum. The superintendent and members of the school board are especially important in this phase of the planning, as well as those people who participate in the previous two study activities.

4. A strong information and involvement plan for readying the community for the change can be undertaken by the professional staff, selected laymen, and parents. Members of the press, radio, and television are included. Besides PTA meetings, coffee klatches and continental breakfasts are scheduled occasionally. Every opportunity is capitalized on to appear before civic clubs or other groups to explain the concepts of the middle school.

5. A continual orientation plan is maintained after the school opens. Newcomers to the community, instructional personnel from other schools within the system, or visitors from other systems will want to know about the program. A slide-tape presentation may be developed that orients visitors to the program before they are taken on a tour.

6. A plan for involving resource people is a very important component of a community relations program. A questionnaire or survey identifies interests among the students or members of the community, and workshops are scheduled during the school day or in the evenings. Parents and teachers or older students conduct these workshops in, for example, flower arranging, arts and crafts, or bowling.

7. A planned community relations program continues year after year to keep the community informed about the progress of the program and to seek continuing community participation in program development.

PLANNING FOR CONTINUOUS PROGRESS

Goals. Continuous progress plans are built on learning activities that are determined only after data on all phases of growth are considered. These activities are provided on the basis of individual needs, interests, and abilities and are paced at the individual's own rate of learning. Flexibility is a necessity.

Plans:

1. The first step in the process is the preparation of a statement of goals for each curriculum area and for the skills of continued learning.

2. After the overall goals are written, a list of learning objectives is formulated. If learning objectives are already available in some areas, the faculty or team may wish to adapt and adopt them.

3. After objectives are written or selected, teachers find out which objectives pupils have achieved by administering tests keyed to the objectives. Alternatives to tests might be work samples or activities designed to check specific objectives.

4. Appropriate activities for accomplishing the objectives are then planned, involving the use of media, space, equipment, and personnel.

5. Reassessment or postassessment can take the form of a completed project, a teacher-pupil conference, a written test, work samples, or teacher observation as the students are working on activities.

6. A system of multidirectional communication among the teacher, the learner, and the parents for reporting the learner's progress is a task for the faculty, with parental and student help. It may take the form of some type of written report or a parent-student-teacher conference, or both.

7. Adequate record-keeping systems that describe where a student is on a continuum of skills facilitate the reporting to students, parents, and other staff members.

8. Organizing the school into teams facilitates planning. Each team of teachers can zero in on a specific student population, and with common planning time scheduled, they can discuss the students' performance in all areas and develop instructional units that meet the needs and interests of the students on their team and capitalize on each others' strengths.

9. Assigning students by age, with a range of two to four years, is a promising alternative to a graded system. After securing parental consent, put some 10-, 11-, and 12-year-olds together; some 11-, 12-, and 13-year-olds together; and some 12-, 13-, and 14-year-olds together. At the end of the year, compare this procedure for assigning students with the traditional grade level assignment procedure. If steps 1–7 have been followed in the curriculum planning process and if a good teaming relationship has been established, the result is a plan for continuous progress that parents and teachers will like and accept.

EVALUATING LEARNING AND SCHOOLING

Goals. Evaluation in the middle school is a continual process by which information is gathered to find out how well the goals of the organization are being achieved. Some questions to be answered in the evaluation process are: a) How well are the developmental needs of the between-agers being filled? b) How much individualization of curriculum and instruction is being achieved? c) How well is the curriculum providing a planned sequence of concepts in the basic knowledge areas, a major emphasis on interests and skills for continued learning, a balanced program of exploratory experiences, and services for personal development? d) How much continuous progress and smooth articulation is there between the several phases and levels of the total educational program? e) How well are the personnel and facilities available for continued improvement of schooling being used?

Plans:

1. Periodic testing, individual student self-report files, and teachers' and parents' reports provide data to evaluate how well the program is helping the personal development of the transescents.

2. An evaluation team randomly selects student cases throughout the year, determining how much the program is being individualized and adjusted to these students' needs and how much articulation between the different phases of the program is being achieved for each student. Student schedules are checked periodically to discover imbalance.

3. The curriculum coordinator and a curriculum committee maintain a continuing evaluation of the total program, based on the school's stated objectives and utilizing data from the previously mentioned evaluation procedures, plus polls of students, parents, and faculty on specific issues.

4. A personnel and space utilization study is periodically conducted to identify unused, overused, and poorly used resources and facilities.

5. Until teacher preparation programs provide adequate skills in measurement and evaluation, an inservice education program helps teachers acquire the knowledge and skills they need to participate effectively in the planning and evaluation process.

6. Follow-up data are secured from the high school on the continued learning skills of former middle schoolers and on their high school interests, successes, and difficulties. This information is used as basic data for the continuing evaluation outlined in item 3.

RENEWING THE PROGRAM AND STAFF

Goals. Renewal of the program and staff takes two common forms: conversion of a faculty from another, more traditional type of program to a middle school program; and the year-by-year renewal of a regular middle school program and staff. In either case, this period of renewal can be greatly affected by the degree of advance planning that has taken place.

The very nature of the middle school calls for continual planning, whether it takes the form of an annual updating of a regular program or a more basic change from a departmentalized, textbook-centered curriculum to an individualized, continuous progress middle school program. Middle school programs are not fixed but are continually evolving. The changing nature of the learner at this age is paralleled by continual faculty planning.

Basic to changes that involve new staff and programs is planned preparation that allows time for the acceptance of the middle school concept, for teachers' input into the planning and implementation stages, and for an overall emphasis on change at the classroom level.

Plans:

1. Any successful program of renewal spells out in concise language the regular procedures for curriculum development. The role of each contributing part, such as advisory groups and curriculum councils, is detailed.

2. Teachers who will be affected by the change are given sufficient lead time to understand the proposed program and to prepare themselves to become active participants in the change process.

3. Sufficient time and resources are provided so that curricular planning and teacher input are of value to the effort. Resources can take such forms as teacher aides, consultant help, the provision of space and materials, a professional library at the school level, and easy access to duplication services.

4. The scheduling of teacher planning time, if effective, includes the provision of daily team planning periods and some provision for long-range planning.

5. The timing of the transition period is aided by consideration of the change process as a whole, rather than from the perspective of many unrelated parts. For there to be effective coordination of the change effort, a minimum of one year of advance planning is called for.

6. Included in any planning for conversion to the middle school concept is visiting existing middle schools; visits are usually planned to see particular programs and features, and time is provided for interaction with the personnel of the school visited.

7. An effective change effort builds in a regular and organized method of evaluation. Vital to the evaluation program and process is the possibility that the program will reverse itself if it does not seem to be working as planned.

8. Special summer workshops are used to renew existing middle school faculties and for the pilot study of programs envisioned by new middle schools. To be effective, such summer workshops have direct access to children attending regular classroom sessions.

9. Before middle schools are adopted on a systemwide basis, a pilot study utilizing one middle school is conducted. Such pilot studies can prevent large-scale mistakes. Furthermore, within the individual middle school, many new programs, such as activity periods, exploratory courses, team teaching, multiaged grouping, and problem-solving laboratories, are piloted in individual situations before being adapted for schoolwide use.

SEARCHING FOR MIDDLE SCHOOL IDENTITY

Goals. The middle school is a distinct unit in the educational system, bridging the elementary and high schools. As a bridging unit, it has some characteristics of both schools; yet it cannot, and must not, be merely an upward or downward extension of either. Its program must provide for the immature learner, who needs the close guidance of a single teacher, and for the mature learner, who needs the challenge of many specialists; thus the learning opportunities, organization, and schedule must be as flexible as these guidelines have proposed in order to accommodate all the differences in its students. Such a school cannot be classified, accredited, and evaluated by standards designed for the upper or lower schools. Instead, the standards must also accommodate the variety of provisions essential in the bridging school. Its personnel require special training and certification related to the goals of the middle school. But despite the necessary accommodations for its unique goals and programs, the middle school cannot rightly stand as a wholly separate organization. As a bridge that promotes continuity of education, the middle school must be carefully planned and interrelated with both elementary and high schools so as to maintain a single system of continuous schooling.

Plans:

1. The state department of education officially recognizes the middle school, and accreditation programs have been specifically designed for middle schools.

2. Teacher education programs provide special preparation for teachers at the middle school level. These programs include such unique features as a study of theory and research and case studies of transescent children, an extended experience in a good middle school through practicums and internship, competence in more than one subject area, and basic training in the teaching of reading and other learning skills.

3. Where regional accreditation is required of the middle schools, the plan for accreditation is based on unique criteria related to middle school objectives.

4. Middle school planning groups include personnel representing the elementary and high schools, so as to advance continuous schooling aims and maintaining the unique characteristics and objectives of the middle school.

5. Personnel in the middle school continually clarify the definition and program of middle schools and work to eliminate all activities and practices not consistent with the concepts and objectives of the program.

6. Parents and laymen are involved in middle school programs, because their recognition of the concept will eventually legitimize the identity the middle school seeks.

7. Budgetary priorities for the middle school program reflect the objectives of the middle school.

8. The programs of professional organizations provide specific sections for middle school personnel.

USING THE GUIDELINES

The burgeoning middle schools are as yet without special accrediting standards and other fixtures of the established elementary and high schools. This fact should encourage experimentation and flexibility, although it also leaves the middle school with less identity and sanction. To guide experimentation and aid professional organizations and other sanctioning groups to understand and assist the new school organizations, an orderly process of continuing preparation, review, and modification of such guidelines as these seems essential.

This set of guidelines is intended as a possible aid to middle school faculties and other planning groups seeking bases for planning and evaluating their middle schools. They are not intended to be prescriptive or authoritative, but illustrative of the thinking of one planning group about the goals and plans of middle schools. It is hoped that many such guidelines will be developed and shared as a means of moving the middle school program toward identity and sanction.

ADDITIONAL READINGS

ALEXANDER, WILLIAM M., and others. *The Emergent Middle School*. Second edition. New York: Holt, Rinehart and Winston, 1969.

DEVITA, JOSEPH C., PUMERANTZ, PHILIP, and WILKLOW, LEIGHTON, B. *The Effective Middle School*. West Nyack, N.Y.: Parker Publishing Co., 1970.

EICHORN, DONALD H. *The Middle School*. New York: The Center for Applied Research in Education, 1966.

HANSEN, JOHN H., and HEARN, ARTHUR C. *The Middle School Program*. Chicago: Rand McNally, 1971.

MOSS, THEODORE C. *Middle School*. Boston: Houghton Mifflin Co., 1969.

STOREN, HELEN F. *The Disadvantaged Early Adolescent: More Effective Teaching*. New York: McGraw-Hill Book Co., 1968.

Learning and Maturation in Middle School Age Youth

Hershel Thornburg

Of all studied areas of human development, the stage of preadolescence has long been the most neglected. This age range, typically described as 9 to 12 or 10 to 13, is a uniquely awkward range that somehow bridges the gap between childhood and adolescence. It has been expressed as the period of time when the nicest children begin behaving in a most awful way (17).

Children of this age are difficult. Their unconventional mannerisms and their unpredictable behaviors make them a very difficult group to research. Teachers find them uncooperative. Parents find them annoying. In general, it is easier to deal with youth that are either younger or older than with the preadolescent. Yet, this should not fail to make us recognize the need for more knowledge about children within this age range.

Some hope for recognizing and meeting the needs of preadolescents may be found in the emerging middle school. By definition the middle school is a school built to cover the developmental range of late childhood, preadolescence, and early adolescence. It may best be thought of as a "phase and program of schooling bridging but differing from the childhood and adolescent phases and programs (2, p. 5)."

Those who support the middle school feel that the failure of the junior high school to function as a bridging school between childhood and adolescence has forced educators to seek out an alternative. The faults inherent in today's junior high system appear to be twofold: (1) The ninth grade has tended to maintain its philosophical and practical ties with the high school. (2) Many seventh and

From *Clearing House* XLV, no. 3 (November 1970): 150–155. Used by permission of the author and publisher.

eighth grades have still followed an elementary format such as the older 8-4 organizational plan used (7). One additional problem has resulted throughout the years of the 6-3-3 plan. The junior high school has tended to model after the high school. Extracurricular activities, interscholastic athletics, cheerleaders, bands, banquets, and proms, all activities enjoyed during high school, have become a way of life in many junior high schools. There is increasing support by several proponents of the middle school (5, 7, 15) to have the middle school function as a transitional school and leave the above-described activities to the high school.

Eichhorn has tried to justify the middle school organization by advancing the concept of transescence.

> Transescence is the stage of development which begins prior to the onset of puberty and extends through the early stages of adolescence. Since puberty does not occur precisely at the same chronological age in human development, the transescent designation is based on the many physical, social, emotional, and intellectual changes that appear prior to the puberty cycle to the time when the body gains a practical degree of stabilization over these complex changes (7, p. 111).

Granted, there is no specific line separating childhood and adolescence. Rather there are gradual developmental and learning changes involving the physical, intellectual, and social life of youth. Through such maturation and learning, the well-knit pattern of childhood personality is considerably loosened as youths experience identifying behaviors with other youths, and thus move toward adolescence. Alexander (1) found from a sample of middle school programs now in operation that 44.6 percent stated "to provide a program specifically designated for students in this age group" as a reason for establishing such a school. It is not the intent of this article to justify the middle school or describe reasons for its existence. However, since the concept of the middle school program is an increasing one, several developmental and learning tasks which youths encounter during preadolescence are presented to give proponents of the movement a basis to more realistically realize an educational program based on meeting student needs.

(1) DEVELOPING AND ORGANIZING KNOWLEDGE AND CONCEPTS NECESSARY FOR EVERYDAY FUNCTIONING

At ten and eleven years children develop interest in highly organizing and structuring their knowledge. The preadolescent develops a "mode of intellectual functioning" (9, p. 43). The child initially operates toward the end of Piaget's stage of concrete operations. During this stage the individual is capable of reasoning about concrete objects experienced within his environment. By the fifth and sixth grade the preadolescent is not as dependent on immediate concrete objects in systematizing and understanding basic ideas about relevant phenomena and objects. Once the meaning of an object is established through experience, the 10- to 11-year-old is capable of comprehending it without any current reference to the concrete object. Therefore, the intellect has developed to the point where it is increasingly independent of concrete objects, which suggests that the individual is ready for more advanced intellectual thought.

Within the structure of the middle school, learning experiences can be guided for youth so that there is easier transition to advanced stages of thought.

Thus, by grades seven and eight, most students should be capable of reasoning about hypotheses and deducing conclusions, two characteristics of Piaget's stage of formal operations. Now all information which was ordered, organized, or structured within the mind is characterized by more flexible thinking and sets the basis for the ability to deal with reality.

One of the things that facilitates these increasing intellectual functions is an enlargement of interests within the preadolescent. Through his own intellectual curiosity, the preadolescent now becomes an experimenter. Particular academic subjects interest a youth and he has increasing tendencies to check them out. This promotes moving out of the realm of fantasy and questioning, and into the realm of experimentation and reality. Thus, his social and physical world take on increasing significance.

How may the middle school provide for a greater realization of this task with youth? First, ten- and eleven-year-old's intelligence functions on a junior high school level more so than on an elementary plane. Therefore, if students ages 10 to 13 fall within the same general period of intellectual development, it seems reasonable to develop an educational program in a manner more suitable to their needs and abilities. Thus, a middle school program with a more highly organized curriculum, staffed with teachers who are specialists in their discipline (5), can better realize student needs and abilities.

(2) ACCEPTING INCREASING CHANGES IN ONE'S PHYSIQUE

Preadolescents begin experiencing several physiological changes during the transitional period of childhood to adolescence. The term "pubescence" is applied to such changes and indicates that the body is rapidly approaching puberty which is characterized by sexual maturation.

Physically the average girl has her growth spurt after 10 with the peak being reached around 12. Girls experience the beginning of breast development about 10.5 years, pubic hair development around 11, and menarche about 12. Approximately 80 percent of all girls reach menarche between 11.5 and 14.5 years (14). Boys initially experience growth in the testes and penis around 12 and pigmented hair at 13. Involuntary rigidity of the penis and irregular seminal emissions may be experienced at this age. All such activities are part of the male growth spurt which begins about 12.5 and peaks around age 14 (20).

Throughout the age range represented by the middle schools virtually all youths will experience significant physical changes. To reduce anxiety, it is helpful if they have an awareness of what physiological changes will take place. Research has shown that they are concerned about their height, weight, fatness, thinness, and facial features. Of special concern to girls is largeness or smallness of the hips and breasts. Boys are similarly concerned about the largeness or smallness of the genitals (3). If preadolescents are made aware that different rates of growth are not abnormal, they can learn to accept their physique better. The middle school could help them learn this if it can put physical and physiological changes into a normal developmental context for its students.

(3) LEARNING NEW SOCIAL-SEX ROLES

Our culture sets patterns of accepted social behaviors throughout childhood and adolescence. In early childhood, this has meant aggressiveness in boys and dependency in girls. Boys are expected to be rough, active, adventurous, and rugged. On the other hand, girls are expected to be docile, ladylike, and interested in household or domestic type activities. Through perpetuation the sex roles unfolded into the traditional work role for men and the wife-mother role for women.

In today's society, some varying social-sex roles are being suggested. By preadolescence most youngsters have had exposure to role behaviors that are not as distinctly masculine or feminine as they once were. The hair of little girls is shorter and of little boys is longer. Both have learned to play and accept mannequin dolls, i.e., G.I. Joe and Barbie. In the case of girls, Barbie represents a sexy teen-ager who is involved in all types of social events as her diversified and descriptive wardrobe indicates. While it is hardly fair to give Barbie credit for accelerating female social interest, it is true that one's fantasies may later be transferred more readily to reality if such fantasies have been rewarding.

What today's 10- to 13-year-old is faced with is an increasing unisexuality, and an accelerated flexibility for women in American social structure. The effect has been felt in the emergence of one's sex role. Now less distinct masculine-feminine roles exist in our society. Most positively affected has been less emphasis on the developing girl to accept the traditional wife-mother role.

It is not intended to minimize the importance of identifying with contemporaries of the same sex. But, it is suggested that preadolesence is not the period of quietly accepting one's own sex role as it was once. Earlier socialization has brought about change. The most accelerated has been female aggressiveness (18) and earlier heterosexual involvement. Havighurst (12) suggested that around 13 or 14 most boys and girls become preoccupied with social activities with more intimate companionships, i.e., double-dating, with couple-dating following. Still, there are increasing indications that today group social activities begin around 11 or 12 with more selective dating following (19). Research indicates that many preadolescents are feeling pressures from their parents and peers to be involved heterosexually by grade six (13). Perhaps the task of learning new social-sex roles is more difficult for girls than boys. While it is quite obvious that learning appropriate social-sex roles will not be totally realized during the middle school period, there is no doubt that what is learned during this period will have significant effects on the emerging adolescent and eventually emerging adult.

It is quite possible that the middle school movement may contribute to earlier adolescent socialization. While it is not possible to determine what the social impact might be, it is certainly possible that having 10- to 13-year-olds together will increase earlier socialization (19). This effect will be most likely determined by the philosophy of the school district. If the intent is to build a mini-high school, then it is most certain that earlier socialization will result. On the other hand, if the middle school emerges as a new school geared to the social, educational, and physical needs of its pupils, then early socialization will not be accentuated and emerging social-sex roles may be more realistically realized.

(4) DEVELOPING FRIENDSHIPS WITH PEERS

Most peer relationships that are formed during preadolescence are with those of the same sex. Typically boys express a dislike for girls, and girls shows a general lack of concern that boys are in their environment. Most close friends are of the same sex. With this group preadolescents learn to get along. On a general basis "they form teams, committees, and clubs and are very much aware of the personalities of people their own age" (11, p. 121). The importance of pre-adolescent peer groups should not be underrated. They, too, feel many of their behaviors being shaped by their peers. "Even though children may resist inwardly or feel threatened, they attempt to produce the behavior they think the group expects of them" (10, p. 223).

The initial stage of peer development is formed among isolated unisexual cliques. It is considered isolated in terms of any relationship with corresponding groups of the opposite sex. Dunphy (6) suggests that this represents the persistence of the preadolescent gang into the adolescent period. As preadolescents move into grades seven and eight, their peer associates may begin becoming heterosexual, although on a more limited basis than in later adolescence. Such heterosexual interaction is often done cautiously and is often only undertaken within the security of group settings where members of the same sex are also present.

The middle school could provide a structural framework where its students can develop meaningful and cooperative relationships with peers. This can be facilitated by (1) stressing the importance of socialization with members of the same sex and (2) by allowing heterosexual group activity to evolve out of the students own natural development and personal interests. It seems important that in forming peer relations pre- and early-adolescents feel they are not being forced into such roles. Within the conceptualized middle school it may be possible to create this kind of environment better than in the existing junior high school where many social activities approximate high school behaviors.

(5) BECOMING AN INDEPENDENT PERSON

This task has been described by Havighurst (11) as the time when pre-adolescent youth are expected to become physically independent. He stresses that this should not be equated with emotional independence but that it is strictly physical independence. Havighurst asserts that such independence is obtaining the ability to be away from home at night or go to a summer camp without being terribly homesick or needing mother in his environment.

The preadolescent should begin looking upon himself as a maturing in-dividual and look upon adults as adults. He should see his parents in a new relationship. While maintaining such emotional dependency, the preadolescent should not exercise blind faith in his parents such as he did during childhood. In the process of normal development he gradually begins exercising his right to make choices. While his behavior may become increasingly independent of adults, such behavior should not be misconstrued by adults to think that he is independent and does not need guidance and continued support. Rather adults, i.e., teachers and parents, should recognize the preadolescent's growing concern of making choices and provide for him suitable experiences that allow the gradual acquisition of independence.

How might the middle school help its students with this task? First, by definition, it should provide a more independent and complex structure than the elementary school. Secondly, since its functions are transitional, it should provide a less complex model than the existing junior high school although it may be highly departmentalized. Havighurst (11) makes an important point here. He has observed that not all youngsters 10 to 12 years have enough self-control to get along in this structure. He sees the middle school requiring of its students the ability to adapt one's behavior to a variety of situations. Therefore, quite realistically, Havighurst has pointed up one real test for the middle school—the ability to solve the problems of motivation and method so that this complex structure might aid in the process of becoming an independent person.

(6) DEVELOPING ELEMENTARY MORAL CONCEPTS AND VALUES

As the preadolescent begins identifying more with his peers, and adult identity declines, there is a shift in the way in which conscience develops. Children between the ages of 10 and 13 can make much progress in reasoning, sympathy, esthetic sense, love, and morality. These youth can now learn a greater regard for truth and fairness, especially within the activities of peer groups. Then as youths move out of preadolescence into adolescence, they can better begin assuming increasing self-responsibility and increasing responsibility to peer, school, and community activities.

In today's society much stress is being placed on individuality. Accompanying individuality should be self-responsibility. The middle school is in a good position to assist students in this task. Through departmentalization, students can learn responsibilities through many different academic and social approaches, since they are exposed to several different teachers and students in one day's time.

Probably the most detrimental factor to the student's learning this task is the effect of adult moralizing. Many teachers attempt to deal with stealing, lying, laziness, cruelty, and bullying by moralizing with the student. "Good" wins rewards and "bad" suffers consequences. If teachers are really interested in helping youths develop moral concepts and values, they might better help children "(1) make free choices whenever possible, (2) search for alternatives in choice-making decisions, (3) weigh the consequences of each available alternative, (4) consider what they prize and cherish, (5) affirm the things they value, (6) do something about their choices, and (7) consider and strengthen patterns in their lives" (16, p. 47). The flexibility of the middle school potentially makes this possible.

CONCLUSION

Discussion has focused on the physical, intellectual, and social development of 10- to 13-year-old youths during their transitional period from childhood to adolescence. Six maturational and learning tasks have been described as occurring during this age range. The ability for the middle school child to cope with these tasks and realize as many of them as possible should strengthen his ability to acquire increasingly more complex maturation and learning tasks during adolescence. Learning to cope with bodily changes, exercise a new mode of intellectual functioning, and taking steps to be a person in his own right presents a tremendous challenge to the youngster from 10 to 13. The challenge is significantly as great to the emerging middle school to develop and implement an educational program which will foster greater maturation and learning on the part of its students.

BIBLIOGRAPHY

(1) ALEXANDER, WILLIAM M., "The Middle School Movement," *Theory into Practice*, 1968, 7(3), 114–117.

(2) ALEXANDER, WILLIAM M., EMMETT I. WILLIAMS, MARY COMPTON, VYNCE A. HINES, and DAN PRESCOTT, *The Emergent Middle School*. New York: Holt, Rinehart and Winston, 1968.

(3) ANGELINO, HENRY, and EDMUND V. MECH, "Fears and Worries Concerning Physical Changes: A Preliminary Survey of 32 Females," *Journal of Psychology*, 1955, 39, 195–198.

(4) BRECKENRIDGE, MARIAN E., and E. LEE VINCENT, *Child Development*. Philadelphia: W. B. Saunders, 1960.

(5) DI VIRGILIO, JAMES, "Switching from Junior High to Middle School?" *The Clearing House*, 1969, 44, 224–226.

(6) DUNPHY, DEXTER C., "The Social Structure of Urban Adolescent Peer Groups," *Sociometry*, 1963, 26, 230–246.

(7) EICHHORN, DONALD H., "Middle School Organization: A New Dimension," *Theory into Practice*, 1968, 7(3), 111–113.

(8) EICHHORN, DONALD H., *The Middle School*. New York: Center for Applied Research in Education, 1966.

(9) FLAVELL, JOHN, *The Developmental Psychology of Jean Piaget*. Princeton: Van Nostrand, 1963.

(10) GORDON, IRA, *Human Development: From Birth Through Adolescence*. New York: Harper and Row, 1962.

(11) HAVIGHURST, ROBERT J., "The Middle School Child in Contemporary Society," *Theory into Practice*, 1968, 7(3), 120–122.

(12) HAVIGHURST, ROBERT J., *Developmental Tasks and Education*. New York: Longmans, Green, and Company, 1952.

(13) MARTINSON, FLOYD M., "Sexual Knowledge, Values, and Behavior Patterns of Adolescents," *Child Welfare*, 1968, 47, 405–410.

(14) MEREDITH, HOWARD V., "A Synopsis of Puberal Changes in Youth," *Journal of School Health*, 1967, 37, 171–176.

(15) OESTREICH, ARTHUR H., "Middle School in Transition," *The Clearing House*, 1969, 44, 91–95.

(16) RATHS, LOUIS E., MERRILL HARMIN, and SIDNEY B. SIMON, *Values and Teaching*. Columbus, Ohio: Charles E. Merrill, 1966.

(17) REDL, FRITZ, "Pre-adolescents—What Makes Them Tick," *Child Study*, 1944, 21, 44–48.

(18) REISS, IRA L., *Premarital Sexual Standards in America*. Glencoe, Ill.: Free Press, 1960.

(19) THORNBURG, HERCHEL D., "Adolescence: A Re-interpretation," *Adolescence*, 1970 (in press).

(20) WINTER, GERALD D., "Physical Changes During Adolescence," in *The Young Adult*. G. D. Winter and E. M. Nuss (eds.). Glenview, Ill.: Scott, Foresman, 1969.

Values Clarification in Junior High School

Mildred W. Abramowitz
Claudia Macari

Do I have to go to the streets to get changes?
Does it make any difference to our government what I do?
Does religion have any meaning for me?
Should I follow what my parents do in religion?
How can I make school more meaningful?
How can I make better use of weekends?
How do I know where to draw the line on a date?
What is there to talk about in my family?
Jack was a close friend. Now we pass each other without a word to say. What
   happened?
How can I get money to work for me instead of my working for it?
What should I believe about drugs? diet? eggs? meat? mercury?
How should I wear my hair? Should I grow a beard?

These are just a few of the questions young people are asking today, and, of course, they are not just for the young but for all of us.

If young people were to come to you for help with these questions, could you answer them?

They are the big questions in our lives, and only we can answer them for ourselves. Schools have not been very helpful. They have not given us the tools to answer them. The *values clarification* approach is one attempt to give young people the tools to answer—a chance to shape their lives.

THE KEY QUESTIONS

Adolescents are living in a very confusing world where they must continually make choices regarding their attitudes and actions in politics, religion, work, school, leisure, love and sex, family, friends, spending of money, health, and personal taste. These are all areas of confusion and conflict for them, because things are changing so fast that they have great difficulty in looking to the past for the "proper" way to behave. They have few established models. They are asking questions; and as they weigh what their parents say and do, what their friends say and do, and what their teachers say and do, they find uncertainty, incon-

Mildred W. Abramowitz and Claudia Macari. "Values Clarification in the Junior High School." *Educational Leadership* 29(7):621–26; April 1972. Reprinted with permission of the Association for Supervision and Curriculum Development and Abramowitz and Macari. Copyright © 1972 by the Association for Supervision and Curriculum Development.

sistency, and even no answers at all to the key questions of their lives. They flounder for answers by themselves, and our schools have not been very helpful in developing the processes to help them get the answers.

Traditionally, schools have tried to impose values, or they have tried to ignore the whole problem, or they have said that it is not an area of their concern but that of parents and the church. Yet in this day of rapid change, adolescents are confronted with many different points of view, and they are then left to sort them out. The purpose of the values clarification approach is to give pupils experience in valuing to enable them to answer the questions that really concern them. It is important to pupils that schools are concerned with what they regard as personally important to them, as well as with their traditional role of passing on the achievements of the past.

Values are not readily transmitted, but they can be learned. If one accepts the idea that values cannot effectively be taught, but that they can be learned, one moves from moralizing and inculcating toward a process of value-clarification. Value-clarification involves a series of strategies which are not guilty of forcing one set of right values down the throats of all students. Instead, the process tends to raise issues, to confront the student with inconsistencies, and to get him to sort out his own values, in his own way, and at his own pace. The practice of this approach and the theory on which it is based have been developed over a number of years by Louis Raths, Merrill Harmin, and Sidney Simon. A full presentation can be found in the book *Values and Teaching*[1] and in *New Strategies in Values Clarification.*[2]

In our school we are interested in values clarification teaching as one way to help our pupils know what they feel about what happens to them in the course of a day. We believe that thinking is accompanied by feeling, and we would like to experiment with ways of taking advantage of this so that pupils can be helped to answer the questions: Who am I? Where am I going? What do I care about? Is this what I want to do? What alternatives do I have? Which choice is wisest for me? We think that being able to answer such questions would make life more meaningful to our boys and girls, and in the process would help to make school a place where they would grow and where their lives would be affected.

Sidney Simon says that "it turns out that most people have very few values."[3] Values clarification teaching is based on the seven criteria for the determination of a value developed by Louis Raths. Raths' contribution was unique, in that he was not interested so much in the content of the value (whether materialistic or spiritual) but was interested in the process whereby a value came about. He said a value started with a belief you were proud of and were willing to affirm, where you had chosen it from alternatives with regard to possible consequences and free from outside pressure to choose any particular thing, and where you had taken action on this belief other than to talk about it and had done this in a

[1] L. E. Raths, M. Harmin, and S. Simon. *Values and Teaching.* Columbus, Ohio: Charles E. Merrill Publishing Company, 1966.
[2] S. Simon et al. *Values Clarification: A Handbook of Practical Strategies for Teachers and Students.* New York: Hart Publishing Co., 1972.
[3] Sidney Simon. "Promoting the Search for Values." *Educational Opportunity Forum* 1 (4):84; Fall 1969. Special issue on Psychological Humanistic Education. Albany: New York State Education Department.

regular pattern, not just at sporadic times. Value-indicators are people's beliefs, attitudes, morals, activities, interests, feelings, goals, and aspirations; but they are not values unless they meet the seven criteria. We may have many value-indicators, which are certainly good things to have, but very few values.

The theory further states that people with very few values tend to be con-forming, apathetic, inconsistent, and often very ambivalent, all of which seems quite sad when one realizes the extent to which values should guide a man's life. This argues strongly for the school's taking a more active part in the clarifi-cation of values. There are few areas in the affective domain about which there is so much talk and so little action as there is with values. The valuing process weaves together critical thinking and affective education in a functional and relevant program.

Our ideas, methods, and inspiration were given to us by Sidney Simon of the University of Massachusetts and his colleague, Howard Kirschenbaum, the director of Adirondack Mountain Humanistic Education Center. We attended several of their workshops and worked with five classes and ten members of our faculty during the school year 1970–71. This current school year (1971–72) we are conducting a teachers workshop in our own school during the school day, and we are also working with three classes for demonstration and practice pur-poses. One of these classes was with us last year, and we are planning to continue with this class for a third year.

William W. Niles Junior High School is located in a disadvantaged area in the Bronx. The student body is 60 percent Puerto Rican and 40 percent Black, and the pupils are familiar with the problems of perpetual mobility, broken homes, absent fathers, drugs, and violence in the streets and in the home. Achievement is low in reading, writing, and oral expression. Admissions and dis-charges result in a one-third turnover in the course of a school year. Literacy in any language is a problem. The boys and girls are, on the average, more than two and a half years retarded in reading and in mathematics when they come to us from elementary school. The school is well thought of and well liked in the community because it has a concerned faculty that works hard at teaching and at establishing warm relationships with children and parents and to foster self-discipline so that teachers can concentrate on teaching.

Specific structured techniques have been designed to accomplish the goals of values clarification teaching. Some of these are described here.

STRATEGIES

The strategies which were presented to our students were employed for the purpose of stimulating thinking and of making them aware of the processes of values clarification. Students were encouraged to take a stand on what they be-lieved, declare it publicly, make their choice freely, and to act upon it. However, the right of the student to "pass" on any strategy was respected and protected. It is necessary to have the right not to say anything. Whatever was said by the student was accepted with no sign of condemnation, rejection, or ridicule. The task of not commenting or of controlling one's facial expression is the most dif-ficult of all. It is only in a free and relaxed atmosphere of mutual respect and acceptance that the pupils can express themselves and think about where they stand and how they feel and how they will act upon issues that affect their lives.

The following strategies are some examples of those used in our classes:

1. *I love to do.* Students were asked to write 20 things they love to do. (Incidentally, all written work is absolutely private and is only shared with others if the student wants to.)

The procedure that followed was:

1. Star the five things you love to do best of all.
2. Place a check after the things you love to do alone.
3. Place a cross after the things you love to do with other people.
4. Circle the things that cost you less than $3 to do.
5. Write the date of the last time you did each of these 20 things.

This strategy gives the student some insight into what is important to him. It reveals his needs for companionship or his lack of it, pleasures which may cost very little, and helps him to evaluate the way he spends his time.

2. *Alternative search.* There are times when our students are stymied and frustrated by situations and incidents in their lives. They are overwhelmed by the feeling that they do not know where to go or how to act and that they inevitably have to bow to circumstances or fight without direction or reason. Students must be trained to examine a situation and consider all possible alternatives.

For example, the following problem is given to the students as a strategy for alternative search:

You are walking home and as you approach the building in which you live, you see a man and a woman standing in a doorway. They are arguing loudly and violently. Suddenly the man pulls the woman by the hair and slaps her face, punches her in the eye. She screams again and again and calls for help.

Directions: Form a group of three people. Each person will say in turn one action he would take in this situation. One person will record what is being said. All answers are to be accepted without comment or criticism no matter how ridiculous or impossible they may seem. This is a way of brainstorming. Do not judge or evaluate the ideas given in this search for alternatives.

After this is done, we ask the person who has recorded the alternatives to share with us what has been said by the trio.

It is through this that students realize that people may think and act in the same manner, or that there are many different ways to try to resolve a problem, or that there are always possible solutions to every problem if we consider alternatives. It will also indicate to what extent a person will allow himself to become involved with other people and what feelings and ideas he is protecting.

3. *Values voting.* This is a strategy that allows a student to indicate his feelings and thoughts publicly on any questions asked of him and to see how others feel about the same things. It emphasizes that people differ. This is a time when he can give an answer without being told that he is right or wrong.

His opinion on an issue is respected. The value of this strategy in the development of self-confidence is immeasurable.

Directions: The teacher explains that a vote will be taken on 10 questions and each student will show how he feels or thinks about the subject by doing the following: positive answer—raise hands; negative answer—thumbs down; neutral or pass—fold arms.

If the student feels strongly about the subject, he may shake his hand vigorously up or down as the case may be.

All questions must begin with "How many of you." Some examples of questions are:

1. How many of you follow a religion?
2. How many of you are happy in school?
3. How many of you are honest all the time?
4. How many of you have a best friend?
5. How many of you are in favor of war?
6. How many of you choose your own clothes?
7. How many of you feel loved?
8. How many of you think sex education should be taught in school?
9. How many of you would like to live the rest of your life where you are living now?
10. How many of you think a family should be limited in size?

After the questions have been asked, the teacher can ask several students to share their feelings about a particular question and give reasons for voting as they did. This, of course, is on a voluntary basis. This strategy is a learning experience for the teacher because he is in close contact with feelings and ideas and values that his students are revealing. It is also a form of public affirmation of what he prizes or cherishes. It is up to the teacher to incorporate these in his teaching. Those questions where big differences occur can lead to good class discussions. After the first session, students are encouraged to bring in their own questions to have the class vote on them.

4. *Continuum.* The continuum is another device to get our students to examine how they stand or feel about issues at a particular moment in time. This shows how people are the same or differ, and that there are many different positions on an issue. The position a student chooses on a continuum is not fixed. A student may change his mind due to certain experiences and reexamination of his feelings. In that case he will change his position on the continuum.

Directions: A line is drawn and two opposite ideas are put on each end of the line. Pupils take a position on this line which represents where they stand on the issue at that moment. They may not use the center—this is reserved for "compulsive moderates."

For example, if the subject is School Marks, the continuum may appear as follows:

Mable Marks.........☐..........Gradeless George

The student is told to put his mark at the place he stands on this line.

Continuum on Draft Dodger Dan..........☐..........Eager Egbert

Continuum on Medicine Pillbox Pauline..........☐.......... Natural Nell

Students are encouraged to think about their answers and to make any changes in position they wish to at subsequent sessions. They are made to feel free to change their position as they weigh more evidence. The value here is that students may see how their peers think and feel. Sharing the same experience draws the group together and gives it the comforting feeling of not being alone. This strategy can be the forerunner of exciting discussions.

5. *Rank order.* This strategy involves decision making, evaluating, weighing consequences, judging, in a very realistic way. The student has to become totally involved in the problem at hand because he has important choices to make.

> *Directions:* The student is given three statements and he must choose which would be hardest for him to do or tolerate as a first choice; second choice, less hard; third choice, easiest for him to do or tolerate.
> 1. Three "things" that some men do that people do not like:
> a. A man who always interrupts his wife, finishes her story, contradicts her.
> b. A man who lies around watching TV all day.
> c. A man who smokes a pack of cigarettes a day.
> 2. You are on a Congressional Committee in Washington, D.C. $10,000,000 has been given for three worthy causes. Which would you do first, second, third? You must spend all the money on one thing.
> a. Use the money to clean up rivers, garbage, sewage, pollution.
> b. Train those who do not have jobs.
> c. Divide the money among 10,000 needy families.
> 3. Which would you find hardest to do?
> a. Drop a bomb on Vietnam?
> b. Electrocute a man who has been judged to die in the electric chair?
> c. Run over someone who is threatening you with harm while you are driving your car?

This strategy allows the student to compare his thinking to that of his classmates. If they feel as he does, he feels reinforced. If the thinking is different from his, he can examine the issue and reevaluate his own thinking if necessary.

A variation of this strategy is to have the students list what they think might be other types of behavior that men practice that they do not like; or to list other worthy causes on which to spend $10,000,000. Any of the Rank Order Strategies might be the takeoff point for a social studies lesson, a science lesson, or an English lesson.

The few strategies we have used for demonstration purposes are just a sample of the many that have been developed. It is through these devices that our students learn to think critically in deciding what their values are. They learn to accept them, and, at the same time, to respect and tolerate other people's values.

A BETTER RAPPORT

We have been working with the values clarification approach for only nine months, and yet we see many benefits for pupils, teachers, and administrators.

Pupils have felt warmth and there has been evidence of the development of mutual trust. Students like the personal attention, the relaxation, the period of "fun," the freedom to express their ideas and feelings. Discipline problems seem to disappear. Pupils feel important and they see their teachers and administrators as human beings with the usual "ups" and "downs" of human beings. They hear that other pupils have the same problems and confusions and conflicts that they do. They hear their ideas and thoughts being accepted without either praise or condemnation.

Teachers and administrators have experienced a better understanding and a better rapport with each other and with pupils whom they can see as fellow humans. They have shared experiences with each other and with pupils and have become more aware of each other. Teachers have many opportunities to really "listen" to each other and to pupils and to build a group feeling among themselves and pupils.

Our main problem has been to contend with "killer" statements—efforts by some pupils to put each other down by ridicule, laughter, or jeering. Since we are living in a "put-down" society where all of us find it difficult to speak openly and freely of a person's strong points, we have really had to do much thinking about how to stop this at least during class time. We are also living with a society that has had the biblical ethic that "pride goeth before a fall" ingrained in it, so that all of us think that to be proud of something will hurt us; and even if we do feel proud, we keep it to ourselves. We are working on how to handle this and have seen enough success to encourage us. "Put-down" remarks and lack of self-esteem are both very characteristic of the kind of children we are working with, and this, of course, intensifies the problem.

There are authorities who doubt that values clarification work can be done with ghetto children at all. The feeling is that until basic emotional needs are met, pupils will not be able to look at their values. We understand this point of view, but we feel we have seen enough success of the type described in the previous paragraph to continue our experimentation with enthusiasm. Perhaps we will not be able to go as far with our youngsters as we could with middle class children, but we will have begun the difficult process of getting pupils to decide for themselves what they value and take steps to live the lives they would like to live.

Our Eighth Graders Tackled Air Pollution

Julie Brown Coleman

"What can eighth graders do about air pollution?" queried my American history class. We devoted a day each week to current events, and my students were becoming increasingly disturbed about the pollution problem. However, they also felt that no one would pay any attention to their ideas on the subject.

I indicated that I would show them how they could do something effective about air pollution *if* they were willing to assume extra work in addition to their regular assignments. The class voted unanimously in favor of a special pollution project, and we started work immediately. (This group also had me for English, and, because our English class came just before lunch, and history, immediately afterward, we could spend two-and-a-half hours a day together.)

First, the class divided into four groups. One was to create an overall plan for our project; the second, to secure outside consultants on air pollution; the third, to supervise letter writing; and the fourth, to coordinate poster-making activities.

The results of our first day's meetings almost made me wish we had not undertaken the project. The planning group suggested that we go to see some sources of pollution. They reasoned that since we were together for two-and-a-half hours a day, we should be able to leave the school and visit establishments in our area that were spewing large amounts of pollutants into the air.

Usually, outside trips were not undertaken at our school because pupils scatter each period to pursue individual schedules. However, I agreed to speak to the principal and found that he was so enthusiastic about the project that he was willing to obtain a school bus for the trip.

Much to our delight, the mayor of Billings, the first outside speaker we contacted, agreed to come to school and spend an hour talking about the pollution problems in our city. After his talk, the class planned a trip to the next city council meeting so that they could see for themselves the lawmakers of our city.

Students had to find their own means of transportation to attend this meeting, since the council meets at night, but attendance was good, nonetheless. We went early in order to consult with the city sanitarian about the severity of pollution in Billings and to see slides showing specific pollution problems.

The next consultant who spoke to the class was an ardent conservationist, a professor from Eastern Montana College. He is a dynamic speaker, and when he had finished talking, the students were so enthusiastic about fighting pollution

From *Today's Education* LIX, no. 2 (February 1970):60–61. Used by permission of the author and publisher.

that they were primed for some activity. At the time, the citizens of Billings were trying to establish an Air Pollution Control Board with Yellowstone County and Laurel, and our speaker suggested that students pass petitions door-to-door to gain support for the project.

I cringed as he spoke. What would some parents say about their children circulating petitions? I was almost hoping everyone would forget about the idea, but the next day a stack of petitions arrived, and the students were eager to start getting signatures.

I decided to have in hand a written permission slip from a parent before allowing any student to circulate a petition. Only two parents refused to let their children participate, and most were enthusiastic about the idea. One mother of a slow achiever wrote that her daughter ". . . gets up eagerly these days and no longer dreads going to school. She can't wait to see what the class is going to do next."

While circulating petitions, the students learned some valuable lessons. They were amazed to find out that many adults don't know and/or don't care about pollution. Some children and their parents had spirited discussions at home, and one reported, "I told my dad I didn't care if he wanted to sit back and do nothing. I don't want my children growing up in an atmosphere where they won't even be able to breathe."

In English class, we turned to letter writing, and the students eagerly sought assignments. The Letter-Writing Committee drew up a list of people to contact, including the editors of newspapers, automobile and airplane manufacturers, oil refiners (we have three refineries in our area), the manager of the local steam plant, city councilmen, school board members (some of the schools still use incinerators), the governor, and the President.

Names generated more names. The Secretary of the U.S. Department of Health, Education, and Welfare was added to the list. So was the Surgeon General. The class researched further in the library so that they could write to more people involved with air-pollution control on the state and federal levels.

When answers started to arrive, we soon had a bulletin board full of letters with impressive signatures and a great deal of worthwhile information, which we later donated to the library.

Then, the committees decided that we were ready for our trip to a local oil refinery and the steam plant. In order to make these visits in two-and-a-half hours, we took sack lunches and gulped them down on the bus between stops.

When the students learned that the oil refinery's pollution-control equipment wasn't working the day we visited and that the manager of the steam plant felt his company's lack of pollution-control devices was justified on the grounds of economy, they asked some pointed questions. At the steam plant, the public relations man, who was sitting next to me, wondered aloud defensively, "What has history got to do with air pollution anyway?"

After our field trip, the poster committee went to work. Members assigned each student the task of drawing three posters, which they then placed in stores and offices all over town.

The final assignment of the unit was a compilation and evaluation of the project. I had asked each student to keep a diary to record his activities during the project, and they used these in writing evaluations of our study.

Not only did the students have fun working on our air-pollution project, but they acquired a proficiency in planning, in letter writing, and in understanding our governmental structure. They also became avid newspaper readers.

After school started this past fall, a stream of students trailed into my room to report about events related to air pollution that had occurred during the summer. And when a local refinery announced a million-dollar expenditure for pollution-control devices, one of the boys came running to me, crying, "Look what we did!"

Individualized Science for the Slow Learner

Therald P. Quayle

David returned the laboratory kit to the shelf. He had just completed the last laboratory activity listed on his guide sheet. He and three of his classmates then moved quickly to a conference area to review their objectives in preparation for the self-test on the unit.

As I observed this happy group going about their activities, I reflected back to other less fortunate "Davids" of a few short years ago. David and those with him today are all considered slow learners. But in our present science program, they don't have to keep up with the "average" pace, as determined by the teacher. They move at a rate that is comfortable to them, and thus they aren't bewildered or overwhelmed by the content of the material or by the pace required to cover it.

In an attempt to help our slow learners, we in the Science Department first tried ability grouping but abandoned it because we found that the students who were pigeonholed in the slow learner group began looking on themselves as "dummies."

Again we tackled the problem, and our discussions led us to agree that it would be inadvisable to lump all slow learners into one group. We found considerable fluctuation in the achievement of many of the individuals classified as slow learners: Students so classified one year were able to do regular work the following year.

As a result of our findings, we began a team teaching project aimed at providing a unified, concept- and laboratory-centered program for science in grades 7–9. By so doing, we hoped to overcome the problem of freezing a student into a particular level or grouping. And we set up a track system to allow students to work at various ability levels, using last quarter's grades as a criterion for placing students on specific tracks.

From *Today's Education* LIX, no. 3 (March 1970):50–52. Used by permission of the author and publisher.

When evidence kept cropping up that the track system was only partially successful (our criterion for placement proved faulty), we finally realized that we were still grouping the students. Then and there we decided to enable the students to do their own grouping by placing them in a program where they could progress at a rate and level commensurate with their ability.

In our initial attempts to set up an individualized program, we found the need for a guide that could be placed in the hands of each individual student. After many trials and revisions, we devised the following model for our present student guide sheet: title, behavioral objectives, reading, notebook, laboratory activities, conference, evaluation, supplementary and enrichment activities.

The specific behavioral objectives listed on the student guide sheet follow the criteria as outlined by Robert F. Mager in *Preparing Instructional Objectives:*

1. What the learner should be able to do at the completion of the guide sheet
2. The conditions under which he will be examined
3. The extent (or level) to which he will be required to achieve.

Essentially, this program allows each student to become involved in the processes of science in such a manner that he will enjoy a reasonable degree of success and thus develop an enthusiastic, confident attitude.

Reading frequently presents a formidable hurdle to many students, who either cannot read at all or tend to shy away from it. To overcome this, instead of using a regular textbook, we have many books available for use in the classroom and, through our science curriculum center, for use at home. In addition to the books, we have tape-recorded excerpts from the textbooks for the slow readers so that each may then follow along in the text while the voice on the tape reads the words. We also make available to the slow learner a wide variety of colorful pamphlets that appeal strongly to him.

The notebook is designed to be easy for students to keep up and concentrates on developing concepts by use of a few key questions and/or important vocabulary words.

The heart of the program is the laboratory, into which the student moves after a brief amount of reading and notebook work. He completes his laboratory activities with a group of two or three other students who are at the same point in their work. We plan to have some of the more difficult laboratory activities take place in carrels where students can hear tape-recorded instructions and follow them.

In addition to the laboratory, conferences provide an opportunity for small groups of students to interact. We encourage students to discuss with each other the problems they encounter. The behavioral objectives on each guide sheet provide fuel for such discussions. These informal conference sessions usually involve from two to six students. The teacher's role is to assist, to instruct, and to pose problems to the students as needed. It is here that students receive most of their formal instruction, which is geared to what they need when they need it.

In all of their activities, the students have help and guidance. Informal evaluation is an ongoing process. The teacher can compliment a student for handling equipment properly or he can point out any mistakes that are being made. Formal evaluation consists of two parts. First, whenever a student is ready, he takes a self-test and corrects it with an answer sheet. (The answer key is correlated with the objectives, so that the student may evaluate his own learning problems.) Second, the teacher makes a post-test evaluation to determine if a student is ready to go on to the next guide sheet.

Supplementary and enrichment activities include a wide variety of optional activities that may help the student to gain an understanding of the unit materials. These include filmstrips for individual viewing; audio-tutorial programs (film loops and flip charts accompanied by audiotapes); and pamphlets, paperback books, or special articles or reprints on related areas.

Each student follows an outlined basic procedure on any guide sheet, as illustrated in the chart above.

After the conference the student reenters the regular program as directed by the teacher on the basis of the student's needs.

The pretest serves to (a) determine if the student has already achieved the objectives of the unit (being able to bypass some of the material provides a great boost to the slow learner), (b) make the student aware of his competencies, incompetencies, and background for the unit, and (c) arouse an interest or curiosity to help motivate the student toward the unit.

In this type of program, the teacher ceases to be the key figure in the classroom and becomes a director of learning. The student accepts the responsibility for learning.

With the individualized approach, each student follows his guide sheet, and this allows the teaching staff to spend more time with those who most need help. Thus the slow learner receives help when he needs it.

As we stand today and pause to look at the past and at our present program, we also have a vision of the future. On the basis of what we (and others) have learned about individualized instruction, our goals now include—

1. Being able to evaluate more fully the skills and abilities (including reading, math, and reasoning abilities) of students when they enter the course
2. Determining each student's interest and background in science
3. Developing a wide variety of individualized laboratory activities within each conceptual scheme
4. Developing an extensive list of behavioral objectives for each conceptual scheme, so that on the basis of our pretests, we can select the specific objectives that each particular student should accomplish
5. Developing an adequate pretest for each conceptual scheme
6. Obtaining or developing a wider variety of audio-tutorial programs at different levels of difficulty
7. Devising a method of oral evaluation, especially for the slow learner
8. Providing a program that will challenge and allow success for all students.

Someday, we hope to arrive at the time when we can realistically ask, What is David ready for in science? instead of Is David ready for what we offer in science? and then be prepared to provide all the Davids with whatever they need.

A Nongraded Middle School

Robert J. McCarthy

Liverpool, New York, is a suburb of Syracuse with a pupil enrollment of approximately 9,000. Until recently, its schools were divided into three traditional units—elementary, junior high, and high school. Under the clear light of analysis, such arrangements were not entirely satisfactory. The graded junior high school approach, in particular, did not seem to be as effective as it might be in reaching children in the 11 to 15 age bracket. Ninth graders seemed to be intellectually and socially alienated from the younger junior high school students; sixth-grade youngsters appeared to have more in common with seventh and eighth graders.

The ideal solution would have been to group all grades, K–12, in one large building. This would have allowed an ungraded approach to function in a supportive setting. But such an arrangement was out of the question at the time for the Liverpool school district, so we chose what seemed to be the next best alternative—an ungraded middle school.

The Liverpool district's 7–8–9 arrangement was failing to meet the social, emotional, and curricular needs of its ninth-grade pupils in a number of ways. For example, we did not have enough personnel and equipment for in-depth laboratory investigations in various fields of science which ninth-grade level students were ready to pursue. We could provide only a limited choice of foreign languages in the junior high schools, and we lacked adequate vocational and professional programs. Moreover, we clearly faced certain limitations in remedying the situation.

We realized that it would be far too costly to duplicate the facilities and the program offering of the existing junior high schools for a single grade. And while it would be physically possible to develop numerous challenging programs in the four-year high school with its enrollment of 2,200 pupils, it was out of the question for the ninth grade. Furthermore, we realized that our elementary schools were not able to satisfy the demands of our sixth-grade pupils, particularly in science, industrial arts, home economics, foreign languages, and physical education.

In view of all these factors, we decided to place the sixth grade with seventh and eighth grades and to create a middle school. Liverpool's middle school attempted to develop an organizational framework well suited to the young adolescent. This necessitated combining much of the elementary school's concern for the "whole" child with that of the secondary school's emphasis on achievement in content areas—no easy task, but one that had to be done. An ungraded approach plus the interdisciplinary teaming of teachers and students helped us

From *The National Elementary Principal* XLVII, no. 3 (January 1968):15–21. Copyright © 1968 National Association of Elementary School Principals. All rights reserved. Used by permission of the author and publisher.

accomplish this goal by guaranteeing the flexibility necessary for developing an individualized program for each student.

WHY UNGRADED?

Parents know that each of their children is unique. And administrators and teachers have always recognized that every child comes to school with a different background, different experiences, different interests, different perceptions, and different abilities. Although few will dispute this contention, little has been done to organize our schools in such a way that each student will have a different program—one suited to him and his needs. We tend to build the master schedule and then try to fit the child to the program. This condition will probably prevail as long as we adhere slavishly to the graded approach.

The graded system is based on the assumption that each child progresses at almost the same pace as other children of the same age. Following this line of reasoning, all students should profit from taking the same subjects, in a set order, year after year. But various forms of psychological testing, as well as the personal experiences of every teacher, have proved this assumption to be false. Also, youngsters learn in a variety of ways and in a variety of patterns, alternately spurting ahead and slowing down as their minds and bodies develop at different rates.

Such variations in physical and intellectual growth patterns must be reflected in programs being developed for these students. Some youngsters may best pursue a concept or develop certain skills by means of a sequential approach; others may comprehend similar concepts or develop similar skills by utilizing a somewhat disjointed intuitive approach to the topic. The important thing is that the students be permitted to learn in ways which are most suited to their current operational patterns.

Realizing that much of today's traditional organizational pattern is neither adequate nor fair to many of our students, the Liverpool school system decided to change rather than perpetuate error by remaining with an outmoded graded system. Ungradedness is necessary if American educators are to meet the challenge of educating masses of children while at the same time providing instruction which enables each student to learn at his own rate and which takes into account each student's interests and abilities.

Once outside the school, children associate with other children of all ages. They do this because of mutual interests and desires. But as soon as they enter our schools, these associations are broken up by artificial grade barriers. Teachers attempt to regroup within the various grades and classes, but the fragmentary "grade" organization makes this extremely difficult. Ungradedness provides the vital ingredient of flexibility which is needed to develop individual programs for students.

Our ungraded program attempts to form groups of students on the basis of their needs in various areas. With this approach, for example, a so-called sixth level youngster with a talent in the area of mathematics might be placed in a mathematics class with the most advanced and mature students in the middle school, but he would still remain with many of his own age group for some or all of his other program. The student is placed with new groups when his progress indicates the need for reassignment.

At this point, it cannot be emphasized too strongly that the students are studying various concepts and skills in the areas of English, social studies, art, music—*not* seventh-grade English, sixth-grade mathematics, and eighth-grade music. There is really no such thing as sixth- or seventh- or eighth-grade English. Educators refer to it in this way because it happens to be listed this way in a state syllabus or curriculum guide. In an ungraded structure, the student will study English concepts and skills, and progress as rapidly as he can along a pattern of development that is most appropriate for him. Some may move through a sequence rather quickly; others may need substantially more time. But to have this continuous progress you need nongradedness.

To summarize, an ungraded approach recognizes that:

1. Each child is different.
2. Each child can benefit from a program built especially for him.
3. Learning is a process involving certain steps which may vary in their complexity and may not follow a fixed pattern.
4. The order in which these steps are taken and the rapidity of movement from one step to another will vary with the individual.

The student in our ungraded, individualized program is allowed to grow in many ways according to his unique talents, abilities, and interests, without the interference of the "grade" barrier. To enable him to make continuous progress in his educational development, the student is guided by his counselor and his instructional team.

INTERDISCIPLINARY TEAMING

In order to facilitate ungradedness in the Liverpool Middle School, six interdisciplinary teams were established for the 1966–67 school year. Except for changes in personnel, the structure has remained the same for the second year of our middle school operation. Five of these teams consisted of one English, one social studies, one mathematics, and one science teacher per team. Because we identified approximately 45 youngsters who had severe learning problems but possessed normal intellectual capabilities, we also set up a special three-member team composed of talented individuals who were interested in working very closely with these students.

Teachers were assigned to teams on the basis of inter-personal compatibility as well as balanced intellectual strengths. A series of conferences was held in January 1966 with members of the staff who would be working in our middle school. The discussions were frank. Our leadership team, which consists of the principal, the instructional consultant, and the pupil personnel consultant, wanted to find out from the staff themselves not only what they thought about inter-disciplinary teaming but also how they felt about working with some of their colleagues.

It was obvious that the only workable basis for the teaming of teachers was their willingness to work together, and their desire—or lack of it—to attempt the "new." Alternately teams were created that were either "experimental" or "traditional" in their approaches to education.

When interviewing candidates, we specifically sought individuals with "young" minds—people who felt that they did not have the answers to everything but who were willing to try to find some good answers. Our screening process immediately eliminated from consideration those candidates who were primarily subject matter oriented. Since the primary function of the interdisciplinary team was to develop a close personal relationship with the students, it was essential that we secure the services of individuals who would initiate programs to fit the students, rather than force youngsters to conform to a previously established curriculum pattern unrelated to their needs, interests, and abilities.

Each interdisciplinary team, with the exception of the previously mentioned three-member team, was responsible for the instruction of approximately 110 students in the areas of English, social studies, mathematics, and science. Members of each team were also responsible for developing the reading skills necessary for comprehending the ideas being developed within the team. All members of a particular team had the same students, and also served as the homeroom teachers for these students.

Originally we thought that a team leader would be essential to the proper functioning of each team. But, as the year progressed, it became evident that such a position was unnecessary; various members of each team were assuming leadership positions as situations dictated.

In order for each interdisciplinary team to function effectively, it was necessary for team members to have a great deal of information at their disposal regarding all of the children on their team. A questionnaire completed by the previous year's teachers, plus valuable information obtained by our guidance department from test scores and parent-teacher conferences, was presented to the team to give them a fairly comprehensive picture of each individual student. Before school opened, our youngsters were placed with teams on the basis of the data that had been gathered.

GROUPING

At this point, it seems appropriate to compare the methods we used for grouping students during our first year as a middle school with our new grouping procedure.

Initially teacher ratings were used to categorize pupils as 1-excellent, 2-good, 3-fair, and 4-poor in the areas of mathematics, science, social studies, and English. Having accomplished this, and having decided upon the makeup of each interdisciplinary team, it then became necessary to determine which teams could best handle certain groups of youngsters. Such decisions had to be made if the program was to be successful.

The eventual team and student assignments are summarized below. Note that the summary shows ability levels, and grade levels as traditionally conceived.

Team 1   ability levels   1–2–3

                                                  experimental

               grade levels   6–7–8

Team 2	ability levels	2–3	
	grade levels	6–7	experimental
Team 3	ability levels	1–2–3	
	grade levels	6–7–8	experimental
Team 4	ability levels	2–3–4	
	grade levels	6–8	traditional
Team 5	ability levels	2–3	
	grade levels	7–8	experimental
Team 6	ability levels	2–3–4	
	grade levels	6–7–8	traditional

These numerical data regarding student rating and team capabilities, combined with the choices students made in the elective areas of art, music, home economics, industrial arts, band, orchestra, chorus, French, and Spanish, were fed into a computer. Students were then placed with what, at the time, seemed to be their appropriate team and in those elective subjects which were open to them. As the year progressed, we found the operation to be anything but satisfactory. We were attempting to develop a personalized program of instruction and yet we had grouped youngsters in a manner that led to the very antithesis of what we were striving to achieve.

In June 1967, we asked each teacher to write a detailed evaluation of each of his students in terms of the progress made during the year. Our leadership team, guided in large measure by these evaluative reports and their own recommendations gained from counseling sessions with the students, worked for six weeks during the summer prior to the start of our second year to place each student individually with the interdisciplinary team most capable of working with that particular individual. In addition to this, we scheduled each youngster individually in those elective resource areas that he had an interest in and that would be of benefit to him. This was an exhausting operation but an essential one, and it was definitely in keeping with our educational philosophy. We did, however, make use of our district's data processing center to print out team and homeroom lists, plus student listings for the various resource areas.

Once teachers and students had been assigned to teams, a host of other situations had to be created in order for the interdisciplinary team to function effectively. We had to provide time during the school day for the team to meet and discuss their students and their programs. We had to give content or subject matter teams the opportunity to coordinate all that was going on in the various interdisciplinary teams. Finally, we had to set aside time for the students to work with their teachers on a one-to-one basis.

Since it was the responsibility of each interdisciplinary team to constantly group and regroup its students in the four major subject matter areas, it was obvious that a common planning room and a common planning period were essential. This would serve as the team's headquarters where all meetings would take place. The teachers could arrange the room any way they wished. Each facility was initially equipped with four desks and four chairs, file cabinets, a large closet, and several soft lounge chairs and/or a sofa.

Teams 1, 2, and 3 had their planning periods in the afternoon; teams 4, 5, and 6 had their meetings in the morning. Initially our building leadership team had to urge teachers to regroup pupils on the basis of the students' interests, ability, achievement, competency in various areas, maturity, and the special needs of the individual. As the year progressed, more staff members began to see the necessity for this and took the initiative themselves.

In September 1966, all our youngsters were grouped in their various subject matter areas and computer scheduled into specific rooms for definite times with members of their team. This was done to minimize confusion for our staff and for the students new to our building and our program. As we began our second year in September 1967, this became unnecessary because our district had set aside sufficient funds to support a one-week building workshop for the entire staff. In addition to this, all teachers new to our school and to the district were involved in a four-week professional development program that explored such concepts as nongradedness, continuous progress, independent study, individualized instruction, and the philosophy and psychology of teaming. Sufficient time was allotted to staff for reviewing all information pertinent to the students assigned to their team. Each team was then able to develop preliminary individual pupil schedules, groupings, and room assignments before the youngsters arrived.

In initial meetings of teachers and students, diagnostic pretesting took place. This enabled us to further identify groups of students, regardless of age, who were at a similar point in learning for a particular discipline area. Once students with such similarities were identified, along with the various levels of understanding that they had achieved, the team could begin to create the types of programs these students needed. Thus, after evaluating the strengths and weaknesses of their pupils, the team would create classes in which pupils would be working with others who had arrived at approximately the same level of proficiency and maturity in a certain subject matter area.

The members of each interdisciplinary team also serve as the homeroom teachers for their students, thus building an even closer bond between students and teachers. Much has been published about teaming, and the greatest stress has been laid upon large group and small group instruction, seminars, and the use of audiovisual materials. Many of the studies have neglected to mention one of the prime reasons for teaming a group of teachers—to help them get to know their students. By establishing interdisciplinary teams, by using these same team members as homeroom teachers, and by providing time during the day for students to meet with their teachers individually or in small groups, a climate was created whereby the teacher could act as counselor and advisor to the student.

Another significant reason for the formation of interdisciplinary teams was to help to correlate and integrate various subject matter areas. This eliminated needless duplication of effort on the part of staff and, more important, allowed students to see definite relationships between subject matter areas. By teaming teachers from various subject matter areas, we also enabled each staff member to see what was going on outside his own specialty area. We could then integrate topics and concepts so that the student and the teacher received a total view of what was taking place. Such knowledge and such an approach to learning could only improve our educational program. The mechanical operations of the team can be illustrated further by two team schedules:

Team 1

7:50– 8:25	Content teams. Planning sessions.
8:30– 8:45	Homeroom.
8:50–11:50	Interdisciplinary team teaching in English, social studies, mathematics, science, and reading. Staff arranges the time and the place where the pupils will receive instruction.
11:55–12:35	Lunch.
12:40– 1:35	Interdisciplinary team planning period.
1:40– 2:40	Individual pupil instruction period. An extra help session.
2:45– 2:55	Homeroom.

Team 4

7:50– 8:25	Content teams. Planning sessions.
8:30– 8:45	Homeroom.
8:50– 9:45	Interdisciplinary team planning period.
9:50–10:50	Individual pupil instruction period. An extra help session.
10:55–11:35	Lunch.
11:40– 2:40	Interdisciplinary team teaching in English, social studies, mathematics, science, and reading.
2:45– 2:55	Homeroom.

The team usually meets with students for a three-hour block of time each day. The teachers, however, have the freedom to do what they wish with those three hours. This is essential if the team is to be able to regroup students constantly for various instructional purposes. It would have been simple to divide the three hours into four 45-minute segments—and such an arrangement did prevail during the first week of school while the children were adjusting to their new teachers and to a new building. But such unimaginative calculations are not typical nor are they encouraged

After the first few days it was expected that, with the students, each team would develop its own schedule. This had to be done to create optimum conditions for the showing of films in their entirety, to conduct lengthy laboratory experiments, and to have the opportunity to listen to and talk with visitors to the schools. Once having agreed on the schedule to be employed for a day or for a week, it was essential that the students be informed of this decision. Since the members of the team were also the homeroom teachers of these students, it appeared that this could be accomplished rather easily during the homeroom period by giving the pupils a copy of their new schedule.

As school began last fall, each interdisciplinary team had:

1. Its own planning room
2. A common planning period for all members of the team

3. A period of time set aside during which the teachers could meet on an individual basis with their students
4. The freedom to arrange the three-hour block of time as needs dictate
5. The encouragement to constantly regroup students within the team and to transfer them to other teams when this seemed desirable
6. The go-ahead to develop individualized programs for students, based on the results of initial pretesting and student interests
7. Time to meet with other interdisciplinary teams and with their own subject matter or content teams.

Each team is assuming a considerable amount of responsibility, and the staff is being given clearance to tackle a great many of the problems that directly affect them. Teachers have an opportunity to operate in this way because we believe that for any organization to function effectively, the members of that organization must be willing to assume leadership in certain activities under the guidance of the leadership team. Since schools exist for students, these youngsters could and must influence the programs we offer. It follows that teachers, who help to educate these youngsters, should also influence the operation of the school. No administrative team could run the whole show itself and shouldn't try to.

CONTINUOUS PROGRESS REPORT FORM

With the implementation of an interdisciplinary team, nongraded, continuous progress approach to students and instruction, the inadequacies of our A-B-C-D-F report card were very much in evidence. Members of our staff, along with the leadership teams of the other two middle schools in the district, decided to launch an attack on the problem. The results of their six-month study led directly to the board's adoption of a continuous progress reporting system to students, their parents, and future teachers.

In analyzing the existing reporting system and developing plans for a new one, the staff felt that a system should be devised that:

1. Is used by individual teachers when appropriate and not just at uniformly prescribed times such as every five or ten weeks
2. Describes the student's program
3. Indicates the student's present achievement in terms of his ability
4. Recognizes that neither ability nor achievement is necessarily static and that both may change as the student matures physically and intellectually
5. Acknowledges achievement in terms of the student's self-development, rather than just in terms of a letter grade.

By allowing each teacher to issue this report when the exploration of a particular concept or topic has been completed, the staff no longer will be under the gun to have their grade sheets in the principal's office by a certain date. If a teacher is writing only ten or twenty reports at a time, he will be able to devote more time, effort, and thought to his evaluation of the individual's progress. This is exactly what the report is designed to do. The focus of our program and our reporting system must be the individual student. Although staff members are expected to complete at least one such report on each of their students during each ten-week period of the school year, teachers have the opportunity to select the most appropriate time for its issuance.

By employing a three-part form we were able to provide the student and his parents, the guidance counselor, and the interdisciplinary team with a thorough picture of the youngster's program and his progress in terms of the program, as related to the student's own ability. As much as possible, we also attempt to schedule parent conferences when such reports are issued.

It is our belief that this system has these advantages over many other reporting systems:

1. It provides ample space for teachers to make appropriate comments concerning each student, rather than relying on the trite clichés available on most checklist reporting devices.
2. It provides teachers with enough time to do a careful job on each report, since not all of the reports will be prepared at the same time.
3. It provides parents, students, counselors, and future teachers with some idea of the concepts that the student has worked with and the degree to which these concepts have been grasped.

The interdisciplinary teams, the flexibility with which they can operate, and the responsibility given to staff to both develop and evaluate individualized student programs exist for one major purpose: to allow the Liverpool Middle School to seek continually for new and better methods that will enable each youngster to progress according to his own ability, interest, talent, and drive.

SECTION 7   ADDITIONAL LEARNING ACTIVITIES

Problems and Projects

1. Why is a special curriculum or program of education needed for transescents and early adolescents? While preparing your answer to this question, refer to the articles by the White House Conference on Education, Havighurst, and Rowland and McGuire in Section 2 and the article by Thornburg in this section. What social forces are particularly significant for learners at this age level?

2. What social and psychological influences have led to the development of the middle school? Refer to the article by Van Til in this section for assistance in answering this question. How would you answer this question raised by Van Til: "Are the forces fostering the middle school as powerful as the forces which fostered the junior high?"

3. Use the bases and criteria of curriculum planning to examine the proposals for the middle school made in the article "Guidelines for the Middle Schools We Need Now," in this section. Which of the four curriculum bases have been used extensively in this proposal? Were any of the four bases not used in planning this proposal? Also examine the proposal in terms of continuity, provision for individual differences, balance, and flexibility. Discuss your ideas about the guidelines with others. Suggest improvements in the guidelines. Are there trends that have been overlooked in these guidelines?

4. Could you use the "values clarification approach" in teaching (see "Values Clarification in Junior High School," in this section)? Do you want to? What do the authors of this article mean when they say that "values cannot effectively be taught, but that they can be learned"? What learning theory is being used in the teaching described in this article? Evaluate the teaching and curriculum described in this article in terms of objectives and the four curriculum bases. Compare your evaluation with that of others who are studying this topic.

5. Eighth-grade students and their teacher made a current social force an important part of their curriculum through student-teacher planning (see "Our Eighth Graders Tackled Air Pollution," by Julie Brown Coleman, in this section). Evaluate this curriculum and teaching in terms of the other bases: human development, learning theories, and knowledge. What other social problems and social forces might be equally interesting and challenging to transescents and early adolescents as part of their curriculum? You might consider developing a teaching plan regarding another social problem for learners at this age level. If you can try out your plan, you might consider writing an article for possible publication concerning your experiences.

6. Talk with a group of transescents and early adolescents about the social forces of concern to them in the school, in their community, or on a national level. Share your findings with your fellow students.

7. What teaching and curriculum procedures are used by Quayle (see "Individualized Science for the Slow Learner") to provide for individualized learning? Examine the teaching and curriculum described in terms of objectives and the four bases of curriculum. On the basis of this analysis, suggest other ways in which the teachers working with this plan might provide for individualization.

8. Examine the middle school program described by Robert T. McCarthy in terms of the guidelines presented in "Guidelines for the Middle Schools We Need Now." Would you make suggestions for changes in the middle school at Liverpool, New York, in the light of the guidelines? Do the plans and practices at Liverpool suggest any changes in the guidelines?

9. If you have been developing a "case problem" about a middle school or a junior high, examine practices at the school in the light of the trends and in-

novations studied in this section. Should your school incorporate any of these trends in its curriculum and teaching? Your suggestions should be based on:

(1) Examination of the trend in light of objectives, the curriculum bases, and other criteria.

(2) Examination of present practices at the school to determine if the suggested trend would improve what is now done to provide for the learners' needs, and social goals.

Slide-Tapes

The DeSoto Middle School Story, color, 30 mins. Slide-tape production featuring an innovative middle school program in Florida. Includes a description of interdisciplinary team teaching and special interest courses designed for the transescent learner. Write to DeSoto Middle School, Arcadia, Florida 33821.

Filmstrip and Recording

Del-Mar Middle School, 80 frames, color. Describes the Del-Mar Middle School in Belvedere-Tiburon, California. Distributed by Reed Union School District, 1155 Tiburon Blvd., Belvedere-Tiburon, California 94920.

Visits to Schools

One of the best ways to study curriculum planning and teaching is to visit schools to observe teaching or to participate in teaching. It is useful to have an appointment with the principal, the curriculum director, or some other leader in the school.

You may want to ask your instructor or someone else to suggest a school or teacher that you might visit.

While visiting or while planning the visit, try to obtain information about the school's social setting, the learners in the school, teaching practices in the school, and the content and organization of the curriculum so that you can examine what you see and study in the school in terms of objectives of education, the four bases of the curriculum, and curriculum criteria such as balance, individual differences, flexibility, and continuity. It is important to try to learn what the school considers to be its objectives and/or what the teacher considers his objectives to be (when observing a particular teacher). Compare these objectives with objectives of education as you view them, and objectives for the grade level or curriculum area being observed.

Also, you may find it useful to consider whether current trends or innovations at the particular school level or subject area might be used to advantage at the school being visited.

After your visit, discuss your analysis of what you saw with others. Try to plan a small group discussion with others who have visited the school.

Books to Review

A number of texts have been written on the middle school. The following are sources the reader might want to review:

Alexander, William M.; Williams, Emmett L.; Compton, Mary; Hines, Vynce A.; Prescott, Dan, and Kealy, Ronald. *The Emergent Middle School*, 2nd ed. New York: Holt, Rinehart and Winston, 1969.

Bondi, Joseph C. *Developing Middle Schools: A Guidebook.* New York: MSS Informational Corporation, 1972. See especially the sections relating to Special Interest Courses and Middle School Organization.

Hansen, John H., and Hearn, Arthur. *The Middle School Program.* Chicago: Rand McNally and Company, 1971.

Howard, Alvin W., and Stoumbis, George C. *The Junior High and Middle School.* Scranton, Pennsylvania: Intext Educational Publishers, 1970.

Overly, Donald; Kinghorn, Jon; and Preston, Richard. *The Middle School: Humanizing Education for Youth.* Worthington, Ohio: Charles A. Jones Publishing Company, 1972.

Popper, Samuel H. *The American Middle Schools: An Organizational Analysis.* Waltham, Massachusetts: Blaisdell Publishing Company, 1967.

Richardson, Elwyn S. *In the Early World.* New York: Pantheon Books, 1964.

Storen, Helen F. *The Disadvantaged Early Adolescent: More Effective Teaching.* New York: McGraw Hill, 1968.

Stoumbis, George C., and Howard, Alvin W. *Schools for the Middle Years.* Scranton, Pennsylvania: International Textbook Company, 1969.

Stradley, William E. *A Practical Guide to the Middle School.* New York: The Center for Applied Research in Education, 1971.

Van Til, William (*et al.*) *Modern Education for the Junior High School Years,* 2nd ed. Indianapolis: Bobbs-Merrill, 1967.

Pamphlets

Pamphlets are also sources of information. The reader might examine the following:

Center for Urban Education. *The School in the Middle: Divided Opinion on Dividing Schools.* New York: Center for Urban Education, 1968.

Kohl, John; Caldwell, William; and Eichhorn, Donald. *Self-Appraisal and Development of the Middle School.* University Park, Pennsylvania: The Pennsylvania School Study Council, 1970.

Lounsbury, John H., ed. *The Junior High School We Saw.* Washington, D.C.: A.S.C.D., 1964.

McCarthy, Robert, and Goldman, Samuel. *How to Organize and Operate an Ungraded Middle School.* Prentice-Hall Successful School Administration Series. New York: Prentice-Hall, 1967.

Curriculum Guides

Guides are valuable sources of information. The reader might want to obtain the following:

Fordham University, School of Education. *Occupational Awareness in the Urban Middle School.* New York, 1972.

Lee County School District, Middle School Guides in Science, Mathematics, Social Studies, Language Arts, Music, Art. Ft. Myers, Florida, 1970.

Trauschke, Edward, ed. *A Guide to the Middle School in Florida.* Tallahassee, Florida: Florida Courses of Study Committee on the Middle School, Florida Department of Education, 1973.

Journal Articles

Alexander, William M. "What's the Score on Middle Schools?" *Today's Education* 60:8 (November 1971), p. 67.

Brown, Joan G., and Howard, Alvin W. "Who Should Teach at Schools for the Middle Years?" *Clearing House* 46:5 (January 1972), pp. 279–283.

Chiara, Clara, and Johnson, Elizabeth. "The Middle School: Is It Doomed for Failure?" *Today's Education* 60:1 (January 1971), pp. 288–292.

Clarke, Sanford, "The Middle School: Specially Trained Teachers Are Vital to Its Success," *Clearing House* 46:4 (December 1971), pp. 218–222.

DiVirgilio, James. "Our Middle Schools Give the Kids a Break," *Today's Education* 60:1 (January 1971), pp. 31–32.

Flinker, Irving, and Pianko, Norman. "The Emerging Middle School," *Clearing House* 46:2 (October 1971), pp. 67–72.

Howard, Alvin W., and Phillips, William. "Results of a Four-State Survey of Junior High Schools," *Clearing House* 45:2 (October 1970), pp. 120–124.

"The Middle School," *National Elementary Principal* 51:3 (November 1971), *entire issue.*

Moss, Theodore C. "Characteristics of a Good Middle School," *NASSP Bulletin* 55:357 (October 1971), pp. 71–74.

Viewpoints 47:6 (November 1971), *entire issue.*

Journals
   The following journals are particularly good sources:

The Bulletin of the National Association of Secondary School Principals
Clearing House
Educational Leadership
The National Elementary Principal (see especially the November, 1971 issue "The Middle School")
Nation's Schools
Phi Delta Kappan
Today's Education

Education for Middle Adolescents

PREREQUISITES

1. Reading and studying of the Introduction to this book, and Sections 1 through 5.
2. The development of, and ability to utilize, a set of curriculum criteria to describe and evaluate a curriculum plan. You must be able to use this set of criteria in order to critically analyze and make curriculum or teaching decisions regarding programs described in this section.

RATIONALE

All curriculum planners and teachers should be acquainted with the goals and trends in education at all levels, regardless of the level of the program of education at which they plan to work. You should know about goals and trends in education for middle adolescents whether you plan to work at this level or not. You will be able to be a better curriculum planner or teacher at one of the other levels if you have this information. This view is based on such curriculum criteria as continuity in learning, balance in the curriculum, and provision for individual differences.

This section is now called "Education for Middle Adolescents" rather than The High School. In keeping with the definition of *curriculum* presented in the Introduction, the focus will be on programs of education rather than exclusively on school programs. The title is intended to focus attention on a group of learners and their needs rather than on a school program.

In the Introduction to Section 7, adolescence in our society was described as the period from approximately age thirteen to age twenty. In that section introduction, transescence and early adolescence were described as spanning approximately ages ten to fifteen. Therefore, middle adolescence is the period from approximately age 15 to 18, the high school years.

Middle adolescents are beginning to seek some assurance of eventual economic independence of parents and other adults. They sense their possession of new intellectual powers and they need to develop cognitive skills. Their dominant motivation most frequently is to achieve social status in the adolescent community, according to their peer world expectations. They often have a duality of orientation: engaging in behavior approved by adults versus engaging in behavior approved by peers. Middle adolescents, according to Erikson, seek a "sense of identity" and the development of values to have as one's own. According to Bennett Berger, sociologist at the University of California at Davis, adolescence is one of the ways that culture violates nature by insisting that, for an increasing number of years, young persons postpone their claims to the privileges and responsibilities of common citizenship. It is useful, at this point, to review the theories of Williams, Otto, Havighurst, Erikson, Piaget and others by turning to Section 2.

The American high school has been under heavy pressure during recent years. It has been plagued by strikes by students, rioting, physical attacks on teachers, and other violence. A study in New York stated that these crises result from the high school's massive size, monolithic structure, and authoritarian lines. This report stated that students expressed underlying negativity and tension toward their teachers. Some students find their school experience painful, and many find it unenjoyable. Minority students feel they receive differential treatment. In general, students ask for more openness and mutual respect. Neither students nor teachers see students as influential in school policy. Many students do not feel they are learning very much. The high school typically does not use the rich resources of the community.

In 1969, Frederick Wiseman recorded similar data in his documentary film, *High School*. (See a complete reference to this film under Problems and Projects at the end of this section.) The film showed students eager to try new things—and the school responding with rules and regulations. The students want to participate, and the teachers hurry to leave with the last bell. Of course there are many instances of curriculum and teaching practices much different from these, but the student's image of the high school today is too often like that just described. It is at this high school level that the need for programs of education rather than programs of schooling comes into perspective most clearly.

To meet the needs of middle adolescents, most American educators advocated the *comprehensive high school* during the 1950s and 1960s. A truly comprehensive high school would provide needed learning opportunities for all the normal adolescents from the slow learner to the gifted and talented. Its purpose would be to enable each learner to develop to his greatest potential for his own success and happiness and to make a maximum contribution to the American society of which he is a part. This would necessitate that the school affect positively the behavior of students now, as adolescents and unique human beings, and later, as adult wage earners, citizens, and family members. Such a school would have to offer a curriculum with breadth and depth, individualized instruction, and many functional learning opportunities. And it must have teachers who are not overburdened and harassed, who can enjoy working with middle adolescents, and who attempt to see the world from the students' point of view. It is clear that we have a long way to go before it can be said that most American high school boys and girls are attending a comprehensive high school.

The comprehensive high school of the 1970s, even if generally attained, is inadequate for the program of education needed by many adolescents. This fact is evident from the following list of trends at this level. It is also shown in the new models for education for middle adolescents described in "High School with No Walls," "The John Dewey High School Adventure," "An Innovative High School in a Midwestern Suburb," "McGavock: A Model School," and "Portland's Personalized Educational Program," all in this section. These high schools demonstrate ways in which programs of education can be made more personal and interesting if time, resources, and energy are dedicated to these purposes.

What *objectives* should guide programs of education for middle adolescents? At this level, the objectives would include the following:

1. Helping learners in career development, whether it be through vocational education or additional academic development.
2. Offering learners many opportunities to grow in citizenship skills, understanding, and responsibilities.
3. Aiding students to grow in self-direction in study and learning.
4. Assisting learners in many ways toward self-realization and identity.
5. Encouraging the development and practice of critical thinking.

Other statements of objectives are provided by Havighurst and Ohme in this section. And Cohen and Richards present the important concept of *youth advocacy* as an aspect of programs of education for adolescents.

Continuity of learning and the great variety of individual differences in learners suggest the need for the reader to reexamine the objectives stated for education for early adolescents in the introduction to Section 7. And because some middle adolescents will be advanced in their development socially, emotionally, or cognitively, you may wish at this point to look ahead to Section 9 to consider the discussion in that introduction of objectives of programs of education for late adolescents and young adults.

To better provide for the attainment of objectives at this level, the following *innovations* are being proposed and tried. This list of *innovations* and trends in education for middle adolescents includes references to pertinent articles in this section.

1. De-schooling program ("Portland's Personalized Education Program")
2. Nongraded schools ("The John Dewey High School Adventure"; The Case for the Small High School'; "Steps Toward Relevance: an Interest-Centered Curriculum")
3. Differentiated staffing ("McGavock: A Model School")
4. Self-pacing materials, learning activity packages (LAPS) (UNIPACS) (see reference under Problems and Projects at end of this section)
5. School-within-a-school ("McGavock: A Model School")
6. Comprehensive high school ("McGavock: A Model School")
7. Continuous learner progress ("The John Dewey High School Adventure")
8. Phasing and mini courses ("Steps Toward Relevance: An Interest-Centered Curriculum"; "The Case for the Small High School"; "McGavock: A Model School")
9. Schools with no walls ("High School with no Walls—It's a Happening in Philadelphia")
10. Alternative curricula and schools ("McGavock: A Model School"; "Port-

land's Personalized Education Program"; see also "Options for Students, Parents, and Teachers" in Section 5)
11. Flexible scheduling ("The John Dewey High School Adventure")
12. Interest-centered curriculum ("Steps Toward Relevance: An Interest-Centered Curriculum")
13. Instrumental and expressive education ("High Schools for the Future")
14. Modular scheduling ("The John Dewey High School Adventure")
15. Career education ("McGavock: A Model School")
16. Education for parenthood ("Exploring Childhood")
17. Independent study ("What Is Independent Study All About?")
18. Student oriented curriculum ("An Innovative High School in a Midwestern Suburb")
19. Team teaching ("McGavock: A Model School)
20. Student teacher planning ("An Innovative High School in a Midwestern Suburb"; "High School with No Walls—It's A Happening in Philadelphia")

OBJECTIVES

Your objectives in studying education at this level as part of the curriculum should be as follows:

1. To be familiar with the objectives, current innovations, and recent trends in education for middle adolescents.
2. To be able to explain the functions and goals of education at this level as part of the total curriculum.
3. To be able to use the objectives of education at this level, the curriculum bases, and other criteria in making curriculum and/or instruction decisions regarding present programs as well as regarding proposed innovations and trends.
4. To be able to suggest improvements in middle adolescent curriculum plans through the decisions made in number 3.

PREASSESSMENT

1. Identify the innovations and trends listed in the Rationale above, and discuss their implications for education at this level.
2. Evaluate each of the trends in terms of objectives, bases of curriculum, and curriculum criteria that you regard as appropriate.
3. Select any middle adolescence curriculum plan and describe and analyze it in terms of objectives, the four curriculum bases, other curriculum criteria, and innovations and trends at this level of education.
4. Suggest improvements or changes in the curriculum plan in number 3 in the light of your analysis.

In answering numbers 3 and 4 of the preassessment, you might choose to analyze the curriculum plans described in the following articles in this section:

1. "High School with No Walls," by Resnik
2. "McGavock: A Model School," by Burns
3. "Portland's Personalized Education Program," by Boss.

LEARNING ACTIVITIES

Articles in this section will help you to understand the purposes and functions of education for middle adolescents as an important part of the curriculum. They will also acquaint you with the problems, as well as the innovations and trends, of programs of education for middle adolescents.

Other learning alternatives are suggested at the end of this section.

POSTASSESSMENT

After attempting the preassessment you may do *one or more* of the following:

1. Ask your instructor whether you are ready for a postassessment evaluation on education for middle adolescents. Most students will need further work on this curriculum base.
2. Read the articles on education for middle adolescents in this section and try to determine how the problems, goals, trends, and innovations being discussed in each article should be considered in curriculum planning and teaching.
3. Choose additional activities and readings or films and videotapes from those listed at the end of this section.
4. Look in your library or media center for other films, books, or articles on middle adolescent education programs and teaching.
5. Discuss the reading you have done and the films you have viewed with your fellow students. The key questions: How should the goals, innovations, trends, and suggestions you've studied affect a school's curriculum? How should they be considered in planning for teaching?
6. When you are ready, ask your instructor for advice on a suitable postassessment for you for this topic. Satisfactory completion of numbers 4, 5, and 8 under Problems and Projects at the end of this section might be one possibility. Or satisfactory written completion of the preassessment for this section, after completing other learning activities, might be a satisfactory postassessment. Consult your instructor about this. You can evaluate your ability to do these postassessment activities before seeing the instructor.

High Schools for the Future

Robert J. Havighurst

In looking ahead at the future of secondary education in this country there are two possible positions which one may take. One is the position which stresses the *problems*—the schools in the slums of the big cities, and the small schools in

From *Bulletin of the National Association of Secondary-School Principals* LII, no. 328 (May 1968):117–125. Used by permission of the author and publisher.

the small villages. This is a familiar approach, but it is not the one I am going to take in this paper. The other is the position which stresses the opportunities of the high schools in a rapidly developing society. This latter is the approach I will follow.

This is an optimistic position. It assumes that we are solving our domestic problems of social integration and of metropolitan area cooperation between central city and suburbs. As we solve these problems, the future will present us more and more urgently the problem of the wise use of leisure, and the high schools will have the opportunity and the responsibility of contributing in a major way to resolving this problem.

There are two interrelated characteristics of our system of producing goods and services which result in an increase of free time and a growth in our ability to use free time wisely. The first is the remarkable increase in economic productivity due to automation and cybernation. The man-hour productivity in 1960 was three times that of 1900, in the United States. The American people elected to produce more goods and many new products with this increasing productivity. At the same time they elected to shorten the work week from about 60 to about 40 hours. Every American has more leisure (time free from work) than his grandfather had, if he wants leisure time. Nobody is forced by iron necessity to work as long as his grandfather did at the beginning of the century.

The second characteristic is the increasing ratio of white collar to manual workers. In the year 1956, the white collar workers first outnumbered the blue collar workers in the United States. Now white collar workers have a five to four preponderance over blue collar workers. With increased proportions of white collar workers goes more flexibility in the use of free time. For blue collar workers, as a general rule, free time is a time for rest and relaxation and the simplest forms of recreation. For white collar workers there is a greater tendency to use free time in a variety of forms of action.

The various forms of action can be seen in three major categories:

Service—unpaid, freely chosen activities for the welfare of the family or the community
Study and Contemplation
Play—activities which are enjoyable in themselves.

THE GROWTH OF LEISURE

What people do with their free time is the major human concern of our society. How they use space is incidental to their use of time. Thus time is the arena or the stage on which the drama of human development unfolds in our society. Free time is a promontory of the future jutting into the present—a kind of concrete, present utopia. In Thomas More's Utopia, people worked only six hours a day. We have now reached that state.

The goal of a highly productive society is to set the stage for the wise consumption of the goods and services that the society produces. As the task of production is accomplished more and more fully, the task of consumption becomes more important and more complex. How shall we use our time and our resources in our highly productive society? This question dominates the situation.

With the present level of life expectancy, the present norm of retirement at about age 65, and the present length of the work year and the work week, the average American has something like 20 years of leisure more than his grandfather had.

This leisure time may be used for a variety of kinds of action, some of which are more strenuous mentally or physically than most work is. We shall increasingly speak of higher and more liberal forms of work and action rather than of work and nonwork.

If the business of life is living, with work just one form of living, then the old ethic of work on which our society has rested since the Reformation must be replaced by a broader ethic of the use of time.

Any system of ethics must have standards of better or worse. Accordingly, we must develop standards of better or worse that apply to use of time. These standards will be more flexible, more varied than the ethical standards that have been developed to apply to work.

The new ethics of the use of time should include not only moral standards but also esthetic standards.

INSTRUMENTAL AND EXPRESSIVE EDUCATION

There are two basic aspects of education, both of which are essential for lifelong learning. They are the instrumental and the expressive. Instrumental education means education for a goal which lies outside and beyond the act of education. In this form, education is an instrument for changing the learner's situation. For example, the learner studies arithmetic so as to be able to exchange money and to buy and sell things and to become a competent scientist or teacher. Or the learner as a young adult studies in his vocational field so as to get a promotion, or studies cooking so as to become a better housewife. Instrumental education is thus a kind of investment of time and energy in the expectation of future gain.

Expressive education means education for a goal which lies within the act of learning or is so closely related to it that the act of learning appears to be the goal. For example, the learner studies artithmetic for the pleasure of learning about numbers and quantities. The learning of arithmetic is its own reward. Or the learner as a young adult studies the latest dances so as to enjoy the dances he and his friends go to. He learns to dance "for fun," and not to become a teacher of dancing or even to make new friends. Expressive education is a kind of consumption of time and energy for present gain.

In a changing society a competent person needs to make a combination of instrumental and expressive learning at every stage of his life.

He cannot confine learning to one or two stages of his life. Not long ago it was customary to divide the life cycle with a period of infancy and childhood for play, of childhood and adolescence for study, of adulthood for work, and old age for play again. Today nobody can live that way and be a competent member of contemporary society. Rather, the life cycle should be conceived of as a rope with parallel strands of play, study, and work each extending all the way through life, but with the work strand having greater thickness in adulthood, while the study and play strands have greater thickness in childhood and adolescence.

John Maynard Keynes, one of the great thinkers about the economics of a productive society during the present century, saw this coming when he wrote his essay on "Economic Possibilities for Our Grandchildren." Writing about the high school students of the next decade, he said, "It will be those people who can keep alive, and cultivate into fuller perfection, the art of life itself and do not sell themselves for the means of life who will be able to enjoy the abundance when it comes."

The high schools of the coming decade will be the principal instrument for these changes in the American way of life. This will result in major changes in the high school curriculum.

THE CURRICULUM AND EXPRESSIVE EDUCATION

We may expect a drastic shift in high school curricula which will tend to place the arts and humanities in balance with the sciences and mathematics. Just as the decade of the 1960's will go down in educational history as the decade when the instrumental aspects of the high school curriculum were reformed and strengthened, the decade of the 1970's will come to stand for the strengthening of the expressive aspects of the high school curriculum.

As the curriculum develops, we will come to recognize a new type of successful student—the student with a high Expressive element. This person will be somewhat different from the highly Instrumental student who is the model of the successful student today. There will be four combinations of the Expressive and Instrumental factors, as shown in the following chart:

		Expressive Values	
		High	Low
Instrumental	High	A	B
Values	Low	C	D

The C-type, high in Expressive and low in Instrumental values and attitudes, is one who will come into greater favor in the decade ahead.

"Innovations in the High Schools" was the topic of the April 1967 issue of *Nation's Schools.* This reported a national survey in 1966 of 7,237 accredited high schools by the North Central Association of Colleges and Secondary Schools, to find out what innovations had recently been made. A list of 27 innovations was used in checklist form. Of eight curriculum innovations, seven were in science or mathematics and one was titled "Humanities Course." There were seven technological innovations, all of instrumental character. There were twelve innovations in the category of organization. Only one of them was clearly expressive in character, namely "Cultural Enrichment Programs," but some others would lend themselves to expressive activity, including "flexible scheduling," "honor study halls," "optional class attendance," and "student exchange program." Thirty-one percent of the schools reported that they had introduced cultural enrichment programs, while 18 percent reported that they had a humanities course, combining instruction in art, music, literature, photography, and history.

The coming upsurge of interest in the arts and humanities is not yet visible in this kind of survey, but it is seen clearly in the current grants being made by the U.S. Office of Education under Title III of the Elementary and Secondary

Education Act. A strikingly high proportion of these grants are going for cultural enrichment programs.

ESTHETIC STANDARDS AND EXPRESSIVE EDUCATION

A controversy will no doubt develop among the leaders of expressive education over the extent to which the arts and humanities can be taught effectively to the mass of high school students. What is the place of esthetic standards in such a program? This writer's view is that esthetic standards can and should be taught, but also that esthetic standards will evolve through the experience of many people with a variety of ways of using their free time.

However, there will be people who contend that high school courses in the arts and humanities should be limited to a minority of students who demonstrate a high level of skill or appreciation in these courses. This was illustrated in a conference on *Humanities and the Schools* held in 1965 at the University of Kentucky, under the chairmanship of Harold Taylor. One group of speakers, including the chairman, argued that all kinds of students can and should participate in the arts and in creative activities. There were others who insisted on the importance of maintaining standards. For example, Stanley Kauffmann, the film critic, said:

> In this matter its is important to start with a clear, unsentimentalized view, free of democratic fallacies. A very small proportion of any country's population has at any time had a strong interest in art. I think it is a dangerous mistake to assume, as a dynamics in the teaching of humanities, that that proportion must be increased. If it happened to be increased, that would be lovely. What is much more important is, first, that it be maintained and, second, be continually refined. . . .
>
> I am much more concerned with the touching of the few who will respond to art than with dabbling every member of the class with a little art vaccine. Of course one cannot reliably know in advance who the responsive few will be, and therefore the approach must be to the whole class. What I am concerned with is the intent of the approach; so that when those few are reached, they are given help instead of—as often happens— hindrance that may take years to overcome. It is culturally more important that those few get some glimmer of the mysteries and uncertainties of art than that the majority be given a few facile certainties to make them feel they have a grip on the subject.

Edgar Friedenberg, a facile critic of public education, argues that all youth could enjoy and participate in the arts, if, only the educational establishment would permit it. He says:

> What I want to see happen is for youngsters to experience the private vision that any one, to the degree that he is an artist, must start with; the discipline, derived from the properties of his medium and from the nature of the available symbols, to which the artist must submit; and the growth and development of that vision under discipline. But a public school, socializing young Americans to enjoy the Great Society, is not a very promising *ambiance* in which to try to bring this confrontation about.

The American society offers major resources for the pleasurable use of free time that are now in full course of development. These are: the outdoors, television, the performing arts, and a fourth agency, the National Foundation for the Arts and Humanities.

1. Use of the Outdoors

As the population increases and society becomes more urbanized, the outdoors will become increasingly precious as a leisure-time resource; at the same time, the outdoors will be increasingly threatened by the incursions of urbanism and technology. Air and water pollution threaten to make the outdoors unsafe in many areas. Industrial exploitation of rivers, lakeshore, seashore, and mineral deposits endanger the recreational use of the outdoors.

There is need for a clear statement of the functions of leisure activity and a policy of using the outdoors to serve these functions. Three functions of leisure in a crowded urban society are:

to give isolation, at times, amid the shoving and sprinting and raucous activities of the city

to reduce nervous tensions, through an effective combination of physical with mental activity

to provide a setting for the experience of awe and reverence for things that are not man-made

2. Television

Mr. Lee Loevinger, a member of the Federal Communications Commission, told the twentieth convention of the New Jersey Broadcasters Association:

It seems to me that television is the literature of the illiterate, the culture of the low-born, the wealth of the poor, the privilege of the underprivileged, the exclusive club of the excluded masses. . . . Television is a golden goose that lays scrambled eggs. And it is futile and probably fatal to beat it for not laying caviar. Anyway, more people like scrambled eggs than caviar.

This view of TV as an element in the mass culture will be challenged as the federal government moves to establish "public television" which will be separate from the advertising business. The Carnegie Corporation comments:

What commercial television cannot do because of its need to reach mass audiences, noncommercial television cannot do because it lacks the money, facilities, and personnel. Hence in the technologically most advanced society in the history of man, the greatest technological device for informing, delighting, inspiring, amusing, provoking, and entertaining remains pitiably unexploited, and the American public is the loser.

With the Ford Foundation also interested in making noncommercial television a force for better use of free time, it is clear that there will be a public television network financed at a level of at least $100 million a year. This network will assist the 124 existing educational television stations and will provide programs that go beyond the bounds of what is ordinarily called educational television.

3. The Performing Arts

It is generally claimed that there has been a kind of "cultural explosion" in the United States since World War II. The number of symphony orchestras has doubled in 20 years, to a total of more than 1,400. The number of groups presenting opera doubled to 754 in the decade before 1964. Much of this growth was in the amateur sector. Of 1,401 symphony orchestras, only 54 were composed predominantly of professional musicians. Two economists looked at the phenomenon with a critical eye and concluded that much of the increase between 1946 and 1963 was because of growth in population and increase in prices as well as in real income, rather than because of increased interest in the arts compared with interest in other activities. It is concluded that substantial subsidy from the federal government is needed to give the performing arts the kind of development they deserve.

4. National Foundation for the Arts and Humanities

The bill that was signed into law on September 29, 1965, may go down in history as the most important piece of legislation for that year and perhaps for that decade. Thus the national government acknowledged responsibility for the state of the arts and for the functioning of the arts in the improvement of the mass culture. Before that time, a number of states had set up State Councils on the Arts with programs that included sponsoring touring groups in the performing arts, art exhibitions, conferences on music, and providing technical assistance to local community groups that supported museums, galleries, theater, and music groups. While the amounts of money provided for the State Councils have been modest and the budget of the Foundation for the Arts and Humanities is only $12 million in its second year, the money has already set in motion some promising programs.

The level of federal government support for the performing arts will certainly advance to at least $100 million a year within the next decade, and this will support work in major regional centers in addition to assisting the State Councils in their programs.

THE HIGH SCHOOLS AND THEIR RESOURCES

The high schools will be related to leisure-time resources in two ways. First, the schools will make increasing use of them. Especially in the area of the performing arts, we will find the high schools taking a big part in the spread of active participation in local musical and dramatic activities. Wherever there is an adult theater or chorus or orchestra, we will find the high school carrying on a youth theater or chorus or symphony, as a junior version and a preparation for adult participation.

Second, the schools will be studying the matter of social policies for use of leisure. Young people will be getting ready to act as citizens on behalf of conservation of recreational areas. They will be advising their Congressmen about government appropriations for public television and for the National Foundation for the Arts and Humanities. The wise and pleasurable use of leisure will become recognized as a major social goal in the United States, to be studied and discussed by high school students as part of their preparation for citizenship.

Youths As Advocates

Donald Cohen

Catherine V. Richards

America often forgets about its youth until there is trouble. When we talk about developmental programs for children, the picture of lively preschoolers usually comes to mind. But it is urgent to consider the special, developmental needs of youth, and to recognize the significant contributions that young people can make to the well-being of the nation. Such consideration may well lead to the renewal of some of our major social institutions.

Youth advocacy raises critical issues about the ways in which youth relates to institutions and adults. Perhaps when we think and talk about child advocacy programs, we should also discuss the roles youths can perform as child advocates, and some of the qualities needed to be an effective advocate.

Advocacy is a special relationship with two basic ingredients: the summons by someone or some cause in need of help and the acceptance of this responsibility by someone else. An advocate speaks, pleads, intercedes. Let's think about some of the people who could be considered effective advocates—people such as Martin Luther King, Jr., Eleanor Roosevelt, Ralph Nader, Jane Adams, Mahatma Gandhi and Abraham Lincoln. What characteristics are shared by effective advocates such as these? This is not a simple question, because advocacy is a complex activity. But there are some essential features of advocacy.

An effective advocate is able to form a trusting relationship with someone or some group for whom he speaks. He knows what the person or group needs, and he knows what has to be done to reach his goal. The advocate is skillful in working with available resources but, equally important, he is able to mobilize new resources. He is able to keep his eye on the eventual target but to detour, accept frustrations, and tolerate delays as he progresses toward his goal. Effective advocates are not those who accept the *status quo*; rather they are assertive, competitive, and able to respond to a setback with a new, more forceful plan of action. And they are not detached—they function most successfully when they are deeply committed to their cause.

How does a young person develop the qualities needed for advocacy, and how does being an advocate further his personal development?

BECOMING AN ADVOCATE

Parents are a child's first advocates. They are committed to his welfare and they are entrusted by nature, society, and the child himself to care for the child.

From *Children Today* I, no. 2 (March–April 1972):32–34. Used by permission of the authors and publisher.

Our culture strongly defends the concept that parents are spokesmen for the fulfillment of a child's needs and rights.

From this relationship with parents, children learn a great deal about the mutual responsibilities involved in advocacy. If he has received good care from his parents and community, a child entering his school age years is able to speak for himself about his own needs and rights. Later, when he enters adolescence, he may become an advocate who speaks on behalf of the well-being of others and for the principles to which he is committed.

Obviously, youths generally do not have all of the characteristics of mature advocates, such as philosophical perspective, planning abilities, judgment relating to alternatives and delays, or essential knowledge about the complexity and relationships within systems and operational procedures. Yet, many adolescents display some of the most important features that an advocate needs to be effective: idealism, energy, personal involvement, ability to think logically, and human trust.

The types of vigorous and forceful behavior that are involved in advocacy are a sign of healthy, personal development. This capacity to feel with others and to act in their behalf is an essential aspect of development in preparation for parenthood.

WHAT ADVOCACY DOES FOR YOUTH

At adolescence, a youth begins to feel that he has a personal history, one that influences him and which he can, in turn, determine. This sense of destiny with different possible outcomes accounts in part for the inner confusion, intense feelings, and ideological vigor that characterize adolescence. A chance to be an advocate helps an adolescent clarify his feelings.

As an advocate, the youth must use his cognitive abilities to evaluate abstract principles and decide between different, and perhaps conflicting, principles that may guide his action. In the process of thinking about and speaking for causes and other people, a young person may test his own beliefs and values, define his personal strengths, and shape himself into the kind of person that he admires. As he speaks for others, a youth brings his own values into sharper focus.

Often, the cause for which a youth speaks is relevant to his own needs, feelings, and desires—factors that also make for an effective advocate. However, it is also true that few people are more capable of altruism and self-effacement than the adolescent.

An adolescent asks: "What am I ready to stand up for? What do I believe? I know what other people *think* I am and what they say I *should believe and do* with my life. But who am I really?

An adolescent, like a nation, defines his identity piece-by-piece in the course of partial solutions to the issues of advocacy.

WHAT ADVOCACY DOES FOR SOCIETY

Advocacy can be an essential social instrument in the developmental experiences of youth. It is apparent that there must also be advocacy to assure provisions and support for youth involvement in community activities. One aspect of the relationship between youth and society is defined by the extent to which the society meets the physical, intellectual, and social needs of maturing young people. Another aspect is described by the degree to which the society clearly makes evident its needs for the energies and abilities of youth. These needs should be significant to the society, call upon the talents and energies of young people, and provide youth with real experiences with the difficult policy issues involved in deciding the course of human affairs in their community.

The profound questioning and occasional activism that marks advocacy by young people may arouse strong feelings in adults and their institutions. A youth may accuse his parents of hypocrisy because they say they are concerned about economic inequality and then complain about low-income housing ruining property values in their neighborhood. Through such advocacy, a youth defines his views about status and class. How does his advocacy affect the adults in his life?

First, advocacy by youths may be totally unacceptable to adults or it may anger them. Second, adults may shut off their true feelings and display compliance. Or, they may listen and learn. The willingness of adults to respond to young people with honesty and flexibility is essential if young people are to develop into fully mature adults and skilled advocates.

It is almost a truism that the youthful advocate should be heard and taken seriously by adults and institutions. But, to be taken seriously does not mean that adults should weakly comply. For example, adult professionals who adopt the speech, clothing, and style of the youths with whom they work may reflect a simple accommodation rather than a serious appreciation and personal assimilation of the meaning of youthful advocacy. Youths, of course, generally recognize this accommodation as not reflecting real change in the adult's understanding of the need for the social changes they are advocating.

Advocacy by youth—as well as by adults—has little meaning if it does not meet with a resistance to test it. In general terms, what the youthful advocate requires, and what can only be provided by adults, is the perspective of history, tradition, and the continuity of culture. When adults are willing to stand up for their own traditional beliefs, youths can have the freedom to advocate to the limits of their energy and idealism. On the other hand, adults who are unclear about their own identities, or who abdicate their responsibilities, are likely to give in too quickly or resist too strongly. In either case, youths then hold back.

Where adults are unsure of themselves, youths' sense of self-preservation inhibits advocacy. This, in turn, blocks one road to personal growth. For example, the violent campus disturbances and the extreme quietude that many observers now sense on the same campuses may be traced, in part, to the difficulties experienced by many adults in clearly knowing and articulating what they truly believe, what they will stand up for, and what they feel they can do in redress.

Vigorous youth advocacy requires vigorous adult advocacy. A well-functioning, integrated society provides the arenas (through legislative bodies, courts, negotiating tables, and families) where this type of healthy aggression among advocacy groups can be modulated and channeled into meaningful collaboration.

WHERE CAN YOUTHS BE ADVOCATES?

An effective advocate works in an area that is personally meaningful because of his self-interest and first-hand knowledge. Union leaders traditionally work to improve conditions for workers, political leaders work to improve government for the governed, and leaders of racial and religious organizations strive to eliminate bigotry for the oppressed. These leaders and these organizations do not aim at abstract changes. Different groups—workers, the governed, and the oppressed— unite to work for important changes in their immediate life situations. Of course, life is complicated, and an individual may thus belong to or have his cause supported by several different advocates. (For example, he may be both a worker and belong to a racial minority).

An accepted principle in relation to advocacy groups is that *the advocate optimally attempts to transform those institutions which shape his own life.* This is far less clearly applied to youths, whose advocacy is often channeled by adults towards more distant, and sometimes abstract, causes. It is more consistent with psychological development and our social principles to allow youths to fully participate as advocates in shaping the institutions which, in turn, shape their lives. Giving the vote to 18-year-olds was one step in the direction of giving youths a voice in shaping major institutions.

Outside of the family, a major social institution which affects the personal development of children and youths is the school, which society entrusts to convey its highest values and beliefs about the democracy, equality, and freedom on which this nation is founded. Yet, schools have often become ineffective in conveying social values, at best, and dangerously oppressive, at worst.

One reason for the difficulties of educational institutions is the separation in schools between the schooled and the schoolers, between the taught and the teachers, and between the school and the community. There were times when these divisions were considerably more narrow. Socrates learned from the questions and assertions of his students, with whom he argued. The questions of a youthful friend and student inspired Maimonides to write his *Guide for the Perplexed.* To what degree today do elementary and high school teachers feel comfortable in discussing ideas with students, admitting ignorance, or in showing that they, too, are still studying and learning? To what extent are advocates invited into the school, or are students asked to consider matters of mutual concern in the community?

Socrates might say that the only programmed instruction from which a student could really learn—in a way that changed his character—was a program that the student himself helped to write. It is in this way that advocacy and instruction intersect. The renewal of educational institutions requires dramatic changes in the quality of school social relations. By advocating for the principles and causes that affect them, students can help create educational institutions of new vitality. To make this possible, however, the adults must feel secure enough about their own competence and personal worth to be able to acknowledge personal doubts, needs, and values. Today, the pre-conditions for advocacy are not met in most schools, for there is little coming together between adults and young people.

This analysis of schools is equally applicable to social institutions which affect youth: community centers, boys and girls clubs, youth organizations, athletic centers, sites of employment, churches, etc. The value of these institutions for the people they are meant to serve has often been reduced by the division between the provided and those provided for. Allowing young people to be advocates in institutions which are meant to serve them will not only benefit these youths directly. It will also bring new vitality to the institutions which serve them now and in which they will participate as adults in the future.

Steps Toward Relevance: An Interest-Centered Curriculum

Herman Ohme

> *A painter whose end object is a picture on a canvas, becomes interested not only in canvases, but in easels, in art exhibits, in paints, in the chemistry of color mixing, in light and shade, in other painters, in subjects for painting, etc.*
>
> > Samuel Tennenbaum,
> > William Heard Kilpatrick,
> > Trail-Blazer in Education

INTRODUCTION

There is little doubt that the traditional high school curriculum fails to provide the type of relevance that students need if they are to derive any real benefit from the great amount of time they spend in and out of the classroom in pursuit of an education.

Neither is there much doubt that the highly respected and widely publicized innovative practices fail to provide any real advance toward the development of a relevant curriculum. In secondary education the term "innovation" usually implies some form of modular scheduling, large or small groupings of students, independent study, team teaching, and some newer concepts such as "pontooning." Except for certain types of independent study, most of these innovative improvements offer little more than changes in organization or structure. When shorn of their new labels, they involve, simply, regrouping of students, varying allotments of class time, and some modifications of teacher roles. The curriculum content and the curriculum processes remain basically the same. After the initial break-in period, the novelty wears off, leaving the problems still unsolved and still demanding attention. Again, teachers and administrators are faced with the irrelevance of the traditional curriculum and the realization that, in spite of their heroic efforts at innovating, the problem has remained intact. As one frustrated principal observed, "The same old medicine has been put into a new bottle."

Educators who have attempted to provide relevance in the curriculum have

From *The Journal of Secondary Education* XLV no. 9 (Nov. 1970):299–304. Used by permission of the author and publisher.

discovered that a teacher may readily accept changes in the number of students he must meet on any given day, or the amount of time he must spend in delivering a lecture to a large group, or he may work well on a team with another teacher. Nevertheless, he will be extremely reluctant to accept the idea that changes should be made in the course he teaches—he rejects the idea of changing the course content, the homogeneous class, the grade level at which it is taught, the number of weeks required to teach it, the procedures for evaluating students, and the unquestioned importance of the course in the total curriculum. Few significant changes have been made in these areas, for to contemplate such changes is to invite attack from every teacher who looks upon any disruption of his well-ordered classroom routine as a call to arms. Under such circumstances, there can be little doubt as to the outcome of any attempt to introduce curriculum changes that are truly innovative.

Consequently, the reason why organizational and structural changes accomplish so little and usually result in such costly failure, is precisely this: the cart is put before the horse. The *form* (the schedule) has been redesigned in remarkable ways, but little significance has been attached to the *function* (the curriculum). It is as simple as that. Meaningful changes in the curriculum content and the process of learning must come before the mechanics of structuring can be considered. Before effective scheduling techniques can be devised, curriculum content must have been modified from the results of in-depth evaluation. The great need, therefore, is not for prepackaged "flexible scheduling," but for new approaches in developing and implementing curriculum content and process—for relating what is to be learned to the needs and interests of students.

An Interest-Center Curriculum in English

One such approach was initially implemented during the 1967–70 school year at North High School in Torrance, California. It is best described as an interest-centered English curriculum. Although begun in the English department, the concepts are applicable to any area of the curriculum. It is based on two major premises: (1) students take courses as electives from a broad range of selections high in interest value, and (2) teachers develop courses they want to teach, drawing from their own areas of interest and specialization.

The chief features of an interest-centered curriculum are these: It offers short-term courses, usually nine weeks in length; it allows for natural grouping of students according to interests; classes are nongraded, 10–12; and teachers serve as program counselors in their own subject areas.

Short-Term Electives

Essential to the interest concept is the short-term elective. This eliminates the semester or year survey-type course, so heavily weighted with fact and convention that spontaneity and enthusiasm are difficult to generate and impossible to sustain.

The short-term elective requires acceptance of the philosophic concept that one of the major goals of instruction is to develop skills and provide knowledge primarily so that the student will desire and be able to proceed on his own after he has completed the course. It is literally impossible to "cover" all of the material in a history or English literature class in a semester or even a year. What happens is usually an extremely uneven coverage of about fifty percent of the material up to the last few weeks, then a dash through the last half of the book without regard for students' interest, or the fact that the most important material of all, the current scene, has not been reached.

Short-term courses lend themselves to high interest levels because time is an important factor in sustaining interest. It cannot be wasted in study sessions, busy work, or too frequent testing.

Short-term courses also allow for greater variety in selection. A student has the opportunity to take at least four interest courses during the year, instead of one long dreary survey. It gives the teacher the unique opportunity to involve students in suggesting and even assisting in the development of courses. This not only makes for more enthusiastic teaching, but the teacher acquires a much greater understanding of the curriculum and the learning process.

Short-term courses are designed to integrate basic skills into the course content, and not treat them as isolated entities as is done so often in the traditional curriculum. Knowledge does not exist in a vacuum, and should not be taught in one. This is the quickest way for a student to lose interest.

The following are some examples of course titles offered to students, together with brief descriptions of course content developed by teachers and students at North High School for the interest-centered English curriculum:

Contemporary scene. Stop! Hear! Read! Think! How does man fit into our twentieth century world? What do Simon and Garfunkle have to say? And Rod McKuen? This course will tune in on what's happening now—where we're at—and what it's all about. It will explore all types of books and songs, including those chosen by the student which reflect modern man and the world he grooves in.

Prerequisite: Sincere interest in taking a look at the world around you.

Sports in literature. Discover the place of sports in literature today by exploring the lives of famous athletes, and by looking in on teams as they start championship drives. Although reading will comprise the backbone of the course, oral expression and composition will also be stressed.

Advertising: The miracle worker. Is advertising a demon or friend? This course will examine how advertising affects American life. Emphasis will be on writing and preparing printed radio and TV advertising.

Prerequisite: C average or better, 10th grade reading ability, and a curiosity about writing.

Journey into terror and the unknown. A coffin lid creaks open; airy mist floats down the stairs; a man screams in terror while being walled in. This is part of the journey into the atmosphere of the gothic. Other works in which astrology, ESP, witchcraft, ghosts, and psychic phenomena are the chief characteristics will be explored. There will also be journeys into the fantastic—worlds of the future, of the imagination, and of the unexplainable.

The full range of electives offered include the following categories: Adventure, Composition, Drama, Gothic-Bizarre-Mystery-and-Science fiction; The Hero; Humor, Language, Mass Media, Mythology, Short Story, Twentieth Century Man, Reading, and Television Production.

The selection process is closely related to the counseling done by the teachers, and the concept of natural grouping.

Natural Grouping

Students have always been grouped in classes either homogeneously—according to predetermined criteria, or heterogeneously—at random, usually by grade level.

Natural grouping, unlike either of the above, is grouping by common interest in a manner similar to the structure of society itself. The principle has rarely been utilized in learning.

The artificial and arbitrary "convenience" grouping done in most schools is closely associated with the traditional curriculum, and can only be altered when the curriculum itself is changed. It may well be that most of harm we do to students results from the arbitrary labels we pin on them, sometimes as early as kindergarten. These labels are in essence "success" and "failure" tags which the students usually manage to incorporate into their lives and their personalities.

In high schools the groups are often identified by a number, or as "college," "general," or "remedial." Coupled with this inappropriate categorization of students is a staff seniority system in which the longer-tenured teachers demand and get the college-bound students, while the less-experienced teachers get the remedials. As idiotic as this may seem, it is nonetheless true. The disastrous effects of this type of grouping attribute to the development of a chain that includes such other links as truancy, misbehavior, willful disobedience, suspension and dropout. Ultimately the burden comes to rest on the shoulders of parents and taxpayers.

It is significant that in the interest-centered curriculum there is no artificial or arbitrary assignment of students or teachers. The students are free to choose their courses from a broad range of offerings. In making their choices, they group themselves according to their own needs, interests, course content, and teacher recommendation. The courses they choose are designed to motivate them and to appeal to them. While students are often advised, they are never coerced. They choose. This freedom of choice is essential to the development of responsibility. It is active rather than passive participation in the learning process. It allows for enjoyment and a much greater possibility for success.

The role of the teacher in the process is also unique. Not only has he developed the course he will be teaching, he also becomes the program counselor.

The Teacher as Counselor

Developing an interest-centered course does not necessarily mean that it will be taught. Enough students must want to take it. This necessitates involving students in curriculum matters. It necessitates seeking their ideas and having dialogue with them as to what they would like. It makes it possible for teachers to gain insight into students, their needs, desires, likes, and dislikes. It requires the teacher to be the real expert in program counseling in his own subject area. It also makes it necessary for the teacher to communicate with his colleagues more frequently, and to know the content and objectives of the total curriculum in his department.

With the number and variety of interest-centered courses to be offered, and the frequency of choice resulting from the shorter term of the courses, the teacher becomes the ideal person to do the program counseling. This also benefits the guidance personnel by providing them with more time to do personal and vocational counseling.

Nongraded Classes, 10-12

The principles of the nongraded class are best exemplified in an interest centered curriculum. Differences in maturing are inconsequential when interest and enthusiasm in the subject are high. It is possible that in certain classes, the maturity level of students may actually be more homogeneous because of the fact that the class is nongraded and naturally grouped. Age can often be the least important factor in the maturity range of a given group.

It also becomes possible to offer a broader selection of electives. In some classes a prerequisite may be a necessary screening device, but grade level itself should not be a selection criterion.

Cost

Interest-centered classes need not cost significantly more than regular classes. Additional costs may arise from a greater need for clerical assistance, and a greater variety of instructional materials. In cases of limited budgets, the program can be started in a modest way, at almost no cost. As the staff becomes more sophisticated, differentiated duties, use of teacher aides, student assistance, and other unrealized potentials may make it possible to allocate more funds for the necessary materials and clerical time. A great deal will depend on teacher and administrator ingenuity, as well as cooperation and desire.

Expected Outcomes from an Interest-Centered Curriculum

The initial outcome from an interest-centered curriculum is a notable change in attitude on the part of both teachers and students. Students find that school ceases to be a place of drudgery, boredom, and captive audiences. Emphasis tends to shift from grades to a desire to learn; from fear of tests to continuous progress through a variety of evaluations that includes self-evaluation; from school regulation to the acceptance and recognition of individual responsibility; from apathy to involvement.

This is what relevance is all about. When a curriculum can help to bring about results such as these, then it has become a relevant curriculum. More specifically, the interest-centered curriculum tends to produce fewer failures and fewer behavior problems. Teachers, sparked by the enthusiasm of the students, find new interest in their work. They also acquire skills in curriculum development and in the understanding of the learning process which further augment their classroom effectiveness. This is a real step in the direction of meaningful differentiation in staff classification.

The motivation of learning itself, tends to ignite a chain reaction. For example, a course in environmental pollution might begin with an overview of the sociological problems involved. This, then would proceed to the physiological, economic, political and philosophical implications. All of these approaches would tend to cut across traditional secondary school departmental lines, and in turn could lead to the evolvement of a more relevant structural pattern that would bring about greater integration of the academic divisions and greater cooperation among teachers.

Under the stimulus of interest-centered courses, it follows that schedule modifications, decisions regarding class time allotments, personnel and facility utilization will become more relevant to the goals and the real needs of students and teachers. In such a curriculum, *form* will indeed follow *function*.

One rather painful outcome might result from this type of highly motivated program. It involves the weak teacher. In an interest-centered curriculum in which students have freedom of choice, the less effective teacher tends to stand out in an unfavorable light. Students who are free to choose, are also free not to choose, and assuredly they will not choose courses taught by teachers whose skills they do not admire. The less favored teachers are known to their colleagues, to parents, to administrators, as well as to the students. They are often protected by laws which originally were not intended to provide such protection. The interest-centered curriculum may motivate some to work harder and become more effective, it may force others to leave the profession, or the school. It may also create some problems that require new types of solutions.

In general, the interest-centered curriculum in any subject area cannot help but excite and motivate students and teachers. It offers great promise.

A total high school curriculum, entirely interest-centered, carefully planned and evaluated stage by stage, with a staff committed to the concept, could become the most significant and relevant curriculum that has yet been developed.

What Is Independent Study All About?

Donald W. Empey

In recent years considerable attention has been focused on student independent study by both elementary and secondary teachers.

Basically, independent study is the pursuit and acquisition of knowledge and skills by students with limited assistance from their classroom teachers. This is in contrast to the imparting of knowledge from teacher to student as is provided through lectures, demonstrations, and discussions. For some students independent study may be limited to acquiring understanding through seeking the answers to problems posed by teachers. For others, independent study may involve a self-directed learning activity completely divorced from any course requirements. It places emphasis on self-responsibility and self-regulation for learning. It can in-

From *Journal of Secondary Education* XLIII, no. 3 (March 1968): 104-108. Used by permission of the author and publisher.

volve research in the library, construction in the shop, or investigations in the laboratory.

Much of the professional literature pertaining to independent study is found in descriptions of such organizational plans as team teaching and flexible scheduling. Independent study need not be limited, however, to such plans. Schools with traditional programs can provide opportunities for independent study. To take full advantage of the opportunities available in team teaching and flexible scheduling, however, both teachers and students must know what independent study is all about.

Self-direction is one of the most important objectives of education. By the time a student graduates from senior high school, he should have developed a high sense of self-direction and motivation. Unfortunately, much of the education in our schools today consists of teachers talking and (hopefully) students listening. If pupils are to have an opportunity to develop self-direction, they must have an opportunity to experience it through independent study.

We live in a world of change in which the amount of knowledge is accumulating very rapidly. Much of what students learn today will be obsolete in the near future. Much of what they will need to know as adults is not yet known by anyone. The Educational Policies Commission of the National Education Association states that the average high school graduate today will have to be reeducated at least three times during his lifetime just to keep pace with the acceleration of knowledge. It is obvious that one of the primary functions of education is to help students "learn how to learn."

Independent study is psychologically sound. An individual learns best what he discovers for himself. Much of what is known about the learning process suggests that there may be altogether too much emphasis in schools placed on the teacher "transmitting knowledge." Valid research indicates that learning is better acquired when the teacher creates situations whereby the student can discover knowledge for himself.

At Arcadia (California) High School independent study has been divided into four phases. The distinction has been made as a convenience for teachers to help clarify the objectives of various types of independent study projects. It is realized, of course, that all aspects of independent study do not fit neatly into these compartments but the following classifications have proven to be helpful.

Phase One (the lesson for tomorrow). This level of independent study is initiated by the teacher. It is the customary daily or weekly homework assignment. The assignment may be an open-end or a closed-end activity. Drill or practice experiences, routine in nature, are examples of closed-end activities. Homework assignments may be left open-ended, thus helping the student learn how to use information in an orderly and creative way. For example, the assignment may call for the student to compare two characters in a literature selection, or see how many different ways a problem in mathematics can be solved.

To be truly effective, homework should be individualized; that is, the assignments given to pupils should be based on the student's need to acquire certain information or develop certain skills. In some cases, however, it may be an assignment that all students in the class are to complete. While the scope of the daily or weekly homework assignment is limited, it has a definite place in the total plan of independent study when used properly by teachers.

Phase Two (the self-instruction package). Phase two of independent study is also teacher initiated but wider in scope than phase one. Suppose the teacher is planning a unit on the Civil War. As part of this plan the teacher might prepare a package of materials to guide the student through various independent study experiences. Part of this package might be distributed to the student in the form of directions, guide questions, and statements of problems. Much of the package would be kept in the library or learning resource center to be used by students during time reserved for independent study. Part of the student's instructions might call for the use of reference books, periodicals, and pamphlets. The student might be asked to listen to recordings of music of the Civil War period. He might be asked to study maps, to view slides, video tape recordings, films, and filmstrips concerning various facets of the war.

This type of independent study calls for a much wider range of instructional materials than has been used in the past. Learning takes place better when various channels of communication can be used. Since some students learn best by reading, some by viewing, and some by listening, the multi-media approach to independent study can be effective.

Phase Three (the project). This phase of independent study may be initiated by the teacher or by the student and is very open-ended in nature. The student, upon his own initiative or upon the request of a teacher, selects a project to develop in some depth. Next, the student will do the necessary reading, viewing, listening, computing, examining or building. He will subsequently report the results of his work in some type of presentation to the class or to the teacher. This phase of independent study provides an opportunity for the student to be creative and self-directing in completing the project.

Care must be taken by the teacher and the student in outlining what the project will involve so that it does not become "busy work." So many classroom projects are the "cut and paste" variety, which has very limited learning value. The objectives of a project need to be well defined in advance.

Phase Four (individualized research). Phase four is the highest level of independent study. It is student-initiated and self-directed with limited assistance from the teacher. It begins with the student selecting a topic of interest and value to him. He then asks a teacher to be his advisor and together they outline the objectives of the project, the procedures to be followed, and the system for reporting and evaluating the project. Such an activity may extend over an entire semester or year with the student reporting his progress to the teacher periodically. The project need not be in conjunction with a course in which the student is currently enrolled.

This type of independent study activity might involve a student in science research utilizing the facilities of the science laboratory and the assistance of the science staff. It may involve a research paper for a student of history. It may involve the construction of an engine or the making of clothing for students in the practical arts.

Often, the quest for knowledge will lead the student outside the confines of the school. With assistance from the student advisor, it may be possible for interviews to be arranged with experts in the field of interest. The pupil doing research in science, therefore, may receive advice and assistance from staff members from a nearby university or industrial establishment. The student studying the problems of urbanization may spend time assisting staff members in a Head Start project.

So often teacher planning focuses on classroom presentations and discussions. Actually, as the teacher plans, consideration should be given to at least four types of learning activities. First, the teacher should consider what types of experiences need to be provided through presentations by the teacher. Second, the teacher needs to plan experiences which provide an opportunity for interaction among students. Third, consideration should be given to activities involving laboratory experiences. Finally, the teacher needs to determine what kinds of activities can be pursued by the student on his own.

As teachers consider the placement of activities into the four categories presented above, many are surprised at the number of things that are now being done in the classroom for all which could be done independently. As students assume more responsibility for their own learning, the role of the teacher, of course, changes considerably. He becomes an expert in helping pupils discover knowledge for themselves. Most independent study thus becomes a very integral part of the total learning strategy developed by the teachers. Its planning involves attention equal to that which is given to preparing for lectures and discussions.

One of the most difficult tasks facing educators today is the selection of materials to assist teachers and students in independent study. During the past five years, considerable emphasis has been placed on the manufacturing and acquisition of equipment. Much of this equipment, such as the teaching machine, has great potential for utilization in independent study. However, the "software" to be used in these machines is lacking.

In the past, educators have placed most of the emphasis in independent study on the use of printed materials. There is, however, great potential in the proper utilization of a wide variety of media. Materials for independent study include not only books and periodicals but also such items as tape and disc recordings, filmstrips, slides, and videotaped programs. Recent developments in the use of 8mm film are particularly applicable to individual study. Programmed learning has, perhaps, its greatest potential in the area of independent study. If a student is having difficulty in a particular segment of a course, or if he wishes to engage in enrichment work within that course, programmed learning materials have been and can be written to be of assistance to him.

Independent study takes many forms. Facilities for such learning also vary. Independent study may take place at a student's desk, at a study center within a classroom, at a library or at a resource center.

School libraries must be more than book collections. Space and equipment should be made available for listening and viewing stations. The use of audiovisual materials cannot be limited to the classroom only. These materials must be made available to students in the school library or instructional materials center.

The study carrel, equipped with facilities for viewing and listening, has a place not only in the library or instructional materials center, but also in certain classrooms. Primary grade teachers have found that students can benefit from viewing and listening in independent study carrels.

As the concept of independent study grows in a school, the library may be inadequate. Learning resource centers and open laboratories located throughout the school will provide additional areas for individual study. Resource centers for social science, English, and mathematics, as well as laboratories for science and industrial arts, will provide opportunities for independent study to become an integral part of the total instructional program. Such centers will be supplied with the necessary apparatus, supplementary textbooks, periodicals and pamphlets. Resource centers may have library books and audio-visual materials pertaining to particular topics assigned on a temporary basis. The centers should be equipped with tables and chairs, bookcases, study carrels, and listening and viewing stations. Experimental programs are under way in some school districts which will provide an interlocking system of informational retrieval in the resource centers, the library, and classrooms, through dial access.

The Case for the Small High School

Aaron Cohodes

The notion that anything small can be done better by anything big is an insidious part of our current society. Small firms are gobbled up by larger firms and larger firms are digested by even larger firms. To make it these days is to be crowned with the current supreme accolade: super.

Well, maybe bigness in itself is really not so hotsy-totsy, although it may be a little late in the day for some schoolmen to take this position. What has happened is that, virtually without exception, every school that is big tries to find ways of appearing smaller. And most schools that are small try to find ways of appearing bigger. For heaven's sake, as Burke told Congress, satisfy somebody.

The cult of bigness is producing a new race of nomads, Alvin Toffler points out in *Future Shock*. There is, Toffler writes, a definite tendency for the more nomadic children to avoid participating in the voluntary side of school life—clubs, sports, student governments, and other extracurricular activities. The bigger the school, the less likely they are to be involved.

In *The Greening of America*, Charles A. Reich provocatively examines the revolt by our younger generation against what he calls the impersonal corporate state.

In still another assessment of the so-called classroom crisis, Charles E. Silberman makes a convincing case for more humane classrooms, although in the process he makes it clear he prefers the British method of administration, where principals teach as well as manage.

From The Bulletin of the National Association of Secondary School Principals LV, no. 355 (May 1971):106–111. Adapted from an article that originally appeared in *Nation's Schools*, September 1970, written by Stanton Leggett, Arthur Shapiro, Aaron Cohodes, and C. W. Brubaker. Used by permission of the author and publisher.

ENDORSEMENTS OF THE HUMANISTIC APPROACH

I commend all three of these books to you—*Greening of America, Future Shock,* and *Crisis in the Classroom*—if only as defense against some of the literate parents of your students who you may be sure will read them and take immediate positions on what their high school should or should not be doing. The books do have several things in common. For one thing, they are interminable. For another, they all prescribe, or seem to endorse, a humanistic approach to education, where students can find themselves at their own rate without always being in a competitive crowd.

The best place for this kind of education is in a small high school. But up to a few years ago, if you asked most educators to think small instead of big about secondary school education, the chances are they would frown—especially if they were weaned on the Conant dictum that high schools of fewer than 750 students don't count.

The thing to keep in mind is that few first-rate schools across the country are big. But a lot of big schools across the country are not first-rate. "There is something about largeness that attracts more problems," admitted one high school principal. "But we continue to build larger and larger schools."

The fact a lot of people seem to ignore is that a frightening number of urban high schools provide essentially custodial care. Their services are for the most part remedial or disciplinary and education is the ingredient that fills the time between the rumbles. You don't need a study to prove this, although there are some. You only need eyes.

Well, of course, there is something about smallness that attracts problems, too, of a different kind. The trend toward school consolidation in rural areas is unremitting, according to *The New York Times* and the NEA, in large part because of the increased recognition that all kids should have an equal shot at being prepared for college. You consolidate, in short, to get calculus. But there are some who contend you can have all the values of small size and calculus too.

EVERYONE IS NEEDED

Possibly the best argument for reconsidering prevailing strictures on the size of high schools, as I have tried to suggest, comes from the kids themselves. When a school is small, each student is really needed. This is an important counterbalance to our impersonal culture. At least one prominent educational consultant, Stanton Leggett, argues that new curriculum developments, which take into account reorganized programs and human talent, can help make the small school workable and desirable. Not long ago, in the *Nation's Schools*, an article making the case for a small high school[1] used the premise that small schools can compete successfully with larger ones and provide an effective range of experiences for students under two conditions: (1) that the teaching model be shifted and (2) that four organizational devices now being used be synchronized.

---

[1] By Leggett, Arthur Shapiro, C. W. Brubaker, and myself. The educational ideas in this paper are based largely on material developed by Stanton Leggett & Associates, Inc., Chicago.

THE TEACHING MODEL

In the "Smallway concept," the teacher must shift his approach and become a guide to learning, foregoing the satisfaction of transmitting facts. Under this model, a class of at least 20 students is not necessary to make offering a course worthwhile. Approaches in which students learn at their own speed make it possible to offer advanced placement physics or calculus, for example, to one, two, or ten kids. Using this kind of thinking, a high school could handle 250 students with only 10 faculty members plus a combination principal/counselor and a librarian/teacher. This group could offer 70 or more courses each year with more flexibility than larger schools.

When teachers would be selected for Smallway, the idea would be to start with the variety of talents wanted. This would determine the size of the staff and in turn the approximate student population. An increase in desirable teachers would increase the population accordingly. Here, rather quickly, are the talents that should be represented on the faculty: artist, businessman, communications and literary expert, home economics specialist, language instructor, mathematician, musician, scientist, social scientist, technologist, and several teachers interested in athletics. A key suggestion here is that one good general scientist may be worth a number of specialized ones. One scientist, whatever his specialty, who understands scientific procedures and processes and can transfer these concepts to students is really what we're looking for.

The community, of course, must pitch in. Smallway depends on specialists in the area who can widen student knowledge and provide them with a kind of apprenticeship in specific fields. What scientist or doctor or engineer or musician will turn down a sincere invitation to "come out and help the kids"? Quite probably, some of these local resources can be persuaded to work with the school staff on some sort of subcontracting basis that makes them responsible for a given portion of the curriculum.

ORGANIZATIONAL PATTERNS

Here are the four organizational devices that make Smallway feasible:

Phasing—A proposal that all students of the school study one major curriculum topic at a time. Phasing assumes a nongraded structure; it questions the validity of having a ninth-grade course that is different from one for tenth-grade students. Who are schools kidding? In the area of social studies, the school might offer three major courses: American history, world studies, and government. These are scheduled in different years, and all students take them at the same time.

Short-term minicourses reject the theory that in order to "take a subject" you have to spend a year or more at it. The inoculation period, in fact, may be nine or as few as three weeks.

As we've suggested, the nongraded approach is basic to Smallway. Whenever we do anything that counts in education, we upgrade, mixing the experienced with the inexperienced.

Uncommitted time in the learning schedule is the fourth guidepost in our organizational patterns. A considerable amount of time should be left open for students and teachers to use at their own discretion.

We hope we're not giving the impression that the small high school is an irresistibly attractive concept. It has both advantages and disadvantages. Only a fool is certain and assured, as Montaigne has observed. One of the problems we face in education is that, by definition, we can't be sure of what will happen when we experiment with the curriculum and organization pattern. And when we promise more than we can perform, a lot of the true values in the new program get lost in the criticism that "You didn't do all that you said you would do."

Here, then, are some of the disadvantages of the small high school that simply won't go away:

1. Since we tend to equate efficiency with large size, there may be a public credibility gap.
2. In a small high school, kids can't get lost in a crowd. Sometimes, this kind of protection is most useful.
3. Smallway can't have large-scale football, cheerleading, marching bands, etc.
4. The school is so small that failure of any component is clearly visible.
5. Resources, such as software and audiovisual equipment, will be costly in proportion to the number of students.
6. Some degree of staff specialization is lost.

In contrast, here are the education advantages:

1. Teachers cannot hide behind the ceremonial system of a large school.
2. What students are really like will make a difference.
3. Parents can be more involved in a small school. In a large school, the power source may be surrounded with a smoke screen of ceremonial systems.
4. It costs very little more to be small—if the teaching system changes.
5. A huge program, based on and tailored to the needs of the students, is feasible.
6. At Smallway, everyone is needed. No one is left out. All can participate wisely.

Will the Smallway concept work?

We think so. Bits and pieces of it have been tried. We think a careful and extended trial is warranted at the very least on the grounds that what now is available is not conspicuously successful.

The air is filled with public rebukes of education. When a community explodes over such issues as race, the high school principal sits—if he can squirm past the placards and protesters—in the middle of a mess that has festered since the Civil War. It is a mess he did not make, but nobody cares about that. What everybody does care about is having the mess cleaned up. Now. Right away. Instant accomplishment.

Not long ago, I was involved in a presentation before some teachers; and, as usually happens in such situations, I didn't spend much time on what was good about the teachers, but I spent a lot of time on ways they might consider improving their performance. One teacher approached me afterwards with a kind of pained look on his face and said, "Mr. Cohodes, you may never have an ulcer, but you certainly are a carrier."

All of us involved in education, I submit, must be classified as carriers even though this may not stop the ulcers.

THE PRINCIPAL MUST BE CUCKOO

The way things stand, anybody who wants to become a high school principal these days must be just a little cuckoo. He must guide the teaching staff while appearing to be guided. He must negotiate with everyone in the community above the age of six. He must steer clear of unreasonable indebtedness and move relentlessly toward improved educational opportunities for all students—while following encrusted policies that are often unsound or illegal or insane. If he is to hang around a while, he must accomplish these hazardous assignments with the tacit if not enthusiastic support of all groups involved, many of which, by the nature of his job, he must frequently rebuff or outrage. And, of course, he must expect his background, his pedigree, and his motives to be questioned regularly in the crudest possible terms.

The wonder is that there aren't more high school principalships going begging. This is the Age of Aquarius, but it is also the age of the activists. Citizens, students, and teachers who are mad no longer stew over it. They make themselves heard. For the high school principal, it would seem there are compelling reasons, and advantages, for reaching out, instead of digging in, to try new approaches in an intelligent and, indeed, an aggressive fashion. The definition of a leader is one who leads.

Exploring Childhood: A New Way for High School Students to Learn

Marilyn Clayton

Peter B. Dow

Can high school students learn from working with preschool children? A few years ago most educators would have smiled at the proposition, or regarded it as appropriate only for courses in "homemaking" or "family life." But today teenagers in increasing numbers—both boys and girls—are invading day care centers, Head Start programs, preschools, and even formal kindergartens, seeking opportunities to care for, teach, and learn from the very young.

In a barrio section of Houston, for example, an enthusiastic group of black, Chicano, and "Anglo" students have taken over two prefabricated classroom buildings adjacent to their high school and are running a nursery school with the help of their home economics teacher, a community social worker and a group of neighborhood parents. With the strong support of their social studies teacher,

From *Children Today* II, no. 2 (March–April, 1973), pp. 8–13. Used by permission of the authors and the publisher.

an equally motivated group of 86 high school students in Boston combed their community, as well as two neighboring school districts, to locate day care centers and kindergartens where they could spend up to a whole day a week working with preschoolers.

Sparked by this growing interest in young children on the part of adolescents, educators are becoming increasingly excited about the potential for new learning that involvement with the young can bring about. "Cross-age" tutoring programs —where older students work with younger ones in all areas of the curriculum— are found with increasing frequency in the nation's secondary schools. Activities that take students out of the school are less widespread and more difficult to administer; but the growing popularity of "open" and "flexible" campus programs in many high schools is making it feasible for teenage students to create work-study programs for themselves, and to have apprenticeship experiences outside of the classroom.

One effort to develop and extend the possibilities for using work with young children as a way for high school students to develop new skills is the "Exploring Childhood" program. This combination of field and course work is being designed by the Social Studies Program of the Education Development Center in Cambridge, Massachusetts, under grants from the Office of Child Development and the National Institute of Mental Health. The program, which is being piloted this year in seven school systems and is scheduled for testing in 200 sites next fall, asks high school students to use their experiences with children as a way of learning about human growth and development.

The program has many goals. For some students, working with children is fascinating because—although they may not want to talk about it—they expect to be married shortly and have families, and they would like to know how to provide a healthy environment for their children's growth. (An increasing number of high school students, in fact, are parents already and are in special need of information about child development.) For others, studying childhood is a new way of learning about themselves. Many of the issues preschool children face as they begin spending time away from their families are similar to the stormy problems adolescents encounter as they prepare to leave school for employment, college, or to start their own families. For still another group, the importance of "Exploring Childhood" lies in the way it helps them think about possible careers that relate to working with the young: education, health care, social work, and even some areas of business and the law.

But perhaps the central purpose of "Exploring Childhood" for all students is to help them understand that there are valuable links between learning and living. For example, we recently visited an informal center for preschoolers in a Boston YWCA, which is being run by an older woman with the help of several high school students. The children range in age from toddlers to 4-year-olds. The high school students have been encouraging the children to draw and have begun to assemble a rather impressive collection of children's art, ranging from a child's first scribbles to colorful and carefully drawn pictures of people, houses, and trees. At the same time, they are taking "Exploring Childhood" for three hours a week.

Among the topics students examine in the course is children's art. The course material traces the development of line, shape, and symbol in children's drawings, discusses cross-cultural differences in the content of children's art, and shows at what age those differences emerge. By comparing the drawings made by the pre-schoolers they know with the class materials on children's art, students are quickly able to identify the emergence of line, shape, and symbol in the children's drawings. This comparison leads naturally into a discussion of the development of motor control and intellectual growth.

But physical and cognitive development are only two aspects of what can be observed in children's art, and the course material also raises questions about emotional and social growth. Recently one teacher, after completing a discussion of representation in children's art, asked his group of all white, mostly working class students, "Have you ever seen the drawings of black children? What kind of faces do they draw?" After a pause, one girl answered: "I used to work in the kindergarten and there were some black children there. The faces they drew were always white." The class went on to discuss why this might be so.

Still another dimension of "Exploring Childhood" is suggested by the children's art unit. High school students, like all of us, find that telling younger people what to do is irresistible. Therefore, it is not surprising that some students have tried to influence their children's drawings. During our visit to the YWCA pre-school, the following dialogue took place.

Visitor: "Why is that fence in the drawing?"

Student: "Well, the child was making grass but got tired of it, so I suggested that she put a fence in instead."

Visitor: "Isn't it curious the way the tree is placed so close to the flower? I wonder what the child meant by that?"

Student: "She had already drawn the flower and we suggested that she include a tree, so she put the tree next to the flower."

The classroom issue that may follow is not, "Should we or should we not shape children?" but rather "When do we shape children?" and "What are the consequences?" For shaping is always present in human interactions, and particularly in such environments as schools and preschools.

In summary, the unit on children's art exemplifies that major features of the "Exploring Childhood" program. Our goal is to provide ideas and information that will capture the interest of a diverse group of students, whether they are headed for college, work or raising their own families. It is designed so that learning proceeds from the direct experience of working with children and the "knowledge" presented in class is organized to support that first-hand experience.

The course views childhood from many perspectives and has been developed with the help of scholars from a variety of disciplines, including Dr. Jerome Kagan, T. Berry Brazelton, M.D., and Dr. Urie Bronfenbrenner. Emphasis is not placed on presenting particular theories about child development but on helping teenagers learn to become explicit about two aspects of the way they think about children: the goals and values they hold for what a human being should be like, both as a child and as an adult, and their own theories about how much a child can be shaped by other people.

The pedagogy of "Exploring Childhood" depends heavily on the students' experience in working with young children. Activities are designed to allow students to move from the concrete to the conceptual—deriving ideas, problems and questions for the classroom from work in the field.

Respecting the experience many students have had with children is particularly beneficial for students who have previously had no academic success. Many students come to "Exploring Childhood" with expertise. They have been baby-sitters for neighbors; they have interacted with, and been responsible for, brothers and sisters; they have ideas, suggestions, and experiences that matter to their class-mates. This class may mark the first time anyone has listened to them as if they had something worthwhile to say. A pedagogy that uses both the experience of working with children and the feelings that result from this work as a source of ideas about human development creates a classroom context in which feelings and intellect are not separated but mutually respected.

"Exploring Childhood' 'is being designed to be adopted by schools as either a totally new course or as a supplement to ongoing programs. In either case, the subject areas under which the program may be adopted are many: home eco-nomics, guidance, family living, child development, psychology, and so on. Simi-larly, the field sites that provide the students' work experience may range widely in purpose and structure: preschools, nursery schools, Head Start programs, child care centers, kindergartens, and laboratory schools in junior and senior high schools. In addition, the young children, as well as the students, come from a nation whose population is characterized by an enormous diversity of cultural traditions, values and goals concerning the task of rearing children. Our approach to the challenge of preparing teenagers to be responsive to such diversity in methods and values is to avoid teaching specific childrearing techniques and practices, and to emphasize (a) apprenticeship to the teacher of young children and (b) observation of how the world looks and feels to a child.

The course is made up of a variety of materials organized around three general content areas: cross-age helping, child development and socialization. During the first month the program concentrates on cross-age helping issues. This is designed to give students some initial competence before they go to their field sites, and to build the class into a supportive group prepared to share members' successes, failures, ideas and insights throughout the year. Students observe at field sites, report back to the class, and compare and contrast their experiences. Booklets in storyboard format, audio-tapes and films allow students to sharpen their observation skills and develop ways of working together in problem-solving.

Once students have started working with children, the second large unit of class work begins: study of the basic patterns of child development. Through their observations at field sites, activities conducted with young children and class study and discussion, students build a working background of ideas organized around three questions: What are the universal patterns of development? How does human diversity develop? What is necessary to support development?

To help students develop a concrete sense of what a young child is like, they are asked to record their observations and identify the major features of children's development, based upon their own reactions, inferences and generalizations. A film that juxtaposes children of different ages is used for studying the sequence of development and for examining behavioral differences in children of the same age.

In addition to the children's art unit, topics for study include children's play and children's developing perceptions of other people. Students begin work on "A Child's View of People" by reflecting on their experiences at field sites and by considering such questions as, "Do you think the children see you as you are?" At the field site students look at the way children's drawings portray mothers and fathers, other children and themselves. They play games with children that help them see a child's egocentrism. The use of picture cards, for example, and of books that children consistently "show" upside down to someone across the table, illustrate the difficulty a child has in understanding the perspective of another person.

In the second half of the year, after students have explored numerous aspects of development in depth and have a sense of the filter through which a child experiences the world, they begin to study socialization. First they explore a child's immediate world and examine what happens in his daily interactions with friends, family and other people. Film is used here as the major medium of instruction, showing students a series of families at breakfast and enabling them to see commonplace interactions and to ask such questions as, "What values are being transmitted?" "What is the child learning about men, about women?" Again, the focus is on overall patterns in the ways families express love and care for their children, show authority, handle conflicts and foster autonomy.

Students then look at the larger context of society. What kind of support do families need in caring for their young? How do various societies meet these needs? Films will show them examples of societies organized in ways different from our own.

Students are frequently given opportunities and techniques for evaluating their own learning in the program—an important ability if they are to continue to learn after the course is over. In addition to questionnaires and exercises for self-evaluation, students keep journals throughout the year that relate what they are learning about children to what they are learning about themselves.

Teachers of the program have many roles in addition to that of conducting the high school class. They are counselors, program organizers and "teacher" trainers. Frequently these teachers do not have a strong background in the field of child development, but they can bring other people into the classroom as a supporting resource: a preschool teacher, a pediatrician, a social worker, parents of the young children and other community members.

At monthly seminars, the preschool teachers meet with the high school teachers to work through major course concepts and share their views on what students and children are experiencing in the program. The teacher education component of "Exploring Childhood" is being designed to review the important issues that students deal with in the course. Teachers will be helped to become explicit about their goals for students and their concept of learning, and to think about how the experience of watching their students teach and care for small children develops their own views about the learning process. The program offers both teachers and students a chance to grow, through aiding and experiencing the growth of others.

Although "Exploring Childhood" is still in the formative stages, it has already stimulated a good deal of interest around the country. The growing concern of high school teachers and administrators for providing productive work-study situations for their students, coupled with the nation's expanding interest in the preschool child, has provided a very favorable reception for programs of this kind. The major problems, of course, are finding sites that will accept students in apprenticeship roles and overcoming the organizational and logistical barriers which might hinder the establishment of effective working partnerships between community agencies and the schools. So far these obstacles have been minimal, due to the limited scale of the program this year. Our experience next year, when we attempt to introduce the program on a nationwide basis, should yield more information. How many school systems and communities will endorse a style of learning that assumes that direct experience with young children is a necessary part of a course in child development? For those who do agree that learning and living must be organically linked, "Exploring Childhood" may provide an important model for reform in all areas of the social studies curriculum.

High School with No Walls—It's a Happening in Philadelphia

Henry S. Resnik

In the great jungle of public education, the high schools are open game these days, and the onslaughts of the critics, from respected academics to long-haired student activists, are having a devastating effect. The severest criticisms define the typical American high school as a prison-and-factory, but even establishment insiders have admitted that most high schools are several generations behind the times. Everybody, it seems, is looking for alternatives, and the school system of Philadelphia has found what many educational reformers consider a truly exciting possibility: an experimental high school called the Parkway Program.

A year-round happening, the program is a school without grades, marks, arbitrary rules, authority figures, a building—or, its advocates claim, boredom.

The locale is in and around central Philadelphia: in offices, museums, science centers, hospitals, theaters, department stores; in luncheonettes, in the Automat, on street corners, and stairways. Students can opt for such courses as: law enforcement at the administration building of the Police Department, library science at the public library, and biology at the Academy of Natural Sciences. In fact, with all of Philadelphia as a resource, Parkway students are free to study just about anything that may interest them.

When most administrators want to boast about a new high school, they produce drawings of a $14-million edifice that took three years to build; the best picture of the Parkway Program is an aerial view of Philadelphia's Center City. The program is named after the Benjamin Franklin Parkway, a mile-long boulevard lined with cultural institutions that begins at City Hall and culminates in the Greek-revival Museum of Art on a hill overlooking the Schuylkill River. The Parkway Program brushes aside the traditional notion that learning must be acquired within four-walled boxes called classrooms and acknowledges that life and

From *Think* XXXV (November–December, 1969):33–36. Reprinted by permission from *Think Magazine*, published by IBM, copyright © 1969 by International Business Machines Corporation.

learning are all part of the same ongoing process. The city itself is the classroom, and the life of the city is the curriculum.

NO LID TO BLOW

There are no dropouts here. Parkway students linger long after scheduled classes are over and often volunteer to come in for various weekend activities. As far as the program is concerned, no administrators are worried that "the lid will blow." There *is* no lid.

Perhaps most important, the program is structured to acknowledge the value and uniqueness of every individual. For most of the people the program serves— teachers and students as well—school has become a portal to self-fulfillment.

Philadelphia's "school without walls" began as a brilliant gimmick for decreasing overcrowding—at virtually no cost to the school system—and publicizing the climate of innovation that a new Board of Education had been trying to establish since the beginning of 1966.

According to local legend, a board official looked out his office window in the board's Parkway headquarters one day, saw the huge palaces of culture—the Free Library, the Franklin Institute, the Art Museum and dozens of others—that line the Parkway for most of its length, and said, "Why not use all this as the campus of a high school?" When the proposal was announced in February 1968, it was the talk of Philadelphia—the combination of economy and novelty lent the idea an almost irresistible magic. Several leaders of Parkway institutions complained that they had not been consulted and that their participation was far from guaranteed, but these objections were lost amid the general din of rosy publicity.

Old guard administrators at the Philadelphia Board of Education still maintain, as they did at the beginning, that the program is no more than a good job of public relations on the part of the reformist board and the liberal administration of Superintendent of Schools Mark Shedd. It is indeed good copy, but more than any other single experiment in Philadelphia's huge reform movement, the Parkway Program delivers the basic educational changes that Shedd promised when the Board hired him early in 1966. Although the program has a good deal of surface glitter and seems so much a merely slick idea, it questions basic assumptions about the structure of schools. Its supporters believe that its potential for effecting change is virtually unlimited.

"THE RIGHT MAN"

In retrospect, it is clear that the possibilities of the proposal might never have been realized if it had fallen into the wrong hands. For months after the board's announcement, traditionalists within the school system limited their reaction to questions about how administrators could ever coordinate the activities of so vast and sprawling a campus. For them, the proposed "Parkway High School" was merely a difficult exercise in scheduling, a nightmare vision of shuttle buses jamming the parkway, and harried vice principals imploring systems analysts to help them out of the mess. If this attitude had prevailed, the program could easily have amounted to a bizarre variation on the usual humdrum theme.

But then, in June 1968, the board announced the appointment of 42-year-old John Bremer as the program's director. An Englishman and a born rebel, Bremer had roughly twenty years of educational experimentation to his credit. Nine of these he had spent in England, principally in connection with the Leicestershire Schools, which are now being widely hailed as models for reform in elementary education throughout the United States. Most recently, after emigrating to America and teaching education at the university level, Bremer had been unit administrator of New York's Two Bridges district, a tempest-torn effort at decentralization and community control. Bremer was so soft-spoken and mild-mannered that some observers within the central administration wondered in the beginning whether he could handle the politics of the job. Soon, however, their fears were set firmly to rest, for it became clear as time went on that, in the words of an educational consultant close to the program, Bremer has been "the right man in the right place at the right time."

Typical of Bremer's approach was his insistence, from the earliest days of his appointment, that, contrary to popular belief, there would be no shuttle buses connecting the various parkway institutions—students would have to find their own way of getting from one place to another, no matter what the distance. The decision reflects a philosophy that has come to dominate the program and to determine its basic shape and style: Bremer is committed to individual growth, creativity, and autonomy; he is an enemy of bureaucracies that tell people exactly what to do and think (or how to get to a destination); he delights in public criticism of the educational establishment. At the opening of the summer session in July 1969, he told a group of students entering the program for the first time, "In terms of behavior and attitudes, you're going to have to unlearn everything you've learned in your public school education so far, as quickly as possible."

The pilot "unit" of the Parkway Program opened in February 1968, with approximately 140 students, among whom half were black and 20 were from Philadelphia suburbs; nine full-time teachers; another ten or so student-teachers or undergraduate interns; and a huge second-story loft headquarters two blocks from City Hall. A second unit was opened, in rented office space five blocks from the first, at the beginning of the summer session, enrolling another 130 students. In September 1969, a third unit, about ten blocks from the first, was opened in an old school building. This consists of an elementary school for 130 children in kindergarten through fourth grade, modeled on the libertarian British infant schools that Bremer helped to pioneer, and a high school for 130 students who participate in and study, among other things, the entire operation of the elementary school. A fourth unit, again with 130 high school students, has just opened. The original plan called for a high school of 2,400 students, and although Bremer has considered such modifications of the plan as a "nongeographical school district" encompassing much larger numbers of students throughout the city, each unit in the growing program has been modeled on the same basic pattern.

One of the greatest attractions of the Parkway Program for students is the tremendous freedom it allows—some observers believe that the program is merely chaotic. Bremer insists, however, that he has provided a tight "internal" structure. While each unit has taken on a distinct character of its own, any any rate, certain structural elements are common to the entire program:

LIKE A FAMILY

Tutorial Groups

These groups of about fifteen students and two teachers are the principal base, rather like a family, of each student's Parkway career. In the tutorial group, which meets for two hours four days a week, the student plans his schedule, receives personal counseling, and makes up deficiencies in such basic skills as reading and math. Some tutorial groups plan parties and outings; others organize informal athletic events; others agree to study a subject of mutual interest. The tutorials are also responsible for the extensive written evaluations of both students' and teachers' work that take the place of grades.

Selection by Lottery

One of Bremer's educational axioms is, "Anything that can be measured is educationally worthless." Consequently, the Parkway Program bypasses standardized tests as a basis for admission and favors the totally random method of drawing names from a hat. There were 10,000 applications for the 130 places in the second unit; some teenagers burst into tears when they missed their chance at the public drawing.

HOW TEACHERS ARE CHOSEN

Faculty Selection by Committee

Most teachers in the Parkway Program are selected by committees consisting of university students, parents from the community, visiting teachers, and students and teachers from other units. After the initial interviews, a few dozen of the most promising applicants are assigned the task of deciding what process of elimination they should use in filling the limited number of openings, and are then observed by Bremer and key advisers as they thrash out the problem.

Institutional Offerings

Each unit is responsible for enlisting the aid of the various downtown institutions, both public and private, in the form of courses and other projects, which range from discussion and planning groups to paid employment. So far, each unit has managed to line up more than thirty offerings. The Parkway catalog lists 90 "cooperating institutions."

Faculty Offerings

Since the program operates only within general requirements for the high school diploma in the State of Pennsylvania, the permanent faculty members have been able to explore many subjects and courses of study that the traditional high school would never allow. During the first session, for example, students could choose from such unusual fare as: "Psychology and Personal Problems," "Multimeda Journalism," "Filmmaking," "Vagabond Sketching," "Kite-flying," numerous workshops in creative writing, and courses in 10 languages.

Town Meetings

Sometimes shouting sessions, sometimes orderly public debates, the program's weekly town meetings have emerged as the principal form of government in each unit. Discussions range from such basic questions as what kinds of rules and philosophies the unit should adopt to such mundane matters as the filling out of forms, but the emphasis throughout is on total participatory democracy.

"EVERYBODY'S YOUR FRIEND"

What may be the most important factor in the program's success, however, is the emphasis on community that has come to motivate the behavior of most participants as if it were a religious force. The various structural elements have certainly encouraged this sense of community, but it seems to derive as much from Bremer's inspiring, almost charismatic vision as any other single factor. According to Mario Fantini, the program's liaison with its initial sponsor, the Ford Foundation, "John Bremer made the program *human*." Most teachers are known, at any rate, by their first names only, and students usually describe the warmth and intimacy of the program as if they can scarcely believe they have found such things in a place called school. "Here you get the feeling that everybody's your friend" is a typical reaction.

Bremer insists that the almost random selection of students and faculty has neutralized his power to create a private fiefdom; nevertheless, it is clear to any visitor that he has set the tone for the entire operation and that this tone is almost always informal and spontaneous. Members of the first unit were so friendly and drew so close, in fact, that they may have inadvertently perpetuated a certain anti-establishment cliquishness.

"The first day of the program," reports one teacher who had had more than a decade in the traditional system, "one of the students said 'What do you want to be called? Some of the teachers are called "Mr." or "Mrs." Some are called by their first names.' I said You call me 'Mrs.' After 10 days' time I didn't want anybody calling me 'Mrs.' again."

Another teacher defines what seems to be the most important factor in the self-education of everyone in the Parkway community: "One of the things I've gotten," he observes, "is a sense of power. In the regular school situation you have it within the confines of the classroom, but here I'm really in control of myself and the program as it affects me and the people I'm working with. There's always the sense that the kids are teaching you and you're teaching the kids."

"My kid had already dropped out, even though he was still going to school," says the father of a Parkway student. "They discouraged him at his old school; they discouraged his musical talent, one of his main interests. He's a much different person now—he's interacting with the other kids and the faculty to a far greater extent. . . ."

Constantly attracting such testimonials from throughout the city, the Parkway Program flaunts its own inability to be evaluated in traditional terms.

"It's founded on a new principle of what education is," says Mario Fantini, who is also one of Ford's leading educational theorists. "The existing system isn't working. If you look at the student unrest as a symptom of the inability of the educational system, forged in another century, to be responsive to the concerns of this generation, it seems that many of those concerns would be addressed in a Parkway-like school."

MORE PARKWAY PROGRAMS

Some educators across the country seem to agree. By the fall of 1969, similar programs were under way in at least four major cities; several community groups in Philadelphia were eager to align themselves with Bremer and his philosophy; the Board of Education had voted to increase the size of the student body in 1969 to 700; and Bremer had a pledge of $500,000 from the school system's operating budget. For once, it seemed, a school had managed to please just about everybody.

There have been critics, of course. The program has been attacked as just another of the board's fancy experiments and there have been threats to block city funding. Yet the Parkway Program costs no more than what the board would need to educate the Parkway students in regular high schools.

Some observers argue that despite his emphasis on individual initiative, Bremer has often been hypocritically, arbitrarily authoritarian. A few teachers contend, moreover, that the most important advantage of the program is not its structure but the intimacy provided by a smaller teacher-student ratio—an intimacy that Bremer may have trouble maintaining as the program grows.

Though riding the crest of a wave, Bremer appreciates what he often refers to as the "messiness" of learning. He is almost proud to admit that the first sessions were not without their problems. Principally, too many students have not received the training in basic skills which is supposed to be a primary function of the tutorials. He is confident, however, that the problems will be solved—solving educational problems, is, after all, what the program is about.

The John Dewey High School Adventure

Sol Levine

Modular scheduling." "Schools without walls." "Schools within schools." A new jargon indicative of administrative tinkering—or substantive change in the process of secondary education? Proponents of reform search earnestly for answers to the all-too-evident problems of our schools: disruption, racial conflict, tuned-out students, and curriculum irrelevance. Nationwide, there has been a mushrooming of educational experiments designed to provide answers. John Dewey High School, located in the borough of Brooklyn, is one such experiment. Or, as the school brochure hopefully describes it, John Dewey High is "an adventure in education."

From *Phi Delta Kappan* LII, no. 2 (October 1971):108–110. Used by permission of the author and publisher.

THE DESIGN

When it opened in September of 1969, John Dewey High represented a major departure from the traditional New York City high school. The blueprint for Dewey, drawn up by a committee of New York City educators with educational savvy and foresight, included the basic concepts of flexible modular scheduling, cyclical programming, learning for mastery, and independent study. The committee envisioned a new school with distinctive characteristics:

It abolishes grade levels, discontinues the Carnegie Unit as a measure of progress, breaks the five-period-per-week lockstep, abandons the distinction between major and minor subjects, provides instruction in practical arts for college-bound as well as work-oriented youngsters, incorporates extraclass activities into the curriculum, involves the classroom teacher in guidance, utilizes new methods and modern technology to supplement conventional instructional procedures, and makes use of a longer school day.

This blueprint became the basis upon which the educational program of the school was structured. Inherent in the program are some of the goals of the school:

1. Enabling students to learn at their own rate.
2. A vast array of course offerings designed to meet the needs and interests of students of all ability levels.
3. Individualization of instruction and a serious attempt to avoid the impersonalization of large, overcrowded schools.
4. The development of a sense of self-reliance and independence among students and an ability to learn on their own outside of the formal classroom.
5. Teacher and student involvement in the development of the educational program.

IMPLEMENTING THE DESIGN

The goals and ideals are lofty. To what extent has the philosophy been translated into program?

One parent, making her way uncertainly through knots of students relaxing on campus grounds, commented, "This looks like Woodstock." She saw students strumming guitars, playing frisbee, and otherwise relaxing. But after a tour through the building she sat down and wrote a letter expressing admiration for the school's relaxed and open atmosphere.

Student reaction is typified by one who said, "It's unbelievable. I'm experiencing the kinds of things no other school could give me." As part of his high school program, this student works one day a week helping a professor at the New York University Dental School. John Dewey's planners believe that learning can take place outside of the formal classroom.

All students elect to attend John Dewey High School. There is no special examination for admission into the school. Students need only apply for admission. Every effort is made to maintain an integrated school (approximately one-third of the students are black and Puerto Rican) and to have a broad spectrum of student ability levels. The school population is typical of Brooklyn academic high schools.

The teaching staff is young and exciting. By agreement with the United Federation of Teachers (the union has been superlative in its cooperation with this experiment) 50% of the school staff is chosen by the principal without regard to seniority status. All remaining teachers transfer into the school voluntarily. Teachers new to the school are required to attend a summer orientation institute. Much of the time in the summer program is spent in developing curricula and teaching materials. The overall success of this orientation program is reflected in the staff's dedication to and enthusiasm for the experiment.

From an organizational point of view the essential ingredients in the Dewey program include the following:

1. *An Eight-hour Day.* Teachers and students alike have an eight-hour day to enable students to learn at their own rate. Approximately 25% (varying with the daily schedule) of the student's day is spent on independent study. Students can accelerate in all subject areas by taking DISKs: Dewey Independent Study Kits. DISKs are self-contained courses taken outside of the formal classroom. Department advisers are available to help and guide students working on DISKs. Students can get course credit by passing examinations (written, oral, or laboratory) designed to determine mastery in a DISK.

2. *Independent Study.* The independent study program is nondirective. That is, the student need not account for this time. Students have the option of going to department resource centers, using the school library (generally packed to capacity), involving themselves in club activities (built into the school day), or relaxing on campus grounds. Resource centers are a vital focal point of the independent study program. The centers are equipped with all sorts of software and hardware related to individual subject areas. Moreover, teachers are always available at the center to help students having difficulty or to assist those who are advancing more rapidly than the average. Each teacher spends approximately one hour and 40 minutes a day in his departmental resource center.

3. *Flexible Modular Scheduling.* The eight-hour day is broken into 20-minute time periods, better known as modules. Courses can be programmed to meet for two, three, or more modules. For example, social studies classes generally meet on a 2-3-2-3 basis four times a week. That is, they meet for 40 minutes on Mondays and Wednesdays and for an hour on Tuesdays and Thursdays.

4. *Cyclical Programming.* The Dewey year is divided into five seven-week cycles with an optional sixth summer cycle. Students are reprogrammed every seven weeks. (The school programming is done in affiliation with the Brooklyn College computer center.) A Dewey term generally ends on a Friday, and on Monday students receive their new programs and start the new term. Despite the fact that officials are very liberal with program changes, a total of fewer than 500 changes (out of a possible 16,000) were completed in three days. The efficiency of the programming system is astounding. Courses are designed to last for one, two, or more cycles. This "mini-term" concept has enabled Dewey to help students avoid the "long corridor of failure" associated with annual or semiannual organization.

5. *A Broad Array of Course Offerings.* The mini-terms facilitate the development of an unusual number of course offerings in all subject areas. By way of illustration, the English department offers well over 35 courses to students. E.g., Introduction to the Novel. The American Dream (an interdisciplinary course), The Bible as Literature, The Generation Gap in Literature, Literature of Protest,

Literature of Science Fiction and Fantasy. Thus a student can select, cafeteria style, those courses of interest to him. To assure a "balanced diet," Dewey students must meet the minimum requirements established for all New York City high school students. However, Dewey has one of the highest curriculum indices (number of subjects taken per student) in the city; most students take between seven and eight subjects in each cycle. This means that students will graduate early or will be in a position to take additional electives. A Dewey student's program might include: transportation (the automotive shop is one of our six shops), sculpture, the modern novel, consumer economics, brass ensemble, typing (all students must show proficiency in typing), marine biology, and algebra.

6. *An Extensive Guidance Program.* There are seven full-time guidance counselors with a student load of 300 each. This enables counselors to provide omnibus counseling—educational, vocational, and college counseling as well as "crisis" counseling. We also have the part-time services of a psychologist and social worker.

7. *Learning for Mastery.* Dewey students do not receive numerical grades, inasmuch as an underlying concept of the school program is that students learn to achieve mastery. Students receive four basic grades: M (for mastery), indicating sufficient mastery to move into the next phase of work; R (for retention), indicating need to repeat the course due to a failure to achieve mastery; MI (for mastery in independent study), indicating mastery in the DISK program; MC (for mastery with condition), indicating marginal mastery with specific areas of weakness. This grade enables us to provide for "prescriptive teaching." All students receiving MC or R have an educational prescription form sent home which explains specific areas of deficiency. These prescriptions are available to the new teacher and are also available in the resource center. Teachers can help students overcome deficiencies in both the classroom and resource center. The language department requires students to take supportive DISKs (with teacher assistance) where a student has received an MC.

The question most frequently asked concerning the John Dewey grading system is, Will it permit students to be admitted to the colleges? Extensive meetings and communication with college admissions officers have yielded an overwhelmingly favorable response. College admission will represent no serious problem for our students. In fact, at this writing one of our 10 graduates (graduating after two years in our school) has already been accepted by a private college.

8. *Innovations in Teaching Techniques.* The area where the most work remains to be done is that of teaching methodology. Dewey rooms have folding walls, permitting us to operate a number of team-teaching programs. We are hopeful that this program will be expanded. The marine biology program (an extensive and exciting one) makes full use of the surrounding beach areas and the Coney Island Aquarium. Interdisciplinary courses are being developed. For example, a metal sculpture class is a combined effort of the fine arts and industrial arts departments.

One of the more exciting programs we have instituted on a pilot basis is our "4-1 Program." This involves students in an educational experience outside of the school one day a week. As of last March, Dewey students were studying anthropology in the Museum of Natural History, art students were studying in the Brooklyn Museum, science students were working in a number of medical fields at the Brooklyn Downstate Medical Center, and a number of other students were pursuing projects in areas of their particular interest. For example, one student was working as a free-lance reporter for a local newspaper. Students receive course credit for work done in this program.

ELIMINATING THE GENERAL TRACK

"Tracking" or homogeneous grouping does not exist in John Dewey High school. We hope thus to come to grips with the glaring inadequacies associated with the "general diploma"—a course of study which is essentially a hodge-podge of courses leading, in my view, to few educational or marketable skills. In English and social studies students who receive an R can opt for an alternative course, thereby avoiding the failure syndrome associated with repeating courses. In sequential skill subjects, such as mathematics and foreign language, we have provided for a series of attenuated courses. That is, students can take algebra in the normal five-phase span (one year), in a seven-phase span (one and one-half years), or in 10 phases (two years). There is frequent movement within the 5-7-10-phase courses, depending upon teacher-counselor recommendations.

SUCCESS OR FAILURE?

It is obviously too early to evaluate the success or failure of the Dewey program definitively. Ongoing formal and informal evaluations will continue. Yet there are certain basic indications of apparent successes and problems.

Do students use their independent study time productively? While one can quibble over the meaning of the term "productively," there is evidence that most of the students do use their study time in an educationally positive man-ner. The school library is generally filled to capacity (a beautiful sight when one considers the underutilization of many high school libraries), and the resource centers are used on an average of 75% of capacity. The sight of teachers working with students on a one-to-one basis or in small groups is a delight to an educator's eye.

The DISK program is extremely popular. During the first three cycles, 559, then 1,138, and finally 1,174 students signed up for DISKs. The completion ratio during Cycle II averaged approximately 40%, while approximately 30% of the students received credit for courses on DISKs. Our experience indicates that the highest rate of passing (in the DISK program) is among those who have taken out multiple DISKs. There have been obvious problems with the DISK program, however. As might be expected, the overwhelming number of subscribers for DISKs are advanced students; relatively few students who receive R's are involved.

"Coming to Dewey was like moving from a prison to freedom," remarked one student. While he was doubtless overstating the case, nevertheless his com-ment reveals a problem. Students coming from traditionally structured school environments often find it difficult to adjust to the large blocks of independent study time. A relatively small percentage of students spend too much time in the cafeteria, failing to avail themselves of the school's superb facilities. Continued counseling, parent consultation, and ongoing orientation have led to some lim-ited success with these students.

Has the generally relaxed atmosphere led to an improved student-teacher and student-student relationship? We believe it has, although atmosphere is hard to measure. Nearly all the visitors to Dewey cite the "excellent tone" within the school. The frequent reprogramming of the school has led to an improved teacher-student relationship. During the course of a year, teachers meet many students and form strong educational associations. A very small percentage of the students can still be classified as alienated, but the overwhelming number get along quite well.

A long list of pluses and minuses would, at this point, serve little purpose. A formal evaluation is being developed with faculty, student, and parental assistance. John Dewey High School is experiencing all of the growing pains and excitement associated with a new educational undertaking. While many of the innovative aspects of the school program can be found in other experiments throughout the country, what makes it particularly exciting is the commitment of one of the largest educational systems in the world—the New York City schools—to this venture into educational alternatives. It is my own view that one of the answers to the problems of large urban school systems is the development of an increasing number of educational alternatives for students. When students can elect to go to the school of their choice, a major step forward will have been taken. I look forward to the creation of additional John Dewey High Schools located in each of the five boroughs of New York City.

An Innovative High School in a Midwestern Suburb

Bill Ray Lewis

"The Shawnee Mission Northwest community is dedicated to creating an awareness of each individual's self-worth."

To the nearly 1,700 students enrolled at Shawnee Mission Northwest High School in Shawnee Mission, Kansas, these words are becoming reality. The suburban Kansas City school has become a laboratory for living.

The "spirit of Northwest" derives from a philosophy of personal commitment and involvement. Guided by that philosophy, students, parents, and staff members are part of a distinctively innovative and exciting school—a microcosm of the community which supports it, a place where all can feel needed, productive, and worthy of recognition.

From *Phi Delta Kappan* LIII, no. 2 (October 1971):105–107. Used by permission of the author and publisher.

Of course an innovative high school is a particular mixture of specific innovative practices, few of which are likely to be completely new. At Shawnee Mission Northwest, for example, much of the instructional program is built around the concept of independent study and a media-oriented resource center. It draws its major strengths from the involvement of students and parents, from the teachers' reevaluation of their roles, from a flexible curriculum, and from the benefits of outstanding physical facilities.

"Northwest is 'Number One' because it puts us first. What more could one ask? Students feel a tremendous sense of belonging and think of school as *them*—not simply an inanimate building."

The 16-year-old girl who expressed this satisfaction with Northwest is the recipient of a wide range of student-oriented innovations in curriculum and schedule planning. She and her classmates, with the staff, have cooperatively developed a "variable schedule" which permits great flexibility in each day's activities. Two days a week the six traditional 60-minute class periods are operative. On alternate days, three 90-minute class periods are scheduled. The extra-long periods allow teachers freedom in planning and conducting their classes, providing time for extended field trips, lab experiments, or projects requiring more than an hour. This scheduling also permits an optional half-hour activity period before classes begin and, after the third class of the day ends at 1:45 p.m., an optional 75-minute period for makeup work, conferences, work in the resource center, or extracurricular activities. Professional faculty meetings are scheduled as needed during part of this period; optional pep assemblies, regular student assemblies, and departmental meetings are all included in the regular school day, as well.

At Northwest, the student's choice is the guideline for class assignments. During registration, he indicates his preferences for a subject, the time it is offered, and the instructor he wishes. Should a first-choice become overcrowded, a second choice will be honored. The advantage of this method is summed up in one student's comment: "I have no one to blame but myself if I don't like all my courses and teachers."

She would have a chance to register criticism, however, because the school has instituted an informal student evaluation of the instructional program. Developed by a joint student-faculty committee, the appraisal form allows the student to express his opinion about the teacher's subject matter preparation and the classroom environment, about any learning difficulties and recommendations for improvement of the course. Because the evaluation is intended only to help the instructor appraise his teaching effectiveness, he need not disclose the results to his administrator.

Evaluation at Northwest is a two-way process. One goal of the staff is to assist each individual student to develop his ultimate potential. To do so, evaluation and individual counseling take place in each classroom. Staff members work closely with the guidance deans to diagnose both learning and behavior problems and to prescribe possible alternatives for their solution.

"It's so different here. The whole thing is based upon trust, and the vast majority of kids readily respond to this 'humane' treatment. Vandalism is very slight in our building, and we've even had student volunteer committees formed to assist in cleaning up the parking lot, halls, and restrooms. Kids just plain care!"

The "kids" might well agree with this senior student, for at Northwest they have good reason to care. They are invited to weekly rap sessions with the administrative staff and they are given a say in the hiring of teachers. They have a commons area, planned for the students by the students, and they have a voice in determining what new courses are offered in each department.

As part of the effort to involve students in their school, each week the administrative staff meets with a group of randomly selected students to discuss Northwest problems and issues. Each student's attendance is requested by formal letter. "The kids love these meetings, and so do we," says the principal, Merlin Ludwig. "It gives us a chance to let our hair down and talk straight from the shoulder. We discuss everything from the caliber of the instructional program to the type of dance bands our students prefer." A large measure of the students' satisfaction with these meetings comes from the chance to express themselves. "Our students don't expect us to implement every suggestion," Ludwig says, "but they really appreciate being given the opportunity to be heard."

Student comments are further welcomed by an administration which is interested in their evaluations of teacher applicants. Students are included in the applicant interviews, and their reactions are factored into hiring decisions. Explains one administrator, "We are looking for teachers who really love kids—and who, better than the kids, can help us find them?"

"Northwest's student-centeredness is evidenced by the existence of the student mall."

The mall, a cavernous enclosure separating the academic wing from the industrial arts, music, and crafts classrooms, serves as the student commons. The commons area is the hub of all student activity and provides the students of this innovative complex with an area somewhat like an immense living room. This vital area is a place to visit with friends, hold a committee meeting, work on an assignment, or grab "40 winks" in a relaxed atmosphere. A carpeted "rap center" at one end of the commons is used for informal chats with guidance deans or for browsing through vocational planning literature. There are soft drink and snack dispensers and a "breakfast bar" which offers fresh rolls, doughnuts, cookies, and hot chocolate during the early morning periods. Plans are afoot to landscape an area next to the building, to extend this popular relaxing and study area to an outdoors environment.

Another essential facility in the Northwest plant is a spacious and carpeted resource center equipped with a touch-tone retrieval system. The center features 80 individual study cubicles, 37 of them equipped with television monitoring sets, headphones, and touch-tone selector mechanisms for instantaneous recall of audio or video program tapes. The resource center was built and equipped to accommodate both the students who thrive on independent study and those who prefer more structured programs. Microfilm readers, tape recorders, record players, filmstrip projectors, magazines, and books are all available there for student and faculty use.

Teachers are further aided by a ready supply of materials and technical assistance in a well-equipped media preparation room, enabling them to prepare tapes, transparencies, posters, and dittoed and mimeographed copies of needed materials. A secretarial assistant and student assistants working under an approved distributive education program are also available to help with the preparation of media.

Instructors are also provided with departmental offices complete with desks and filing space. In place of the conventional desks, classrooms are equipped with adjustable teaching stations. Retractable walls in several classrooms permit large-group instruction and a team-teaching approach when the situation requires.

"We're considered as professionals, and being professional carries with it an inherent responsibility of thought, research, and implementation."

Teachers who can express this kind of professional confidence are likely to perform their instructional roles with courage. In addition to receiving excellent logistical and staff support, the Northwest faculty is encouraged to experiment. They are in a continual quest for innovative ideas that will better help them in relating ideas to young people. "We know that if one idea doesn't work, we will be encouraged to try another," says Roxy Yowell, foreign language chairman.

Among the experiments in progress at Northwest are independent study units, a "school without walls," and a series of "mini-course" electives. One of Northwest's science classes provides a good example of how the individualized approach to learning is stressed at the school. At the start of each unit of work the instructor distributes a course outline which includes the proposed expectancies for the various grade levels to be achieved. Each student selects his academic goal and proceeds at his own pace. He is graded on each unit as it is completed and may correct his mistakes and retake the examination if he wishes to raise his grade on the unit's work.

A sociology instructor supervises a "school without walls" which permits students to gain firsthand experience by visiting and researching segments of the surrounding community.

Both the language arts and the social science departments currently offer "mini-courses" with students and faculty often working together to develop a relevant offering. Language arts has featured such provocative topics as "The Age of Rock," "The Spirit of Christmas," and "The Magic of Superstitions." Ranging from three to six weeks, these short electives are only part of a program which combines them with team planning and "free" classroom days. The "free" days are set aside for production of original plays, lengthy presentation of research projects, or in-depth study of selected authors or periods of literature.

"Instead of students asking me what we're going to do today, I should be asking them: What are you going to do today?"

This is the attitude expressed by a teacher who feels she has benefited from the freedom and flexibility of the language arts program just described. It is only one example of the priority Northwest gives to humanizing education and introducing a spirit of relevancy into the curriculum. Working with such a priority, Northwest instructors quite naturally see their roles as educators changing.

Rather than be "dispensers" of facts, staff members believe they can best assist the student by serving as "mediators." No longer the all-knowing god-teacher, the Northwest instructor takes the role of educational guide. The mere presentation of facts is not enough. He encourages students to seek answers independently, to question, to weigh evidence, and only then to make decisions.

Implementing the Northwest philosophy has been a challenge to staff members, who in turn feel an obligation to make learning more of a challenge for their pupils. A great part of the effort is to instill a feeling of self-worth in every student.

"The difference filters back to the parent. The teen-ager's outlook is constructive, rather than harassed. My young people feel trusted, and they respond to that enthusiastically. They study harder. They feel they are a part of the society they live within. They try to contribute. . . ."

Many parents reflect the differences fostered by the Northwest program. One of the ways they are involved with students in an essential relationship is through a somewhat unique parent-student-teacher association. Operating under the guidelines of the National Congress of Parents and Teachers Association, this vital organization serves as a key link between the school and the home. It assists the school in fulfilling its obligations to the student and parent and has tremendously helped parent as well as student morale.

Students belonging to this organization have full voting rights, pay dues, and may be elected to executive positions. One of the organization's most important objectives is the encouragement of a close-knit family relationship. Parents and students thus work together for common goals, and both are afforded the opportunity of relaxed communication as they intermingle.

Parent involvement in Northwest activities is certainly a prime objective of school officials. They have encouraged weekly parent "roundtable" discussions with opportunities to tour the building, visit classes, eat lunch, and ask questions concerning school policies and activities. Because of the success of the weekly roundtables, monthly sessions are now held at night for parents who cannot attend during the day, and satellite roundtables have begun meeting in various homes and public buildings throughout the school's attendance area. Similar sessions are being planned for senior citizens and other people in the community who do not have children in the school.

"Difficulty has arisen when patrons have assumed that a 'student-oriented school' was a 'student-run' school."

Educational traditionalists have referred to Northwest as a "country club" and as a school which is completely dominated by student thought and opinion. As pacesetters for innovative practice, we anticipated this criticism, knowing that the basis for negative comment is usually a misunderstanding of the school's philosophy.

Better communication seems the most logical weapon in removing obstacles to better education, at Northwest as elsewhere. We continue to try to involve all concerned in the planning of changes and to eliminate the element of misunderstanding and suspicion. We have had to explain terms like "free time" and "student-centered" to help reorient parents and even some faculty members who have admitted they once thought schools were for them rather than for students.

Some students adjust to Northwest's "freedom" slowly or with difficulty. Being responsible for their actions for possibly the first time in their lives, they may find they are ill-equipped to discipline themselves for study, attendance, or personal behavior. But the results of a recent student opinionnaire reflect success in achieving many of our goals: Students feel trusted, they are proud of their school, and most of them feel that they are learning more at Northwest than they would at a more traditional school.

The Northwest school community faces the future with an enthusiasm born out of creating a school for "kids." Ahead lie plans for a 12-month school year, a pass-fail grading system, and an exploding curriculum. As long as youth has first priority, Northwest will be a "Number One" school.

McGavock: A Model School

James A. Burns

Recently, U.S. Commisioner of Education Sidney D. Marland has called for a total reformation of secondary education that would blend curricula and students into a single strong comprehensive secondary system. The Metropolitan Public Schools of Nashville, Tennessee, began to move in this direction about five years ago with the planning of McGavock Comprehensive High School, which opened in September 1971.

McGavock is the first of eight or nine large senior high schools which will eventually enroll all the high school students in metropolitan Nashville. The McGavock model has important implications for changing conceptions of professional personnel. Program development and models of teacher-pupil interaction demand different roles for professional personnel in this kind of school.

There is 448,000 square feet of space in the McGavock building, which was constructed at a cost of nearly $9 million. The school site is adjacent to a 400-acre public park which has facilities for baseball, softball, golf, tennis, track, and picnics. The school system and the Metropolitan Park Board have cooperated in the development of these adjacent athletic, recreational, and aesthetic facilities.

The school is designed for implementing a truly comprehensive secondary

James A. Burns. "McGavock: A Model School. *Educational Leadership* 29(6):529–33; March 1972. Reprinted with permission of the Association for Supervision and Curriculum Development and James A. Burns. Copyright © 1972 by the Association for Supervision and Curriculum Development.

school program. The plans for this two-story structure feature an open theatre auditorium, a horticulture area with greenhouse, learning centers, a planetarium, a data processing lab, graphics and photography labs, and a communication skills laboratory.

Special attention has been given to the development of unique vocational-technical facilities which will promote the comprehensiveness of the school. Facilities have been included for child development careers (including a nursery), health related professions, aircraft mechanics, commercial food preparation, commercial art, data processing, plus extensive facilities for experiences and training in welding, refrigeration, automotive mechanics, electronics, sheet metal, electricity, and shop machines.

Approximately 2,700 students were enrolled in McGavock in the fall of 1971 with a maximum eventual enrollment of approximately 3,200. Because of the special programs which are available, students attend McGavock from throughout the metropolitan area although the school basically serves one attendance area.

PHILOSOPHY

McGavock Comprehensive High School is designed to serve a diverse student population with different needs, backgrounds, and career development goals and patterns. The McGavock purpose includes the development of learning experiences which not only prepare students for college, but which also are relevant to other groups of students and their needs. The facilities and the size of the student population at McGavock make possible the development of curriculum programs which will meet the needs of all groups of students. This idea has not been limited to the development of additional programs, but involves building increased depth, flexibility, and relevance into traditional curriculum areas.

The general goals of the McGavock School are:

1. Curriculum programs for students of differing career patterns
2. Increased emphasis placed upon career development for all students, not just terminal students
3. Programs relevant to students of varying achievement and socioeconomic backgrounds
4. Increased emphasis on specialization and in-depth study within all areas of the curriculum
5. Personalized "small school" approach to guidance, administrative, and extracurricular programs
6. Community school programs which serve the entire community as well as the student population
7. An exemplary model school for secondary program development for the Metropolitan Nashville School System.

ORGANIZATION

The McGavock organizational structure is designed to place special emphasis on program and curricular development through the positions of coordinator of program and staff development, coordinator of vocational-technical education, and teacher leadership positions. Administration, pupil personnel services, and community relations are the responsibility of the executive principal and four "small school" principals.

Each subject area department at McGavock is organized on a "team" basis, with departmental planning and coordination a high priority. Each department has a team leader who has designated responsibility for leadership. The larger departments have lead teachers who are the leaders of teams of teachers working on a particular phase of the program. These teacher leaders are paid small supplements. This kind of differentiated staffing arrangement plus an emphasis on in-house program direction place professional personnel in new and more responsible roles regarding curriculum development at the local school.

The "small school organization" at McGavock is a compromise modification of "school-within-a-school" versus departmental organization plans. The "small school organization" utilizes a decentralized administration and pupil personnel focus while maintaining departmental organization for curriculum development. Four different small school teams, each composed of a "small school" principal and two counselors, are responsible for creating and maintaining a personal, concerned atmosphere for the 700 students the team services through administrative, guidance, and extracurricular functions.

Students are, however, scheduled in classes on a schoolwide basis. This organizational pattern is an effort to emphasize personalized aspects of the program while maintaining the benefits of schoolwide curriculum organization. The planners of this school felt that the "school-within-a-school" organization was not feasible for this school at this time. As secondary personnel become more adept, flexible, and open toward completely individualized instructional programs, the school-within-a-school organization will have enhanced potential.

CURRICULUM DEVELOPMENT

The McGavock curriculum plans were based on the idea that an instructional program should focus on "the way it should be and not how it has been done." This has resulted in a curriculum different from other high schools in Nashville. Perhaps the central thrust of the curriculum model has been diversity of program to fit diversity of student needs and interests. There is little remaining of the conventional wisdom that a segment of content is necessary and good for *all* students.

Students at McGavock have a variety of options available. Students make choices according to their own interests, needs, and backgrounds. The options include a variety of courses or programs which are not normally available—such as astronomy, geology, probability, statistics, advanced sociology, vocational-technical programs—but also a variety of options *within* particular courses.

Science, social studies, and English curricula are characterized by phase-elective options. This means that students have options to choose within particular phases of these curricula. For example, the social studies curriculum is basically designed in six-week segments. Students have a choice during one six-week segment of World Studies of studying one of three topics: (a) Religious Movements; (b) Revolution: Military and Social; or (c) Major Political Movements. During one six-week segment of American Studies I, the student will choose one of three topics: (a) The Al Capone Era; (b) Yesterday, Today, and Tomorrow (1940–19??); or (c) War and Peace.

Phase-elective options in English are organized on a semester basis. Eleventh and twelfth grade students have available 28 different semester length courses which they may take in lieu of traditional junior and senior English. These 28 options include more traditional segments of English such as "The Structure of English" and "Survey of American Literature." Other more exotic electives such as "Media Study," "Media Production," "Film Making," "Vocational Reading," and "Theatre Arts: Improvisation, Acting" are also included. The English curriculum and scheduling are the responsibility of the English Team so that the options are not taught as completely separate segments. Program design specifies that portions of each student's week are planned on a departmental basis, so that the program is not simply 28 courses but rather the 28 options are one major part of a total program.

The phase-elective curriculum in science at McGavock includes separate courses for the general, the terminal, and the especially interested science student. The biology program offers General Biology, Applied Biology, and two versions of Specialized Biology (BSCS Yellow and BSCS Green) as well as Advanced Biology.

The same is true of other sciences. Students choose phases of each of these courses on a six-week basis. In addition, students have a selection of three-week science experiences to choose from as a part of any of the biology courses. Many of these experiences are designed with career development patterns, such as the following: "Science for Laboratory Technicians," "Science for Cosmetologists," and "Science for Food Service." Other three-week experiences are more general, such as "Population Explosion," "Pollution," and "Drug Abuse."

The various options within the phase-elective approach have been developed by the McGavock faculty and are taught according to the faculties' abilities and interests. Many teachers have been enthusiastic about working with specific options relating to themselves as individuals. Certainly this type of curriculum implies that teachers cannot be treated as interchangeable parts in a factory model and that individual differences of professional personnel are an important factor in curriculum development.

EVALUATIVE DESIGN

McGavock's role as a model for secondary curriculum development requires systematic program evaluation. Evaluation has been a major component of the McGavock effort since its inception. A Task Force for Evaluation has been organized which works with the McGavock staff in defining, measuring, and evaluating school progress. Each department and/or program thrust has been developed with specifically measurable performance objectives. Evaluation is focusing on process as well as product and will be a continual part of the school's development. Through the evaluative effort, the Metropolitan Schools hope to be able to better make decisions as to modifications or adjustments that are needed and as to what aspects of the McGavock program should be replicated in other schools. Certainly future directions for high school program development in Nashville will begin with the McGavock effort.

Portland's Personalized Education Program

Richard Boss

Many critics of contemporary education claim the secondary schools of America are too highly structured, inflexible, and too much like college preparatory institutions. Some claim the high schools are completely out of tune with the times. They say that the courses taught are not relevant to a modern space-age world.

In Portland, Oregon, the Board of Education and chief school administrators have tried to do something about such charges. They decided to set up alternate routes for completing the educational requirements for the high school diploma.

The district made an extensive study of the "student with special needs," and a variety of programs have been started to provide services that will more suitably and appropriately educate the children of *all* the people.

One of these exciting alternates in the Portland Public Schools is the "Personalized Education Program" (PEP). This program tries to design opportunities for an educational experience for each student that will take into account his or her needs, interests, and potential. The central idea of PEP is to shape the school to fit the students' needs instead of fitting students to the school.

Some of the more important concepts of PEP took shape in the development of the Vocational Village, a school for dropouts, and the Residential Manpower Center (RMC), a modern Job Corps. The author of this article was the chief administrator in both schools. It was determined at the beginning of each program that the goals of secondary education needed to be brought into focus for each student. Each student needs a PEP plan which spells out his personalized goals for employability, further education, or other specific needs.

A road map needs to be designed that will show each student how he can achieve these goals through education. Once an adolescent can be shown how to identify personal goals, and to see methods of obtaining these goals, half the problem has been solved. The remaining half deals with procedures and student-teacher relationships.

MOTIVATING YOUNG PEOPLE

The author's experiences with the Portland PEP philosophy have been primarily with high school dropouts and disadvantaged youngsters. Many procedures

Richard Boss. "Portland's Personalized Education Program." *Educational Leadership* 29(5): 405–407; February 1972. Reprinted with permission of the Association for Supervision and Curriculum Development and Richard Boss. Copyright © 1972 by the Association for Supervision and Curriculum Development.

were utilized to free teachers so they could actually teach and have more time to spend with individual students. Other practices were tried to motivate young people to accept school and learning as a meaningful and worthwhile experience.

It is important to note that both the Vocational Village and the Manpower Center operate with facilities outside the structure of the regular schools. The Village is housed in a storefront business-warehouse facility. The RMC is housed in three separate buildings, including a former private junior college and hotel downtown, and a former seminary 20 miles outside Portland, in a rural area.

Alternative forms of schooling can and should permit students with special needs to attend classes in facilities separate from the regular school. The able and ambitious youngster has just as much right to an appropriate educational experience as the disadvantaged. Far too many educators believe that one must change the "establishment" to accommodate all young people at the same school building.

There is no real evidence to prove that one needs to "water down" or change what is well done to start something one does not now do at all. In other words, why ruin a perfectly good high school which is efficient, effective, and by all accredited standards doing a good job with 75 percent of the eligible enrollees? Can the American high school be all things to all people?

ALTERNATE FORMS OF SCHOOLING

The phrase "alternate forms of schooling" means that other programs, curricula, activities, and/or educational experiences should be designed to educate appropriately the student with special needs. Some of the procedures which have worked well with, and have been made a part of, the Portland PEP philosophy are the following:

1. No grades or grade levels are identified. Students commence work at their proficiency level, and proceed at their own rate. Performance evaluations are made periodically to determine achievement.
2. Courses are not required. Students are encouraged to come to grips with their own deficiencies and make rational decisions about corrective measures.
3. Positive reinforcements are used as often as possible to give the students awards for success. It is more fun to be a winner. The students feel good about themselves, and miracles begin to happen.
4. Teachers are taught to be managers of the learning environment as opposed to being a source of knowledge. They become less frightened about the fact that they do not know everything; they loosen up and become real people.
5. Students in this age group (ages 14 through 21) are given greater responsibility to make decisions which will determine their destiny. They sometimes make mistakes—so what? They need practice in making decisions and living with the results.
6. Classrooms are operated with maximum flexibility. Many times no two students are working on the same project, problem, or lesson. Small class size should be maintained so that each student will receive personal attention.
7. The more advanced student can and should become an effective aide in reaching the student having the greatest difficulty. Many times the advanced student can accelerate learning this way.

8. Teachers are taught to demonstrate and to show students how to do something rather than simply to lecture.
9. Teachers are encouraged to utilize the community as a learning laboratory; to take the student to "where the action is."
10. Teachers are taught to identify and teach only those things which relate to behavioral outcomes. Performance evaluations are made indicating achievement. When the student can learn and do, he is maximizing his benefits at the school.

ADMINISTRATION OF DISCIPLINE

Probably the most important element of the PEP philosophy is not a procedure so much as a frame of mind. This deals with the administration of discipline in the school setting. As shown above, students and teachers alike are given greater latitude to establish a learning environment. The misguided administrator is the one who does not know one cannot give freedoms unless one also holds people responsible. The student and teacher can do as they like, but they must do something, and this something must be constructive.

Tied to discipline, and equally important, is the element of acceptance. Unless the adult can really accept each and every youngster for what he is, nothing else really ever works. The student must be able to approach an adult who can "say it straight," be warm and understanding. This means every employee from the custodian to the school administrator must be selected as a person who loves or cares for young people, and feels comfortable in working with them.

SECTION 8 ADDITIONAL LEARNING ACTIVITIES

Problems and Projects

1. Read "Learning Activity Packages: An Approach to Individualized Instruction," by Richard V. Jones, *Journal of Secondary Education* XXXXIII, No. 4 (April, 1968), 178–183. This article is also available in Hass, C. G., and others, *Readings in Secondary Teaching*, Allyn and Bacon, Inc., 1970, pages 403–410. This article describes self-pacing materials now in use for individualized instruction including both LAPS and UNIPACS. It seeks to answer the question: How is the teacher to survive in a classroom full of students, each progressing at different rates within individualized programs?
Write to Nova High School, Fort Lauderdale, Florida, for LAPS in your area of teaching, or to Marine City, Michigan, for UNIPACS. Perhaps your library or teaching materials center will have some LAPS or UNIPACS.
Discuss these curriculum materials with your fellow students.

2. Refer to Hass and others, *Readings in Secondary Teaching*, Allyn and Bacon, Inc., 1970, for articles on "The Teacher's Roles," pp. 190–251. Twenty-seven articles present different aspects of this topic. You may find the following particularly valuable:
   (1) "The Teacher as a Curriculum-Maker," by C. R. May, pp. 201–206.
   (2) "Two Approaches to the Teaching Process," by Ned A. Flanders and E. Amidon, pp. 201–206.
   (3) "Can We Measure Good Teaching Objectively," by Arthur W. Combs, pp. 206–210.
   (4) "Teachers and the Socially-Disadvantaged Pupil," by Robert J. Havighurst, pp. 336–347.
   Another section of this book deals with "Skills Needed by the Teacher," pp. 380–504.

3. "The average American has something like twenty years of leisure more than his grandfather had." Havighurst makes this statement in "High Schools for the Future," in this section. He states that in the near future the "wise and pleasurable use of leisure will become recognized as a major social goal of the United States." What changes in the curriculum should be made if this is true? What does Havighurst mean by "instrumental and expressive education"?

4. What is meant by "advocacy" (see "Youths as Advocates")? Why does Cohen believe that advocacy is an important experience for middle adolescents? What does advocacy by youth do for the society? Examine this concept in terms of the goals of education for middle adolescents and the four curriculum bases.

5. What does Ohme mean by an "interest-centered curriculum" ("Steps Toward Relevance: An Interest-Centered Curriculum")? Why are short term electives important in this curriculum? Examine this curriculum in terms of objectives, the four bases of the curriculum, and provision for individual differences. Which of the four bases are emphasized in this curriculum proposal?

6. What are the advantages of a small high school (see "The Case for the Small High School")? Do you agree with Alvin Toffler that the "cult of bigness is creating a new race of nomads"? Discuss this proposal with others who are studying education for middle adolescence.

7. Read "Chicago's School Without Walls," by Edgar G. Epps, in *Models for Integrated Education*, edited by Daniel U. Levine, Wadsworth Publishing Co., 1971, pages 32–42. Compare Chicago's school with Philadelphia's school without walls (see "High School with No Walls—It's a Happening in Philadelphia"). Discuss and examine these new programs of education with your fellow students.
8. If you have been preparing a case problem about a high school in connection with your study of Sections 1 through 5, decide which innovations and trends presented in this section should be incorporated in the school you are studying. Use objectives of education and the four bases of the curriculum to support your decisions.

Films

High School, black and white, 75 mins. A documentary film by Frederick Wiseman. Presents a series of formal and informal encounters between teachers, students, and parents, in classes, sex education lectures, school entertainments, gym, cooking lessons, a simulated space flight, and disciplinary proceedings. The *American Library Association Booklist* for May 15, 1971, stated that "the probing camera reveals bad teachers, stifling student-counselor encounters, and frustrating parent-teacher conferences; it also shows good teachers and excited students . . . but the overwhelming tone is one of dullness, student boredom, teacher boredom, and the futility of individuality." Articles about this film have appeared in *Saturday Review*, April 19, 1969; *Newsweek*, May 19, 1969; *The New Republic*, June 21, 1969; and *The New Yorker*, October 18, 1969. If you cannot see the film you may find it useful to read these articles as a basis for discussion. Distributed by Zipporals Films, Inc., 54 Lewis Wharf, Boston, Massachusetts 02110. Minimum rental, $100.00. Prints are available for five year long term lease.
The Improbable Form of Master Sturm, color, 13 mins. Presents the nongraded high school, which places emphasis on young people as individuals. Filmed at Melbourne High School, Melbourne, Florida. Distributed by Institute for Development of Educational Activities, Melbourne, Florida 32901.
High School Team Teaching: The Ferris Story, color, 26 mins. This film is an excellent springboard for further investigation and study by persons interested in team teaching and flexible scheduling. Explains the planning and stages preceding the initiation of team teaching at Ferris High School in Spokane, Washington. Distributed by Bailey Film Associates, 11559 Santa Monica Blvd., Los Angeles, California 90025.

Visits To Schools

Visit a school to observe teaching or to participate in teaching. It is useful to have an appointment with the principal, the curriculum director, or some other leader in the school.

You may want to ask your instructor or someone else to suggest the school or teacher that you might visit.

While visiting or while planning the visit, try to obtain information about the school's social setting, the learners in the school, teaching practices in the school, and the content and organization of the curriculum so that you can examine what you see and study in the school in terms of objectives of education, the four bases of the curriculum, and curriculum criteria such as balance, individual differences, flexibility, and continuity. It is important to try to learn what the school considers to be its objectives and/or what the teacher considers his objectives to be (when observing a particular teacher). Compare these objectives to objectives of education as you view them and objectives for the grade level or curriculum area being observed.

Also you may find it useful to consider whether current trends or innovations at the particular school level or subject area might be used to advantage at the school being visited.

After your visit discuss your analysis of what you saw with others. Try to plan a small group discussion with others who have visited the school.

Books to Review for Additional Information

Alexander, William M., ed. *The High School of the Future: A Memorial to Kimball Wiles.* Columbus, Ohio: Charles E. Merrill Publishing Company, 1968.

Alexander, William M.; Salor, J. Galen; and William, Emmett L. *The High School Today and Tomorrow.* New York: Holt, Rinehart and Winston, 1971.

Clark, Leonard; Klein, Raymond; and Burks, John. *The American Secondary School Curriculum,* 2d ed. New York: The Macmillan Company, 1972.

Gorman, Burton W. *Secondary Education: The High School America Needs.* New York: Random House, 1971.

Hass, Glen; Wiles, Kimball; and Roberts, Arthur. *Readings in Secondary Teaching.* Boston: Allyn and Bacon, 1970.

Tanner, Daniel. *Secondary Education: Perspectives and Prospects.* New York: The Macmillan Company, 1972.

Unruh, Glenys, and Alexander, William M. *Innovations in Secondary Education.* New York: Holt, Rinehart and Winston, 1970.

Journals Featuring Articles on Education for Middle Adolescents

The Bulletin of The National Association of Secondary School Principals
The Clearing House
Educational Leadership
The Journal of Secondary Education
Today's Education

Education for Late Adolescents and Adults

PREREQUISITES

1. Reading and studying of the Introduction and Sections 1 through 5 of this book.
2. The development of, and ability to use, a set of curriculum criteria to describe and evaluate a curriculum plan. You must be able to use this set of criteria in order to critically analyze and make curriculum decisions regarding programs described in this section.

RATIONALE

All curriculum planners and teachers should be acquainted with the goals and trends in education at all levels, regardless of the level of the program of education at which they plan to work. You should know about goals and trends of education for late adolescents and adults whether you plan to work at this level or not. You will be able to be a better curriculum planner or teacher at one of the other levels if you have this information. This view is based on such curriculum criteria as continuity in learning, balance in the curriculum, and provision for individual differences.

This section is now called "Education for Late Adolescents and Adults" rather than "Community College," the title in the last edition. In keeping with the definition of "curriculum" presented in the Introduction, the focus will be on programs of education rather than exclusively on school programs.

The community college, a new educational institution, developed in America and has been a major element of the American system or free public education. It evolved from the junior college, but it has been designed to serve many more social purposes.

The community college serves the community with an adult education program in a variety of fields. It provides a college-parallel program for those who wish to transfer to four-year colleges or universities after two years. It offers terminal education in many vocational, technical, and commercial subjects for those who will go no further in formal education programs. A number of states have developed master plans to provide community colleges within commuting distance of all high school graduates.

The community college has grown from one serving a limited number of students to one providing education for all youth not in four-year colleges and for many adults and senior citizens.

The community college serves many young people who are late maturers or "late bloomers" who wouldn't be permitted to enter a four-year college or university on the basis of high school grades. Many students who need remedial work in basic skills get such work in "guided studies" non-credit programs. Success in such work enables them to continue in other areas of study.

Today community colleges often offer five types of programs:

1. *A Junior College Transfer Program.* This is the equivalent of the first two years of undergraduate college work in a four-year college. It leads to the associate of arts (A.A.) degree. For many students the community college, located near home, may be a better place to take this work than at a larger, often more impersonal, college or state university.
2. *A Technical and/or Vocational Program.* There are many jobs important in a technological society for which the needed preparation can be completed in two years or less. Such preparation provides outstanding opportunities for many young people. The United States Office of Education, in cooperation with many large corporations, publishes a pamphlet entitled "Twenty-Five Technical Careers You Can Learn in Two Years or Less." It lists technicians in varied fields such as air conditioning, commercial flying, electronic data processing, police science, and oceanography.
3. *An Adult Education Program.* This program serves the whole community. Classes are formed according to interest and demand. The program can be particularly important for our growing number of senior citizens.
4. *Remedial Programs.* These programs serve all students whose previous background may prevent them from successfully completing academic or technical education. In 1970, eighty percent of the public community colleges had special provisions for students who had not satisfactorily completed traditional academic requirements in high school. Moore discusses this type of program in "Opening the College Doors to Low Achievers."
5. *Community Service Programs.* These programs focus on programs of education rather than programs of schooling, in keeping with our definition of curriculum in the Introduction. "Multi-service Outreach Programs," extension centers, in-plant training, and programs for the disadvantaged are examples. The college goes to the community with instruction and programs when and where they are needed. Harlacher describes these program developments in "New Directions in Community Services."

Late adolescence in our society is a period of life that is critical in the development of ego-identity. It is a period when the young person moves from one age grade to another. It is important for psycho-social identity, work or role-related success in terms of the achievement values of the society, and integration into the life of the local community. According to Havighurst, late adolescence and early adulthood is a period full of tumult in our society. It is a time when the individual is questioning values, military service, courtship and marriage, and new status as worker, parent, or citizen. The period may cover five or ten years of highly individualistic life in which the young person may tend to grow into alienation, loneliness, or ruthlessness with little feeling for the values of community life. According to Havighurst, early adulthood is the period most full of teachable moments. In the past it has been "emptiest of efforts to teach." This is one of the challenges to community college programs. Larsen discusses teaching opportunities in "The Community College and Human Potential," in this section.

More than any other educational institution, the community college is being shaped by its present curriculum planners. They have the opportunity to plan in the light of objectives sought and all curriculum bases and criteria—to plan adequate programs of education rather than just programs of schooling for late adolescents and adults.

What should be the *objectives* of programs of education for late adolescents and adults? Many goals might be suggested; some are derived from social forces, some from human development and learning theories, and some from theories about knowledge and cognition. A review of the five types of programs offered in community colleges reveals that the programs relate to vocational preparation, development of citizenship skills, and self-realization. These colleges are geared to meeting the needs we all have as a result of rapid changes in the American life style—needs for new *vocational, leisure-time,* or *personal* knowledge and skills. Meeting such needs is a major objective of the institutions.

Trends, plans, and programs recently used to meet the goals of education for late adolescents and adults include the following. (References to pertinent articles in this section accompany each item.)

1. Move to non-campus colleges ("The Big Move to Non-Campus Colleges")
2. Remedial education ("Opening the College Gates to the Low Achiever")
3. Technical education and occupational programs ("Curriculum Trends and Directions in American Junior Colleges")
4. Community services programs ("New Directions in Community Services"; "Curriculum Trends and Directions in American Junior Colleges")
5. Community counseling ("New Directions in Community Services")
6. Cultural centers ("New Directions in Community Services")
7. Institutional synergism ("New Directions in Community Services")
8. Developmental programs ("Curriculum Trends and Directions in American Junior Colleges")
9. Informal curriculum ("Curriculum Trends and Directions in American Junior Colleges")
10. Adult education ("Thirty Million Adults Go to School")
11. Peer group programs ("Curriculum Trends and Directions in American Junior Colleges")
12. No-failure grading practices ("Opening the College Gates to the Low Achiever")
13. Mini-unit organization ("The Big Move to Non-Campus Colleges")
14. Career education ("Advancing Career Education")

Can the community junior college serve the diverse needs of the late adolescent, young adult, and other age groups it seeks to serve? Can it successfully provide programs as diverse as college transfer, remedial, adult, and community service? Herein lie both the problems and opportunities of this institution and its teachers.

OBJECTIVES

Your objectives in studying education at this level as part of the curriculum should be as follows:

1. To be familiar with the objectives, current innovations, and recent trends in education for late adolescents and adults.
2. To be able to explain the functions and goals of education at this level as part of the total curriculum.
3. To be able to use the objectives of education at this level, the curriculum bases, and other criteria in making curriculum and/or instruction decisions regarding present programs as well as regarding proposed innovations and trends.
4. To be able to suggest improvements in community college curriculum plans through the decisions made in number 3.

PREASSESSMENT

1. Discuss the implications of each of the fourteen innovations and trends listed in the Rationale.
2. Evaluate each of the trends in terms of objectives, bases of curriculum, and selected curriculum criteria.
3. Select any curriculum plan at this level and describe and analyze it in terms of objectives, the four curriculum criteria, and innovations and trends.
4. Suggest improvements or changes in the curriculum plan in number 3 in the light of your analysis.

In answering numbers 3 and 4 of the preassessment, you might choose to analyze the curriculum plans described in the following articles.

1. "Advancing Career Education," by Martin
2. "Opening the College Gates to the Low Achiever," by Moore

LEARNING ACTIVITIES

Articles in this section will help you to understand the purposes and functions of education for late adolescents and adults. They will also acquaint you with the problems, as well as the innovations and trends, of programs of education at this level.

Other learning alternatives are suggested at the end of this section.

POSTASSESSMENT

After attempting the preassessment you may do one or more of the following:

1. Ask your instructor whether you are ready for a postassessment evaluation on education for late adolescents and adults. Most students will need further work on this curriculum base.

2. Read the articles on education for late adolescents and adults in this section and try to determine how the problems, goals, innovations and trends being discussed in each article should be considered in curriculum planning and teaching.
3. Choose additional activities and readings or films and videotapes from those listed at the end of this section.
4. Look for other films, books, or articles on educational programs for this age group that are available in your library or media center.
5. Discuss the reading you have done and the films you have viewed with your fellow students. The key questions: How should the problems, goals, trends and innovations you've studied affect a school's curriculum? How should they be considered in planning for teaching?
6. When you are ready, ask your instructor for advice on a suitable postassessment for you for this topic. Satisfactory completion of numbers 5, 6, 7, 8, or 9 under "Problems and Projects" at the end of this section might be one possibility. Or satisfactory written completion of the preassessment for this section, after completing other learning activities, might be a satisfactory postassessment. Consult your instructor about this. You can assess your ability to do these activities before seeing your instructor.

Curriculum Trends and Directions in American Junior Colleges

Raymond E. Schultz

Curriculum trends and developments in the American junior college have paralleled closely the dramatic growth and development of this type of institution. It is no exaggeration to state that no other educational institution in the United States has experienced as much curriculum change during the past 15 years as has the junior college. This article describes those developments.

There is some difficulty in treating curriculum trends and directions of private and public junior colleges together. The focus of this article is on the public institutions. However, in the areas of general-liberal studies and pre-professional programs the situation described is applicable to private junior colleges. This is much less true for the other types of programs discussed.

Several organizational approaches might be employed for an overview of curriculum trends and directions. None is completely satisfactory and none is without merit. In any such scheme there is overlapping and some areas may not receive the attention which they deserve. The primary emphasis in this article is on formal learning experiences organized around the following areas:

From *Peabody Journal of Education* XLVIII, no. 4 (July 1971):262–269. Copyright © 1971 by the *Peabody Journal of Education*. Used by permission of the author and publisher.

1. General-liberal studies programs
2. Occupational programs
3. Developmental programs
4. Pre-professional programs
5. Community service programs.

This treatment does not do justice to the many informal educational experiences which junior colleges provide for students. That important area is treated in summary form only.

GENERAL-LIBERAL STUDIES PROGRAMS

Before discussing curriculum trends and directions in this area so far as the junior college is concerned, attention needs to be given the term *general-liberal studies* as used in the context of this article. As far as basic purposes are concerned, it is generally agreed that this aspect of a student's education should serve both his personal-human and his social needs. Until quite recently, the predominant view has been that the most effective way to accomplish these ends was through the traditional liberal arts. This approach emphasizes the cultural heritage of Western civilization and is strongly book oriented. That position began to be challenged after World War I with the advent of the general education movement. Advocates of the movement urged that more emphasis be given to the contemporary scene and that a student's learning experiences not be limited so completely to reading books. They urged that more emphasis be placed on other types of learning experiences.

Since World War II there has been an amalgamation of the traditional *liberal arts* and the *general education* points of view outlined above. While both terms are still found in institutional catalogs, they have lost their original distinct meaning. This writer uses the term *general-liberal studies* to reflect the amalgamation which has occurred.

Insofar as junior colleges are concerned, their offerings in general-liberal studies still closely parallel those of the senior colleges and universities to which their students transfer. In substantial degree this is because senior colleges and universities impose such requirements on junior colleges.

Since junior college general-liberal studies programs have been tied so closely to senior institutions, it is hardly an exaggeration to say that junior colleges have not had a soul of their own in this matter. That might not be necessarily bad except that senior institutions differ in their requirements not only from one another but among schools and colleges within a single university. For example, one college or school within a university may require six semester hours of Western Civilization and two courses in Chaucer. Another may require a course or two of United States history and American literature. This has too often resulted in a nightmare insofar as the junior college is concerned. It has forced them to proliferate their curriculums to accommodate the whims and inconsistencies of senior institutions. This is both expensive and demeaning for junior colleges. And, in the end, the intended purpose of this *hoop jumping* is frequently not served because students make belated changes in programs and institutions.

But, changes are occurring. Measures have been or are being taken in several states to remedy such problems. These measures are basically of two types. One type is represented by Florida where a compact has been entered into by the public two-year and senior institutions. The essence of the compact is that each institution has been given the authority to develop its own program of general-liberal studies for bachelor degree seeking students. That program must include a minimum of 36 semester hours representing studies in certain broad fields. Once a program is developed and printed in a junior college's catalog, students receiving the associate of arts (transfer) degree are not held responsible for the senior institution's general-liberal studies requirements after transfer. However, even in states like Florida where public junior colleges have been given a great deal of latitude in the development of their general-liberal studies programs, many of them have made little use of their freedom. Their curriculums still look very much like those of nearby senior institutions. One gets the impression that they love their shackles.

The other type of measure is found in states such as Georgia and Texas. In those states, a basic general-liberal studies core of courses has been identified which is required of all bachelor degree seeking students during the first two years whether enrolled in a public junior college or senior institution.

To this point no reference has been made to general-liberal studies for students enrolled in non-transfer occupational programs. Until quite recently there was a pronounced difference of viewpoint as to what, if any, emphasis general-liberal studies should receive in occupational programs. While there still exist differences of opinion, leaders in occupational education usually recommend that a segment of general-liberal studies be included in all two-year occupational degree programs. Their recommendations as to the minimum that should be devoted to that end cluster around 25 to 30 percent of the total credit hours. This is misleading, however, because in practice this amount usually includes skill courses in writing and mathematics. While most occupational degree programs now require a course or two in the social sciences and frequently applied psychology, few include even a single course in the humanities.

While the overall picture of general-liberal studies in the junior college is one of parroting senior colleges, there are notable exceptions. Some institutions have developed new courses which represent major departures from the traditional departmental courses. Among these are courses which are focused on other than Western European culture. These include courses on Asian and African cultures and Negro history. Courses in music, art, and literature which treat the contributions of Blacks in these areas have also made their appearance in the curriculums of public junior colleges. One also finds courses which focus on contemporary problems and needs such as courses in ecology, pollution control, current social problems, and contemporary art forms. Some of these courses have been copied from senior institutions but others are the creation of junior colleges. Stimulus has been given to this and other curriculum areas by the formation of junior college consortiums which share ideas and work cooperatively to develop better educational programs for their students.

OCCUPATIONAL PROGRAMS

The term *occupational education* is used here to represent those programs which are designed to prepare the graduates to go directly into employment.

They include a spectrum ranging from short courses of a few months to two calendar years. As with highly specialized bachelor degree programs, an increasing number of so-called two-year occupational degree programs are requiring more than two academic years for completion. Within a relatively short time, three-year occupational programs in the junior college may be common.

The growth of junior college occupational programs during recent years has been nothing short of phenomenal. To illustrate this the writer selected at random two institutions (which were operating in 1954–55) from each of 10 states representing a broad geographic distribution. A comparison was made of the number of occupational programs offered by these 20 institutions during the 1958–59 and 1970–71 academic terms—a twelve-year interim period. The results were as follows:

Occupational Programs	1958–59	1970–71
Average number of programs offered	9.2	36.4
Least number offered by an institution	2	9
Largest number offered by an institution	23	80

Numerous public junior colleges which did not exist in 1960 already have occupational programs in such number that they exceed the 1970–71 average of institutions represented in the above analysis. A combination of related factors accounts for this growth. Major among them has been a growing awareness on the part of both public policy makers and educational leaders that there exists a need in the work force for personnel with specialized preparation below the professional level. Further, they realized that a void existed in our educational system for meeting this manpower requirement. To resolve the problem, one state after another created a system of community colleges or expanded an already existing system. With this came funds, both state and federal, to develop programs, employ staff, and to build and equip the facilities needed for alleviating this need.

Other factors have played a role in the expansion of occupational programs in junior colleges. Not the least of these has been an effort on the part of professionals to look critically at their fields to determine how better use can be made of their specialized talents. This has resulted in an increased awareness of the need for and the desire to utilize support personnel. The health-related professions represent a good case in point. In recent years these professions have put a great deal of effort into this restructuring. As a result, new opportunities are opening up for supportive personnel in the allied health fields and existing programs are being expanded. Junior colleges have become the primary agency for preparing personnel for the allied health fields.

Greater acceptance by parents and youth of careers which require less than a bachelor's degree is also contributing to the growth of occupational programs in the junior college. It is becoming easier to attract students to these programs. This acceptance is also growing on the part of junior college faculty, counselors, and administrators. Young people and their parents are becoming increasingly aware that while there is a growing oversupply of professional personnel in many fields, employment opportunities are good for graduates of most occupational programs offered by junior colleges.

In addition to the allied health occupations to which reference has been made, expansion is also occurring in other areas. Among these are the public service occupations, especially such areas as traffic management, law enforcement, and pollution control and sanitation. Opportunities for junior college graduates in business-related occupations remain good, particularly in the secretarial and mid-management occupations. New programs are being established by junior colleges to meet the need for personnel in service occupations such as food preparation and the tourist-related area. The recent rapid expansion of programs in the industrial technician occupations has recently leveled off. However, some new programs are being developed in that area as others are terminated in keeping with changes which are occurring in technological developments.

A recent significant trend in occupational preparation at the junior college level has been cooperative education. This is by no means a new concept. A few colleges and universities have employed it for a long time, e.g., Antioch College and Northwestern University. The concept has also been utilized by high schools in distributive occupational programs. Only recently, however, has cooperative education received serious attention by junior colleges. But interest seems to be growing rapidly. A recent report identifies over 60 two-year institutions with cooperative education training programs.[1]

DEVELOPMENTAL PROGRAMS

Here again, terminology is a problem. A variety of terms is employed to describe what are referred to here as *developmental programs*. Basically they refer to those efforts made by institutions to assist students who have specific educational needs and/or for whom standard educational offerings of the institution are inappropriate.

A great deal of effort has gone into this area during recent years. Several factors account for this. One is growing evidence that most of our past efforts in remedial education can only be described as colossal failures. They simply have not achieved their stated or implied purpose of preparing students to succeed in a regular college program, e.g., a transfer curriculum in most cases. Another factor has been an increasing enrollment of students from economically and educationally deprived backgrounds. Related to the factors just mentioned has been a growing sense of responsibility for developing realistic learning opportunities for the full range of students who enter these open door admission policy institutions.

A variety of practices and programs is replacing the former remedial bonehead English and mathematics courses. Any such changes are likely to be a gain since these courses have typically been looked upon as *Siberia* assignments by instructors and crosses to be borne by students. In summary, few conditions for success are found in most traditional remedial courses. Because of the number and variations of approaches now being employed in developmental programs, enumerating them is difficult. A brief review of the types of changes which are occurring follows.

One change is a growing realization that a group of students who are deficient in a given area such as reading differ greatly from one another in the specific nature of their problems. Consequently, a remedial course which gives them all the

[1] Robert L. Brown, *Cooperative Education* (Washington, D.C., 1971).

same treatment is almost certain to miss the target for many. As a result, tions are individualizing their remedial programs. A student's weaknesses are diagnosed and specific activities are planned to remove them as quickly as possible and/or as the student chooses.

Another change related to the one just described is a belated recognition that individuals vary in their learning styles. As a result, a variety of materials, techniques, and types of presentations is being employed. One result of this has been the increased use of film, filmstrip, recordings, and other type media and technological aids.

Some institutions are experiencing success in assisting students with educational deficiencies by keeping them in regular courses and providing them special assistance. One method of doing this, which has been found to be quite successful in several experimental settings, is to employ students as tutors. Others use lay assistants or teacher aides to provide individual assistance and some offer extra class sessions for such students.

Another approach which some institutions are finding more satisfactory than remedial courses in skill subjects is a general program for high risk students. The rationale here is that many of these students will remain at the institution only a short time and that the best way to serve them is by providing experiences which will assist them in their day-to-day lives. Among the variations used are block time periods with team teaching, courses which cut across subject fields, and innovative methods of presenting materials. An effort is usually made to get these students enrolled in occupational programs in which they can succeed and which will qualify them for employment.

In all of these approaches, the importance of student motivation is receiving increased recognition. As a consequence, greater care is being taken in staffing. Institutions are recruiting faculty specifically trained to work with such students and are selecting volunteer instructors from among those already on the staff. The added cost of many of these programs is of great concern to administrators. Few states provide extra funds for this purpose. Federal funds have helped in some cases but that represents fair weather assistance of short duration.

PRE-PROFESSIONAL PROGRAMS

The reader will probably have noted that this article contains no section on transfer programs per se. This is because of the increasing difficulty of specifying in advance what is, in fact, transferable to senior institutions. More and more courses and programs which were neither intended nor represented by junior colleges as being transferable are being transferred. For example, occupational programs developed to prepare junior college graduates for immediate employment are frequently accepted in total or in major part by senior institutions.

Because of this and other forces which are at work, the time is near when the transfer issue as we have known it will no longer exist. The associate degree will be accepted by senior institutions at face value just as the high school diploma is now. Students presenting the associate degree will categorically be classified as juniors. A student's program at the senior institution will be determined by the major selected and its relationship to the courses previously completed. In many cases he will be able to earn a bachelor's degree in two additional academic years whereas in other cases additional time will be required. Already in states with well developed junior college systems it is not uncommon to find senior institutions where the junior class is comprised of more transfer than native students. Before long this will be the norm. Consequently, senior institutions have an increasing stake in the pre-professional programs offered by junior colleges. Several trends are occurring as a result.

One trend is to move professional courses into the upper divisions, i.e., junior and senior years. Nevertheless, those responsible for professional programs at senior institutions are taking more initiative to work with their junior college counterparts. Among other things this has resulted in articulation conferences at the division and department levels. One outcome is better agreement and understanding of courses and course content. Another outcome is greater awareness by those in senior colleges that changes in their professional requirements must be communicated promptly to their feeder junior colleges. To facilitate this communication, senior institutions are creating special offices under such titles as Office of Junior College Relations and Office of Two-Year College Affairs. Where there have been serious efforts to articulate pre-professional and professional preparation an interesting concomitant development has occurred. Senior institutions have come to recognize the need to agree among themselves on professional requirements. This is alleviating one major articulation problem encountered by junior colleges—variations in requirements for the same major among senior institutions.

COMMUNITY SERVICE PROGRAMS

Whether or not community service programs represent a distinct curriculum area is a matter of viewpoint. From one perspective those programs are encompassed in the other curriculum areas treated in this article. Considered in that light, the distinguishing features are to whom, when, and where these educational opportunities are provided. From another perspective these are programs in their own right. That is, they represent offerings which are not found elsewhere in a junior college. Regardless of the point of view held, this is a rapidly growing area of educational endeavor in many two-year colleges. Its importance is reflected by the fact that many such institutions are now officially called *community colleges*.

An important characteristic of community service programs is adaptation. Such programs vary in length from a day to an academic term. They are offered at times and places convenient to those they are intended to serve be it at 11:00 p.m. in a factory for a group of workers on a swing shift or during midmorning in a community center for a group of elderly citizens.

In this brief treatment suffice it to say that things are happening in the area of community services. Forward looking directors of junior college community service programs have as their stock in trade the *extended campus* and the *college without walls* concepts. Their programs are reaching people from all walks of life. Many of the activities mentioned in the next section are encompassed in community service programs. This area is just coming into its own so far as the junior college is concerned.

THE INFORMAL CURRICULUM

The informal curriculum has more impact on students than many curriculum planners realize or are willing to acknowledge. Consequently, it has been sold short at all levels of education. There are, however, notable exceptions to this general condition among junior colleges and indications that the blackout is being lifted.

Among the activities that constitute the informal junior college curriculum are student government, publications, special interest and social organizations, cultural programs, intramural and intercollegiate sports, recreational programs, and numerous informal endeavors. The fact that many public junior colleges have no residence facilities has had a bearing on the development of their informal curriculums. They are adapting to this situation in a number of ways. One of these is in facilities planning. Places are being provided where students can meet informally and where they can engage in recreational activities. Another approach being employed increasingly is the involvement of students in the planning of such activities.

As public junior colleges address themselves to their role of community oriented institutions, the informal curriculum is reaching far beyond the regular student body. Adults of the community from all walks of life increasingly participate in the social, cultural, recreational, and public service activities on junior college campuses. With the current emphasis on informal education, exciting developments exist for community oriented junior colleges. No other type of educational institution is as well suited to serving all people in all ways.

Opening the College Gates to the Low Achiever

William Moore, Jr.

Since I grew up in the ghetto, was a two-time high school dropout, was in the lower tenth percentile when I enrolled in college, and was graduated third from the last in my undergraduate class, I can justifiably describe myself as having been academically unsuccessful. Add to these credentials the fact that I am a Negro, and I believe you will agree that I can speak with authority and conviction on the subject of the educationally disadvantaged student.

Each year thousands of low achieving students enter adult society with "worthless" high school diplomas. Many of these students have been sold on the

From *Today's Education* LVII, no. 9 (December 1968):38–40. Used by permission of the author and publisher.

purported value of the diploma, but they will not receive any reward for acquiring it. For a few good students, the diploma is a passport to college; for some others it leads to a union card and the world of work; but for far too many, particularly Negroes in the cities, it is no more than an attendance prize. Its holder cannot get into college or into desirable areas of the work world. Such students, who are denied additional schooling, who cannot go to work, and who are vulnerable to the draft, are potential dynamite.

Though the academically unsuccessful come from all races and social classes, a disproportionately large number come from minority groups, especially from the Negro race. They often live in ugly cities. They come from broken homes, dilapidated housing, seething streets, and crippling schools. Only a few of them are motivated toward education. Most of them feel rejected, almost all of them have experienced some failure, a considerable number have been poor, and few of them have had a second chance at an education.

Many people say that our institutions of higher learning are shutting out or flunking out too many kids in a society in which the number of unskilled jobs remains about the same while the number of unskilled persons continues to increase. In addition to producing trained professionals, is higher education turning out enough other people with different marketable skills?

With all its resources and all its expertise, higher education has shown little concern for disadvantaged youth. College people have insisted that they are doing what they are supposed to do. They have rejected the awesome burden of trying to salvage students who are "unqualified" for higher education. Traditionally, they have recommended that some other "more appropriate" educational agency should try to reach students judged academically unsuccessful. Only a few have asked soul-searching questions—and found challenging answers.

In this decade, what constitutes a bona fide educational opportunity for the socially and economically disadvantaged that would be beneficial both to the student and to society? It certainly cannot arise from the traditional attitude of higher education that says to these young men and women, "This is what we have to offer—take it or leave it." Few of the inept can take it; too many of the unmotivated leave it. And educational experience for these students has to be significant.

The disadvantaged—by the sheer magnitude of their numbers and the insistence of their voices—have created a climate where higher education can no longer remain comfortable with its habitual position of scholarly detachment. Consequently, a social and academic revolution is beginning to affect higher education. In its vanguard are new theories and techniques for dealing with the marginal students. As a result of the increased emphasis on higher education for the masses, community colleges are springing up at the rate of 50 per year. And some are stressing an open-door policy—one that will admit students who were underachievers in high school, those with limited ability but high motivation, and those who are culturally and economically disadvantaged. This is a dramatic change for higher education, although Negro colleges have long provided educational experiences for such students. Upward Bound and similar groups are also operating on many college campuses, but the fact that such programs are too few needs no documentation.

Believing they had a responsibility to serve the marginal student, Forest Park Community College's board of trustees, president, administrators, and faculty decided to accept the open-door policy and the challenges it presents.

(Such a policy *must* have commitment from the top down.) Assisted by grant funds from the Danforth Foundation, they structured a truly imaginative program —the General Curriculum: A Program for the Educationally Disadvantaged— which attracts financial aid from public and private sources.

General Curriculum is an experimental program developed on the premise that the student who enters it will need simultaneous assistance in the basic academic skills (reading, mathematics, grammar, and composition), and personal enrichment and adjustment to self and society. The program provides this assistance through programmed learning, general education classes, and guidance techniques—including careful and proper placement (into college curriculum, an existing training program, or directly on a job).

Located between the city and the suburbs, the college's General Curriculum Division attracts both Negro and Caucasian students from both directions. Poor and affluent students alike are assigned to this program on the basis of two criteria: high school rank at graduation and percentile rank on the School and College Ability Tests (SCAT). *These ranks must be in the lower third and the tenth percentile or below, respectively.* To be assigned to the General Curriculum, the student must meet both criteria. He is not, however, locked into the program. If he makes satisfactory progress (B—) after a semester or a year in the program, he may move into the transfer, technical, or career programs.

To solve the basic skills problem, the college offers a multimedia approach to programmed instruction. All instruction in our Programmed Materials Learning Laboratory is individualized. Each student proceeds at his own rate and works only on those skills in which he is deficient. His periodic examinations are spaced for maximum reinforcement; he always knows at what level he is working and where he must go to reach his objective. We place on him the burden of responsibility for assimilating the material. (The present Laboratory has auxiliary laboratories in writing, mathematics, and reading. And we have added a psychologist to the PMLL staff to diagnose learning problems and to prescribe remedial procedures appropriate to the student's learning style.)

Forest Park Community College readily observed that educationally disadvantaged students know little about events beyond their day, beyond their age group, beyond their neighborhood. Thus, they lack both an understanding of the total contemporary culture and a basic historical frame of reference. Therefore, for personal and cultural enrichment of these students, two teams of teachers developed (and continue to develop and evaluate) a one-year program of general education designed to provide their students with a stimulating and successful classroom experience. These teams have interest and experience in working with low achievers.

The marginal student is frequently antagonistic, hesitant, and indifferent to the educative process. These attitudes are compounded when the curriculum content fails to touch him in a direct way. For these reasons, material for the general education courses is chosen in terms of its relevance. (Students would be unmotivated either to understand when Ptolemy lived or to appreciate the influence of his cosmological theory. According to one General Curriculum student, "Ptolemy goofed with his theory of the universe, anyway—so why be bothered with him?")

We use no textbooks in these courses. Instructors choose their materials from current articles and other supplementary readings that are interesting, timely, and provocative. The content of one course is not isolated from the content of other general education courses. Rather, each course is structured around five broad headings: orientation, self, self and society, human relations, and values.

Each team has a weekly conference, which gives its members an opportunity to evaluate a student's progress with every other member of the team, including the counselor who works with the student. Every teacher also has a chance to determine whether his material correlates adequately with the content other team members are presenting. He also can discuss, compare, and exchange teaching techniques that have been effective in instructing General Curriculum students.

In guidance—one of the most cohesive factors in this program—a low student-counselor ratio ensures that students can be seen at least once a week or daily if necessary. Students attend guidance classes two class periods per week —to appraise their attitudes and their abilities. The counseling program is student- and community-centered rather than institution-centered. This implies that counselors are trained to know intimately all facets of the community so that its total resources are at the disposal of the educationally disadvantaged student. People from business, industry, the professions, labor, and management meet with our students, answer questions, and provide information about requirements for employment and opportunities for advancement.

Other features of the Forest Park General Curriculum program include:

A deliberate plan to work with the deprived community
Provisions for articulation between the high schools, community, and the college
Remission of fees (tuition, books, and so forth) for needy students
Employment of a full-time social worker
Internships (with stipends) for prospective college-level teachers of the disadvantaged
Continuing workshops for in-service personnel and workshops on a national basis for those interested in learning techniques of the program
Access to expertise (in terms of consultation) and funds to experiment and develop a model program for the educationally disadvantaged across the nation.

The essence of our program cannot be captured in this short article. It is more than an educational program. It is people—creative people who have endured the frustrations, conflicts, dilemmas, and dynamics of human interaction. It is the long hours, coffee-stained tables, overflowing ashtrays, skipped lunches, and forgotten dinners; the endless meetings, conferences, memos, reports, and deadlines. It is the persistent challenge of *doing* what we didn't know could not be done.

And it is also the conversion of an English teacher into a programmed-learning expert by trial and error, the small successes, the blundering into a new technique or procedure that worked, and unsolicited letters from students who said they were helped. All these are the human ingredients.

At this point, we lack definitive research that will tell us exactly where each student has gone and how each has performed after involvement in the General Curriculum. But we do know that many students now view education and their individual abilities in a positive light, that they no longer perceive education as an experience of frustration and failure.

Even though the St. Louis humidity is unbelievable, grandmothers who have deferred their education for many years come to learn. Fathers, after the day's work, come to perform the computations in fractions that the fifth graders they leave at home have already mastered. Some come because they want to earn more money on their jobs. Others come because they are bored. Somehow, they will accept the inconvenience. Neither the blond kid who cannot master decimals nor the black one who consistently fails to make subject and verb agree complains. And this makes it all worthwhile.

New Directions in Community Services

Ervin L. Harlacher

The community college is fast becoming a dynamic force which affects the thought processes, habits, economic status, and social interaction of people from every walk of life, in every part of the country. More and more, it is becoming the most important element of this nation's educational structure.

The community college in implementing its full community dimension is breaking, once and for all, the lock-step of tradition, i.e., college is four walls, college is semester-length courses; college is credit; college is culturally and educationally elite.

It seems inevitable that the community college will place even greater emphasis on its community dimension in the decade ahead. The community college will demonstrate, to an extent even greater than it has to date, that college is where the people are, and that community services are designed to take the college program out into the community as well as bring the community to the college.

In its most significant role, the program of community services constitutes what might be called "Operation Outreach." Peter S. Mousolite has suggested that, "We emulate the English minstrel, the French jongleur, the Spanish trovador, the Chautauqua enterprise so popular not so many years ago," and through the use of mobile units move out into the community and create the program there.[1]

THE NEXT GREAT THRUST

While the full potential of the program of community services has not yet been realized by all institutions, there is reason to believe that the next great thrust of the community college development will be in the direction of com-

From *Junior College Journal* XXXVIII, no. 6 (March, 1968), 12–17. Used by permission of the publisher.

[1] Mousolite, Peter S. *The Edge of the Chair*, remarks presented to National Conference on Vocational and Technical Education. Chicago: May 16, 1967.

munity services. The American Association of Junior Colleges therefore authorized the present study.

In conducting this study the author during the summer and fall of 1967 visited thirty-seven community college districts in thirteen states, representing the small and the large, the rich and the poor, and the urban and the rural community college. He also corresponded with administrators of twenty-eight additional college districts in twelve states, with trustees and presidents of newly organized community college districts, and with officials of state agencies concerned with the governance of community colleges. The sixty-five community college districts participating in this study operate 104 college campuses in nineteen different states.

The community college is dedicated to the proposition that, important as are formalized curriculums offered for youth and adults within its classrooms, informal education provided on a continuous basis throughout the community for all of the rest of the people is of equal importance in building the character of the citizens who make up the state.

The program of the community college may be conceptualized in two dimensions—formal education and informal education. Through its formal dimension, sometimes characterized as schooling, the community college provides transfer, occupational, general education, and guidance and counseling programs for youth and adults enrolled in regularly scheduled day and evening classes on the campus.

But it is through its community dimension that the junior college truly becomes a community college. Chancellor Samuel B. Gould of the State University of New York, has underscored the importance of this dimension of informal education:

It is my conviction that a college, in addition to its more readily accepted intellectual dimension, should have the dimension of community that offers a place for the general life enrichment of all who live nearby: young and old, artisan and farmer and member of profession, college graduate and comparatively unskilled. Thus many of the gaps or weaknesses that the new pressures of numbers are bound to create in formal education can be filled or strengthened as a college opens its doors and its resources to all in a friendly and informal fashion, without thought of credits or degrees or anything more than to assist the burgeoning of understanding in the individual as a member of a personal, physical, political, economic, artistic and spiritual world.[2]

The philosophy that the community college campus encompasses the length and breadth of the college district, and that the total population of the district is its student body, makes it possible for the community college, in a massive and untraditional way, to broaden the base for higher education. This philosophy also makes it possible to ease the problems of access to higher education by taking the college to the people. Furthermore, it offers freedom from the traditional image of the American college and university which sees college primarily, if not entirely, as an institution concerned with educating youth.

[2] Gould, Samuel B. "Whose Goals for Higher Education," remarks prepared for delivery before 50th Annual Meeting, American Council on Education, Washington, D.C., October 12, 1967.

While the addition of community services has revolutionized the role of the community college, actually the community services concept is as old as Socrates —possibly older. Socrates first exemplified it by taking his wisdom into the streets and the market place and there created a student community representative of the people and actively concerned with the social and moral issues of the time.

By the eighteenth century, however, the idea of providing higher education for all the people had been abandoned, and the universities became storehouses for factual knowledge and retreats for the idle rich or select few.

The first step toward providing community services in this country was taken in 1826 by Josiah Holbrook when he established the American Lyceum. In later years, after the lyceum died out, chautauqua, initiated in 1874, carried forward the lyceum "spirit" and became a symbol of education and culture until its peak year in 1924.[3]

MORRILL ACT

Another step in the development of community services was the establishment of agricultural extension as a function of American universities under the Morrill and Smith-Lever Acts. The philosophy of agricultural extension focused on "helping people to help themselves."

The community services function as defined in this study, i.e., educational, cultural, and recreational services above and beyond regularly scheduled day and evening classes, is completely foreign to the traditional idea of college education but it is the manifestation of what the community college was created for. The community college recognizes that by definition it has an obligation to: (1) become a center of community life by encouraging the use of college facilities and services by community groups when such use does not interfere with the college's regularly scheduled day and evening programs; (2) provide educational services for all age groups which utilize the special skills and knowledge of the college staff and other experts and are designed to meet the needs of community groups and the college district at large; (3) provide the community with the leadership and coordination capabilities of the college, assist the community in long-range planning, and join with individuals and groups in attacking unsolved problems; and (4) contribute to and promote the cultural, intellectual, and social life of the college district community and the development of skills for the profitable use of leisure time.

A COMMUNITY SERVICE AGENCY

The original idea of the community college was one that involved a "grass roots" approach. In theory, at least, everyone connected with such an institution would look around, find educational gaps, and help fill the gaps. The community college faculty and staff—teachers and doers in the broadest possible sense—would

[3] Jones, Bertis L. *The History of Community Development in American Universities With Particular Reference to Four Selected Institutions.* Unpublished Ed. D. dissertation, University of California, Los Angeles, 1961, p. 329–332.

undertake to solve human problems in the community around them or point out the needs to other educational groups in the community to care for.

Rooted in the soil of the district community it serves and drawing its students and strength from that community, the community college is particularly suited as a community service agency:

1. The community college is a community-centered institution with the primary purpose of providing service to the people of its community. Its offerings and programs are planned to meet the needs of the community and are developed with the active participation of citizens.
2. The community college claims community service as one of its major functions and, according to Thornton, ". . . . the scope and adequacy of these services determine whether or not the college merits the title of community junior college. . . ."[4]
3. Since the community college is usually a creation of citizens of the local community or area, and since it is most frequently governed by a board of local citizens, the community college is readily capable of responding to changing community needs.
4. Most community colleges are operated by a local district which encompasses several separate and distinct communities. The ideal locale for a program of community services is one "in which there are numerous communities and subcommunities with natural and compelling interrelationship. . . ."[5] The program of community services welds these separate communities and groups together.
5. The community college is an institution of higher education, and as such can draw upon the advanced resources of its staff in assisting in the solution of the problems of an increasingly complex society.
6. The community college, as a relatively new segment of American education, is "unencrusted with tradition, not hidebound by a rigid history, and in many cases, new and eager for adventure." Thus, it is able, without duplicating existing services in the community, to tailor its program to meet local needs and conditions.

At least seven directions which this major emphasis on the community dimension will take, seem safe to predict at this point:

I. *The community college will develop aggressive multiservice outreach programs designed to truly extend its campus throughout the entire college district.*

Through the use of extension centers, empty stores, portable units located on vacant land, mobile units, churches, schools, libraries, museums, art galleries, places of business and other community facilities, the community college will establish communications links with all segments of the college district community, encouraging a free exchange of ideas and resources. The community college, stable yet unfettered by the performance of buildings, will move in physical location in response to shifting needs.

[4] Thornton, James W., *The Community Junior College.* New York: John Wiley and Sons, 1960, p. 66.
[5] Seay, Maurice F., and Crawford, Ferris N., *The Community School and Community Self-Improvement.* Lansing, Michigan: Clair L. Taylor, Superintendent to Public Instruction, 1954, p. 144.

Extension centers. Pasadena City College in California offers short courses, lectures, and forums in sixty-five different sites in every part of the six unified districts which compose the college district, which includes a unique course for wives of prisoners. And 600 students are enrolled in college credit courses offered by Miami-Dade Junior College, Florida, in a variety of community locations, including public agencies, hotels, airlines, the Miami Beach Center, and a local Air Force base.

In-plant training. Perhaps the most extensive in-plant training program in the country is operated by New York City Community College, resulting in pretraining or in-service training for 180 newly appointed building inspectors, 300 building inspectors, 320 dietary aides from eighteen hospitals, 1,000 nurses' aides, and 700 municipal employees. Top management training courses conducted by El Centro College in Texas for a Dallas hospital, including basic management, work simplification, problem solving and goal setting, reportedly saved the hospital $750,000 operating costs during the first year. And the in-service training program developed for federal employees by Cuyahoga Community College in Cleveland, Ohio, is expected to attract some 500 initially, with the federal government paying tuition.

Mobile and portable units. Hudson Valley Community College in New York last summer utilized effectively an "Opportunity Van" in two disadvantaged Albany neighborhoods, recruiting students for its urban center. Another excellent example is the community science outreach program being developed by Oakland Community College in Michigan, in cooperation with a local institute of science, and featuring mobile exhibits and demonstrations, traveling museums and short courses.

II. *The community college will place increased emphasis on community education for all age levels and all age groups.*

Increasingly, community education services are not limited to youth just out of high school or to adults of the community, but are provided for citizens of all ages—including elementary and secondary school youngsters—with varying interests and points of view, and are provided at all social and economic levels. More and more these educational services embrace the whole gamut of community life with the objective of preparing citizens to cope with rapid and sweeping social, political, and technological change.

Short courses. The Center for Community Educational Services, established by the State University of New York Agricultural and Technical College at Farmingdale, offered 720 workshops, seminars, institutes and conferences last year, accommodating 32,000 persons. Since 1940 Abraham Baldwin Agricultural College in Georgia has offered 743 short courses for 98,699 farmers, stressing the latest techniques in farming and related fields.

In-service training. Suffolk County Community College in New York has developed, in cooperation with Civil Training Council, twenty-two county-financed in-service training courses for county employees, offered during the working day at seven different locations.

Baltimore Junior College in Maryland, under its new careers program, trained some 300 disadvantaged persons, twenty-two and up, with job problems as psychology aides, home visitation aides, government service aides, data processing aides, etc. Some 1,100 disadvantaged adults and young adults are enrolled in the East Bay Skill Center, funded under MDTA and operated by Laney College in California. Big Bend Community College in Washington provides, on a contractual basis, training programs in licensed practical nursing, nurses aide, and mechanics, i.e., riveting, for a local Women's Job Corps Center. And Oakland Community College's project SERVE, funded under Title I of the Higher Education Act, stimulates active participation of senior citizens in community affairs through a three-part program: free counseling and placement service for those needing additional income; a volunteer placement bureau; and carefully tailored short courses.

Meeting community needs. "The Destroyers," a forum on the illegal drug traffic, sponsored by Ceritos College in California in cooperation with fourteen local school districts, resulted in a change in the curriculum for the fifth and sixth grades.

III. *The community college will utilize a greater diversification of media in meeting community needs and interests.*

No longer can it be said that the community college fulfills its community responsibility by merely offering a new course "anytime ten or more citizens want it, if teachers, space, funds, and equipment are available." Increasingly, the class is only one of a plethora of media utilized in the program of community service: telecommunications; seminars and symposiums; performing groups; self-instructional packages; educational and cultural tours; workshops and conferences; counseling and consultative services; research and planning, recreational activities; science experiments and exhibitions, facility usage; leadership, coordination, and advisory assistance; public lectures, and fine arts events.

Short courses. Even short courses offered under the program of community service take on a different format. Especially designed as in-service training for personnel of paleontology laboratories located in the area, the biostratigraphy seminar, sponsored by Bakersfield College in California, is now in its sixth year and continues to fill a need for the petroleum industry.

Telecommunications. Chicago City College's TV College, on the air approximately twenty-six hours per week, since 1956 has permitted 100,000 persons to take seventy different credit and noncredit courses in their homes, generating 170,000 enrollments. Using FM radio, Long Beach City College in California serves 100,000 kindergarten through twelfth grade students of the Long Beach Unified School District. In order to provide educational opportunities in five outlying areas of its 2,600 square mile district, Los Rios Junior College District in California is developing the concept of the Little Red Electronic Schoolhouse, equipping the one-room facilities with thirty carrels for audio-tutorial study.

Tours and field trips. During August of 1967, a week-long nature study field trip into the Minarets area of the Sierra Nevada was organized by Foothill College in

California for thirty-six members of the community. And an imaginative program of field studies in Mexico and South America has been developed by the College of San Mateo in California including "pre-Columbian civilization" in Mexico City; and "Mayan civilization" centering on the Yucatan peninsula and Guatemala; and a people-to-people exploration of Central and South America.

Community performing groups. The Music Makers of the Foothill Junior College District in California encompass three community performing groups; a 140-voice community symphonic choir, the Schola Cantorum; a select chamber ensemble, the Master Symphonia; and a ninety-piece symphony, the Nova Vista Orchestra.

Consulting services. A program of technical assistance to industry, including bulletins, newsletters, and general consultative services, is being developed by New York City Community College in the areas of optics, data processing, and numerical control.

Community counseling. Cuyahoga Community College's project SEARCH for the culturally disadvantaged of the Hought section of Cleveland features a counseling center to help individuals identify realistic educational and vocational goals for themselves. North Florida Junior College provided the leadership for the development of an area guidance center, where twenty counselors serve elementary schools, high schools, and junior colleges in six rural counties by providing 115 hours of guidance time daily.

IV. *The community college will increasingly utilize its catalytic capabilities to assist its community in the solution of basic educational, economic, political, and social problems.*

In the process of becoming an educational resource center, the community college is dynamically relating its programs to the existing and emerging needs of its district community. Through action programs aimed at closing ravines now dividing the inner city from the outer community; baseline data from community studies; the leadership and advisory assistance of college personnel in the mobilization of community resources; long-range planning; workshops, institutes and conferences; and the organization of community coordinating councils and other needed groups, the community college is becoming an agency for social change.

Programs for the disadvantaged. During the past year, 192 disadvantaged students have participated in the Neighborhood Youth Corps program at Westark Junior College in Arkansas, spending approximately half of their time in remedial reading, writing and arithmetic, and the other half in automobile mechanics, automobile body and welding programs. Baltimore Junior College has developed two programs to motivate youngsters from culturally disadvantaged sections of Baltimore to stay in school and seek college goals: (1) an Upward Bound program for promising tenth and eleventh grade students; and (2) Operation: College Horizons for junior and senior high school students and their parents. The Peralta Colleges in California are developing an extensive program for the culturally disadvantaged who remain in the inner city, which features a student service corps, community development centers offering educational and counseling services, a cultural enrichment program, and a scholarship assistance program.

Community leadership. In order to give maximum service to its community, Abraham Baldwin College initiated project SURGE (Systematic Utilization of Resources for Growth and Efficiency) for Tifton and Tiff County in 1964, utilizing fourteen committees, representing every aspect of community life and an annual "town hall" type meeting.

Workshops, institutes, and conferences. An extensive program of community workshops and seminars to provide information and education about local government, planning renewal, community organization, etc., has been developed by Essex Community College in Maryland.

Organization of community groups. New York City Community College has proposed the establishment of an economic training institute to be designed by a task force in response to problems identified by the South Brooklyn Community Progress Center's clientele as well as its professional staff.

V. *The community college will be increasingly concerned about the cultural growth of its community and state.*

That this trend is already taking shape has been evident in many communities for some time. A survey of development in California four years ago, for example, resulted in this conclusion: "California communities from the Sierra to the sea, and the Siskyous to the Mexican border are experiencing a cultural, social, and intellectual renaissance. And much of the credit for the community rebirth is due California's seventy-one public junior colleges and their programs of community services."[6]

Cultural centers. Flint Junior College in Michigan has developed a cultural center which includes an intimate theater, auditorium, an art center, planetarium, museum, and a public library. Del Mar College in Texas has become a cultural center for the entire college district through its extensive cultural program which includes community performing groups—a chamber orchestra, a chorale, choral ensemble, and a full symphony orchestra; and festivals and series presentations. Rockland Community College in New York has taken a number of steps to join forces with community groups in creating a cultural center for the community which would feature an on-campus museum, a theater and/or auditorium, and a planetarium. A most ambitious and extensive composite of performing arts activities was initiated in the spring of 1967 by Bucks County Community College, Pennsylvania, when it undertook a multifaceted program of experimental theater, children's theater, elementary and secondary school visitations, an art festival, and a college-sponsored professional repertory company.

Arts councils. Delta College in Michigan was instrumental in the formation of a forty-member arts council which is housed on the college campus and publishes an annual calendar, functions as a "clearinghouse" for the scheduling of events, operates a central arts activity over the colleged-owned educational television station.

[6] Harlacher, Ervin L. "California's Community Renaissance," *Junior College Journal,* XXXIV (May, 1966).

VI. *The community college will place greater emphasis on interaction with its community.*

Increasingly, it is being recognized that the effective program of community services is built upon (1) a solid foundation of citizen participation and college-community interactions and (2) a thorough understanding of the community. Citizens actually participate in the planning, maintenance, and evaluation of the program; and the college, recognizing that it must be of the community and not just in it, participates in community life. In such a way, mutual interaction is achieved.

Institutional synergism. This term has been defined as simultaneous action of separate agencies, which together have a greater total effect than the sum of their individual efforts. Illustrative of this term is the concept of the "Health and Education Campus" being developed by Essex Community College in Maryland, the Franklin Square Hospital, and the Baltimore County Health Department, and featuring the sharing of physical facilities and human resources, the joint development of paramedical curriculum, and development of continuing education programs for patients and the community through television. Rockland Community College is developing a college library as a strong community-serving central reference and research library to complement existing library services in the county, and a media center capable of sending programs to all schools in the county. Approximately one hundred paintings of Chautauqua County Society artists are constantly on display in hallways and offices throughout the campus of Jamestown Community College in New York, making the entire campus an art gallery. And thirty-three companies cooperate with Rock Valley College in Illinois in the promotion of and recruitment for its unique Career Advancement Program which is permitting 174 company-employed students to work half-time and spend half-time in class.

Advisory committees. Ceritos College in California is aided in the planning and implementation of its program of community services by a citizens' advisory council and nine advisory committees, including adult education, business, civic responsibilities, community research and development, community volunteer services, fine arts, professions, recreation and youth.

Community councils. Vincennes University Junior College in Indiana has organized a council of top managers of industry in the area which plans educational programs for the welfare of industry.

Community-college sponsorship. Joining forces with a community organization, North Florida Junior College has created the North Florida Junior College-Madison Artist Series Association for the purpose of planning and financing high-level artist series programs for the college and the community.

VII. *The community college will increasingly recognize the need for cooperation with other community and regional agencies.*

In order to avoid unnecessary duplication of services, a greater effort is being made by community college personnel to coordinate the community college program of community services with programs of other community and regional agencies, i.e., public schools, recreation districts, governmental agencies, museums, art galleries, libraries, and four-year colleges and universities.

Community college cooperation. The San Mateo and Foothill Junior College Districts in California have entered into a special training program, co-sponsored by the Junior League of Palo Alto, for the purpose of training unpaid volunteers for the public schools. And seventeen junior colleges of Los Angeles County, California, are cooperating in the offering of a two-unit health education course over a local commercial television channel.

Cooperation with four-year colleges. The College of the Redwoods and Humboldt State College in California are cooperating in the extension of concerts and lecture series programs to local communities in northern California. The Community College of Philadelphia and thirty-six other two- and four-year colleges are participating in a consortium, the College Bound Corporation, to provide admission counseling for community high schools. Big Bend Community College is coordinating with four other colleges and a public school district in a nine-county area in the state of Washington, a unique program designed to upgrade Japanese migrants to a fifth grade reading level and offering prevocational and vocational programs.

Cooperation with public schools. Oakland Community College during the past year offered some eighty credit and noncredit courses in twenty-nine different centers in the college district, in cooperation with local public schools.

Regional cooperation. Approximately eighty colleges in California, including a few four-year colleges as well as community colleges, have organized the College Association for Public Events and Services for the purpose of block-booking lectures, artists, and exchanging package programs and experiences. CAPES organizations have also been organized in Arizona and Michigan.

CONCLUSION

Through imaginative programs of community services, community colleges are beginning to assume their natural role as a catalytic force—providing the leadership, coordination, and cooperation necessary to stimulate action programs by appropriate individuals and groups with the community. The reciprocal relationship between the community and the community college is such that the community college both reflects and effects changes in the structure of its community, and the life patterns of its residents.

More and more, the community college is inserting into the life stream of its people forces that can change, revise, unify, and stimulate the individual, the organization, and ultimately, the tone of mind of the entire community.

30 Million Adults Go to School

J. Eugene Welden

In the waning days of World War II, military aircraft design advanced so rapidly that by the time a model was in production a much better one had already appeared on the drawing boards. "If it flies, it's obsolete," was the popular way of expressing it. Today one could almost apply that same observation to a college student: "If he graduates, he's obsolescent."

During the four years a student labors amidst the cloistering ivy, the mushroom cloud of the knowledge explosion swirls by. The embryonic scientist, engineer, or business administrator may find, as he steps out of college and into his first job, that many of the techniques and much of the theory he learned have been superseded by better ways and fresher thoughts. He will then realize that it is no longer possible to conceive of a completed education that will satisfy the needs of modern man. Education must be a continuing, lifelong process.

Indeed, a central issue of our times is the impending obsolescence of man. Many Americans attempt to preclude or at least delay this obsolescence and to learn to deal with not merely the changing demands of their jobs, but with the increasing complexity of their own domestic problems and the social problems of their communities as well. Add to these incentives that "divine discontent" which spurs to further learning those who are not content with what is, but who pursue what could be. The resulting picture: 30 million American adults, with and without degrees, engaging in systematic, planned instructional programs.

The contemporary "system" of continuing education has its roots in the basic notion that knowledge and skill are means both for self-improvement and for the solution of societal or community problems. Perhaps continuing education can best be defined through the purposes it proclaims to serve. Although there are no neat compartments for categorizing its purposes and programs, five areas of general purpose are used in this article for discussing the various activities.

First comes fundamental literacy education which is a prerequisite for all other kinds of continuing education for adults. This is often referred to as remedial education, because it provides for those who were unable, at the normal school age, to acquire the basic skills of reading, writing, and computing.

"I got tired of just listening to other people. I wanted to read for myself to see if what that preacher said was true," said 81-year-old Locus Tucker, a retired merchant mariner in New Orleans. Through a public school remedial program, Tucker now reads at the sixth-grade level after a lifetime of illiteracy.

Second is education for vocational, technical, or professional competence. This prepares an adult for his first job, helps him get a better job, or keeps him up to date on new developments in his occupation or profession.

From *American Education* V, no. 9 (November 1969):11–13. Used by permission of the author and publisher.

Carl Barnes has taken 15 courses in the U.S. Department of Agriculture Graduate School since he went to work for that Department. By combining continuing education and job performance since he left college at the end of his second year, he has moved up over the years from classification clerk to manager of data processing to his present position, director of personnel.

Third is education for health, welfare, and family living which includes activities related to planned parenthood, consumer relations, and child care.

In Bisbee, Ariz., the County Council of Young Women's Christian Associations organized a family life education program for young wives of men employed in the mines. A series of meetings included such topics as family finances, understanding your husband, child care, nutrition, and mental health. A registered nurse led discussions based on Marion Hilliard's book, A Woman Doctor Looks at Love and Life. This program helped a group of young adults to deal with problems of immaturity and insecurity.

Fourth comes education for civic, political, and community competence, including all kinds of programs related to government, community development, public affairs, political education and the like.

The Bloomington, Ill., experiment of several years ago is a good illustration of activities in this category. The city was generally down at the heels: Among other ills, its educational programs and facilities were lagging, its sewage system was antiquated, and it had more substandard housing than it cared to admit.

A group of civic-minded and concerned citizens organized themselves into the Better Bloomington Committee to see what they could do about these conditions. They formed study groups to learn how their sewage system, local educational programs, and other community services functioned and how to improve them. They drew on the expert knowledge of the faculty from Illinois State University in neighboring Normal. They brought in consultants for special studies. They enlisted the PTA, civic clubs, the League of Women Voters, the Jaycees, and other organizations in a cooperative effort to improve the economy and well-being of the community. Though it lacked the tight structure usually associated with education per se, the committee and its activities composed a very real educational experience.

The effort was hardly a full-circle success in that not all the goals were reached. But today, as a result of the labors of its Better Bloomington Committee, the city has a new sewage system, new schools, an extensive adult education program, and a new building code.

Fifth is that broad area of education for self-development, in which people pursue individual interests or improve their skills. Associate Justice Byron White, for example, took a course in reading improvement just before he joined the Supreme Court. He is one of literally thousands of Americans who seek to increase their reading speed and comprehension in order to cope with the knowledge explosion.

For many people, continuing education means re-engaging in study for a personal and specialized reason: to get a better job, to pass a test, to socialize, to acquire new skills in dealing with family life problems, or to pursue an avocational interest. Therefore, education is actually episodic rather than continuous for the adult, and is usually continuing only for the institutions that offer it.

Among the institutions offering continuing education programs, colleges and universities are acquiring more and more recognition for the substantial part they have assumed in educating adults for self-improvement and for more responsible action on the social and economic problems that face communities, States, and the Nation. More than 300 colleges and universities are currently participating in community service and continuing education programs provided under title I of the Higher Education Act of 1965. These local or regional projects, which involve an estimated 400,000 persons, are ". . . for the purpose of assisting the people of the United States in the solution of community problems. . . ."

California's Humboldt State College has emphasized land-use and urban-rural community planning. The University of Florida's urban counseling and research service has assisted in recreational programs for the elderly, given courses for members of planning commissions, and provided demographic surveys and analyses. Washington University helps low-income families in St. Louis understand and use community resources and legal processes for improving housing; tenants, property owners, realtors, local government personnel and community organizations are involved in these efforts.

The continuing education division in many universities is a complex of programs presented during the day or evening, lasting from one day to 15 weeks, and for varying tuition costs. St. Louis University's bulletin describes 79 different courses ranging from "Government Contract Negotiation" through "Turmoil in the Mid-East," to "God and Man in the Modern World."

In 1914 continuing education in colleges and universities received a big boost when the Cooperative Extension Service was established by the Smith-Lever Act. This act appropriated Federal funds to land-grant institutions to provide instruction and practical information for the people living in the area served. The Cooperative Extension Service was, and still is, based on the management of agriculture—production, marketing, and distribution—and has the largest staff of educators of adults in the country: Some 15,000 agricultural agents, home economists, and other specialists compose an experienced resource for continuing education.

Since the massive migration from the farm to the city, however, the Service has added major efforts for community resource development, public affairs, and the wise use of natural resources in conservation and environmental programs. This is all part of the newer general extension programs in higher education which, unlike the purely agricultural services, aim to reach wider segments of society by becoming more and more urban oriented.

The concept of continuous learning activity was again expanded in 1951 with the establishment of a permanently staffed facility, the Center for Continuing Education at Michigan State University. The W. K. Kellogg Foundation played a major role in that experiment and later supported centers at the universities of Georgia, Oklahoma, Nebraska, New Hampshire, Chicago, and Notre Dame.

Current efforts are now being directed to the development of community or junior colleges as continuing education institutions. According to the American Association of Junior Colleges there is reason to believe that a future role of these institutions will be to provide ". . . a special program of community services that becomes a catalytic force—not the passive role of classes for adults—to supply the leadership, coordination, and cooperation necessary to stimulate action programs by appropriate individuals and groups within the community."

As might be supposed, continuing education takes place in a wide variety of settings besides colleges and universities. It is offered under the auspices of public schools, business and industry, voluntary and professional organizations, government agencies, labor unions, libraries, museums, and religious institutions. The history of continuing education indicates that when there is a collective goal that involves a number of people, social agencies and voluntary organizations tend to be the medium of educational exchange. When individual goals are paramount, the learner tends to turn to the traditional educational agencies that were created mainly for the education of children and youth.

Public school adult education programs have traditionally served the broad individual interests of those living in the immediate community. In the past few years they have been addressing themselves to the increasingly complex industrial-technical needs of business and industry.

The Helena, Mont., school system provides adults with instruction in advanced farm and ranch management. Adults and industry benefit from a Cincinnati program that stresses the convenience of neighborhood adult education centers, Saturday morning academic high school classes for adults, and training programs conducted in cooperation with employers. When Amsterdam, N.Y., lost a major industry, the city's public schools launched a retraining program to prepare individuals for work in other industries already established there or newly arrived. The schools also cooperated with an employment service to open new job opportunities for the unemployed.

Beyond manpower-oriented education, leisure-time education still is offered by a majority of the more than 20,000 public school districts in the United States. A most provocative experiment in community adult education was launched in 1935 by the Charles Stewart Mott Foundation, in cooperation with the Flint, Mich., public schools. Still going strong, the program today includes more than 1,200 classes for adults along with youth services, a school-community health program, and community activities for families at each school.

Before an adult can be trained for a job or prepared to appreciate leisure time he must have a fundamental grounding in reading, writing, and simple number computing. Latest estimates indicate that some 17 million American adults who lack an eighth grade education are now in need of such basic education. In 1968, with Federal support under the Adult Education Act of 1966, approximately one-half million adults were enrolled in basic education classes in the public schools. In this regard schools are contributing to the repair of social and economic cleavages between ill-equipped adults, trapped without education, and the rest of prosperous, aspiring America.

Professional organizations have also mounted the continuing education bandwagon. Recognizing the need for their individual members to engage in a continuing educational process, the professions have frequently turned to higher education institutions for assistance. For example, the *Journal of the American Dental Association* lists regularly a host of programs conducted at colleges and universities throughout the country specifically for the benefit of practicing dentists. In Kentucky 37 percent of the State's dentists have attended at least one course in the State university's continuing dental education program. A recent survey indicates that more than 50 percent of California's dentists may be attending courses in that State's universities. The 5,000-member Academy of General Dentistry exists principally to foster continuing professional education.

The Joint Committee on Continuing Legal Education of the American Law

Institute and the American Bar Association has presided over efforts to keep the attorney's knowledge current in the ever-changing field of law. This aim is being assisted largely through cooperation between voluntary groups and State university law schools. Voluntary organizations for continuing legal education have blossomed in the 1960's and today exist in more than 30 States.

The American Medical Association reports that 139,752 physicians registered during the 1967–68 school year for continuing education programs at the 67 medical schools which participated in an AMA survey. Through radio and television courses and participation in other institutional programs—often directed to problems in the delivery of health services—an estimated 150,000 additional men of medicine are continuing their education.

The Federal Government's efforts to train its own employees are dramatic for their magnitude and diversity. In fiscal year 1968 there were 1,034,793 instances where individuals enrolled for such training at a total cost of $30,757,899. Courses and subject areas included astrogeophysics, watershed and timber management, shorthand refresher courses, and high reliability soldering. Purposes were almost as varied as the courses themselves. Yet there was a unifying element to all of the training programs. Their objective is to achieve a Federal service of both heightened quality and responsiveness to serve better the changing physical and social needs of all Americans.

Public libraries fit comfortably into the field of continuing education. Whether called readers' advisory services, or continuing education, the libraries' objective has been to reach individuals of every age, education, philosophy, occupation, economic level, ethnic origin, and human condition. Though the book is still the basic tool, public libraries have sponsored discussion groups, added audio-visual collections, and created new and interesting facilities.

Through its public affairs program the Detroit Public Library increases the citizens' understanding of local issues and stimulates more rational community action. Recent programs focused on urban renewal—the architect's role in city planning, demolition, public housing, new municipal facilities, and such. The library presented a series of lecture-discussions, supported by a reading list of popular titles and exhibits, and proposed city-wide "Most Beautiful Building" contests.

"Composers Conferences" co-sponsored by the Dallas Public Library and Dallas Symphony Orchestra have provided many young musicians with an opportunity for public performance of their works. Symphony goers avidly attend the programs in which critics, composers, and laymen participate in discussion groups to learn about new trends in music and relate them to earlier traditions.

As in other lands, education for American adults has frequently been linked to religious purposes or institutions. However, the Sunday Bible class with its teacher-patriarch lecturing on the Old Testament to an audience of the half-sleeping faithful has all but disappeared. To relate to men caught in change, religious education programs are now organized to meet the demands of the times and with new understanding of how adults learn.

Organized adult Jewish education has become an integral part of the American Jewish educational scene since World War II. The heritage of Judaism has always centered on study and scholarship as an individual goal. More recently, the general purpose of several organizations has been to seek knowledge of the contemporary status and problems of the American Jews, and of Jewish cultural tradition in relation to today's society.

Participation in continuing education is still largely sporadic and unsystematic. A recent analysis of programs and agencies by Wilson Thiede of the University of Wisconsin, however, proposes formation of a new community agency which would offer a total curriculum to serve adults. Sequential learning experiences would replace the occasional offerings presently available and permit an individual to pursue in depth a subject of personal concern. The educational program would be relevant both to community life and to the lives of individuals. Emphasis would be placed on the solution to a dilemma in affluent America: How properly to balance entertainment and instruction in the regimen of men.

At present, the adults who crowd into classes to seek new information, knowledge, and skill do so by and large of their own volition. However, a British cybernetician, Sir Leon Bagrit, said recently, "Such rapid change permeates every sphere of human activity that we may anticipate the beginning of compulsory education for the middle-aged and elderly." Who knows—the middle-aged dropout may, within the next 20 years, find himself running from a truant officer.

The Big Move to Non-campus Colleges

Ernest L. Boyer

George C. Keller

In this financially alarming but comparatively strife-free year for American colleges and universities, perhaps the single most dramatic development has been the announcement of several plans to enable students to earn academic credits and even college degrees without having to live on a campus, or even attend classes there.

The new plans have propellants within them that could trigger one of the most significant shifts in the structure of American higher education since the introduction of large-scale, federally financed research during World War II. Phrased in the muffling jargon of educational prose the new proposals may not appear radical, but they do share certain broad assumptions about what higher education really is all about.

For years, the word "college" has to most Americans meant four uninterrupted years in one institution, in a place removed from the diversions of ordinary life. It conjures up nostalgic memories of classroom lectures, fraternity and sorority parties, glee clubs, football weekends, hectic final exams, term papers,

From *Saturday Review* LIV (July 17, 1971):46–49, 58. Copyright © 1971 Saturday Review, Inc. Used by permission of the authors and publisher.

trips home for the holidays, beery bull sessions, and romance beside the Virginia creeper. More recently it has also meant protest marches, extracurricular volunteer work, and rock concerts with Joe Cocker or Sly and the Family Stone. In short, it has been the physical and social aspects of campus life that have traditionally defined "going to college."

Central to most of the new non-campus programs, however, is the assumption that the fundamental process of acquiring a college education need not be dependent upon the familiar campus setting. Not where or for how long a student goes to college, but what actually happens to him intellectually during his collegiate years is what counts. Many innovators believe that the preoccupation with the physical and social context of higher education has obscured the more crucial questions, which concern what is happening inside the student's head.

A second, and closely related, assumption is that the parietal element in higher education has been far too heavily emphasized. Too many colleges still implicitly operate on the premise that they are dealing with reluctant, lazy children who must be continually prodded and threatened if they are to learn anything. The process of higher education too often has borne disturbing similarities to the force feeding of geese destined to contribute to the world's supply of pâté de foie gras. While explicit parietal rules and social regulations have been liberalized or abolished, the fundamental structure of college education has remained implicitly coercive.

The new assumption is that the individual's own motivation, his desire to learn and to grow, should play a more central role in the formulation of educational policy. Ideally, the acquisition of a college education should represent a positive act of individual volition rather than passive acquiescence in an institution's routines and requirements. A closer approximation of this ideal is what the innovators are striving for.

In the conversation and writings of those responsible for the new proposals, one finds the conviction that genuine intellectual competence, and not some magic number of "years in residence" or "credit hours," should be the single most important criterion for the baccalaureate degree. What a person knows, not how many courses he has taken, should be the fundamental concern toward which all academic planning is directed.

The various off-campus and non-campus schemes that spring from these shared assumptions and concerns generally fall into four broad categories.

The first, and least radical, represents the continued development and extension of efforts that have long been made by many American colleges and universities to increase the opportunity for off-campus learning experiences within the broad framework of the traditional pattern of campus residency. For decades, undergraduates have enjoyed a "junior year abroad" or participated in various types of work-study interludes. The newer programs add such possibilities as a hitch in VISTA or a semester in a ghetto, a museum, or a specialized school, such as a dance studio. The programs may be quite highly structured, such as Chapman College's "World Campus Afloat," which offers undergraduates courses on a ship that travels around the globe with field trips ashore; or fairly loose, as at those institutions where gifted students are allowed as much as a year off to write a novel, study French literature, or pursue other special interests—all for academic credit.

These off-campus extensions of the curriculum are not without problems.

For example, how many academic credits should a student receive for forty hours of tutoring migrant workers? And how does one maintain "quality control" and prevent a genuine, if unconventional, learning experience from degenerating into a merely frivolous and self-indulgent frittering away of time?

But far outweighing such practical difficulties is the fact that all such efforts represent a movement toward a concept of higher learning that is far more in tune with the conditions and opportunities of contemporary life—a concept which recognizes that we have erected too high a barrier between the campus and the real world "out there." For the proponents of such off-campus programs, the individual college campus remains an essential intellectual base, but it is also seen as only one element in a far broader educational environment—an environment that includes the ghetto, the threatened wilderness, the polluted lake, the industrial laboratory, the social service agency, the city halfway around the world.

A second category of off-campus plan, the largest and most familiar, is to permit conventional academic work to be done off-campus, often over a time period longer than the usual four years and often through programs designed chiefly for adults.

The prototype is the famous external-degree program of London University, which has for decades enabled students from Nigeria, Australia, the Bahamas, or India to work toward their degree in any manner they wish, and in any part of the world, so long as they passed the required examinations set by the university.

Since 1961 working adults from all over America, unable to take the time to live or attend classes on a campus, have been studying in the University of Oklahoma's pioneering B.A. program in liberal studies, which combines independent home study, correspondence work, and annual three-week residential seminars at the university. Recently Syracuse University, the University of South Florida, and the State University of New York at Brockport have established similar programs, sometimes supplemented by television and on-campus laboratory work in the sciences.

Two interesting new versions of these adult programs are Britain's "Open University" and the U.S. Navy's smaller program for "Afloat College Education." The Open University is Britain's attempt to democratize its traditionally elitist university programs quickly, with limited resources. The hope is to allow vast numbers of housewives and other adults with jobs to earn academic degrees in three to six years at a total cost to the student of less than $1,000. Last January, coal miners and clerks, salesmen and schoolteachers began enrolling in the Open University. There are six degree programs: humanities, science, social studies, technology, education, and mathematics. Thousands are listening to radio lectures, going through correspondence course packets, watching television courses, and reading in local libraries in preparation for examinations they will take at one of the 250 local study centers, where they also meet with some of the 2,500 tutors and counselors who are acting as study assistants and advisers. They will also attend a week of summer school at one of the twelve regional centers or at one of England's established colleges.

In the U.S. Navy's program, ship crewmen can earn up to two years of college credit at one of five colleges (Harvard is among them) by passing examinations based on heavy on-board reading, mastery of filmed courses, and attendance at lectures and seminars conducted by professors who visit their ship while it is in port. Under this program, the Navy has even flown professors to remote bases in the antarctic.

The most unusual program in this category is the recently initiated "University Without Walls," whose founding father is Samuel Baskin, an imaginative professor of psychology at Antioch College in Ohio. Professor Baskin had been seeking support for his plan for several years before recently obtaining a U.S. Office of Education planning grant of $415,000 and a Ford Foundation grant of $400,000. What he envisions is an innovative educational program confined mainly to the campuses of nineteen cooperating institutions, including such diverse schools as the large University of Minnesota, the small Staten Island Community College, the University of South Carolina, the predominantly black Howard University, the Quaker Friends World College, and the Catholic Loretto Heights College.

Within each of these institutions, forty to one hundred interested students will pursue a distinct academic program with guidelines established by the University Without Walls, a kind of academic holding company with little in the way of formal staff or administrative bureaucracy. Part of the time these students may take conventional courses at their own colleges, but they may also move about to one or more of the cooperating colleges or universities; serve supervised internships in businesses, hospitals, or museums; or study independently with the aid of reading lists, televised lectures, records, and tapes. Professor Baskin's program clearly rejects the traditional concept of college education with its exclusive stress on single-campus residency, classroom lectures, and narrow departmental majors. It also widens our conventional notion of "the faculty" to include experts and talented individuals from the "outside world"—artists, businessmen, musicians, or government officials.

The third off-campus "category" is in reality a single program: the New York State Education Department's unique new external-degree program, through which the associate in arts and bachelor of business administration degrees will be awarded to anyone who passes a set of comprehensive examinations. (Unlike the "Open University" program, this will involve no actual instruction, simply the administering of examinations and the awarding of degrees.) This program, with the aid of a joint planning grant from the Carnegie Corporation and the Ford Foundation, will permit persons who have studied on their own, in whatever fashion, to receive a sheepskin without ever enrolling at a college, setting foot on a campus, or paying a penny in tuition.

This category may expand, though. At a recent meeting of the American Association for Higher Education in Chicago, Jack N. Arbolino, executive director of the Council on College-Level Examinations of the College Entrance Examination Board, proposed a "national university" that would, like the New York State Education Department, grant degrees to anyone in the nation who passed its degree examinations. The program that Mr. Arbolino heads already has made a small start in this direction by administering tests in two dozen different subjects, from American government to data processing, for which the student, upon passing one or more of them, may request academic credit from his college.

The fourth and last of these varied approaches to off-campus education is the State University of New York's new Empire State College, which is in the active planning stage. This experimental "college without a campus" (supported by a $1-million joint grant from the Carnegie Corporation and the Ford Foundation) will be similar in some respects to other programs we have described. It certainly owes much of its inspiration to innovations at other colleges, in other countries, and within the State University itself. But it also will have certain distinctive characteristics of its own. Unlike most external degree programs, for example, it will retain the opportunity for occasional on-campus study. It will encourage a close student-teacher relationship and will offer a wide variety of educational options to the student.

Because New York has placed all its public institutions of higher education under a central leadership, the State University is particularly well suited to undertake such an experimental venture. SUNY is actually a single entity made up of seventy separate institutions, including liberal arts colleges, specialized schools (in agriculture, forestry, engineering, etc.), community colleges, and four major universities. This means that New York already has in its State University a kind of multi-faceted consortium of institutions with widely varied characteristics and resources.

The central idea of Empire State College is to create an academic program that will free the student of the restraints of residence on a single campus and make available to him the resources of the entire university system. A combination of home study, off-campus work-study experiences, educational films, cassettes, correspondence courses, and periods of study elsewhere in America or abroad will enlarge enormously the options open to each student. While some may elect to do half or two-thirds of their work in residence at one or more of the State University's institutions, others will spend most of their time studying off-campus. Time limits, too, will be freer. A college degree may be attained in two, three, four, or eight years, depending on the individual student's specific circumstances and individual capacity for academic work.

But Empire State College is not conceived as a "do-your-own-thing" institution. A small core faculty at a central headquarters, with resident tutors at twenty regional study centers to be set up around the state, will design and direct the programs, prepare the correspondence courses, approve each student's plan of study, and counsel with students by telephone, mail, and in periodic personal meetings. In short, the educational experience of the student will be guided and evaluated at every stage by trained and committed scholars. While the student will complete assigned papers, reports, and examinations, he will be largely freed of grade pressures (grading probably will be on a pass/fail basis) and of specific credit-hour requirements. He will be able to concentrate more on his own education and less on the requirements of a specific institution.

Implicit in the design of Empire State College are several notions—rooted in the more general educational assumptions mentioned earlier—that seem alarmingly simple to some and simply alarming to others:

1. Formal classroom instruction, while still important, is no longer the sole or even the principal means of acquiring information and ideas at the college level.
2. Given the present wide variety of students, the continuing explosion of knowledge, and the emergence of new fields of academic concern, the curriculum no longer should be the exclusive concern of the faculty. Responsibility for its design and content should be shared by faculty members and students.
3. Residency on a single college campus is no longer a requisite for quality

education. (One-fifth of America's college students already study at more than one institution during their undergraduate careers.)

4. Four years, and certainly four consecutive years, are not an inviolate block of time essential to an undergraduate degree. Longer or shorter periods of study, possibly interrupted by other activities, do not damage—and may actually improve—the net effectiveness of collegiate study.

5. While frequent and intimate contact with mature scholars is vital to a good college education, no faculty member can any longer be regarded as simply a purveyor of factual knowledge, even in his field of specialization. Increasingly, professors must act not only as sources of information but as sensitive intellectual guides, as concerned questioners of personal and social actions and values, and as provocative stimulants urging students to discover their own capacity for critical and creative thought.

None of these assumptions, taken singly, is entirely new. But taken together, and taken seriously, they add up to a new vision of what the college experience can, and should, entail.

To some skeptics, all these new schemes for off-campus learning are chiefly the brainchildren of presidents, faculty committees, and foundation officials who, desperate about the present financial crisis in higher education, are blindly stabbing at ways to process more students for less money.

Undeniably, a search for economy is a factor in the development of the new programs. A resident college education next fall will cost parents about $4,500 a year at most of the nation's leading private colleges and universities, and close to $3,000 at many public colleges and universities. By 1980, the charges could be $8,000 and $5,000 respectively. To anyone seriously concerned about providing some form of higher education to every American who desires it and can benefit by it, the economic situation is patently serious. It is neither shameful nor contemptible to be searching for new modes of providing high-quality education at a lower cost.

But there are, we think, more fundamental and long-range reasons for the current interest in the radical restructuring of American higher education. These derive from quantitative and qualitative changes in American youth, in the character of American society, and in present trends within higher education itself.

Disgruntled souls who shake their heads and mutter that young people aren't what they used to be are, as a matter of fact, absolutely correct. Young people *have* changed appreciably, and not just in the more publicized and superficial ways.

Physically, young people are larger and healthier than they were fifty years ago. Girls and boys are about three inches taller and ten pounds heavier than they were in 1920, principally because of advances in nutrition and medicine. Childhood diseases that used to stunt and maim, and even fill the cemeteries, have almost been wiped out. (The chief cause of death for persons under 21 is now accidents, primarily automobile accidents.) These same advances in nutrition and medicine have also caused adolescents to mature physiologically much earlier than in the past. In the United States the onset of puberty for girls has dropped from an average age of 14 in 1920 to 12.4 today, and, for boys, from 15 to 13.5.

Today's young people differ intellectually as well as physically. Kenneth Keniston of Yale, among others, has noted that the average American sixteen-year-old today has had five years more schooling than his counterpart in 1920.

A recent U.S. Census Bureau study revealed that the number of young adults with high school diplomas has doubled since 1940, while the number with college degrees has tripled.

The average student today scores approximately one standard deviation above the student of a generation ago on standardized tests of intellectual achievement. A level of performance that places a student in the middle of his graduating class today would probably have placed him in the top 15 percent thirty years ago. Or, to put it another way, in achievement, a teenager today is approximately one grade ahead of his parents when they were his age.

In the more amorphous psychological realm, numerous observers have noted the new mood among contemporary youth, the sense of generational uniqueness, the imagination and audacity, the impatience, the social concern, the disdain for history and authority. One can only speculate as to causes. Television, which began commercially in 1948, entered most homes fifteen to twenty years ago. Thus, as has been widely noted, this is the first college generation raised on television practically from infancy. According to surveys, many young people in college today watched television about twenty hours a week when they were children, for an annual total greater than the number of hours they spent in school.

In addition to the ubiquitous tube, such factors as greater mobility, affluence, and longevity have also contributed to a different psychological state. For instance, because of the low life expectancy of former times—47.3 years in 1900—it was not unusual for a young person to lose one or both of his parents before reaching college age. Today, with the average life expectancy almost seventy years, orphanage has virtually been wiped out. Now, ironically, it is the continuing lively presence and pressure of both parents that many young persons perceive as a serious problem.

Yet, while young persons now are significantly different from those of fifty or even twenty years ago, American higher education is structurally much the same. Our colleges and universities (not to mention our grade and high schools) urgently need to recognize these important facts, and to redesign their programs accordingly. To keep nearly one-third of our young people occupied in an institutional setting that effectively segregates them from the world of "grown-ups" for seven to ten years beyond the onset of puberty appears a more untenable arrangement with each passing year.

Another major force affecting the colleges has been the knowledge explosion itself. New technologies and sciences have burgeoned—from cybernetics to marine botany; new social problems—the urban crisis, the population explosion, pollution—have generated new study areas. Campus faculties have multiplied, splintered, and regrouped under the impact. Advances in photography, sound engineering, optics, communications, and transportation have revolutionized the movement of information, ideas, and people themselves. They make possible such things as a telephone seminar in astrophysics among scientists from several countries, a short intersession of anthropological study in West Africa or Peru, or the study of Eskimo culture through films.

In the face of all these changes, the old yardsticks of higher education—faculty-student ratios, years in residence, credit-hours for courses, and grading—become increasingly difficult to apply. The notions that there is a fixed "body of knowledge" to be delivered to the young, that college faculties necessarily know what is best for students, and that the departmental major is the only desirable method of organizing intellectual inquiry, are seriously challenged.

Moreover, we are at the beginning of a second admissions boom—that of older persons re-entering college. Until the end of World War II, colleges catered chiefly to the privileged and the gifted. College admissions was the art of keeping people out. Since 1945, however, admissions policies have expanded until currently half of all high school graduates—two out of five of all young Americans—go on to college. Now, with technological change, increased leisure, new conceptions of womanhood, and greater affluence encouraging and requiring changes in career and life-style, continuing education is emerging as a new frontier of higher education. Most colleges and universities, especially public ones, are trying to help people in rather than screen them out. And as colleges admit greater numbers of students from more varied socio-economic backgrounds, their curriculums have altered in order to serve effectively the expanded new clientele with its broader range of preparation and aspirations.

To shift one variable, such as the kind of students served, while attempting to hold constant all the rest of the components of the university structure is to court disaster, as too many institutions have learned. Likewise, to try to accommodate the knowledge explosion on the campus, with the increased research, field work, and specialization that it demands, without re-examining the traditional "liberal education" requirements is irresponsible.

As the recent Carnegie Commission report *Less Time, More Options* suggested, today's college and university clearly must offer many tracks, many options, and many different programs to serve the new variety of students and to assist in the exploration of new areas of intellectual inquiry. Large universities may have to break up into several colleges. Smaller colleges may have to establish links with other colleges and other kinds of learning institutions in society. And all will have to allow increased opportunities for independent and off-campus study.

It is these profound transformations—in our young people, in our society, and in higher education, as well as the grave financial condition of the colleges—that compel radical changes in the venerable but outmoded patterns of American collegiate study. The many proposals for off-campus or non-campus study contain many details to be worked out and objections to be overcome. But they represent serious efforts to experiment with fresh patterns of undergraduate education. The alternative is a continuing and ever louder dirge about the poverty, disruption, and "irrelevance" of our campuses.

It would be tragic if the social institution that has contributed so much to our civilization should fail to respond vigorously to the challenges that confront it at this crucial moment. The present crisis is assuredly one of dollars. But even more, it is one of will, of creative energy, of new ideas. Higher education is in a period of painful transition. The greatest need is to act boldly, with fresh vision, in the face of new conditions. The training of the mind and sharpening of the sensibilities are still the best hope of mankind.

Advancing Career Education

Marie Y. Martin

An educator whose responsibilities involve a fair amount of travel in the United States quickly becomes aware that American education is today undergoing a major shift in direction. The potential impact of this phenomenon doubtless will not become fully apparent for many years, but that a fundamental change is occurring there can be no question.

At its core is a new view of education's function. In every section of the country, a significant number of schools and colleges are seeking to reorient and broaden their purposes. Their common goal is to respond to the student's specific, immediate educational needs in a manner that serves his long-term aspirations for a satisfying and meaningful life after his schooling is ended. This is career education, a concept which recognizes that learning is more than an intellectual exercise—that in stretching people's minds and honing their sense of values, the schools and colleges have the further obligation of preparing them to launch successful working careers.

Nowhere is this thesis better illustrated than in our community junior colleges. Career education is in fact as current as the newest of these institutions and as old as the first of them. And with the stimulus of The Education Amendments of 1972, the community colleges will be called upon to play an even larger role in spreading the career education concept. From their beginning, the two-year colleges have emphasized programs that are responsive to the needs both of their students and of the society in which those students will live. Given that approach—plus what would appear to be a growing pragmatism among students, a determination to weigh their schooling in terms not of a degree as such but of its application to the job market—it is not to be wondered at that Census Bureau reports show these institutions as accounting for almost all of the increase in college freshman and sophomore enrollments between the years 1966 and 1971. Expectations are that this year the overall community college student body will exceed 2.5 million—something in the order of 30 percent of total undergraduate college enrollments.

Many will of course be in a transfer status that enables them to go on to a four-year college or university. Even among these students, however, there is a sharply increasing trend toward combining transfer programs with occupational courses. The net result is still further stimulus to a revolutionary overhaul of education, evidenced by such developments as the wide departure from standard curriculum, flexible scheduling, the acceptance of work experience for college

From *American Education* VIII, no. 7 (August, September 1972):25–30. Used by permission of the author and publisher.

credit, new approaches to counseling, novel methods of teaching, unconventional types of facilities, the varied background and experience of the faculty, and many others.

Given the current widespread interest, it is surprising how recently career education has emerged as a national movement. The concept clearly touched a vital chord. Its beginnings reach back only to January of 1971, to a speech made by Dr. Sidney P. Marland, Jr. a few weeks after he had been sworn in as the 19th U.S. Commissioner of Education. As Dr. Marland pointed out on that occasion, despite American education's unquestioned accomplishments, it can take little credit for its performance in making sure that no one leaves school unequipped to get and hold a decent job. Just about half our high school students, he said—in the order of 1,500,000 in any given year—are involved in schooling that prepares them neither for careers nor for college. And of the three out of ten high school graduates who go on to higher education, a third will drop out and a depressing proportion of the remainder will emerge with degree in hand but no clear-cut idea in mind of what to do with it.

In subsequent meetings with educators, students, representatives of business and labor, leaders of various professional associations, members of ethnic groups, State and local government officials, and many others, Dr. Marland has continued to urge consideration of the career education concept: "education that prepares one to think and to care about social responsibility and personal intellectual fulfillment, but education that also equips all learners, at whatever age, with satisfying and rewarding competencies for entering the world of work in the field of one's choice."

The climax in establishing career education high on the Nation's agenda came when President Nixon made the concept an important element in his 1972 State of the Union message to Congress and established it as a White House priority. The discussion has by now become nationwide, and so has the move to translate ideas into action. In an increasing number of educational institutions and at various levels of the school experience, career education is proving to be a systematic way of 1) helping students gain an understanding during the course of their academic studies of the many careers available in the United States— something over 20,000—and 2) preparing them for the career of their choice.

The leadership being exerted by the community colleges in exemplifying and strengthening these principles is particularly noteworthy. Hundreds of such institutions in hundreds of localities have initiated programs that merit the study of educational decision-makers at every level. The character of their innovations and practices can be illustrated by focusing on six of these colleges, located in various parts of the country. The summaries that follow are based on personal observation; extensive interviews with administrators, faculty, and students; and materials supplied by the individual institutions.

Pasadena City College in Pasadena, California, offers no less than 64 career-oriented courses—from commercial airline pilot training to metal processes technology. Such courses engage about half of its 14,000 students, with the other half taking transfer courses in preparation for entering four-year colleges. Among Pasadena's instructional staff are many of its own graduates who have gone on to universities, received degrees, worked in various career fields, and now are regular or part-time members of the faculty. As with many community colleges, Pasadena seeks to recruit a faculty that is representative of the makeup of the student body, and it encourages them to reach beyond the college itself and work with other groups in the community.

Typifying the stress placed on interdisciplinary cooperation between the academic and "practical" skills, each year at Pasadena the students build and sell a model home to the highest bidder—enlisting as they do so the interest and cooperation of representatives of the professions, labor, and business. Students studying architecture develop a range of designs, with the best being chosen on a competitive basis. Students in architectural specifications then take over, drawing up the specs and making sure they are followed by the students in construction classes. Students of interior design select the color schemes to be used and decide upon the drapes and furnishings. The printing and lithography students prepare advertisements and brochures. Business classes participate in preparing bid specifications. And helping from the sidelines at every step is an advisory committee composed of practicing architects and experts from the construction unions, trade associations, utility companies, and furniture stores, some of which donate materials for the project.

Pasadena has 71 off-campus educational sites—in churches, schools, parks, vacated factories, and the like—where classes are offered in courses ranging from power sawing to grocery store operations. A key component of this PCC community action program is a mobile career guidance unit. Moved from place to place in low-income neighborhoods, it serves as a center for job aptitudes testing, counseling, and information about subjects available at PCC's main and satellite campuses.

New York City Community College of the City University of New York is located on a small site in Brooklyn and serves an ethnically mixed student body of 8,000 men and 7,000 women in 34 different career education and college transfer courses. About 80 percent of the students have chosen one or more of the career courses, which are offered both day and evening. The overall career program has three components—general education, orientation, and training in specific skills, with the curriculum for the latter being determined largely by the entry level requirements of industry or by the State's licensing boards. Provisions also are made for training in skills and general education requirements needed for advancement in jobs beyond the entry level.

Student needs and industry demands have an important impact on NYCCC's offerings. Located as it is near the center of the advertising industry, for example, the college has developed programs responding to the continuing demand for people trained in commercial art, graphic arts, and advertising technology. New York is also rich in opportunities for graduates in hotel and restaurant management, and chefs from the college hold their own in the face of top competition and frequently start their first job at a salary of $8,000 a year. Of some 150 students participating in cooperative education programs in engineering technologies, data processing, and accounting, better than 80 percent were offered permanent jobs by the companies with whom they had been gaining experience.

Supportive services offered by the college include an aggressive outreach to students who need counseling by experts in specific fields and the establishment of advisory committees which help develop and update programs, arrange for the availability of advanced equipment, and serve as major resources for job placement. In addition, there is a Special Services Tutorial Project funded by the U.S. Office of Education and an Anti-Drug Use Program funded by the State.

Various career programs operated by the college's Office of International Development and Recruitment send increasing numbers of counselors into local high schools, and the Division of Continuing Education sponsors courses at local senior citizens centers. Other community-based programs are provided in low-cost housing complexes, and NYCCC recently has experimented with the idea of offering credit courses at a community church to give adults an opportunity to "try out" college before making a commitment to enroll at the main campus.

Central Piedmont Community College in Charlotte, North Carolina, never closes its doors on the 8,000 students it serves—56 percent of whom are men and 44 percent women. Its instructional program runs around the clock, partly to make full use of expensive facilities and handle heavy class loads, and partly to accommodate students who have jobs during the day. (Thus an automobile mechanics course, for example, gets under way at midnight and runs until 7 a.m.) For these same reasons, Central Piedmont is a year-round institution, and about 70 percent of the students who attend during the regular academic year enroll in summer classes to complete trade and vocational courses.

In all, Central Piedmont offers 34 occupational programs. One of the most recent to be added to the curriculum is a Human Services Associate degree program geared to employment in day care centers, nursing homes, orphanages, and other welfare-related service agencies. President Richard Hagemeyer is particularly proud of the new career education building being constructed in part with support from the Office of Education. "As in every community," he points out, "Charlotte's greatest educational need is in the occupational area—preparation of students for gainful employment."

Moraine Valley Community College, located in the southwest suburbs of Cook County, Illinois, is attended by about 3,800 students, of whom 42 percent are formally enrolled in career education programs, though in fact virtually the entire student body is engaged in some courses relating to careers. The college currently offers 27 programs leading to an Associate degree in applied science or to a one-year certificate. In addition, a number of continuing education classes are provided for people seeking to improve themselves professionally or simply to enrich their lives, and the college sponsors seminars, workshops, and institutes for nearby municipalities, industries, and others.

In an exemplary program in Industrial Engineering Technology devised by MVCC faculty and one of its community consultant committees, each student individually pursues specified, measurable objectives organized according to particular job factors. This means that if a student completes only part of the program he will still be qualified for a job in one of the industrial technology fields (though of course at a lower level) because he has mastered at least some of the required skills. The program is organized in such a way as to make it possible for all students to be working on different tasks at the same time and to select among alternative approaches to learning those tasks.

In general, MVCC seeks to reflect the collective educational needs of the community and to exercise leadership in meeting those needs.

Community College of Denver has 7,200 students enrolled on its three campuses, and of them 64.4 percent are participating in career programs. The average age of CCD's students is 27, and 75 percent hold full- or part-time jobs. As a response to this unusual student body, the college has defined career education as education which meets the needs of the individual as determined by the individual himself. Particular help in making that determination is provided by a career center which operates on the theory that the individual's chance of choosing a satisfying career is directly proportional to the number of occupations he knows about and understands. In developing the informational material necessary to serve that purpose, the center has become a major learning resource not only for the students and faculty but for high school and junior high school counselors and for the community at large.

Recognizing that many students need experiences in many career fields before they can intelligently settle on one, the college allows students to develop schedules that permit them to try out introductory courses in a number of different occupations, moving at any time from one program to another if they find that their initial choice proved unsuitable.

One of the basic elements in CCD's effort to assist individuals with career choices is a group of instructional laboratories covering basic skills. Most instruction is either individualized or carried out with very small groups. Some students enroll in the instructional laboratory and at the same time pursue their career program, while others concentrate on acquiring basic skills before they enter the program.

Lane Community College in Eugene, Oregon, was established to serve as the career education center for the quarter million people living in the State's southern Willamette Valley and its environs. Business, civic, and educational leaders give enthusiastic support to this college, which serves nearly 20,000 full- and part-time students each year. Lane offers more than 42 separate career-oriented fields, each designed to lead directly to employment at the end of a one- or two-year period of preparation. A lower division transfer curriculum is also offered.

Lane is a place of change, not in its definition of career education but in how that definition is translated into action. Courses are added or deleted to reflect shifts in the job market, and the emphasis of instruction has moved to a concentration on the personal needs of the individual. A key step in achieving that goal has been the development of more than 850 "VIP's"—Vocational Instructional Packages designed by the faculty with the assistance of experts from business, labor, industry, and the professions.

An open-entry/open-exit instructional strategy allows the student to enter a program at any time, accomplish his objectives at his own rate, and exit from the program no sooner and no later than he can meet the requirements of the job he is pursuing. Placement services are provided, and the college maintains constant liaison with the business community and with the Oregon State Employment Office, enabling students to receive up-to-the-minute information about job opportunities and current wage levels. All students receive on-the-job experience before completing their programs, thanks in large part to cooperative arrangements with local firms.

At Lane—and at Pasadena, New York City CC, Central Piedmont, Moraine Valley, and Denver—career education is a vital force. The same can be said of hundreds of others among the more than 1,100 community colleges in the United States and its territories. These institutions have much to offer, not only to their students but to people interested in exploring the career education concept. I am sure that all of them, and particularly the six I have discussed, would welcome your inquiries and would be glad to have you visit them.

SECTION 9 ADDITIONAL LEARNING ACTIVITIES

Problems and Projects

1. Good teaching for adults must take into account past negative school experiences, remoteness of past schooling, and the self-doubts of adults. It must provide at the earliest possible time for encouragement and for successful experiences. A detailed statement of "Good Teaching for Adults" with a list of ten principles may be obtained by writing to Andrew Hendrickson, Center for Adult Education, Ohio State University, 1945 High Street, Columbus, Ohio 43210.

2. Only one in six couples married in 1916 could expect to reach their golden wedding anniversary together. Today, one couple in three may expect to reach their golden anniversary. What implications does this have for education for adults? What implications does it have for community college programs? Discuss with other students.

3. Read "The Coming of the Common Colleges" by Wallace Roberts, *Saturday Review*, June 21, 1969, pages 67, 82. Can a *common college* succeed? What are some of the problems facing such an institution?

4. It is estimated that one in four of all the occupations that will be in existence in 1980 in the United States doesn't even exist today. What are the implications of this statement for curricula in community colleges and high schools?

5. The 1972 Report of the National Advisory Council of the Education Professions, "People for the People's Colleges" indicates that pre-service programs for junior college teachers are "grossly inadequate." It states that the disciplines in the universities are inflexible; the colleges of education are unsure and unpracticed; and the available instructors are either narrow subject matter specialists or secondary-school oriented college of education graduates. Neither, according to the report, is prepared to instruct at the community college level. (Write to the AACTE, One Du Pont Circle, Washington, D.C. 20036 for additional information about this report.) Using objectives for education for late adolescents, the four curriculum bases, and criteria such as flexibility, individual differences, continuity, etc., propose some general guidelines for a pre-service program for community college teachers. Discuss with others.

6. Discuss "Opening the College Gates to Low Achievers," by William Moore, Jr. (who was himself a "two-time college dropout"). Do you agree that present high school diplomas are worthless for thousands of low achieving students? How do you feel about the new techniques being used to deal with marginal students that are described in this article? Appraise this program in terms of objectives and the four curriculum bases.

7. Examine the "system of continuing education" described in "Thirty Million Adults Go to School" in terms of objectives, the four bases, and individual differences.

8. What is the particular value of the "university without walls" described in "The Big Move to Non-Campus Colleges"? In the same article the "external degree program" is described. Evaluate both of these programs in terms of objectives and the four bases of the curriculum.

9. If the "case problem" that you may have developed in Sections 1 through 5 is about a community college or other post-high school institution, develop the case further by relating the trends and programs described in this section to the present program.

Audio-Tapes

How Can Our Colleges Best Meet the Demand for Higher Education? 26 mins., 3¾ track audio tape. Discusses issues in higher education in the United States. Distributed by National Tape Repository, University of Colorado, Boulder, Colorado 80302.

Junior College Development and Facilities in the Space Age. 3¾ IPS, 1 track audio tape. B. Frank Brown discusses junior college development and facilities in the space age. Distributed by University of Minnesota, Audio Visual Education Service, Room 55, Westbrook Hall, Minneapolis, Minnesota 55455.

Educational Records

Community College and Its Function. 33⅓, 12 inch record. Discussion of the function of the college in the community. Distributed by Educational Record Sales, 157 Chambers St., New York, New York 10007.

Visits to Schools

Visit a school to observe teaching or to participate in teaching. It is useful to have an appointment with the community college dean, the curriculum director, or some other leader in the college.

You may want to ask your instructor or someone else to suggest the college or instructor that you might visit. While visiting or while planning the visit, try to obtain information about the school's social setting, the learners in the college, teaching practices in the college, and the content and organization of the curriculum so that you can examine what you see and study in the college in terms of objectives of education, the four bases of the curriculum, and curriculum criteria such as balance, individual differences, flexibility, and continuity. It is important to try to learn what the college considers to be its objectives and/or what the instructor considers his objectives to be (when observing a particular instructor). Compare these objectives to objectives of education as you view them and objectives for the community college or curriculum area being observed.

Also, you may find it useful to consider whether current trends or innovations at the community college level or subject area might be used to advantage at the college being visited.

Try to determine whether the college you are visiting has the five types of programs listed in this section introduction and how extensive each one is.

After your visit discuss your analysis of what you saw with others. Try to plan for a small group discussion with others who have visited the college.

Books—Community College

Barzun, Jacques. *The American University: How It Runs and Where It Is Going.* New York: Harper and Row Publishers, 1968.

Berg, Ivar. *Education and Jobs: The Great Training Robbery.* New York: Praeger, 1970.

Cohen, Arthur M. *Dateline '79: Heretical Concepts for the Community College.* Beverly Hills, California: Glencoe Press, 1969.

Cohen, Arthur M., and Brawer, Florence B. *Confronting Identity: The Community College Instructor.* Englewood Cliffs, New Jersey: Prentice-Hall, 1972.

Gleazer, Edmund J. *This Is the Community College*. Boston: Houghton Mifflin Company, 1968.

Graham, R. William. *Instant College*. Boston: Branden Press, 1971.

Johnson, B. Lamar. *Islands of Innovation Expanding*. Beverly Hills, California: Glencoe Press, 1969.

Medsker, Leland L., and Jillery, Dale. *Breaking the Access Barriers*. New York: McGraw-Hill, 1971.

Ogilvie, William K., and Raines, Max R. *Perspectives on the Community Junior College*. New York: Appleton-Century-Crofts, 1971.

Organizations

Two states have completed comprehensive plans for the establishment of community colleges. They are California and Florida. By writing the State Department of Education in those two states the reader should be able to obtain a wealth of information on state planning for community colleges.

The American Association of Junior Colleges and the American Association of Higher Education are two organizations that the reader should be familiar with if he wants to find additional sources of information on education for later adolescents and adults.